Listening

Listening

An Introduction to the Perception of Auditory Events

Stephen Handel

A Bradford Book
The MIT Press
Cambridge, Massachusetts
London, England

First MIT Press paperback edition, 1993
© 1989 Massachusetts Institute of Technology

Printed and bound in the United States of America by Maple-Vail, Inc.

Library of Congress Cataloging-in-Publication Data

Handel, Stephen.
  Listening: an introduction to the perception of auditory events/Stephen Handel.

  p.   cm.
  "A Bradford book."
  Includes bibliographies and index.
  ISBN 0-262-08179-2 (HB), 0-262-58127-2 (PB)
  1. Auditory perception. 2. Hearing. 3. Music—Psychology. 4. Speech perception.
5. Music—Acoustics and physics. 6. Auditory pathways. I. Title.
BF251.H27   1989
152.1'5—dc19   88-22502
                                                                               CIP
                                                                               MN

To Mary Ann, Mark, and the bowling-ball cat

Contents

Preface

Listening puts me in the world. Listening gives me a sense of emotion, a sense of movement, and a sense of being there that is missing when I am looking. I am more frightened by thunder than by lightning, even though I know that thunder is harmless and lightning is deadly. I feel far more isolation living with ear plugs than living with blinders. Listening is centripetal; it pulls you into the world. Looking is centrifugal; it separates you from the world. Helen Keller (1954) has reflected on the profoundness of being deaf.

It is the immediacy of the auditory world that led me to write this book about the perception of auditory events. I use the term *events* in a broad way; it includes individual music and speech sounds, musical and speech phrases, thunderclaps and hand claps, the sounds of objects breaking, and the sighs of contentment and the sighs of exasperation. The events covered most extensively are human: music and speech. I will argue throughout that there are basic commonalities in the perception of music and speech. From production to perception, music and speech share acoustic, physiological, and cognitive/organizational processes and constraints.

No book can be complete, and this one is no exception. My interests have led me to emphasize the connection between the physical properties of the sound wave and the percept. Unless we can understand what there is to hear, we can not understand perceiving. This emphasis reflects the theoretical views of J. J. Gibson, who has consistently sought an ecological analysis of the perceptual world. My beliefs have led me to emphasize the perception of events (of whole units) within a context. The context changes the production and transmission of the acoustic sound wave, and the listener must retrieve the event despite the surface variation. This second emphasis reflects the varying theoretical views of M. Wertheimer, W. Kohler, F. Allport, E. Brunswik, W. R. Garner, and J. J. Gibson, who, in spite of their differences, were all interested in the perception of structure. Given these interests and beliefs, many topics are untouched. There is very little discussion of cross-cultural differences, perceptual development, or the aesthetics, meanings, and emotional connotations of music and speech.

This book is written for novices—no prior knowledge is assumed. I have avoided the use of musical scores and have supplemented technical measurements with simpler numerical ratios. Moreover, there is a glossary of terms to help readers skip around the chapters. Suggestions for further reading are listed at the ends of some chapters to supplement the references in the text.

The book is organized roughly into two parts. Chapters 1–6 concern sound production, and chapters 7–13 concern sound perception. All the chapters are relatively self-contained so that readers with different interests may pick and choose among them. I would recommend that every reader begin with chapters 1 and 2. Chapter 1 (A point of view) provides a general orientation. Chapter 2 (The production of sound) provides the technical acoustic material for the rest of the book; it is the key chapter. The rest of the chapters are a mixed bag. Some are primarily about music: chapter 4 (Sound generation by musical instruments); chapter 10 (Grammars of music and language). Some are primarily about speech: chapter 5 (Sound generation by voice: Speaking and singing); chapter 9 (Phonemes: Notes and intervals). Some compare music and speech: chapter 6 (Commonalities: Physical and perceptual); chapter 8 (Identification of speakers, instruments, and environmental events); chapter 11 (Rhythm). And some concern auditory perception in general: chapter 3 (The environment of sound); chapter 7 (Breaking the acoustic wave into events: Stream segregation); chapter 12 (The physiology of listening).

A reader solely concerned with music might read chapters 1, 2, 4, 6, 7, 8, 10, and 11 (chapters 3 and 12 optional); a reader solely concerned with speech might read chapters 1, 2, 5, 6, 7, 8, 9, and 11 (chapters 3 and 12 optional).

This book has been written according to the Peter Principle: it is at the level of my incompetence. I would like to acknowledge the help of several reviewers who saved me from myself and significantly improved the manuscript: Albert Bregman, McGill University; W. J. Dowling, University of Texas at Dallas; Fred Lerdahl, University of Michigan; and Bruno H. Repp, Haskins Laboratories. I would also like to acknowledge individuals who unbeknownst to themselves served as role models: T. Cornsweet (1970) and A. Benade (1960 and 1976), whose books serve as models of writing; the large number of researchers whose ideas have forged my understanding of perception; and the editors of the magazine *The Absolute Sound*, who convinced me that there was more to hear than I heard. I would like to thank Wynne Brown at Brownline Graphics, who skillfully transformed my sketches into figures. Finally, I would gratefully like to thank Connie Ogle in particular, Ann Smith, and Sandy Anderson, who constantly assured me that the book would be finished, assuaged my guilt about causing the clear-cutting of forests, and were able to produce correct text out of colored lines crisscrossing a page.

Listening

Chapter 1
A Point of View

If you had to choose, would you prefer to be deaf or blind? Without taking time to reflect, most of us would prefer to be deaf, to see rather than hear. Now imagine going about your day-to-day life deaf or blind. Blind individuals can make it. They communicate, laugh, and joke with blind and sighted individuals; they listen to music and so on. Deaf individuals make it only with extreme difficulty and are generally restricted to the friendship of other deaf individuals. They are cut off from others; they are isolated. In our culture, I would much prefer to be blind than to be deaf.

In this book I concentrate on those parts of human experience that are primarily auditory: (1) the perception of an object's location in space by sound alone; (2) the perception of nonspeech sounds, particularly music; and (3) the perception of speech. These experiences seem to be part of every human's experience. All cultures have evolved language, all cultures have evolved some type of musical expression; and even newborn infants judge whether a sound comes from the left or right. It seems reasonable to expect that there should be a match between the physical properties of sound, psychological experience, and the physiological properties of the auditory system.

There are basic similarities in the three phenomena. All are concerned with identification of events, ranging from the identification of an individual by voice over a telephone to the identification of a musical instrument (a clarinet as distinct from an oboe). All are concerned with the perception of patterns, ranging from a sentence or song to a melody or the movement of a fly buzzing around your head. And all are concerned with the perception of rhythm. After all, we dance to sounds; we do not dance to lights.

Auditory events tell us about the surrounding world. What is characteristic about these events is that they are spatial and temporal; the information specifying the event consists of variations in the sound over both short and long time periods. These variations often occur almost instantaneously (the changes in loudness, quality, and timbre of a note when a violin is initially bowed); they may also occur in short time periods (the changes in pitch, duration, and timbre for a syllable or a note) or occur in long time periods (the changes in loudness, duration, order, and rhythm among elements of a sentence or a musical phrase and the changes in position for a moving object).

What will make the analysis difficult is that what happens in the short time intervals affects what happens in the long time intervals and vice versa. We should not think of independent acoustic units that are butted together. Rather, in combining consonants and vowels to form syllables, the articulation forces the acoustic properties of each to invade the other so that both consonant and vowel come out physically different from what they would be if paired with a different vowel or consonant. We hear the same "d" sound in the syllables [da] and [du], although the acoustic signal for "d" changes dramatically. The lack of correspondence between the sound wave and the percept is greater in longer segments. When we listen to an utterance, we hear a sequence of sounds (roughly letters, termed *phonemes*) in which one begins when the previous one ends; each one appears to be conveyed by a discrete packet of sound. Again, this is not the case: there are no units in the acoustic pressure wave clearly separated by physical breaks that correspond to each discrete perceptual unit. The spelling of the word cat is "c" followed by "a" followed by "t." If, however, we try to cut out the "c" part from a tape recording, no unique section can be found. The "c" permeates the entire word acoustically, albeit not perceptually. Similarly, the rhythm of a sentence does not merely come from the accent on each syllable but depends simultaneously on the individual syllables, on the individual words, and on the meaning of the sentence as well. For example, even if each word in the phrase "the white house" were equal as measured by an electronic meter, a listener might report hearing "THE white house" if the utterance specified one of the possible white houses, or "the WHITE house" if the utterance specified the President's lodging, or "the white HOUSE" if the utterance specified which white object. The context as a whole, not each word separately, determines the rhythm and meaning. Unfortunately, it *is* as complicated as it sounds.

The relationship between the physical stimulus and the phenomenal perception is not clear-cut. The phenomenal world of the acoustic events of a listener is not necessarily that described by the physical properties of the sound energy. There is no sound pressure–variation that will always lead to one and only one perception. Similarly, there is no perception that always comes from one and only one pressure variation. If the converse were true—if for every different sound percept there were a unique pattern of sound pressure and if each different sound pressure pattern led to a unique percept—then the problem of auditory perception would be solved, and not by psychologists. It would be solved by physicists who could accurately measure the sound pattern. Perceiving would become rote memorizing; all that would be necessary would be associating each sound pattern with its name or meaning.

This is not the case. Listening is not the same as hearing. The physical pressure wave enables perception but does not force it. Listening is active; it allows age, experience, expectation, and expertise to influence perception. It is often helpful to illustrate how the ear is like a microphone or how the eye is like a camera. It is a mistake, however, to equate the ear with listening or the eye with looking, or to equate the faithful recording of sound energy or light energy with hearing or seeing. We hear and see things and events that are important to us as individuals, not sound waves or light rays (e.g., Noble 1983). Nonetheless, we must measure the physical signal so that we can begin to understand the relationships between the signal as measured by a meter and the event the listener hears. The study of listening must take place within the context of the environment in which listening evolved, since it is the product and reflection of that environment. After all, in spite of the complexities, understanding music and speech comes naturally to all of us.

This orientation should be contrasted to the classical view of sensation and perception. The earliest Greek philosophers held that the mind experiences the external world through the senses. The Greek philosophers, attempting to explain the truthfulness of perception, believed that objects give off little replicas of themselves—eidolas—that when conducted to the mind, allow us directly to perceive the object due to their similarity to that object. In this case, the sensation is the perception. Today we know that acoustic and visual energy stimulate nerves and that it is the nerve firings that are transmitted to the brain. Each nerve responds to one type of energy, and the firing of that nerve is presumed to result in one sensory quality, regardless of the way it was stimulated. These qualities are the sensations, the simple conscious experiences like red, salty, or high pitch. The sensations are the bits and pieces of the perceptions, the blobs of color on a French Impressionist painting, the discrete light bulbs in a scoreboard, or the individual whistles in a bird song. These sensations become the basis for perception. However, many objects will yield the same set of sensations; and conversely, the same object will yield differing sets of sensations, depending on context. Perception is the necessary second stage, the process by which these elements are bound into objects and events. During perception, the conception of an external event is constructed. Perception is based in part on experience, and only through that experience is it possible to make sense of the ambiguous, discrete sensations.

Psychologists have long believed in this dichotomy between sensation and perception. It has led to research that has attempted to determine the sensitivity and accuracy of each sense organ. If the ear is only a microphone, then what is the softest sound it can hear? How sensitive is it to changes in loudness or pitch? How much distortion can it detect? The important point is that this experimentation used the simplest situations, with sounds that were simple and unchanging. It precluded the discovery of the possibilities for perceiving events and objects. On the whole, the results of this research, ably summarized by Yost and Nielsen (1985), Green (1976), and Moore (1982), will not be presented here.

What I will do is emphasize the perception of events. This first requires a detailed analysis of the physical characteristics of sounds themselves. Most natural sounds are not constant; they change more or less continuously from start to finish, with all parts interacting with one another. Only after the acoustic input is described can we ask questions about the relationships between the physical input and the perceived events. The relationships found between the physical and psychological worlds will motivate and suggest how to look at the physiological world. Here we will ask what sensory and physiological mechanisms exist to explain the psychological, phenomenal experiences. If, for example, we find that many sounds are perceived and identified because of a rapid increase in intensity, then we should look for physiological mechanisms that "fire" to increases in sound pressure or loudness. This organization is consistent with the view that the perceptual systems evolved to cope with the possibilities of environmental stimulation.

This short chapter sets the foundation for the study of listening. Auditory events are set in time and they are perceived in time. For this reason the changes in the characteristics of sound from onset to decay must be explicated. If an understanding of our experiences is possible, it must be correlated to the temporal characteristics of sounds. Before this is possible, however, the basic physical principles underlying sound production must be understood, and this is the topic of the next chapter.

Further Reading

I General Perceptual Theory

Allport, F. H. (1955). *Theories of perception and the concept of structure.* New York: Wiley. Though slightly out of date and eccentric, it is the book I always refer to.

Boring, E. G. (1942). *Sensation and perception in the history of experimental psychology.* New York: Appleton-Century-Crofts. This book, along with Boring's *A history of experimental psychology* (1950), are the standards for historical background.

Rock, I. (1975). *An introduction to perception.* New York: Macmillan. A good introduction; the focus, however, is visual perception.

II Specific Perceptual Theories

A Ecological Theory   The ecological approach to perception developed by Gibson is the dominant theme throughout this book. Michaels and Carello provide an introduction, and Gibson's two books are the "bibles."

Gibson, J. J. (1966). *The senses considered as perceptual systems.* Boston: Houghton Mifflin.
Gibson, J. J. (1979). *The ecological approach to visual perception.* Boston: Houghton Mifflin.
Michaels, C. F., and Carello, C. (1981). *Direct perception.* Englewood Cliffs, N.J.: Prentice-Hall.

B Information Theory

Garner, W. R. (1962). *Uncertainty and structure as psychological concepts.* New York: Wiley. A rewarding discussion of structure.

C Gestalt Theory
Koffka's *Principles* is the textbook of gestalt psychology and Kohler's *Task* provides a recent summary by one of the founders.
Koffka, K. (1935). *Principles of gestalt psychology.* New York: Harcourt, Brace, & World.
Kohler, W. (1969). *The task of gestalt psychology.* Princeton: Princeton University Press.

D Phenomenology

Ihde, D. (1976). *Listening and voice: A phenomenology of sound.* Athens: Ohio University Press.

E Comparisons between Audition and Vision

Geldard, F. A. (1970). Vision, audition, and beyond. In W. D. Neff (ed.), *Contributions to sensory physiology.* Vol. 4 (pp. 1–17). New York: Academic.
Julesz, B., and Hirsh, I. J. (1972). Visual and auditory perception: An essay of comparison. In E. E. David and P. Denes (eds.), *Human communication: A unified view* (pp. 283–340). New York: McGraw-Hill.
Marks, L. E. (1978). *The unity of the senses.* New York: Academic.

Chapter 2

The Production of Sound

The production of musical, vocal, and environmental sounds can be conceptualized as arising from several interacting processes. The first process involves the initiation of a vibration. This vibration can be started by bowing a string, striking a metal bell, blowing through a mouthpiece, or expelling air through the vocal cords. This energy brings about the vibration of the string or the bell or the vibration of air molecules within a clarinet or within a vocal tract. To produce audible sound, the vibrating string or the air vibrating within a tube must transfer its energy to a sound body that is more effective in transmitting the vibratory pattern to the air medium. However, the method of connection between the vibration and the sound body and the physical properties (the resonances) of the sound body transform the vibration. The vibration of the sound body is not identical to the original vibration. The vibration pattern of the sound body that is propagated through the air toward the listener is modified further by the objects in the environment. The environment thus imposes its own properties on the sound reaching the listener.

To provide a glimpse of what will follow, this chapter will emphasize two concepts common to all types of sounds. The first concept is that the complex vibration patterns that occur on violin strings, within the vocal tract, or on the wooden back of a guitar can be conceptualized as the combination of many simple vibrations. Thus, we can analyze any complex vibration pattern into a set of component vibrations, each of which "moves" independently. The complex vibration that occurs is determined by the physical construction of the object as well as by how it is played (e.g., plucked as opposed to bowed; whispered as opposed to shouted). The second concept is that the degree to which the vibration on one object (e.g., on a string) can transfer its energy to another object (e.g., the wooden body of a violin) depends on the strength of coupling between the two as well as the match between the natural vibration frequencies of the two. Unless the physical processes in sound production are understood, it is impossible to grasp the potentials for perceiving. After all, to design a boat, you would need to understand wind, water, waves, and so on. More important, you would need to understand the boat in the medium of water;

its stability in water is much different than on land. In thinking about sound production, it is useful to begin by considering the simplest vibrations, and then build more complex vibrations from these building blocks.

2.1 Simple Harmonic Vibration

The simplest vibrations have been termed *harmonic motion*. Harmonic motion is created by an elastic restoring force: if an object is moved from its resting or equilibrium point, the force acting to return it to equilibrium is proportional to its displacement (or distance from equilibrium). Nearly all vibrating systems we will consider—strings, wooden blocks and plates, vocal cords, air—are elastic, and therefore all undergo harmonic vibration.

Harmonic motion can be modeled by means of balls, meant to represent simple masses or objects, and springs, meant to represent the elastic forces tending to pull or push the masses back to their initial positions. Consider one mass connected by a spring to a rigid post, as shown in figure 2.1. At one point the ball will be in equilibrium (point E). If the ball is pushed to the left, compressing the spring, the force exerted by the spring will be proportional to the amount it was compressed. When released, the spring acts to push the ball to the right, and because of momentum the mass shoots past the equilibrium point at maximum velocity (time 2). The spring now stretches and creates a force tending to pull the mass back to the left. The ball slows down as the rightward movement stops at maximum stretch, and the movement begins to the left (time 3). The speed of the movement to the left is slow at first, and then reaches its maximum at the equilibrium point (time 4). The movement then slows down as the spring compresses, and creates a rightward force. The mass finally stops at the left displacement point (time 5). Now the movement begins again as the spring expands.

The result is a harmonic oscillation of the mass about the equilibrium point. The graph of the position of the mass at different times is also included in figure 2.1. These vibrations or oscillations are represented by *sinusoid* curves or waves. Sinusoid vibrations (harmonic motion) arise in an immense variety of mechanical systems, from masses connected to springs, to tines of tuning forks, to stretched strings of pianos and violins, to air molecules within clarinets and vocal tracts. In all these cases, the restoring force is proportional to the displacement (i.e., the restoring force on air molecules acts to equalize their distribution in space). Moreover, according to Fourier's profound mathematical theorem, any vibration or oscillation that repeats itself indefinitely can be built up from (or is analyzable into) a set of pure sinusoid waves. Harmonic motion is thus the building block of acoustics. The details of this procedure will be discussed later in this chapter.

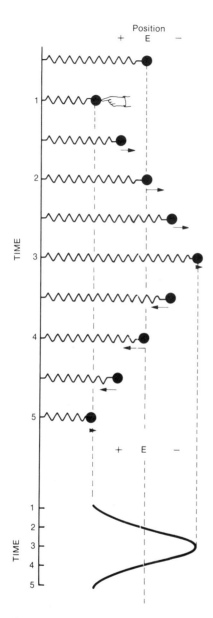

Figure 2.1
Harmonic motion is generated by the elastic compression and expansion of a spring. The velocity of the mass is maximum at the equilibrium point and minimum at the "turnaround" points. The velocity at each instant is denoted by the length of the arrow.

The sinusoid wave generated by harmonic motion is redrawn in figure 2.2. Imagine the sinusoid wave (position against time) being created by the movement of a radius around a circle. This representation facilitates the definition of several important terms referring to sinusoid waves in particular and wave motion in general. In each case the definition is stated first for simple harmonic motion and then for general wave motion.

- *Amplitude* is the maximum distance from equilibrium through which a vibrating element moves. Unless restrained in some fashion, the distance in one direction will equal the distance in the other direction.
- A *periodic* vibratory pattern is one that repeats itself over and over again. Obviously sinusoid movement is periodic, but the vast majority of periodic movements, being more complex, are not sinusoid.
- A *cycle* includes the displacement of the vibrating body from its equilibrium to its maximum in one direction, then to its maximum in the opposite direction and then returning to the equilibrium point. We can define a cycle only for a periodic wave. For complex vibrations, a cycle in general refers to one repetition of the wave pattern. Typically this wave pattern will be irregular and can cross the equilibrium point many times within one cycle.
- *Frequency* and *period* represent alternate ways of timing a single cycle. Frequency (F) is the number of cycles per second; period (T in sec) is the time needed to complete one cycle. If the frequency is 50 cycles/sec, then the period is 2/100 sec (0.02 sec or 20 msec). In equation form:

$$F \text{ (in cycles/sec)} = \frac{1}{T} \text{ (in sec/cycle)}.$$

The unit for frequency is Hertz (Hz).
- *Wavelength* is the distance between corresponding points of the wave as it is propagated through some medium. Wavelength and frequency are reciprocal:

Wavelength (m/cycle) × Frequency (cycles/sec)

= Speed of sound (in m/sec).

If we assume that the speed of sound is 340 m/sec, then the wavelength of a 680 Hz vibration is 0.5 m/cycle.
- *Phase* is the progression of a wave through one cycle, which can be represented as the movement through one 360° circle. Phase is measured in degrees; by convention, the cycle begins at equilibrium at 0°, the maximum displacement in one direction is at 90°, equilibrium is at 180°, and maximum displacement in the reverse direction

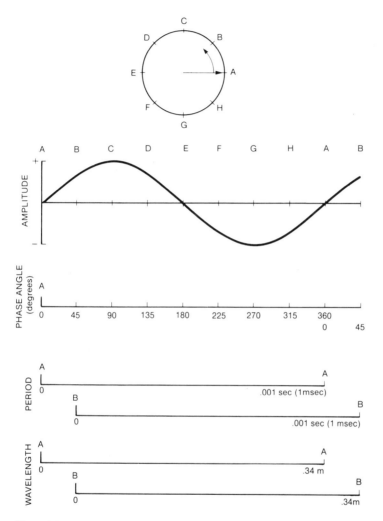

Figure 2.2
The representation of phase angle, period, and wavelength for harmonic motion. A single period is equal to a 360° change in phase angle (one rotation around the circle). The period and wavelength can be measured between any pair of equivalent points on the wave. Two possibilities are shown.

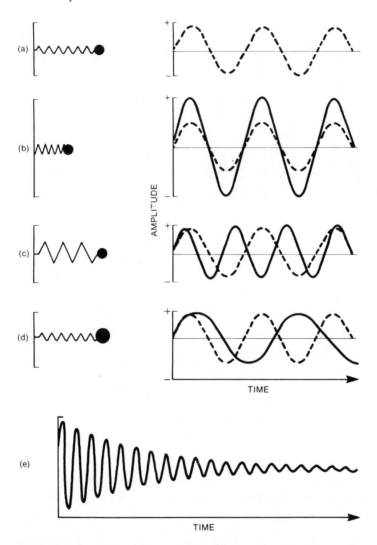

Figure 2.3
The mass and stiffness of the spring control the amplitude and wavelength (frequency) of
harmonic motion. The harmonic motion resulting from a standard spring and mass is shown
in (a). Increasing the displacement changes the amplitude but not the wavelength, shown in
(b). The dashed curve, shown in (a), represents the original motion. Increasing the stiffness
of the spring decreases the wavelength (i.e., increases the frequency), shown in (c). In
contrast, increasing the mass increases the wavelength (i.e., decreases the frequency), shown
in (d). The decay of harmonic motion is depicted in (e). As the motion decays in amplitude,
the frequency remains constant: the amplitude peaks remain equally spaced in time.

is at 270°. Phase is often used to specify the relation between two waves.

With these definitions in hand, suppose that we pushed the mass further to the left, thereby further compressing the spring. The mass, when released, will shoot out to the right, and both the leftmost and rightmost positions are going to be farther from the equilibrium point. Thus, the amplitude of the movement will be greater but the period (or frequency) will not change, because the period is determined only by spring stiffness and mass. If we employ a bigger, stiffer spring, the period wil be shorter (although the amplitude may not change). The bigger spring will whip the mass back and forth. If we used the original spring but increased the size of the mass, the period would increase; this measly spring is going to have a hard time moving that big mass. All these possibilities are illustrated in figure 2.3.

The initial vibration will soon die out. Friction in the spring and air resistance will dissipate the original energy. One of the most important properties of simple harmonic motion is that as the amplitude decays, the period remains the same. In other words, the displacement becomes smaller and smaller, although the time for each cycle remains constant. It is for this reason that a musical note seems to remain at the same pitch as it gets softer. The decay is also shown in figure 2.3.

Superposition of Waves
One of the most important characteristics of harmonic vibration is that the combination of two or more waves is merely the sum of the amplitudes at each time point. This allows us to decompose any complex sound into simpler waves, which when recombined will generate precisely (in reality, closely approximate) the original complex wave.

Examples of the additivity and superposition of two simple harmonic waves are shown in figure 2.4. The resulting sound wave is simply the arithmetic sum of the magnitudes of the amplitudes of each wave at corresponding time points. In the first three cases, the two waves have the same frequency and amplitude. What differs among the cases is the phase relationships: (a) the two waves are *in phase*, both start at 0°; (b) the two waves are 90° *out of phase*; (c) the two waves are 180° *out of phase*. In the remaining two cases, the two waves have different frequencies (in the ratio of 4:3). In (d), the waves are in phase; in (e), the waves are 90° out of phase. In all five cases, the resultant sound wave is always the sum of the individual amplitudes.

When sounds add together, many different outcomes are possible. The sound waves can reinforce each other and lead to a wave with twice the amplitude, or the sound waves can interfere with each other and cancel out.

I. IDENTICAL FREQUENCIES

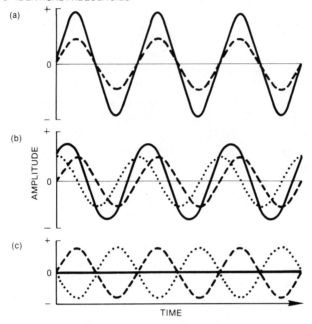

II. DIFFERENT FREQUENCIES

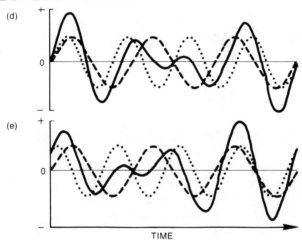

Figure 2.4
The superposition of two or more sound waves gives rise to a combination wave that is the sum of the individual waves. In (a), the superposition of two identical waves (both are represented by the same dashed line) forms a wave with twice the amplitude. In (b), the superposition of two identical waves 90° out of phase (the dotted and dashed lines) forms a wave with the same frequency but different phase angle and amplitude. In (c), the superposition of two identical waves 180° out of phase forms a flat, zero-intensity wave because the amplitudes always cancel completely. The superposition of two waves of different frequencies forms more complex, but still periodic, waves. In (d), the waves are in phase; in (e), the waves are 90° out of phase.

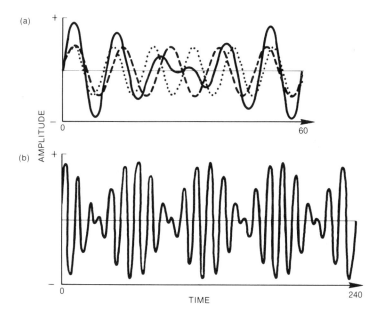

Figure 2.5
Superposition of two waves with similar frequencies causes beats. In (a), the addition (superposition) of the dashed and dotted waves creates a wave that oscillates in amplitude. One period is shown. In (b), the regular oscillation in amplitude can be better seen across four periods.

Alternatively, the sound waves can sum and yield a wave with a different pattern. Even more complex outcomes occur when many sounds of different frequency combine.

The additivity of sound waves can be used to understand beats, shown in figure 2.5. Combine two sinusoid waves at similar but not identical frequencies. Quite arbitrarily, use the frequencies of 166 Hz and 200 Hz. The sum of the two sound waves will yield a periodic sound wave of average frequency (equaling (166 + 200)/2 = 183 Hz), having a regular oscillation in amplitude (shown in figure 2.5). This oscillation is termed a *beat* and is heard as a regular fluctuation in loudness. The amplitude oscillation is a sinusoid wave, and the frequency of the fluctuation is the difference between the two frequencies, in this case 200 Hz − 166 Hz = 34 Hz. Panel (a) illustrates the superposition in a short time span, and panel (b) illustrates the amplitude oscillation over a longer time span.

Beats can be used to tune musical instruments, because very few individuals can adjust the frequency of each note precisely. A piano tuner, using a tuning fork or electronic instrument, can simultaneously play the correct frequency and the corresponding key of the piano. If the piano note is mistuned, beats will arise from the differing frequencies of the tuning instrument and piano. The tuner brings the note into tune by adjusting the string tension of the piano until the beats disappear. When this occurs, the frequency of the tuning instrument and the piano note will be identical, and the note will be correctly tuned.

Breakdown of Complex Vibrations into Sinusoid Vibrations: Fourier Analysis
Up to this point I have considered what occurs when two or more sound waves are added together. I argued that complex sound waves arise from the superposition and additivity of simple harmonic (sinusoid) waves. What about the reverse direction? How and when can we take a complex sound wave and break it into sinusoid waves such that those waves will re-create the original complex wave when they are added together? Moreover, are there stable relationships among the sinusoid waves?

The answers come from Fourier's theorem. There are two complementary cases. The first concerns sounds that are periodic and that may be considered to be steady state. The second concerns sounds that are nonperiodic: sounds that are very brief or are continuously changing and do not repeat at constant time intervals. For example, a hiss and a sharp click are nonperiodic sounds. It is simpler to begin with periodic sounds.

Periodic sounds   Any periodic waveform, no matter how complex, can be analyzed, or decomposed, into a set of simple sinusoid waves with calculated frequencies, amplitudes, and phase angles. The phase relationships do not appear to have a great effect on the perceived sound, and therefore we will consider the amplitude spectrum but not the phase spectrum. The frequency of each sinusoid is an integer multiple of one fundamental frequency determined by the period, the time between successive repetitions of the entire wave. For example, suppose a complex wave repeated every 0.005 seconds, or 200 times per second. This would mean that the lowest frequency sinusoid would be 200 Hz, and the other sinusoid waves necessary to re-create this complex sound would be multiples of 200 Hz: 400 Hz, 600 Hz, 800 Hz, 1000 Hz, etc. Each sinusoid is termed a *harmonic*, and by convention, the fundamental is called the first harmonic; the sinusoid that is twice the fundamental is termed the second harmonic, and so on. The amplitude of each harmonic will differ, depending on the strength of that component in the vibration of the complex wave (the amplitude of one harmonic might even be zero). The mathematics of Fourier analysis allow us to calculate each amplitude.

Let me summarize the complementary nature between additivity/superposition and the Fourier analysis. We start with a graph of the vibration amplitude against time; this shows the actual displacement of the vibration at each point in time. Using Fourier analysis, we can calculate the amplitude of each harmonic. Typically, the results of Fourier analysis are represented by a graph with the frequency of the harmonics on the x-axis and the amplitudes of each harmonic on the y-axis. The harmonic/amplitude representation is termed the *frequency* (or *line*) *spectrum*. Remember that each vertical line represents one sinusoid vibration at a particular amplitude.

In figure 2.6(a), the pressure-time wave is the sum of the first three harmonics. The Fourier spectrum contains three lines, one for each harmonic. We can break apart the original wave into the three harmonics, and each harmonic can be represented by a Fourier spectrum with one harmonic. Due to additivity/superposition, it is possible to combine the harmonic vibrations to reproduce the original complex wave and to combine the Fourier spectra to reproduce the original spectrum. The symmetry is indicated by the double arrows: additivity/superposition and decomposition by Fourier analysis are two sides of the same coin.

Other examples of Fourier analyses are shown in figure 2.6(b) and (c). A rather simple periodic wave with instantaneous right angle changes is seen in (b). For obvious reasons, it is called a square wave. The Fourier spectrum of the square wave is made up of the fundamental and all the odd harmonics—3, 5, 7, 9, ... (to square off the wave). The amplitudes of these harmonics are proportional to their frequency: the third harmonic is one-third the amplitude of the first harmonic, the fifth harmonic is one-fifth the amplitude of the first harmonic and so on. Adding higher harmonics changes the shape of the sound wave to approximate that of a square wave, as shown in figure 2.6(b). The second is termed a ramp, or "sawtooth," wave, seen in figure 2.6(c). The sawtooth wave is made up of all harmonics. The amplitude of each harmonic is proportion to its number (e.g., the fourth harmonic is one-fourth the amplitude of the fundamental). The square and sawtooth vibrations, the result of the higher-order harmonics, sound much sharper and piercing than the sinusoid. The last two examples come from a harp and an English horn. For each of the instruments, the sound pressure wave and corresponding Fourier spectrum are shown. The "sound" of any instrument is determined, at least in part, by the number, intensity, and distribution of the harmonics. For example, an instrument that contains only the fundamental sounds mellow and soft. If strong harmonics exist, the sound is more shrill.

I would like to pause to give a physical interpretation of Fourier analysis. As it stands now, it seems merely a mathematical abstraction, but it is really a physical statement of the strength of all the vibrations that are actually occurring. For example, suppose I plucked a string. The string soon settles down into a complex yet periodic motion. Although this motion does *not* look harmonic, it is the result of the superposition of sinusoid vibrations: the fundamental and all harmonics. It is critical to understand that these sinusoid vibrations occur simultaneously and occur independently of each

18   Chapter 2

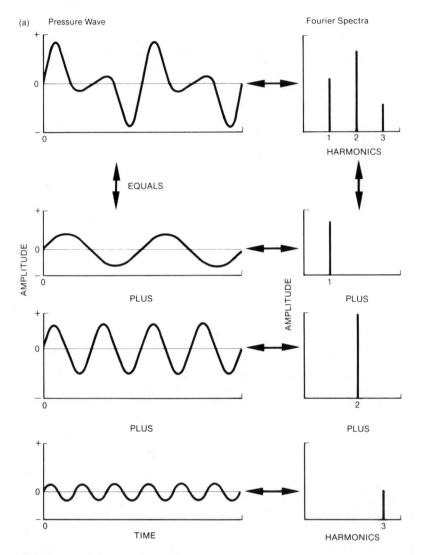

Figure 2.6
The Fourier analysis of periodic sounds results in a set of discrete harmonics. Fourier
analysis and additivity (superposition) are complementary. In (a), a periodic wave is shown
that can be analyzed into the sum of three harmonics. The superposition of the three
harmonics reproduces the original waves. In (b), a square wave is built up by summing the
odd harmonics. At every stage, there is a match between the pressure wave and the Fourier
representation. In (c), the Fourier representation of a sawtooth wave, a harp, and an English
horn note are shown (adapted from Culver 1956).

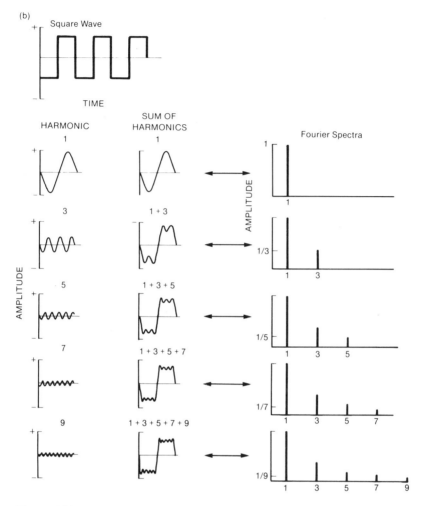

Figure 2.6(b)

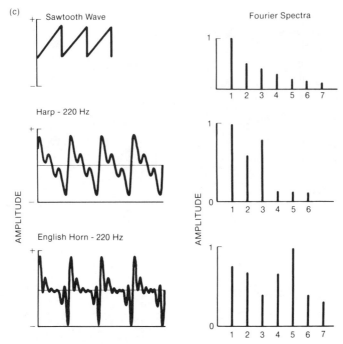

Figure 2.6(c)

other. The Fourier spectrum is therefore the representation of these simultaneous vibrations; the spectrum specifies the frequency, amplitude, and phase of each harmonic. Each harmonic vibration on the string can produce an air pressure wave of its own frequency that is propagated through the air. The complex sound wave reaching our ears can thus be represented by the Fourier spectrum, being the sum of all the component harmonics.

Nonperiodic sounds   Nonperiodic sounds can also be decomposed into sinusoid waves according to the Fourier theorem. The spectrum is more complex, however, because the energy is spread over frequency bands, and there may be an infinite number of frequency components. Each sinusoid has a specific amplitude, so the amplitude-frequency spectrum representation would be continuous (as opposed to the discrete line spectrum for a periodic sound). White noise, sounding like a hiss, is one extreme example of a nonperiodic sound. White noise is a random event; at any instance each frequency has an equal probability of occurring, and moreover the amplitude of each frequency will vary from instance to instance. Over a very long time period, there will be equal energy at every frequency. Thus the spectrum is continuous, with an equal amount of energy at every frequency. A short click is another extreme example of a non-periodic sound. If the click is infinitely short (a hypothetical event), the Fourier spectrum is continuous, with an equal amount of energy at every frequency (exactly like white noise). Because of the spread of frequencies, the click does not have a tonal quality. In intermediate cases like a single pulse of 10 msec or a single cycle of a sinusoid wave of 100 Hz, the Fourier spectrum is continuous except for null frequencies, at which the amplitude is zero. The null frequencies occur at multiples of one, divided by the duration. In this example, the null frequencies would be multiples of 100 Hz, i.e., 200 Hz, 300 Hz, and so on. As the duration is increased, say to 100 msec, the null frequencies become multiples of 10 Hz, and more of the energy occurs at the fundamental frequency. Examples of this are shown for a sinusoid wave in figure 2.7. At durations considerably longer than the period, we can assume that all of the energy is at the fundamental. It is important to remember that as a sound becomes shorter (with respect to its period), the Fourier spectrum becomes more continuous over frequencies; individual frequencies cannot be resolved.

The sounds around us have both periodic and nonperiodic components: an instrumental note will increase and then decrease in amplitude, or a soprano will sing the notes of a scale, gliding across frequencies. In each of these cases, one Fourier representation cannot adequately portray the sound across time. Instead, the time-varying signal is broken into time segments or "windows," and a Fourier analysis is performed on each time sample. Each analysis yields the amplitude of the component sinusoid vibrations in one time segment, and stringing the segments together will portray changes in frequency and amplitude across the duration of the sound. A second way to conceptualize this process is to imagine a set of meters; each meter continuously measures the amplitude of one frequency. Thus, the output of any meter will track the amplitude of one frequency across time. The outputs across all the different meters will show the amplitude variation of all the frequency components.

Two alternative representations have emerged, one more appropriate for the analysis of sounds that change in intensity, the other more appropriate for the analysis of sounds that change in frequency. Each will be discussed in turn below, and these representations will then be used in subsequent chapters.

Representation of amplitude variation   A simple sinusoidal vibration shown in figure 2.8 is increasing in amplitude throughout the time period t_1 where energy is being added. Then the displacement remains constant for the time period t_2 where the energy added equals the energy lost to friction, and finally the displacement dies out during time period t_3 where energy is

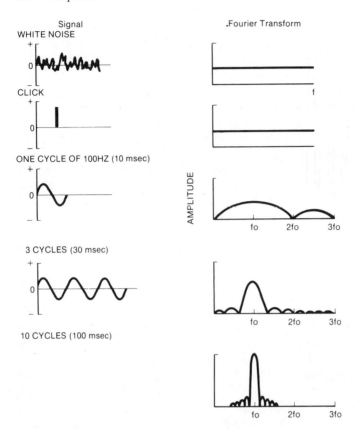

Figure 2.7
Fourier analyses of nonperiodic sounds result in continuous frequency spectra. The Fourier spectra of white noise and a infinitely short click are flat: equal amplitude at all frequencies. The Fourier spectrum for short tone bursts is continuous except for null frequencies. As the duration of the tone burst increases, more of the energy becomes concentrated at the fundamental frequency.

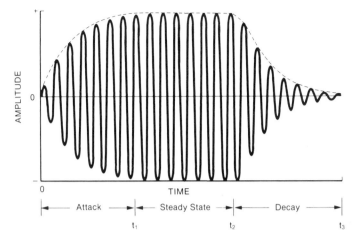

Figure 2.8
The attack, steady-state, and decay of a sound wave. The dashed line is the amplitude envelope (also termed the amplitude contour).

lost to friction. The time interval in which the amplitude is increasing is called the *attack*, or onset transient; the interval in which the amplitude is constant is termed the *steady state*; and the interval in which the amplitude is decreasing is termed the *decay*, or offset transient. It is best to think of this time-varying sound as having two components: (1) a steady sinusoidal vibration and (2) an amplitude envelope that represents the onset, steady-state, and decay displacement. The envelope is portrayed as the light line touching the peaks of the vibration. If a harmonic remains at one frequency. it can be represented by the positive side of the amplitude envelope: a graph of displacement as a function of time.

A complex sound will consist of several harmonics. Each harmonic typically will have a different initiation point and different attack, steady-state, and decay timing as well as a different maximum amplitude. As long as the frequency of each harmonic is constant (and this is roughly true for instruments), we can represent each harmonic by its amplitude envelope. An example composed of three harmonics is shown in figure 2.9. The top panel illustrates the pressure wave. The wave is sampled at four time points, and the Fourier spectrum at each time point is shown. Then, the amplitudes of each harmonic are combined across all the time samples to create the amplitude envelope of each harmonic. This is illustrated in the third row for the first harmonic. The amplitude envelope is a shorthand way of illustrating the actual harmonic, which is shown directly below the envelope. Comparisons among the amplitude envelops of each harmonic display the temporal relationships.

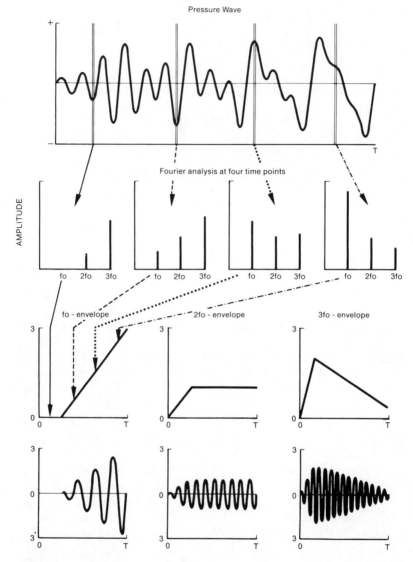

Figure 2.9
The Fourier analysis of a time-varying sound wave is accomplished by analyzing the wave at different time points and then combining these analyses. The sound wave and the four time "windows" are pictured in the top row. One period (time = T) is shown. For each time window, a separate Fourier analysis yields the amplitudes of each harmonic (shown in the second row). To create the amplitude envelope for each harmonic, the amplitudes across all time points are combined. To avoid clutter, this is shown explicitly only for the first harmonic in the third row. In a real analysis, the windows would be adjacent or overlapping and a truly continuous amplitude envelope would be created. The amplitude pattern of each harmonic is depicted in the bottom row.

Representation of frequency variation   Now consider a set of sounds that vary in frequency—for example, a singer running up the scale. To display the frequency variation clearly, sounds are plotted as frequency (y-axis) against time (x-axis). The amplitude is shown, with less accuracy, by the thickness or blackness of the drawn line. This representation is termed a spectrogram. Spectrograms of sounds varying in frequency and amplitude are shown in figure 2.10. The left side illustrates the vibration pattern; the right side portrays the spectrogram representation.

Each of these two graphical schemes to portray the amplitude and frequency variation of common sounds is based on the essential idea of Fourier analysis: to represent any sound as the sum of the component harmonic vibrations. The Fourier analyses at consecutive (or overlapping) time periods can then represent the amplitude and frequency variation across time. Much of present-day theorizing about sounds makes use of Fourier analyses. In addition to providing mathematical tools for the speci-fication of sounds, it has been argued that Fourier analyses have a physio-logical and psychological rationale. As early as the 1840s, George Ohm hypothesized that the human ear and nervous system "performed" a Fourier analysis on sounds and that this analysis was the basis of auditory perception. We now know that this contention is not literally true; never-theless, Fourier analyses provide a useful guide to both acoustic and psy-chological theories.

Sound Pressure and Intensity

When an object undergoes harmonic motion, it produces a change of pressure in the surrounding air medium. Although our naive experience is that air does not exist, it is necessary to remember that air is composed of molecules that are in constant motion and that this motion produces a constant static pressure in all directions. Pressure is defined as the force (push or pull) applied to each unit of area. It represents the concentration of force. In air, the static pressure is determined by the collisions among the air molecules, and the number of collisions is determined by the speed, mass, and density (number of molecules in a volume) of the molecules. As long as the air molecules are undisturbed, they move in random directions, which creates a static pressure that is uniform in all directions. This uniform pressure provides the medium through which sound propagates but, being uniform, does not generate any sound itself.

A sound is a relatively rapid change of pressure superimposed on this uniform static pressure, much like a flash bulb in a lighted room. The harmonic movement displaces the adjacent air molecules so that they are alternately pushed closer together and pushed further apart. This creates higher pressure regions (where the air molecles are pushed together) and lower pressure regions (where the air molecules are pushed apart). The

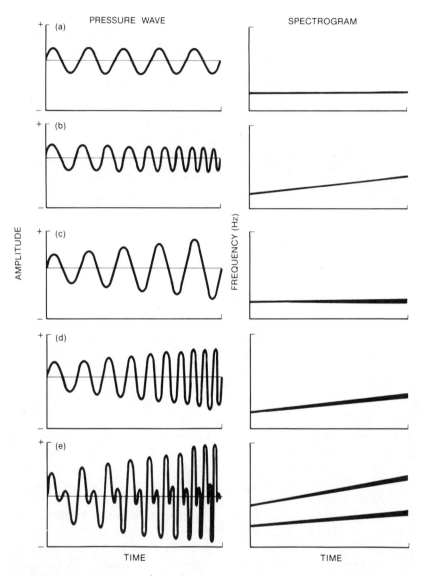

Figure 2.10
The representation of frequency and amplitude variation using spectrograms. In (a), the frequency and amplitude are constant; the spectrogram representation is a horizontal line (constant frequency) of uniform thickness (constant intensity). In (b), the frequency increases; the representation is a rising line of equal thickness (intensity is constant). In (c), the intensity increases; the representation is a horizontal line (frequency is constant) that increases in thickness. In (d), both frequency and intensity increase; the representation is a rising line of increasing thickness. In (e), the sound wave consists of two harmonics that both increase in frequency and intensity. Each harmonic is represented by a rising line of increasing thickness.

molecules within these regions move in order to return to static pressure, and this movement results in pressure differences being propagated through space. (Sound propagation will be discussed in chapter 3.)

Imagine that the harmonic motion is initially to the right, where it will compress the air molecules into a smaller region and thereby create a region of higher pressure. The molecules within the higher pressure region flow out to reduce the pressure, and this rightward flow produces a new higher pressure region further to the right. The higher pressure region continues to move rightward at the speed of sound, 340 m/sec. Meanwhile, the harmonic motion, passing through the equilibrium point and moving to the leftmost point, has reversed. This leftward movement creates a region of lower pressure because molecules have been pushed out of the region. The flow of molecules into this lower pressure region creates a new lower pressure region further to the right, and a lower pressure region moves to the right at 340 m/sec. The harmonic motion continues with the object moving through equilibrium to the right creating another higher pressure region. This second higher pressure region also propagates to the right. This generates an air pressure wave: higher pressure (movement to extreme right), equal pressure (movement to the left through equilibrium point), lower pressure (movement to extreme left), equal pressure (movement to the right through equilibrium point), higher pressure (movement to extreme right), and so on (see figure 2.11).

Now it is possible to connect frequency and wavelength. If the harmonic vibration frequency is 100 cycles/sec, then the time between equivalent higher pressure regions (between rightward extremes) is 1/100 sec (10 msec), and the distance between equivalent regions (i.e., wavelength) is 340 m/sec × 1/100 sec = 3.40 m. If the frequency is 200 cycles/sec, then the time between equivalent pressure regions is 1/200 sec (5 msec), and the wavelength is 340 m/sec × 1/200 sec = 1.70 m. As the frequency increases, a higher (or lower) pressure region travels a shorter distance before another equivalent pressure region is generated (because of the more rapid back-and-forth harmonic motion). Thus the wavelength decreases.

Intensity depends on sound pressure, and the sound pressure depends on how tightly air molecules are compressed together. The farther a sound body moves, the greater the displacement and compacting of air molecules and thus the greater the pressure increase within a cycle. To measure intensity, we can arbitrarily choose one value of sound pressure as a reference value and then measure all sounds by how many times each is greater than the reference pressure. The only problem is that the range of audible sounds is so large—the loudest sounds are 100,000,000 times more intense than the softest ones—that it is awkward to use the actual ratios. To achieve smaller numbers, the ratios are converted to the logarithms of the ratios. Using logarithms, sound intensity is measured in

(a) 100 Hz

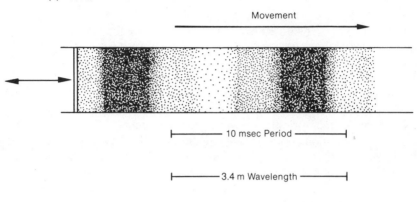

(b) 200 Hz

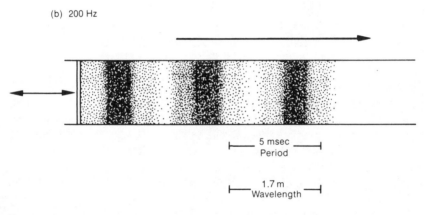

Figure 2.11
Sound waves propagate as alternating regions of higher pressure (dense texture) and lower pressure (light texture) areas. As the vibration frequency increases, the regions of higher and lower pressure become more compact.

decibels:

$$\text{Decibels (dB)} = 20 \text{ logarithm } \frac{P_1}{P_2}$$

$$= 20 \,(\text{logarithm } P_1 - \text{logarithm } P_2),$$

where P_1 is one pressure to be measured and P_2 is a second pressure. (Logarithms are in the base 10.) Using this formula, any *two* tones that have a pressure ratio of 10 to 1 (dB $= 20 \log P_1/P_2 = 20 \log 10 = 20 \times 1$) will differ by 20 decibels, any two tones that have a pressure ratio of 100 to 1 will differ by 40 decibels, and any two tones that have a pressure ratio of 1000 to 1 will differ by 60 decibels. What is important to remember is that differences of 20 decibels mean one tone has 10 times the pressure of the second, irrespective of the overall pressure, and that each additional 20 decibels indicates another 10 times greater pressure. Thus, 80 dB results from 20 + 20 + 20 + 20, meaning 10 × 10 × 10 × 10, or 10,000 times more pressure. Adding decibels is the same as multiplying pressures. Throughout the text, the actual pressure ratio as well as decibels will be presented.

It is possible to measure all sounds against a common reference. The common reference pressure is 0.0002 dyne/cm², which is approximately the lowest pressure necessary for the average human to hear a 1000 Hz tone. Sounds measured relative to this reference are labeled dB SPL. In table 2.1, the loudness in dB SPL of some common sounds are listed. A common

Table 2.1
The Sound Pressure Level (dB SPL) of Typical Sounds

Sound level (dB SPL)	Pressure (dynes/cm²)	Sound
200	10^6	Normal atmospheric pressure
180	10^5	
160	10^4	Threshold of pain
140	10^3	Jet engine
120	10^2	Threshold of feeling
100	10	Subway station; very loud music (*fff*)
80	1	Busy street; loud music (*f*) average conversation
60	0.1	Quiet conversation; soft music (*p*)
40	0.01	Quiet room
20	0.001	Soft whisper
0	0.0002	Threshold of audibility

complaint is "the music is so loud that I can't hear myself think. My experimental attempts to measure this loudness have always failed. Introspections of my colleagues suggest that loud sounds attract attention, but with a shift of attention one can always hear oneself think.

It is important to note that sound intensity decreases as the square of the distance traveled. Thus, at distances of 2, 3, and 4 meters, the sound pressure is 1/4, 1/9, and 1/16 as great. This will become important when considering the effects of the environment on the sound reaching the listener.

2.2 Sound Production

At this point we come to the heart of the chapter. Sound production involves several overlapping processes in which vibration energy is transferred from one object to another—for example, the vibration of the violin string created by the performer is transferred to the wooden front and back plates. The vibration of the sound body creates most of the sound that reaches the listener. Our discussion will begin with the vibration modes of a stretched string and then consider the vibration modes of air columns, wooden panels, and enclosed rooms. Later sections will outline the way vibrations are transferred between coupled objects and the radiation of sound into the air.

Modes of Vibration

To understand and describe all the possible vibration patterns for simple and complex objects, the best strategy is first to identify the various simple vibration patterns (the vibration modes). If we can do this, then by Fourier analysis and additivity/superposition we can analyze any complex vibration into the sum of these simple modes.

Stretched strings   A stretched string anchored at both ends might appear to be continuous and uniform, but it is helpful to conceptualize this string as being made up of discrete masses strongly interacting with one another. The masses can be imagined as interconnected by springs anchored at the ends (a stretched string under tension acts like a spring, because the force to return to the equilibrium position is proportional to displacement). We start with a string with only one mass, then consider a string with two masses, three masses, and so on. In the process we will induce general rules about the number of ways a string can vibrate.

Imagine the simplest case: one mass connected by springs to rigid mounts (see figure 2.12). If we begin to move one of the mounts up and down in a sinusoidal movement, the mass also begins to move in a sinusoidal wave motion because of the elastic forces imposed by the springs.

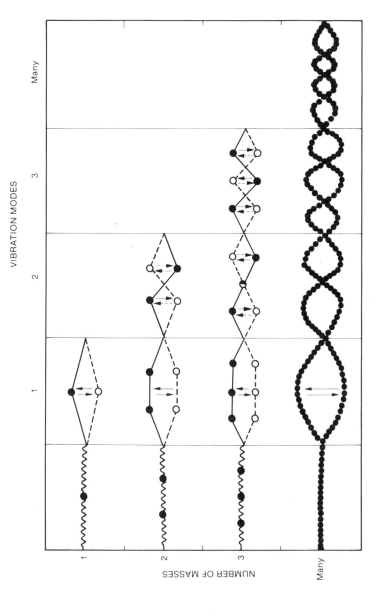

Figure 2.12
The possible vibrations of a stretched string are determined by the number of masses. With one mass, only up-and-down movement can occur. With two masses, both masses can move up and down together, and in addition, the two masses can move up and down out of phase. With three masses, there are three possible independent and additive movements. With an infinite number of masses, as would be true for a real string, there are an infinite number of independent vibration modes (adapted from Benade 1960).

What is critical to understand is that only one type of motion is possible. The mass can only move up and down. The frequency of movement depends on the stiffness and mass of the system: making the string stiffer increases the frequency, and making the mass bigger reduces the frequency. As described in the section below on coupling, the amplitude of movement will depend on the match between the frequency of shaking and the natural frequency of the mass/spring combination.

With two masses, there are two possible modes of vibration. In the first mode, the two masses move up and down together and the pattern of movement is shown in figure 2.12. In the second mode, the two masses move in opposite directions. It is as if there are two mode 1 vibrations occurring in the left and right halves, with each oscillation having a common point in the middle that does not move. Each mass moves in sinusoidal motion with twice the frequency of mode 1. If in mode 1 the masses move back and forth 1000 times per second, then in mode 2 each of the masses would move back and forth 2000 times per second. (Actually, the exact frequency of mode 2 depends on the nature and spacing of the springs and masses. If the masses were placed at 1/3 and 2/3, the frequency would be 1732 Hz.) A picture of mode 2 is also shown in figure 2.12.

For a three-mass chain there are three characteristic modes of vibration: (1) all the masses vibrate back and forth together; (2) there are two regions of vibration—masses 1 and 3 oscillate out of phase and bypass each other, mass 2 is stationary; and (3) there are three regions of vibration—masses 1 and 3 vibrate in phase, mass 2 vibrates out of phase. The first two modes are equivalent to the first two (and only) modes for a two-mass system. What the third mass does is allow the emergence of an additional vibratory mode in which there are three vibrating segments.

This process can be generalized to ten, twenty, and thirty masses. For any chain the number of different modes of vibration equals the number of masses. For all chains, in the first mode all the masses move up and down together. In the second mode, there are two regions of oscillation. In the third mode, there are three regions of oscillation, and so on (shown in figure 2.12). In mode 2 the frequency of vibration is twice that of mode 1; in mode 3 the frequency of vibration is triple that of mode 1, and so on.

The final step is to consider a continuous chain made up of an infinite number of infinitesimal masses, much like a real stretched string. Since there are an infinite number of masses, there should be an infinite number of possible modes of vibration. In mode 1, the entire chain would vibrate as a unit; in mode 2, the chain would vibrate in two sections, and so on for the remaining modes. For this system, the ratios of the frequencies of the successive modes are $1:2:3:4:5$, or the frequency of mode n = (frequency of mode 1) $\times$ n. It is these vibration modes, and only these, that are possible in a continuous string anchored at both ends. It should be noted that this simple result is true only for perfect strings. The vibration modes of real-life strings are not perfect multiples. We will return to this problem.

Using additivity and superposition, it can be argued that any possible overall pattern of vibration will be made up of combinations of these possible modes, and similarly, any possible vibration must be analyzable into these modes. In other words, this analysis provides the total possible range of allowable vibration modes. If I pluck or bow a string, certain of these modes will occur, and the vibration motion of the string will be the sum of the amplitudes of these modes, nothing more and nothing less.

Suppose we looked at a vibration mode from the side. What you would see is that sections of the chain are going up and down (in sinusoidal movement, actually), but the sections are stationary; they do not travel either left or right. For this reason, this type of vibration is termed a *standing wave*. The individual points oscillate, but the wave profile does not move. A *node* is a point or position on a standing wave that is stationary; an *antinode* is a point or position on a standing wave that undergoes maximum displacement.

Why and when do standing waves occur? When you "shake" the string at any point, it creates sinusoid waves that travel in both directions down the string. At the fixed ends, each wave is reflected backward. Each wave retains its shape and travels back toward the other end. If you continue to shake the string, there will be a series of waves moving toward the two fixed ends and a series of reflected waves moving back from both ends. All the waves will add because of superposition. If the frequency of "shaking" is correct, the original and reflected waves will be in phase and yield a large vibration movement that leads to a standing wave vibration mode. On the other hand, if the frequency is not correct, then the original and reflected waves will be out of phase, the two waves will cancel, and a vibration mode will not appear. In sum, a vibration mode is a standing wave pattern. Each vibration mode is independent, and any combination of modes yields a complex vibration pattern equal to the sum of the amplitudes of the standing waves.

Air columns   In discussing the vibration modes of a string, we built up the string, mass by mass. It is possible to proceed in the same way in order to induce the modes in an air column. This account is based on Benade's elegant book, *Horns, strings, and harmony* (1960).

Imagine a bottle with a cork that can slide up and down in its neck. We push the cork down. The cork will compress the air in the bottle, and the air will act like a spring to push the cork back up to its equilibrium point (like compressing a balloon). The momentum of the cork, like the momentum of a mass attached to a spring, will make the cork overshoot the equilibrium position. Now the pressure inside the jar is less than the atmosphere and the outside air will act to push the cork back into the jar. Again there will be an overshoot—the cork will compress the air in the bottle and the oscillation will begin anew. The oscillation will be sinusoidal because the restoring force is proportional to the displacement from equilibrium. More important, there is only one possible mode of vibration; the cork can only move up and down. To convert this model to air, simply think of the cork as a slug of air that is oscillating up and down.

Now consider a system made up of two interconnected jars. There are two masses (i.e., corks), and just like a string with two masses, there are two vibratory modes. In the first mode, both corks move up and down together; in the second mode, the corks are out of phase, as one moves up, the other moves down and vice versa (see figure 2.13). Now imagine that the number of jars is multiplied thousandfold and that the resulting pipe is smoothed out. This is analogous to a continuous string with an infinite number of masses. For this pipe, there are an infinite number of "air masses" and therefore an infinite number of vibration modes.

What are these modes? It is best to consider the movement of air molecules within the pipe. Assume that the pipe is closed at one end and open at the other. A vibration mode is a standing wave, and it will result from the superposition of traveling waves of air molecules that are reflected from the ends (exactly like standing waves in a string). Starting at the closed end of the tube, suppose we push the air molecules together to create a region of higher pressure (termed a *compression*); this region will propagate down the tube until it reaches the open end. Here the compression overshoots and leaves behind a region of lower pressure (termed a *rarefaction*) at the end, which in turn travels back up the tube. At an open end, a compression is reflected as a rarefaction (and vice versa). The net pressure will be zero: the compression is balanced by the rarefaction; it is a node. At a closed end, however, a rarefaction is reflected as a rarefaction, and similarly, a compression is reflected as a compression. The pressure alternates between maximums; it is an antinode. This is easiest to see for a compression; the densely packed air molecules, when spreading out to relieve the higher pressure, bounce back from the closed end, re-forming the compression, and as a result it is the compression that travels back the tube. For a pipe closed at one end and open at the other, it takes four trips along the length to produce one complete sinusoid wave. This movement of the higher and lower pressure regions is diagrammed in figure 2.14. The wavelength is four times the pipelength and the frequency is the speed of sound divided by the wavelength (i.e., four times the pipelength).

The pressure variation is shown in figure 2.15. At the open end there is no net pressure change, since a rarefaction is always balanced by a compression. At the closed end, there is a pressure change over time due to the alternation of high pressure compressions and low pressure rarefactions.

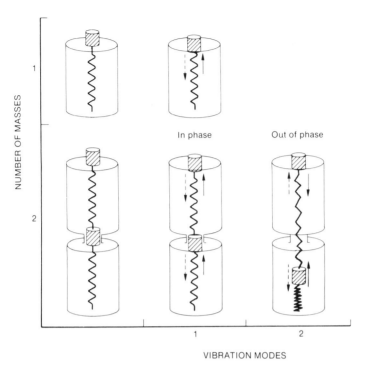

Figure 2.13
The possible vibration modes of an air column are determined by the number of masses of air. With one air mass, the mass can go only up and down. With two air masses, both masses can move up and down together in phase, and in addition can move up and down out of phase. With an infinite number of masses, as would be true for a real air column, there are an infinite number of independent vibration modes (adapted from Benade 1960). The vibration modes of an air column are therefore analogous to the vibration modes of a string.

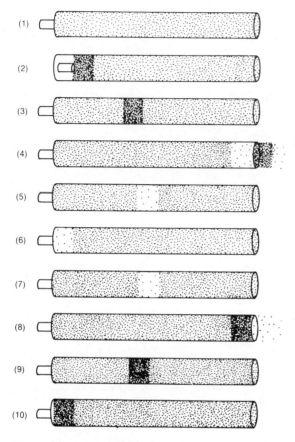

Figure 2.14
Propagation of a pressure wave in a tube open at one end. Inward movement of the piston creates a region of high pressure that travels down the tube (2 and 3). At the open end, the high pressure region overshoots, creating a low pressure region (4). The low pressure region travels back up the pipe (5), where it reflected as a low pressure region at the closed end (6). The low pressure region then travels down the pipe (7) until it overshoots at the open end (8). This creates a high pressure region that travels back up the pipe (9), where it is reflected at the closed end as a high pressure region (10). The movement would then start all over again.

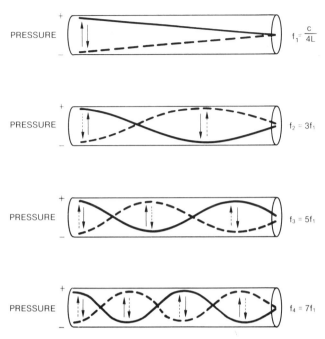

Figure 2.15
The variation in pressure is maximum at the closed end of a pipe and zero at the open end. This means that only odd harmonics can occur.

For any higher vibration mode to occur, there must be zero net pressure variation at the open end and maximum pressure variation at the closed end. This is possible only for odd harmonics. (Even harmonics would require the two ends to have equal pressure variation, which is impossible and thus cannot occur.) For this reason, the possible vibration modes in a tube closed on one end are the odd harmonics of a fundamental frequency whose wavelength is four times the tube length. The frequency of the second vibration mode, f_2, is three times the fundamental frequency, and the frequency of the third vibration mode, f_3, is five times the fundamental frequency. This outcome is true for a *tube* closed on one end. For a *cone* that flares to a tip, all harmonics are possible. Clarinets support only odd harmonics; saxophones, oboes, and bassoons are cones supporting all harmonics. Trumpets, because of their flaring bells, also support all harmonics.

How can we make an instrument out of a tube? The lowest note would be the frequency of the lowest vibration mode. The next possible note without changing the tube would be the next vibration mode (the third harmonic). For the trumpet, the player can "lip" to the higher mode by changing the vibration frequency of the lips. For the clarinet, the reed is floppy and its movement is controlled and dominated by the standing waves in the bore. The higher vibration mode cannot be achieved by lipping alone; the clarinet needs special register holes that degrade the amplitude of the fundamental so that changes in lipping can produce the higher modes. For both instruments, the notes between the mode frequencies are produced by changing the length of the bore. For brasses, extra lengths are added to step down from the higher to lower mode. To play trumpet notes, one shortens the instrument, lips to the higher vibration mode, and lengthens the instrument to play the intermediate notes. For clarinets, finger holes are opened, which effectively shortens the instrument to the length between the mouthpiece and open hole. To play clarinet notes, one lips the lower mode and moves up the scale by opening finger holes to shorten the tube. In summary, each vibration mode of the tube provides for a range of notes, which are achieved by varying the length.

The vocal tract can also be modeled as an open tube, closed at one end by the vocal cords and open at the mouth. But the vocal tract is almost like a rubber tube; the complex shape of the vocal tract changes the vibration mode frequencies so that they are not simply the odd harmonics. Moreover, the vocal tract can change in size and shape and further modify the vibration modes. This flexibility yields the tremendous variety of speech sounds, communicating both information and emotion.

Wooden plates   When a string is excited, the vibratory pattern is the sum of vibration modes. In a similar fashion, when excited, the vibratory pattern of a sound board of a piano or the sound body of a violin (a box composed of the top, bottom, and interconnecting ribs) is the sum of the characteristic vibration modes. The important point, however, is that for a complex structure like the violin, there are no simple integer relationships among the frequencies associated with each mode. Moreover, there are so many modes with nearly overlapping frequencies, particularly at higher frequencies, that there are frequency regions of vibration rather than the discrete frequencies of vibrations found for strings. Nevertheless, each of the characteristic vibration modes of a plate has great similarity to those found for vibrating strings. The two-dimensionality of sound boards merely allows new patterns of vibrations to occur.

To measure the vibration modes of a complex plate, we would excite the plate at a point with a sinusoidal vibrator, vary the frequency of the vibrator, and measure the movement of the plate. The plate will always vibrate at the frequency of the vibrator. (This important point will be discussed in detail below.) The maximum amplitude of movement will occur when the frequency of the driving vibrator equals the frequency of one of the vibration modes of the plate.

We know from our analysis of a vibrating string that for the lowest vibration mode, the entire string moves as a unit. This suggests that the first mode of the plate would also be the in-and-out movement of the entire plate. The second mode of a string consists of two vibration sections that are out of phase, with a node at the center. The points of maximum displacement lie between the center and each end. Since our plate has both length and width, there would be two possible modes—one with the vibration pattern along the length and one with the vibration pattern along the width. The next string mode would have three vibrating sections, and by analogy, a vibrating plate would also have three sections, with modes spaced in thirds. Figure 2.16 shows the first four modes of a guitar plate with clamped edges and demonstrates how these modes exist in a real instrument. The "bull's-eye" pictures show the pattern of movement. Each circular line represents a region of equal movement (much like a contour line on a map) and the inner circles undergo greater back-and-forth movement. The center of the bull's-eye has the maximum movement. The plus and minus signs indicate the relationships among the movement areas. Mode 4 has three regions of movement: the top and bottom region move up and down together, and the middle region is opposite. Clearly there will be many varied vibration modes for a complex plate. This in no way creates problems for us (although it makes an instrument maker's task incredibly difficult). At any point in time, the entire vibration pattern is merely the sum of the vibration of the individual modes. Because of additivity, some vibrations may cancel each other; others will reinforce each other.

Enclosed rooms   Another system in which standing waves occur is an enclosed room or auditorium. The wave produced by an instrument or speaker will reflect off the walls continuously and in the process generate standing waves. These standing waves are in principle no different from those formed on vibrating strings, plates, or air columns. Each standing wave is produced by the superposition of traveling waves moving in opposite directions. In common with all other standing waves, there are positions of high pressure variation (i.e., antinodes) and positions of zero pressure variation (i.e., nodes).

It was noted above that the violin sound body is composed of so many vibration modes at irregular and unpredictable frequencies, because of its complex shape, that it appears to have broad regions of maximum vibration. This is also true for a room. A room possesses many vibration modes, particularly at higher frequencies, though in contrast to a violin the frequencies of these modes can be calculated theoretically. The modes arise from multiple reflections from the walls, floor, and ceiling. There are vibration modes that arise from reflections off two opposite surfaces (two

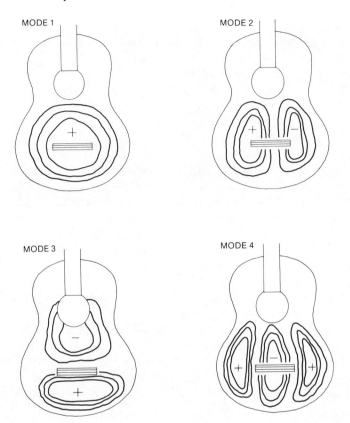

Figure 2.16
The first four vibration modes of the guitar top plate. The vibration modes are analogous to those found for strings and air columns (adapted from Benade 1976).

walls or the ceiling and floor), from reflections off four surfaces, and from reflections off all six surfaces. The frequency of each vibration mode is determined by the effective distance between surfaces. The wavelength of the fundamental standing wave produced by bouncing off two opposed surfaces is twice the distance between the surfaces. For example, if the distance between the two walls is 5 m, the wavelength of the fundamental will be 10 m and the frequency of this vibration mode will be 34 Hz. All the harmonics of this fundamental frequency are also possible, so standing waves of 68 Hz, 102 Hz, 136 Hz, etc., can also arise from reflections between these two same walls. In general, standing waves reflecting off four or six surfaces tend to have shorter wavelengths (i.e., higher fundamental frequencies) and to be weaker than standing waves reflecting off two surfaces. The number of vibration modes within any frequency range increases as the square of the frequency. To provide a more specific example, consider a 3 m × 5 m × 6 m room. There are 3 vibration modes within a 10 Hz band centered around 100 Hz, but there are 286 vibration modes within a 10 Hz band centered around 1000 Hz. Overall, the number of modes increases with the size of the room.

To illustrate the different vibration modes of a room, tones of different frequencies can be played through a speaker and then the vibration amplitude for each frequency can be measured at different points in the room. The amplitude variation is shown as a function of frequency for two positions in one room in figure 2.17. There is a fairly irregular pattern of peaks and depressions. One peak cannot be associated with a single vibration mode, because the vibration modes are too close together in frequency even at these low frequencies. Rather, peaks appear when several vibration modes with the same resonant frequency are simultaneously excited and the amplitudes add. For example, in the 3 m × 5 m × 6 m room, there are two modes with a resonance frequency of 57 Hz: the fundamental across the 3-m dimension and second harmonic across the 6-m dimension. Similarly, minimums appear when simultaneous vibration modes superimpose such that the amplitudes cancel. It is interesting to note that the room response gets more irregular as the room shape gets more symmetrical, because this provides the opportunity for several modes to have the same resonance frequency. It is for this reason that irregularly shaped rooms often have the most accurate sound.

The high points and low points of the sound pressure at one frequency within a room also are determined by the superposition of the amplitudes of standing waves associated with each vibration mode. At one position in a room, the standing waves generated by one frequency might cancel each other, but at a different position the identical standing waves might combine positively. Both of these outcomes occur. Figure 2.17 illustrates

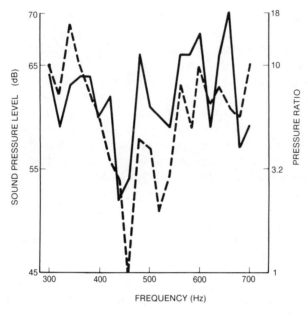

Figure 2.17
The pressure variation at two positions in my living room. One position is represented by the solid line and the second position is represented by the dashed line. At several frequencies, the sound pressure between the two positions differs by 9 dB (pressure ratio = 2.8).

that the sound pressure at one frequency can be very different at two different positions. As the frequency is changed, it is impossible to predict the amplitude at one room position on the basis of the amplitude at another position.

To summarize, a room has a set of possible vibration modes and standing waves that is determined by its size and shape. At lower frequencies there are fewer modes; at each frequency there will be positions of high amplitude and positions of low amplitude. At higher frequencies, there are many overlapping vibration modes; at these frequencies the amplitude will be essentially constant throughout the room.

Clearly, there are similarities in the vibration modes across diverse components and objects. This outcome is the result of the commonality of an elastic medium that brings about harmonic motion. Each of the vibration modes has a natural frequency, and that mode can be maximally stimulated by energy at that same frequency. Each of the vibration modes is independent and can be initiated separately. However, the method of stimulation, the connection between the vibrator and the object, and the position of excitation all effect the time-varying amplitude of vibration. This will be discussed below.

Coupling: The Initiation of Vibration
The degree to which one vibration system can drive another system into vibration depends on two factors: (1) the match between the driving frequencies and the frequencies of the vibration modes of the second system; and (2) the strength of the connection or coupling between the two systems.

Frequency match   The first factor is the match between the driving frequencies and the vibration mode frequencies. Imagine a mass attached to two springs. Suppose the natural frequency of the first vibrating mode of the mass/spring system is 60 Hz. Next, we begin to apply a sinusoidal vibration to one spring. If we apply a 30 Hz motion and continue until the mass settles into a periodic motion, there will be very little vibration. The driving frequency is too different from the natural frequency of the first mode to excite that mode. It is very important to realize that the mass will vibrate at the driving frequency of 30 Hz, even though the natural frequency is 60 Hz. At a driving frequency of 50 Hz, the amplitude of the vibration will be greater; again, the frequency of vibration will be at the driving frequency of 50 Hz. If we set the driving frequency to 60 Hz, the amplitude will be maximum, because that is the natural frequency. The pushes and pulls imposed by the driving vibrator will reinforce the movement of the spring/mass. The forces will be in phase with the movement. A representation of each vibration is shown in figure 2.18. If we increase the frequency of the vibrator beyond 60 Hz, the amplitude of movement will begin to decrease. The plot of vibration amplitude against frequency is termed a *resonance* curve, and the frequency at which the driving vibrator produces the maximum amplitude of movement is termed the *resonant* frequency. It is the natural frequency of a vibration mode. A compelling example of coupling and resonance occurs when a singer cracks a glass. The glass has a resonant frequency at which the vibration is maximum. The singer can discover the resonant frequency by tapping the glass. The tap is analogous to a short click that has energy across a wide range of frequencies (see figure 2.7). The glass will vibrate in response to energy at its resonant frequency. The sound of the tap gives away the resonant frequency. If the singer matches that frequency, then the air pressure wave will set the glass into vibration. If the pressure wave is intense enough, the vibration of the glass will increase to the point that it will shatter.

Now imagine a three-mass string such that the resonant frequencies of the first three modes are 60 Hz, 120 Hz, and 180 Hz. If we again use a single vibrator, then at a driving frequency of 60 Hz the string vibration

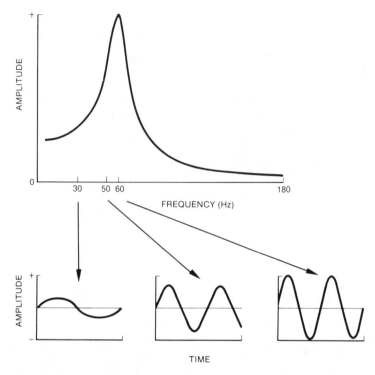

Figure 2.18
The resonance curve for one vibration mode. The vibration is pictured at driving frequencies of 30 Hz, 50 Hz, and 60 Hz. At every driving frequency, the vibration frequency is at the driving frequency. At the resonant frequency of the mode (60 Hz), the vibration amplitude is maximum.

will be that of the first mode, with all three masses moving up and down together. When the driving frequency is 90 Hz, things get more com-·plicated. The driving frequency will initiate vibration of both the first (60 Hz) and second (120 Hz) modes. The initiation of the first mode will lead to all the masses moving up and down together at 90 Hz, and the initiation of the second mode will lead to the first and third mass moving by each other at 90 Hz. The two vibrations will sum together to produce a complex pattern. (Neither vibration mode will have a large amplitude; the driving frequency is too distant from the resonant frequency of either mode.) If the driving frequency is 120 Hz, then the second vibration mode will dominate the pattern: the first vibration mode will disappear and the second vibration mode will increase to maximum amplitude. If the driving frequency is 150 Hz, both the second (120 Hz) and third (180 Hz) vibration modes will be excited (at 150 Hz). The degree to which any mode is excited depends on the match between the driving frequency and the natural frequency of the mode as well as on the strength of the coupling, which will be discussed below. Now imagine that the driving vibration is composed of two harmonics of equal amplitudes at 90 Hz and 150 Hz. Each component of the vibrator can excite each of the vibration modes of the mass/string system. The 90 Hz vibration will excite the 60 Hz and 120 Hz modes, and the 150 Hz vibration will excite the 120 Hz and 180 Hz modes (at 150 Hz).

The important concept is that as a vibration pattern is transferred from one object to another, the frequencies of the vibrations do not change. However, because of the match between frequencies of the driving vibrator and the resonant frequencies of vibration modes of the "driven" object, the amplitude of each vibration will change. A high amplitude harmonic in the driving vibration may be diminished if it is not close to the resonant frequency of any vibration mode, and conversely a weak harmonic may be enhanced if it matches a resonant frequency. The frequencies do not change, only the amplitudes.

Coupling and damping   The second factor is the connection or coupling between the driving vibrator and the driven vibration. In the previous examples, the driving vibrator was connected to the mass by a spring, so that a mass could move somewhat independently of the vibrator. The vibrator and mass are *loosely* coupled. For a loosely coupled system, the amplitude of the second system (the driven system) is maximum at the resonant frequency and decreases dramatically at other frequencies. The driven system "wants" to vibrate at its resonant frequency, and the loosely coupled driving vibrator can bring about a large amplitude vibration only at that resonant frequency. Now imagine a different physical system, in which the mass is more rigidly connected to the vibrator by a stiff link (e.g., a rod). Here the vibrator and mass are *tightly* coupled. If the driving vibrator and mass (or driven vibration) are tightly coupled, then the pattern of the driving vibration will dominate the vibration of the mass. Because of the tight coupling, the mass must follow the movement of the vibrator very closely. The amplitude of vibration is nearly identical to the vibrator movement and thus remains at nearly the same level for all frequencies. Examples of resonance curves for loosely and tightly coupled systems are shown in figure 2.19. The term *quality factor* (Q) is used to describe the degree of coupling; a high Q indicates a loosely coupled system, a low Q indicates a tightly coupled system.

A second important aspect of coupling is how quickly the driven vibrator reaches its maximum amplitude after the driving vibration is imposed (i.e., the attack time), and how quickly the driven vibrator stops vibrating after the driving vibration stops (i.e., the decay time). When a driving vibrator is applied to an object, the object attempts to vibrate at its

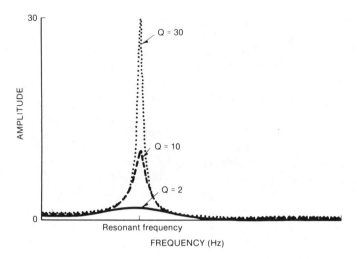

Figure 2.19
The resonance curve for different degrees of coupling. As the coupling becomes tighter (Q decreases), the vibration amplitude becomes more uniform across frequencies.

resonant frequency. On the one hand, if the two are tightly coupled, the vibrator quickly comes to control the frequency of vibration of the object and makes it equal to the vibrator frequency. The natural frequency quickly dies away, and the maximum amplitude is attained rapidly. On the other hand, if the system is loosely coupled, it takes time for the driving frequency to control the object, the natural frequency dies away slowly, and the maximum amplitude is attained slowly. The initial motion is irregular until the driving frequency gains control. When the driving vibrator stops, the object attempts to shift its vibration frequency to the resonant frequency. On the one hand, if the driving vibrator and object are tightly coupled, the object loses vibration energy rapidly because it cannot vibrate independently of the (now stopped) driving vibration. On the other hand, if the system is loosely coupled, the object loses vibration energy slowly because it can vibrate somewhat independently of the driving vibration. In sum, loose coupling (high Q) indicates slow growth and decay; tight coupling (low Q) indicates rapid growth and decay.

To examine some concrete numbers, consider any tone. For decay, if $Q = 3$, then in 1 cycle the amplitude will fall to 36% (of maximum) and in 2 cycles the amplitude will fall to 13%; if $Q = 30$, then in 10 cycles the amplitude will fall to 36% and in 20 cycles the amplitude will fall to 13%. For attack, if $Q = 3$, then in 1 cycle the amplitude will increase to 63% (of maximum) and in 2 cycles the amplitude will increase to 87%; if $Q = 30$ then in 10 cycles the amplitude will increase to 63% and in 20 cycles the amplitude will increase to 87%. Notice that the attack and decay are inverses.

The Q factor is also a measure of the damping. *Damping* simply refers to the resistance, mainly due to friction, that causes the vibration to decay with time. Thus when a mode is heavily damped and tightly coupled (low Q), there is a great amount of resistance; the vibration grows and decays rapidly, and maximum amplitude is relatively constant across frequency. A highly damped system dissipates energy quickly. When a mode is lightly damped and loosely coupled (high Q), there is little resistance; the vibration grows and decays quite slowly, and maximum amplitude occurs at the resonant frequency. Energy is both taken up and given off slowly.

To provide a concrete example for these ideas, imagine that you are pushing someone on a swing. In one case, you are connected to the swing with a very stiff spring, almost a solid rod (tight coupling, heavy damping). In the second case, you are connected with a loose flexible spring (loose coupling, light damping). You move the swing by pushing and pulling on the spring. I think it is easy to see that with the stiff spring, on the one hand, you can readily control the swing. It will move almost in synchrony with your arm movement: it will start when you start and stop when you stop. However, the height of the swing is basically limited by the length of your arm movement and will remain at nearly the same height whether you move your arm at slow or fast frequencies. On the other hand, with the loose spring it will take some time to get the swing moving, and similarly, it will take some time for the swing to stop if you hold your arm steady. But, with the looser spring, if you move your arm at the resonant frequency of the swing, that swing will reach a great height. A heavily damped system sacrifices amplitude of response for speed of response, and a lightly damped system sacrifices speed for amplitude.

One final point: the attack and decay processes are complementary in time. When a driving vibrator is coupled to a driven sound body, the driven sound body attempts to vibrate at its resonant frequency. If the driving frequency matches the resonant frequency, then the sound body vibration mode will build up very smoothly. If the driving frequency does not match the resonant frequency, two things happen simultaneously: (1) the initial vibration of the sound body at its resonant frequency will be damped out (or suppressed), and (2) the vibration of the sound body at the driving frequency will build up. It is as if the energy at the resonant frequency is being shifted to energy at the driving frequency. In this case, the initial pattern will be very irregular because of the two interacting vibrations, and only gradually will the sound body vibration perfectly match that of the driving vibrator. In both cases, the onset interval and ultimate amplitude will depend on the coupling between the driving vibrator and sound body. When the driving vibration ceases, the decay process will be complementary. If the driving vibration was at the resonant frequency, then the decay will be smooth. If the driving vibration was not at the resonant frequency, then the decay will be erratic, because the sound body vibration will change from the driving frequency to its resonant frequency. It is as if the energy at the driving frequency is being shifted to the resonant frequency. In the process, the driving frequency and resonant frequency will occur simultaneously and will therefore interact to produce interference (i.e., beats). Onset and decay are complementary: the processes that occur during the onset portion match those that occur during the decay portion. The very same processes occur in all coupled vibrations— when a sound body is driven by a string or when a room is driven by a human or stereo speaker.

We can see how these tradeoffs occur when comparing a high-fidelity speaker to a violin to a voice. What characteristics should a speaker have? The response should be "flat" across frequencies, and the speaker should start and stop vibrating very quickly to follow any signal. These characteristics occur with a low Q, which implies that the speaker should be heavily damped and tightly coupled. The Q's are about 0.7. The disadvantage is the low amplitude of movement (and thus sound) of the speaker; a high-powered amplifier can compensate for this defect. In contrast, consider a violin. Here one wants volume, plus a persisting rich tone consisting of many harmonics. These characteristics would occur with a high Q, an undamped system. In fact, the Q's in a violin tend to be between 30 and 50. The disadvantage here is that each mode shows a markedly higher response at the resonant frequency. With only one or two vibration modes, the notes of the scale would be of very different loudnesses. In the violin body, though, there are many modes with adjacent frequency peaks. This smooths out the amplitude response of the violin across its frequency range. Thus the requirements for a good speaker (heavy damping) and a good violin (light damping) are almost opposite. A voice represents an intermediate case. We need to speak rather quickly to communicate efficiently. Typical speaking rates are on the order of 160 words per minute, or 5 syllables per second. This would suggest a low Q, damped system. However, the voice must be loud, which would suggest a high Q, undamped system. The Q of human voices is about 10, an in-between value in face of conflicting requirements. (This value also reflects the properties of the damp throat and mouth tissue.)

It should now be clear that the degree to which the energy can be transferred to a sound body depends on how easy it is to induce the sound body to vibrate at the frequency of the "driving" vibrator. The two basic factors are the coupling (or damping) of the sound body and the frequency match between the driving vibration and the resonance frequency of vibration modes of the sound body. It remains to discuss two of the complications.

The first complication occurs because the driving vibration is typically composed of fundamental and harmonic frequencies. Thus a complicated vibration pattern is being imposed on a sound body vibrator with an intricate pattern of vibration modes. Each driving harmonic has the potential to initiate each and every vibration mode. As described previously, additivity and superposition come to the rescue. The complex driving vibratory pattern can be conceptualized as being built up of sinusoidal vibrations. Each of these simple vibrations can excite every vibration mode (although at different amplitudes). The overall sound body vibration becomes the sum of all the effects from each harmonic. The overall motion of the object will be very complex, but it is always decomposable into the characteristic vibration modes. Because of this summation, at certain frequencies and positions the vibrations resulting from each mode reinforce each other, and at other frequencies and positions the vibrations cancel each other. Reinforcement and interference even may occur at different regions at the same frequency.

The second complication occurs due to the temporal pattern of the driving/driven vibration interaction. There are two aspects: (a) each harmonic of the driving vibration may have a different pattern of growth and decay; and (b) each vibratory mode of the sound body has a different rate at which a vibratory mode builds up and decays, because of the coupling (Q). Thus the attack and decay timing of any vibration mode will be due to the joint action of the two time functions. Consider a realistic driving vibration like a violin string. If the string is bowed, the higher harmonics are initiated first, with the fundamental beginning later. It takes a while for the bowing process to become firmly established. But this does not necessarily mean that the higher frequency vibration modes of the violin sound body begin first. The higher frequency vibration modes will begin first only if those modes are tightly coupled. In that case, the high frequency bowing vibration can be rapidly transformed into sound body vibration. If the lower frequency modes are tightly coupled, however, then those modes may begin first even though the lower frequency string vibrations are delayed. In addition to all this, the vibration modes of both the driving and driven vibrations may influence each other; the transfer of energy is interactive. The pattern of the driven vibration modes may feed back to the driving vibration.

To summarize, the two sections concerned with sound production have covered: (1) the concept of vibration modes, the ways in which strings, air columns, plate, and rooms undergo harmonic motion; and (2) the concept of coupling, the process by which a vibration pattern is transferred from one object to another object, for example, from a string to a wooden plate.

The important concept is that the vibration modes of the driven object (the wooden plate) act to change the relative amplitudes and timings of the driving vibrations.

An overarching way to think of sound production in all domains has been termed the source-filter model. The model captures the essential idea that the initial step is the excitation of the source, a vibrating element. The source then transfers its vibration energy to a different vibrating element, which radiates the energy into the air, where it is heard as a sound. This second element acts to modify the original vibration pattern due to the degree of coupling and the resonant frequencies of its vibration modes. The second vibrator thus filters the original vibration and changes the relative amplitudes of the original vibration pattern. For a violin, the source is the vibration pattern on the string and the filter is the wooden body. For a trumpet, the source is the air vibration pattern coming through the player's lips, and the filter is the tubing of the metal body. For speech, the source is the air vibration pattern coming through the vocal cords, and the filter is the vocal tract (throat, mouth, tongue, lips, etc.). For a bouncing ball, the source is the vibration caused by the ball's impact with the floor (the impact is like a click, so the vibration source is a continuous range of frequencies; see figure 2.7) and the filter is (the vibration modes of) the ball (and floor). For an auditorium, the source is any vibration created by an instrument or voice, and the filter is (the vibration modes of) the room.

An Example: A Violin

To clarify these ideas, we will work through a specific example based on the violin. To review:

1. The first step is the application of energy to initiate the string vibration. The way the string is set into vibration determines the strength and temporal onset of each harmonic.

2. The energy of each string harmonic is then transferred to the sound body. The sound body has many distinct vibration modes, and each string harmonic has the potential for energizing one or more vibration modes. The characteristics of each vibration mode (resonant frequency, Q) determine whether a string harmonic can excite that mode and the rate of growth, final amplitude, and rate of decay.

3. The movement of the sound body imparts a complex pattern of compressions and rarefactions to the surrounding air molecules, and this is propagated outward.

Although I have portrayed these processes as one following the other, a more realistic view would be of overlapping processes. The properties of the sound body can work "backward," making it easier or harder to bring forth a note. The coupling between the string and the sound body acts from the string toward the sound body, but it also acts from the sound body onto the string. It is these highly interactive, overlapping processes that have made the violin (as well as other instruments, for the violin is not unique in its complexity) so difficult to study.

Steady-state sounds: harmonics and formants   The steady-state tone is a function of the amplitude of the harmonics of the vibrating string and the amplitude of the sound body vibration modes. To calculate the amplitude of the sound at any frequency, multiply the amplitude of the string harmonic by the amplitude(s) of the vibration mode(s) at that frequency. For striking or bowing a string, the amplitude of each higher harmonic of the driving string decreases by a factor of $1/n$. Thus, the second harmonic is $1/2$ the fundamental, the third harmonic is $1/3$ the fundamental, and so on. Moreover, we will suppose that the violin sound body has three identical main vibration modes, one at about 300 Hz, the next one at about 420 Hz, and the highest at 700 Hz. Assume that each mode has the same damping, so that the resonance curves are identical. To simplify the arithmetic, the resonance curves have been squared off. The width of each mode is 50 Hz and the amplitude is 3. Between the vibration modes, the sound body vibration is small and constant (equal to $1/2$). This is illustrated in figure 2.20.

Imagine that the lowest string (G_3) is excited. This string is tuned to a fundamental frequency of 196 Hz. Assume that the first four harmonics are produced: 196, 392, 588, 784 (shown in figure 2.20). Comparing the vibration frequencies of the string to the resonant frequencies of the vibration modes, only the second harmonic falls within the frequency range of a vibration mode. We can then work out the frequency spectrum by multiplying the string energy of the harmonic by the amplitude of the vibration mode, using the $1/n$ factor for each string harmonic, as shown in table 2.2.

The next whole note would be A_3 at 220 Hz. The calculations would yield the figures shown in table 2.3. Skipping to the whole note C_4 at 262 Hz would yield the calculations in table 2.4. All the harmonics fall between the strong vibration modes (see figure 2.20) so that the amplitude of each harmonic and ultimately the loudness of the note are severely reduced.

Now consider the calculations for A_4—440 Hz—shown in table 2.5. The frequency spectrum differs from note to note as a result of the amplitudes of the harmonics of the vibrating string and the amplitudes and frequencies of the sound body resonances. Two notes, A_3 and A_4, an octave apart (a frequency ratio of 2 to 1), are closely related, and yet the spectra are quite different, as shown in table 2.6. For this reason, an instrument cannot be characterized by its frequency spectrum alone.

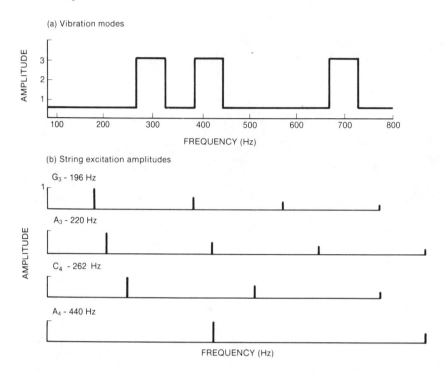

Figure 2.20
The vibration modes and string excitations determine the sound output. In (a) the
amplitudes and resonant frequencies for vibration modes are pictured for a hypothetical
violin. In (b) the string excitation amplitudes are indicated for four notes, assuming a $1/n$
bowing factor.

Table 2.2
Calculation of Frequency Spectrum for G_3

Harmonic (Frequency)		Factor	×	Resonance	=	Amplitude
1	(196 Hz)	1	×	1/2	=	1/2
2	(392 Hz)	1/2	×	3	=	3/2
3	(588 Hz)	1/3	×	1/2	=	1/6
4	(784 Hz)	1/4	×	1/2	=	1/8
TOTAL						2.29

Table 2.3
Calculation of Frequency Spectrum for A_3

Harmonic (Frequency)		Factor	×	Resonance	=	Amplitude
1	(220 Hz)	1	×	1/2	=	1/2
2	(440 Hz)	1/2	×	3	=	3/2
3	(660 Hz)	1/3	×	1/2	=	1/6
4	(880 Hz)	1/4	×	1/2	=	1/8
TOTAL						2.29

Table 2.4
Calculation of Frequency Spectrum for C_4

Harmonic (Frequency)		Factor	×	Resonance	=	Amplitude
1	(262 Hz)	1	×	1/2	=	1/2
2	(524 Hz)	1/2	×	1/2	=	1/4
3	(786 Hz)	1/3	×	1/2	=	1/6
4	(1048 Hz)	1/4	×	1/2	=	1/8
TOTAL						1.04

Table 2.5
Calculation of Frequency Spectrum for A_4

Harmonic (Frequency)		Factor	×	Resonance	=	Amplitude
1	(440 Hz)	1	×	3	=	3
2	(880 Hz)	1/2	×	1/2	=	1/4
3	(1320 Hz)	1/3	×	1/2	=	1/6
4	(1760 Hz)	1/4	×	1/2	=	1/8
TOTAL						3.54

Table 2.6
Comparison of the Amplitudes of the First Four Harmonics of Two Notes Separated by an Octave

Note (Frequency)	Harmonic			
	1	2	3	4
A_3 (220 Hz)	1/2	3/2	1/8	1/8
A_4 (440 Hz)	3	1/4	1/6	1/8

At this point, it is possible to get a better picture of the concept of a *formant*. A formant is a frequency region of high amplitude and is due to the resonances of one or more vibration modes within a frequency range. The formant will enhance any driving vibration lying within that region; it will enhance either the fundamental or any harmonic that falls within this interval. For example, if the formant is between 800 Hz and 900 Hz, it will enhance the eighth harmonic of tones from 100 Hz to 112 Hz, the seventh harmonic of tones from 114 Hz to 129 Hz, the sixth harmonic of tones from 133 Hz to 150 Hz, and so on down to the second harmonic of tones from 400 Hz to 450 Hz and the fundamental of tones from 800 Hz to 900 Hz. Thus any note that falls within 100–112 Hz, 114–129 Hz, 133–150 Hz, 160–180 Hz, 200–225 Hz, 266–300 Hz, 400–450 Hz, or 800–900 Hz will yield an amplitude peak between 800 Hz and 900 Hz. The place of maximum amplitude (the formant frequency) therefore is relatively independent of the driving frequency. For this reason, it may be possible to characterize instruments and speech sounds (e.g., vowels) by formant frequencies, because these frequencies are independent of the fundamental note frequency and of the speaker's vocal cord frequency (see chapter 5).

Attack and decay transients   The above work illustrates the general principles underlying steady-state sounds: selective amplification of the driving harmonics by the sound body vibration modes. It seems much harder to discover general principles underlying the characteristics of the attack and decay transients of a sound, unfortunately, because of the coupling of the many driving string harmonics, each with their own attack/decay timing to the multiple sound body vibration modes. The complications occur because after a string is excited, the amplitude of each harmonic increases at a different rate, so that at every instant each harmonic is transferring a changing level of energy to the sound body. The sound body is therefore vibrating as a function both of the changing string energy and of its ability to absorb this energy because of the coupling between the string and sound body.

Here is a rough analogy. Imagine that you turn on a space heater. The heater slowly heats up to its maximum output. As it is heating up, it is transferring a changing level of heat to the air and the air is similarly transferring a changing level of heat to your cold body. However, there is a lag. The rate at which you warm up is a function both of how fast the heater warms up (the driving vibration) and of the coupling between you and the heater (whether you are close or far away; whether you are wearing heavy clothes).

In the following example, we will make these simplifying assumptions:

1. The fundamental frequency of the vibrating string is 200 Hz, generating harmonics of 200 Hz, 400 Hz, and 600 Hz. The string is bowed so that the $1/n$ bowing factor will determine the maximum amplitude.

2. Most probably, each string harmonic "starts" at different times and grows to its maximum amplitude, moreover, over different lengths of time. The higher harmonics require less energy to activate, so they begin first. (Even before this stable oscillation emerges, there is high frequency noise caused by scraping the bow on the strings.) We will make a simplification and assume that although each harmonic starts at a different time, each harmonic reaches its maximum amplitude all at once. Assume that the highest string harmonic (600 Hz, third harmonic) begins at time $(t) = 10$ msec after bowing starts and that each successive lower harmonic begins 10 msec later: $t(400\ \text{Hz}) = 20$ msec and $t(200\ \text{Hz}) = 30$ msec.

3. As for the decay transient, the most realistic model for the decay of a string would be that after bowing stops, each harmonic decays at a different rate. Measurements indicate that the fundamental decays in about 500 msec, and the higher harmonics decay in less than 100 msec. The decay is probably exponential; in each time period the amplitude probably falls by a constant fraction. We will make the simplifying assumption that after bowing ceases, each harmonic stays at its original value until a certain time and then it decays to zero instantaneously. On the basis of the above data we will assume that the first harmonic (200 Hz) decays 500 msec after bowing ceases, the second harmonic (400 Hz) decays 300 msec after bowing ceases, and the third harmonic (600 Hz) decays 100 msec after bowing ceases. The time pattern of the string is shown in figure 2.21, panel (a).

4. Assume there are three vibration modes in the violin body. The first mode has a resonance at 200 Hz with a Q of 20; the second mode has a resonance at 400 Hz with a Q of 30; the third mode has a resonance at 600 Hz with a Q of 10. A representation of these vibration modes is shown in panel (b). There the attack and decay in amplitude is shown at the resonant frequency as a function of time. The differences in attack and decay time are due to differences in damping and differences in resonant frequency.

The vibration of the sound body is shown in panel (c). The amplitudes are determined by both the string harmonics and the sound body vibration modes. The ultimate amplitude is Q multiplied by the bowing factor. The onset of each body vibration mode is determined by the string vibration onset. The rate at which the amplitude increases is determined by Q, the measure of the coupling. The

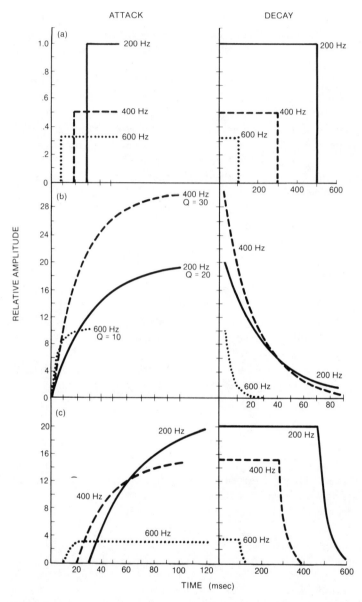

Figure 2.21
The attack and decay transients are a function of the string excitation and the coupling between the string and sound body. In (a), the excitation—attack and decay timing plus amplitude—for each harmonic of the string is displayed. In (b), the attack and decay timing plus amplitude for each sound body vibration mode is displayed. In (c), the resulting attack and decay of each sound body vibration mode is illustrated. It is this pattern that best represents the vibration of the violin.

decay begins when each string harmonic ceases, and the rate of decay is determined by Q. We are assuming that each harmonic drives only the body mode equal in frequency. In general, each harmonic can affect each of the body modes, and this determines the actual transients.

What can be seen, even in this simplified model, is that the attack is characterized by the initial growth of weaker higher harmonics. The growth of the fundamental is slower, but it does ultimately reach the greatest amplitude. During the decay, the higher harmonics fade away quickly; the later part of the tone is relatively pure, consisting only of the fundamental. Two real-life examples of violin notes are shown in figure 2.22. The first (a) comes from older research, and the attack transients quite clearly correspond to this simplified model of initial growth of the higher harmonics combined with slower growth of the fundamental. The second (b) uses computer analysis. The picture here is somewhat different. The onset of the harmonics is roughly simultaneous; the fourth harmonic, however, begins with a sharp peak or spike that then undergoes a more gradual increase and subsequent decrease in amplitude. In addition, the fourth and fifth harmonics reach the maximum amplitude, not the fundamental. (The third harmonic is very weak.) The decay of the harmonics follows the predictions closely: the lower harmonics decay far more slowly than the higher harmonics. There are erratic changes in both frequency and amplitude for each harmonic (which are not shown in the simplified figure); whether these modulations have perceptual consequences will be discussed in chapter 8. The differences between the instruments should not be surprising. The interplay between the strings and sound body generates unique attack and decay transients for any instrument. Each string vibration will tap into a different set of vibration modes and therefore yield a unique pattern of vibration.

2.3 The Radiation of Sound

The vibration of the sound body leads to the propagation of sound. The vibration of a wooden plate or a taut drumhead acts to create regions of higher and lower air pressure that propagate outward. By the same token, the regions of higher and lower pressure within a clarinet or trumpet tube, or within the vocal tract, escape out of the opening and create pressure waves that propagate outward. With complicated shapes, each vibration mode may have a different pattern of spatial propagation. The vibration pattern reaching the listener may thus differ from the vibration pattern in the sound body. The radiation process acts like a filter, changing the amplitudes of the harmonics.

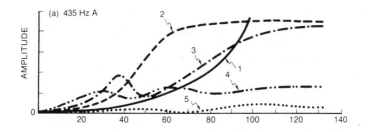

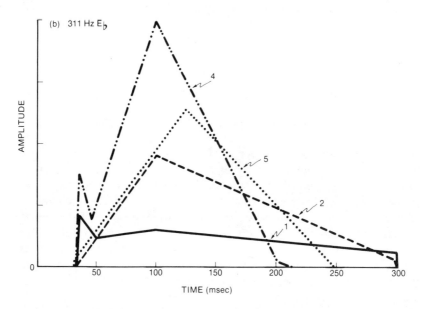

TIME (msec)

Figure 2.22
The growth and decay of each harmonic for a real violin tone undergo a different temporal
pattern. Moreover, different violins may have different temporal patterns for each harmonic.
Each harmonic is labeled by number (a is adapted from Winckel [1960] 1967; b is adapted
from Moorer and Grey 1977a).

This filter effect is particularly striking when sound is propagated from a vibrating air column. The shape of the tubing and the difference in air pressure between the tube and the surrounding atmosphere act to allow certain frequencies to be propagated more easily. The mechanism for sound radiation in the trumpet is by sound waves leaking out of the bell; the mechanism in the clarinet is by sound waves leaking out of the open finger holes. Both the bell and open holes radiate the higher frequencies more efficiently. The bell allows sound waves above a frequency of about 1500 Hz to travel farther out the bell before being reflected back up the bore, so that these waves are able to leak energy out the bell. Similarly, the first one or two open holes of a clarinet act to reflect back the lower frequency waves at that point, while allowing the higher frequency waves to pass down the bore. The higher frequency waves then radiate out of the following open holes, and since there are several of these holes, much of the energy is radiated.

To calculate the amplitude of each harmonic reaching the listener, the strength of the internal harmonic must be multiplied by the percentage of radiation for that harmonic. This percentage increases at higher frequencies, because more energy of the higher frequencies escapes from the instrument. A very simple function would start at 0% radiated at 0 Hz and increase in a straight line to 100% radiated at 1500 Hz. An example of this calculation (harmonic amplitude × percent of radiation) is shown in figure 2.23. The same process occurs when speaking. The higher frequencies are much more efficiently radiated so that the "mouth–air interface" boosts the high frequency content of speech. This boost effectively doubles the sound pressure for each doubling of frequency. Clearly, the relative amplitudes within the instrument or within the vocal tract will not equal those reaching a listener.

In addition to these effects, the vibration modes of the room surround also effect the perceived sound. As stated before, the many vibration modes above 1000 Hz yield a nearly constant radiation of sound and a high frequency boost: the sound pressure doubles for each doubling of frequency. In contrast, at lower frequencies, there are fewer vibration modes so that the amplitude of lower frequency sounds will vary from position to position.

Let me try to put all this in perspective. All of the parts and connections we have discussed to this point are essentially the same. Each part—the source, the sound body, the radiation function, the room surround—can be conceptualized as a set of vibration modes. Each mode has a natural frequency (the resonant frequency). Each connection has a degree of coupling, which determines the shape (flat across frequency or peaked at the resonant frequency) of the resonance curve and the rate at which the vibration increases and decreases. The sound reaching the listener is a

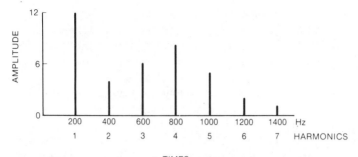

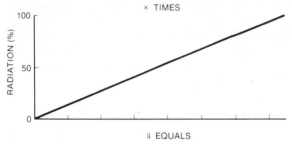

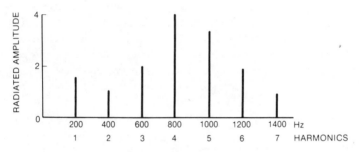

Figure 2.23
The sound radiation reaching the listener can be calculated by multiplying the amplitude of the vibration modes at each frequency within the sound body by the percentage of sound radiation at that frequency. The radiation function can dramatically change the relative amplitudes of the harmonics reaching the listener from that within the sound body.

complex time-varying amplitude pattern, due to the vibration modes and their coupling. This is an overly simplified picture, because we are assuming that each part and connection act independently. This is not actually the case: the components do interact and interfere with each other. Some of these interactions will be discussed in later chapters. To finish this overview, we will consider briefly the ways in which the performer can vary the sound reaching the listener.

2.4 The Performer: Playing and Speaking

To review, the source-filter model conceptualizes sound production as being composed of three overlapping processes: (1) The source is set into vibration by means of external energy—for example, plucking, blowing, or exhaling. (2) The source vibration then is transferred to the sound body, which in turn begins to vibrate. (3) The sound body vibration then sets up air molecule pressure waves that propagate to the listener.

At each step in this chain, the performer can modify the sound to a greater or lesser degree. The performer can change the source vibration (i.e., the relative amplitude of the harmonics) by the force or method used to excite the source; the performer can change the vibration pattern of the sound body by changing its shape physically or by silencing one of the vibration modes; and the performer can change the sound wave reaching the listener by changing the radiation (using a mute), by aiming the instrument, or by choosing a physical position in a room to compensate for standing waves. A complete description of these options is impossible, but the discussion below will highlight some aspects for the violin, trumpet, and speaking.

Violin

There are several ways in which the performer can effect the source vibration. First, the performer can vary the way the string is excited. Consider plucking versus bowing. In general, the maximum amplitude of the n vibration mode (the amplitude of harmonic n) will be $1/n^2$ of the fundamental for plucking and will be $1/n$ of the fundamental for bowing. In other words, the maximum amplitude of the third harmonic for a plucked note will be $1/9$ of the fundamental but will be $1/3$ of the fundamental for bowing. Thus a plucked note will have a weaker harmonic structure than a bowed note.

Second, the amplitudes of the vibration modes can be changed by varying the place on the string that is excited. For any vibration mode, the nodes are stationary and the antinodes undergo maximum displacement. If I excite the string at an antinode (the point of maximum displacement), then that mode will reach its maximum amplitude. Conversely, if I excite the string at a node (the point of zero displacement), then that vibration pattern will not occur; it will be stilled. For a vibration mode to occur, all the stationary points (the nodes) must not move. In general the overall amplitude of the vibration mode is proportional to the relative amplitude of the mode at the point of excitation (e.g., maximum at antinode, zero at node). Following this principle, pianos are constructed so that the hammers strike at one-eighth of the string length (for the lower notes) to still the seventh harmonic, thought to be very dissonant.

Third, the performer can vary the force and position of bowing. When the string is bowed, the string forms a kink shaped like a triangle, which races around the string. The string sticks to the bow until the kink passes under the bow. At that time, the friction decreases and the string slips free. As the bowing continues and the kink passes, the string resticks to the bow and the process is repeated. This has been termed the *slip-stick* process. On the one hand, if the force is maximum, the kink resembles a sharp triangle and the higher harmonics are amplified. On the other hand, if the force is minimum, the kink resembles a rounded triangle and the higher harmonics are softened. Moreover, as the bow is placed closer to the bridge, the required bowing force increases and the kink becomes more sawtooth: the fundamental is degraded and the higher harmonics are further emphasized (termed *sul ponticello* bowing). To achieve a tone rich in the higher harmonics, the violinist should therefore bow near the bridge with maximum force (Schelleng 1973).

The performer can vary the vibration modes of the sound body by the way it is held. The main effect of holding the violin is to decrease the amplitude of the vibration modes (and to decrease Q, suggesting heavier damping). The amplitude may be decreased by 50%. Although there have been no experiments comparing different holding positions, it seems probable that different positions can change the relative amplitudes of the vibration modes.

Trumpet
The vibration source for a trumpet comes from the lip oscillations of the player. In rough outline, the pressure in the mouth pushes the lips out. As the lips open, the pressure drops, until the tension of the lips closes them. The cycle then repeats. The lip oscillation creates alternate regions of high and low pressure, an air-column vibration. The pressure waves are reflected from the end of the flare and tend to act to strengthen the lip oscillation. The trumpeter, by varying the blowing pressure, can vary the strength of the higher harmonics in much the same way that the violinist can vary the strength of the higher harmonics by varying the bowing force. At low blowing pressures, the lip movement produces a smooth, sinusoidal flow; at higher blowing pressures the flow is more abrupt, resembling a triangu-

lar or sawtooth wave. The triangular or sawtooth pressure wave contains stronger, higher harmonics and therefore leads to a brighter, more piercing tone.

The trumpet player can also make use of the radiation properties to change the perceived sound. As discussed in section 2.3, the radiation of sound out of the complex trumpet tube is not identical for all frequencies. Typically, lower frequency harmonics are radiated in all directions equally; the higher frequency harmonics tend to be beamed out the end of the instrument. Thus the player can vary the sound by moving the instrument from directly toward the listener to offset from the listener. The sound will change because the higher harmonics will be relatively lower in amplitude. The performer can also change the radiation properties by placing a mute in the bell. Overall, the mute tends to reduce the radiation of the lower harmonics, and in addition, by virtue of their physical construction, some mutes possess resonances. This can yield a "wah-wah" sound.

Speaking and Singing
We have seen how the performer can affect the source vibration for violins and trumpets. In both cases, the harmonic content changes at different intensities, and in particular the higher harmonics increases more rapidly at higher intensities. The same effect is true for speaking. As the pressure from the lungs is increased, or as the speaker changes the percentage of time the vocal cords remain open, the percentage of higher harmonics increases. Shouting is more piercing (i.e., greater high frequencies) than speaking. At the other extreme, when whispering, the vocal cords never really vibrate; the source vibration resembles white noise, possessing equal pressure at all frequencies.

What distinguishes speaking, however, is the ability to vary the resonance properties of the vocal tract. One interesting case is termed the singer's formant. The sound output of an orchestra tends to decrease at frequencies above 1000 Hz. In order to be heard above the orchestra, male singers modify their vocal tract to produce a vibration mode around 2500 Hz (the singer's formant). This vibration mode, being higher in frequency, allows the singer to be heard despite the orchestra. The singer can also vary the shape of the mouth opening to vary the radiation characteristics (Sundberg 1982).

2.5 The Psychophysics of Audition

The previous sections described some of the processes involved in the production of sound. The goal of the present section is to describe some of the relationships between the physical intensities of frequency and pressure and the psychological magnitudes of pitch and loudness.

Sensitivity of the Ear

Human senses are remarkably sensitive. For instance, it appears that only one unit of light energy—a quantum—is necessary to stimulate a retinal cell. What about audition? It is true that the ear can detect movements of the eardrum about a hundred times smaller than the diameter of a hydrogen molecule, but how close is this to the maximum possible sensitivity? Moreover, what is the sensitivity to change? How much must a tone be increased or decreased in amplitude or frequency in order to hear a difference? It seems easy to imagine how to conduct these experiments. Present softer and softer tones until the subject can no longer hear the sounds (or present louder and louder sounds until the subject can just hear the sound). But there are many other factors to consider. What frequency should be used? What should be the duration? What should be the separation between successive stimuli? And so on.

We can begin by considering the effect of frequency on the minimum sound pressure for perception. The minimum sound pressure as a function of frequency is graphed in figure 2.24. The sensitivity is plotted in decibels with respect to the reference pressure of 0.0002 dyne/cm^2. This figure shows that there is a difference of 70 dB (a ratio of 3000 to 1) in sensitivity

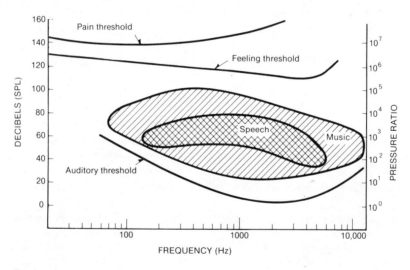

Figure 2.24
Frequency-intensity regions for auditory experience. The auditory threshold represents the minimum intensity at which each frequency is just perceptible (i.e., which is perceived on 50% of the presentations). The feeling and pain thresholds represent the minimum intensity-frequency combinations that result in the perception of feeling the sound and the perception of pain. The typical frequency and intensity regions for music and speech fall between the auditory threshold and the feeling threshold.

between low frequencies and the region of maximum sensitivity between 2000 Hz and 5000 Hz. Also included are graphs of feeling and pain pressures as well as the usual frequency and intensity for sounds of speech and music. Note the fantastic range of the ear: from threshold to pain is about 150 dB (a ratio of 30 million to 1). The frequency range for tonal hearing is usually placed between 20 Hz and 15,000 Hz. Below 20 Hz, the sound no longer has a continuous tonal quality; we do hear sounds below 20 Hz, but they resemble a series of independent thumps. Above 15,000 Hz the tones are very high pitched and most adults cannot hear them (although dogs can).

It is difficult to assess how good this sensitivity is. To hear, one must detect the sound above the noise generated by the random movement of the air molecules themselves. An analysis by Green (1976) suggests that the ear has inertia and that it thus really does not achieve the maximum possible sensitivity. Let me suggest an analogy. We all know from sad experience that it is harder to get a stalled car rolling than to keep it rolling. The difference in force is the inertia of the car. In the ear, it takes more pressure to hear a signal above threshold noise (like starting the car rolling) than pressure to hear a signal above normal listening levels (like keeping the car rolling). The ear is a mechanical system, and the friction must be overcome. Other animals, such as the cat, are more sensitive than humans and may be limited by the movement of the air molecules themselves.

Although the absolute sensitivity of the ear may not compare to that of the eye, it is worthwhile to compare the relative speeds with which the two senses attain their maximum sensitivity. The eye takes more than 30 minutes in darkness before it attains its maximum sensitivity; in contrast, the ear reaches close to its maximum in 0.1 second. As Green (1976) states, "This quick recovery, coupled with an enormous dynamic range, makes hearing a very impressive sense modality, even if it cannot hear the molecules dance" (p. 50).

A second component of sensitivity is the ability to distinguish changes in the sound. Extensive experimentation using pure sounds has measured the change in intensity or the change in frequency required before subjects can judge two sounds as being different. With regard to intensity, for normal listening levels and for frequencies between 1000 Hz and 4000 Hz (where much of speech energy is located), the change in amplitude required to detect a difference is roughly 12%. With regard to frequency, at normal listening levels a detectable change in frequency (in Hz) can be as low as 0.5 Hz to 4 Hz for frequencies up to 3000 Hz. Above 6000 Hz, the ability to distinguish between two tones on the basis of frequency becomes very poor. In fact, above 6000 Hz the sense that tones have a musical pitch is rather weak, and this may explain why the musical scale does not go above

4000–5000 Hz. (This loss is probably due to physiological limitations, discussed in chapter 12.)

Psychophysics of Perception
These data measure the sensitivity of the auditory system, but they do not measure the perceived loudness or pitch, the perceptual variables, as a function of the physical intensity and frequency. For example, does a tone of 500 Hz appear five times higher in pitch than a tone of 100 Hz? This is the province of psychophysics, the relationship between physical values and perceptual magnitudes.

Intensity and loudness   Starting with intensity, we can identify two issues. First, is it possible to judge whether two sounds of different frequency are of equal loudness? Second, is it possible to adjust a sound so that it appears two times louder than another sound? (The "two times" is not important; we could ask the subject to adjust the sound to half the loudness or five times the loudness.) Clearly the first judgment should be easier, because all that is required is an "equal" or "not equal" response. For that reason we will first consider judgments of equal loudness.

We would not expect two sounds of different frequency but equal physical amplitude to sound equally loud. We know from figure 2.24 that the minimum amplitude for hearing (the absolute threshold) differs across frequency, and this would suggest that equal amplitude tones will not sound equally loud. To do this research, the experimenter presents a fixed standard (usually 1000 Hz). The subject is given a control to adjust the amplitude of a second tone of different frequency to match the standard in loudness. After the subject makes the adjustment, a comparison tone of another frequency is presented and the subject again adjusts the amplitude. This process continues until a wide range of frequencies are used. The data consist of the frequencies and amplitudes of tones that sound equally loud to the standard (and presumably to each other). These points can be plotted, with the x-axis as frequency and the y-axis as physical amplitude. All points can be connected by an equal loudness line. This is illustrated in panel (a) of figure 2.25. Then we can set the fixed standard 1000 Hz tone at a greater amplitude and go through the entire process again. This will generate a different equal loudness curve. A set of such equal loudness curves is shown in the panel (b) of figure 2.25. The loudness for each curve is arbitrarily set as the amplitude of the fixed 1000 Hz standard. Thus if the amplitude is 50 dB SPL, that loudness is defined as 50 *phons*. What is important perceptually is that at lower amplitudes, low or high frequency tones must be increased in amplitude in order to sound equally loud. Yet at higher amplitudes, all frequencies sound equally loud, and the gain in loudness is particularly great for low frequencies. This leads to a change in

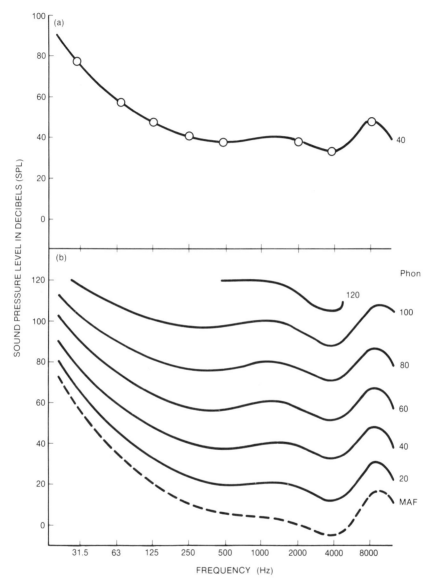

Figure 2.25
The perceived loudness of different frequency-intensity combinations. Panel (a) represents the intensities at which sounds of different frequencies match the loudness of a 1000 Hz tone at 40 dB. For example, a tone of 31.5 Hz must be roughly 40 dB more intense (pressure ratio = 100) to match, and a tone of 4000 Hz must be slightly less intense to match. Panel (b) represents a series of matches to different loudness levels of the 1000 Hz tone (based on International Organization for Standardization Values 1981). The loudness (phon) of the 1000 Hz tone is shown on the right. The number of phons is defined as the dB of the 1000 Hz tone. The 40 dB curve in panel (a) matches the 40 phon curve in panel (b).

the quality (or timbre) of sounds. At higher intensities, the quality becomes "darker," an observation dating back one hundred years to the physicist Ernst Mach.

Now we will consider a psychological scale for loudness: the relationship between perceived loudness (psychological) and the sound pressure level (physical). To do this experiment, the subject is presented with a tone of fixed frequency and fixed amplitude and is required to adjust another tone of the same frequency so that it is a specified loudness ratio of the first. The second tone usually is adjusted to be twice or half as loud as the standard. If we arbitrarily call the first standard tone one unit in loudness, a tone twice as loud is 2 units, a tone twice as loud as the second tone is 4, and so on. We end up with a set of points. Each point has a physical amplitude and a psychological loudness in numerical units. A graph of this sort is shown in figure 2.26. What is clear is that the growth of loudness is not constant and that the growth of loudness is smaller than the growth in

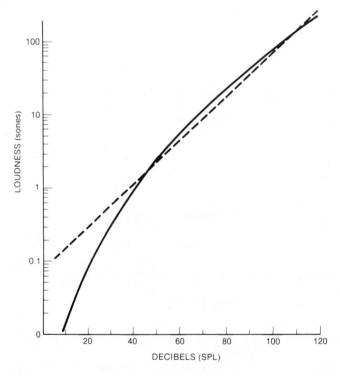

Figure 2.26
The relationship between sound pressure (decibels) and loudness (sounds). The dashed line represents a twofold increase in loudness for every 10 dB (3.16 pressure ratio) increase in sound pressure (adapted from Stevens and Davis 1938).

pressure. To achieve a doubling of loudness, you must increase the pressure of the sound threefold. To increase the loudness 10 times, the pressure must be increased 33 times. Two instruments sound only 1.6 times louder than one.

Frequency and pitch   We can investigate the same relationships for frequency, particularly the relationship between pitch (psychological) and frequency (physical). As with loudness, experimenters begin with a standard tone of fixed loudness and frequency. Subjects are required to adjust a second tone of equal loudness so that it stands in a certain pitch ratio to the standard tone. In these experiments, subjects adjust the comparison to be half the pitch of the standard. The graph relating pitch to frequency is shown in figure 2.27. The pitch of a 1000 Hz tone was set at 1000 (the unit was termed *mels*). What is similar to the results for loudness/intensity is that the change in pitch is not as great as the change in frequency (we must consider ratios here, because this was the basis for judgment). Starting from 1000 Hz, if we increase frequency 9 times to 9000 Hz, the pitch only

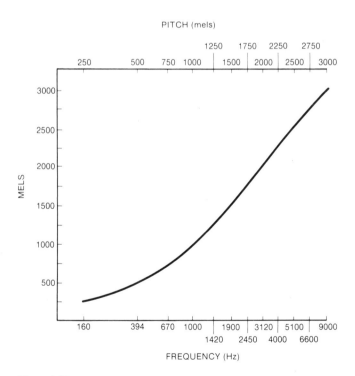

Figure 2.27
The relationship between frequency (Hz) and pitch (mels) (adapted from Scharf 1975).

increases 3 times to 3000 mels. Similarly, if we decrease frequency by 1/6 to 167 Hz, the pitch only decreases by 1/4 to 250 mels. Thus, for both loudness and pitch, the psychological change is slower than the physical change.

Resolution   The ear and the auditory system do not possess perfect resolution; the system combines energy across time and frequency. With respect to time, the energy falling within units of 200 msec is combined. We can understand the integration of sound energy over time by imagining a snowfall on a day so warm that each flake melts after 200 msec (1/5 sec). The actual snow on the ground at any time is made up of all those flakes that fell in the past 200 msec. If the perception is based on the total amount of snow on the ground at one point, then it does not matter whether all the flakes fell within 200 msec, within 100 msec, or within 50 msec. However, if the same number of flakes were to fall over 300 msec, the perception would be smaller, because at any point after 200 msec some of the flakes would have melted and the total number of flakes would be reduced. Flakes are like neural impulses. The auditory system integrates all neural impulses within 200-msec intervals, and the output is the total number of such impulses. Impulses due to stimulation further in the past are "lost."

Moreover, the auditory system integrates tones of similar frequency. For this reason, two tones close in frequency are easier to detect than one tone in isolation. In fact, each of the two tones can be made half as intense and still be heard. However, there are limits to the frequency separation that results in integration. At low frequencies (100 Hz), the maximum frequency separation is about 100 Hz (50 Hz to 150 Hz); at high frequencies (5000 Hz), the maximum frequency separation increases to about 1000 Hz (4500 Hz to 5500 Hz). This frequency separation is termed the *critical band*.

What temporal and frequency summation imply is that two stimuli that arrive within a short time span and are similar in frequency are not resolved into different sounds. Moreover, the existence of critical bands suggests that all the harmonics of one tone may not be perceived individually. For example, consider a tone with a fundamental frequency of 200 Hz. The lower harmonics would be resolved by separate critical bands, but the higher harmonics (e.g., 3000 Hz, 3200 Hz, 3400 Hz) would be integrated, because all fall within a single critical band. We need to be more precise here. There is an overlap in multiple critical bands, for example, 2900–3300 Hz, 2950–3350 Hz, 3000–3400 Hz, and 3050–3450 Hz. Thus all three harmonics might not fall within one critical band, but in no instance will only one harmonic fall within a single critical band.

We must be very careful in trying to discover those aspects of the physical stimulus that are relevant for perception. Changes and differences both within and between stimuli may not be perceptibly different, because of the inability of the physiology to distinguish between them. We will return to this issue in later chapters.

2.6 Overview

The goal of this chapter was to describe sound and some of the processes involved in the production of sound. In addition, a number of basic relationships between physical properties and psychological qualities have been introduced. Many concepts will be used again and again in the following chapters. These are listed below:

1. Simple harmonic motion; sinusoid wave
2. Frequency; amplitude; period; phase
3. Fourier analysis; additivity; superposition
4. Frequency spectrum; sound spectrogram
5. Fundamental and harmonics
6. Periodic and nonperiodic waves
7. Attack; steady-state; decay
8. Vibration modes; sound bodies
9. Coupling: Q
10. Resonance
11. Sound pressure levels; decibels

The next three chapters will deal with some of the intricacies of sound production. Once again, the motivation is to describe the possibilities for listening. To put it another way, to understand the processes by which sound is produced will allow us to make a better prediction about which parts of the sound are most important for perception. We will next turn to the propagation of sound and the changes brought about by the physical surround.

Further Reading

Backus (1977), Benade (1960, 1976), Hall (1980), and Taylor (1976) are strongest in acoustics; Green (1976), Strong and Plitnik (1983), and Yost and Nielsen (1985) are strongest in psychophysics. A. P. Dowling and Ffowes (1983) and French (1971) provide a more mathematical treatment of acoustics, with French being the easier of the two works.

Backus, J. (1977). *The acoustical foundations of music.* 2nd ed. New York: W. W. Norton.

Benade, A. H. (1960). *Horns, strings, and harmony.* Garden City, N.Y.: Anchor Books.

Benade, A. H. (1976). *Fundamentals of musical acoustics.* London: Oxford University Press.

Dowling, A. P., and Ffowes Williams, J. E. (1983). *Sound and sources of sound.* Chichester: Ellis Horwood.

French, A. P. (1971). *Vibrations and waves*. New York: W. W. Norton.

Green, D. M. (1976). *An introduction to hearing*. Hillsdale, N.J.: Erlbaum.

Hall, D. E. (1980). *Musical acoustics: An introduction*. Belmont, Calif.: Wadsworth.

Strong, W. J., and Plitnik, G. R. (1983). *Music, speech, and high-fidelity*. Salt Lake City: Soundprint.

Taylor, C. (1976). *Sounds of music*. New York: Clarles Scribner & Sons.

Yost, W. A., and Nielsen, D. W. (1985). *Fundamentals of hearing*. 2nd ed. New York: Holt, Rinehart, and Winston.

Chapter 3

The Environment of Sound

The propagation of vibration through the air medium of our environment generates the possibilities for perceiving. However, the vibration reaching our ears is not an exact replica of the original pattern. To understand the effects of the environment we will need to cover a diverse set of topics, beginning with the basic issue or sound propagation in air.

3.1 Sound Propagation

To transmit vibrations from one place to another requires some material or medium in the intervening space. It may be in any form—solid, liquid, or gas. Sound will not travel through a vacuum. To model the propagation of vibration, we can imagine a series of masses, each interconnected to its neighbor by a spring (see figure 3.1). The masses stand for air molecules, and the springs stand for the elastic medium acting to equalize the pressure between each pair of masses. Suppose we move the first mass to the right. This compresses the first spring; that spring then will attempt to expand back to its original length. When the spring expands, it will push molecule 1 back to its original position but also force molecule 2 toward molecule 3, which results in the compression of spring 2. The compression between molecules 1 and 2 has been passed on, and now occurs between molecules 2 and 3. Spring 2 now expands, pushing molecule 2 back to its original position and pushing molecule 3 closer to molecule 4 which thereby compresses spring 3. The compression has been moved to the right one more step. The disturbance is passed through the molecules, but each molecule undergoes only a minute, rapid back-and-forth harmonic movement. If the first spring had originally been expanded and stretched by pulling it to the left, it would have contracted, pulling molecule 2 to the left, thereby stretching spring 2, and so on. The expansion would have been passed on to the right. The compression or expansion is propagated long distances, although at slow rates.

Imagining one more step with springs and balls, we can apply a back-and-forth displacement by using a tuning fork or speaker cone to produce a back-and-forth movement. The spring will be alternately expanded and

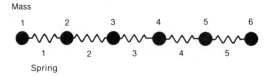

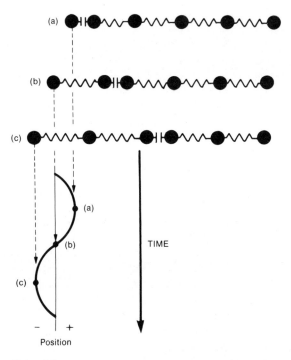

Figure 3.1
The movement of a compression by the back-and-forth movement of individual molecules. The compression (shortening of the spring) is propagated to the right in (a), (b), and (c). Each molecule undergoes only a back-and-forth sinusoidal movement, as displayed vertically at the bottom of the figure.

compressed as shown in figure 3.2. What will be propagated to the right will be expansion, normal (equilibrium), compression, normal, etc. Again, it is critical to remember that each molecule does move back and forth but ultimately remains in the same place; it is the pattern of compression and expansion that is propagated. At the edge of the Atlantic Ocean on the east coast of the United States, the waves breaking on the beach are not bringing water from Europe; individual water drops are stationary. The same phenomenon occurs in a "Slinky" toy. Push one end back and forth. There will be movement running along its length, but obviously each coil remains in the same relative position (see figure 3.3).

Now it is time to trade in the springs and balls for air. Air is a compressible medium, like a spring, and when compressed will act to eliminate that compression. For example, as you pump up a balloon, the compressed air generates a stronger and stronger pressure against the rubber membrane. Imagine a cylinder of air with a flat surface fitting tightly at one end as in figure 3.4. On the average, the molecules are evenly distributed throughout the tube. Push the flat surface in; this will have the effect of pushing air molecules in front of the surface, which creates a compression (i.e., high pressure) of the molecules, exactly like compressing the spring. Now the air molecules will move to the right to dissipate the higher pressure, and in doing so, they create a region of higher pressure immediately to the right. At this point, the molecules again move away from the higher pressure (both to the left and the right) and the high pressure region moves further to the right (the leftward movement of the molecules tends to equalize pressure). In a similar way, if the flat surface is pulled to the left, it creates a region of lower pressure (a rarefaction) that moves to the right. All of our arguments made when modeling with springs and balls are identical when using air molecules.

This oscillation of individual air molecules that results in propagation of pressure differences is termed a *longitudinal* wave. It is the only type of wave possible in air. For a longitudinal wave, the vibrating particles move along the same or opposite directions as the wave. Thus, for a wave traveling horizontally, the molecules move back and forth, left and right. The other type of pressure wave is termed a *transverse* wave. For a transverse wave, the molecules move at right angles to the direction of the wave. Thus if the wave moves horizontally, the molecules move up and down. Transverse waves occur, for example, when a rope is flicked up and down. Sound travels as a transverse wave only in solids. The mathematics of Fourier analysis yields the same results for transverse and longitudinal waves, and thus a transverse wave can always be reconceptualized as a longitudinal wave and vice versa. It is awkward to represent regions of higher pressure by squeezing dots together and regions of lower pressure by separating dots. It is simpler to represent a sound pattern as a graph of

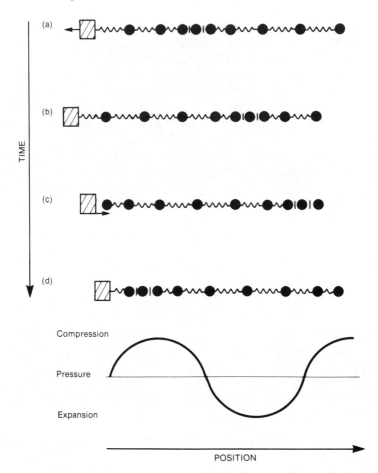

Figure 3.2
The vibratory motion of the block generates an alternating pattern of expansions and compressions. The compression and expansion pattern of the spring at time (d) is depicted at the bottom of the figure.

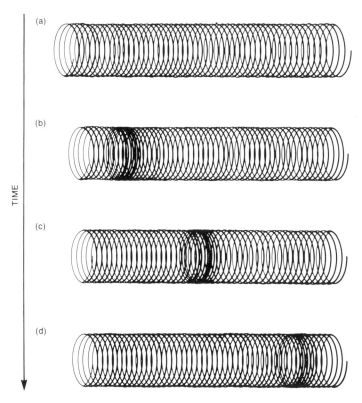

Figure 3.3
Compressing one end of a Slinky leads to the movement of that compression along the
entire length. Each coil undergoes a small back-and-forth movement.

(a)

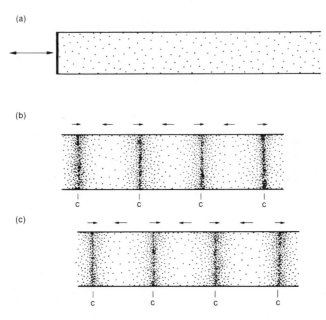

(b)

(c)

Figure 3.4
Propagation of sound waves in air. Originally, the air molecules are distributed uniformly as in (a). The movement of a vibrating object creates regions of higher pressure where the air molecules are compressed together (labeled c), and regions of lower pressure whee the air molecules are spread apart. The air molecules move to equalize the pressure shown by the direction of the arrows in (b). This movement generates new high and low pressure regions slightly to the right of the original ones in (c). It is this continuous back-and-forth movement of the molecules that leads to sound propagation.

pressure across time. In our mind's eye, when pressure is positive, the air molecules are closely packed, and when the pressure is negative, the air molecules are spread apart.

Because of the physical processes involved, sound travels relatively slowly, only about 340 m/sec (1250 km/hr) or 1100 ft/sec (750 miles/hr). In contrast, the speed of light is almost instantaneous (310,000 km/sec; 186,000 miles/sec). This difference allows for the trick of estimating where a storm is by counting the number of seconds between seeing a lightning flash and hearing the thunder. A difference of about 5 seconds indicates that the storm is about 1.7 km or 1 mile away.

3.2 Sound Propagation in the Environment

If we floated in outer space, sounds would be propagated from an instruments or speaker, reach the listener, and then pass on, never to be heard again (assuming we suspend the physical fact that sound will not travel through a vacuum). This is not our natural state, of course. In an environment of trees, buildings, walls, and countless objects, sound waves are reflected and scattered. The sound pattern at the ear thus differs from that at the source. The environment may generate multiple representations of a single signal because of reflection; it may generate a modified spectrum and a modified spatial distribution because of interference from the objects and resonances of an enclosure. In addition, the body itself acts to alter and reflect the sound reaching the listener's ears, and movement of the source or the listener acts to alter the sound in still different ways.

The role of the environment is ambiguous. In one way it introduces error and uncertainty by bringing about changes in the acoustic wave. In another way it aids perceiving by creating multiple yet modified signals that can be related and compared to each other to recover the original signal. I am not sure whether the net effect is positive or negative—that is, whether the multiple signals can compensate for the increased variation in the sound wave or not.

To understand the behavior of sound waves, we will first make the simplifying assumption that sound waves act identically at all frequencies. The sound waves will be conceptualized as directional arrows, and the geometrical consequences will be used to explain reflection, room resonances, and reverberation. Then we will drop this limiting assumption and consider the interactions between the size of reflecting objects and the wavelength of the incident sound waves. The consequences of this interaction will be used to explain the diffraction and interference of sound waves. Following this, we will consider the effect of movement—of either the source or listener—on the perceived sound wave.

Sound Waves as Arrows: Reflection
To understand the reflection of sound waves, we will think of the waves as resembling arrows or rays that travel in a straight line. When a ray encounters an obstacle, the sound bounces off so that the angle of incidence equals the angle of reflection, the same way a ball bounces off a wall.

Reflections off surfaces   In the case of our people dangling in space, there will be but one sound ray from the speaker to the listener—the direct ray. Now imagine that both speaker and listener have their feet on the ground. Here there are two sound rays: (1) the direct one, and (2) the one in which the sound ray reflects off the ground before reaching the listener's ear. The reflected sound wave must travel farther to reach the listener, which means it arrives after the direct wave. For example, suppose the two are 3 m (10 ft) apart and the speaker's mouth and listener's ear are 1.5 m (5 ft) above the ground. If sound travels 340 m/sec (1100 ft/sec), then the direct sound wave will reach the listener in 3/340 sec or 9 msec; the reflected sound that bounces at the midpoint will reach the listener in 4.2/340 sec (12 msec), or approximately 3 msec later (see figure 3.5).

If we now add a ceiling, the number of reflected waves reaching the listener increases. There is the direct sound wave, the "single bounce" reflected wave hitting the floor and the analogous single bounce hitting the ceiling, the "double bounce" reflected wave hitting both the ceiling and the floor, the "triple bounce" reflected wave, and so on. The waves can bounce back and forth many times before reaching the listener, and theoretically there are a limitless number of ways the sound can travel between the speaker and listener (see figure 3.5). Side walls and a back wall add to sound paths, as in figure 3.5(c).

What are the consequences of the reflected sound?

1. The first is that the total energy reaching the listener is greatly increased. Remember that the waves created by the speaker spread out more or less equally in all directions. The energy reaching a point decreases as the square of the distance. The two people suspended in space would have a difficult time hearing each other at a distance of 9 m (30 ft). The direct wave would have attenuated over this distance.

When the two people are standing in a room, many sound rays will be reflected to reach the listener's ears, and the total energy will increase significantly. In fact, back walls or stages and amphitheater shells are designed to reflect "escaping" sound rays back to the audience (see figure 3.5). Notice that any reflected sound ray is going to be less intense than the direct sound ray for two reasons. First, some of the energy will be absorbed by the reflecting surface. Second, the distance traveled by any reflected wave will be greater than the direct wave (each reflection will add to the distance) and the intensity of the sound wave will attenuate further due to air friction over the greater distance.

2. The second is that the listener will be bombarded with a sequence of sound waves, one following the other. The direct wave, the loudest, will reach the listener first. The next set of sound rays, reflected off one surface, will be softer than the direct ray. Subsequent rays will have reflected off two or more surfaces and will be further attenuated. The time interval between the arrivals of sound waves (e.g., between the direct and the first reflected wave) depends on the difference in distance traveled by the two rays, and this difference is related to the number of reflections a sound wave must undergo before reaching the listener's ears.

The temporal pattern among the sound rays affects the sound quality. Blauert and Lindemann (1986) suggest that early lateral reflec-

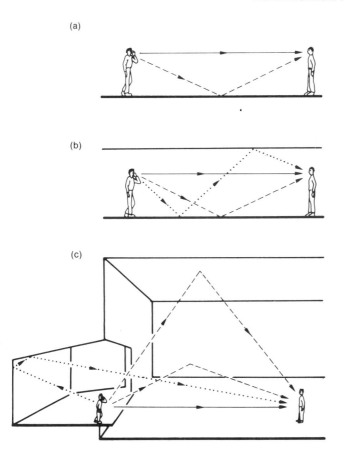

Figure 3.5
Reflections off surfaces generate multiple sound waves reaching the listener. In (a), there is one reflection off the ground (dashed line). This reflection is weaker than the direct wave and reaches the listener after the direct wave. In (b), there are reflections off the ground and "double" reflections off the ground and ceiling (dotted lines). The "two-bounce" reflections off the ground and ceiling are weaker and reach the listener after the single reflections off the ground. (There are single reflections off the ceiling that are not shown for visual clarity.) In (c), there are multiple reflections off back walls, ceilings, floors, and side walls in a typical enclosed room.

tions yield a sense of spaciousness. If the reflected waves that bounce off the walls arrive first (as would happen with high ceilings), the stereo effect is enhanced, and concert halls with this property are preferred by listeners.

3. The third consequence is that the multiple reflections allow sound to penetrate under balconies, into different rooms, and in general to fill up a room. Good architectural design requires that balconies have large openings and small overhangs so that sound can indeed reach all seats.

It is important to mention that the position of a sound source and a recording microphone are interchangeable. That is, if the source is at position A and the microphone at position B, the measured amplitude would be identical to that if the microphone were at A and the source at B. A listener will hear the identical sound if the performer is on the stage and the listener is in a concert hall seat or if the performer is in that seat and the listener is at the performer's position on stage.

The perceptual effects of the multiple reflections will depend on the way the reflected waves are integrated with each other and with the first direct wave. Although these effects can be varied, at this point it is sufficient to note that reflections arriving within 35 msec are not heard as distinct, separate sounds; instead, these reflections combine with the direct sound. This is termed the *precedence* or *Haas effect* and will be discussed at the end of the chapter. It is for this reason that the reflected sound waves are not normally heard as separate sounds. Reflected waves that are delayed for greater time periods may create disconcerting echos. This possibility occurs in high auditoriums where the distance to and from the ceiling creates such a long delay that an echo is heard. Using 35 msec as the critical time, the difference in distance that may yield an echo is 35 msec × 340 m/sec (1100 ft/sec) or about 12 m (39 ft). The floating panels hanging from the ceiling of these auditoriums serve to "cut off" and reflect the sound waves at shorter distances so that echos will not occur.

Reverberation   The traveling waves (the rays) reflect continuously off the walls and in the process generate standing waves and vibration modes. It was pointed out in the previous chapter that these vibration modes are no different than those of any sound body. The coupling or damping of each vibration mode determines the amplitude as well as the rate at which vibration increases and decreases in amplitude. If the mode is heavily damped, it dissipates energy rapidly and will fall in amplitude quickly.

We can now understand the classic concept of reverberation time. The reverberation time is defined as the number of seconds it takes a sound to decay to one-millionth of its original intensity and is nothing more than the decay of the characteristic vibration modes. When the source is shut off, the steady-state vibration, at the driving frequency, disappears rather quickly; the energy at the driving frequency is translated into energy at the resonant frequencies of the vibration modes of the room. These modes then decay due to absorption at the reflecting surfaces and friction among the air molecules. The time for each mode to decay (i.e., the reverberation time) will depend on its reflection pattern, initial amplitude, and rate of damping. A heavily damped mode will dissipate energy rapidly and have a short reverberation time because of the energy absorbed at each reflecting surface.

It is unlikely that the vibration modes at different frequencies will decay at the same rate. For this reason, the reverberation time of a room will be different across the frequency range. The reverberation time is technically defined for 1000 Hz tones to avoid this complication. This allows standardization but unfortunately hides the fact that the reverberation time is not constant. Typically, the higher frequency vibration modes decay more quickly (i.e., have a shorter reverberation time). This arises from two factors. The first factor is that higher frequency vibrations tend to be absorbed at surfaces to a greater degree than lower frequency vibrations, and it is the high frequency vibrations that reflect off four or six sides, as opposed to low frequency vibrations that reflect off two sides. The second factor is that higher frequency vibrations have higher frictional losses in air; for frequencies above 5000 Hz, air frictional losses may equal wall absorption losses.

Sound waves as Interference Patterns: Diffraction
Treating all sound waves as identical directional arrows is a simplification, because there are many aspects of wave propagation that are a function of the wavelength of the sound. We know from experience that sound waves do not act exactly like billiard balls bouncing off cushions. Sounds spread through openings and bend around walls and corners, unlike light waves, which act more like arrows and normally create sharp shadows. We can hear noises behind a building or down a side street. The sounds are weaker, to be sure, but sound waves do bend around corners, and this phenomenon is termed *diffraction*.

To understand diffraction, it is critical to remember that sound travels in waves. The wave movement is one of pressure variation, a series of compressions and rarefactions. When an object vibrates, there will be a series of alternating compression and rarefaction wave fronts that expand outward in an ever-widening circle. (It is like ripples in a pool of water that are created by moving an object back and forth.) The distance between equivalent wave points will be equal to the wavelength. Representations of these

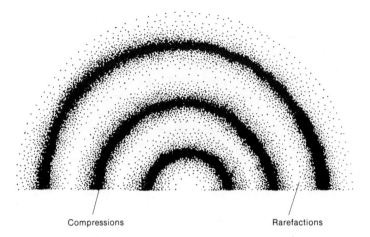

Compressions   Rarefactions

Figure 3.6
Sound propagation consists of alternating regions of high pressure (dense texture) and low pressure (light texture). The sound wave expands in three dimensions; this is a slice through them.

waves utilize expanding concentric circles to illustrate the traveling wave fronts. Each dark outer circle shows one compression wave front. The outermost circles were produced first and have propagated furthest (see figure 3.6). The interspersed lighter concentric circles represent the rarefaction wave fronts. In air, the wave would expand in three dimensions, in much the same way as blowing up a balloon from the middle. This picture shows just one slice through the expanding balloon.

The reflection of sound waves off objects and the propagation of sound waves through openings is symmetrical. For example, the transmission of pressure waves through an opening is exactly the same as the reflection back from an object of the identical shape. In both cases, the ratio between the wavelength of the sound and the size of the object or opening determines the spatial pattern of the sound. The first step will be to discuss simple cases in which the wavelength is much greater than an opening or reflecting object. The second step will be to discuss the more difficult cases in which the wavelength and the size of the opening or object are roughly comparable.

Wavelength longer than object length: equal sound diffusion   Imagine a wall with a tiny aperture. As the sound waves strike the wall, the wave will reflect off the wall with the exception of the point of the sound wave that is incident on the tiny opening. To understand the reflection, imagine that the wave is made up of many particles. Each particle can act like a new

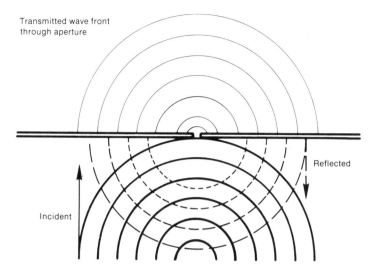

Figure 3.7
Sound reflection off a surface with a tiny opening. The majority of the sound energy is reflected (darker dashed lines). The point(s) on the incident wave that pass through the opening generate an expanding replica wave. This replica wave, drawn in light lines, is much lower in intensity.

source of sound waves. In other words, each point on a wave can generate the entire expanding sound wave all by itself. When the wave collides with the wall, each point will act to generate an identical reflection wave such that the angle of incidence will equal the angle of reflection. As long as the wall is relatively smooth, then the total reflected wave front, being made up of the wave from each point, will be identical in shape and opposite in direction. This, incidentally, is the mechanism by which sound waves are reflected and provides the rationale for our previous assumptions when using directional arrows to simulate wave movement.

There will be one point on the wave that will pass through the opening. That wave point will not pass through the hole like an arrow. Rather, it will act like a sound source and generate a new expanding wave. This new wave will be identical to the incident wave. The point aperture will transmit a copy of the incident wave by generating and propagating a perfect match (see figure 3.7). The intensity of the propagated wave is quite low.

Now imagine a reflector that is a tiny disk (i.e., the material removed from the wall to make the opening). The analogous process will occur when the sound wave is incident on the disk (see figure 3.8). All the sound wave with the exception of the point on the sound wave hitting the disk will pass by the disk; the point hitting the disk will act like a new source,

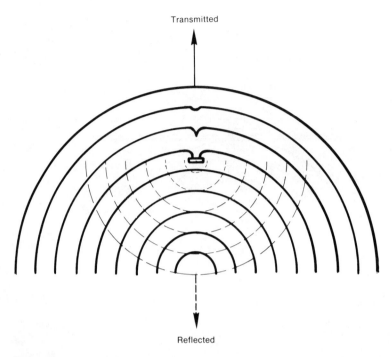

Figure 3.8
Sound reflection off a tiny disk. The points on the incident sound wave that reflect off the disk generate a replica reflected wave (dashed lines) of weak intensity. The points on the incident wave that pass by the disk gradually fill in the gap created by the disk.

reflecting back an ever-widening replica sound wave. Again, the reflected sound energy is just a tiny percentage of the incident energy.

Clearly the wave going beyond the disk will have a gap. However, this gap will be filled in as the wave propagates. The points at the edges of the disk will produce replica, expanding waves, and these will come to merge together. The sound shadow will disappear: the gap will soon become a depression and then disappear at a greater distance as the sound waves expand further, as shown in figure 3.8. This "filling in" will occur almost instantaneously (i.e., adjacent to the disk) because of the very small shadow induced by the tiny disk. (By the same process, the gap in the reflected wave created by the aperture will also be filled by the expanding waves.)

In sum, the reflection off a tiny disk and the propagation through a tiny aperture is a replica of the incident wave for all frequencies. In these cases, the wavelength is much greater than the gap or object. The sound wave is propagated or diffused in all directions equally. A listener behind a wall with a tiny aperture will hear the same sound regardless of position;

similarly, a listener in front of the disk will hear the same reflected sound regardless of position. At the other extreme, the wavelength could be much smaller than the gap or object. This is the case for light waves, where the wavelength is roughly 500×10^{-9} m, or one-millionth of a foot. For light, there would be a narrow beam passing through the gap or reflected back from the object. The light beam is not diffused but remains a narrow beam after passing through the aperture or after being reflected by a disk.

Wavelength equal to object length: directional sound propagation   For openings and disks of intermediate size, sounds of different frequencies are diffracted in various ways. Remember that when sound waves are reflected off surfaces or transmitted through openings, each point on the surface or in the opening can be thought of as generating a sound wave. A pair of points will generate two sound waves. At some spatial locations, the waves will meet 180° out of phase so that the pressures will cancel. At other spatial locations, the waves will meet in phase so that the pressures will add to reach maximum intensity. This process yields spatial *reinforcement* directions of maximum intensity where sound waves are in phase, and spatial *null* directions of minimum intensity where sound waves are out of phase. The specific spatial pattern of intensity (i.e., the number and direction of null lines) will depend on the ratio between the wavelength and the size of the aperture or disk.

A good explanatory system consists of two tiny apertures separated by a perfectly reflecting surface. At each opening, the wave point generates a sound wave that propagates in all directions. Suppose that the distance between the openings is 2 meters and the frequency of the wave hitting the apertures is 340 Hz (the wavelength being 1 m). Destructive interference will occur whenever two waves are 180° out of phase, which is the same thing as being separated by one-half the wavelength (a compression occurs at the same location as the rarefaction). Specifically, interference will occur when a wave that is traveling from one of the two apertures and has traveled 1 m meets a wave that is traveling from the other and has traveled 1.5 m. The two waves then are 180° out of phase: a compression will occur at the same position as a rarefaction. Interference will occur at all points at which the difference in distance between the apertures is .5 m: 2–2.5, 3–3.5, 4–4.5, and so on. All of these points taken together form a null line. Another set of interference points occurs when two waves meet such that one has traveled 1, 2, 3, 4 ... m and the other 2.5, 3.5, 4.5, 5.5 ... m. In this case, it is as if the 2 waves are spaced 1 1/2 cycles apart (1.5 m), again being 180° out of phase. Each set of interference points generates two symmetric null lines. The two apertures are spaced only 2 meters apart so that it is impossible for waves propagated from the two openings to be 2 1/2, 3 1/2, 4 1/2 cycles, or more apart.

Figure 3.9 shows two null lines created by waves separated by 1/2 cycle, and two null lines created by waves separated by 1 1/2 cycles. From any point on a null line, we can calculate the distance to each source. For the inner two null lines, the difference in distance is .5 m (1/2 wavelength) and for the outer two lines the difference is 1.5 m (1 1/2 wavelengths). Between the four null lines are regions of higher intensity. The maximum intensity occurs when the waves are in phase; they are separated by an integer number of wavelengths (0, 1, or 2). The maximum intensity therefore lies midway between a pair of null lines and decreases on either side, reaching zero at the null line. The regions of energy between the null lines are often termed *lobes*. For this particular case, the maximum amplitude of each lobe is identical. This is not true in general: for a large opening or a large object the amplitude of the side lobes falls off rather drastically. As mentioned previously, this is a two-dimensional picture of a three-dimensional process. The center lobe is really like a slender balloon, the other lobes are concentric. This is shown in figure 3.9(b).

Now it is possible to see how the relative sizes of the wavelength and the distance between the two apertures determines the pattern of the radiated sound. First, increase the wavelength to 4 m by using a 85 Hz tone. In this case, interference can occur when the two waves differ by 2 m (1/2 cycle), or 6 m (1 1/2 cycle), or 10 m (2 1/2 cycles) and so on. This only can happen along the line connecting the two apertures (because the separation is only 2 m) so that there is zero radiation left or right. The sound is radiated in all other directions; the maximum amplitude is straight ahead, with the amplitude diminishing at other angles reaching zero along the line connecting the two apertures. In contrast, decrease the wavelength to .5 m (680 Hz). In this instance, null lines occur when the waves are separated by .25 m (1/2 cycle), .75 m (1 1/2 cycles), 1.25 m (2 1/2 cycles), and 1.75 m (3 1/2 cycles). This generates a series of eight null lines; the sound radiation is much more directional since the sound energy is concentrated in the lobes. These two cases are illustrated in figure 3.10.

In general, sound radiation becomes more evenly dispersed or scattered as the wavelength increases (frequency decreases) and as the distance between radiating points decreases, because there are fewer possible cancellation lines. Roughly, when the wavelength is more than four times greater than the separation, the radiation pattern is uniform in all directions. When the wavelength of the sound is less than the separation, the radiation pattern becomes sharply nonuniform, with directions of high energy and directions of low energy. What this means to the listener is that the radiation pattern for a complex tone may differ among the harmonics. The intensity of the lower frequency harmonics will be uniform in all directions, the intensity of the higher frequency harmonics will vary across space.

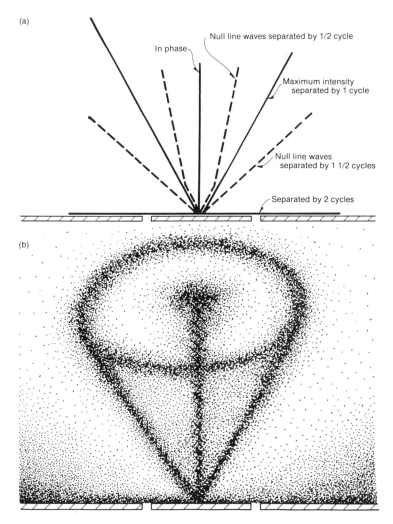

(a)

In phase

Null line waves separated by 1/2 cycle

Maximum intensity
separated by 1 cycle

Null line waves
separated by 1 1/2 cycles

Separated by 2 cycles

(b)

Figure 3.9
Directional sound propagation caused by the superposition of waves. Two waves will create destructive interference when a compression from one wave occurs at the same point as a rarefaction from the other wave. This will occur when the waves are out of phase by 1/2 cycle, 1 1/2 cycles, 2 1/2 cycles, and so on. These zero points occur along four dashed lines (hyperbolas) in (a). In contrast, two waves will sum to maximum amplitude when a compression from one wave occurs at the same point as a compression from the other wave. This will occur when the waves are in phase by 0, 1, 2, 3, or more cycles. The points of maximum amplitude occur along the five solid lines in (a). In three dimensions, each line of maximum amplitude traces out a cone, as in (b). There is a center solid cone surrounded by hollow cones. The high intensity hollow cones drawn darker are separated by interspersed hollow cones representing regions where there is interference—that is, where the amplitudes tend to cancel. If we imagine rotating the solid and dashed lines in (a) around the center in-phase line, we would generate the cones in (b).

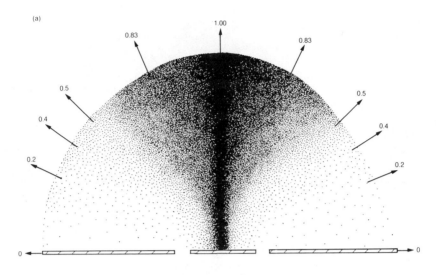

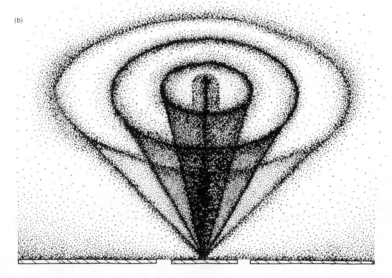

Figure 3.10
Directional sound propagation: Effects of wavelength. The ratio between the wavelength of
the sound and the distance between the two apertures determines the interference pattern.
In (a), the wavelength (4 m) is twice the aperture distance. Null lines occur only left or right,
and there is a "fan-shaped" amplitude pattern. In (b), the wavelength is one-fourth the
aperture distance. This creates eight null lines. In three dimensions, there is an intense solid
central cone, surrounded by hollow cones of alternating low and high intensity.

We can generalize from these results by considering any extended surface as being made up of many adjacent points. Thus, a slit may be conceptualized as being made up of a series of tiny apertures, each radiating sound waves. Because of the duality between an aperture and a disk, a reflector can be thought of being made up of a series of tiny disks, each reflecting incident sound waves. The same general principles outlined above hold for these extended sources. Sound waves that meet 180° out of phase (i.e., that differ by half wavelengths) will cancel and create null lines. Between the null lines, the intensity will be maximum. For extended sources, the secondary side lobes are relatively weak. If the amplitudes of the lobe directly in front of the aperture or disc is said to be equal to 1, then the amplitudes of the first two off-center lobes are roughly 0.20 and 0.13, and the other lobes are even weaker.

The same general rules hold for the diffraction pattern of the reflected sound off the surface surrounding a slit or the transmitted sound bypassing an extended surface. As the wavelength increases (or the size of the slit or reflector decreases), the sound becomes more uniform. In all cases—the reflection off an object, the reflection off the surface surrounding an opening, the transmission through an opening, or the transmission around an object—for the sound pattern to be uniform in all directions, the wavelength must be greater than twice the longest side of the aperture or reflector.

There is one more issue to consider. The radiation patterns we have just explained take some distance to emerge. Directly behind a wide opening, the sound waves will "shoot through" undisturbed, forming a beam; only at a distance will the diffraction pattern form. Similarly, behind a disk there will be a sharp sound shadow, which will be filled in at a distance due to the interference pattern created by the sound waves radiating from the edges of the disk. In the same fashion, the diffraction pattern of the reflection by a surface will form at a distance in front of the surface. Again, it is the relationship between the size of the object and the wavelength that determines the beam or shadow. If the size of the opening or disk equals or is less than the wavelength, then the diffraction pattern will be predominant immediately. If the size of the opening or disk is four times greater than the wavelength, it will take about 16 m for the diffraction pattern to dominate. In this instance, immediately behind an opening there will be a beam, and behind an object there will be a rather sharp, uniform sound shadow. The beam and shadow will gradually transform into a pattern of lobes and null lines at a further distance. In short, low frequencies fill in, and high frequencies create shadows, beams, and interference patterns.

Complex sounds: diffusion and directional propagation   To put all of this together, imagine that you are listening to an orchestra through an open window about 0.5 m × 0.5 m in the middle of a long wall. If you are standing in front of the window, then the vast majority of sound will consist of direct waves from the orchestra, along with additional sound waves resulting from reflections off the ground or adjacent walls, and so on. As you move directly backward away from the window, the sound becomes a mixture of the direct sound through the window and the sound waves propagated from the edges of the window. For an opening 0.5 m on each side, sounds with a wavelength of 2 m or more (170 Hz or less) are radiated uniformly. Thus the intensity will be similar in all directions, even next to the window itself. For higher frequency sounds, say 680 Hz (wavelength is 0.5 m), the waves create interference patterns and the intensity of the sound changes drastically in different directions due to the null regions. The diffraction requires space to develop, however, and thus in the vicinity of the window the dominant characteristic for this frequency (or higher) will be that of a uniform *beam* of sound, with a geometrical shadow around its sides, coming through the window. As the diffraction pattern develops (2 m or more from the window), the majority of the energy will be concentrated in a lobe (beam) about 60° wide. For even higher frequency sounds, this overall pattern—a uniform beam with a shadow near the window transforming into a series of directional lobes—will be even more accentuated. The beam will extend further from the window and the diffraction pattern will be even more directional. There will be more, but narrower, high intensity lobes. If you were to pace back and forth across the room, the sound would change and the manner in which it changed would depend on your position with respect to the window. Near the window you would hear only low frequency sounds until you crossed the window; then you would hear both low and high frequencies. After passing by the window, all that would remain would be the low frequency tones. If you paced a great distance away from the window, the low frequency tones would still be distributed uniformly. However, the beam of high frequency sound would have spread out, generating null lines due to interference, as the diffraction pattern emerged. The intensity would vary according to position (see figure 3.11). In a "real" room, the sound waves coming through the window would reflect off the floor, ceiling, and walls. These reflections, particularly those for high frequency sounds, tend to fill in regions adjacent to the window.

Now imagine that you are standing behind a wall and listening to an orchestra playing in front of the wall. Assume the wall is 0.5 m wide, which means it corresponds to the open window. If you are against the wall, all that you will hear are the low frequency tones that diffract immediately and circle around the wall. There will be a sharp sound shadow for higher frequency tones as the diffraction pattern emerges at some distance beyond the wall. As you walk back from the wall, intermediate

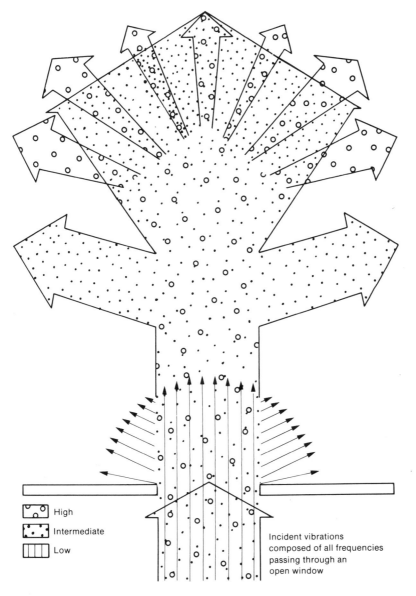

High

Intermediate

Low

Incident vibrations
composed of all frequencies
passing through an
open window

Figure 3.11
Directional sound propagation of a complex tone. If we imagine a tone coming through an open window, the low, middle, and high frequencies will give rise to different spatial patterns. The low frequencies will immediately spread out and continue to propagate in all directions (depicted by arrows). The middle frequencies will create a beam that at some distance from the wall will form broad regions (lobes) of high amplitude. The highest frequencies will form a beam that extends further from the wall. Then the highest frequencies will disperse into relatively narrow high amplitude lobes.

and then high frequency tones will begin to be heard as these waves start to fill in behind the barrier. As this occurs, interference patterns begin to emerge in the same way as described previously. If you walk parallel to the wall at some distance back, the strength of the higher harmonics will change as you walk through the null lines (although there will still be a shadow for the highest frequencies). At still further distances from the wall, the highest frequencies will finally fill in, creating regions of higher and lower intensity.

The prediction of the behavior of sound in a real room can be almost impossible. The transmission, reflection, diffraction, and shadowing effects are intricately determined by the frequency of the sound, the size of intervening objects or openings, and the geometry of the entire room. Only for the most simple conditions are the net effects amenable to calculation. Trying to solve one acoustic problem may produce another. For example, the suspended ceiling panels used in auditoriums serve to minimize echos caused by the long-delayed reflection from the ceiling. But these panels also create a series of apertures and reflecting surfaces that are frequency-sensitive. This in turn changes the frequency spectrum of the reflected sound at different locations. Each seat in an auditorium will have a different sound.

3.3 Movement: The Doppler Effect

Movement, either of the source or listener, changes the wavelength of sound waves. This is termed the *Doppler effect*. It is the Doppler effect that causes the pitch of a train whistle to increase as the train approaches and to decrease as the train recedes into the distance.

To understand the Doppler effect and the resultant change in frequency, imagine that the sound is produced by a device that produces one cycle every second (1 Hz). (Although this is ridiculously low for an auditory signal, it makes the explanation simpler.) Further, imagine that the sound source is moving from left to right at the speed of 170 m/sec, or one-half the speed of sound, and that the observer is standing to the right.

At time zero, the source emits a pressure wave. After one second, this original pressure wave will have traveled 340 m and the sound source will have traveled 170 m. Now the sound source emits a second wave. After another second (the time now equals two seconds), the original wave has reached 680 m, the second wave has reached 510 m (this wave was emitted from the source at 170 m at time 1, and traveled 340 m between time 1 and 2), and the sound source has reached 340 m. Another second later, the original wave is at 1020 m, the second wave is at 850 m, the third wave is at 680 m, and the sound source is at 510 m. Thus, successive waves are separated by 170 m. Because of the movement of the source, the wavelength that would have been 340 m if the source were stationary (since the frequency was 1 Hz) has been reduced to 170 m. This effectively changes the frequency to 2 Hz (see figure 3.12).

Now imagine that the source moves to the left. At time zero, the source emits a pressure wave. After one second, this wave has traveled 340 m to the right, while the object has traveled 170 m to the left. At time 1, the source emits a second wave. By time 2, the initial wave has traveled 680 m to the right, the second wave has traveled 170 m to the right (the source was 170 m to the left and the wave has traveled 340 m to the right), and the source is now at 340 m to the left. After another second, the initial wave is at 1020 m to the right, the second wave is 510 m to the right, the third wave is at the starting point, and the source is 510 m to the left. Again, if we continued to examine the position of the waves at subsequent time intervals, we would find that the wavelength would be 510 m. Here the wavelength has been increased because of the movement. The frequency has been reduced to 0.67 Hz (see figure 3.12).

All of the above analyses are based on the listener being "in line" with the moving source—the source either moves directly toward or directly away from the listener. But this is rarely the case. More often the source passes us some distance away. We might be standing on an observation deck, for example, watching planes land and take off. Without going into the geometry, what determines the size of the Doppler shift is the rate at which the distance between the source and listener changes. When the source is far in the distance, movement toward or away is almost equivalent to the source moving directly in line with the listener: the distance change is rapid and therefore the frequency shift is maximum. When the source is nearly in front, however, the distance between it and the listener changes very slowly, even though the speed of the source does not vary. This slow change in distance produces a much smaller shift in frequency, and the frequency shift disappears altogether when the source is directly in front. Thus, the overall effect is as follows: as the source approaches from a great distance, the increase in frequency is maximum. The frequency increment then decreases as the source approaches (i.e., the sound becomes lower in perceived pitch), and the frequency reaches its true value in front of the listener. As the source moves away from the listener, the frequency decreases slowly and then more rapidly as the source moves farther and farther away from the listener. This accounts for the rather gradual change in frequency as the sound source passes by. To give an example, suppose a sound source with a frequency of 1000 Hz is traveling 100 m/sec (roughly 225 miles/hr) and passes on a line 50 m in front of the listener. Far in the distance the frequency would shift to 1294 Hz. The frequency would then decrease as the source continued to move toward the listener: at 100 m (from the point of being in front of the listener) the frequency would be

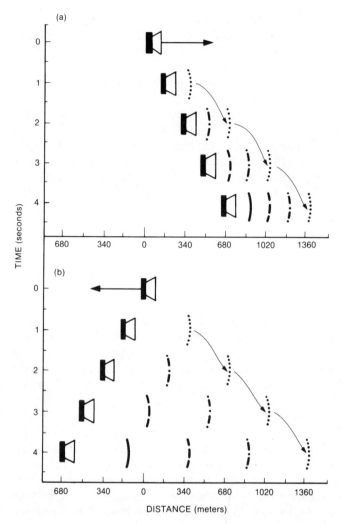

Figure 3.12
Movement of the sound source changes the frequency. In both panels, the object and sound waves are indicated at five time points reading from the top. The position of the object and the position of each successive sound wave are shown at each time point. Each successive sound wave is depicted as a different type of line. Arrows trace the movement of the first sound wave. In (a) the object moves toward a listener to the right. The movement pushes the sound waves together generating a higher frequency. In (b) the object moves away from the listener. The movement spreads the sound waves and generates a lower frequency.

1263 Hz, at 50 m the frequency would be 1210 Hz, at 25 m the frequency would be 1132 Hz, at 10 m the frequency would be 1056 Hz. Directly in front of the listener the frequency would reach the source frequency of 1000 Hz. As the sound source continued past, the frequency would decrease in a similar fashion. In general, the change in frequency is greater as the source approaches than when it recedes particularly at higher speeds due to the inverse relationship between frequency and wavelength (Dowling and Ffowes 1983; Kelly 1974).

Although we have analyzed the Doppler effect in terms of the sound source movement, the same effects would occur if the listener moved while the source remained stationary. That is, if the listener moved toward the source, the listener would cut through a greater number of sound waves in a single time period: the frequency would increase. If the listener moved away from the source, the listener would effectively "outrun" some of the sound waves: the frequency would decrease. In the extreme, if the observer moved faster than the speed of sound, new sound waves would never reach him, and he would overtake any previous sound in reverse order and hear a sequence backwards. Due to the great sensitivity to frequency differences, a movement as slow as 2.1 km/hr (1.3 miles/hr) can cause a perceptible change in frequency, and movement of 135 km/hr (84 miles/hr) can cause a change in one muscial whole note (Kelly, 1974).

Here is another example of the interchangeability between sound source and listener. Although the magnitudes of the frequency shift differ, the qualitative effects are identical. This interchangeability is analogous to the one between aperture and reflecting surface in determining diffraction and analogous to the interchangeability between source and listener in creating the pressure variation in a room.

3.4 Localization and Locomotion

The purpose of all this material has been to describe the various perceptual consequences of the environment. The vibration modes of a room, the reverberation time, the reflection of sound waves, the diffraction of sound waves, and the movement of source or listener all contribute to the auditory world. All of these processes act to modify the sound at the listener's ears from that produced originally. What is most striking to me is the rather unpredictable nature of these effects. Even in walking around a simple room, the pattern of the sound waves changes in irregular ways. It is the stability of our perception and knowledge about the outside world that is quite amazing. In spite of this irregularity, sighted and nonsighted individuals can develop remarkable abilities to make use of the reflected or diffracted sound patterns as well as the Doppler shifts to move around and locate their position in rooms, corridors, and even outdoors. Moreover, individuals can locate moving and nonmoving sound-producing objects as well as non-sound-producing obstacles and can often describe the size, shape, and texture of these objects from the pattern of the reflected and diffracted sound. Clearly, this is a sophisticated, learned skill, but it does demonstrate the potential of this information for understanding the external world.

Locating a sound-producing object is the heavily investigated area. In nearly all the experiments, the stimuli were short-duration sinusoid tones or white noise (hiss) bursts, the investigations were conducted in a "free field" (e.g., on top of a building or in an anechoic chamber) to minimize reflected sounds, and the subjects were instructed to immobilize their head and body. These restrictions tend to make the experimental situation unlike that of normal listening, in which the objects may produce time-varying stimuli of moderate duration, the environment contains surfaces that result in a multitude of reflected and refracted waves, both ears are stimulated many times by the same signal due to different paths and reflections, and the subject is free to move and orient toward the sound. With these constraints in mind, we will begin by considering the various cues to location.

Object Localization

The human body acts to generate the physical cues for object localization. If we were only points in space with central ears, there would be no way to infer the direction of sound. It is the three-dimensionality of our bodies that allows for directional hearing. Moreover, the body is an incredibly complex source of reflected and diffracted sound waves. The shoulders, head, chest, and outer ears are all different sizes and therefore affect sounds of varying wavelengths in contrasting ways. In much the same way that a concert hall imposes changes on the auditory signal, so does the human body before the sound waves enter the ear.

Object localization is a remarkable achievement. Each ear receives a different auditory signal (this will be discussed in detail below), and yet the auditory image is one of objects that appear fixed in the outside world; the objects do not appear to be in the ears or head. In addition, despite head and body movements, the position of the object appears steady, so that the observer must be compensating for the position and orientation of the head.

Two ears seem necessary for adequate localization; individuals with only one functioning ear have grave difficulties. Each ear hears a slightly different signal. Variations in the signal reaching each ear arise from path differences, from the listener's body, and from diffraction due to objects in the environment. It is these differences that underlie the ability to localize. Durlach and Colburn (1978) have asked, tongue in cheek, why do we have *only* two ears? A third ear in a new position would receive a still different signal, and comparisons among the three ears should enhance our perceptual capabilities. At the very least, it surely would have changed the development of stereo equipment.

In the average adult, the diameter of the head is 17.5 cm and the ears are separated by 22.9 cm around the circumference of the head. Behind each ear is the pinna, an elaborately shaped piece of cartilege. The average pinna is 35 mm (1.33 in) wide by 67 mm (2.67 in) long and sticks out about 25.4 mm (1 in). (My ears are exceptionally large: 44.5 mm × 83 mm. In some Adlerian way, this must account for my interest in sound.) Although the head is often assumed to be a simple sphere, it is actually quite unsymmetrical. The head, along with the neck and shoulders, acts to produce time and intensity interaural differences between the sound reaching each ear. Interaural time differences are due to the physical separation between the two ears; interaural intensity differences are due to reflections and shadowing from the head, pinna, and the rest of the upper torso. There are also interaural spectrum differences due to diffraction and reflection that create disparities in the frequency distribution between the ears.

Interaural time and phase differences   The physical separation between the two ears means that a sound wave will reach the near ear before the far ear. The temporal difference or delay will be maximum when the source is located to the left or right of the head; the difference will be zero when the source is located at the front or back; and the difference will be intermediate at other positions. A graph of the interaural time difference as a function of the position of the source is shown in figure 3.13. Note the very small time differences involved due to the small separation between the ears. Even if the source is opposite one ear, the time delay is less than 1 msec. Early investigators were fooled into thinking that this very small magnitude precluded its use as a perceptual cue. This proved to be false, using very short clicks, listeners can detect interaural time differences as short as 0.01 msec, or roughly ten times shorter than the interaural difference at 10° left or right of center.

There is a second consequence: because the sound wave arriving at each ear has traveled a different distance, the phase angle of the sound at each ear will differ. The difference in phase angle between the near and far ear will be a function of the wavelength of the source as well as of the orientation of the source. What is happening is as follows (see figure 3.14). Imagine that the sound source is opposite the right ear and that the distance between the two ears is 0.23 m around the head. In addition, imagine that the sound is 367 Hz, with a wavelength of 0.92 m, four times the distance between the ears. Suppose that the sound arrives at the right ear with a 90° phase angle (maximum positive pressure; see panel a). Then

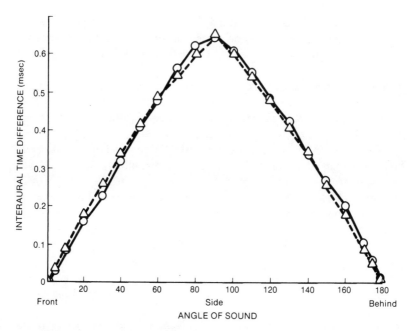

Figure 3.13
The interaural time difference due to the additional time required for the sound to travel around the head. The dashed line with triangles is calculated assuming the head is a perfect sphere. The solid line with circles is from measurements using a head replica (from Fedderson et al. 1957, by permission).

the sound will need to travel another .23 m around the head before it arrives at the left or far ear. When the wave reaches the left ear, the phase angle will still be 90° because of the wave propagation, but the phase angle at the right ear will have increased as the sound wave has progressed. In the time required for the sound to reach the left ear, the sound wave at the right ear will have completed another quarter of a cycle or 90° (distance around head [0.23 m] divided by wavelength [0.92 m]). Therefore, the left ear phase angle of 90° will lead the right ear phase angle of 180°, (panel b). If we think of the left ear first, then the right ear lags the left ear by 270°. The phase angle difference of 90° will be constant as long as the sound continues. For example, when the equilibrium amplitude at 180° arrives at the left (far) ear, then the pressure will be negative at 270° in the right (near) ear (panel c).

The phase angle difference will depend on the wavelength of the sound. If the frequency is doubled, this means that the wavelength is halved and the phase angle difference will be doubled. Thus, the phase angle difference for a 733 Hz (0.46 m wavelength) sound should be 180° (panel d). Simi-

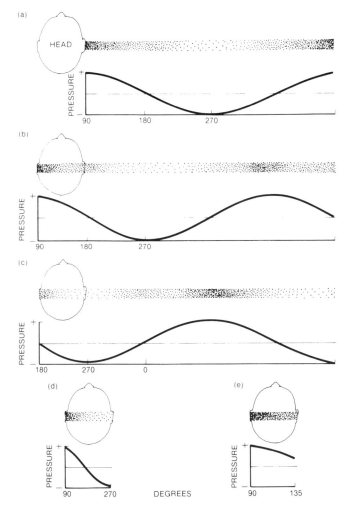

Figure 3.14
Interaural phase differences. Due to the size of the head, the sound pressure will differ at each ear. In (a) the high pressure region of the sound wave has just reached the right ear. The wave then circles the head. The wavelength of the sound is four times the distance around the head. In this case, when the high pressure region reaches the left ear, the pressure of the right ear will have returned to equilibrium, as illustrated in (b). The phase angle difference in pressure between the two ears is 90°. The wave will continue to propagate outward so that when the equilibrium region reaches the left ear, the pressure at the right ear has become minimum, as illustrated in (c). Again, the phase angle difference in pressure between the two ears is 90°. The phase angle difference of 90° will remain constant as the sound wave continues. If the wavelength of the sound decreases, then the phase angle difference will increase, and vice versa. In (d) the wavelength is halved (to 0.46 m); the phase angle difference is doubled to 180°. In (e) the wavelength is doubled (to 1.84 m); the phase angle difference is halved to 45°.

larly, if the frequency is halved (183 Hz, 1.84 m wavelength), the phase angle difference will be halved, or 45°: 0.23 m ear distance divided by 1.84 m equals 0.125, a 1/8 cycle difference, or 45° (panel e).

The phase angle for any specific frequency also depends on the position of the source. For example, if the sound is 45° to the right, then the difference in distance between the source and the two ears is only 0.13 m (not 0.23 m). The phase angle difference for the 367 Hz sound is now 51° (i.e., 0.13 m divided by the 0.92 m wavelength is approximately 1/7 cycle or 51°). The phase angle difference for all other frequencies would change accordingly. It is therefore possible to obtain the identical phase angle difference for sounds of different frequencies and positions. For example, a sound of 208 Hz directly opposite the right ear would also produce a phase angle difference of 51°.

How might a listener use phase angle to judge location? The basic notion is that if the sound is to the right of the listener, the phase angle between the right and left ear will be less than 180° and the phase angle between the left and right ear will be greater than 180°. The reverse would occur if the sound is at the left. The listener localizes the sound on the side to minimize the phase angle. There is an ambiguity when the ear difference equals the wavelength (about 1500 Hz for sounds opposite one ear), because the phase will be equal at both ears. For even greater frequencies in which the wavelength is less than the ear difference, which ear should serve as reference is also ambiguous, since there are positions on either side of the head that produce the identical phase angle difference. In fact, research has suggested that phase angle is an effective cue only for sounds below 1500 Hz.

Interaural intensity differences   Interaural differences in intensity are due to the diffraction by the head, pinna, and other body parts. These act like reflecting disks and create a sound shadow at the far side of the head. From the previous discussion of diffraction, we can point to two effects that relate to localization. The first is that the head will create a sound shadow immediately behind itself for sounds whose wavelengths are roughly equal to or shorter than the size of the head. For a human head that is about 17.5 cm in diameter, the sound shadow will be significant for sounds with frequencies greater than 1500 Hz. The second effect is that the sound waves coming from the edge of the head gradually fill in the shadow and produce diffraction patterns in the process. The interaural intensity differences as a function of the direction and frequency of the sound are shown in figure 3.15.

These intensity curves are not completely regular; the sound shadow is not a simple function of either the direction or the frequency of the sound. Some of these irregularities can be understood in terms of interference

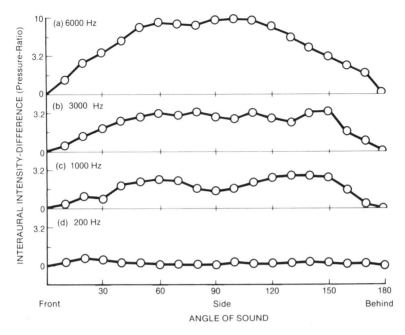

Figure 3.15
The interaural intensity difference due to the sound shadow cast by the head. The difference is graphed for different frequencies at various positions around the head (from Fedderson et al. 1957 by permission).

patterns. For a 200 Hz tone, there is a relatively small yet constant shadow. The wavelength of a 200 Hz tone is roughly nine times larger than the head so that the sound waves are able to circle the head immediately for all orientations. For this reason, there is only a weak, constant shadow. For a 1000 Hz tone, the shadow is slightly greater, and there is a reduction in the strength of the sound shadow at 90°. This seems unexpected, because the maximum shadow should occur when the sound source is directly opposite the shadowed ear. The reason for this dip is that the interference pattern due to diffraction has a maximum central lobe where the waves from the edges converge. The maximum central lobe is identical to the central lobe from two slits shown in figures 3.9 and 3.10. This produces a "bright" spot in the center of the interference pattern directly on top of the far ear and creates the minimum in the intensity difference curve. For a 6000 Hz tone, there is a large, directional shadow. Here, the wavelength is small relative to head size, and there is a sharp shadow next to the surface of the head. Other influences on the interaural intensity difference, such as the interference between direct waves and reflected waves from the shoulder, interference due to the pinna, and the lack of symmetry of the head, also produce various effects.

The traditional theory of sound localization has attempted to integrate all of the potential cues into a duplex theory. At lower frequencies, localization is said to be based on phase (temporal) differences and at higher frequencies localization is said to be based on intensity differences. There is also strong evidence that regular amplitude oscillations, such as those created by beats, are used for localization. On the whole this characterization seems adequate, although it does not answer questions about integrating the information coming from a complex object with a wide range of frequencies (Searle et al. 1976).

The pinna adds additional localization cues, particularly for the front-back position and elevation of the sound (imagine that the sound can be in any position starting directly in front, continuing overhead, and ending directly behind). Until about twenty years ago, the pinna was viewed as a vestigial organ, useful for holding glasses or hats but little else. It was intuitively clear that a cat could improve localization by turning and pointing its ears to maximize the intensity of the sound entering the ears. But the human ear was stationary, and in addition it was shaped in mystifying ways. Surprisingly, however, it is the convoluted shape that provides localization information. One possibility is that the convolutions produce a series of reflected waves that enter the ear canal and strike the eardrum after specific delays. The temporal pattern of the reflected waves entering the ear proper may be a function of the elevation of the object. In particular, the pinna is tipped upward so that there is a delay of only 0.04 msec when the signal is above the horizon, but a longer delay of 0.1 msec when the signal is below the horizon (see Rodgers 1981). A second possibility is that the convolutions generate reflected waves that produce interference with the sounds entering the ear. The direct wave and the reflected wave would be out of phase due to the added distance traveled by the reflected wave. Measurements of this phenomena suggest that if the sound is in front of the listener, there is an amplitude peak at low frequencies (250–500 Hz) and at high frequencies (above 13,000 Hz). As the sound moves overhead, the peak shifts to roughly 8000 Hz, and behind the listener there are peaks around 1500 Hz and around 10,000Hz (Hebrank and Wright 1974). What this means is that the pinna and the ear canal leading to the eardrum form a resonant sound body in which the resonant frequencies depend on the orientation of the incoming pressure wave. The ability to make use of these frequency-dependent amplitude variations to infer elevation depends on the familarity with the sound source. Listeners are much more accurate with known sources because they can compare the frequency spectrum amplitudes to a reference value. Typically, listeners judge unknown sources as being behind (Wallach 1938, cited in Blauert 1983).

The physical principles underlying object localization illustrate all the ways in which the environment can effect the sound. There is a temporal delay between the sound reaching the near and far ear, there are multiple reflection paths that occur in the pinna and produce interference, and there are sound shadows because of diffraction created by the head. In addition to these static cues, there are other cues produced by head movements. For example, if an object is in front of a listener, then turning the head clockwise will increase the left ear sound pressure, but turning the head counterclockwise will decrease left ear sound pressure (people spontaneously rotate their heads to improve accuracy). All of these indices to localization seem to have distinct neurological structures. We will return to this in chapter 12.

Localization in the environment   The vast majority of experiments on localization have made a conscious effort to minimize reflections so that the judgment will be based solely on the initial direct sound. However, we normally perceive in an environment with multiple sources that generate multiple reflections, and this raises two general issues. First, when do sounds from different spatial directions fuse into one signal? If perception were precise, the direct and each reflected sound wave would create a spatially discrete sound. Second, if the waves fuse, is the perception different from that created by the direct wave only? A good review is found in Gardner (1969a).

Let us start with the issue of fusion. Imagine two audio speakers separated by a medium distance. If the sound through each speaker is identical, then all the sound will appear to come from a point between them (a phantom speaker). If we adjust the intensity and timing slightly, the sound moves between the two speakers toward the earlier, more intense one. If the intensity and timing differences are increased further (e.g., if one speaker is moved closer), then all the sound appears to come from one speaker. The position of the second speaker is suppressed (although the second speaker does affect the perceived loudness, spatial extent, and tone quality). The precedence effect occurs even if each ear is presented just one of the sounds, which demonstrates that the position suppression is due to processes in the central auditory system. There is a time limit to the fusion; if two sounds are separated by more than 35 msec they will create two sound images. A striking example occurs for multiple sources arrayed along a line. As the listener moves left to right, the entire output from all the speakers seems to move with the listener and originate from the speaker in front (see figure 3.16). This perceptual tendency has been termed the Haas or precedence effect (Haas 1972; Wallach, Newman, and Rosenzweig 1949).

The precedence effect allows us to understand the fusion of the direct and reflected sound waves from one source. The reflected sound waves

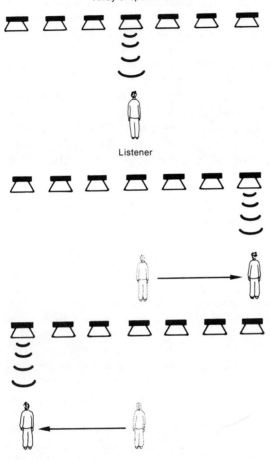

Figure 3.16
The precedence or Haas effect leads the listener to perceive the sound as coming from the closest speaker. If speakers are arrayed in front of the listener, left and right movement gives rise to the perception that the sound is moving with the listener. The sound always appears in front.

bouncing off the ceiling or walls create ambiguity because they suggest spatial positions above or off to the side of the listener. By suppressing localization from these delayed reflected waves, the precedence effect acts to ensure the correct localization of one source. Rapid onset transients strengthen the precedence effect, leading to better localization, and long, slow onsets minimize the precedence effect, leading to rather poor localization. Without rapid onsets to trigger the precedence effect, the interference patterns within a room due to standing waves can create large intensity differences that interfere with localization (Rakerd and Hartmann 1986). However, the precedence effect is not complete. Ceiling and floor reflections aid localization; wall reflections hinder localization (Hartmann 1983). The rationale for these results seems clear. Ceiling and floor reflections "point" toward the source and provide interaural time and intensity cues identical to the direct sound (elevation cues due to the pinna would differ, though). Wall reflections generate interaural cues for a different orientation. However, as mentioned previously, listeners prefer concert halls in which the first sound reflections come from the side walls, which suggests that the sense of being surrounded by music is more important than the sense of being able to localize instruments.

Remember that reflected waves are not identical to the direct waves due to absorption at walls, diffraction, and so on. The perceptual system must continually judge whether two sounds represent one source and its reflection (its echo) or whether the two sounds represent two different sources. It appears that if the two sounds have similar frequency components, although not necessarily identical components, the two sounds will be fused as long as the time delay is appropriate (Divenyi and Blauert 1987). As the direct and reflected sounds or the series of reflected sounds become more different, the perception broadens into an extended, diffuse, but single source. This may occur when a signal is reflected in different ways before reaching the listener. In a reverberant room, the sound waves are moderately related, and this leads to the sense of the sound filling the room. We can further imagine a large object, like a tree, with multiple surfaces (leaves) producing similar but not identical sounds. Based on outcomes using only two speakers, we would expect the perception to be of a rather extended object (Perrott and Buell 1982). In sum, the sense of space achieved by listening depends on slight differences in the waves reaching the ears. These differences may be created by reflection and diffraction or by similar multiple sound sources. (We will consider the organization of sounds into events in chapter 7.) If the sounds become so different that they are unrelated, the perception becomes one of multiple sound sources.

Perceptual judgments about size and distance are based on the frequency spectrum, intensity, and the degree of reverberation. Size is judged by the amount of low frequency energy. This seems to be based on reasonable expectations because low frequency resonances are found for larger objects. Distance is judged by sound pressure, frequency spectrum, and reverberation (Coleman 1963; Mershon and King 1975). As the source moves into the distance, the sound pressure decreases, the higher frequencies diminish more rapidly due to air friction (e.g., the "dull roll" of thunder), and the percentage of direct sound decreases while the percentage of reflected sound increases (in an enclosure). Listeners make use of all these variables in making distance judgments, but they underestimate distance. That is, they judge sources to be closer than the actual physical distance (von Békésy 1949). However, the judgment of distance is relatively crude and susceptible to experience. Experience tends to dominate physical variables. For example, listeners were asked to judge the distance for shouted, normal, and whispered voices. (It was easy to distinguish among the three voices.) Even if the voices were the identical sound pressure, listeners judged the whispered voices closest and shouted voices farthest. Whispers denote intimacy and closeness; shouts denote distance (Gardner 1969b). I am uncertain whether this poor performance reflects the fact that changes in sound waves that may signify distances are inherently ambiguous and inconsistent, or whether it merely reflects an unrefined skill because sight more readily gives distance information for humans.

Although I have emphasized the role of two ears in localization, there are other perceptual consequences of having two ears. First, it is easier to follow one voice or conversation in a crowded room with two ears than with one ear, the "cocktail party effect." With two ears, background noise seems to fade away. Second, imagine a room in which the reflecting surfaces absorb the high frequencies. With one ear, the sound seems hollow, but with two ears the sound maintains its true quality. Third, the "smearing" due to overlapping reflected waves in a reverberant room degrades less with two ears. In all these instances, the ability to compare the signals received by the two ears allows the listener to pick out those parts of the ongoing signal that are related and correlated, and that therefore signify one sound event (Koenig 1950). For example, the sounds from one speaker's voice reaching each ear of the listener are closely related, and the internal comparisons between the ears allow the listener to pick that voice out of the other overlapping voices. What this all means is that although three ears would be somewhat better than two, there is no doubt that two ears are significantly better than one.

Locomotion by Nonsighted Individuals
The ability of blind individuals to move around the environment has been known for hundreds of years. Three major theories emerged to explain this. The first theory was sensory; it postulated increased sensitivity or

heightened response of the skin sense, particularly the face (pressure or temperature), or of the auditory sense (pressure). The second theory was perceptual; it postulated the attachment of new meanings to the usual or ordinary sensory cues. The third theory was occult; it postulated a sixth sense, magnetism, electricity, or a vestigial organ, which was sensitive to the vibration of some hypothetical substance (Hayes 1941).

In all probability, the confusion about locomotion comes from two sources. The first is the introspective reports of the people themselves. Blind individuals rarely realize that they are using auditory information for locomotion. In one study (Worchel, Mauney, and Andrew 1950), only 3 of 34 subjects reported using audition. Instead, most reported a facial or visual sensation such as "shadows or pressures across the eyes" or "a bodily sensation similar to a shadow falling" or reported the feeling that "an obstruction had blocked the wind." The first researchers were misled because the reports were incorrect.

The second source of confusion is that there is no single perceptual characteristic solely used for locomotion. People use auditory cues, but they also use smell, heat, and wind to perceive objects. Moreover, listeners can gain information about the objects and the layout of the environment not only when an object actually produces a sound but also from the effect of an object on sound propagation (remember that most objects are silent). Environmental sounds are of diverse types: (1) short single sounds at particular locations; (2) a "wall of sound" that may be produced by the ocean or a line of traffic; or (3) a trajectory of sound that may be created by a buzzing fly or a receding car. The trajectory leads to changes in intensity (and possibly frequency, because of the Doppler effect). It has thus been difficult, even in careful experiments, to uncover the information used for locomotion. What is characteristic is the dependence on sequential information perceived over time, as opposed to visual scene information perceived at once in a glance (Strelow 1985).

The first studies on locomotion and obstacle sense by blind individuals quickly demonstrated that auditory information was primary (Ammons, Worchel, and Dallenbach 1953). Blind *and deaf* subjects were unable to approach and stop in front of a 1.2 m × 1.2 m barrier without colliding with it; blind *and hearing* subjects were able to do so. If the blind and hearing subjects were forced to use hearing protectors, their performance decreased. These subjects often shuffled their feet and did so more strongly when they were wearing the ear protectors, to compensate for the impaired hearing. In the same fashion, extraneous noise that obscured the sound of their footsteps led to poorer performance. Pressure sensations on the face or ear surfaces were ineffective in defining and perceiving obstacles. Physical analyses suggest that both intensity and frequency change can provide information about distance. Remember that intensity decreases through space by the distance squared. At 4 m the sound is 1/16, at 3 m it is 1/9, and at 2 m it is 1/4. As you approach an object, the amplitude thus increases more and more rapidly. Frequency provides information when a noise signal is reflected from a flat surface. This generates various kinds of interference patterns due to the superposition of the sound waves. One consequence is a sense of pitch as one approaches a surface; the apparent pitch of the noise gradually increases until about 1 m (40 in) from the surface, and then the pitch increases much more rapidly (Bassett and East-mond 1964; Twersky 1951). For both intensity and frequency, it is the rate of change that gives information about approach. As you close in on the object, the increase in loudness and pitch quickens.

Experimental demonstrations that bats and porpoises could locate prey by means of sensing the reflection of self-generated calls (echolocation) led to research aimed at discovering whether humans could locate objects by means of the reflections of self-produced whistles, vocalizations, or finger-snaps. The results from several studies indicate that people can indeed judge whether a flat surface exists and whether two flat surfaces are the same size or the same distance, although the ability to discriminate is not very good. The blind subjects used singsong chants, tongue clicks, hissing, and whistling sounds, all generated a wide range of frequencies. They moved their heads from side to side as much as 45° left and right. By moving their head back and forth, the listeners moved through the various interference lobes of each frequency and thereby accentuated any differ-ences in the reflections. Moreover, some subjects could even distinguish among surface textures; they could discriminate between velvet and denim and between cloth textures and bare surfaces like wood, metal, or glass. It should be clear that this skill is an example of learning to attend to existing changes in the physical sound pattern. Sighted individuals were initially poorer in performance but gained accuracy with practice (Kellogg 1962; Rice and Feinstein 1965).

3.5 *Overview*

This leads to the final point. If we lose sight of the complexity of the perceiver and the environment, then we are likely to be misled about the nature of perceiving. For example, theoretical analyses have often assumed the head to be a perfect sphere floating in space and the ears to be embedded holes in this sphere, much like finger holes in a bowling ball. If this were the case, then any interaural time or interaural intensity difference would be produced at many different locations (and there would be no spectral differences at one ear or between ears). There would be a "cone of confusion," because any sound source located on the surface of the cone would produce the same interaural differences (see figure 3.17). Using the

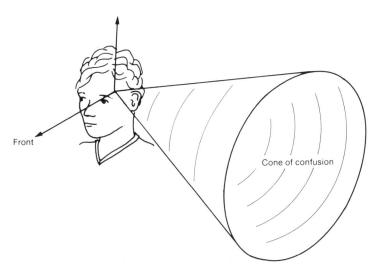

Figure 3.17
The cone of confusion refers to all positions in space that result in the identical interaural time, phase, and intensity differences. This cone is based on a model of the head as a perfect sphere floating in space. This model neglects the effects of other body parts.

ear hole as a reference, a source 45° in front would be equivalent to a source 45° in back, to a source elevated 45°, and to a source lowered 45°. Moreover, points at any distance along each direction would produce the identical differences. This is due to the assumed symmetry and lack of features of the sphere representing the head.

This analysis has led to the notion that the information for sound localization is inadequate, since so many possible locations can produce the identical interaural differences. But this view is dependent on the abstracted impoverished representation of the head and the impoverished description of the possible variations in sound energy. This view has been reinforced by experiments using sinusoid tones in a free-field. However, the head is not symmetrical, the neck and body produce reflection, diffraction and interference, the pinna is asymmetrical and intricately shaped, and even our hair can change the sound reaching each ear. Moreover, the environment generates multiple sound waves. Each of these represents complications from a physical and mathematical standpoint, but each can yield psychological information about the object's spatial characteristics and location. I am returning to the same theme once again. If we look closely at the physical processes underlying perception, we discover a wealth of information. This information may come from complicated interrelationships, but perception is surely not limited by the lack of sufficient information about the world. Rather, perceiving may be limited to the extent that we become overwhelmed by the amount of available information and are not able to select the relevant information.

Further Reading

Beranek, L. L. (1962). *Music, acoustics, and architecture.* New York: Wiley.
Knudsen, V. O., and Harris, C. M. (1978). *Acoustical designing in architecture.* New York: American Institute of Physics.

Chapter 4

Sound Generation by Musical Instruments

The previous chapters have explored the source-filter model of sound production. Conceptually, the source-filter model allows us to deal separately with the excitation and the sound body. We can analyze the excitation vibration into the harmonic (or partials), analyze the sound body into the vibration modes, and then predict the sound output by multiplying the excitation amplitudes of each harmonic by the vibration mode amplitudes (at those frequencies). We assume that the excitation frequencies and amplitudes are constant across time. Similarly, we assume that the resonant modes are passive and constant, and we also assume that the excitation (source) and sound body (filter) are independent. We term this a *linear* model, because equal changes in the excitation amplitudes are assumed to generate equal changes in the sound output amplitudes (e.g., if a change in excitation from 2 units to 6 units generates a change in output of 8 units, then a change in excitation from 98 units to 102 units would also generate a change in output of 8 units).

However, this model cannot cope with the actual complexities of sound production. It fails in nearly all respects. The excitation—the movement of a string due to bowing, the movement of the trumpeter's lips, or the movement of the clarinet reed—is actually nonlinear. Increasing the blowing pressure or the bowing velocity does not lead to a constant increase in airflow or string friction. Instead, at some pressure value, the clarinet reed will snap shut, stopping the flow of air, and at some point the string will jump off the bow. These motions are not symmetrical: opening the reed is not the same as closing the reed; catching the string is not the same as releasing the string. Second, the source (excitation) and the filter (sound body) are interdependent. The properties of the sound body can control the excitation, because they are coupled together. An analogy can be found in driving on ice. The frictional properties of the icy surface (analogous to the sound body) will control to some degree the way power can be applied to the tires (analogous to the excitation). You cannot slam down the accelerator and expect the car to react as it does on a dry surface. Third, this model has great difficulty in predicting the onset and offset transients, because the source-filter model is conceptually constant over time. Amplitude is portrayed as a function of frequency and not as a function of time. Below, the violin, and trumpet, and clarinet will be briefly described to clarify and expand some of the concepts from chapter 2.

4.1 The Violin

Each of the violin-family instruments consists of arched top and back plates joined at the edges by thin strips of wood termed ribs. The top plate contains two elongated cutouts—f-holes—which allow the air enclosed within the violin to propagate any oscillations. The strings are fastened at the tailpiece at one end, at the pegs at the other end, and pass over the bridge that is mounted on the top plate. Over time, the neck of the violin has been lengthened and placed at a greater angle to increase the sound output power. It is through the bridge that the strings act on the violin body. The body thus supports the strings and acts to radiate the string vibrations.

The bridge has two feet. The foot under the treble strings is connected by the "sound post" to the back plate. The sound post serves to create a rigid connection between the top and bottom plates. The sound post restrains the treble side of the bridge so that it acts as a simple lever, rocking at the sound post fulcrum and applying a twisting force at the bass foot over the bass bar. This allows the violin to swell and reduce in volume. Although the sound post rigidly connects the top and bottom plates, its role is not to transmit vibration to the back plate; actually, it creates a null point to still some vibration modes. The sound post is critical to the sound of the violin, and the exact placement is done by trial and error. The French call the sound post the "soul" of the violin, and if removed, the violin sounds like a guitar. Under the other foot of the bridge is the bass bar, a strip of wood glued assymetrically to the underside of the top plate. Structurally, the bass bar serves to reinforce the top plate and also serves to keep the entire top plate vibrating as a whole (the f-holes tend to weaken the integrity of the top plate). Acoustically, placing the bass bar off to one side minimizes the cancellation of sound waves that are 180° out of phase within the body (see figure 4.1).

Vibration Modes

To measure the vibration modes of an assembled violin, we hold the violin loosely and apply a sinusoidal vibration of differing frequencies at various points. At the resonant frequencies, the vibration modes should emerge. These modes are standing waves in wood. They represent the summation of the reflected traveling waves produced at the excitation point. The vibration amplitude will be maximum at the resonant frequency, and the

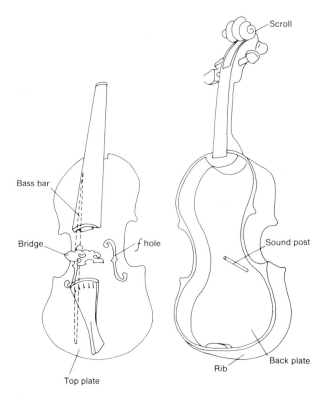

Figure 4.1
A schematic picture of the violin. The position of the sound post and bass bar greatly affect the sound quality.

"flatness" versus "peakiness" of the graph of the amplitude against the frequency yield a measure of the damping (refer to figure 2.19).

Recent research (Moral and Jansson 1982) has suggested that there are several types of vibration modes of the sound body. In the first type, the top and bottom plates vibrate in unison, and the pattern found on individual plates is identical to that found in an assembled violin. At the lowest frequencies, the middle of the violin vibrates out of phase with the two ends. If you imagine a bar, this mode corresponds to the middle of the bar moving up and down (see figure 4.2). At higher frequencies, between 350 Hz and 700 Hz, the two plates still vibrate in unison. The maximum amplitude of the two-dimensional movement occurs at the edges, however, where the plates are connected to the ribs. The fact that there are distinct vibration modes (shown in figure 4.2) results in frequency regions of high-vibration amplitudes interspersed with frequency regions of low-

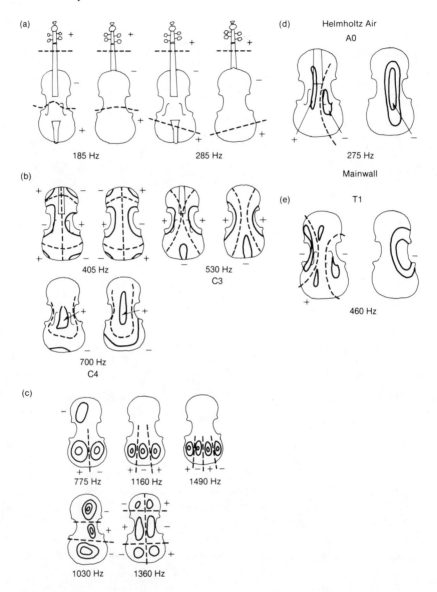

Figure 4.2
Vibration modes of a violin. The dashed lines are null positions, separating up from down movement. The regions of maximum amplitude are indicated by solid lines. The plus and minus signs convey the direction of movement. At the lowest frequencies, the top and bottom plates vibrate in unison (a). At frequencies between 300 Hz and 800 Hz, the plates vibrate in unison, but the amplitude of movement is greatest at the edges (b). At the highest frequencies, the plates do not vibrate together (c). Other vibration modes of importance are the (d) Helmholtz air mode and the (e) main wall vibration model (adapted from Moral and Jansson 1982).

vibration amplitudes. At frequencies above 700–800 Hz, the vibrations often are restricted to either the top or the bottom plate; the plates do not vibrate in parallel. A vibration pattern of the top plate at one frequency may be found in the bottom plate at a different frequency. As the frequency is further increased, there are more vibration modes within any range of frequencies, and the vibration pattern of each plate gets more complicated. This leads to a more uniform response at the higher frequency.

On top of these vibration modes, there is the "Helmholtz air resonance" and the "main wall resonance." The air resonance is created when the top and bottom plates vibrate out of phase so that the volume of the violin body alternately increases and decreases. This resembles an accordian. Air is alternately sucked in and expelled, creating a propagating sound wave of alternating pressure. The main wall resonance occurs from the complex vibration pattern of the top plate combined with an out-of-phase movement of the bottom plate.

These vibration modes represent the sound body possibilities. In order to affect the tone quality, these vibration modes must be excited by the string vibration (otherwise they would not occur during normal performances). To determine the degree to which the string vibration is transferred to the sound body, we vibrate the bridge with a sinusoidal vibration of different frequencies and then measure the vibration of the sound body. The vertical axis (input admittance) measures the degree to which string vibrations are transformed into bridge vibrations and subsequently into sound body vibrations. Below 1000 Hz, the admittance is closely related to the radiated sound. The results of one such measurement are shown in figure 4.3. The curve shows clear peaks at frequencies below 1000 Hz and

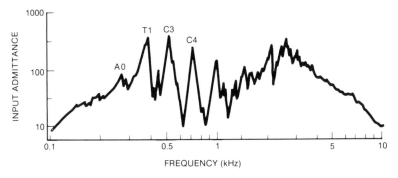

Figure 4.3
Input admittance measures the degree to which the string vibration can set the sound body into motion. The y-axis therefore measures the amount of vibration of the violin body. The vibration peaks at A0, T1, C3, and C4 are the vibration modes shown in figure 4.2 (adapted from Moral and Jansson 1982).

a very broad peak from about 2000 Hz to 4000 Hz. The peaks at the lower frequencies can be identified with the individual vibration modes described previously and illustrated in figure 4.2, while the broad higher frequency peak can be correlated to the overlapping resonance modes of the sound body and the resonance modes of the violin bridge itself. There is thus a strong relationship between the vibration modes of individual plates and the vibration of the violin due to the strings, although not all vibration modes radiate much sound energy (e.g., the lowest modes between 180 Hz and 300 Hz).

Sound Output
These curves of the string–sound body system portray the output for any single frequency. A bowed string, however, excites the sound body with a complex wave composed of the fundamental and harmonics, and each harmonic in turn may excite one or more vibration modes. We could proceed mathematically using the Fourier theorem: the output of the bowed violin would be the sum of the outputs from each harmonic driving each vibration mode. Alternatively, we could proceed empirically by playing the violin as strongly as possible and measuring the level of sound pressure at each note. This curve has been termed a loudness curve (even though we measure sound pressure level), and two examples are shown in figure 4.4.

The "loudness" curve is much smoother overall than the vibration curve. As calculated in chapter 2, the loudness at any frequency is the sum of the sound pressures generated by all the excitation harmonics taken together. The output of each harmonic is equal to the amplitude of the harmonic multiplied by the amplitude of the vibration mode. The harmonics act together to fill in the holes in the vibration curve. Consider, for instance, the loudness peak at about 200 Hz for panel (a). There is no physical vibration mode at this frequency, but it is roughly one-half the frequency of the wood vibration at about 400 Hz. Thus the loudness peak is due to the second harmonic of the note tapping into the wood peak, This is not an isolated event; any note is "supported" by the sum across all the harmonics.

An ongoing research project initiated by F. A. Saunders has attempted to correlate the perceptual quality of a violin to its physical properties. One aspect is the relationship between the frequency of the vibration modes and the musical-note frequencies. For a good instrument, the air resonance falls near the frequency of the second (D) string 294 Hz) and the main wood resonance falls near the frequency of the third (A) string (440 Hz). If the wood resonance occurs at that frequency, it supports or reinforces the second harmonic of the first (G) string (196 Hz). The excellent Stradivarius violin shown in panel (a) conforms to these rules. A poor violin is shown in panel (b); in this instrument the wood mode is too high in frequency, and as a result all the scale notes are of low intensity. Violin makers control the

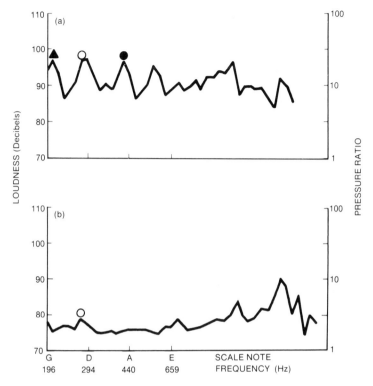

Figure 4.4
Loudness curves for two violins. The top panel characterizes an excellent Stradivarius. The air resonance (open circle) falls near the second string ($D_4 = 294$ Hz) and the main wood resonance (closed circle) falls near the third string ($A_4 = 440$ Hz). The loudness peak at the G string is due to the main wood resonance. The second harmonic of the G string (roughly 400 Hz) excites the wood resonance, and this produces the loudness peak. The second panel characterizes a poor quality violin in which the air resonance does not fall at the appropriate frequency (from Hutchins 1962; copyright © 1962 Scientific American, Inc.).

frequency of the vibration modes by varying the thickness of the wood plates or by varying the strength of the glue connections (Hutchins 1962).

4.2 Trumpets and Clarinets

The wind instruments provide a contrast to the violin family. The vibration is initiated by air pressure, the source excitation is produced by longitudinal airwaves (rather than transverse waves on a string), the input is regulated by a pressure-sensitive mouthpiece, and so on. Nevertheless, the same principles apply, and we will consider the theoretical vibration modes of a tube, the particular vibration modes of these instruments, and the coupling between the player and the instrument.

What is common to both the trumpet and the clarinet is that the mouthpiece is a system that lets in puffs of air when the oscillating air pressure is at a maximum. The maximum variation in pressure at the mouthpiece will occur at the frequencies of vibration modes. For this reason, we can mechanically introduce puffs of air into the mouthpiece at different frequencies and measure the resulting pressure at the mouthpiece. When the frequency of the "puffer" matches a frequency of the vibration mode, then the pressure variation will be high; when the frequency falls between vibration modes, the pressure variation will be much lower. By plotting pressure variation against frequency, therefore, we can identify the vibration modes by the peaks on the graph.

The Trumpet

The evolution of the trumpet can be seen as an attempt to solve two problems. The first is to achieve a series of tones that correspond to the notes of a scale. The second is to make an instrument that is easy to play with a loud, firm sound. The odd harmonic resonances (3, 5, 7, ...) of a tube open at one end and closed at one end must be moved to the musically useful harmonics (2, 3, 4, 5, ...).

The vibration modes of the sound body are determined by three components: (1) the length of the cylindrical tubing; (2) the length and flare of the bell; and (3) the shape of the cuplike mouthpiece. We can measure the frequencies of the vibration modes by starting with only the cylindrical tube, then measuring the tube-flare combination, and finally measuring the entire mouthpiece-tube-flare combination. In this way, the function of each section can be discovered.

In figure 4.5, four curves are presented (Backus 1976). The y-axis is the input impedance. The input impedance is a measure of the pressure variation and is maximum at the resonant frequencies. The x-axis is frequency plotted in terms of frequency ratios. (This is the reason the peaks appear closer at high frequencies.) The second resonance is lined up with the

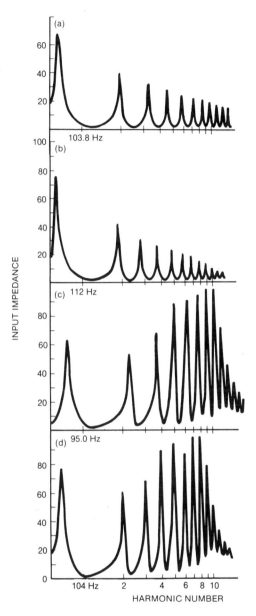

Figure 4.5
Vibration modes of the trumpet. The four panels represent stages in creating a playable instrument: (a) the vibration modes of a straight tube; (b) the vibration modes of a straight tube with a flaring bell; (c) the vibration modes of a straight tube with a mouthpiece and leader pipe; and (d) the vibration modes of a tube plus mouthpiece and leader pipe plus bell (adapted from Backus 1976).

second harmonic, because the second resonance represents the lowest usable vibration mode. Panel (a) presents the pressure variation for a cylindrical tube of the same length as the trumpet. For this cylinder, the pressure peaks occur at the odd harmonics, just as theory would predict. The reduction of the higher harmonics is due to greater frictional losses. There are problems with this tube as an instrument, however. The sound is muffled and of poor quality, because very little of the energy in the tube radiates out. In going from the rather small bore to the huge surrounding atmosphere, most of the energy is simply reflected back up the tube.

These problems are partially resolved by adding the flaring bell. The bell serves two functions. The first is to allow the sound energy of the higher modes to propagate more successfully out the end of the tube. (Incidentally, the megaphones used by cheerleaders perform the identical function. They allow more of the speech energy to propagate into the air.) This can be seen in panel (b) by the great reduction in pressure above 1500 Hz. Nearly all the pressure variation above 1500 Hz is propagated; almost no sound remains to return up the bore to combine with the traveling wave from the mouthpiece to create a standing wave at that frequency. (Remember that these curves are measured within the instrument.) The second function of the flaring bell is to lower the frequency of the higher vibration modes so that they more closely match musical notes. The flare allows the traveling waves to go farther down the bell, particularly for higher frequencies, which increases the wavelength and therby yields a lower frequency. The resonance peaks are closer in frequency in panel (b) as compared to panel (a).

The main function of the leader pipe and mouthpiece is to increase the effect of the instrument tubing on the player's lips. At several points we noted how the pressure variation in the tube "colludes" with the player's lips to bring about a stable standing wave. To influence the lips effectively, the pressure variation due to the standing wave must be high. The leader-mouthpiece serves to couple the player and instrument more closely because of its own natural vibration mode around 900 Hz, which acts as an "amplifier" around those frequencies. It thereby generates the greater pressure peaks in this frequency region (panels c and d).

These pressure curves are generated by varying the frequency of the driving sinusoidal vibrator and measuring the pressure at the mouthpiece. When the trumpet is actually played, the musician takes the place of the vibrator. The puffs of air injected by the musician may be relatively pure, or they may consist of many harmonics. The resulting oscillation within the instrument will be the product of the amplitude of the excitation harmonic generated by the player multiplied by amplitude of the pressure variation (i.e., the amplitude of the vibration mode) at that frequency. It is exactly the same calculation as done for the violin (see the example in section 2.2).

For trumpets, the Q factor or damping is a function of frequency: the coupling is less for higher frequencies (Luce and Clark 1967). At lower frequencies, the majority of sound energy is reflected back to the mouth-piece, which effectively increases the coupling between the player and instrument. On the basis of the coupling, lower frequency resonant modes should have a more rapid attack and decay but a smaller steady-state amplitude. However, the smaller amplitudes of these modes will be compensated by the higher amplitudes of the lower partials generated by the breathing of the trumpeter. These factors balance each other, so that we might expect the lower partials to enter earlier, reach their maximum amplitude more quickly, and have a slightly greater steady-state maximum amplitude. (The harmonics are not exact multiples of the fundamental, so that it is more correct to term them partials.) Analyses of two trumpet notes are shown in figure 4.6. Moreover, as found for the violin, there are amplitude and frequency modulations for all the partials, and there are amplitude "blips" as the frequency of the partials stabilize.

The Clarinet
The same "puffer" procedures can be used to discover the vibration modes of the clarinet (Backus 1974). Consider the graph when all holes are closed (E_3−164 Hz), shown in figure 4.7. The curve shows the odd harmonics, but they are successively lower in frequency than predicted—they are flat. This has the effect of sometimes placing an even harmonic at a resonance peak. For example, the sixth harmonic falls close to the middle of the fourth vibration peak. If the player is producing puffs of air with a sixth harmonic, then it will resonate with the fourth vibration mode and will appear in the harmonic spectrum. This is how even harmonics get produced in the clarinet, where theoretically only odd harmonics should appear: the modes are not exact multiples of the fundamental.

Now consider another lower-mode note produced by opening finger holes, which thereby changes the effective length of the tube (panel b). The effect of the open holes is to reduce the amplitude of the higher modes, exactly as the flare did for the trumpet. What is happening? For a pipe with open holes, the low frequency sound waves are reflected at the highest one or two open holes; due to this reflection, what low frequency energy escapes the bore can only do so from these open holes. In contrast, the higher frequency sound waves can penetrate all the way down the tube. This allows more energy to escape, because it can radiate from all of the open holes. This produces the reduction in amplitude within the instrument shown in panel (b). The lowest frequency at which the vibration wave can penetrate down the entire tube is termed the tone hole lattice cutoff frequency. Benade and Larson (1985), summarizing extensive research, argue that the cutoff frequency determines the perceived quality of wood-

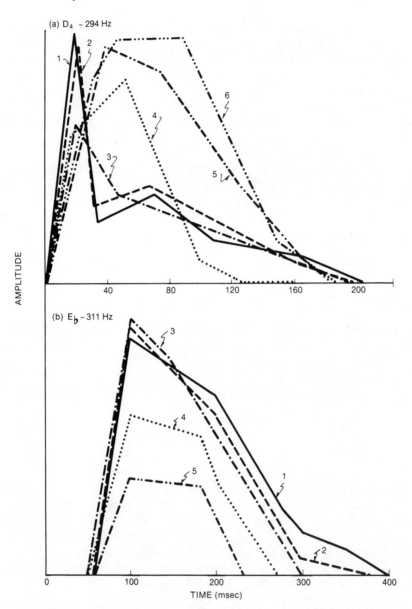

Figure 4.6
Simplified amplitude envelopes for the partials of two different trumpet tones. The amplitude envelopes differ considerably due to different notes, instruments, and players (*a* adapted from Risset and Mathews 1969; *b* adapted from Moorer and Grey 1977b).

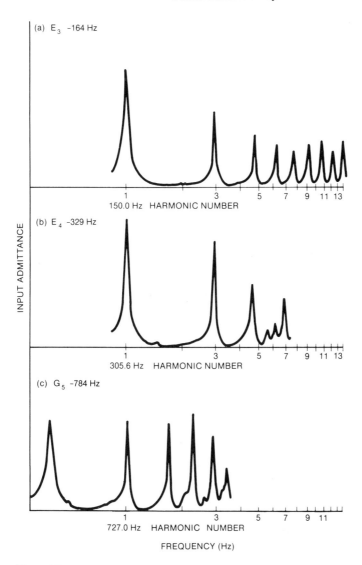

Figure 4.7
The input admittance for three notes of a clarinet. The E$_3$ and E$_4$ notes in (a) and (b) are played in the lower region. The G$_5$ note in (c) is played in the higher register (adapted from Backus 1974).

winds as well as their radiation. Benade (1976) relates that classical musicians prefer a slightly lower cutoff frequency; jazz musicians prefer a slightly higher cutoff frequency.

Finally, consider a higher frequency note that must be produced from a higher vibration mode. To do this, a register key is opened to degrade the amplitude and change the resonant frequency of the lowest vibration mode (panel c). In this register, there is typically little correspondence between the harmonics and vibration modes. In addition to the fundamental, only the third harmonic is close to a resonance peak. Tones in this register are composed mainly of the fundamental, with varying patterns of harmonics. The tone quality thus varies between the two registers.

A detailed analysis of one clarinet note (approximately 311 Hz) is shown in figure 4.8. The first three odd partials are maximum and the even-numbered partials are depressed as predicted. The lower partials seem to have a more rapid attack, indicating a greater degree of damping, much like the trumpet.

The Coupling between Player and Instrument
The player's lipping and the resulting vibration modes of the trumpet and clarinet are interdependent. The mouthpiece acts as a valve, permitting air to enter the instrument when the pressure in the mouthpiece is high and tending to preclude air from entering when the pressure is low. It is an antinode. For the brass instruments, the lips act as the valve; for the woodwinds, the reed acts as a valve.

One outcome of an air valve, which can be easily imagined for a reed, is that the characteristics of the airflow entering the instrument change as a function of the amplitude of the blowing pressure and thereby change the tone quality. Suppose that a player is blowing quite softly. The reed will oscillate back and forth gently, with little movement, and the motion will be almost purely sinusoidal. The air into the clarinet is never completely shut off. As the blowing pressure is increased, the reed oscillation will be larger (although the air still may not be completely cut off at any instant). This has the effect of rapidly increasing the amplitude of the higher harmonics within the mouthpiece. If the amplitude of the fundamental doubles, then the amplitude of the second harmonic increases fourfold, the amplitude of the third harmonic increases eightfold, and so on. If the blowing pressure is further increased, the reed will begin to flap closed against the mouthpiece, a change that the player recognizes as a variation in feel and tone color. This effectively cuts off the air into the clarinet and can amount to 50% of the cycle time. This further alters the relative amplitudes of the higher harmonics and the quality of the sound (Benade and Larson 1985).

In summary, the blowing pressure determines the harmonic structure. Greater pressures lead to a progressive enhancement of the higher har-

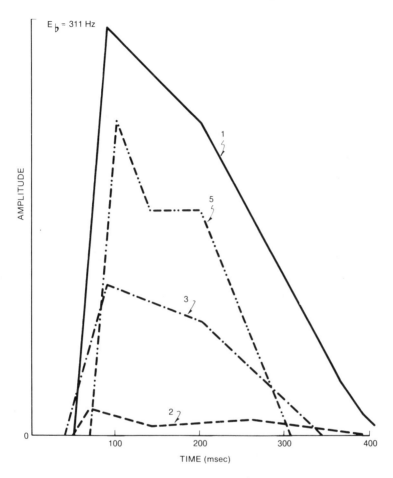

Figure 4.8
Simplified amplitude envelopes for the partials of a clarinet note. The odd harmonics are
maximum (adapted from Moorer and Grey 1977b).

monics. This is true for the trumpet as well as for the clarinet. Increasing the blowing pressure when playing the trumpet leads to more rapid, sharper lip movements and changes the air puffs coming out from the lips. The growth of the harmonics as measured within trumpet and clarinet are shown in figure 4.9.

The first consequence of this growth of harmonics is that it makes playing an instrument easier, because it allows the player to use several vibration modes to support a played note. The standing waves in the tube (due to the vibration modes) can only influence the vibration of the player's lips when there is strong pressure variation. As the player blows more strongly, the pressure variation due to higher vibration modes becomes greater, and this variation reinforces the lower vibration modes. Thus the standing wave in the tube can better control the lip frequency (Benade 1976). Consider an instrument that has its vibration modes at 60 Hz, 180 Hz, 300 Hz, 420 Hz, 600 Hz, 720 Hz, etc. (the odd harmonics of 60 Hz). If the player attempted to play a 60 Hz tone very softly, only the 60 Hz vibration mode would form a standing wave, and it would be difficult for the player to match his or her lip vibration to the weak pressure variation. As the blowing pressure was increased, the "lip valve" would generate stronger harmonics (at all harmonics of 60 Hz: 120 Hz, 180 Hz, 240 Hz, 300 Hz), and each of these stronger higher harmonics produced by the lip valve would drive a higher vibration mode. The 180 Hz third harmonic generated by the player's blowing would drive the instrument's 180 Hz second mode; the 300 Hz fifth harmonic generated by the player would drive the instrument's 300 Hz third mode, and so on. Remember that each of these higher vibration modes has its pressure maximum at the mouthpiece. For this reason, the pressure variation at the mouthpiece becomes greater due to this summing, and it in turn allows the player to better time the air puffs to build up the oscillation to a high level. The same type of collaboration would occur for other notes. Consider the note of 180 Hz. The timing of the pressure oscillation for this note would be reinforced at higher intensities by the instrument's 720 Hz sixth mode, the 1080 Hz ninth mode, and so on. As the relative strength of these vibration modes increased with blowing pressure, they would have progressively greater effects. Notice that it is possible to play a note for which a vibration mode does not exist. A note of 75 Hz could be played by using the vibration modes at 300 Hz, 600 Hz, 900 Hz, etc. The standing waves of these vibration modes would allow the player to vibrate his lips at 75 times/sec to produce that note. (This is most easily accomplished in the trumpet, where the player's lips are somewhat independent of the bore.) This type of collaboration among vibration modes has been termed a regime of oscillation by Benade. A similar effect occurs for bowing. The slip-stick process keeps the higher harmonics strict multiples of the funda-

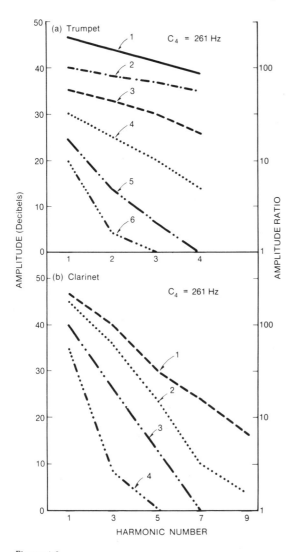

Figure 4.9
As the blowing pressure increases, the strength of the higher harmonics increases relative to the strength of the lower harmonics within the trumpet and clarinet. This can be seen by comparing the lowest blowing pressure (4 through 6) to the highest blowing pressures (1 through 3). As the pressure increases, the amplitude of the higher partials grows most rapidly (adapted from Benade 1976).

mental. This allows the string vibration to control more completely the vibration of the sound body.

Sound Radiation

I have noted that sound waves leaking out of the bell is the basic mechanism for sound radiation in the trumpet and that sound waves leaking out of the open finger holes is the corresponding mechanism in the clarinet. For a trumpet, the lower frequency harmonics tend to "cling" to the surface of the bell and are propagated outward in all directions. The higher harmonics tend to be more concentrated and to be beamed outward from the center of the bell. The behavior of a woodwind is similar, but slightly more complicated. The lowest frequencies are radiated out of the first open holes and spread out uniformly. The higher frequencies are sent out in a conical shape with the axis of the cone along the center line of the instrument. The highest frequencies tend to be beamed along the axis of the clarinet.

Overall, the higher frequencies are radiated most efficiently. As shown in figure 2.23, the percentage of radiation can be represented by a linear function, reaching 100% radiation at 1500 Hz. The strength of the pressure amplitudes within the instrument multiplied by the percent of radiation gives the frequency spectrum reaching the listener. Calculations of this sort are shown in figure 2.23.

As discussed previously, the timbre of an instrument is in part determined by the perceived strength of the harmonics. The perceived strength of each harmonic is determined by the human sensitivity at that frequency (see figure 2.25 for loudness curves) along with the physical intensity of the harmonic. At lower intensities, the auditory system is most sensitive to the middle frequencies, and much of the radiated sound energy is also in that range. The timbre would thus be dominated by the strength of the middle frequencies. At higher intensities, the auditory system roughly is equally sensitive across all frequencies, and the radiated higher frequency intensities become much stronger. In this case the timbre would be determined by nearly the entire range of harmonics. Instruments should "sound" different at different playing levels. This is one example of the fact that the percept is a joint function of the production process and the perceiver.

4.3 Overview

This chapter has commented on many aspects of the sound production of the violin, trumpet, and clarinet. Although each of these aspects yields perceptual information, none is definitive in specifying the instrumental sound; there seems to be no one-to-one correlation between an acoustic configuration and an instrument. Nevertheless, these aspects, both in their number and in their interactions, demonstrate that the listener's world is ever changing. At the same time, we see that there are regularities that cut across instrumental boundaries.

A caution is in order. These aspects are not independent; rather, they are like the strands of a web. Every single aspect of the sound is interrelated to all of the others. Each aspect is changed by the others in much the same way that each filament of a web functions with respect to the others. This means that any one aspect may lead to correct identification of an instrument, because it is determined by all the others. Similarly, an archeologist can identify a species from one bone fragment because the shape of that bone is a reflection of the entire body shape. However, although it is possible to suggest the structural importance of a bone or a strand of a web, it is impossible to point to one and argue that it is more or less important than any other. The strength of the whole emerges from the connections among the parts. The same is true for an instrumental sound: it emerges uniquely out of its interrelated aspects. We may still focus on individual aspects, of course, because though each may provide only one perspective, like one sheet of a blueprint, they may, when taken together, provide a framework for understanding in much the same way that a set of blueprints provides a representation of the entire building. Remember, then, that each of these aspects isolates but one fragment of the sound and that these fragments overlap and interrelate.

F. A. Saunders (1937), who possibly more than any other individual rekindled research interest in the violin, puts it this way:

> Violins have aroused the interest of people of all sorts from several centuries. The beauty of their form, of the wood itself, and of the varnish pleases the eye, their tones charm the ear, and the range of their expressiveness appeals to the souls of artists. The coldly calculating scientific man has paid less attention to them as vibrating systems than they deserve. The strings, the bridge, the two "plates" (top and bottom), and the sides of the violin form a complex system, closely coupled together, in which each part is affected by the others, all with different natural habits of vibration, damping, etc., of their own, but strictly bound by their close relationship and thus forced to give up their individuality for the good of the group. (p. 81)

Further Reading

The books edited by Hutchins (1975, 1976) and Kent (1977) are part of the Benchmark Papers in Acoustics series. Each book contains the original research articles. The article by McIntyre and Woodhouse (1978) is a good summary of research on the violin, and the tutorial article by McIntyre, Schumacher, and Woodhouse (1983) is a mathematical treatment of oscillations in the violin and clarinet. The article by Boomsliter and Creel (1972) could be recommended for any chapter. It is an interesting discussion of sound production and sound perception.

Boomsliter, P. C., and Creel, W. (1972). Research potentials in auditory characteristics of violin tone. *Journal of the Acoustical Society of America*, 51 (6, part 2), 1984–1993.

Hutchins, C. M. (ed.) (1975). *Musical acoustics*. Part 1: *Violin family components*. Stroudsburg, Pa.: Dowden, Hutchinson, & Ross.

Hutchins, C. M. (ed.) (1976). *Musical acoustics*. Part 2: *Violin family functions*. Stroudsburg, Pa.: Dowden, Hutchinson, & Ross.

Kent, E. L. (ed.) (1977). *Musical acoustics: Piano and wind instruments*. Stroudsburg, Pa.: Dowden, Hutchinson, & Ross.

McIntyre, M. E., Schumacher, R. T., and Woodhouse, J. (1983). On the oscillations of muscial instruments. *Journal of the Acoustical Society of America*, 74 (5), 1325–1345.

McIntyre, M. E., and Woodhouse, J. (1978). The acoustics of stringed musical instruments. *Interdisciplinary Science Reviews*, 3 (2), 157–173.

Chapter 5

Sound Generation by the Voice:

Speaking and Singing

The voice is a wonderful instrument. It can cajole, enrage, and seduce others. It can betray oneself. It can whistle, hum, moan, whisper, shout, sing, and imitate an instrument. Its expressive range is greater than any other. The voice creates human interaction.

Yet the voice is fundamentally an instrument no different from the violin or trumpet. Air is expelled through the vocal folds in such a way that a periodic or nonperiodic vibration pattern is generated. In both cases, the vibration is coupled to the vocal tract cavity (e.g., the mouth, lips, tongue, nose), which functions exactly like the sound body of a violin or trumpet. The vocal tract sound body selectively amplifies the harmonic spectrum of the vibration pattern. This "shaped" speech sound is then radiated from the mouth and nose.

It is interesting to note some of the morphological adaptations that seem to make speech natural to humans (Lenneberg 1967; P. Lieberman 1984). First of all, human beings have the most intricate and complex set of muscles to move the mouth and lips. The mouth is relatively small and can be opened and closed quickly. This allows the rapid closure and explosive opening required for sounds like /b/ and /p/. The teeth are regular, even in height, with the top and bottom meeting to form an unbroken barrier. This construction is essential for the production of sounds like /f/, /v/, /sh/, and /th/. The tongue is broad and muscular, as opposed to the long and thin tongues of monkeys. This allows changing the volume and shape of the mouth, which thereby amplifies different harmonics. Finally, the vocal cords are simpler in structure than those of other primates. The system is streamlined so that optimal flow occurs primarily on expiration. This is matched by the human lungs, which can easily change the distribution of breathing in to breathing out with no discomfort. When not speaking, the time to inhale and the time to exhale is roughly equal, and this is true whether relaxing or strenuously exercising. However, when speaking, the time to inhale can be as short as one-fifth of a second and the time to exhale can be as long as 20 seconds.

The speech chain from production to perception entails complexities unknown thirty years ago. Speech seems like a series of individual units that follow each other in time. Each unit appears analogous to an alphabetic letter. Contrary to what we experience, the acoustic physical signal does not, however, consist of discrete packets of energy, each bound to an alphabetic letter. The acoustic signal for any linguistic segment is spread out across several acoustic units. This overlapping of speech sounds is due to the mechanical constraints on the movement of the jaw, tongue, and lips, coupled to the high rate of talking. It has been estimated that the average syllable is 200 msec long and that 2.5 words are spoken per second on average. There are about 100 muscles involved in speaking, so that the rate at which individual muscular events occur (throughout the speech apparatus) is roughly several hundred every second. If each speech sound had to be completed before the next one started, it would be impossible to talk quickly. The production system must cheat in order to get all the sounds out rapidly: movements appropriate to several successive sounds must be made simultaneously, and movements necessary to produce future sounds must be started early enough to ensure that the vocal tract will be in the correct position to make those sounds when they are required. At any given point in time, the sound pressure pattern is the result of what happened in the past, what is happening now, and what will happen. The signal is *context dependent*—the acoustic wave for any speech unit changes because of the surrounding speech units. At any single moment, the signal will have information concerning successive sounds, because of their overlap. This has been termed *parallel transmission*. Although we hear the speech units as discrete entities, like eggs on a conveyer belt, the process of speech production it is like eggs that have been pushed through a wringer. In the resulting mess, the contents of each egg will have flowed and mixed with those of the neighbors. The listener must identify from the bits of shell, yolk, and albumen the nature of the original eggs (this analogy comes from Hockett 1955, p. 210).

The fact that speech sounds mutually influence each other due to articulatory movements has been termed *coarticulation*. The movements do not occur one after the other, as our experience of successive speech sounds would suggest. Instead, they overlap to a greater or lesser degree. Coarticulation changes the resonances of the sound body for each sound from what would have occurred if it had been vocalized alone. (In fact, some consonants cannot be articulated alone.) The acoustic signal is therefore different, and it will differ in various ways as a function of the succeeding and preceding sounds. Coarticulation also occurs across words and therefore blurs any acoustic boundaries between adjacent sounds. Coarticulation leading to context dependency is the rule, not the exception. This overlapping of speech units has the consequence of making understanding easier; it allows us to miss parts of the signal and still retrieve the linguistic units from the surrounding sounds. But it makes understanding speech in terms of fixed unchanging sounds impossible.

A common example of overlapping and context dependency of movements is jumping over a puddle. You make the jump far before you leap: approaching the puddle you vary your stride and shuffle your feet to avoid obstacles and to make the takeoff foot fall at the right point in front of the puddle. Moreover, even during takeoff, you are making anticipatory corrections for the landing. Thus, the movements for takeoff, jump, and landing are occurring at the same time. An example in speech production occurs when making the sound "stru": speakers round their lips to produce the "u" sound even before starting to make the initial sounds.

A speaker intends to convey a message. To do so, the speaker makes a coordinated series of movements in the vocal tract to bring forth the appropriate speech sounds. The unanswered physical and psychological questions concern the form of the speech sound produced by the speaker and perceived by the listener. Do listeners perceive speech in terms of the articulation of the speaker? Should the speech sounds be conceptualized as segments that are produced by movements of the articulators (lips, tongue, etc.) to a specific configuration? If so, can these segments be readily identified in the acoustic signal and are these segments "heard" by listeners? Nearly all of this chapter revolves around the correspondence among the articulator movements in sound production, the acoustic physical signal, and the listeners' world of meaningful speech. These correspondences are subtle and not at all obvious.

Research up to the present has suggested that the way to analyze and understand speech is to start with the articulatory processes by which speech is created. We will review these and then discuss the possible relationships among the articulatory mechanisms, the acoustic signal, and the perceived speech sound.

5.1 The Production of Speech Sounds

Typically, speech has been conceptualized as being the end product of four sequential processes: (1) the airstream process, in which air is expelled from the lungs; (2) the phonation process, in which the air from the lungs is set into vibration; (3) the articulatory process, in which the vibration pattern is modified by the resonances of the sound body formed by the oral and nasal cavities; and (4) the radiation process, in which vibration is radiated into the air. A schematic cross-sectional view of the vocal tract and the vocal cord is shown in figure 5.1.

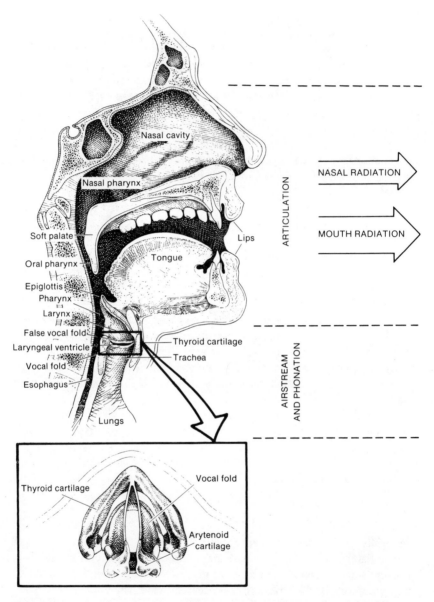

Figure 5.1
A cross-sectional view of the vocal tract and the vocal cords. The airstream, phonation, and articulation processes are sketched. The sound radiation is propagated mainly through the mouth; the nose is a secondary radiator for "nasal" consonants (from Sundberg 1977; copyright © 1977 Scientific American, Inc.).

The Airstream and Phonation Process

The flow of air expelled from the lungs provides the power for speech sounds. The output pressure is relatively constant and can extend for long periods. To produce a sound, the airflow must be converted to an oscillatory flow. This can be achieved by inducing the vocal cords to vibrate, producing a periodic air column; by producing turbulences in the vocal tract by constricting the tract at some point in the mouth; or by closing the tract completely, using the lips or tongue, and then releasing the air pressure suddenly.

The air from the lungs passes through the vocal cords of the vocal folds. The cords that do the actual vibrating are small, muscular, flaplike folds attached to the interior of the larynx. The cords are remarkably flexible and can be positioned in a wide variety of shapes and spacings. When we breathe, they are pulled back out of the way; when we whisper, they are held so that the air flowing through them produces a rushing or hissing sound; when we voice, they vibrate to open and close; and when we murmur, they are slightly apart—they can still vibrate but air flows through.

During normal breathing, the vocal cords are held apart. When speaking is about to begin, the cords are brought together. The high pressure resulting from the airflow from the lungs forces the cords apart, which allows air to move up into the vocal tract. The vocal cords still present a narrowing of the vocal tract, so the air pressure at this point is lower than in the surrounding area. This creates a "suction" (the Bernoulli effect) that tends to draw the vocal cords together. (It is like blowing through a floppy straw with a kink. As you blow, the kink tends to close, stopping the flow.) In addition to the Bernoulli force, the muscular tension of the cords themselves also acts to reclose the opening. Because the cords are initially together, the separation caused by the airflow induces a muscular force to bring them back together. The two forces acting in synchrony overcome the airflow pressure separating the cords, reclose the vocal cords, and the oscillation begins again.

The vibration is that of an air column, as in a trumpet or clarinet. The vocal cords, although they are stringlike, only admit and close off the air entering the tube. The vocal cords are therefore analogous to the lips of a trumpet player or the reed of a clarinet. They are not analogous to violin strings. The vocal tract is a tube open at one end (the mouth) and closed at one end (the vocal cords). The air column vibration creates standing waves.

The frequency of the vocal cord vibration comes from the tension, length, and mass of the vocal cords. From the discussion in chapter 2 on the vibration of strings, we would expect that increasing the tension or decreasing the mass of the string would increase the fundamental frequency, and that increasing the length would decrease the fundamental frequency. Male vocal vords (fundamental frequencies of 80–240 Hz) are both longer and more massive than female vocal cords (fundamental frequencies of 140–500 Hz), which in turn are longer and more massive than those of children, (fundamental frequencies of 170–600 Hz). Surprisingly, the vocal cords lengthen to produce higher frequency sounds. However, the lengthening of the cords produces increased tension and decreased mass, which more than compensates for the increased length.

An amusing demonstration occurs when speaking after breathing helium. The speaking voice is very high-pitched and squeaky. Yet the vocal cord frequency does not change in the less dense gas. What does change is that the resonant frequencies of the open vocal tract tube increase by about 75%. The fundamental resonance frequency equals the speed of sound divided by four times the tube length, and the remaining harmonics are the odd harmonics. The speed of sound increases about 75% in helium, and the resonance frequencies increase by the same fraction. The high-pitched voice occurs because the vocal tract filter supports the higher harmonics of the vocal cord vibration (P. Lieberman 1977).

In addition to being able to vary the frequency of vibration, the speaker can also vary the "kind" of oscillation. At one extreme, the airflow past the cords is gentle, the Bernoulli force is therefore weak, and thus the cords never close completely. The flow pattern looks sinusoidal but slightly askew. The amplitude of the fundamental is far greater than those of the higher harmonics. At the other extreme, the airflow is greater and the Bernoulli force is stronger; the vocal cords consequently remain completely closed for up to 70% of the cycle, and the airflow resembles a triangular vibration. The first five or six harmonics are roughly equal, with higher harmonics rapidly decreasing in magnitude. As the breathing pressure increases, the vibration pattern entering the vocal tract resonator is much richer in higher harmonics. The timbre and color of the voice changes.

Consider some of the similarities among the vibration of vocal cords, violin strings, and a trumpeter's lips. There is an identical relation between tension/mass and fundamental frequency. The vibration frequency of a violin string is varied by the adjustment of tension and mass, the vibration frequency of the trumpeter's lips is varied by changing the lipping tension, and the vibration frequency of the vocal cords is also varied by changing the mass and tension of the vibrator. There is also an identical relation between harmonic content and intensity. For the violin, trumpet, and voice, an increase in intensity is always accompanied by a larger relative growth in the magnitudes of the higher harmonics. The sound gets shriller, more edgy, and again reveals the perceptual problem of identifying an instrument or a speaker in the face of acoustic energy changes.

The Articulatory Process
The air pressure vibration pattern induced by the vocal cords then enters the sound body: the pharynx, connecting the vocal cords with the nasal cavity and the oral (mouth) cavity. The mouth is the most important part of the vocal tract, because its shape and size are the most variable. The mouth can be varied by adjusting the relative positions of the palate, tongue, lips, and teeth. The tongue is the most flexible component: the entire tongue can move backward and forward, as well as up and down, and its tip, edges, and center can be moved independently. As the vocal tract transforms its shape, the resonant frequencies of the vibration modes change. The vocal tract therefore modifies in different ways the relative amplitudes of the harmonics stemming from the vibration of the vocal cords. The vocal cord vibration and the sound body resonances are independent; each can be varied separately.

Vowels provide simple examples. The vowel /i/ is produced by constricting the front of the palate with the tongue and by a small jaw opening. This positioning tends to lower the frequency of the first resonance (about 300 Hz) and increase the frequency of the second resonance (about 2300 Hz). In contrast, the vowel /a/ is produced by constricting the pharynx with the tongue. This positioning makes the first resonance about 750 Hz and the second resonance about 1200 Hz. The response of the vocal tract for three vowels is shown in figure 5.2.

Radiation Process
The final step is the radiation of the sound energy into the air. The mouth acts in much the same way that a trumpet or a clarinet does. Higher frequencies are radiated more efficiently than lower frequencies. It has been estimated that for each doubling of frequency (i.e., each octave), the output increases by two times (6 dB).

Summary of Speech Sound Production
The production of speech sounds is analogous to the production of violin or trumpet sounds. An excitation vibration is produced, the vibration is impressed on a sound body, the sound body is forced into vibration, and the sound body vibration is radiated into the air. Each step modifies the original vibration, changing the relative strength of each harmonic. The spectrum of the vocal cord vibration multiplied by the resonance curves of the vibration modes multiplied by the radiation function yields the propagated sound.

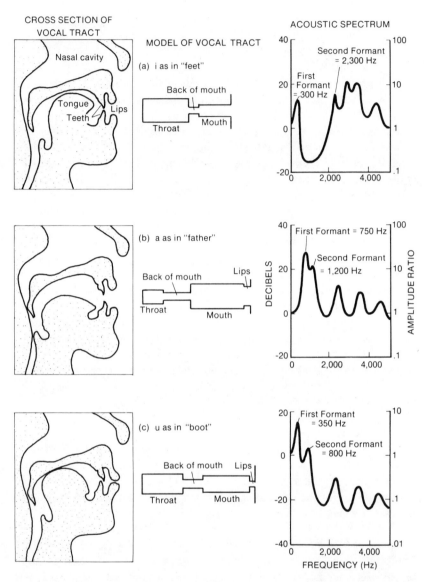

Figure 5.2
The articulatory process. The positions of the articulators can be determined from x-ray pictures. The positions of the tongue, lips, teeth, and jaw create the resonant cavities that generate the resonances of the vocal tract. The resonances of the vocal tract can be calculated on the basis of the cavities, and the theoretical acoustical spectra for each vowel are shown in the right column (adapted from G. A. Miller 1981).

5.2 *Phonetics: Speech Sounds*

There must be equivalences between the production of speech and the perception of speech. It seems reasonable to assume that the driving force in the evolution of speech was the need to convey a wide variety of messages at acceptably fast rates of communication. The bottlenecks, in this case, would be the ability of the human vocal system to articulate the required speech sounds and the ability of the human auditory system to perceive them. The sounds used for speech must necessarily be limited by the mechanical constraints in articulation and by the neural constraints in perception. Sounds that are difficult to articulate and sounds that are difficult to identify are not suitable for speech. On this basis, if we can describe sounds used in language in terms of articulation and in terms of the resulting acoustic signal, then we should be in a good position to understand the processes and difficulties of speech perception.

The most common scheme for describing speech sounds is to characterize each sound as a unique bundle of articulatory features. In view of the great diversity of languages, it is surprising that three articulatory differences have been found universally: (1) the manner of articulation, which distinguishes consonants; (2) the manner of voicing—voiced or unvoiced—which distinguishes among consonants that have the same manner of articulation; and (3) the place of articulation, which distinguishes among vowels and among consonants that have the same manner of articulation and that have voicing. Each feature is characterized by two or more values. There are four different places of articulation, for example. Each sound is therefore described in terms of its value on the three articulatory features.

It is possible to describe the speech sounds on two levels. The first is the *phonetic* or *pronunciation* level. At this level, a full acoustic description is made: each speech sound is defined by all the features necessary to make the sound. For example, the *p* in "pot" and the *p* in "spot" differ phonetically because the *p* in "pot" is made with a slight puff of air, an aspiration, and the *p* in "spot" is unaspirated. The second is the *phonological* or *phomenic* level. At this level each speech sound is defined by only those features necessary to create a difference in meaning. *Pot* differs from *tot* which differs from *dot*; /p/, /t/, and /d/ represent meaning or phonemic differences. The smallest segment of sound that can produce a linguistic contrast is termed a *phoneme* (and is indicated by surrounding slashes). A pronunciation difference generating a linguistic difference in one language may not signal a linguistic difference in another language. Neither /l/ nor /r/ occurs in Japanese, and therefore "I had butterfries in my stomach" is equivalent in meaning to "I had butterflies in my stomach." Phonemes are defined by language use, not by acoustic differences. The various forms of a phoneme are termed *allophones*. Allophones do not change meaning, and the acoustic differences are due to varying contexts and positions within the speech act. We will consider in more detail below the production of phonemes: the vowels and the various kinds of consonants—fricatives, stops, nasals, glides and semivowels.

Vowels

All English vowels are voiced: the vocal cords undergo periodic vibration (/h/ may be an exception; it is really a voiceless vowel). The vocal tract is open, and vowels tend to be rather steady in their sound. Distinctions among vowels are based on: (1) the position of the main part of the tongue; (2) the height of the tongue, which controls the degree of constriction of the tract; and (3) the position of the lips. A classification and pictorial representation of the vowels on the basis of tongue position and degree of constriction is presented in figure 5.3. The labels for tongue position should not be taken literally; they only describe how the vowels sound with respect to each other. The representation is a description of auditory qualities, not articulation (Ladefoged 1975). For example, the tongue is highest in front of the mouth for the vowel /i/ in "heed," highest in the back of the mouth for the vowel /u/ in "who'd," and the lowest for the vowel /ae/ in "had" or the vowel /a/ in "pot." There is a second class of vowels termed *diphthongs* (/ou/ in "tone," /ei/ in "take," /ai/ in "might,"

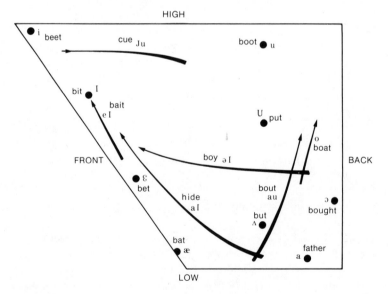

Figure 5.3
Classification of vowels and diphthongs in terms of the height of the tongue and the part of the tongue involved in the constriction (adapted from Ladefoged 1975).

/au/ in "shout," /oi/ in "boy"). Diphthongs are the combination of two simple vowels and are produced by movements from the first to the second; for example the tongue would move from *a* to *u* for the diphthong *au*. Some phoneticians have suggested that /i/ (tongue as far forward and as high as possible), /u/ (tongue as far back and as high as possible), and /a/ (tongue as far back and as low as possible) are "cardinal" vowels, in that they form a yardstick against which other vowels are compared.

This characterization suggests that there are relatively stable articulation positions for each vowel. Each articulatory position results in vibration modes located at different frequencies. Each mode will amplify a range of frequencies (i.e., yield a formant), and much of the research to date has tried to specify each vowel in terms of the frequencies of the lowest two or three formants. We will return to this model later in the chapter.

Consonants
Consonants differ from vowels in many ways. Consonants involve both intensity and frequency transitions, and the vocal tract constriction used to form consonants can create a nonperiodic sound source. However, the constriction causes consonants to be weaker than the more open vocal tract, voiced vowels. The classification of the English consonants in table 5.1 is based on the features of manner of articulation, place of articulation, and manner of voicing.

Stop consonants   Stop consonants begin with a brief but complete blockage of airflow. The blockage may occur at the lips, as in /b/ or /p/; it may occur at the hard palate behind the upper teeth, as in /d/ or /t/; or it may occur at the soft palate, as in /g/ and /k/. Releasing the block creates an initial noise burst due to the rush of air. The frequency spectrum of the burst is determined by the point of constriction. During the same time span, the vocal cords vibrate, and the timing of this vibration is critical to the identification of the consonant. There are at least five variations in the timing between the onset of the stop (or the onset of the initial noise burst) and the onset of the voicing. These variations are shown in figure 5.4. At one extreme (e.g., an English initial /b/), the voicing continues throughout the block, the burst, and the following sound, such as a vowel. In the middle, the vocal cords are resting in a closed position, and voicing begins just prior to or just after onset of the burst. At the other extreme, the vocal cords are held apart, and the voicing is delayed 20 to 50 msec after the release of the burst. The burst is louder and more noiselike, because the open cords allow more air to escape and build up during the block. Phonetically, *voiced* stop consonants are characterized by vocal cord vibration during the actual block, and *aspirated* stop consonants are characterized by noise (lack of cord vibration) during and following the block. The onset of

Table 5.1
The English Consonants

	Position of Articulation							
	Bilabial (lower lip, upper lip)		Labio-Dental (lower lip, upper teeth)		Dental (tongue tip, upper teeth)		Alveolar (tongue tip, gum ridge)	
Type of Articulation	Voiced	Voice-less	Voiced	Voice-less	Voiced	Voice-less	Voiced	Voice-less
Stops	b	p			d	t		
Fricatives			v	f	*th*en	*th*in	z	s
Affricatives								
Nasals	m						n	
Laterals							l	
Semivowels	w						r	

	Position of Articulation					
	Palatal (tongue front, hard palate		Velar (tongue back, soft palate)		Glottal (Vocal Folds, Glottis)	
Type of Articulation	Voiced	Voiceless	Voiced	Voiceless	Voiced	Voiceless
Stops			g	k		
Fricatives	mea*s*ure	*sh*allow				h
Affricatives	*g*yp	*ch*ip				
Nasals			sa*ng*			
Laterals						
Semivowels	y					

the voicing relative to the onset of the burst is termed the *voice onset time*. To create phonemic meaning differences (phonological differences), languages select different points along the voice onset time continuum to form the voiced-unvoiced opposition. Phonologically voiced stops in English (/b/, /d/, /g/) are phonetically similar to (2) and (3), partially voiced or voiceless and unaspirated; phonologically unvoiced stops in English (/p/, /t/, /k/) are phonetically similar to (4), voiceless and aspirated. In contrast, phonologically voiced stops in French are similar to (1), and unvoiced stops are similar to (3). Spectrograms of three stop consonants are shown in figure 5.4. The voicing is represented by the vertical lines.

Fricatives   Fricatives are produced by turbulent airflow that is caused by a partial constriction in the vocal tract. The position of the constriction creates damped vibration modes with resonant frequency regions. The friction of the constriction produces a "hissing" sound that is characteristic of all fricatives. Fricatives like /f/ and /v/ are produced by a constriction at the front of the mouth: raising the lower lip until it nearly touches the

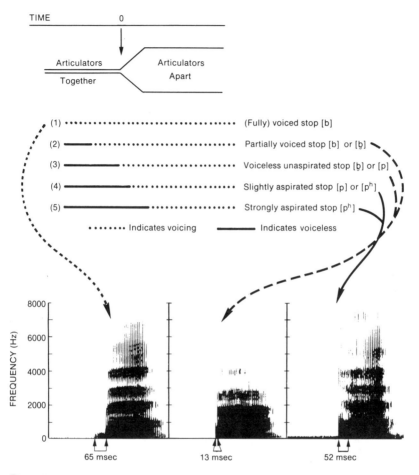

Figure 5.4

Voiced-voiceless feature for consonants. A schematic representation of the production of stop consonants is shown in the top panel (adapted from Ladefoged 1975). The articulators are held together until time 0, when they are released, producing the sound burst. Five variations of voicing are shown: at one extreme voicing may begin before the burst and at the other extreme voicing may begin well after the burst. The symbol [p̥] is a voiceless voiced stop as in "that boy" and [pʰ] is an aspirated /p/ as in "pie". Three actual spectrograms are shown. The voicing is shown by the vertical striations. The spectrogram on the left is a prevoiced consonant resembling (1) above. It represents a negative voice onset time. The middle spectrogram is a voiced [di] resembling (2) and (3) above. The consonant on the right is a voiceless [ti] resembling (4) and (5) above (from Foss and Hakes 1978, by permission of Prentice-Hall, Inc.).

upper front teeth. The airstream passes through some of the space between the upper teeth. This positioning acts to attenuate frequencies below 1500 Hz and above 7500 Hz. The sound contains relatively equal amounts of energy at frequencies between 1500 Hz and 7500 Hz; these fricatives are perceived as a noise "high" in pitch but weak in intensity. Fricatives such as /sh/ as in "she," and /s/ as in "sip" are produced by a constriction at the back of the mouth utilizing the root of the tongue. The air may then be forced over the sharp teeth edge (sip) or forced into a narrow beam due to grooving the tongue (she). This positioning results in a greater contribution of low frequency sounds (down to 700 Hz) and moreover results in peaks of energy, much like vowel formants, between 1000 Hz and 3000 Hz. These sounds seem louder than those articulated at the front of the mouth. For voiced fricatives (*view, than, zoo*), the turbulent airflow is accompanied by a low frequency periodic component (around 700 Hz) because of the vibration of the vocal cords.

Other consonants   Nasals (/m/, /n/, /ng/) are produced by blocking the output of sound through the mouth with the tongue (like stop consonants) and dropping the soft palate so that sound radiation is through the nose. The sound radiated through the nose produces a nasal murmur containing low frequency energy. If you pinch your nose closed, the sound output will be blocked and the nasal will be silenced. The nasal chambers are constant in shape and size, and the nasal resonances are thus the same for all nasal consonants. The closed mouth acts as a second resonant chamber. The place of articulation where the mouth is blocked off determines the particular voiced nasal consonant. The /m/ (my) is produced at the front of the mouth by the lips, /n/ (nigh) is produced by moving the tongue tip to the gum ridge, and the /ng/ (range) is produced by moving the back of the tongue to the soft palate. Thus, although the sound emerges from the nasal cavity, it is the size and shape of the mouth that determines the consonant.

Summary of Phonetics
To produce the speech sounds of a language, the positions and shapes of the articulators are manipulated to yield different resonances. The timing and spatial demands on the articulators (e.g., larynx, lips, tongue, and mouth) required for speech are severe. For example, if the closure of the lips undershoots by as little as one millimeter, then "best" will become "vest": a stop consonant will become a fricative; air will escape through the opening. We can use articulation as a frame of reference against which to explore the generalities underlying speech perception. For example, if we discover differences between the voiced plosives /b/ and /d/ due to the place of articulation (bilabial versus dental, table 5.1), then the same differ-

ences ought ot occur between the unvoiced plosives /p/ and /t/ and between the nasals /m/ and /n/, because each of these sets involves the same distinction in place of articulation.

5.3 The Continuous Speech Signal

With rare exceptions, speech is necessarily coarticulated. This means that the phonetic segments we hear are created by the coordinated movement or gestures of the vocal tract structures. The movements among the structures are so integrated that analysis of any one muscle or structure will prove unsuccessful in describing the acoustic output or in predicting what is heard. For example, to articulate the syllable /bu/ requires movements of the lower lip, upper lip, and jaw, and the movement of the upper lip consists of simultaneous rounding and opening. These overlapping movements create an acoustic wave in which there is no simple correspondence between a perceived phonemic segment and a uniform section of the speech signal. Because of the coordinated movements of the articulators, the acoustic pattern that "signals" the phoneme is distributed over long sections of the acoustic signal and is altered by articulations necessary for the preceding and succeeding phonemic segments. G. A. Miller (1951) describes this succinctly: "The vocal machinery does not produce phonemes the way a typewriter prints letters" (p. 26).

The "overlapping" of the acoustic signal is demonstrated in figure 5.5. The top panel is a schematic representation of the syllable [bag]. The overlap of the phonemes is shown by the shading, and the formants are superimposed. Hardly any part of the acoustic signal can be attributed to only one of the phonemes.

The bottom panel is an analysis of the roughly 1-sec phrase "Santa Claus." A visual analysis of the acoustic spectrogram leads to the conclusion that it can be broken into eighteen distinct segments. But, as can be seen in the lower section, no single acoustic segment represents one phoneme, and moreover every acoustic segment (with the possible exception of numbers 10 and 15) is involved with more than one phoneme. Each phoneme is represented by overlapping acoustic segments.

The realization that there is no simple correspondence between an acoustic segment and a phonemic segment has led to a variety of theoretical approaches to speech perception. All approaches agree, I think, that speech perception is based in some way on the articulation of speech. Some theorists have postulated genetically endowed neural systems that directly perceive speech in terms of the articulation involved in speech production (e.g., Liberman and Mattingly 1985). Other theorists have postulated that though the speech signal is variable, there do exist acoustic invariants, because of articulation constraints, that can be utilized to recover the

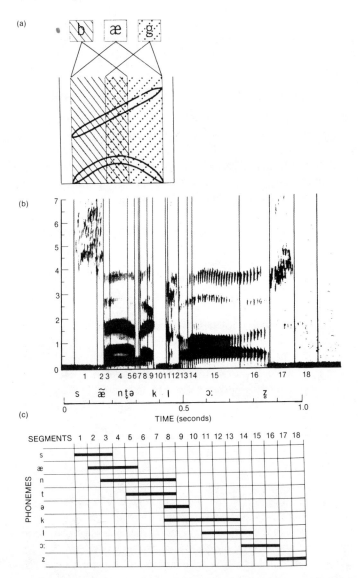

Figure 5.5
In the continuous speech signal, individual phonemes are overlapped acoustically. In the representation of "bag", the properties of the consonants are so intermixed that the initial consonant overlaps the ending consonant (from Liberman 1970, by permission). In the representation of "Santa Claus", 18 acoustical segments can be identified. The 9 phonemes are spread across 2 to 6 acoustic segments. Nearly all acoustic segments are generated by articulatory information from more than one phoneme. There is no one-to-one correspondence between a phoneme and an acoustic segment (adapted from Lenneberg 1967).

segments (Stevens 1972; Stevens and Blumstein 1981). These invariants may be dynamic, and therefore they may not correspond to observable acoustic segments. The common thread in both these views is that co-articulation is regular in some fashion. Phonemic segments do follow each other in the acoustic wave (although they may be overlapping), and the articulatory movements do have similar dynamics (movements) and positions. Without this regularity, perception would be impossible. Some of the consequences of coarticulation will be illustrated below, including the use listeners make of the acoustic changes due to coarticulation for speech identification.

To portray the continuous speech signal, I will use the speech spectrogram, which presents frequency as a function of time. To allow the production of speech for experimentation, speech synthesizers were invented in the 1940s. These took spectrogram-like representations and created speech. The idea is quite simple. Researchers begin with a spectrogram. Black lines represent the frequencies. This picture is pulled under a line of photo cells; each photo cell is connected to an oscillator tuned to a specific frequency determined by the cell's position. A photocell at the bottom of the sheet would connect to a low frequency oscillator; a photocell at the top of the page would connect to a high frequency oscillator. The output of the photocell is proportional to the "blackness" of the line under the photocells, and this ouput in turn determines the amplitude of the oscillator. It is like a musical score (if you imagine that the score is pulled past your eyes): the height of the note determines the frequency and the accent marks (blackness) indicate the intensity.

One can start with a real speech spectrogram, make a guess as to the important parts of the signal, re-create these parts on the synthesizer, and then discover what this simplified re-creation sounds like. It will sound somewhat unnatural, but the important question is whether it is intelligible. By working back and forth between the spectrograph and synthesizer, researchers are able to create patterns that mimic the phonemes.

An example of the interplay between a speech spectrogram and a speech synthesizer is shown in figure 5.6. Both actual spectrogram and the synthesized signal based on the important acoustic energy regions are shown. The original spectrogram is immensely complicated, and that fact again reveals the lack of simple correspondence between the acoustic signal and perceived speech segment. For instance, the silent durations do not segment the words in the phrase "the dog snapped at." The silences within "snapped" are greater than those separating "the" and "dog." It is also clear that the synthesized representations do not capture all of the acoustic variation in the utterance. Obviously, a representation is not intended to capture all of the variation; it is meant to portray the acoustic energy necessary for intelligible speech. It may, however, lead to a conception of

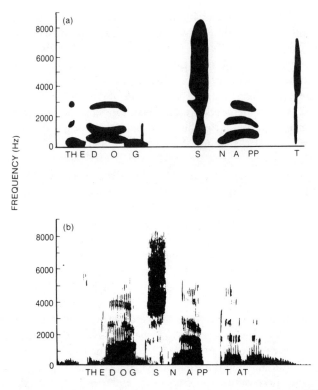

Figure 5.6
A comparison between the spectrogram analysis of a phase spoken in fluent conversation, "the dog snapped at" (b) and the synthesized version of the same phrase (a) (from Foss and Hakes 1978, by permission of Prentice-Hall, Inc.).

segments—bursts, transitions, formants—that is inappropriate. Although this problem needs to be kept in mind, the following material illustrates the effects of coarticulation on the acoustic signal. In particular, different acoustic signals may yield the same percept in different contexts, and conversely, the same acoustic signal may yield different percepts in different contexts.

The stop consonants—/b/, /d/, /g/, /p/, /t/, /k/—demonstrate the lack of a reliable one-to-one relationship between the acoustic signal and the perceived speech sound. The /d/ occurs in nearly all the languages of the world, and it is among the first vocalizations of the child (Liberman et al. 1967). Recall the production of the English stop consonant: (1) there is a silent period during the stop; (2) the stop is released, yielding a burst of sound energy; and (3) the vocal cords begin to vibrate during or immediately after the burst for (English) voiced stops but are delayed for (English) unvoiced stops. However, it is impossible to produce an isolated stop consonant: it has to go or come from somewhere. It is possible to say [up], [ib], [pu], or [bi], but it is impossible to say /b/ or /p/ without implying any other sound. The vocal tract must change from the shape for the consonant to the shape required for the following vowel (or consonant, as in "bread"). The articulators open, and the tongue moves toward and reaches the position for the following sustained vowel (or consonant). For this reason, there is a transition from one set of formant frequencies associated with the consonant shape to the set of formant frequencies associated with the following vocalic sound. These are termed the *formant transitions*.

In an attempt to characterize the /d/ acoustically, research has investigated the formant transitions alone, without the noise bursts. The outcome can be shown by illustrating the transitions that give the "best-sounding" /d/ for three different vowels. As can be seen in figure 5.7, the first (lower) formant is almost identical. However, the second formant transitions are drastically different for each syllable. To give one example, for [di] the second formant transition rises from 2200 Hz to 2600 Hz, yet for [du] the second formant falls from 1200 Hz to 700 Hz. The acoustic information about the place of articulation for the consonant (tongue tip, upper teeth) depends on the vowel. The /d/ percept does not come from the transition itself. If the transition is reproduced alone, it sounds like a chirp or whistle. We can try to sneak up on the /d/ by progressively cutting off the steady-state part from the right, working left. This does not uncover the /d/, because we hear either the whole consonant-vowel syllable or a nonspeech sound. There is no point at which a pure /d/ appears. Because of coarticulation, the formant transition is determined by both the consonant and the vowel. They are overlapped in articulation and in the acoustic signal, although we hear them following one another. Different acoustic signals may thus be classified as the identical phoneme when they convey information about similar articulation.

In slightly more complex vowel–stop consonant–vowel utterances, the formant transitions from the initial vowel to the consonant may be changed by the articulatory requirements for the final vowel. Moreover, the formant transitions from the consonant to the final vowel may be changed by the initial vowel (Öhman 1966). This can be seen for the stop consonant /g/ in figure 5.8. The formant transitions out of the initial vowel /a/ change because of the final vowel (looking down the middle column), and the formant transitions into the final vowel /a/ change because of the initial vowel (looking across the row). Even in these simple utterances, the acoustic signal (i.e., formant transitions) for the identical stop consonant can change dramatically.

In words, even the stop can change. Zue and Laferriere (1979) demonstrated that if the stop precedes a stressed vowel in the middle of a word

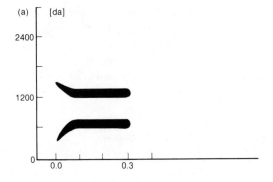

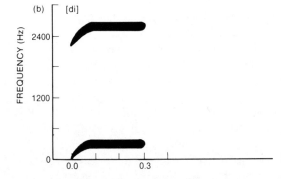

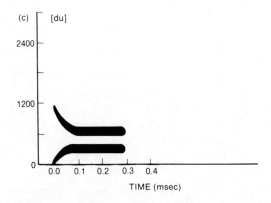

Figure 5.7
Formant transitions generating the "best" /d/ for three different syllables. The first formant is nearly identical: all the formant transitions are in the same direction. However, the second formant differs for each syllable; the formant transition can move upward or downward (adapted from Liberman et al. 1967).

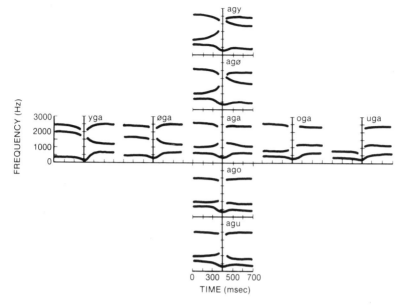

Figure 5.8
Formant transitions for vowel-/g/-vowel utterances. The formant transition into the consonant from the initial vowel varies as a function of the following vowel (middle column). Likewise, the formant transition into the final vowel from the consonant changes as a function of the initial vowel (middle row). The vowel–stop consonant–vowel cannot be conceptualized as a sequence of three independent phonemes (adapted from Öhman 1966).

(e.g., reduce, addition), there is a clean stop and release. However, if the stop consonant follows a stressed vowel (e.g., raider, madder), the stop becomes a "flap" produced by briefly touching the tongue to the ridge of the mouth. Because of coarticulation, speech production cannot be understood as a series of independent, one after the other, articulatory movements or gestures.

There are other ways in which the continuous speech signals yield information about discrete phonemes. In particular, the same acoustic cue can lead to a different percept because of the surrounding context. The voiced-voiceless feature was described above. For the voiced stop consonants /d/, /b/, and /g/, the voicing (vocal cord vibration) begins before or immediately after the release of the noise burst; for voiceless stop consonants /t/, /p/, and /k/, there is a time delay of 20 to 50 msec accompanied by aspiration before the voicing begins. As noted, the time differential has been termed the voice onset time. Listeners are remarkably sensitive to these small time differences. An increase in voice onset time of as little as 10 msec will change a sound from being heard as a voiced /b/ to an unvoiced /p/.

Note the problem in continuous speech. The voice onset times will be shorter for individuals who articulate quickly and longer for those who articulate more slowly. Whether a specific value of the voice onset time implies a voiced or unvoiced consonant depends on the articulation rate, and it should be the temporal properties immediately surrounding the stop consonants that count the most. Experiments that vary the articulation rate demonstrate that listeners "correct" for rate. A voice onset time delay of 30 msec that is heard as the voiced [ba] when embedded in slow articulation is heard as the unvoiced [pa] when embedded in rapid articulation (Summerfield 1981).

Now consider the glides and semivowels—/w/, /j/, /r/, and /l/. Following the same procedures of using spectrograms to discover the relevant acoustic parameters and the speech synthesizer to model these parameters, O'Connor et al. (1957) have generated representations of these sounds. In some ways they are similar to stop consonants: (1) formant transitions are followed by steady-state sections; (2) the first formant is relatively constant and is a cue for the glides and semivowels; and (3) the second and third formants serve to distinguish among /w/, /j/, /r/, /l/. Glides and semivowels differ from the stop consonants in that there is no stop and burst at the beginning of the sound. Instead, there is a steady-state segment lasting between 50 and 70 msec (see figure 5.9). Without this steady-state section at the onset, these sounds would be heard as stop consonants, reflecting the constriction of the vocal tract that creates the period of silence before the stop consonant burst and subsequent formant transition.

Although the duration of the formant transition does not distinguish among glides and semivowels, it does differentiate them from stop consonants and vowels. If the transition is shortened to less than 50 msec, glides and semivowels become stop consonants; if the transition is lengthened to more than 150 msec, glides and semivowels become vowels of changing color, like diphthongs. Once again, this cue is not invariant; it depends on the rate of articulation. If we take one specific transition rate and construct a series of sounds in which the steady-state vowel segment increases, then in a relative sense, the transition seems to be getting shorter and its rate to be increasing. The perception is what changes; increasing the vowel duration will lead to the perception of the stop consonant. The transition itself has not been changed, however; only the context has altered (Miller and Liberman 1979).

To further illustrate the possibility that the same acoustic signal can yield differing percepts, we will again turn to the silence produced when articulating a stop consonant and consider the effect of silence on the acoustic signal typical of a fricative (see figure 5.10). The fricative-vowel

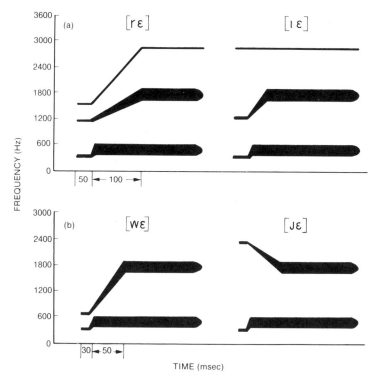

Figure 5.9
Hand-painted simulated spectrograms of glides and semivowel syllables. Glides and semi-vowels are distinguished by a short, steady formant that becomes the transition into the following vowel (adapted from O'Connor et al. 1957).

syllable [sa] consists of patch of noise associated with the fricative, followed by the formant transition characteristic of the vowel /a/. (The formant transition for /s/ is also appropriate for the voiced and unvoiced stop consonants /t/ and /d/, which have the same place of articulation.) Removing the noise produces the perception of a stop consonant syllable /ta/. If the noise is shifted in time to create a 50 msec silence, the percept shifts to /sta/; the stop becomes embedded in the fricative. What the silence is doing is telling the listener that the speaker has closed the vocal tract long enough to have produced a stop. The silence is used to make an inference about the articulation, and the inferred articulation in turn is used to generate the perceived sound (Liberman and Studdert-Kennedy, 1978).

Although it is no surprise that consonants are context dependent, phoneticians have long argued that vowels are the same in all syllables. The same implicit assumption has been made here in discussing the con-

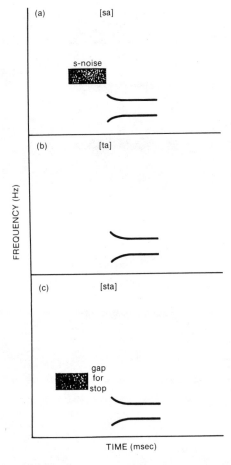

Figure 5.10
What syllable is perceived may be understood in terms of the articulatory constraints. The perceptual effect of a silent interval will be a function of the ongoing acoustic signal. Liberman and Studdert-Kennedy (1978) argue that the silence gives information about the articulation of the speech sound. A silence between the noise and the formant transition is an articulatory cue for the production of a stop consonant (adapted from Liberman and Studdert-Kennedy 1978).

sonant as the dynamic component of speech, the formant transition flowing into a steady-state set of invariant vowel formants. Each vowel is thus
acoustically defined by the frequencies of the first two or three formants
determined by the resonances of the vocal tract.

However, the belief in the invariance of vowels seems to be based more
on tradition than on fact. Consider some of the difficulties.

> 1. Variations in vocal tracts among speakers change the positions of
> the formants. Frequencies that characterize a vowel for one speaker
> may characterize a different vowel for another speaker (Peterson and
> Barney 1952).
>
> 2. The rate of articulation changes the formant frequencies. In rapid
> speech, the articulators do not have time to reach the positions re-
> quired for the idealized vowel (Gay 1978). They undershoot and do
> not reach the steady-state formant frequencies (see figure 5.11). The
> listeners correct for articulation rate and resulting undershoot; they
> report the vowel that would have occurred if the sound had been
> completed, not the "closest" vowel to the actual acoustic signal (Lind-
> blom and Studdert-Kennedy 1967). Vowels, therefore, are not different
> than consonants in the sense that their perception is corrected for the
> articulatory changes due to the overall rate of speaking.
>
> 3. The coarticulation of the consonant-vowel syllable affects the
> vowel as much as the consonant. The effect is two-way: the imprint
> of the vowels pervades the entire syllable as it determines the formant
> transition; in turn, the consonants produce reliable changes in the
> acoustic parameters of the vowels. For example, the distinction be-
> tween the phoneme /d/ in "rider" and the phoneme /t/ in "writer" is
> brought about by changing the duration of the preceding vowel, not
> by changing the consonant. There is no acoustic invariant that char-
> acterizes a vowel in running speech. Nonetheless, the coarticulation
> between consonants and vowels does not interfere with the identifica-
> tion of vowels. The identification of isolated vowels and the identifi-
> cation of vowels in a consonant-vowel-consonant context is quite
> accurate even if the speakers change randomly from trial to trial
> (Rakerd, Verbrugge, and Shankweiler 1984).

These considerations led Jenkins, Strange, and Edman (1983) to argue
that vowels can be specified by time-varying spectral properties as well as
formant frequencies. For example, vowels differ in duration: /ɪ/ (bit) and
/ʌ/ (but) are shorter than /ae/ (bat) or /ei/ (bait). In addition, vowels differ
in the shape of the formant transitions into and out of the more steady-
state, central part of the vowel. Vowels like /a/ (father) have relatively
short symmetrical onglides and offglides; vowels like /ʌ/ (but) have much
longer offglides. Thus, the invariant properties of vowels are stretched

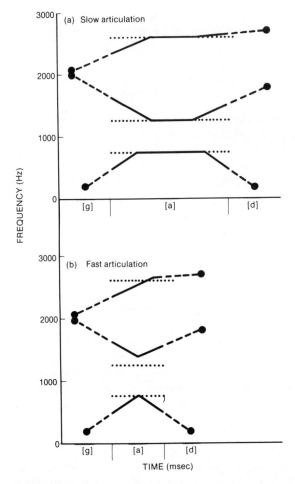

Figure 5.11
The effect of speaking rate on coarticulated vowels. At faster rates, speakers may not reach
the target frequencies of the vowel formants. Nonetheless, listeners correct for the under-
shoot created by the speaking rate and report hearing the vowel that would have occurred
(adapted from Holmes, Mattingly, and Shearme 1974).

across the acoustic signal so that they can be perceived in terms of articulatory and spectral change, by integrating the acoustic signal over time (Verbrugge and Rakerd 1986).

The notion that the vowel is relatively constant in different contexts had been used to explain how speech is understood. Briefly, the theory argues that since the vowel is constant, it can be used to decode the more variable consonant phonemes. The listener uses the vowels to calibrate for overall frequency, rate, dialect, and so on. Some have suggested that the cardinal vowels serve as the referents because their acoustic pattern can be related to a unique vocal tract area function (Joos 1948; Stevens 1972). However, if the vowels are as changeable as suggested above, then the vowels cannot be the "codebook" for speech.

What this means is that the acoustic signal is a puzzle that must be solved by the listener. Linguistic units—phonemes, syllables, words—that are heard as discrete entities are not found as discrete entities in the acoustic signal. Because of coarticulation, there is a mutual interaction among successive parts of the utterance. Linguistic units produced in isolation may be far different than the same units produced in context. The acoustic energy for each unit is merged with the energy for other units, and all diffuse through the acoustic signal. The amount of overlap depends on context, rate, and language. The same phonemic segment can be represented by far different acoustic cues in different contexts, and the same acoustic cue can represent different phonemes in different contexts. On top of these difficulties, there is variation induced by articulatory changes due to rate of speaking, variations of accent and dialect within a large language community, idiosyncratic speech, imitation, emotional state, fatigue, and physical disease. Communication usually succeeds, which indicates that listeners are sensitive to these articulatory changes and recover the articulatory gestures.

Instead of considering these contextual variations as speech noise to be filtered out and ignored, it might be better to conceptualize the variations as "lawful" (Elman and McClelland 1986; Pisoni and Luce 1987). These lawful variations provide "systematic" acoustic-phonetic information. For example, /t/ in a syllable-initial position (ten) is aspirated but /t/ in a syllable-final position (bet) or in a consonant cluster (step) is rarely aspirated. Thus, in a sentence discussed by Pisoni and Luce (1987), "did you hit it to Tom?" the lack of aspiration would suggest that the two /t/'s in "hit" and "it" do not begin syllables, and the presence of aspiration would suggest that the /t/'s in "to" and "Tom" do begin syllables. Although it is still unclear how much of the potential contextual information in the speech signal is utilized by listeners, the presence of contextual regularity suggests once again that perception is not limited by an ambiguous impoverished stimulus.

One reasonably good analogy to speech is a jigsaw puzzle. Objects in the puzzle are like phonemic segments; pieces of the puzzle are like acoustic segments. Each piece of the puzzle may contain parts of several adjacent objects in the puzzle, much like the fact that each acoustic segment may contain cues to several adjacent phonemic segments. Each object in the puzzle picture is made up of several pieces, much like the fact that each phonemic segment can be made up of several acoustic segments. Moreover, each puzzle piece can be interpreted and utilized only in relation to the surrounding pieces. In much the same way, each acoustic segment can be interpreted and utilized only in relation to the surrounding segments. The analogy breaks down, of course, because the puzzle pieces are more rigid and unchanging than the acoustic segments. For the analogy to continue, the puzzle piece would have to be amoeba-like, with pseudopods extending and retracting.

5.4 Models of Speech Perception

A model of speech perception that matches phonetic elements with spectrogram representations does not lead to a simple view of the perceptual process. If we believe that perceptual processes are based on discovering invariants, no matter how complex, then it would be appropriate to question whether this conceptualization is adequate. It is possible to question both sides of the equation. Namely, is speech perception truly based on the recovery of phonetic units as previously defined? And is the acoustic signal as portrayed in a spectrogram the correct representation for an understanding of perception?

In seeking answers, we can start by questioning the reality of phonetic segments. The segmental nature of speech sounds has been taken for granted. The segments are assumed to be the building blocks for speech communication. The appeal is to "objective observation"; experts can hear these segments in the speech signal, so they must exist in the acoustic wave and must exist prior to that in the articulation. This assumes that there is a "true" segment. However, "true" segments have never been observed in the acoustic wave, because segments are so overlapped that it is virtually impossible to isolate one in the acoustic signal. Every time the segment is uttered it comes out differently. To explain the different acoustic realizations of the phonetic segment, it has seemed necessary to hypothesize coarticulation. But coarticulation has never been observed; it was hypothesized in order to account for the variability. We thus have a curious circularity of objective definition. Neither segments nor coarticulation can be defined without the other, and the evidence for one depends on the existence of the other.

One possible way of breaking out of this circularity is to argue that segments do not exist physically and to propose instead that they are derived by the listener. They are the end product of a complex perceptual/ cognitive process. In this sense, segments are mental categories (Hammarberg 1976; Repp 1981). However, even if the notion of phonetic segments needs to be abandoned, there are invariants or resemblances in the articulatory gestures. There must be links between the articulatory gestures, the acoustic signal, and the perception.

In order to discover these links we may need a representation of the speech signal in terms other than a spectrogram. As already mentioned, the spectrogram tends to lead us to think of independent cues to discrete segments. As illustrated in figure 5.5, each phonetic segment is made up of several acoustic segments, and each acoustic segment, in turn, stems from more than one phonetic segment. It may be that these cues and segments are inappropriate representations to explain the percept. A more straightforward representation might require going back to the study of the articulatory gesture (movements) to discover the invariant acoustic outcomes. One alternative is that phonetic segments are coproduced (Diehl 1986; Fowler 1986). Both Diehl and Fowler suggest that the temporally overlapped articulatory movements corresponding to phonetic segments are nevertheless separate and context independent. The overlapped movements are perceivable as separate events because they have different temporal and dynamic patterns. For example, vowels involve relatively slow, continuous changes in an open vocal tract; consonants involve short, discontinuous changes in a constricted vocal tract. The perception of interspersed vowels and consonants, in this view, is based on the organizational principles of the auditory system that partition the continuous signal into events (see chapter 7 for a discussion of stream segregation).

Articulation is compensatory; the undershooting of one articulator may be compensated by the movement of another articulator (Kelso, Saltzman, and Tuller 1986). We produce intelligible speech with our mouths clenched, with the jaw immobile, and while chewing gum. It might be useful to concentrate on the changes in the acoustic signal due to the coordinated movements required for articulation. This moves away from the current characterization based on static phonetic features like position of articulation and focuses on the dynamic properties of the signal. For example, several investigators have focused on the movement from the burst to the voicing onset for stop consonants (Lahiri, Gewirth, and Blumstein 1984). They have argued that the relative changes in the distribution of energy at high and low frequencies around that point in time may provide a stable cue to the identification of the place of articulation of a stop consonant. The cue is dynamic because it occurs over time, and the cue is relative because it involves the relationships among the amplitudes at different frequencies. It is too early, however, to assess the ultimate value of this approach.

To summarize: The inability to discover invariants in the acoustic signal that underlie the phonetic percept has led to two alternative views. The first argues that phonetic perception is a unique perceptual/cognitive event requiring specialized brain circuitry and processes. This suggests a special correspondence between the articulatory gestures in production and the sensory processes in listening (Fodor 1983; Liberman and Mattingly, 1985). I will argue against this view. The second view argues that the acoustic signal does indeed contain the information for speech perception. The research problem is to discover new ways of analyzing the signal to uncover the invariant information. From this point of view, speech poses in no way a unique perceptual problem (Massaro 1987).

5.5 Overview

The speech production system is coupled in two ways. The first is the acoustic coupling between the source and filter in sound production. The second is the kinematic and functional coupling among the articulators required for speech. Through coarticulation, the articulators move to reach a desired configuration. The coupling allows for compensation; if one articulator is constrained, the remaining ones change their positions to yield the desired acoustic signal. Because of the coordinated movements in articulation, acoustic "cues" to the identity of each segment are spread through time. Each cue in isolation is more or less sufficient for the correct percept, but no single cue is necessary, because of the presence of all the others. This multiplicity and equivalence of acoustic information is inherent in speech production and perception. Since one cue can compensate for variation in another (as will be discussed in chpater 9), it seems almost impossible to define phonetic categories in fixed acoustic terms. We may be able to define phonetic categories in terms of higher-order dynamic acoustic variation, but this effort is just beginning. The resolution of the issue is still to come.

Chapter 6
Commonalities: Physical and Perceptual

Audition, hearing, and listening; vision, seeing, and looking: Each sequence suggests differences in the degree of personal involvement in perceiving. Each sequence portrays the paradoxical nature of the senses; in one way they are passive physiological systems, yet in a different way they are active information-seeking and information-reducing systems under the control of the motivational needs of an individual. I think sound perceiving best illustrates this mosaic of opposites.

On the one hand, hearing may be said to be the most active of the senses because of the temporal continuum in which hearing occurs. Hearing must bridge the interval between beginning and end. It is almost impossible to take a "snapshot" of an auditory event, so that the totality is available at one time. Sound perceiving must always be anticipating, hearing forward, as well retrospecting, hearing backward. The "present" gets its meaning from both preceding and succeeding sounds. It is a bit like solving number progression puzzles (1, 4, ?, 16, 25); both the included and missing numbers get their meaning from all the others. On the other hand, hearing may be said to be the most passive of the senses; it is always "on." You do not have to turn to listen, in contrast to the active movements required for looking.

There is a faithful match between the temporal nature of hearing and the inherently temporal nature of life. Events occur in time and objects exist in time. Temporality, however, is not a uniquely auditory quality; it forms the background to all human functioning. The apparent stability or rigidity of the spatial visual world is due to the lack of change over time. There does seem to be a special temporality to hearing and listening (Ihde 1976). Anecdotal reports from people who have lost their hearing describe the loss of the dynamic, ongoing, time-varying, characteristics of the world. This loss is felt not merely in the auditory domain but in all domains. It is the fear of this loss, as well as the fear of being cut off from friends, that led me to state in chapter 1 that I would rather be blind than deaf.

Many aspects of the auditory world have appeared in chapters 2–5. It is useful here to list the possibilities and commonalities. These emphasize the what and how of perceiving and illustrate some of the ways in which the physical "backdrop" supports the temporal nature of listening.

6.1 Commonalities in the Physical World

Sound Production

The stages in all kinds of sound production are the energy required to initiate the vibration, the vibration itself, the transfer of the vibrator energy to the sound body or resonator, the vibration of the sound body, and the propagation of the sound wave. For an instrument, the energy can be supplied by blowing, bowing, tapping, or plucking. The vibration can be that of a string, a drumskin, or an air column. The sound body or resonator can consist of a hollow wooden box, an elaborate metal or wood tube, or a soundboard. For the human voice, whether speaking or singing, the source of energy is the air expelled from the lungs. The vibration can be a standing wave air column produced by the periodic opening of the vocal cords, or the vibration can be turbulence consisting of the vibration of many frequencies. The resonators are the oral and nasal cavities. For an enclosure, the vibrator energy comes from the imposed vibration—an instrument, a voice, or a hammer. The resonator or sound body consists of the vibration modes possible on the basis of the physical size and shape of the enclosure.

The stages are coupled together, and the degree of coupling or connectedness determines the attack/decay transients and the steady-state spectrum. For tightly coupled stages, the attack and decay transients are very rapid, but the maximum amplitude of vibration tends to be low; for loosely coupled stages, the attack and decay transients are slow, but the maximum amplitude at the resonant frequency can be high. This is true for the coupling between the string harmonics and the resonances of the violin sound body, the coupling between air column harmonics induced by lip vibration and the resonances of the trumpet's tubing, the coupling between the air column harmonics induced by the vocal cords and the resonances of the mouth and nose, and the coupling between the harmonic amplitudes of the imposed sound and the vibration modes of a room.

The energy→vibration→resonator→output model is left to right. In other words, the causal effects are thought to work in one direction only: the application of energy causes the vibration; the vibration in turn causes the buildup of resonance modes; the resonance modes cause the sound to be propagated with specific amplitudes. There is a time progression—each process precedes the next. This is not a true representation, because the processes also work right to left, metaphorically "backward in time." The vibration of the strings and air columns as well as the resonance modes of sound bodies all act to influence the way the energy can be applied (recall the discussion of the effect of the tube on the clarinet reed and on the trumpeter's lips). In the same fashion the initial energy and the sound body resonances act to restrict the possible string and air vibration modes. The processes are coupled together. The intertwining in the production process molds each part to conform to the others and to the whole.

What Is There to Hear?
In the following description of the aspects of sound common to music, speech, and environmental events, the goal is to portray the richness of the acoustic world, not to catalogue the cues to perception. There is no fixed set of cues and there is no unique cue to an event, because the sound is the end product of a set of interdependent processes.

Frequency   The frequency range of an instrument or speaker does, in part, characterize it (see figure 6.1). In terms of playable musical notes, the organ has the widest range, a bass tuba can play notes from 41 Hz to 233 Hz, and the piccolo can play notes from 500 Hz to 4000 Hz. Other instruments fit within these ranges. In addition, there are percussion instruments without a definite pitch (e.g., snare drums and cymbals). The lack of pitch, as compared to percussion instruments with a tunable pitch (e.g., kettledrums and xylophones), is thus another component of frequency.

The range of the fundamental frequency of the vocal cords of a speaker can supply information about the person's sex and age (as described in chapter 5) and possibly about the person's emotional state. The fundamental frequency of voiced sounds is varied by changing the tension of the vocal cords. For normal speech, the ratio between the highest and lowest fundamental frequency is about 2 to 1; for singing the ratio is greater, about 3 to 1.

In addition to pitch differences associated with individual sounds, pitch differences may be used to accent syllables or to indicate overall sentence structure. An accented syllable tends to have a higher fundamental frequency. This can be shown with two-syllable words that can be accented on either syllable and thereby change from a noun to a verb. Compare "That's an INsult" to "Don't inSULT him" (the accented part is capitalized). When speakers uttered each sentence, in a comparison of the syllable "in" stressed in INsult and unstressed in inSULT, the stressed syllable had a higher fundamental frequency. In addition to pitch effects on syllables and words, pitch changes over long segments often distinguish between statements and questions. A declarative statement usually involves an overall decrease in frequency; a question usually involves an overall increase in frequency (e.g., Couper-Kuhlen 1986; pitch accents will be discussed further in chapter 11).

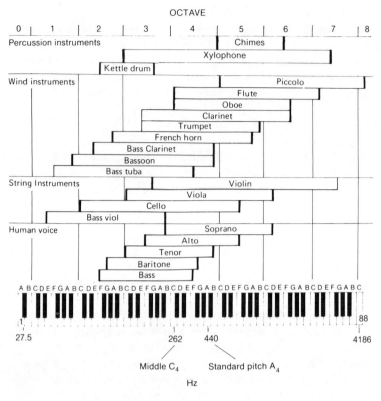

Figure 6.1
The frequency range of human voices and various instruments. Notes are labeled in terms of the note and octave. The black notes of the piano are the sharp and flat notes. The 88-note range of the piano is from A_1 to C_8 (adapted from McBurney and Collings 1984).

Thus, frequency (pitch) effects are found at all levels of the speech signal. Even so, the use of pitch is restricted in English. Other languages use pitch variation to signify different syllables or words. These are termed *tone* languages. Pitch can determine semantic meaning. Kutsherā is "to draw water," and kutshera is "to dig" in Shona, spoken in Zimbabwe (an underline signifies low pitch, an overline signifies higher pitch). Pitch can also determine syntatic meaing (the word for "jaw" in Igbo, spoken in Nigeria, is agba, but to signify the jaw of a monkey, pronunciation shifts to agba). The concept of possession ("of") may be expressed by a high tone on a syllable. Other languages make use of tone glides or contours in which meaning is associated with pitch changes rather than with discrete pitches. It is interesting to note that even in tone languages, there are context effects in which the tonal realization of a sound depends on its surrounding context (Ladefoged 1975).

Duration   Instruments break into two classes: (1) those in which the method of excitation allows for the continuous application of energy and therefore extended notes (bowed violin, trumpet, clarinet); and (2) those in which the method of excitation is essentially a short, impulsive initiation (drums, piano, guitar, plucked violin). In the latter case, the duration consists of a typically short attack time plus a decay time that can range from about 1.5 sec for a xylophone, to about 2.0 sec for a piano, to about 10 sec for orchestral bells.

Duration plays a far more important role than pitch in speech, and significant differences occur at all levels of the speech signal. At the level of individual vowels, there are differences in duration. The vowel /i/ (as in b*ee*t) is longer than /ɪ/ (as in b*i*t); /e/ (as in locate) is longer than /ɛ/ (as in b*e*t). The length of the vowel is changed, however, by the consonant that precedes and follows it. Vowels are always longer before voiced consonants than before voiceless consonants. It is important to note that differences in vowel duration in these contexts are not obligatory consequences of articulatory constraints. Rather, these differences appear to be learned and to represent pronunciation (phonetic implementation) rules specific to English. In English, variations in vowel duration do not differentiate between linguistic units, but in many other languages (e.g., Korean, Danish, Arabic) durational differences signify different vowels. Moreover, as discussed previously, the duration of silences, transitions, and steady states all affect the perception of consonants. These durations act relatively; a specific duration is interpreted with regard to the articulation timings of adjacent segments. In addition to phonemic effects, at the word level, duration indicates stress. Stressed words tend to be extended. At the sentence level, duration indicates sentence structure: the final syllable is often extended.

Intensity   Absolute intensity, per se, must be of secondary importance, because it is too variable. The distance of the source, the source itself, the performer's or speaker's intention, the environment, and so forth will grossly affect the perceived loudness. Nonetheless, instruments and speech sounds do have different intensities and their relative intensities provide some perceptual information. The brass instruments are most powerful, with maximum amplitudes of 75 dB SPL. Reed instruments (e.g., oboe, clarinet) generate sound pressures one-fifth as strong (10–15 dB lower). It is for this reason that the brass instruments are placed at the back of the orchestra and are seated to play "sideways"; otherwise they would overpower the other instruments. In speech, intensity differences can be used to distinguish among consonants. For example, the fricatives /s/ (*s*in), /sh/ (*sh*in), /z/ (lei*s*ure) have more acoustic energy than /f/ (*f*in), /θ/ (*th*in), /ɣ/ (*th*at) and /v/ (*v*im).

The ambiguity of absolute intensity can be seen when listeners judge the loudness of vowels. The perceived loudness depends on the speaker's apparent effort, not on measured physical energy. If speakers pronounce /i/ (b*ee*t) and /a/ (h*a*d) with equal emphasis, listeners will judge them equally loud, although the measured physical intensity of /a/ is greater than the intensity of /i/. If the speaker expends more effort in pronouncing /i/ so that the physical intensities of /i/ and /a/ become equal, listeners now judge that /i/ is louder. The listeners are judging loudness with respect to the effort of production, and not with respect to the intensity of the acoustic wave. As well as being a cue for phoneme and syllable identification, intensity can also be used to indicate stress at the word and sentence level. A stressed syllable is not only longer and of higher pitch, as mentioned above, but also tends to be greater in peak and average amplitude.

We have noted several times how the intensity changes the spectra of instruments and voices. At low intensities the source excitation consists mainly of the fundamental. At higher intensities the excitation consists of a greater percentage of higher harmonics. Thus as the loudness increases, the sound of the instrument and voice changes, becoming more piercing at higher intensities. The same interaction is true for the attack and decay transients. The intensity affects the overall duration of the transients as well as the transients of individual harmonics. (It may be that the relative strength of the harmonics along with the loudness provides information about source distance.)

Noise   Noise refers to rather broad frequency regions of high energy that often occur when the excitation energy is first applied to the vibrator. For example, when hitting bells, triangles, or cymbals, there is a characteristic metallic sound; when bowing a violin, the bow initially scrapes against the string, producing a high frequency "scratch," before initiating the slip-stick process. In speaking, both fricative and stop consonants begin with a brust of energy containing energy at different frequencies. The magnitude of the energy burst, the frequency range, and the timing between the burst and surrounding segments determine the perception of the specific consonant. The magnitude and frequency of the burst are determined by the place of articulation. It may not be the noises themselves that are important; the change in sound from the noise to the attack transient may be the perceptual cue.

Noise can give an instrument or a voice a particular quality. There may be a constant noise associated with an instrument, such as the breathy sound of a flute. The husky, sultry voices of 1940 and 1950 female screen sirens are the result of noise produced by the lack of complete closure of the vocal cords during speaking.

Traditionally, the physical variables of frequency, duration, intensity, and noise have been discussed as independent, absolute cues applicable to individual elements. Clearly, this is not accurate. All four variables are relative, and listeners must interpret durational information in terms of other temporal information. In the same fashion they must interpret frequency and intensity information for a single segment in terms of the frequency and intensity values spread across the entire sound event. Nor are frequency, duration, and intensity independent. Loudness, for example, depends on the combination of frequency and intensity as illustrated by the equal loudness curves (figure 2.25), and the ability to perceive frequency changes depends on the duration and timing of the tones (discussed in chapter 9). The information is typically spread over several elements so that the listener must integrate or analyze the changes over longer time frames.

The variables affect the acoustic signal at all levels; they influence individual notes and phonemes, intervals and syllables, phrases and words, and passages and utterances. The frequency, duration, intensity, and noise characteristics are built out of contributions at lower levels, which are of different sorts: some are the result of physical and articulatory mechanisms, some are the result of musical and grammmatical class, some are the result of type of sequence, and some are even the result of the performer's inferences about the listener. In speaking, novel knowledge is often stressed, thus changing the articulation of these phrases. Yet listeners appear to be sensitive to the information at each of these levels.

Timbre: harmonic spectra, formants, and transients   Timbre is the characteristic quality or "color" of a sound produced by an instrument or voice. The most common definition is by exclusion: that attribute of a tone by which a listener can judge that two sounds of the same loudness and pitch are dissimilar (ANSI 1973).

Traditionally timbre has been thought of as an independent but acoustically measurable property. Each note of one instrument would be characterized by that property, and timbre differences among instruments would be created by different magnitudes along that property. Historically, timbre has been defined in terms of the amplitudes of the harmonics of the frequency spectrum of a steady tone. It has become clear, however, that this conceptualization is inadequate in two ways. Acoustically, timbre is a function of the attack and decay transients as well as of the frequency spectrum. Experimentally, timbre does not appear to be reducible to an acoustical property that automatically yields a clarinet note or a violin note. The transients and steady-note frequency spectra change dramatically from note to note across an instrument's playing range, and still the same timbre is heard (to be discussed further in chapter 8). With this caveat in mind, some conceptualizations of timbre are described below.

a. *Harmonic spectra* Timbre has been defined in terms of the relative amplitudes of the harmonics of a steady-state tone. To do this analysis, one tone would be played continuously and uniformly, and the amplitudes of the harmonics measured. See figure 2.6 for examples of two different instruments. Because the timbre of an instrument sounded the same across the playing range, researchers expected that the spectra would be identical for all notes. Different notes, however, generate dissimilar patterns of harmonic amplitudes. An example worked out toward the end of section 2.2, showed that two notes an octave apart could generate contrasting spectra. In general, harmonic spectra differ across notes and cannot yield a representation of timbre. The harmonic spectra of some instruments, nonetheless, are unique and consistent. For example, the flute spectrum is nearly pure, consisting only of the fundamental. Moreover, struck percussion instruments have nonharmonic partials. In these cases, the lack of a harmonic spectrum might provide perceptual information.

b. *Formants* A modern approach to specifying timbre makes use of formants. As discussed in section 2.2, a formant selectively amplifies a range of frequencies because of one or more similar vibration modes of the sound body (e.g., the violin body, the tubing of wind instruments, the vocal tract). For instruments and the vocal tract, depending on the damping (i.e., the flatness of the resonance curve), each vibration mode can amplify one or more harmonics and can amplify a range of frequencies for noiselike sounds as well as unvoiced or fricative speech sounds. (The damping is greater for the vocal tract than for instruments, and therefore speech formants tend to contain a wider range of frequencies.) The formants of instruments (and of speech sounds) are therefore high-intensity frequency regions consistent across notes and speakers.

The formants of each instrument are created by the sound body and are assumed to be unchanging across its musical range because of the rigid construction. The formants for any instrument can be discovered by identifying the frequency regions of maximum intensity after averaging the frequency spectra across the playing range. In the same way that we can define the formants of our instrument, we can define the formants of different speech sounds, particularly vowels. The formants of each speech sound are usually assumed to be unchanging across speakers because of the common positioning of the articulators. Here differences in sound between /a/ and /i/, for example, are described as a difference in timbre. The formants for any speech sound can be discovered by identifying the frequency regions of maximum intensity after averaging the frequency spectra across different speakers. We might measure the formants for an individual speaker (analogous to an instrument) by averaging the frequency spectra across utterances.

Formants can occur only when there are consistent vibration modes that amplify a fixed range of frequencies. If the frequency spectra are identical for all notes, formants will not occur. Consider an instrument in which the frequency spectra for each note consist of three harmonics with amplitudes of 1, 1/2, and 1/4. Because the spectra are identical for every note, then the overall energy at each frequency averaged across notes would be identical. Across all frequencies, each frequency would occur at times as a low amplitude third harmonic, at times as a medium amplitude second harmonic, and at times as a high amplitude fundamental. For example, all organ pipes can have the same spectrum, which would mean that formants would not occur. Only if the harmonic spectrum is not consistent across notes will formant regions exist.

Formants can furnish several kinds of perceptual information:

1. The frequency of the formants themselves may specify musical and speech information. Vowels have been convincingly synthesized by using two or three formants. The frequency of the formants specific to each vowel has been related to vibration modes because of the positioning of the vocal tract, as described previously. Some instruments are marked by clear fixed formants; the violin is a prime example.

2. The presence or absence of formants can specify phonemic information. The difference between nasal and non-nasal consonants is cued by the presence of formants due to nasal vibra-

tion modes. Similarly, the liquids and glides are cued by initial formants, which lead into formant transitions.

3. The temporal relation between the formants can specify phonemic information. The difference between voiced and unvoiced stop consonants is cued in part by the time difference in onset between the first (voicing) and second formants.

Although the attempts to describe music and speech sounds in terms of formants appears to be more useful than describing these sounds in terms of harmonic spectra, there are many limitations. In speech, the formants relate to the physiology of the vocal system. Children, women, and men have vocal tracts of different sizes and shapes. Therefore, the relationships among the formant frequencies,either in terms of ratios or differences, will change. It is interesting to note that when children are learning to talk by imitating adult speech sounds, they do not try to achieve the formant frequencies of an adult. Instead they generate the frequencies "scaled up" according to the smaller size of their vocal tracts. Each speaker can produce the same vowel at different vocal cord vibration frequencies, and because of the complex shape of the vocal tract this too can change the relationship among the formant frequencies. In addition, the intensity of vocalization will change the magnitude of the higher harmonics and thus change the intensity of each of the formants, and we would also expect that this increased exertion and tension would change the shape of the vocal tract and thus change the frequencies of the formants. Finally, in rapid continuous speech, subjects may not reach the articulatory targets before moving to the next articulatory movements, and this will alter the formant frequencies. In music, the amplitude of the formants for instruments also is a function of intensity. As shown for the trumpet and clarinet (the same outcome, but less dramatically, occurs for the violin), the strength of the harmonics grows with intensity, and for this reason the relative strength of formant regions must also change. It is clear that the absolute frequency and absolute intensity of the formants are not invariant perceptual cues. The formants must be perceived with respect to the ongoing context.

c. *Attack and decay transients* Instrument identity and the sense of timbre are determined in part by the transitions of the harmonics. The attack and decay transients can be conceptualized overall as the time for the sound to grow to full amplitude and the time for the sound to decay to inaudibility. A characterization of this sort tends to lead to the perception of a class of sounds. For example, Schaeffer (1966; cited in Risset and Wessel 1982), argues that a fast attack followed by a slow decay gives a "plucked" quality to any sound, irrespective of harmonic content. Analyses of instrumental tones, however, suggest that merely specifying a single attack and decay time is not sufficient to portray and synthesize an instrumental timbre adequately. Each harmonic has its own temporal evolution, offset in time to all the others. It is this interplay of the changing intensities of the harmonics that yields a sound of changing quality and warmth.

The violin example in section 2.2 illustrated why the attack and decay of each harmonic differs: There are many vibration modes, each with a different Q factor, and therefore there will be large differences among the attack/decay times and amplitudes of each vibration mode. The fundamental and harmonics of each note will excite different vibration modes and thus the amplitudes as well as the transients of each harmonic will vary. Different notes will excite other vibration modes so that there will be little correspondence in harmonics across the playing range.

Instrument transients are not invariant, note by note, duration by duration, frequency by frequency, or intensity by intensity. Nor are speech formant transitions invariant. Rather, formant transitions vary as a function of starting frequency, speaking rate, dialect, duration, and so on. What might be perceptually relevant is not the transients per se, but the transients in the context of the ongoing sound. An attack/decay transient may signify one event when the sound level is low and a different event when the sound level is high. A formant transition may signify one consonant (or articulatory movement) at one rate and a different consonant at another rate. The word [tu]—to, too, or two—can be understood only in the context of a sentence. In the sense that a word can be understood only in the linguistic context of a sentence, I am suggesting that the attack/decay transients can be evaluated only in the acoustic context (e.g., timing, intensity, frequency).

d. *Summary of timbre* It is clear that timbre cannot be conceptualized as an invariant acoustic property that is found for all notes of one instrument. Instead, the timbre is the result of many changing and interacting acoustic properties. There is no single acoustic reason why a clarinet and trumpet sound different (and there is no single acoustic reason why one violin sounds better than another).

Timing and rhythm The temporal nature of the auditory world lends a special importance to time and the timing of sounds. Time provides a framework for auditory events—events are ordered in time; and the timing of acoustic change defines the properties of auditory events. For example, the rate of the formant transitions distinguishes stop consonants from glides. In particular, the onset and offset of sounds define events. This is analogous to the visual world, where sharp changes in color, texture, or shading occur at boundaries of spatial objects. The timing of repetitive sounds often specifies events. For example, the rhythm of engine sounds allows mechanics to diagnose automobile failures, the rhythm of footsteps allows us to make guesses about the terrain and allows doctors to detect anatomical irregularities, and the rhythm of speech leads most of us to make inferences about the speaker's personality, emotional state, truthfulness and so on. Sounds that occur at regular intervals are usually perceived as the same event (the dripping of a faucet); irregular sounds can be perceived as a different events.

Much of the remaining chapters deal with the issue of time in auditory event perception. We should be aware, however, that audition is a spatial sense as well as a temporal sense. Even though the pressure waves at our ears are the summation of sound radiated from many sources (e.g., the instruments of an orchestra), we hear distinct events spread out in space. The ability to localize and thereby distinguish among sound sources is critical to our ability to perceive individual events. It may be true that we do not hear spatial configurations of sounds, a sound square as opposed to a sound diamond, but I believe that the spatial differentiation is crucial to listening. Thus we can argue that time is fused with space to provide the framework for listening and that the rate of change temporally and spatially specifies the events themselves.

Inharmonics   For almost every instrument discussed here, the vibration frequencies of harmonics are not precise multiples of the fundamental. Because of their stiffness, violin and piano strings are sharp: the frequencies of the upper harmonics are higher than would be predicted. The vibration modes of the trumpet are sharp; the vibration modes of the clarinet are flat. This inharmonicity affects the preferred tuning. Imagine two tones in which the fundamental frequencies are an octave apart: 200 Hz and 400 Hz. Sounding these notes together would produce beats between the sharp second harmonic of the 200 Hz tone (say 402 Hz) and the 400 Hz. For this reason, tuners "stretch" octaves (to maybe 401 Hz) to minimize beating.

The inharmonicity is another factor that gives instruments a characteristic warmth. The differences between the harmonics change over time, and this creates a time-varying sound. Instruments that are created electronically with absolutely regular harmonics sound rigid, hollow, and synthetic.

Another effect of inharmonicity occurs when several instruments play together. Each instrument will have been tuned slightly differently, and as a result beats will occur between all the harmonics (see figure 2.5). The intensity oscillation due to the beats gives the overall tone added richness. This is termed the chorus effect. The same effect occurs in one piano. Many of the notes are generated by two or three identical strings that are hit simultaneously by a hammer connected to one key. Each of the "identical" strings will have been tuned to a slightly different frequency, and therefore the hammer stike will create beats for each note and thereby change the sound quality. It is interesting to note that this lack of perfect tuning is what allows the piano tone to decay so slowly (Weinreich 1979). It is somewhat ironic that the instrumental "flaws"—initiation noise and the inharmonics—should prove to be so critical perceptually. But indeed they do, although the experimental evidence will be presented in chapter 8.

Vibrato   Even during the so-called steady-state portion of a sound, there may be frequency variation caused by the performer for aesthetic reasons. This is termed *vibrato*. For a violin, the vibrato is achieved by rolling the finger holding the string against the fingerboard. This effectively shortens and lengthens the string and thereby changes the fundamental frequency. In singing, vibrato on the vowels appears to be due to variation in the muscles controlling the tension of the vocal cords, which changes the vibration frequency. It is rarely found in normal speaking.

For music and singing, it is not the frequency change itself that is important but the fact that the frequency change induces a different amplitude modulation for each of the harmonics. The amplitude of one harmonic may increase and the amplitude of another may decrease during one part of the vibrato, and the reverse may occur during the remaining part. To understand these amplitude changes, it is useful to start with the simplification that the source vibration (string or air pressure through vocal cords) is harmonic. However, the vibration modes of the sound body will be at unpredictable frequencies. Figure 6.2 is a simplified picture of this, superimposing the regular source harmonics on the irregular sound body vibration modes. The height at which the harmonic frequency "hits" the vibration mode amplitude will determine the intensity of that frequency. If the source frequency increases when the player shortens the string, the output intensity due to the first vibration modes decreases, the output of the second mode increases and then decreases as it moves across the resonance curve, and the output of the third mode decreases dramatically. If the source frequency decreases when the player lengthens the string, the output intensity due to the lowest vibration mode will increase slightly and then decrease slightly, the output of the second mode will decrease drastically, and the output of the third mode will increase and then decrease. The changes in output from each vibration mode are unrelated. When the second mode output increases, the third decreases and vice versa. These varying patterns of changes give the tone a pleasing richness. Note that it is the amplitude changes, overlaid on top of the frequency changes, which give the vibrato its sound. Neither alone would be sufficient.

VIBRATION MODES

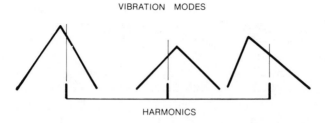

HARMONICS

(a) Increase harmonic frequencies

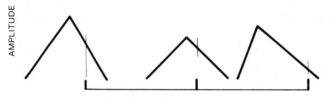

(b) Decrease harmonic frequencies

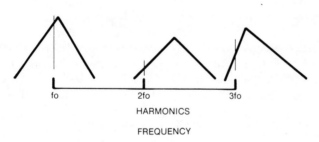

HARMONICS

FREQUENCY

Figure 6.2
Vibrato is created by varying the fundamental frequency of the excitation. Three vibration modes are denoted by simplified "triangular" resonance curves at irregular frequencies. The three harmonics are denoted by vertical tick marks. The degree of excitation of each vibration mode is indicated by the light vertical lines from each harmonic. As the frequency oscillates, it "passes through" the vibration modes, and thus the amplitude of each harmonic changes. Typically, the amplitude change of each harmonic is out of phase with the others. It is the amplitude modulation along with the frequency modulation that creates the overall perceptual effect.

For both music and singing, the frequency of the vibrato is about 6 Hz. The amount of frequency change for singing and music is about one semitone (the difference between two adjacent piano keys). The fact that the vibrato rate is the same for music and singing is somewhat surprising; it may reflect an underlying commonality.

The acoustics of singing are fascinating. One striking example occurs in singing falsetto. What happens here is that the vocal cords shift to a different vibration mode. The amplitude of vibration is small, the vocal cords do not close completely, and at higher frequencies the vocal cords begin to "zipper" together along part of their length, which allows only part of the cord to vibrate. This produces a sound that is more breathy and lacking in harmonics. This change in vibration mode at the higher frequencies seems quite analogous to the register keys of the clarinet, which allow higher frequency vibrations to emerge. In similar fashion to the clarinet, the falsetto has a different color than the lower register, and a great deal of practice is needed to obtain a smooth transition between the two types of vibration.

Context   In a real sense, everything we have said about the music and speech acoustic signal involves context. The rate, duration, intensity, environment, and physical structure (e.g., gender, age) in which sound is produced creates a context that influences each individual sound. Context dependency occurs in the overlapping, interconnected parts of the signal that influence the transitions between sounds. In addition there is the context of the "performance," the emotional state, the intention, the sentence structure, the dialect, to name a few.

It is impossible to discuss the entire gamut of context effects. I will mention here characteristics that extend over several notes or syllables: general stress, intonation (melodic), and rhythm rules (chapter 11 is completely devoted to these issues). For example, "melodic" features express differences in meaning and emotion. A long upward-gliding *yes* can mean, Oh, is that really true? A short upward-gliding *yes* can mean, OK, I'm listening. A downward-gliding *yes* means, Yes, I agree. A long drawn out *yes* can express impatience or boredom.

A possible rhythm rule that extends over many units hypothesizes that there should be equal intervals between stressed notes or stressed syllables. To the extent that such equality is not achieved on the basis of stresses due to frequency, duation, and intensity, other devices are used to approach it more closely. The accent may be shifted to another note or syllable, duration may be increased or decreased, or an extra note or syllable may be introduced whose sole function is to carry the stress. Martin (1972) has suggested that the equality of intervals enables a listener to extrapolate ahead, which thereby increases the intelligibility of what is being said. In speech, stressed syllables are often the most important, and thus the listener can know when to expect the syllables and words neceesary for comprehension.

Radiation and propagation   The sounds we hear are the function of the spatial radiation of sound generated by a speaker or instrument as well as a function of the physical environment (including the listener).

One effect of the physical surround is to create multiple representations of the same auditory event, although each representation will differ to some degree. These representations arise for diverse reasons. First, the listener has two ears; the sound at the each ear will differ in arrival time (phase), intensity, and/or spectra. Second, the shape of the pinna seems to result in a temporal pattern of multiple signals because of the sound wave ricocheting off the ridges. Third, the direct and reflected paths by which the sound wave reaches the listener will result in multiple representations. Simple reflections off a long wall and complex diffractions off a smaller surface or through an opening will change the spectrum reaching the listener.

This means that a listener is assaulted by a temporal series of sound waves coming from the same source. Environments like anechoic chambers, in which all reflections are suppressed, seem eerie. Although we are not consciously aware of the multiple signals as they coalesce with the direct signal because of the Haas effect, they do provide information about the sound source (e.g., spatial characteristics) and the world around us. This is true for musical sounds, speech sounds, and the sounds of automobiles, laughing, crying, and so forth.

Instruments, including the voice, have characteristic radiation patterns that change across the frequency range. Typically, low frequencies are radiated in all directions uniformly, and higher frequencies are more beamed or funneled along the instrumental axis. The violin is more complicated because of its shape and the performer's body. The radiation of the violin plus performer is shown in figure 6.3. If we walk around a performer, the quality of the sound will change.

In sum, the physical characteristics of the sound waves coming from musical and speech events depend on the listener's position. The radiation of different instruments varies across notes and the radiation of speech sounds varies across frequency. These spatial differences are further modified by the physical characteristics of the surounding environment. Thus, the energy reaching a listener may be only part of the entire acoustic pattern, but the listener must compensate for this in order to achieve the correct percept.

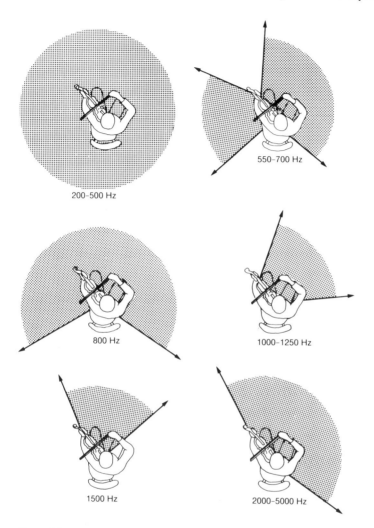

200–500 Hz

550–700 Hz

800 Hz

1000–1250 Hz

1500 Hz

2000–5000 Hz

Figure 6.3
Sound propagation from a seated violinist. The regions of high intensity are shaded (from Meyer 1972 by permission). The radiation pattern is a function of the violin as well as the player.

Summary of Physical World Commonalities
The above list should give you a feel for the number of different aspects of
a sound and their interrelationships. The interpretation of any aspect depends on the interpretation of another aspect and vice versa. It is a reciprocal and circular pattern. The initiation noise resolves into the onset
transient; the onset transient bleeds into and determines in part the steady-
state component. Yet all of these are variable, as functions of frequency,
intensity, duration, and context. The steady state is affected by vibrato and
the inharmonicity of the instrument. The performer can further vary the
steady state (as well as the transient) by the position of excitation of the
string, by the vocal cord vibration, and by the shape of the vocal tract. Yet
the perceptual effect of any change is a function of the frequency, intensity,
duration, harmonic spectrum, and transients of the sound. Moreover, all of
these change as a function of the context, and what the listener hears is a
function of his or her position and the characteristics of the environment.
     The complexities of single sounds are matched or exceeded by the
complexities of sequences of sounds. Because of the continuous nature of
speech and music, the acoustic energy at any single point in time is a fusion
from preceding, present, and forthcoming sounds. The speech articulators
constantly move from one position to another, and these movements "cut
across" phoneme boundaries and drastically alter the acoustic wave that
might uniquely correspond to a phoneme. A melodic or rhythmic line may
require instrumental notes to be so close in time that the transients of
surrounding notes overlap to such a degree that any characteristic acoustic
patterning of a note is destroyed. Parallel transmission, resulting in the
restructuring of the acoustic waves, precludes any invariant one-to-one
relationship between a phoneme or note and an acoustic element.
     Given the degree of complexity at both the level of individual sounds,
where every aspect is a function of the others, and the level of sequences
of sounds, where the acoustic signal is restructured due to the surround, I
am almost led to predict that perception cannot occur. And yet perceiving
does occur, with an ease and immediacy that disguises its difficulty.

6.2 Commonalities in the Perceptual World

As I commented at the beginning of this chapter, audition (and perception
in general) has a passive quality, notable for its immediateness, directness,
and naturalness. Austin (1962) stresses the transparency of perception to
the physical world. We are not aware of our ears, nerves, and brain
interceding between the world and ourselves. Brunswik (1956) pointed out
the rapid, but possibly only approximate, attainments of perception. He
imagined perception to be a relatively autonomous yet primitive system.

What do we hear? We do not hear at only one level; it is not that we hear melodies but not notes, or notes but not harmonics. Similarly, it is not that we hear words but not phonemes, or phonemes but not formants, or formants but not transients. Rather, we can listen at all levels; sometimes we listen at one level at the expense of others, other times we listen at all levels at once. Sometimes each level illustrates only one facet of an event; other times each level illustrates a different reality. Possibly the question "What do we hear?" is a poor one, because it suggests one answer to a reality that admits many.

At one level we hear the various physical features of the sound: an intensity, a duration, a pitch, a vibrato, a frequency, and so on. The list of such features was identical across speech and music, yet some seemed more germane to one domain as opposed to another. For example, pitch (or frequency) seems more important for music; the overall frequency of a speech sound does not affect the meaning of the phoneme or syllable (at least in English). In contrast, duration of acoustic segments may be more important for speech, in which small changes often signify phonemic distinctions.

At a second level, we hear features of a sound that are not directly translatable into physical measures. These are features like warmth, roughness, hollowness, brightness, and so on. With diligence, subtlety, and luck, it is sometimes possible to discover complex relationships among simple physical measures that are correlated to these impressions, but most appear elusive.

At a third level, we hear objects. I am thinking of "violinness," "President Carterness," "President Reaganness," and "airplaneness." What is characteristic is that the sounds seem directly perceived as objects. Gibson (1979) has used the term *affordances*.

At each level, sounds yield meanings, and these meanings represent abstractions, reflections, or translations of the actual physical energies. When listening to speech sounds, we hear the same phonemic unit despite large variations in the acoustic signal, although we can make those acoustic distinctions in other situations. In the same fashion, we understand identical meanings despite different speakers, different rhythms, and different grammatical constructions. Similarly, we hear the same musical interval or chord despite large variations in the note frequencies; we hear the same melody despite many different transformations.

Each level represents an abstraction, an after-the-fact attempt to specify the characteristics of that event. The magnitudes or values at each level are meaningless in themselves; rather, they achieve their meaning (and I am loosely suggesting that an intensity or a duration may have a meaning) only within the interrelationships among the levels. These magnitudes are roughly analogous to the "clues" of a crime. A clue like a muddy footprint takes on meaning within the modus operandi—motive, method, opportunity. Without a context or frame of reference, in a real sense the clues do not exist.

Meanings cannot arise without intensities or durations, without rhythms or textures, and so on. In circular fashion, intensity, pitch, duration, rhythm, and so on are perceived within the structure provided by the meaning. The parts and wholes coalesce into one percept; it is not that the whole determines the parts as the Gestalt psychologists argue. Allport (1955), pointing out that the whole at one level may be a part at a different level, has termed this the inside-outside problem. It is rare to be able to understand any single level as being the synthesis of elements at a "lower" level or as being the analysis of elements at a "higher" level. All levels coexist simultaneously. There is an interchangeability that allows perceiving to function in several ways.

Given this complexity, it is no wonder that no single theory of perception can answer the phenomenal question, "How do things appear?" let alone the question, "Why do things appear as they do?" There are general classes of theories primarily concerned with one of the levels, but no theory successfully bridges the levels.

Yet there is one aspect of the perceptual world that is so compelling that it usually escapes notice. The perceptual world is one of events with clearly defined beginnings and endings (although there are continuous events without onsets and offsets; e.g., air rushing through ducts). An event becomes defined by its temporal boundary. But this impression is not due to the structure of the acoustic wave; the beginning and ending often are not physically marked by actual silent intervals. This has been discussed extensively for speech and language, and the same phenomenon also occurs, although possibly in weaker form, for music.

It is for this reason that the division of the ongoing acoustic signal into meaningful units is a significant perceptual accomplishment. Although the acoustic signal can be broken up into units in a limitless number of ways, only one is meaningful. The division of the stream of acoustic energy into events must depend on the interpretations at the various levels, but the interpretations (the magnitudes and values) at each level must rest on the identification of a unit of analysis. We have here, once again, the kind of circularities we have encountered previously.

Given this perplexing state of affairs—that the interpretation of levels depends on unit formation and vice versa—the remaining chapters will be organized by levels and events. The goal of each will be to describe the correspondences between the discrete units of the phenomenal psychological world and the continuous sound waves of the physical acoustic world.

6.3 Overview

Although the preceding chapters on instruments and voices are similar in form, they are quite different in content. The instrument chapter is physical in orientation; the voice chapter, though discussing speech production, is essentially psychological in orientation. This difference, it seems to me, reflects the beliefs surrounding each domain.

Music is assumed to be perceived in terms of the notes themselves. The notes generate melodies, rhythms, scales, and so on, but the meaning and emotional content of music comes from the perception of the relationship among the notes. In contrast, speech is assumed to be perceived in terms of the meanings of the sounds, and yet the relationship between speech sounds and the meanings of those sounds is arbitrary. Speech perception is thought to be further removed from the acoustic world; there is a search for meaning in speech perception that is absent in music perception.

This difference must at best be one of quantity, not of kind. The idea embodied in this book is that an object or event, not an array of sensations, is perceived. When we look at a face, we see John with a new pair of glasses, or Aimee with a Band-aid on her nose. In the same way, when we listen to music we hear themes, harmonies, melodies, and rhythms. We hear a pattern, an organization that arises from both the notes and the listener. Musically trained observers hear fugues, canons, blues, bebop, chromatic changes, variations on a theme, major and minor triads; they listen to the dialogue of the music. Music is a sound gesture. Speaking is a sound gesture. What I am suggesting is that the understanding of music has the same arbitrariness between sound and content, and the same search for meaning, that occurs in the understanding of speech.

In addition, the problem of context dependency is not unique to speech perception. The same difficulty occurs for music perception. In fact, the sensory data coming from any object or event will change dramatically as a function of the context. The light rays that bounce off an object and reach an observer's eye will depend on the lighting and position of the observer. Yet the same perception will normally result. The movements involved in motor acts also change dramatically as a function of the context. Walking up a hill and down a hill involves quite different movements, yet the same gait is seen. Psychologists have termed these phenomena *constancies* and have made extensive investigations into the way they are achieved. How do people achieve size constancy in spite of the varying distances between the object and perceiver? How do people achieve shape constancy in spite of the changes in shape at different orientations (e.g., a circle is shaped like an ellipse when it is at an angle although it still "looks" like a circle)? And so on. Most psychologists will ruefully admit that these sorts of questions are still unsolved.

Moreover, the problem of the interleaving and interweaving of sensory information is not unique to speech. In nearly all types of motor behavior, the movements are interlocked in time. Throwing a baseball involves a coordinated and simultaneous set of movements of finger, arms, legs, torso, head, and so forth. Similarly, walking involves a set of interwoven actions, and as pointed our above, the patterning of these actions changes as a function of the context.

On these bases, I do not believe that musical production and perception is any different in kind than speech production and perception. I believe the commonalities are so numerous and compelling that it is counterproductive to argue that speech sounds (and language in general) are somehow unique or that musical sounds (and nonspeech in general) are somehow unique. Rather, I believe that both possess the same structural features and that the differences merely represent alternative ways of realizing that structure. Both speech and music depend on the interweaving and the interaction among the component vibration patterns across time. I further believe that when a perception phenomenon is found for speech but not for music, or vice versa, then the sounds were not commensurate. In some way one of the signals was more appropriate, and this led to the apparent perceptual differences. I would argue that the differences found in the listener were due to differences in the stimulation. I do not believe that music and speech perception are fundamentally different domains.

Chapter 7

Breaking the Acoustic Wave into Events:
Stream Segregation

At any point in time, we are being bombarded with acoustic energy from many sources. Right now, I hear a fan blowing, at least four people conversing, and a lawn mower. What we hear is determined by the acoustic wave that reaches our ear. But the acoustic wave is a smear, because of the additive superposition of the sound waves generated by each event. Each event contributes a time-varying frequency and intensity pattern, but the integrity and connectedness of each pattern is lost physically among the other patterns in the overall wave. The acoustic wave is thus inherently ambiguous, because each event loses its identity when it is woven into the acoustic wave. Any segment of the acoustic wave can come from one or more sources. To disentangle the acoustic wave and capture each event, listeners use relationships among parts of the wave at one time point and relationships among parts of the wave across time points. We partition or parse the acoustic wave into events, and it is this ability that allows us to hear overlapping instruments and voices.

From this perspective, to investigate any of the common psychological questions underlying speech and music perception, we first have to answer how parts of the acoustic wave are assigned to one speech or one music event. To hear a sound as a clarinet note or a stop-consonant syllable requires that we assume the components of the sound wave come from one source. And in the same fashion, to hear a sequence of sounds as one melody requires that we assume the successive sounds come from one source. Bregman (1978a) sets up the perceptual question as "deciding how many sources, deciding what is each source, and deciding where is each source." (To which I might add the uniquely human question, "Why" each source.) It should be clear that the how many, what, and where answers are interactive. For example, the *where* decision influences and is influenced by the *what* decision. Listening is "making sense," trying to come up with the simplest and most plausible percept.

I believe that the principles underlying event perception must be similar across different modalities. Thus the perceptual dispositions, rules, and strategies that lead visual elements to be seen as one or more events must be similar to those that lead auditory elements to be heard as one or more events. If this belief is true, it will prove very useful, because the Gestalt psychologists started investigating the articulation of visual "scenes" into events in the early 1900s, sixty to seventy years before similar research began for auditory "scenes." We can use the insights gained from the Gestaltists in visual analysis to guide our thinking about auditory analysis.

The most characteristic concept of Gestalt psychology is that perception is of whole units, sets of related elements segregated from the rest of the elements (this has been called figure-ground organization). The whole is not merely the sum of the individual elements. The whole (the event) has a meaning that is not predictable from the elements. The Gestalt psychologists argue further that the meaning of each part comes from the meaning of the whole. Short curved lines become lips in a picture of a face, rocker legs in a picture of a chair, and fenders in a picture of a car.

We are still left with the problem of what determines which event will emerge. The Gestaltists argued metaphorically that the event is always as good a figure as possible. A good figure will be regular, simple, and organized. Perceptual systems assign elements to construct visual and auditory events out of the aggregate of elements in order to generate the most coherent perceptual events. On the whole, elements belonging to one event are maximally similar and predictable, whereas elements belonging to different events are maximally dissimilar. This has been termed the law of Prägnanz.

Prägnanz is a very difficult concept to pin down. At what level of a figure should Prägnanz occur: in small units of a complex figure, or in the entire global figure? Moreover, does Prägnanz refer to an abstract simplicity or merely to a statistical likelihood (i.e., the event most probable to occur)? Visual perception theorists have been able to generate counterexamples to any sort of precise definition for Prägnanz, which obviously leads to questioning the validity of the concept. Even though a rigorous definition is impossible, we will use it as a general guiding principle: perceptual organization strives toward the most coherent set of events (see Pomerantz and Kubovy 1981, for a discussion of these issues).

Yet perception is of the entire scene. Elements are perceived as belonging to events in order to make all the events coherent. You cannot "throw away" parts of the visual field because they do not make sense. The elements are seen in differing ways until a coherent whole emerges. Organization thus occurs over time; it cannot be instantaneous. Let me provide an analogy. Imagine that you are given a jumble of letters that when unscrambled must produce two words. It is not sufficient to use the letters to form one word, because the leftover letters may not form a second word. What you must do is assign the letters so they produce two words. You may have to give up the first word you make in order to generate two words. In the same way, event perception requires trades—

one element and one event may be perceived differently (and possibly as less structured) if "moving" one element of the acoustic signal over to another event makes both events become coherent.

The Gestalt psychologists described several organization principles that underlie the organization of the visual field. These organizational principles include: (1) similarity: elements that are similar in physical attributes tend to be grouped together; (2) proximity: elements that are close together in space or time tend to be grouped together; (3) continuity: elements that appear to follow in the same direction tend to be grouped together; (4) common fate: elements that move together tend to be grouped together; (5) symmetry and closure: elements that form symmetrical and enclosed objects tend to be grouped together. These organizational principles provide the basis by which elements are grouped into events that maximize Prägnanz. From the Gestalt perspective, we can expect the parts of the acoustic wave that group into one perceptual event to be similar (e.g., in frequency, timbre, intensity), to be in spatial and temporal proximity, and to follow the same time trajectory in terms of their frequency, intensity, position, rhythm, etc. These rules of organization make sense in terms of events in the environment. Sounds coming from one event are likely to be continuous, to be similar, to be in close spatial proximity, and so on.

Experimentally, we can investigate the operation of these organizational rules by placing them in conflict. For example, we can place four open dots at the corners of a square and determine whether viewers tend to group the top two dots against the bottom two dots or tend to group the left two against the right two. By filling two dots (say, the top two) we can induce grouping by similarity: the two top filled dots in one group and the two bottom open dots in another group. By separating the left two from the right two dots, we place similarity in conflict with proximity: similarity organization is top versus bottom; proximity organization is left versus right (see figure 7.1). By pulling the two left and two right dots farther apart, it is possible to determine the point at which the two opposing principles balance, and in this way we can measure the strength of each. This is the basic strategy used in studying auditory organization. Grouping principles are placed in conflict, and the listeners judge which elements appear to go together. The relative strength of each organizational rule is inferred from the percentage of listeners who group the elements in that way.

The organizational rules underlying listening must serve to organize the acoustic wave in two overlapping time spans. First, there is the organization that occurs in short time periods. This refers to making sense of the smeared acoustic wave at an "instant in time." Does the sound wave represent one event (i.e., a note or speech sound) or is it the sum of two or more events? Second, there is the organization that occurs across longer

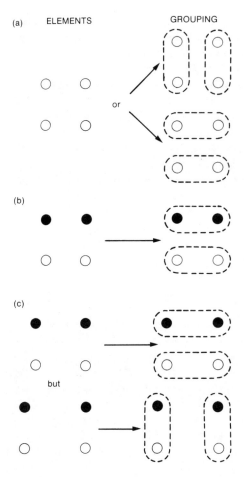

Figure 7.1
Competition among grouping rules. For the four open dots in (*a*), the grouping is equally likely to be done vertically or horizontally. If the two top dots are filled as in (*b*), there will be a strong tendency to organize horizontally, placing the two filled dots in one group and the two open dots in the second group. If the two left dots are physically separated from the two right dots as in (*c*), there will be a point of separation at which the grouping shifts to left versus right. In nearly all instances, it is possible to increase the probability of one kind of grouping by increasing the dissimilarity between stimuli along that dimension.

time spans. This involves making sense of the acoustic wave as it changes in time, each instant being a small part of the entire pattern. Does the overall pattern seem to come from one instrumental or vocal source, or does the overall pattern seem to come from more than one source, and if so, which parts of the acoustic wave arise from each source? The organizational processes occurring within shorter time spans and over longer time spans support each other. Notes can be utilized to uncover sequences, and vice versa.

It is the fact that short time spans are embedded in longer ones that makes it difficult to study one at a time. To study the organization of a single sound into one or two sources, investigators have varied the attack transients and harmonic frequencies of components of single sound bursts. To study the organization of a series of sounds into one or many sources, investigators have varied the frequency, intensity, and timing of the individual sounds. Below, each type of organization will be discussed separately and then in combination.

7.1 Stream Segregation

The perceptual organization of the acoustic wave into events has come to be called *stream segregation*. Each event becomes one separate stream. The term *stream segregation* seems most apropos when considering an ongoing event in which the wave is parsed into simultaneous interwoven streams (e.g., a singer and accompaniment), but we will use it generally to refer to any organization into separate events.

The first experiments seeking to understand stream segregation were motivated by the question of selective attention: under what conditions could a listener attend to one of several competing messages? It is quite clear that we can listen to one conversation in the midst of other conversations and noise. This has been colloquially termed the "cocktail party effect."

Difference in perceived location is one of the major bases for stream segregation (Broadbent 1958). The parts of the acoustic wave that have consistent interaural differences (e.g., phase, timing, and intensity) are "taken out" of the wave, are located at a point in space, and are perceived as one sound source. It is considerably harder to follow one conversation if the localization information is eliminated—that is, if all the sound is recorded and played back through one speaker. As will be described in chapter 12, the auditory neural pathways "compute" the interaural differences in specific brain nuclei and then overlay information about localization with information about the spectral and temporal properties of the signal.

In addition, this research demonstrated that other aspects of the signal could lead to stream segregation if spatial location information were equalized. For example, listeners could attend to one message on the basis of the harmonic spectra (e.g., a speaking voice limited to low frequencies as opposed to a voice limited to high frequencies) and intensity differences (Neisser 1966). Moreover, Cherry (1957) created an experimental situation in which one reader recorded two messages, and both messages were presented simultaneously over headphones. In this case, speaker quality and spatial location differences are eliminated. Nevertheless, a patient listener can identify both messages by using knowledge of the syntax of language and knowledge of speaking habits (e.g., clichés, rhythms).

This research pointed out the diversity of ways that listeners could zero in on one message. The emphasis was on the process of attention, and little work was aimed at discovering the auditory grouping rules. The aim of the research described in detail below has been to isolate these rules. Therefore, given the prepotence of spatial organization, such research has minimized or eliminated interaural differences.

Organization of a Single Sound
Typically, a sound from any source consists of a time-varying pattern of harmonics. When sounds from different sources overlap, all of the harmonic components are intermixed in time and frequency. A listener can use the timing relationships among the components, the harmonic relationships among the components, and/or the amplitude and frequency modulation relationships among the components to parse the sound wave into discrete component sources.

The synchrony of the frequency partials is perhaps the most important cue. For a simple complex tone made up of two partials, offsetting the low and high components so that each had a different time course led to the perception of two tones rather than one fused tone (Rasch 1978). The necessary time difference between the partials was about 20 msec to 30 msec. Even though there was a unique percept at the onset and offset of the partials, listeners did not hear two tones offset in time. Instead, they heard two tones extending in time. The listeners could use the timing asynchrony to distinguish one tone from two tones, but they did not use the asynchrony to distinguish that one preceded the other. Differences in rise time among the partials also affects the probability of forming one complex sound. For example, a long attack time of the lower pitch tone coupled with a short attach time of the higher pitch tone led to the perception of two tones. Different possibilities are illustrated in figure 7.2, panel (a).

The synchrony of the partials is also important for the fusion of partials in more complex sounds, such as simulated vowels. A frequency partial

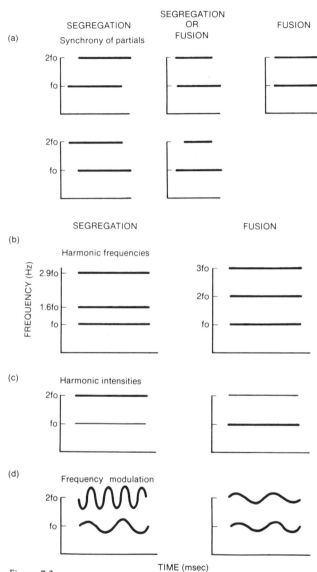

Figure 7.2
Factors that influence the fusion of partials into one complex tone. The most important factor is the onset and offset asynchrony (a). The segregation of the partials into two separate tones is maximum when there are both onset and offset asynchronies; the fusion of partials into one complex tone is maximum when the onset and offset are synchronous. Other factors that influence segregation appear in (b)–(d), left column. The partials have a higher probability of segregating if (b) the partials are not strictly harmonic; (c) the higher partials are more intense; and (d) the frequency modulation is uncorrelated. In contrast, as shown in the right column, the partials have a higher probability of fusing if: (b) the partials are harmonic; (c) the lower partial is more intense; and (d) the frequency modulation is correlated.

that is asynchronous is less likely to be integrated into the vowel. The asynchronous partial forms its own stream and thereby changes the vowel quality (Darwin 1984). Differences in onset result in a stronger sense of segregation than differences in offset.

The harmonic structure also affects the probability that the sound will be perceived as one or more tones (or events). In general, the more closely the partials resemble a natural event, the more likely they are to fuse into one tone. For example:

1. Partials are more likely to fuse if they are harmonic. Octave-related partials are most likely to fuse; out-of-tune partials are more likely to form separate notes (figure 7.2, panel b). Harmonics out of tune by as little as 3%–5% will appear as a separate tone (Moore, Glasberg, and Peters 1985). For complex sounds, the partials are grouped so that they form harmonic series that would have come from tones of different fundamental frequencies. For example, a set of frequencies like 80 Hz, 100 Hz, 160 Hz, 200 Hz, 240 Hz, 300 Hz, and 320 Hz is likely to be perceived as two sources: 80 Hz, 160 Hz, 240 Hz, 320 Hz; and 100 Hz, 200 Hz, 300 Hz (Duifhuis, Willems, and Sluyte 1982).

2. Partials are more likely to fuse if the higher partials are less intense than the lower partials (figure 7.2, panel c). This intensity pattern is characteristic of most environmental sounds and human voices.

3. Finally, intensity and frequency modulation affect stream segregation. Partials are more likely to fuse together if they have the identical amplitude and frequency modulation (figure 7.2, panel d). Even and odd harmonics with different vibrato patterns lead to the perception of two simultaneous tones, one an octave higher (the evens) than the other (the odds) (McAdams and Bregman 1979). Kubovy (1981) has demonstrated another example of intensity modulation leading to stream segregation. Imagine a chord composed of several notes. One note is reduced in intensity for about 0.1 sec and then returned to its original value. When the note is restored to its value, the chord does not merely sound the same as before. Rather, the note stands out against the background of the chord. Kubovy describes it as a chime. The intensity modulation produces segregation.

The rules that underlie the fusion of partials into a complex tone or the fission of partials into separate tones are linked to environmental properties of sounds coming from one source and can be subsumed under the Gestalt laws. Tones that are harmonically related and that have an identical temporal pattern are fused together. Tones that undergo the same changes (i.e., intensity changes because of the amplitude envelope, frequency changes because of vibrato or glides, etc.) are fused together (by common fate). It is easy to overlook, but sounds that do not change over time are assumed to be the same events, which is another aspect of common fate. Perceived continuity of a sound through time is a powerful cue to event organization (Weintraub 1987). Sounds from one source are likely to fulfill these requirements (as well as provide consistent localization cues), and the results show that listeners are sensitive to all these environmental characteristics.

Organization of Sequences of Pure Tones

A sequence of sounds can be organized into one coherent source, or the sounds can be partitioned into two or more overlapping sources. If the sequence is perceived as coming from one source, then each sound represents one part of an event. If the sequence is perceived as coming from two or more sources, then sounds from each source are intermixed; one event might arise from every other sound and a second event from the remaining sounds.

Two research methodologies have emerged. In the first, a sequence of tones is recycled very quickly, usually between 5 and 20 tones per second. Here, the entire sequence may appear to be coherent or the sequence may seem to split into subsequences such that the elements in each subsequence appear to be coherent. If the elements form subsequences, then the elements in each subsequence stream have been conceptualized as being more similar to each other than to elements in other streams. The rationale is that "similar" elements are likely to have come from the same source or event. The various bases for this grouping or segregation into streams can give insights into the rules and strategies listeners use in normal situations to parse sounds into events. In the second methodology, sequences of sounds are presented at slower rates that deliberately place organizational rules in conflict, and the empirical question is which rule do listeners follow in their perception.

Although the actual sound sequences are very different, the two methodologies converge to the same generalizations. For this reason, instead of reviewing the results for each methodology, they can be organized by the following two issues: (1) what factors influence the splitting up of a sequence of elements into two or more streams? In other words, when do we hear all the sounds as coming from one event, and when do we hear the sounds as coming from separate events? The conflict is between coherent perception based on temporal proximity and segregated perception based on one type of element similarity. (2) When sounds do split into streams, what factors or attributes determine how the elements split up? For example, do the elements form streams on the basis of frequency similarity or on the basis of spatial proximity? The conflict is between segregated perception based on one stimulus attribute and segregated perception based on a different stimulus attribute.

One stream or two (or more) streams   In the typical experiment, listeners are presented a sequence of alternating pure tones (e.g., H[high]L[low]HL ... or L[left]R[right]LR ... or L[loud]S[soft]LS ...) and are instructed to report whether the tones form one coherent sequence (an alternation or trill) or whether the tones form two separate but overlapping sequences, one of low tones, the other of high tones, or one of left tones, one of right tones, etc.

Starting with frequency, as presentation rate or frequency separation (i.e., the ratio between the frequencies of the two tones) increases, there is a higher probability of hearing the H's and L's as forming different streams (termed *frequency streaming*). Conversely, as the frequency separation or the presentation rate decreases, there is a higher probability of hearing the H's and L's as forming one alternating stream. At intermediate values of frequency separation and presentation rate, the tendency to hear the notes as forming one coherent stream or as forming two streams can be determined by the listener's attention. Thus there are three regions defined by combinations of presentation rate and frequency separation, as shown in figure 7.3.

1. For presentation rate and frequency separation combinations in the upper right (over the top solid line), elements always form two segregated streams. The boundary line represents the inverse relationship between tempo and frequency separation. If the tones are presented at a 10 elements/sec rate, a frequency ration of 1.25 or more will lead to separate streams, but if the rate is reduced to 5 elements/sec, a frequency ration of 2.25 (roughly an octave) or more will be required to generate separate streams.

2. For combinations in the lower part (below the bottom solid line), elements always form one coherent stream. If the frequency separation is less than 10%, the listeners hear one coherent stream for all presentation rates.

3. In the middle (between the solid lines), above the coherent one-stream boundary and below the segregated two-stream boundary, listeners can hear elements form either one coherent or two segregated streams. By shifting attention, listeners can "make" the two tones go together or separate. In contrast, attentional shifts have little influence in the other two regions.

The same relationship between frequency separation and presentation rate determining stream segregation is true for speech sounds (Nooteboom, Brokx, and de Rooij 1978). For example, the fundamental frequency of alternate vowels in the sequence—a u i a u i—can be increased to yield:

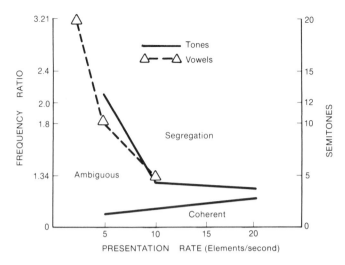

Figure 7.3
The segregation of repeating sequences of sounds into streams. In experiments with tones (solid lines), there is a segregation region in which all combinations of frequency ratio and presentation rate yield two streams. There is also a coherent region in which all combinations yield one stream. In between these two is an ambiguous region composed of frequency ratio and presentation rate combinations that listeners can perceive either as one coherent stream or as two segregated streams (adapted from Van Noorden 1975). For vowels, there is a similar segregation region in which all combinations of frequency rate and presentation rate yield two streams (adapted from Nooteboom, Brokx and de Rooij 1978). (Due to a different methodology, data from the vowels did not distinguish between the coherent and ambiguous regions.)

| high frequency: | | u | | a | | i | | u | |
| low frequency: | a | | i | | u | | a | | i |

The results demonstrate that there is a region of coherence and a region of segregation based on the inverse relation of rate and frequency separation, and the values are comparable to those for tones. The results for vowels are also shown in figure 7.3. Frequency streaming occurs for presentation rate/frequency separation combinations above the dotted line; coherence occurs for combinations below the dotted line. Moreover, at high presentation rates, even a single syllable may break into streams. The fricative [sha] may form a [sh] noise stream and a [da] stop consonant syllable stream.

At faster presentation rates, "narrower" streams will form. Imagine a repeating sequence composed of four tones differing in frequency. At slow rates, listeners might hear one coherent sequence. As the rate increases, the frequency separation among some of the elements will fall above the two-stream boundary and the sequence will split into two streams—higher frequencies versus lower frequencies. As the rate increases still further, all the frequency ratios will fall above the two-stream boundary and each element will form its own stream: high highs, low highs, high lows, low lows. This is illustrated in figure 7.4.

It is critical to realize that the frequency separations and presentation rates that determine streaming are not fixed or unchangeable. They depend on the context, and they are sensitive to other parts of the signal that give additional information about the possible events. For example:

1. Elements that form an increasing or decreasing frequency progression tend to remain more coherent than the identical elements in an angular or random order. Progressions are good continuations; the elements are more predictable and easier to "track." The progression might imply that the elements came from the one source. In music, predictable notes are integrated into the melodic stream; notes that involve large, unpredictable jumps are more likely to form individual streams (Heise and Miller 1951).

2. Adjacent elements connected by frequency transitions that glide into each other are more likely to form a coherent stream (see figure 7.5). The glide connecting the disparate frequencies is a cue that the two notes come from the same source (by good continuation) and are thus more likely to be integrated. In speech, vowels connected by plausible formant transitions are more likely to form a coherent stream; phonetically impossible formant transitions do not lead to a coherent stream (Bregman and Dannenbring 1973; Dorman, Cutting, and Raphael 1975).

3. The timbre of the notes in a sequence can affect the probability that the elements will form separate streams. (I am using the term *timbre* to represent tone quality.) The timbre is physically changed by modifying the harmonic spectra, adding or removing harmonics. Suppose we alternate a low frequency tone (A) and a high frequency tone (B) at frequencies and rates at which the percept is ambiguous. If we add a harmonic to A similar to the frequency of B, the tones have a greater tendency to form one stream. Although A and B are more dissimilar because of the timbre dissimilarity, they sound more similar in pitch quality (because of the higher frequency harmonic of A), and this precludes their streaming. If, on the other hand, the identical harmonic is added to tone B, the probability of each tone forming its own stream is increased. The high frequency harmonic added to B makes it more different in pitch quality as well as in timbre and this increases the probability of stream segregation. In addition, it is possible to bring about streaming between two similar frequency tones that normally would not stream by adding nonadjacent harmonics

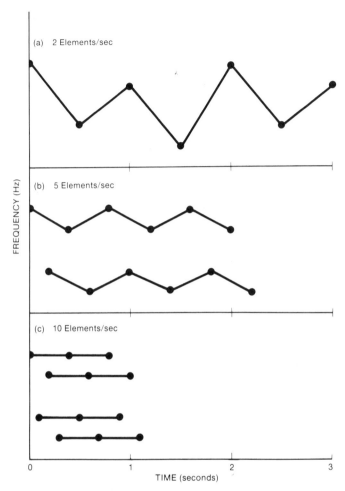

Figure 7.4
As presentation rate increases, streams become narrower in frequency and eventually may yield one stream for each individual note. At slow rates (a), the four tones form one stream. At intermediate rates (b), the two high tones and the two low tones form separate streams. At the fastest rates (c), each high tone and each low tone form a separate stream.

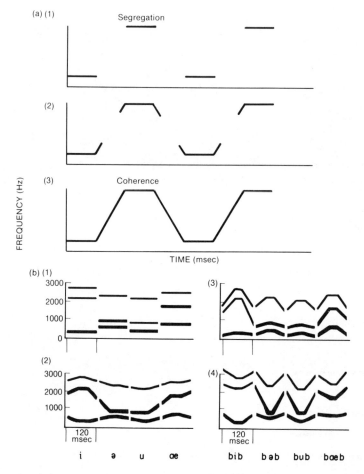

Figure 7.5
Frequency transitions lead to the perception of one coherent stream. In the top three panels, two unconnected tones are normally perceived as two separate streams. Frequency transitions that point toward the tones lead to a higher probability of hearing the two tones as forming one stream, and transitions that connect the two tones lead to the perception of one coherent stream (after Bregman and Dannenbring 1973). In the bottom four panels, simulated vowels and consonant-vowel-consonant syllables used to investigate the effect of formant transitions on streaming are illustrated. In (b1), vowels are *not* connected by transitions; /i/ and /u/ form one stream, and /ə/ and /ae/ form a second stream. Listeners cannot identify the order of the vowels for sequences in which there is an alternation of the first formant frequency (as in b1). In (b2), vowels are connected by formant transitions; all four vowels form one coherent stream and listeners can identify the order of the vowels. In (b3), vowels are connected by formant transitions associated with the consonants; all syllables form one stream and listeners can identity the order of the syllables. In (b4), the vowels are connected by impossible formant transitions created by making the normal consonant transitions upside down. Listeners are unable to identify the order of the sounds (adapted from Dorman, Cutting, and Raphael 1975).

to each tone. This generates timbre differences, which increases the probability of streaming (McAdams and Bregman 1979).

4. Another factor that influences stream segregation is the timing between elements. Elements that are separated by equal intervals are more likely to form a stream than the identical elements when they are unevenly spaced. The auditory system infers that equally timed elements are more likely to have come from a single source (Handel, Weaver, and Lawson 1983).

Frequency separation provides one of the dominant bases for organization into streams. But this does not mean that frequency organization (higher pitch versus lower pitch) is automatic. Frequency streaming is affected by the many other factors detailed above. Moreover, as will be discussed in the next section, whether two frequencies join within a stream is a function of all the other frequencies in the sequence. These other frequencies can capture a frequency into one stream, or they can provide a contrast that "pushes" a frequency into a different stream.

For other attributes, such as intensity differences and spatial position differences, that imply that the sounds come from different sources, there is also an inverse relationship or tradeoff between the intensity (position) difference and presentation rate. For example, at moderate rates of presentation, between 2.5 elements/sec and 10 elements/sec, an intensity pressure difference of 25% to 50% (2–4 dB) between two tones of equal frequency will result in stream segregation (Van Noorden 1975). Stream segregation will be stronger if the intensity difference and/or presentation rate increases, and a decrease in presentation rate can be compensated by an increase in the intensity difference. In similar fashion, stream segregation will be stronger if spatial separation and/or presentation rate increases, and a decrease in presentation rate can be compensated by an increase in the spatial separation between tones (Judd 1979).

We have seen that a sequence of elements can be partitioned into discrete streams of elements that seem to represent one source or event. Each element is assigned to one and only one stream. There are many bases for the assignment into streams. For recycled sequences of tonal elements, pitch similarity may be the dominant organizational attribute (i.e., high pitch tones versus low pitch tones). However, pitch segregation is not absolute; instead we should conceptualize pitch, timbre, intensity, and spatial position as competing for supremacy. For example, Singh (1987) demonstrated that frequency and timbre differences could be traded. Increasing the frequency difference or decreasing the timbre differences led to a greater percentage of frequency streaming; decreasing the frequency differences or increasing the timbre differences led to a greater percentage of timbre streaming. Stream segregation is not rapid; it builds up over time.

The auditory perceptual system considers each possible grouping in parallel, before settling on the most probable organization of the elements into events (Bregman 1978b).

Competition among organizations   The above results suggest that various attributes compete to determine stream organization. The stream segregation is a function of all the elements. The simplest illustration of this occurs for recycling sequences of four elements. Four (or more) elements are used, rather than two, to allow a greater range of organizational possibilities. For example, Bregman (1978c) first constructed sequences of two alternating tones separated by a frequency ratio of 1.8 (sequence 1: 2800 Hz/1556 Hz; sequence 2: 2642 Hz/1468 Hz). Both sequences were heard as coherent despite the rather wide separation between the two tones. After this demonstration, Bregman combined the four original tones into a recycling sequence: 2800 Hz, 1556 Hz, 2642 Hz, 1468 Hz, 2800 Hz, 1556 Hz.... Remember that when presented as an alternating two-tone sequence, the 2800 Hz + 1556 Hz tones and the 2642 Hz + 1468 Hz tones formed two coherent streams. On this basis we might expect the sequence 2800 Hz, 1556 Hz, 2642 Hz, 1468 Hz to break up into a 2800 Hz + 1556 Hz stream and a 2642 Hz + 1468 Hz stream (or to form one coherent stream). Another reason to expect this segregation is temporal proximity, because the 1556 Hz element follows the 2800 Hz element and the 1468 Hz element follows the 2642 Hz element. The outcome was quite different, however. There was a perceptual reorganization so that the pairs of similar frequencies streamed together. The two streams were 2800 Hz + 2642 Hz and 1556 Hz + 1468 Hz, even though this cut across the temporal proximity organization.

Thus what forms are streams with the simplest structure: tones with maximally similar frequencies are perceived to be in one stream, and tones with maximally dissimilar frequencies are perceived to be in different streams.

Subsequent work has also demonstrated that stream formation is a function of the quality of all the elements in a sequence and cannot be predicted on the basis of the similarity within each pair of elements (McNally and Handel 1977). At the presentation rate used (5 elements/sec), previous work would suggest that any pair of sinusoid tones separated by an octave (a 2:1 frequency ratio) would form two streams if the two tones alternated. Two tones separated by three octaves—750 Hz and 6000 Hz —clearly would form two streams. These two sinusoid tones (750 Hz,

6000 Hz), were combined with a white noise element sounding like *shhh* (all frequencies within a 10,000 Hz range) and a rumblelike sound (40 Hz sinusoid wave) to form a four-element repeating sequence: 750 Hz, *shh*, 6000 Hz, rumble, etc. In this sequence, the 750 Hz and 6000 Hz sinusoid tones joined into one stream, in opposition to the white noise and rumble sound. Thus even though 750 Hz and 6000 Hz tones if alternated will form separate streams because of the frequency difference, when mixed with elements of different "quality" they will combine into one stream because of their timbre (tonal) similarity. We can demonstrate further the effect of context by forming four-element recycling sequences of pure tones separated by octaves: 750 Hz, 3000 Hz, 1500 Hz, 6000 Hz. Remember that any pair of such tones would form two streams if they were alternated. Yet together, the four tones remain coherent and form one stream. The simple harmonic relationship among each pair of tones probably brings about the coherent stream.

Acoustic properties that influence the type of stream segregation   These results show that the overall context determines stream segregation. However, they do not directly place alternative organizational principles in conflict to determine the relative strengths. One procedure to test this has been devised by Deutsch (1975). In her initial studies, she placed frequency organization in conflict with spatial position organization. In this technique, pairs of notes are synchronized so that one note is presented to the left ear at the same time that a second note is presented to the right ear by means of headphones. One ingenious example is illustrated in figure 7.6. In this case, there is an ascending frequency progression in which the notes are alternately presented to the left and right ears. Simultaneously, there is a descending frequency progression in which the notes are also alternately presented to the left and right ears (panel a). (Remember, at each instant in time, the left and right notes are synchronous.) There are three basic ways of organizing the elements. The first, shown in panel b1, organizes by ear, or spatial position. Elements in the left ear form one stream and elements in the right ear form a second stream. To do this, listeners must place high and low frequencies in the same stream, which creates a "jumpy" unmusical tune and violates the frequency organization principle. The second, shown in panel b2, organizes by frequency. Higher pitch elements form one stream, lower pitch elements form another stream. To do this, listeners must place left ear and right ear elements in the same stream, creating a reversing frequency progression and violating the spatial organization principle. The third, shown in panel b3, organizes by frequency progression, or good continuation. Elements that form a descending progression become one stream, and elements that form an ascending progression become a second stream. To do this, listeners must place high and low

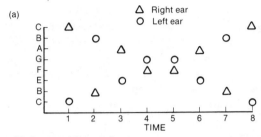

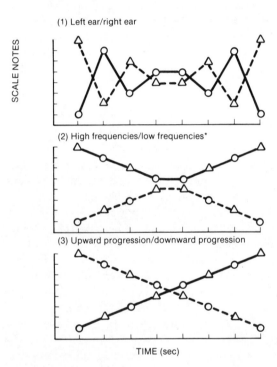

Figure 7.6

Conflict among alternative organizations. In Deutsch's method, two tones are presented simultaneously, one to the left ear and one to the right ear. The tone sequence is pictured in (a). Listeners can organize the tones in one of several competing ways. (b1) Listeners can group the tones in the left ear and group the tones in right ear; (b2) listeners can group the high frequency tones and group the low frequency tones; or (b3) listeners can group the tones forming an upward progression and group the tones forming a downward progression. The preferred organization was (b2), marked by an asterisk.

pitch elements in one stream as well as place left ear and right ear elements in one stream to create a straight progression, which violates the frequency and spatial organization principles. Deutsch (1975) reported that when asked to attend to each ear separately, approximately 75% of the subjects perceived alternative b2. Right-handed listeners, at least, heard the higher pitch tones localized in the right ear and the lower pitch tones localized in the left ear. This illusion seemed to suggest that pitch was the dominant organizational principle.

Subsequent work using the same experimental situation has extended but substantially refined these conclusions. First, Judd (1979) pointed out that although the presentation to two ears was supposed to place spatial organization by ear in conflict with pitch organization, the cues to spatial organization were very weak. If two different tones close in frequency are simultaneously presented to the ears (one tone to left, one tone to right) it is extremely difficult to localize each tone, because both tones are localized on the side of the subjectively more intense tone. Judd therefore argued that if localization cues were enhanced, then place/ear organization (alternative b1) would become a more preferred organization. The results supported that contention. Judd's work therefore demonstrates that this experimental situation produces competition among possible organizational rules like localization, similarity, common fate, and good continuation.

Later, Smith et al. (1982) performed a series of variations that further illustrated competition among the organizational rules. The variations used and the percentages of each type of organization are shown for nonmusicians and musicians in figure 7.7.

The first condition (top panel) replicates that used by Deutsch—strong pitch cues and weak place cues. Although the results were more variable, they resembled those found by Deutsch: listeners tended to hear the lower pitch tones in one ear and the higher pitch tones in the other ear. (Parenthetically, it is critically important to be able to replicate the original results. Only then is it legitimate to argue that subsequent changes in results are due to the changes in stimulus conditions.) In the second variation (middle panel), cues to localization were enhanced by changing the timbre of tones presented in each ear. The sequence in the left ear could be a simulated piano; the tones in the right ear could be a simulated saxophone. In this case, nonmusicians tended to organize by ear/timbre; musicians organized either by ear/timbre or by pitch. In the third variation (bottom panel), cues to organization by progression were enhanced by presenting the elements forming the descending progression using one timbre and by presenting the elements forming the upward progression using a second timbre. In this case, nonmusicians invariably organized by scale progression/timbre, but musicians organized by all three possibilities equally often.

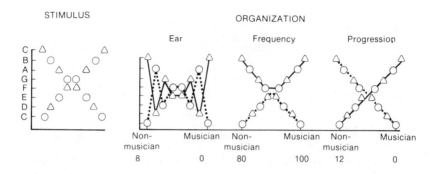

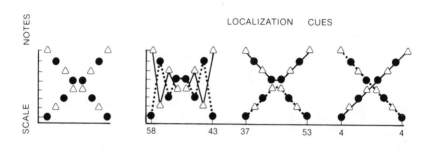

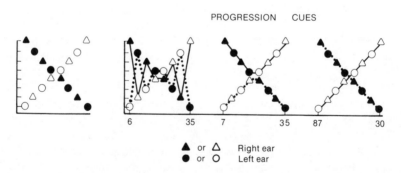

Figure 7.7
Organization is determined by stimulus characteristics and musical experience of the listener.
The percentage of ear, frequency, and progression organizations is indicated separately for
nonmusicians and musicians. In the top panel, the notes in each ear were the same timbre.
In the middle panel, the notes in the left ear were a different timbre than the notes in the
right ear. In the bottom panel, the notes forming the upward progression were a different
timbre than the notes forming the downward progression.

Davidson, Power, and Michie (1987) argue that familiarity with Western tonal music can help explain the outcomes. They hypothesize that classical musicians have a musical bias against organization by ear because it results in tunes that have large jumps between notes, and the tunes are thus "unmusical." Moreover, classical musicians have a musical bias against organization by scale progression, because straight-frequency progressions are not common in music. These musicians would have a bias toward pitch organization, because this results in a reversing-frequency progression tune that is more typical of classical Western music. To explore this possibility, Davidson, Power, and Michie (1987) presented the sequences to contemporary composers who do not follow traditional melodic rules. These composers heard the sequences faithfully, that is, by ear. The authors proposed that training in the analysis of music and familiarity with nontraditional tonal sequences allowed the contemporary composers to break out of the expectations created by lifelong experience with classical music.

These results reinforce my contention that the auditory organization is the outcome of competition among alternative possibilities. The outcome is determined by physiological processes, inherent perceptual processes, stimulus characteristics, and the experiences and strategies of each listener.

Organization of Sequences Composed of Complex Tones
The final type of organization to consider occurs when each tone in a sequence is composed of several harmonics. There are many possible organizations, because the harmonics in each tone can form separate streams. The actual organization will depend on many interacting factors.

Let us start by considering the alternation of two sounds as shown in figure 7.8. Tone A is composed of one harmonic; tone B is composed of two harmonics. If the tones are alternated there are several possible organizations: (a) tone A and tone B form a single coherent stream; (b) tone A would form one stream and tone B form a second stream; (c) tone A strips the higher frequency B_2 component from B and and forms one stream A-B_2-A-B_2, and the lower frequency B_1 component forms a second stream. The A-B_2 stream appears to be going twice as fast as the B_1 stream.

The discussion thus far gives insights about the stimulus conditions that lead to each alternative:

Alternative a: We expect a single coherent stream (1) if the presentation rate is slower than a certain value; and/or (2) if the frequencies of A and B are similar; and (3) if the B-tone partials are synchronous in onset and offset to create the perception of a single complex tone.

Alternative b: We expect an A-tone stream and a B-tone stream (1) if the presentation rate is rapid; and/or (2) if the frequency of the A tone is

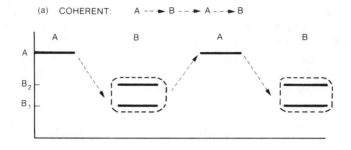

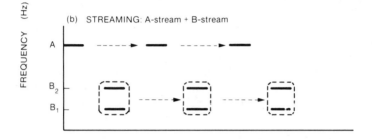

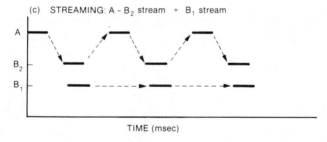

TIME (msec)

Figure 7.8
Possible organizations for repeating sequences composed of complex tones. In (a), there is one coherent stream. In (b), there are two streams: an A stream and a B stream composed of both partials of the complex tones. In (c), there are two streams: an A-B_2 stream composed of the similar frequency A and B_2 components and a B_1 stream. Note that the presentation rate portrayed in (a) is slower than that portrayed in (b) or (c).

quite different from either of the frequencies of the B-tone partials, which creates the frequency separation necessary for stream segregation; and (3) if the B partials are synchronous in time.

Alternative c: We expect an A-B_2 stream and a B_1 stream (1) if the presentation rate is rapid; and (2) if the frequency of A is similar to the frequency of component B_2 to create a frequency stream; and (3) if the two harmonics of the B tone are asynchronous in time to create the perception of two simple tones.

Experimental results confirm these expectations. Bregman and Pinker (1978) constructed a sequence composed of a single sinusoid tone (A tone) alternating with a complex tone composed of two sinusoid tones (B tone). The frequency similarity between the two tones determined the tendency to form a coherent stream, and the temporal synchrony determined the tendency for the partials to fuse, forming a complex-timbre B tone. If the two components of tone B have the identical temporal pattern, there is a strong tendency for the components to fuse into a single complex tone, regardless of the frequency similarity to tone A. As the temporal asynchrony between the two components of B increases and as the single tone and high component of the complex tone become more similar in frequency, the probability increases that the pure A tone and the similar frequency component of complex tone B will form a sequential stream (i.e., figure 7.8, panel c).

To show that these effects occur for different kinds of tonal stimuli, Steiger and Bregman (1981) used glide stimuli that increased (or decreased) in frequency by 41% (e.g., 724 Hz to 1024 Hz). Glide stimuli simulated the formant transitions so important in speech perception. The single glide alternated with a complex tone consisting of two glides (see figure 7.9). In this experiment, the onset and offset timing of the glides in the complex tone was identical.

The probability of the single glide forming a stream with the higher frequency glide of the complex tones was greatest when the glides were similar in frequency and when the glides had the same orientation, both either ascending or descending (see figure 7.9, panel a). The probability was intermediate when the glides pointed in opposite directions (panel b). Surprisingly, the probability was lowest when the single note and component glide followed the same path or trajectory (see figure 7.9, panel c). In this case, although the two glides created good continuation, the glides were more different in frequency and thus, because of frequency dissimilarity, did not tend to form a stream.

The auditory system is constantly faced with the problem of making sense out of overlapping (in frequency and time) acoustic signals coming from two or more sources or events. The physical signal can be broken up

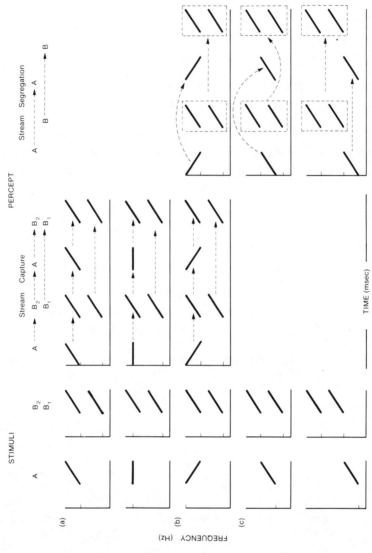

Figure 7.9
Possible organizations for repeating sequences composed of complex glide stimuli. In (a), the A stimulus is either identical to one glide of the B stimulus or the A stimulus is the average frequency of the higher frequency glide of the B stimulus. In both instances, there is a strong tendency for the A and B$_2$ component to form one stream. In (b), the A-stimulus glide has the reverse direction from the B$_2$-stimulus glide (although the frequency range is identical). Both kinds of organization occur. In (c), the frequency of the A-stimulus glide differs from the corresponding B-stimulus glide even though they share the same trajectory. In this case, the A stimulus and B stimulus form separate streams because of the frequency dissimilarity.

in a large number of ways. What the auditory system does do is based on reasonable intuitions about events in the world. The acoustic elements of events in the world tend to have similar frequencies, similar temporal patternings, similar spatial positions, similar intensities, and so on. Listeners make use of these relationships to parse the ambiguous physical signal into the elements composing plausible events. Any single relationship will not always lead to the true representation of the world. But as Bregman (1978a) writes, "No one heuristic will necessarily always succeed, but if there are many of them, competing or reinforcing one another, the right description should generally emerge" (p. 64).

7.2 Psychological Consequences of Streaming

We have discussed to this point the relationship of physical factors in the acoustic signal to stream formation. The formation of streams has several perceptual consequences, both in terms of the organization within a stream and in terms of the organization between streams.

Organization within Streams

Events in the real world overlap and "compete." The acoustic energy from one event may be masked or obliterated by louder sounds or noises (e.g., lawn mowers, screaming children) in the environment. Given this occurrence, the perceptual system must infer whether the event has truly ceased, or whether the noise has "hidden" a continuing event; in the latter case the perceptual system must judge what the missing part of the event was. The context leads to knowledge and expectations about the ongoing events in the environment, and it is this context that leads the listener to expect one signal and not another. If the "masked" acoustic signal at a point tends to suggest that the event did occur, listeners will "hear through" the noise to perceive a signal that possibly did not occur (Warren 1984). This has been termed auditory *restoration* or auditory *induction*.

Suppose a constant frequency tone is presented to listeners. If the signal is interrupted by a silent interval, achieved by snipping out part of the signal, listeners hear a distinct gap or break (see figure 7.10, panel a). However, if a segment of louder noise is inserted in place of the silent interval, listeners report hearing a continuous tone (panel c). The identical tones surrounding the noise generate the expectation that the tone was continuous. Now consider a frequency glide. If the glide is interrupted by snipping out a fragment, listeners hear a distinct gap (panel b). However, if a segment of noise replaces the fragment, listeners report hearing the tone going smoothly from the pitch at the noise onset to the pitch at the noise offset (panel d). The perceptual system "tracks" the signal and hears the change that should have occurred within the noise.

210   Chapter 7

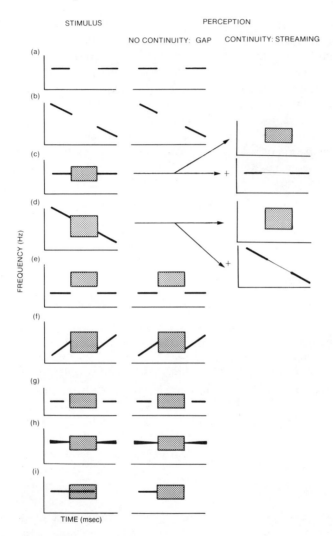

Figure 7.10
Auditory restoration: the perception of continuity induced by a masking sound. In (a) and
(b), a tone is interrupted by a silent interval. The perception is veridical (correct): listeners
hear two tones separated by a pause. In (c) and (d), the gap is filled by a noise stimulus in
which the frequencies match those of the tone and glide. The perception is nonveridical:
listeners hear a continuous tone plus the noise. The noise and tone form separate streams.
In (e), the gap is filled by a noise that does not have frequency components at the tone
frequency. Listeners do not hear a continuous tone. In (f), the frequency glides have a
different trajectory on each side of the noise. Listeners do not hear a continuous glide.
Conditions (e) and (f) suggest that only "plausible" restorations will occur. In (g) and (h),
the tone either ends before the noise or decreases in intensity before the noise. In both cases,
listeners do not hear a continuous tone. Finally, in (i), the tone continues into the noise but
ends simultaneously with the noise offset. Listeners report that the tone appears to end at
the noise onset, a nonveridical percept.

The degree of restoration depends on how likely it is that the noise could have masked the tone or glide. Imagine noise with acoustic energy from 1200 Hz to 3600 Hz. This noise would mask an 1800 Hz tone, and for this case listeners report a high degree of confidence that an 1800 Hz tone was continuous. Because of the lack of frequency overlap, this noise would not mask a 300 Hz tone, and listeners tend not to report that a 300 Hz tone was continuous (panel c). Imagine a glide that progresses from 1000 Hz to 1500 Hz in 500 msec, is interrupted by silence for 200 msec, and then progresses from 1700 Hz to 2200 Hz in an additional 500 msec. In contrast, imagine a glide that progresses from 1000 Hz to 1500 Hz in 500 msec, is interrupted by silence for 200 msec, and then progresses from 1300 Hz to 1800 Hz in an additional 500 msec (panel f). If noise replaces the silence, auditory restoration is much stronger in the first case, because the common trajectory of the glides before and after the noise implies one continuous source (Ciocca and Bregman 1987). The perception of continuity depends on the sounds on both sides of the noise. The listener cannot extrapolate the initial sound through the noise but must use the sound after the noise to induce the continuity.

When auditory restoration occurs (figure 7.10, panels c, d), listeners report the noise but cannot locate its position in the signal. The noise forms one stream and the tone or glide forms a second stream. When stream segregation occurs, as will be discussed below, listeners cannot position the elements of one stream with respect to the elements of the second stream.

This effect is not confined to tones; it occurs in striking form for speech stimuli. In one demonstration, Warren (1970) removed a segment of the speech signal and replaced it with a cough. For example:

The state governors met with their respective legi♯latures convening in the capital city. [The eliminated segment is indicated by the ♯.]

Listeners believed the sentence was intact, were unable to identify which section of the sentence was removed, and were unable to locate the position of the cough. The cough appeared to occur along with the sentence but did not have a fixed location. The cough formed a separate stream exactly like those instances of auditory restoration in which a noise formed a separate stream (figure 7.10, panels c, d). Samuel (1981) subsequently showed that the degree of restoration was determined by the fit between the type of masking sound and the type of speech sound. Remember that fricatives are characterized by a noise spectrum, and vowels are characterized by a periodic (formant) spectrum. In Samuel's experiment, if a noise masker replaced a silent interval in a fricative or a vowel, there was more restoration in the fricative than in the vowel. If a 1000 Hz tone replaced the identical silent interval, there was more restoration in the vowel than in the fricative. (Overall, the noise led to more restoration, which demonstrates the importance of the overall frequency similarity.) This supports the conclusions drawn from tones that when the masking element closely matches the expected component, restoration is more likely to occur.

In another demonstration, Warren and Sherman (1974) showed that sentence context determined the illusionary percept. They presented three sentences:

was on the orange.
It was found that the ♯eel was on the table.
was on the axle.

For each sentence, the surrounding segments were identical; only the final word varied. Listeners reported hearing *peel, meal,* or *wheel* as a function of the context. This effect is not merely due to coarticulation, because mispronunciations do not destroy the illusion. Bashford and Warren (1987) further demonstrated the effect of context by showing that there was more restoration for a sentence read forward than for the same sentence read backward. Eliminating the sentence meaning and grammar reduced the perception of continuity. In a different domain, Sasaki (1980) reported that listeners "filled in" missing notes of a familiar melody played on a piano when those notes were replaced by noise.

Suppose we conceptualize this illusion of continuity as caused by stream segregation based on the belief that the signal is truly continuous. We may then hypothesize that any acoustic evidence that the signal has terminated or changed prior to the noise would weaken the illusion (Bregman and Dannenbring 1977). There are several pieces of evidence supporting this hypothesis:

> 1. If the signal does terminate before the onset of the noise so that there is a short silent interval between the signal and noise, the illusion of continuity is lost. (We are assuming that the signal reappears after the noise; see figure 7.10, panel g.)
> 2. If the signal changes amplitude before the onset of the noise, the illusion is weakened (see figure 7.10, panel h).
> 3. If the signal does not appear after the noise, the signal does not seem to continue into the noise (see figure 7.10, panel i).

What this all points out is the problem-solving aspect of listening and the general tendency toward event perception. In natural situations, there are probably specific changes in energy that specify that an event has terminated. Without evidence of this sort, listeners will have a tendency to believe and to hear events to be continuous, "behind the noise," and thus will fall prey to continuity illusions.

Organization between Streams

If stream segregation occurs, listeners are unable to attend to both streams at once. It is possible to attend to one stream composed of high frequency tones or to attend to one stream composed of low frequency tones, but it is nearly impossible to attend to both streams at the same time. Often attention seems to shift spontaneously from one stream to the other. Because of listeners' inability to hear both streams at the same time, we find:

> 1. If stream segregation occurs, listeners are unable to report the order of the elements in the overall sequence, although they can correctly report the order in each stream. For example, suppose we present the repeating sequence: A3B2C1A3B2C1, etc., where A, B, C represent three low pitch tones that form one stream, and 3, 2, 1 represent three high pitch tones that form the second stream. Listeners correctly report the element order in each stream (e.g., A-B-C-A-B-C as opposed to C-B-A-C-B-A, and 3-2-1-3-2-1 as opposed to 1-2-3-1-2-3, where the hyphens indicate a silent interval between elements in each stream created by the formation of two streams) but they cannot interweave the two streams. Thus, listeners cannot report whether the sequence was A3B2C1, or A2B1C3, or A1B3C2. This result occurs regardless of the basis for streaming: frequency, spatial location, or intensity (Bregman and Campbell 1971).
>
> 2. If stream segregation occurs, properties of individual elements may be lost as they become integrated into a stream. For example, suppose we present two left-ear tones, two right-ear tones, and one to both ears, a middle tone. If the middle tone is captured by the left-ear stream (possibly due to frequency similarity), then that tone will appear to come from the left ear. The reverse localization will occur if the middle tone is captured by the right-ear stream. The localization of the middle tone is dominated by the stream segregation. Results of this sort suggest that judgments of "what" and "where" are interdependent. The formation of streams, "the what," depends on the perceived location of elements, "the where," and simultaneously "the where" depends on "the what" (Bregman and Steiger 1980).
>
> 3. If stream segregation occurs, listeners cannot judge the interval between elements in different streams. Different streams are not integrated, and therefore judgment of the interval between elements in different streams is much poorer than judgment of the interval between elements in the same stream (Thomas and Fitzgibbons 1971).

The consequences of stream segregation are severe: listeners can no longer integrate a series of elements into the correct sequence, and if the fusion of partials into one complex note does not occur, then correct identification will be impossible. Stream organization thus imposes restrictions for auditory communication—in both speech and music—but it also allows for creative improvisations.

Music and Speech
Stream segregation in music   Stream segregation affects music perception at several levels: timbre perception for individual notes, perceptual coherence of adjacent notes, and the emergence of melodic lines.

The rich changing quality of instrumental timbre is created by differences among the partials: differences in onset and offset, differences in intensity envelopes, and differences in the frequency modulations. Yet it is harmonic and temporal similarity among the partials that leads to the perception of one complex tone. Thus the tendencies toward stream segregation constrain the acoustic properties of an instrument. For example, the partials cannot be too asynchronous. It is difficult to arrive at a specific estimate of the allowable asynchrony, but work by Rasch and by Bregman suggests that the asynchrony should not exceed 30–40 msec. At that point, each partial may be heard as a separate tone. In the same way, although the timbre may sound more rich if the partials are not strictly harmonic and do not follow the identical frequency modulations, the constraints on fusion of the partials limit the allowable variation among them.

Performances of musical soloists and groups also reflect these constraints. Soloists—instrumentalists and singers—must be heard over a more intense orchestra. To do so, both vary the output spectrum or vary the onset to avoid being fused into the background. Instrumentalists often play sharp (a few hertz above the correct note) to create a set of inharmonic frequencies that leads to the perception of separate tones. Singers change their vocal tract resonances to create a strong resonance at higher frequencies, and this leads to perceptual segregation. Alternatively, soloists may vary their timing to segregate from the background sound.

Musical groups face a more difficult problem. When playing together, each instrument must be heard separately, and this is easily achieved by playing slightly asynchronously. But the percept must be of simultaneous notes; the notes should not be heard as starting at different times, which would be a sloppy performance. Remember that at time differences of 30–40 msec, two tones are heard separately, but they are not perceived as beginning at different times. At greater time differences, about 60–80 msec, two tones appear asynchronous. One seems to begin before the other. These values therefore set a limit on the allowable time differences among the players—above 30 msec to achieve two-tone perception but below 70 msec to avoid the perception of onset time differences. Measurements by Rasch (1981) of classical music trios and quartets found that the majority of time differences between players fell within the 30 msec to 70 msec range. Rasch also found that the synchronization was more strict for instruments with short rise times (e.g., recorders) and more lenient for instruments with longer rise times (e.g., violins).

The tendency to form a melodic stream is affected by many variables: frequency and intensity similarity, the continuity between adjacent notes, and so on. To ensure that the notes are heard as belonging together, both the composer and the performer must not stray beyond the limits imposed by stream segregation. As discussed in chapter 10, the majority of changes between adjacent musical notes in a melody are only one or two musical steps (i.e., one or two semitones), which makes segregation unlikely. If notes are typically separated by greater frequency ratios, then the tempo must be slowed down, or the timbre (or spatial) similarity must be enhanced, or one note should smoothly slur into the next. All of these compensations represent tradeoffs to ensure a coherent melody.

Finally, when constructing simultaneous melodic lines, principles underlying stream segregation are critical. Composers have often used stream segregation to create the illusion of two simultaneous melodies being played on a single-note instrument like the flute. Two melodies written in different octaves are intermixed so that the low and high pitch notes alternate. Because of the sudden jumps between very different elements, the low and high frequency melodic lines form separate streams and are heard in parallel. Musically, this has been termed *pseudopolyphony*. Although large pitch differences lead to the perception of different melodic lines, the converse is also true. If two melodic lines of similar pitch range are intermixed, it is extremely difficult to hear each melody separately. The notes combine into a single coherent melodic line because of pitch similarity. The theory of musical composition termed *counterpoint* suggests that musical lines not overlap in frequency, so that one line cannot capture the elements of the other line (Piston 1947). In order to perceive each tune, the notes of one melody must be raised in pitch until the notes of each melody do not overlap (Dowling 1973a). Dowling and co-workers also point out that if listeners know what melody to listen for, they can attend to it even if it is intermixed with the other notes by making use of rhythmic and pitch expectancies (Dowling 1973a; Dowling, Lung, and Herrbold 1987). This outcome is similar to that described previously, in which listeners could make use of English syntax and semantics to disentangle two simultaneous messages (Cherry 1957).

Stream segregation in speech   For speech production and perception, the major difficulty at all levels is overcoming the tendency for streaming: the formants are widely spread, the trajectories differ, and the rate of production is very high; there are rapid alternations among voiced, unvoiced, fricatives, and silences as well as rapid alternations in intensity. All of these factors should lead to a confusing segregation of speech sound segments into competing streams.

The production of a stop consonant–vowel syllable involves a noise burst, onset of voicing, formant transitions, and steady-state formants. What holds all these components together into one sound, given that the noise burst has a distinct timbre, one formant transition may increase in frequency although another may decrease in frequency, and the formant frequencies may be quite widely spaced? One acoustic factor leading to the coherence of the syllable is the relative degree of temporal synchrony of the formant transitions. On the whole, the "allowable" asynchrony for a coherent perception of 30–40 msec is not exceeded. A second factor leading to coherence is the existence of continuous frequency transitions, which provide the necessary continuity for each one of the formants. If the transitions are eliminated electronically, then the syllable breaks apart; the noise becomes one stream, the vowel becomes a second stream, and any fricative noise (as in *the*) might form a third stream. These transitions, which are a consequence of coarticulation, provide the glue for coherence. They fuse the formants (Cole and Scott 1973). It should be noted that durations of silent intervals play an important role in many phonemic contrasts. Work on stream segregation suggests that the accuracy of duration judgments decreases drastically when surrounding elements are perceived in different streams. It is a necessity that streaming does not occur.

Listeners can make use of their knowledge of articulation to partition the sound wave. For example, Darwin (1984) started with a simulated vowel and then added energy at harmonic frequencies of the first formant. Listeners did not integrate all this additional energy into the vowel percept if this yielded a vowel that violated articulatory constraints. Some of the energy must have been perceived as stemming from a different source.

The ability to separate utterances from two speakers depends on the segregation into streams. The differing fundamental frequencies and vocal tract resonances (both of these depend on the physiology of the vocal system) of different speakers lead to the segregation of overlapping utterances. On top of fundamental frequency differences, the gradual changes in pitch characteristic of discourse (e.g., statements as opposed to questions) provide additional cues to assigning speech sounds to the correct source and tend to promote the coherence of a long sentence.

7.3 Overview

This chapter began by pointing out that the superposition of sound waves coming from different sources creates a difficult perceptual problem (one that has not been solved by artificial systems). The listener must be able to take bits and pieces out of the signal to construct one or more events. The rules that listeners use are analogous to those used for visual perception and are parallel to the classic Gestalt perceptual rules of similarity, proximity, good continuation, and so forth. I have argued that the rules and processes used for speech, music, and environmental sound perception ought to be equivalent, and by the same token the principles underlying listening and looking ought to be mirror images (or perhaps a more apt metaphor would be echoes) of each other. Some rules seem to apply to all sounds; other rules seem to make use of specific properties of one class of sounds. It should be noted that we also use nonauditory information to make sense of an acoustic signal. Visual information from a speaker's articulatory movements or a musician's breathing and motor movements can be critical for stream segregation. Tactual information from an object's vibration can also be used for stream segregation.

It is important to remember that the principles underlying the partitioning of the acoustic signal are the same ones that lead to the perception of ongoing coherent sources. It is easy to focus on the splitting apart and forget that the results are distinguishable auditory events. The following chapters deal with these events (e.g., phonemes, intervals, melodies, rhythms). The identification of each event is an endproduct of the ongoing perceiving process. Without rules to segregate elements, events could not be perceived.

Chapter 8
Identification of Speakers, Instruments, and Environmental Events

I have always been fascinated by the ease with which we can identify a caller over the telephone. The telephone is not a high-quality transmission system, and yet we can recognize the caller within a few words. It may be confusing when the caller is whispering, or eating a carrot, but we usually make the correct identification. In the same fashion we can identify an instrument in different acoustic environments, in different orchestral groups, at different loudness levels, and at widely different frequencies. Moreover, we can identify motorcycles, doors slamming, missed hammer swings, and gum chewing despite the immense variation in these events. We are able to "capture" an event despite the continuous and possibly contradictory changes in the acoustic signal. Our perception is so direct and immediate that we often forget that we make the identification solely on the basis of the sound reaching us. We need to search for the acoustic information that is unique to the particular speaker, instrument, or event, because it is this information that must provide the basis for identification.

Surprisingly, research on event identification is fairly recent. Little work was attempted until 1940. At that point, motivated by legal issues in criminal identification, research was begun on speaker identification. Specifically, could a witness accurately judge that two voices were identical? Could a sound spectrogram of one individual's speech be used like a fingerprint to identify that individual? Could individuals successfully disguise their voices? More recent research has been motivated by the desire to achieve automatic speaker identification by computer. To do this accurately, empirical work has aimed to discover speech parameters that reliably differ across individuals and to discover whether these parameters are utilized by human listeners. (It is my impression that the most accurate recognition schemes make use of the computational capabilities of even small computers and do not attempt to model human strategies; see O'Shaughnessy 1986 for a review.)

Research on instrument identification has followed a similar course. Until 1960, investigations were sporadic. More recently, research on timbre and instrument identification has become motivated by the related issue of electronically simulating an instrument. The first attempts at electronic simulation led to dull and lifeless instrumental sounds. Research was initiated to discover what acoustic properties make an instrument sound as it does (i.e., its timbre). Along with the need for accurate synthesis, there was the desire to create new instrumental sounds. Without computers this research would be impossible; it would be impossible to perform the Fourier analyses that provide a detailed temporal analysis of each partial, it would be impossible to synthesize a tone by combining different partials to test the accuracy of the timbre analysis, and it would be impossible to make frequency and temporal changes to assess the effect on perceived timbre.

Research on the identification of environmental events has been even more spotty. Although this lack of research may be due to a belief that hearing is ill suited to event identification (although even a brief consideration of the issue would reveal that this contention is false), it is more likely that the inability to analyze and simulate sounds before the advent of high-speed computers stymied researchers.

8.1 Sound Attributes and Identification

Section 6.1 contains a list of acoustic factors that characterize instruments and voices. This list was constructed to highlight the similarities between music and language. The items range from characteristics of individual sounds (e.g., duration, frequency, intensity and vibrato), to contextual characteristics (e.g., rhythm) to mechanical characteristics (e.g., radiation). Although it is true that these attributes characterize any sound, we can expect that the unique characteristics of music and speech (and natural events) will determine the relevance of each attribute for instrument and speaker identification.

We can make a rough three-way categorization: (1) attribute that are used directly for identification; (2) attributes that are used primarily in speaker, instrument, or event identification; and (3) attributes that are not widely used for identification but characterize sound sources in general. Let us consider each in turn. The goal at this point is to provide an orientation, not to describe the results of experiments or to hypothesize that one attribute is prepotent.

1. The spectrum (spectral energy) of a sound (e.g., the frequency and intensity of each partial or formant) and its temporal properties (e.g., initiation noise, attack/decay transients, modulations) create the sense of timbre for speakers, instruments, and events and therefore may be used to identify and characterize individual events. The spectrum and temporal properties are the outcomes of the excitation vibration acting on the vibration modes of the sound body. Both the excitation

pattern and the vibration modes are a function of the physical shape and construction of the sound source. To the extent that individuals, instruments, and other sources possess stable yet different physical characteristics, the frequency spectra and temporal properties will differ reliably among speakers, instruments, and environmental events.

2. Other attributes seem more useful for speaker, instrument, or event identification. For example, frequency and frequency range may be useful for identifying a speaker because an individual's physiology constrains the possible variation in the fundamental vibration frequencies of the vocal cords. Frequency and frequency range are less useful for specifying an instrument, however, because an instrument is designed to play a range of notes. In the same way, duration and rate may be useful for identifying a speaker because of a characteristic speaking style, but depending on the composition, an instrument may be played slowly or quickly, staccato or legato. In contrast, rhythmic patterning may be useful for identifying an environmental event (the repetitive nature of hammering or knocking versus the continuous nature of sawing or scraping) but not useful for identifying a speaker or an instrument. Clearly these differences are a matter of degree and are not absolute: instruments do differ in their frequency range and in their temporal characteristics—drums, for example, cannot play extended notes. Nonetheless, we might expect to find differences in the degree to which these attributes are utilized for different types of events.

3. Finally, there are attributes that seem unlikely to be useful for identification. For example, the sound radiation characteristics of different sources depend on their physical properties. Moreover, the sound radiation pattern will change as a function of frequency. Although there may be large differences in the spatial radiation pattern for different sources, this cue would be difficult to use. (Changes in spectrum might be useful in judging movement and location, however.)

Given the multiplicity of stable and time-varying sound attributes, it is unlikely that any one attribute or combination of attributes uniquely determines identification or timbre. This view differs from the historical belief that timbre is attributable to relatively simple acoustic variables. However, from what we know about the mechanics of sound production and player-instrument interaction, it seems unlikely that the timbre of any instrument or voice can be uniquely specified even by a set of relative values (e.g., the rank order of the harmonic intensities of the frequency spectrum). The usefulness of any perceptual attribute must depend on the values of the other attributes. The social and musical context, as well as the performer's and listener's intent, can grossly alter the bases for timbre perception. The identical openness occurs for instrument, speaker, and event identification.

Each aspect of a sound is a potential means of identification. This is the same theme advanced in chapter 6. There are two parts to this argument.

First, there is no "smoking gun." There is no single cue with which individuals can achieve 100% accuracy and without which identification will be reduced to the level of chance. Rather, any single cue will afford some accuracy, and any single cue when combined with another cue will improve identification. This statement will be true for cues as diverse as the steady-state frequency spectrum or speaking rhythm. Moreover, any ranking of the cues in terms of effectiveness will change as a function of context. In speaker identification experiments, for example, four contexts are typically chosen—isolated vowels, isolated syllables or words, prepared reading passages, and extemporaneous speech. Although formant frequencies may be the most important cue in identifying speakers of isolated vowels, rhythm may be more important when identifying speakers reading prepared text.

The reason that one single cue is not necessary and sufficient for identification is the interactive and context-dependent nature of sound production. The attributes of a sound are not independent. The vibration patterns, resonances, vibrato, and so on are interactive; each aspect of sound production influences another. This influence spreads across a broad time span, and thus each aspect has an imprint on all others. For example, speaking rate and duration influence coarticulation and the harmonic spectrum. To isolate a cue, therefore, is not to study that cue in a "pure" form. There are no pure forms. It is merely to study that cue as realized in one particular sound.

Second, it is possible to uncover potential cues in one experimental context, but we cannot state definitively that human listeners use that cue in "natural" listening situations. In natural situations, we might expect a person to be opportunistic, to use any information that is maximally predictive in that context or among that set of individuals. One speaker may be identified by rate; a different speaker by monotone pitch. Moreover, Sam may be identified by fundamental frequency among one set of individuals, but Sam might be identified by "breathy" sounds among a different set. There has been relatively little experimental work on event identification, and we know hardly anything about strategies in differing situations.

8.2 Perceptual Constancy

It will be helpful to take a step back at this point and look at the problem of identification in more general terms. As stated earlier, the basic difficulty is that of contextual variation. At different times one event will produce physically different acoustic waves, and in addition to variation because of the source, the environment imposes an additional transformation on the physical wave, which further modifies the stimulus from moment to moment and from instance to instance. The problem of achieving constancy, of being able to identify the source despite the variation, becomes the pivotal issue in perception. There can be no simple translation program. To provide a conceptual framework, I will briefly outline four approaches to the problem of constancy.

1. The first approach may be termed the *prototype* or *template* solution. An individual is assumed to develop "ideal" representations and compare each sound with these representations. The similarity between any sound and each ideal is calculated in some fashion, and the representation that most closely matches the sound becomes the percept. The incoming sound may need to be "preprocessed." The sound may be standardized with respect to intensity, duration, or frequency to match the prototypes more closely. Although it may intuitively seem that we sift through the possibilities trying to match a sound, there are several difficulties with this. One is that the differentiation of the idealized representations is hard to understand. How could you initially decide if two sounds were merely variants of one sound and not two different sounds? The traditional solution is to invoke information from a different modality to provide the "true" percept. However, though vision may teach audition about the sounds of page flipping, what teaches audition about speech? Another difficulty is that it would be almost impossible to create a small set of unambiguous templates. Instruments, speech, and event sounds are so context dependent that it appears we would need a different template for each instance. No single template could yield the appropriate categorization.

2. The second approach may be termed the *feature* or *attribute* solution. Here, the identification of sounds is based on abstracting critical features that distinguish among the possibilities. The features may be of various sorts: noises composed of a broad range of frequencies, frequency spectra, attack transients, voicing, durations, rhythms, and so on. Every sound source is characterized by a value on each feature. Each feature has been assumed to be abstracted and signaled by independent and simultaneous neural circuits. The values for each of the features represent the specification or definition of the incoming sound. The sound source specification that most closely matches the incoming sound specification becomes the identification. The effect of learning (and correction) is to emphasize certain features in the matching process. There are sounds that are identified by specific features: the continuous, constant energy spectrum of air rushing

through a duct or the relatively pure spectrum of the flute. Nonetheless, feature models do not explicitly consider the patterning of the features, particularly the timing among the features that is so critical for all sounds. In addition, proposed features are always a mixed bag. Some seem relatively simple and capable of being calculated neurologically; others seem so complex that it would be difficult to imagine a physiological representation. As will be described in chapter 12, there is little evidence that there are feature detectors of the sort hypothesized.

3. The third approach may be termed the *higher-order variable* solution. This solution postulates that there are time-varying, complex acoustic properties that uniquely specify an event. The sound production—the constraints, couplings, and continuities—of the event itself make consistent acoustic energy patterns inevitable. To the extent that listeners can make use of these higher-order variables, we can assume the direct perception of the sound source. Only when the acoustic wave does not unambiguously specify an event are listeners reduced to the properties (intensity, frequency, modulation) of the sound wave. From this perspective, perceptual learning is the uncovering of these variables and not the calculation of acoustic properties. The difficulty here is that it is extremely hard to isolate unique higher-order variables for each source and event. When faced with a formidable perceptual constancy, it requires an act of faith to believe that a higher-order variable can be discovered.

4. The fourth approach is based on innate systems. The idea here is that there are distinct brain structures that decode the acoustic signal to yield the invariant percept. For example, the motor theory of speech perception hypothesizes that the acoustic speech signal is decoded by reference to the articulatory movements that were necessary to produce the acoustic signal. Often these innate systems are thought to be autonomous and independent of other perceptual processes.

8.3 Methods for Studying Event Identification

Three general types of experiments have been used to study identification. Although the focus of each type of experiment is identical, the goals and rationales differ. Moreover, one type of methodology is used predominantly for speaker identification; a second methodology is used predominantly for instrument identification. The three experimental methodologies will be outlined below, and the specific outcomes will be discussed in detail in section 8.4.

The first type of experiment may be characterized as a rating scale methodology. Subjects are presented with a single sound and are asked to rate the sound on scales such as slow-fast, rough-smooth, or hard-soft. The first goal is to discover whether these kinds of perceptual characteristics are useful for describing timbre and for distinguishing among instruments, voices, and natural events. If these perceptual characteristics do describe sounds, the second goal is to identify the acoustic (physical) properties that appear to underlie those characteristics. For example, one perceptual characteristic might be breathiness, and the physical characteristic correlated with judgments of breathiness might be the intensity of a particular frequency band. Voices judged breathy would be marked by high intensity in that band; voices judged nonbreathy would be marked by weak intensity in that band. The rating scale methodology is most useful if there is a wide variety of potential sounds. Starting with a relatively small initial sample, this method can evolve a classification system for timbre suitable for all possible sounds. For this reason, it has been used most extensively for voice quality.

The second type of experiment involves the direct comparison or direct identification of instruments, voices, or events. In comparison experiments, the listener is presented two instruments or two voices at one time and is required to judge the similarity between them. In identification experiments, the listener is presented one unknown event and attempts to identify it. Although these methods look very different on the surface, the intent of both is to abstract the dimensions of timbre. The direct similarity judgments are analyzed to identify clusters of perceptually similar events. Errors in identification experiments are also used to identify clusters of perceptually similar events: instruments (e.g., clarinets and oboes) or voices that are often misnamed and confused are assumed to sound alike, to be perceptually similar. Conversely, two instruments or two voices that rarely are confused are assumed to sound quite different. Following the analysis of the perceptual judgements, for both procedures researchers attempt to characterize the differences among events in terms of acoustic features (as in the rating scale methodology). This method is most suited to cases in which one wants to describe the differences in timbre among a specific small set of events; for this reason, it has been used mainly for describing instrumental timbre.

The third methodology is more complex technically and involves the manipulation of the acoustic signal. For example, formant frequencies might be raised or lowered, or the attack and decay of the formants changed. Alternatively, the resonance function of one instrument may be combined with the vibration pattern of a different instrument (e.g., imposing violin string vibrations on the resonances of a bassoon tube). The timbre will change because of these manipulations, and the experimental question is whether these changes are predictable from a knowledge of specific acoustic properties underlying timbre. The ability to manipulate (and synthesize) timbre provides converging evidence that the analysis of the perceptual characteristics was correct.

The perception of timbre and the identification of an event can come about only from the patterning of acoustic energy. The acoustic patterning creates perceptual differences among events, and it is by means of this patterning that identification is possible. In order for identification to occur, the difference among several instances of one instrument, one speaker, or one event must be less than the differences between different instruments, speakers, or events. This need not be true for all attributes, but it must be true for one attribute or combination of attributes. Only if we can determine what acoustic information reliably signals one event as opposed to another in each context will it be possible to model how a listener can make a correct identification.

8.4 Determinants of Timbre and Identification

Perceptual Attribute Judgments

To ensure that all possibly relevant perceptual characteristics are included, investigators have started with a large set of characteristics previously used to study word meaning. Each characteristic is represented by a scale labeled from one end to the other. For example, the scale for intensity would be constructed with "loud" at one end of a horizontal line and "soft" at the other end of the line. (These are termed bipolar scales.) The listener indicates a judgment by placing a checkmark at some point along the line (e.g., for a medium intensity, the check would be placed at the center of the line). All listeners judge each sound source according to each one of the characteristics (with 5 instruments and 6 characteristics there would be 30 judgments).

The second step would be to analyze subjects' responses in order to reduce the entire set of scales to a smaller number that represent the perceptual characteristics that distinguish among speakers. There are two parts to this process. First, scales are eliminated that do not distinguish among speakers. For example, the scales "left-right" or "beginning-end" may have no relevance for speaker identification. This can be detected if listeners rate every speaker in the middle of the scale or if listeners give unreliable, inconsistent responses. Second, scales are combined that appear to measure the identical perceptual attribute. For example, suppose the scales "clear-hazy" and "deliberate-careless" covary. That is, when a speaker is judged clear that speaker is also judged deliberate, and in addition, when a different speaker is judged hazy that speaker is also judged careless. Here the two scales are giving the identical information, because knowledge of the judgment on the first scale allows prediction of the judgement on the second scale with almost 100% accuracy. It suggests that listeners are making their judgments on the basis of the same part of the acoustic signal. On the other hand, the scales clear-hazy and deliberate-careless may not covary, and instead they may be independent scales. In this case, when two speakers are judged equally clear, one speaker may also be judged to be deliberate but the second speaker may also be judged to be careless by the same listeners. If scales are independent, this suggests that listeners are using a different aspect of the acoustic signal in making the clear-hazy and the deliberate-careless judgments. Therefore, the two scales should be kept separate.

To review, we must start with an exhaustive set of perceptual characteristics. Listeners judge each speaker against each characteristic. The data analyses consist of eliminating attributes that do not distinguish among speakers and combining qualities that appear to measure the same perceptual property (i.e., covary) into superordinate categories. The qualities within each category are related, but the qualities within one category are not related to qualities in a different category. The categories can then be used to generate a classification scheme. Although the statistical techniques are largely automatic (see Schiffman, Reynolds, and Young 1981 for a survey of methods), the skill of the researcher influences the interpretation of the categories and the resulting classification scheme.

In one of the first studies, Voiers (1964) used a list of 49 scales ranging from loud-soft, belligerent-friendly, dry-wet, fast-slow, and rough-smooth to clean-dirty. There were 16 different speakers and 32 judges. Each judge scored all 16 speakers on each of the bipolar scales. Following the experimental procedures outlined above, Voiers concluded that four categories were sufficient to describe speakers' voices. The four categories, along with representative scales, are: (1) clarity, with scales like clear-hazy, deliberate-careless, clean-dirty; (2) roughness, with scales like rough-smooth, scraping-gliding, loud-soft, labored-easy; (3) magnitude, with scales like rumbling-whining, deep-shallow, heavy-light, masculine-feminine; and (4) animation, with scales like fast-slow, disturbing-reassuring, tight-loose, agitated-serene. The four categories could be used to create a classification scheme. For instance, we could classify one speaker as clear/smooth/light/fast and a second speaker as clear/rough/light/slow. We would predict that two voices that have the same characteristics would be difficult to tell apart and that two voices with very different characteristics would be easy to tell apart.

Unfortunately, the connections between derived perceptual categories and acoustic properties of speech are very tenuous. Subsequent research combined bipolar scale judgments of voices with physical measurements (amplitude of voiced and unvoiced sounds, fundamental frequency of vocal cord vibration, and rate). The question remains whether there are physical measurements that are related to the perceptual categories based on the bipolar scales. For example, suppose deep-shallow, a derived perceptual category, covaried with fundamental frequency, a physical measurement. Then speakers judged deep would posses a low fundamental frequency and those judged shallow would possess a higher fundamental frequency; fundamental frequency would lead to judgments of deep as opposed to shallow. The perceptual scale judgments do not systematically vary with the physical measurements, however. A perceptual category of clarity (intelligibility) covaried with the physical measure of averaged voiced amplitude; a perceptual category of evaluation (clearn-dirty, good-bad) covaried with the changes in amplitude of voiced sounds and with speech rate; and a perceptual category of high-low covaried with fundamental frequency. Except for the last one, these connections are not obvious and could not be replicated in further work (Holmgren 1967).

Using a slightly different approach, Clarke and Becker (1969) began by selecting six perceptual attributes that seemed useful for characterizing speaker differences. The six attributes were pitch, pitch variability, sibilant intensity, clicklike elements, breathiness, and speaking rate. The goal was identical: to determine whether these attributes covaried with physical measurements. Subjects judged a set of voices according to these six speech attributes, and Clarke and Becker measured the physical characteristics of the same voices. Only the perceptual judgements of pitch and speaking rate covaried with the equivalent physical measurement (fundamental frequency and syllables per second). These results illustrate the difficulties involved in searching for simple physical properties that underlie complex perceptual attributes.

There has been much less use of direct judgments from predefined scales for the study of instruments. One study has used bipolar scales to describe more "abstract" sounds (von Bismarck 1974). All sounds were the same fundamental frequency but differed in the number, frequency, and amplitude of the harmonics. A frequency-amplitude representation of each sound is shown in figure 8.1. Some sounds contained discrete harmonics (e.g., tones); others contained a continuous range of harmonics (e.g., noises). Subjects judged each sound on 28 scales. Many of the scales were identical to those used previously for characterizing speakers.

These sounds could be represented by two major attributes. The most important may be termed "sharpness" and was indicated by verbal scales like sharp-dull, hard-soft, bright-dark, unpleasant-pleasant, and tense-relaxed. The second most important attribute may be termed "compactness" and was indicated by scales like compact-scattered, narrow-broad, boring-interesting, and closed-open.

As before, an attempt was made to relate the derived perceptual qualities to the acoustic properties of the sounds. "Sharpness" was found to be

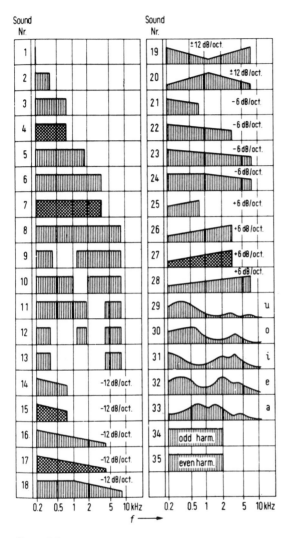

Figure 8.1
Spectral envelopes of abstract sounds. The frequency is depicted along the horizontal axis, and the intensity at each frequency is represented along the vertical axis. Sounds made up of discrete harmonics are symbolized by the vertical hatching, and sounds made up of a continuous frequency range are symbolized by the cross hatching. The increase or decrease in intensity for sounds 14 through 28 is labeled in terms of decibels per octave (i.e., -12 dB/oct. means that the sound pressure decreased by a factor of four each octave: the pressure of three successive octaves would be 1.0, .25, .0625) (from von Bismarck 1974 by permission).

determined by the energy concentration of the frequency spectrum rather than by the shape of the spectral envelope (e.g., rising or falling spectra). Sounds with considerable energy at high frequencies were judged sharpest (nos. 26, 27, and 28); sounds with little or no energy at high frequencies were judged least sharp (nos. 14, 16, and 21). An intuitive picture of sharpness can be gotten by imagining the pictures of the spectra as teeter-totters (seesaws). Imagine where the board would balance; spectra that appear sharper would balance at a higher frequency. Equal perceptions of sharpness could occur by balancing higher frequency harmonics with lower frequency harmonics. For example, compare sounds 13, 19, and 20, which lead to equal perceptions of sharpness. "Compactness" was found to be determined by the distinction between the discrete harmonics of tones (compact) and the continuous harmonics of noises (scattered).

A more recent study has used bipolar scales to evaluate fifteen natural events, such as howling dogs, crying babies, and wind in leafy trees (Björk 1985). The first and most important quality was related to the scales of tense-relaxed, unpleasant-pleasant, dark-bright, and cold-warm. The second quality was related to the scales of dull-sharp, low-high, mellow-harsh, and hazy-clear. The perceptual tense-relaxed quality covaried with the degree of amplitude modulation (i.e., roughness): the highly modulated cawing of birds was perceptually tense, the low modulated bubbling of the sea was perceptually relaxed. The perceptual dull-sharp quality covaried with frequency: the low frequency bubbling of the surging sea was dull, the high frequency bird songs were sharp. It is interesting to note that sound qualities tend to be emotionally loaded. The environment can directly affect emotional state.

It is tempting to try to compare the outcomes across speakers, instrument-like sounds, and natural events. The comparison is ambiguous, because the dimensions found for speakers, tones, and events are not always identical. For example, the "sharpness" tone dimension found for instruments and events cuts across two or three voice dimensions. This leaves us in a quandary. Are the dimensions actually the same and are the empirical differences merely due to the particular speakers, particular instrumentlike tones, and particular events chosen? Or, are there different perceptual dimensions for each type of event? I believe there is a relatively small fixed core of dimensions across all events, but that there is also a relatively large set of unique dimensions evoked for specific events and contexts. At present the issue is unresolved.

The same problem of generality occurs when assessing the overall usefulness of bipolar scales. Are the results determined by the original scales chosen, or would the same outcomes occur from a different set of scales? The evidence suggests that the repeatability of the studies is not very high.

Thus, although rating scale studies are helpful in defining the relevant factors to study, they do not lead to stable or definitive answers.

Similarity and Identification Judgments
The second methodology utilizes the perceived similarity between two speakers, instruments, or events to induce the perceptual qualities (i.e., the timbre). Subjects typically are presented with two sounds and are asked to judge their similarity. Subjects are free to use any criteria they wish as long as they base their judgments on the sound properties. On the basis of the similarity judgments, statistical procedures are used to place the stimuli in a geometric configuration. The distance between each pair of sounds in the configuration is proportional to the perceptual dissimilarity of the two sounds—that is, the more dissimilar the sounds, the greater the distance between the sounds. The kind of configuration that emerges allows the researcher to infer the number of attributes along which the stimuli differ perceptually. The final step is to explain each attribute in terms of the acoustic properties that distinguish instruments, speakers, or events at one end of the attribute from those instruments, speakers, or events at the other end. The main advantage of this procedure is that it is not necessary to know beforehand the ways in which the stimuli differ; similarity judgments are used to discover the perceptual qualities listeners use.

Multidimensional scaling   It will be useful to consider several examples of this procedure. In figure 8.2, I have made up three matrices that represent the similarity among four stimuli. We read each matrix by finding the similarity for each "cell" defined by a row and column. For example, in matrix (a) the similarity (or distance) between sounds A and C is 7 and the similarity between sounds C and D is 1, which indicates that sounds C and D are much more similar than sounds A and C are.

Using matrix (a), we can understand how the mathematical analysis occurs. Start with sound A; sound B is 2 units away. Since we do not know the direction, we can represent all the possibilities by a circle with a radius of 2 with A as the center (see figure 8.3). Similarly, all the possibilities for C and D are represented by circles with radii of 7 and 8 with A as the center. Now consider sound B; sound B is 5 units from C and 6 units from D; all the possible distances of C and D from B can be represented by dashed circles. If we place B at one point on the AB circle, we can then draw the dashed BC and BD circles. As can be seen, there is one point at which the dashed BC circle crosses the solid AC circle and one point at which the dashed BD circle crosses the solid AD circle. These two points satisfy the simlarity among the four sounds. Finally, place C at the intersection of the AC and BC circles; the distance between C and D is one unit and this circle is drawn with lighter dashed lines around C. D can be placed

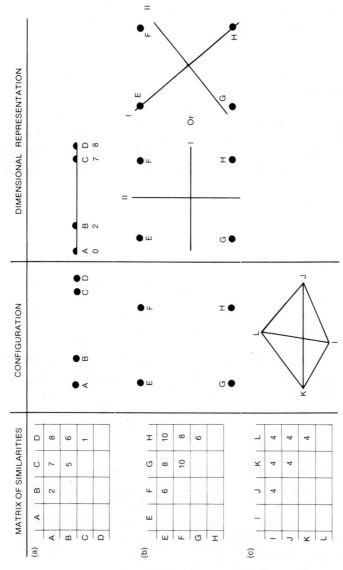

Figure 8.2
Multidimensional scaling: Similarities, spatial configuration, and dimensional representation. The similarity matrices represent the similarity or the distance between any pair of stimuli. Low numbers indicate high similarity between the two stimuli, and therefore these stimuli should be close together in a spatial configuration; high numbers mean low similarity between two stimuli and therefore these stimuli should be far apart in a spatial configuration. (We assume that similarities are symmetric: the similarity of A to B equals the similarity of B to A.) The configurations represent positions of the stimuli that fit the similarities or distances. The dimensional representation is a way of placing the configuration in a one-, two-, or more dimensional space. The dimensional representation is chosen so that dissimilarity between the stimuli can be measured by the differences along each dimension.

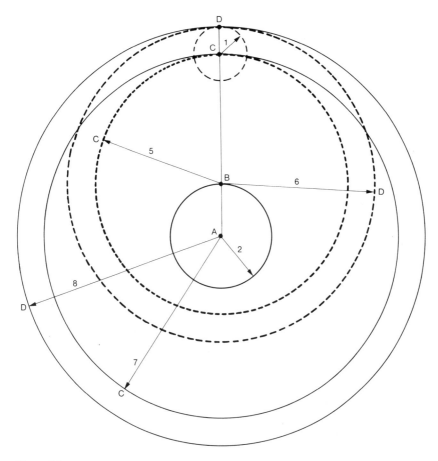

Figure 8.3
Generation of a spatial configuration from the similarity matrix. Each similarity defines a distance between two stimuli. If we arbitrarily place one stimulus at a point, the similarity to another stimulus can be represented by a circle whose radius equals that distance. By successively placing each new stimulus at one point on the circle and drawing additional circles to represent other similarities, the positions of other stimuli may be fixed and determined. Stimuli will be located at points where the similarity circles intersect. In nearly all experiments, it will be impossible to fit the points exactly. For example, if the similarity between A and D is 9, the points will not fit perfectly on a line. To achieve a one-dimensional configuration (i.e., a line), the position of each stimulus is adjusted slightly until all points fit on the line. None of the distances along the line may be exactly identical to the similarities, but each will be a close match.

at the intersection of the three circles (i.e., of AD, BD, CD). This set of similarity judgments can be represented by sounds placed on a line since the points of intersection among the circles lie along one straight line. Sound A is placed at position 0, sound B at 2, sound C at 7, and sound D at 8 (see figure 8.2). If we do this, then the similarity between B and C should be 5 (7 minus 2), the similarity between B and D should be 6 (8 minus 2), and the similarity between C and D should be 1 (8 minus 7), and in fact these are the similarities. This means that each pair of sounds differs along only one attribute, since we can represent the sounds as lying along a one-dimensional line. We infer that listeners are making their judgments on the basis of one difference among the sounds.

Now consider matrix (b). The sounds cannot be fitted along one line, because the similarities among them do not work out. However, we can represent sounds E, F, G, and H as being the corners of a rectangle as shown in the configuration in figure 8.2. Any set of three sounds in this matrix forms a 6, 8, 10 right triangle. What this means is that two dimensions are necessary to represent the judgments. Any pair of sounds can differ along one or two attributes.

The similarity judgments uniquely determine only the geometric configuration, in this case a rectangle. The differences among sounds are interpreted according to theoretical perspectives or intuitions. Suppose we restrict the two attributes to cross at right angles. We could, as shown in the first dimensional representation in figure 8.2, orient the two attributes so that E–F as well as G–H differ only with respect to attribute I, because E and F have the same value on attribute II and G and H also have the same value on attribute II (although it is a different value). In the same fashion, E–G as well as F–H differ only on attribute II, since they have the same value on attribute I. Finally, E–H as well as F–G differ on both attributes. We could also orient the two attributes as shown in the second dimensional representation in figure 8.2. Then, E and H differ only on attribute I, but the other five pairs differ on both attributes. Mathematically, each representation is equally good. Without knowing something about the characteristics of the four stimuli, it is impossible to determine which pair of attributes is appropriate and what each attribute might represent. Suppose the frequency and duration of the four stimuli were: E (1000 Hz, 250 msec); F (1000 Hz, 500 msec); G (2000 Hz, 250 msec); H (2000 Hz, 500 msec). For these stimuli, the first pair of attributes would be appropriate. Attribute I would then represent duration, and attribute II would then represent frequency. It is important to keep in mind that the meaning of an attribute derives from the differences among the elements. Attribute I represents frequency only because E and F differ from G and H in frequency. In choosing these attributes, we are implying that they are perceptually relevant. If a different pair of attributes is chosen, then those attributes will have another meaning. In the second case, attributes I and II do not represent frequency and duration; what they represent would be based on other differences among the sounds. In other words, the differences among stimuli along an attribute act to fix the meaning of that attribute.

Now consider matrix (c), in which all of the sounds are equally dissimilar. The only way these sounds can be geometrically represented is by a pyramid in three dimensions as shown in figure 8.2. What this means is that any pair of sounds can differ along one, two, or three attributes. Again, the positioning of the attributes is mathematically arbitrary. The choice of attributes must be based on the stimulus properties and represent the physical and perceptual differences.

To review, the similarities represent the distance between stimuli and create a geometric configuration among the sounds. The researcher then tries to make sense of the differences among sounds by placing straight lines (usually at right angles) through the configuration to represent the attributes on which the sounds differ. Making the attributes meet at right angles implies that the attributes are independent. The position of the sound on one attribute does not affect the position on any other attribute. The physical differences between sounds often serve as the guideline for the choice of attributes or axes and the subsequent interpretations. The choice of attributes represents a theoretical decision, because it argues that listeners use these attributes in perceiving and judging sounds.

Musical timbre   Grey (1977) investigated musical instruments in an experiment utilizing 12 instruments and 16 notes. (Nine instruments each provided one note, and there were 2 saxophone notes, 2 oboe notes, and 3 cello notes produced by different bowing techniques. Each note was approximately 311 Hz (E-flat above middle C). The notes were recorded and then reproduced by computer to achieve precise equalization of perceived pitch, loudness, and duration. The duration of each note was about a half second, typical of a musical note. Twenty experienced musicians judged the similarity between 2 notes chosen from any of the 16.

The averaged similarity judgments across the 20 subjects represented the distance between any two notes. A statistical procedure found the best configuration of the instrumental notes so that the calculated distance in the configuration was closest to actual similarity judgments. With many tones and only two or three attributes, it is impossible to fit the similarity judgments exactly. A reasonable statistical goal is to preserve the rank ordering: if A and B are judged more similar than B and C, then A and B should be closer than B and C in the configuration. The "best fit" procedure suggested that listeners were using three attributes to make their judgments. This configuration is shown in figure 8.4. The instrumental notes are

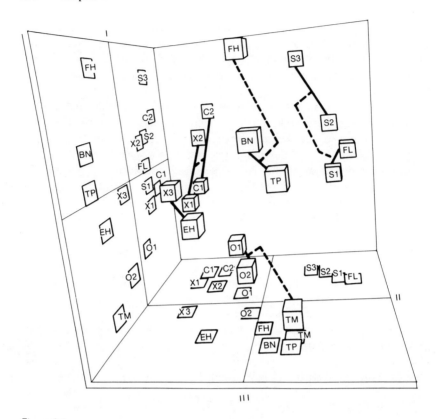

Figure 8.4
A three dimensional representation of the similarities among 12 instruments (16 notes).
Instruments (or notes from one instrument) that are highly related are connected by solid
lines, and instruments that are strongly related are connected by dashed lines. The values on
each of the three dimensions can be determined by looking at the position on the "floor"
and the position on the "left" wall. Key: O1, O2 = oboes (different instruments and
players); C1 = E-flat clarinet; C2 = bass clarinet; X1 = saxophone, medium loud; X2 =
saxophone, soft; X3 = soprano sax; EH = English horn; FH = French horn; FL = flute;
TM = muted trombone; TP = trumpet; BN = bassoon; SI = cello, bowed near bridge
producing nasal brittle sound (sul ponticello); S2 = cello, normal bowing; S3 = cello, bowing
very lightly over the fingerboard producing a flutelike effect (sul tasto). (Adapted from Grey
1977.)

represented by cubes in the three-dimensional space. (The geometric term *dimension* is used in the same sense as attribute or axis.)

The next step is to attempt to provide a perceptual and acoustic rationale for the configuration. To do this the researchers constructed frequency-amplitude time representations for each note and proposed three attributes that seemed to determine the similarities among the notes. The instrumental notes are shown in figure 8.5 according to their ranking on attributes I, II, and III.

Attribute I is a measure of energy distribution. At one end, the French horn and muted bowing cello have a restricted frequency range, and most of the energy is located at low frequencies. At the other end of the attribute, the muted trombone and oboes have a wide frequency range, and a significant amount of energy is located at the upper partials. This dimension is analogous to the sharpness attribute, isolated by the rating scale technique, found for complex sounds and natural events. Attributes II and III appear to reflect the temporal variation of the notes. One end of attribute II represents the woodwinds (saxophones, clarinet, English horn), which are characterized by upper harmonics that enter, reach their maxima, and decay at the same times. The other end represents the strings, brass, flute, and bassoon, which are characterized by upper harmonics that have differing patterns of attack and decay. On the whole, this dimension separates woodwinds, with the exception of the bassoon and flute, from other instruments. Subjectively, this aspect of timbre reflects a static (woodwinds) versus dynamic (brass, strings) quality through the tone duration. One end of attribute III represents instruments that have low amplitude, high frequency energy in the initial stage of the attack segment (e.g., clarinets). Subjectively, these instruments have a buzzlike but softer attack. The other end represents instruments that have dominant lower harmonics and that seem to have a more explosive initial attack (e.g., trumpets).

This research is notable for its emphasis on the temporal attributes of instrumental timbre. Other research using similarity judgments among instrumental notes has found dimensional representations in which the attributes appear to reflect only the harmonic amplitudes of the frequency spectrum. For example, Wedin and Goude (1972) found three attributes: (1) generally high level of partials—"overtone richness"; (2) successively decreasing intensity of the upper partials—"overtone poorness"; and (3) low intensity of the fundamental frequency and increasing intensity of the first few harmonics.

It is clear that all of the outcomes converge in demonstrating the importance of the distribution of harmonic intensities. The outcomes differ with respect to the temporal properties. The reasons for the difference are unclear. The tones in various studies are different durations; perhaps shorter tones emphasize the temporal qualities and longer tones empha-

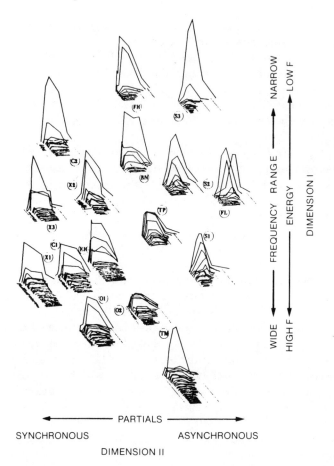

Figure 8.5
Spatial representation of timbre dimensions. Each instrument is represented by a simplified spectrogram. For each spectrogram, low frequencies occur at the top (*upper left*), high frequencies occur at the bottom (*lower right*). Time is portrayed along the horizontal. Onset is at the left. The amplitude of each partial at each time point is represented by the vertical height. In (*a*), dimension I, represented vertically, is combined with dimension II, represented horizontally. In (*b*), dimension I is combined with dimensional III, represented horizontally (from Grey 1977 by permission).

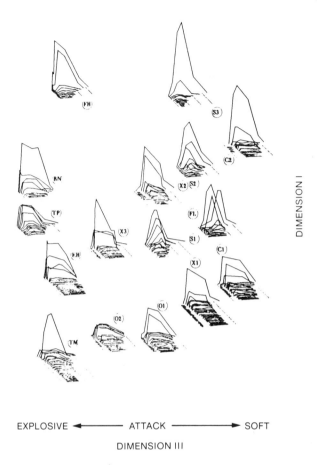

EXPLOSIVE ◄────── ATTACK ──────► SOFT

DIMENSION III

Figure 8.5 (continued)

size the partial/harmonic structure. Grey (1978) and Kendall (1986) have pushed this argument even further. They point out that the majority of investigations of timbre have used isolated notes and that this is hardly representative of typical musical contexts. By choosing only one note, some instruments are forced to play a note at the extreme of their range and therefore yield nonrepresentative timbres. In addition, the relevant perceptual information may exist in the overlap between two notes when they are played without interruption (termed *legato*). It may be the changes in sound that provide the perceptual information, and not an individual note in isolation. In addition to the perceptual information provided by notes in differing regions of an instrument's range, the very act of playing successive notes introduces articulator changes, temporal performance constraints, and overlapping tones that may introduce unique acoustic differences. Grey illustrated the importance of those factors by demonstrating that differences in clarinet and trumpet timbre were easiest to perceive for isolated notes, but differences in bassoon timbres were equally easy to perceive for isolated notes, simple melodies, or simple multivoice melodies.

The results from studies on the accuracy of instrument identification are inconsistent and reinforce the notion that single-tone presentation may be a poor context in which to study identification and timbre. First, the overall level of identification varies greatly from experiment to experiment. Across four different experiments (Berger 1964; Grey 1977; Saldanha and Corso 1964; Wedin and Goude 1972), the percentage correct ranged from 33% to 85%. Second, the rank order of difficulty of identifying the various instruments changes dramatically across experiments. If the rank ordering were consistent, then we could explain the large difference in overall accuracy as being due to the experience of the listeners, recording quality, and so on. Unfortunately, this is not the case; the difficulty of identifying specific instruments changes from experiment to experiment. To pick some striking examples, in one experiment (Berger 1964), the percentages correct for a clarinet, oboe, flute, and trombone were 90%, 97%, 43%, and 47%, but in a different experiment (Wedin and Goude 1972), the percentages correct for a clarinet, oboe, flute, and trombone were 38%, 18%, 40%, and 14%. The oboe was easiest in the first experiment, second hardest in the second; the flute was hardest in the first but easiest in the second. There are numerous examples of this sort; they provide some idea of the difficulties in obtaining general conclusions.

The direct scaling of instrument similarity seems to be a valuable approach to detailing instrument timbre. The research reported here isolated both temporal factors and harmonic factors that appeared to underlie the perception of timbre. Unfortunately, the results do not seem to converge to overall conclusions. First, the attributes of timbre are a function of the experimental context and the specific note(s) chosen. The values on the temporal and spectral measures that seem useful for describing instrument timbre at one note are not consistent across an instrument's range. It is not possible to analyze one note and then use those attack/decay transients and harmonic spectrum to produce a range of different notes—the notes will not sound like the same instrument. Second, the ability to identify any instrument successfully depends on the experimental situation. This may be a simple consequence of the fact that the timbre of an instrument changes as a function of context. One cannot simply say that one instrument is easier to identify than another.

Speech timbre   The difficulties in using similarity judgments to discover timbre characteristics are magnified for speech. For music, there is a small set of instruments. For speech, however, there are limitless numbers of individuals who could be compared with each other. We would expect that there would be inconsistencies in the derived attributes as a function of the set of speakers. Moreover, given the degree of coarticulation in speech, the attributes of voices will also be a function of the speech material chosen.

In a typical experiment (Matsumoto, Hiki, Sone, and Nimura 1973), the stimulus materials were 0.5 sec segments of the Japanese vowel /a/ presented at different fundamental frequencies (120 Hz, 140 Hz, and 160 Hz). The speakers were 8 males ranging from 20 to 35 years in age. Two sounds were presented together, and the subjects judged whether the sounds were spoken by the same person. The measure of (dis)similarity was the percentage of times subjects judged two voices as being different. In addition to the psychological judgments, the experimenters measured fundamental frequency, magnitude of harmonics, fluctuation of fundamental frequency, and vocal tract resonances (the frequency of the lowest three formants) for each vowel.

As was done in investigations of instrumental timbre, the similarity judgments among the 24 vowels (8 speakers at 3 different frequencies) were analyzed to uncover the underlying attributes, and then the physical measurements were related to the psychological (perceived) attributes. The results indicated that the similarity among the vowels could be explained by two characteristics. The most important factor was fundamental frequency. Approximately 50% of the difference between two sounds was due to the difference in fundamental frequency. The second most important factor was the formant frequencies. The differences in formant frequencies, combined with the differences in fundamental frequency, accounted for 81% of the variation in perceived differences between vowel sounds.

In an attempt to generalize these results, the authors used the same procedures for other Japanese vowels. In these cases, however, the fundamental frequency was held constant in order to evaluate more clearly the contribution of other characteristics. Here, differences in the vocal cord vibration—the amplitudes of the harmonics and the frequency fluctuations of the fundamental—predicted the perceived differences between any two vowels better than the differences in the frequencies of the first three formants. These two outcomes illustrate that the set of sounds influences the importance of acoustic variables. In a set of vowels in which the fundamental frequency varies, the differences between formant frequencies is quite important. In contrast, when the fundamental frequency is constant, formant frequencies are less important.

Subsequent research using this methodology has met with only moderate success. Walden et al. (1978) used monosyllables consisting of a voiced stop, a voiced fricative, a nasal, and a vowel. They found that four attributes were used in the judgments of speaker similarity. Even though they made extensive physical measurements, however, only two of the four dimensions from the judgments could be interpreted. One attribute corresponded to fundamental frequency (as found in the study cited above on Japanese vowels), and the second attribute corresponded to word duration, an indication of the speech rate. The third and most important attribute, however, was not related to a physical attribute: it was termed "quality" and seemed to relate to the "richness" of the voice. The fourth attribute corresponded to the speaker's age. Obviously, listeners were not judging on the basis of age itself; they were responding to some voice quality that changed as a function of age. At present, the acoustic properties that lead to the perception of age are unknown.

The same maddening inconsistencies were found in work that studied male and female speakers uttering sustained vowel sounds and spoken phrases (Murry and Singh 1980). The goal of this research was to distinguish voice attributes in a variety of contexts, to discover whether listeners judge male as opposed to female voices according to different attributes, and to determine whether listeners judge voices uttering sustained vowels, as opposed to phrases, according to different attributes. As in previous research, listeners judged the similarity between pairs of voices within one of four groups: male-vowel, female-vowel, male-phrase, female-phrase.

The results were extremely variable. Only the difference in vocal cord fundamental frequency was an important determinant of perceived differences between voices for all groups. The other attributes used to make the judgments differed among the four groups. For example, differences in the frequency separation between the first two formants (F_2/F_1) was a determinant of perceived difference for male-vowels, male-phrases, female-vowels, but not for female-phrases; differences in nasality was an important determinant only for the female-phrase condition.

Vocal cord fundamental frequency turns out to be the most important factor in perceived voice quality. The other voice qualities that contribute to perceived differences change from condition to condition, experiment to experiment. Many factors can be responsible: different speakers, different recording techniques, different utterances, and so on. I have argued that listeners *should* make use of any differences that occur; different attributes will be used in altered situations and different attributes will be used for diverse individuals. At this point, instead of being able to specify a small set of voice qualities that are predominant, all we can do is provide a partial catalogue of the possible cues.

To study the perception of natural events, Van Derveer (1979) tape-recorded events like hammering, whistling, finger snapping, crumpling paper, and walking up and down stairs. The sound of each event was presented, one after the other, and at the end the judges grouped similar sounds together. The most important sound quality was the gross temporal patterning. Hammering and knocking were similar because of their rhythmic, repetitive sound. Sawing, filing (wood), and shaking a pin box were similar because of their continuous, rough sound. Shuffling cards, crumpling bags, and crumpling and tearing paper were similar because of their crackling, which makes up a continuous sound. Jingling keys and jingling coins were similar because of their irregular metallic sound. Two drinking glasses that clinked together several times and a spoon that clinked against a china teacup were similar because of their bouncing, repeated ringing tones that soften in intensity.

In these events, the rhythm and continuity of the sound have the major influence on perceived similarity. Frequency was not important, probably because the sounds lacked tonal qualities. We might wonder whether the judged similarity among events was due to the acoustic properties or whether it was due to the events themselves. Listeners can identify shuffling cards, crumpling paper, and tearing paper by sound alone, and perhaps they judge similarity in terms of the actions and not the sounds. Van Derveer argues that this misses the important point: events and actions that are similar will generate sounds that are similar. This correspondence is necessarily true because of the physical nature of sound production. What this means is that event similarity and sound similarity are alternative ways of describing the same world. We can emphasize the sound (i.e., the proximal stimulus at the ear) or the event (i.e., the distal stimulus at a distance), but they are equivalent.

Listeners can build up incorrect expectations about the relationship between acoustic variables and events. For example, listeners expect male hand-clapping to be slower, louder, and lower pitched than female hand-clapping. This expectation may stem from the obvious fact that males generally have larger hands and arms. But surprisingly, there are no gender differences in clapping; differences in clapping sounds are due to the way one hand hits the other (Repp 1987).

At this point any comparison between the categories of instruments, voices, and events is ambiguous. Clearly, the timbre of all sources depends on the amplitudes of the harmonics. Results from instruments suggest a sharpness dimension based roughly on the energy distribution across the partials. Results from voices suggest a primary attribute based on the fundamental vibration frequency of the vocal cords and a secondary attribute based on the frequency of the second and third formants. Results from natural events demonstrate that metal objects can be distinguished from wood or glass objects, and this suggests that the resonance frequencies are an important attribute. Just as clearly, the timbre of all sources must be dependent on the temporal changes in the frequency components. This conclusion has been demonstrated for instruments in which the synchrony of the partials as well as initial, high frequency energy determine timbre and perceived similarity. This conclusion, however, has not been demonstrated for speakers. None of the reported studies has identified a "temporal" attribute beyond that caused by speaking rate. Intuitively, it seems clear that timing among formant transitions, voice onset times, and so on is going to affect voice quality. Yet no investigator has attempted to determine if any speaker quality dimension covaries with a temporal variation. As discussed in chapter 5, recent work has emphasized the dynamic aspects of speech production and perception; the temporal domain should be investigated more fully in the future. For events, the temporal attribute can distinguish events with extremely fast attacks (explosions) from events with slower onsets (clapping) and can in the same way distinguish among events with different decays. What is probably more important for natural events is the patterning of the component "impulses" across longer time spans. Speech and music also make use of rhythmic patterning, mainly to emphasize meaning or express emotion. If expressions of irony as opposed to expressions of surprise, both brought about by temporal patterning, are different events, then there is a parallel in the use of temporal information. It is thus impossible to chart the parallels between instruments, speakers, and events, because corresponding analyses have not been done in all the domains and because the levels of analysis differ among the domains.

Synthetic Production of Instrumental and Vocal Sounds
The two judgment techniques discussed above provide a set of potential timbre variables that can be used to describe sounds and to distinguish among different sources. However, the experiments do not determine which cues are most important or demonstrate that listeners actually use these cues in a realistic situation (Clarke and Becker 1969). To attempt to answer these questions, experiments have altered the sound artificially. For example, a formant frequency can be raised or lowered, the onset transient of a tone can be eliminated, or a sound can be presented backward to

distort temporal changes but maintain the harmonic amplitudes. If any one of these changes significantly alters the percept, then this is supporting evidence that the altered component is important in creating timbre. If the changes do not alter the percept, then this is evidence that the component is of minor importance.

The sounds of instruments, voices, and events can be conceptualized in two ways. Each, in turn, leads to a style of experimentation.

1. The first is in terms of the properties of the acoustic sound wave that reaches the listener. From Grey's analysis of instrument notes, we can identify an initiation period, an attack transition for each partial, a relatively steady-state section for each partial, and a decay transition for each partial. Following this conceptualization, experiments have artificially changed and simplified the acoustic signal. The simplest example is to make a tape recording of an instrument note and then snip out sections of the tape for experimentation. For example, we could cut out the attack transitions and present listeners with either the attack transitions alone or the steady-state and decay sections alone. More complex manipulations are possible, but for each the rationale is identical: can we determine, by removing parts of the acoustic signal, the aspect of the acoustic wave that is basic to the characteristic timbre of a sound source? If we remove a critical aspect, then the identification of the instrument (or voice) may show a large decrement.

2. The second is in terms of the process of sound production. In simplified terms there are two factors: (a) the imposed vibratory pattern described by its harmonic spectrum, bearing in mind that the harmonic frequencies are not perfect multiples of the fundamental frequency, and (b) the vibration modes created by the physical construction of the sound body. The sound body modes selectively "react" to certain of the imposed vibrations, and it is this output that is radiated to the listener. Following this conceptualization, experiments have created hybrid instruments or voices by joining the vibratory pattern of one instrument or voice to the resonance of a different instrument or voice. One can create a viosoon or bassolin—a violin vibratory pattern coupled to the resonances of the bassoon or a bassoon vibratory pattern coupled to the resonances of a violin. Does the timbre of the hybrid most resemble the source of the vibratory pattern or does it most resemble the source of the resonance pattern?

Simplification of timbre   We will begin with the "simplification" experiments using instruments. The amplitude-frequency-time graphs of various instruments in this chapter as well as in chapter 4 reveal an extremely complex picture. Each partial has a unique overall amplitude envelope.

Moreover, there are rapid small changes in amplitude superimposed on the overall amplitude envelope (i.e., amplitude modulation), and in addition each partial undergoes small frequency changes (i.e., frequency modulation) as the partial grows and decays. Although traditionally a note is charac- terized as made up of the attack, steady-state, and decay portions, this does not adequately portray the temporal properties. Each harmonic undergoes continuous change; even in the "steady state" there is a constant shift in relative amplitude and dominance among the harmonics (see figures 4.6, 4.8, 8.4, 8.5, 8.6, 8.9). We will continue to use the term "steady state" to label the middle part of the note, but it is important to be aware that there is hardly any part that is "steady."

In a series of experiments, Grey and Moorer (1977) progressively simpli- fied instrumental notes to discover the determinants of timbre. The first simplification smoothed out the amplitude modulations for each partial. Each partial thus consisted of a series of six to eight linear segments, without the small amplitude oscillations. The second simplification retained the linear amplitude variation and in addition eliminated the initial low amplitude energy of the upper harmonics, which is the physical measure correlated to the third dimension of the similarity judgment configuration described in the musical timbre section. The third simplification retained the linear amplitude variation and in addition eliminated the frequency modulation of each partial, so that all the time-varying amplitude and frequency changes that might be thought to give each instrument its unique richness were removed. Each of these three simplifications was made for 16 instruments. One representative sample, the bass clarinet (C2), is shown in figure 8.6.

Surprisingly, the simplifications did not fundamentally change the tim- bre of any instrument, but instead resulted in changes that could occur in playing the same note with slightly different styles. For this reason, sub- jects were asked to judge the differences between the various simplified versions of each instrument in terms of the perceived quality of articulation or playing style. The results indicated that the line-segment approximation of the amplitude envelope closely resembled the original tone (figure 8.6, panel b). The elimination of the initial noise or the constant frequency modification yielded timbres that were judged to be poor in quality. How- ever, each simplification brought about a different sort of change. For example, clarinets that contained low amplitude, high frequency noise were greatly changed by the initial low amplitude energy simplification (figure 8.6, panel c); and the soprano saxophones that contained frequency modu- lation were greatly changed by the constant frequency modification (figure 8.6, panel d). Overall the elimination of the initial low amplitude energy was judged to lead to a greater timbre change than did the constant frequency simplification.

Charbonneau (1981) has continued in this tradition, constructing instrumental tones that maintained the overall structure of the note while simplifying the amplitude and frequency microstructure of the individual partials. The first simplification involved the amplitude of the harmonics; each partial was constructed to have the exact same amplitude envelope, although the relative peak amplitude and original offset and onset time points were maintained. Because the original time points were maintained, each partial could become strongest at differing times. Taken together, the simplified partials re-created the overall time-varying amplitude of the note (see figure 8.7).

The second simplification involved the frequency of the partials. A simplification in which each partial stays at a constant frequency is too drastic: the partials must undergo some frequency change to give a good simulation of instrumental timbre. (Grey and Moorer, however, did use this condition.) Charbonneau modified each partial so that it had exactly the same frequency modulation as the fundamental. What was lost, therefore, was that part of the timbre that was due to the differing timings and differing amounts of frequency modulation for each partial.

The results indicated that amplitude simplification had the greatest effect. It is the different prominences of the partials that are critical for timbre. However, as found previously in all similar research, the magnitude of each simplification was a function of the instrument. The flute, trombone, saxophone, and trumpet were most affected by the amplitude simplification, because those instruments are characterized by differing amplitude curves for each partial. In contrast, the French horn was mainly affected by the frequency simplification, because it is characterized by wide frequency fluctuations in the attack of all the harmonics.

These results point out that timbre does change due to acoustic wave simplifications. Do the same sorts of simplifications alter the difficulty of identification? Several studies (Berger 1964; Kendall 1986; Saldanha and Corso 1964; Wedin and Goude 1972) have used a task in which an instrument is played in isolation, and listeners attempt to identify that instrument. In an often-cited experiment, Saldanha and Corso (1964) compared the identification of 10 instruments under five conditions: (1) attack transient + long steady state + decay transient; (2) attack transient + shortened steady state + decay transient; (3) attack transient + shortened steady state; (4) shortened steady state only; and (5) shortened steady state + decay transient. (The middle section "steady state," of course, still contains the amplitude and frequency modulations of each harmonic.) Overall the results indicated that the first three conditions led to equally correct identification of the instrument (about 45%). Given the attack transient plus a segment of the steady state, the length of the steady state or the decay transient did not affect identification. The remaining two

248   Chapter 8

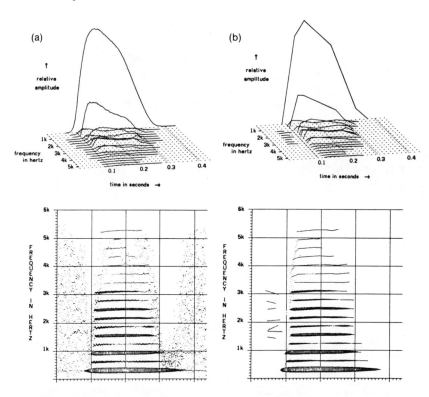

Figure 8.6
Simplification of timbre. The original tone is illustrated in (a). A three-dimensional representation of the amplitudes of all partials as a function of time is shown at the top. A spectrogram of the same tone is shown below. The thickness of the line representing each partial in the spectrogram denotes the amplitude. The first simplification, smoothing out the amplitude fluctuations of each partial, is illustrated in (b). Compared to (a), the simplified version eliminates the small variations in amplitudes as the partial undergoes the attack, steady-state, and decay phases. The second simplification, eliminating the initial low amplitude energy as well as smoothing the amplitude fluctuations, is illustrated in (c). Compared to (b), the elimination of the initial low amplitude energy can be seen by the absence of energy (relatively flat lines in b) between 1.0 Hz and 3.5 Hz during the first 0.1 sec in the three-dimensional representation and by the absence of the thin sloping lines in the first 0.1 sec in the spectrogram. The third simplification, eliminating the frequency modulations or fluctuations as well as smoothing the amplitude fluctuations, is illustrated in (d). Compared to (b), the effect of eliminating the frequency modulations is most easily seen in the spectrograms. The frequency modulations in (b) are depicted by the sloping up or down of the partials (easily seen for the initial energy). The elimination of the frequency fluctuations makes each partial perfectly horizontal (i.e., at one frequency). (From Grey and Moorer 1977 by permission).

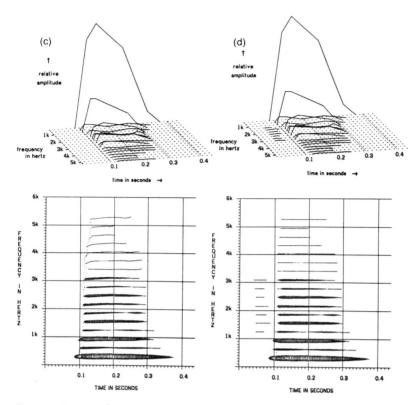

Figure 8.6 (continued)

conditions, which did not include the attack transient, led to poorer but equal performance (32%). Given the steady-state spectrum, the decay transients did not affect identification. From these results we can conclude that both the attack transient and the steady-state spectrum do influence identification. The authors point out that the relative percent of identification for each instrument changed as a function of the conditions and that in addition the difficulty of identification depended upon the note played and whether vibrato was used.

In a similar experiment, Berger (1964) constructed four conditions: (1) the entire note; (2) the entire note played backward: the attack and decay transients are eliminated as perceptual information because the timing is reversed, although the relative amplitudes of each partial during the steady state are maintained; (3) the "steady state" portion, achieved by deleting the first and last half second; (4) the entire note played through a low-pass filter, which effectively transmitted only the fundamental frequency. The

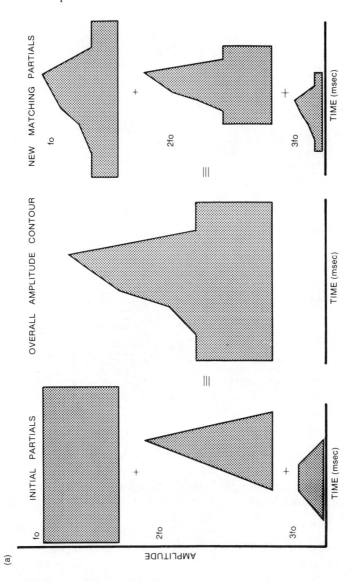

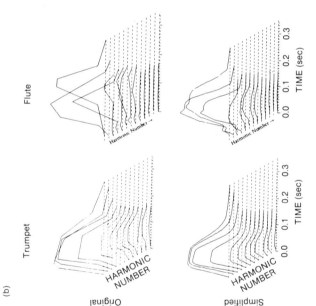

Figure 8.7
Simplification of instrumental timbre. The first simplification involves making the amplitude envelope identical for all partials. An example of this using three partials is shown in (*a*), on the facing page. The original partials are shown on the *left*. Combined, they yield the overall amplitude contour shown in the *center*. In the simplified timbre (*right*), each partial has the identical amplitude contour, although the original onset, offset, duration, and amplitude are maintained. Two examples used by Charboneau (1981) are illustrated in (*b*), on this page. The original trumpet and flute timbres are portrayed at the top, the simplified timbres underneath (from Charboneau 1981 by permission of author).

percentage correct for the unaltered tones was 59%, the percentage correct for the backward tones was 42%, the percentage correct for the steady-state portion was 35%, and the percentage correct for the filtered tones was 18%. Wedin and Goude (1972) have compared the entire note to the steady-state portion. In this work, the percentage correct for the entire note was 33%; the percentage correct for the steady-state section with the attack and decay deleted was only 20%.

Recently Kendall (1986), comparing instrumental identification (clarinet, trumpet, violin) using single notes and whole phrases, has refined these results. For single notes, Kendall's results mirror those above: transients were as important as the steady state in instrument identification. For musical phrases in which notes were slurred together, the results were quite different. Here transients were relatively less important than the time-varying (amplitude and frequency modulation) steady-state signals. Kendall contrasted the time-varying musical signal with a simulated note in which each cycle was identical; that is, the frequency and amplitude modulation of each harmonic had been removed. A static tone led to poorer identification, whether or not the transient was included. (Charbonneau [1981] also found that frequency variation of the harmonics was necessary for a realistic timbre.) It could well be that transient information is more important when playing staccato phrases with short, discrete notes. This possibility was suggested previously when considering the results of Grey (1978).

It is clear that conclusions drawn from similarity judgment experiments and conclusions drawn from identification experiments reinforce each other.

1. The energy spectrum of the partials in part determines timbre and identification. Changing the amplitude envelope of the partials significantly changes the perceived timbre, and eliminating the frequency and amplitude variation of each harmonic changes the timbre and yields poorer identification. Moreover, the steady-state segment of the note is sufficient for correct identification, whether the note is played forward or backward. The identification performance using the steady-state segment is roughly two-thirds the performance using the entire signal.

2. The initial noise segment and the attack transient also in part determine timbre and identification. The elimination of the initial low amplitude energy leads to large changes in perceived timbre, and studies of single notes have shown that the complete attack transient plus steady-state segment leads to better identification than the steady state alone. No experiment seems to have used only the transient information. Possibly the transients by themselves do not lead to a sense of timbre. Transients appear less important in slurred musical

phrases because of the availability of other information. Detailed predictions involving individual instruments are often contradictory. For example, instruments displaying low-intensity, high-frequency energy during the initial segment (strings, flute, clarinet, saxophone) ought to be maximally affected by eliminating the attack transition. In some experiments this is the case, but it is not consistently true.

It must be kept in mind that these results are based on an extremely limited set of instruments and notes. At present we do not know the generalizations beyond these results. Other musicians, instruments, notes, blowing intensities, auditoriums, and so on may lead to very different outcomes. Charbonneau (1981) writes: "We have to remember that the specifications obtained for each instrument by the various types of simplification cannot be considered generally valid for all the notes playable on the instrument. It is an important property of timbre that the analysis of one instrumental note is rarely sufficient for synthesizing a note of differing pitch, intensity, or duration" (p. 18).

We now turn to voice identification. Although the focus for instruments was the description of timbre, the focus for voices has been identification accuracy. This difference is a reflection of the goals: for instruments it is to develop an adequate simulation, for voices it is to develop data for recognition and identification systems. Thus the voice simplification experiments are more concerned with decreases in identification performance than with the description of voice-quality changes.

The most widely used technique to modify a speech signal is to utilize a low-pass filter or a high-pass filter. A low-pass filter does not attenuate frequencies below its setting (i.e., it passes lower frequencies) but does progressively attenuate frequencies above that setting. For example, frequencies two times greater might be attenuated to one-tenth the intensity and frequencies three times greater might be attenuated to one-hundredth the intensity. A high-pass filter does not attenuate frequencies above its setting (i.e., it passes high frequencies) but progressively attenuates frequencies below that setting.) The low-pass filter can be utilized to restrict the voice signal to the fundamental (or fundamental plus other low frequencies); the high-pass filter can be utilized to restrict the voice signal to the upper partials and formants. As described above, low-pass filtering for instruments reduced identification to nearly the change level: instruments cannot be identified by their fundamental frequency. The results are different for voice identification: on the whole it is possible to restrict the frequency range severely and still maintain relatively good identification. If the best performance is 80% correct (chance performance is 50% correct), using a very restrictive 500 Hz low-pass filter or a 2000 Hz high-pass filter still resulted in 60% identification (Pollack, Pickett, and Sumby 1954). The

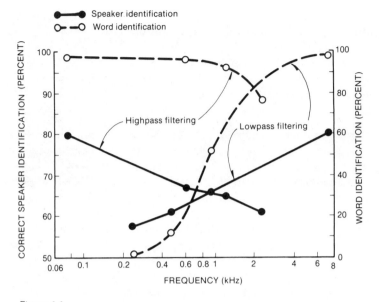

Figure 8.8
The effect of low-pass and high-pass filtering on speaker and word identification. Voices can be identified in spite of very restrictive low- or high-pass filtering. In contrast, words cannot be identified with restrictive filtering (adapted from Hecker 1971).

frequency range for the best speaker identification was roughly between 1000 Hz and 3000 Hz. These results are shown in figure 8.8. Although filtering consistently hindered identification, there were large differences among listeners in their ability to identify speakers. Some listeners might have normally used cues for identification that were impaired by the filtering and were unable to switch their attention to more useful cues in this context. Other listeners might have normally used cues that were relatively unaffected by the filtering or were able to switch their attention to other cues in this case.

It is interesting to note that filtering affected simple word identification far more than voice identification, particularly for low-pass filtering. For low-pass filtering, the pecentage correct in a word identification test ranged from chance, when all frequencies above 200 Hz were attenuated, to perfect (100%), when all frequencies above 8000 Hz were attenuated. In contrast, the percentage correct in a two-alternative speaker identification test ranged from 60% to 80% for the same filter conditions. In addition, there were only small differences among listeners in word identification, as opposed to large differences among listeners in speaker identification.

To investigate the contribution of the dynamic aspects of articulation, researchers have used backward speech or have used only prolonged vowels that minimize articulatory movements. As described previously for instrument identification, playing a note or voice segment backward maintains the identical spectrum (fundamental frequency and variation in fundamental frequency) but reverses and thus effectively eliminates dynamic cues. This will destroy articulatory information about consonants, diphthongs, and syllables and will distort temporal information about duration and timing. Backward presentation lowers speaker identification, a 10–15% drop in percentage correct (Bricker and Pruzansky 1976; Van Lancker, Kreiman, and Emmorey 1985). Van Lancker and colleagues using 4-sec passages of famous voices, make the interesting observation that some voices are easy to recognize backward but others are nearly unrecognizable. For example, if presented normally, correct identification for Bob Hope and Ronald Reagan occurs about 80% of the time. However, if presented backward, the percentage correct for Bob Hope drops to 30%; the percentage correct for Ronald Reagan remains at above 75%. Van Lancker, Kreiman, and Wickens (1985) also investigated recognition of the same voice when the voices were sped up 33% or slowed down 33% (without changing frequency). As found for the backward speech, altering speaking rate produced a roughly 10–15% drop in correct recognition. More important, as was found for backward speech, the effect of rate changes was not the same for all voices. For example, Jack Benny was recognized correctly above 90% of the time for all rates; John F. Kennedy was recognized correctly 88% of the time at a normal speaking rate, 74% of the time at a sped-up rate, and only 17% of the time for slowed-down speech.

These results led Van Lancker and colleagues to argue that the voice signal has a set of possible cues from which the listener can select a subset useful for recognizing a particular voice. The cues employed for one voice may be useless and inappropriate for another. Moreover, the usefulness of a cue for one voice depends on the values of the other cues. Some cues will be distorted by being playing backward and other cues will be distorted by changing rates. On the one hand, if listeners depend on those cues for certain voices, then identification of them will decrease dramatically. On the other hand, if listeners depend on other cues for the voices, then identification will be roughly stable. It is for this reason that identifications of only some voices are affected when they are played backward and only some are affected by rate changes. There is no fixed set of voice features that is used across the board for identification (and by analogy, for timbre). This may help explain the inconsistent results from scaling experiments. Each set of voices will have different salient cues. (This argument is probably true for instruments as well, which explains the inconsistent results across experiments.)

To give a general overview, the same changes in the transient and steady-state sections of a note affect both instrument and speaker identification. It is possible to eliminate transient information by snipping out the transient, playing the sound backward, or using only a steady-state note. All of these simplifications bring about a reduction of identification performance and thus indicate that the transient is a cue for identification. It is possible to eliminate or simplify steady-state information by using low- or high-pass filters or by eliminating the differential amplitude and frequency modulation of each partial. Each of these simplification will also impair identification, and this therefore indicates that the steady-state part of the signal is a potential cue for identification. Identification rarely drops to the chance level, particularly for speakers, which indicates the substitutability of the various possible cues for identification. The cues may be substituted for each other because they are interdependent: the transients cannot change without affecting the steady state and vice versa. For longer musical passages or utterances, there is also substitutability of cues. There are production constraints even at this level in terms of rhythm, fluency, and rate. In addition, there are cues spanning several units (termed *prosodic cues*), such as intonation, which provide alternative kinds of information about the instrument or speaker.

Synthesis of hybrid timbre   The other approach to isolating the cues for identification is to synthesize a hybrid sound. Here, one uses a model for sound production in which a vibratory system (e.g., vocal cords, violin strings, instrument reeds) is set into oscillation by an external force, and this oscillation is imposed on a sound body (vocal tract, violin body, instrument tube). The basic procedure is to take the vibratory system from one source and combine it with the sound body from a second source.

For instrumental tones, one important aspect of timbre is the spectral energy distribution, i.e., the time-varying amplitude pattern of the harmonics. In one study, Grey and Gordon (1978) exchanged the relative amplitudes of each harmonic between two instruments but did not exchange the onset, attack, and decay timings. A simple example using two harmonics is shown in figure 8.9. In the example, the maximum amplitudes are exchanged with the equivalent harmonic of the other instrument, while the timing and envelope of each harmonic for each instrument remains identical. In the experiment, Grey and Gordon exchanged four pairs: trumpet-trombone; oboe—bass clarinet; bassoon—French horn; and normal bowing cello—sul ponticello bowing cello. The trumpet-trombone exchange is shown in figure 8.9, panel (b).

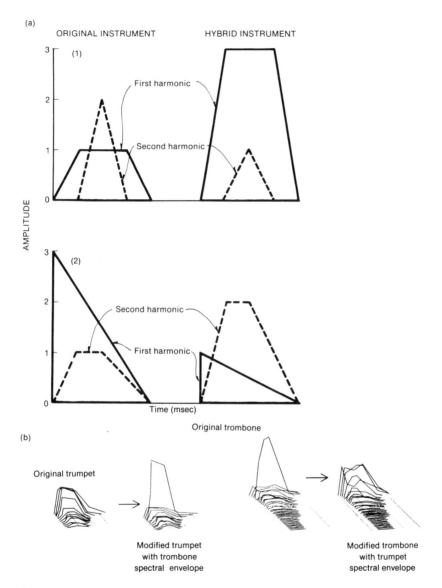

Figure 8.9
Generation of hybrid instruments by exchanging the maximum amplitudes of the harmonics. A simplified example is depicted in panel (a). The two harmonics of the original instruments are shown to the *left*. Each hybrid instrument retains the shape and timing of both harmonics, but the amplitudes are exchanged between the two original instruments. Thus, for instrument (1), the amplitude of the "triangular" second harmonic changes from 2 to 1 in the hybrid because the amplitude of the second harmonic in instrument (2) is 1. An example using a trumpet and a trombone is shown in (b) (from Gordon and Grey 1978 by permission).

This spectral amplitude exchange produced the predicted results: the perceived timbre of the hybrid changed along the spectral energy dimension. The trombone-trumpet exchange took the muted quality of the trombone and imposed it upon the trumpet. The bassoon–French horn exchange yielded a bassoon with the highly explosive attack of a brass instrument and a French horn with the "rounder" attack of a reed instrument. These results illustrate that instrumental timbre arises from two interdependent acoustic processes; it is possible to modify the perceived timbre by interchanging the imposed vibration and sound body modes.

Research on speaker identification has used similar methodologies. For example, Miller (1964) made the first attempt to evaluate the relative contributions of the vocal cord vibration pattern and the vocal tract resonance characteristic. Did a hybrid sound (a vocal cord vibration pattern from one speaker paired with a vocal tract resonance from another speaker) more resemble the speaker defined by the vocal cord vibration pattern (i.e., the relative amplitudes of the partials) or more resemble the speaker defined by the vocal tract resonance functions? In the first experiment, vocal tract vibration modes were exchanged between two speakers. The word "hod" was used, and both speakers had the same duration and fundamental frequency. Listeners judged that each hybrid more closely resembled the speaker whose vocal tract was represented. In three other experiments, vocal tract resonance functions measured from real speakers were paired with artificially generated, but realistic, vocal cord vibrations (e.g., triangle wave forms, pulses, or sinusoids). For example, six speakers produced isolated versions of the vowel /a/, and the vocal tract resonances were calculated. Then each of the six tract resonance functions was paired with two of the artificial vocal cord vibration patterns. In all instances, judges felt that speaker identity was determined by the vocal tract resonance functions. Differing vibration patterns of the vocal cords yield obvious changes in speech quality, but listeners felt that each was produced by the same speaker. Matsumoto et al. (1973), using Japanese vowels, also found that vocal tract resonance functions were dominant in perceived voice quality: hybrid voices tended to be judged closest to voices having the same resonance/formant functions.

Other methods have been used to uncover the roles of vocal cord vibration and vocal tract resonance patterns. For example, studies have eliminated vocal cord vibration information by using a mechanical larynx, by requiring speakers to whisper, or by using noisy fricative sounds. In all cases, subjects were able to identify speakers at better than chance level (see Bricker and Pruzansky 1976). These results demonstrate that vocal tract formant frequencies are sufficient by themselves to support identification. It is also possible to eliminate vocal tract formant information by directly recording the vibration pattern of the larynx. These recordings preserve fundamental frequency, normal variation in fundamental frequency (the contour), and normal variation in timing within each speaker. The results indicate that the vocal cord vibration pattern can be successfully used for speaker identification, and for some listeners it is as good a cue as vocal tract formants. Both the average fundamental frequency vibration and the variation in fundamental frequency can be used for identification. Speakers with high and low fundamental frequencies are rarely confused, and when fundamental frequency is removed as a cue, speakers with different frequency contours are rarely confused (Abberton and Fourcin 1978).

The final approach to uncovering the distinctive properties of voices is to change the fundamental voicing frequency and the formant structure artificially. For example, it is possible to record an utterance and then artificially raise or lower the fundamental frequency. Using this technique, Brown (1981) found that differences in fundamental frequency, differences in average formant frequencies, and differences in formant bandwidth (i.e., the range in frequencies present for each formant) determined the similarity among speakers. Kuwabara and Ohgushi (1987) argue that formant frequencies are most important, and that changes of 5% for the lower formants destroy the sense of voice-personality.

Finally, we turn to one natural event, the identification of bouncing objects versus breaking objects. Actually, each piece of a broken object bounces; the distinction between bouncing and breaking is between one bouncing object and many bouncing pieces. When an object (or a piece of an object) bounces, each brief impact imposes a vibration pattern consisting of all frequencies. The impact thus excites all possible resonance modes, and the sound (i.e., the frequency spectrum) is relatively similar for each bounce. The impacts are "damped quasi-periodic": the impacts decrease in intensity, and the time between successive impacts decreases (i.e., the bouncing speeds up). Each object (or each piece of a broken object) has a unique frequency spectrum, because of its resonance modes, and each bounces at a different rate. The acoustic information for bouncing is therefore one damped quasi-periodic sequence, such that each successive sound has an identical spectrum (i.e., it sounds the same). The acoustic information for breaking involves overlapping damped quasi-periodic sequences, where each sequence (representing one piece) has a different frequency spectrum and a different quasi-periodic temporal pattern. Successive sounds will alternate irregularly, because each represents the impact of a different piece. This is shown as the true cases in Figure 8.10.

Warren and Verbrugge (1984) demonstrated that it is the combined temporal and spectral patterning that provides the information needed to distinguish between bouncing and breaking. To do this, they constructed several hybrid simulations that exchanged the temporal and spectral pat-

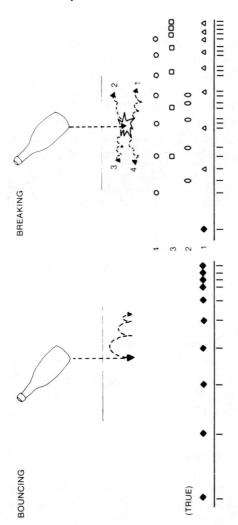

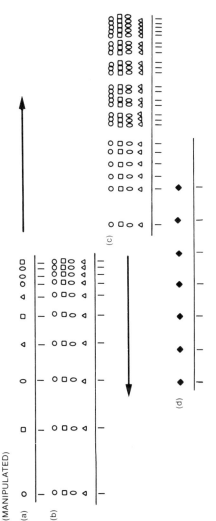

Figure 8.10

Acoustic representation of bouncing versus breaking. When an object bounces, each impact excites all the resonance modes (see facing page). The timing of each impact is quasi-periodic: the impacts decrease in intensity and the time between impacts decreases. This is illustrated in the true condition: the sum of the resonances that occur with each impact are depicted by the filled diamonds. When an object breaks, the first impact excites all the resonance modes (the single filled diamond). The object then breaks into parts and the bouncing of each part gives rise to a quasi-periodic sequence. This is depicted in the True condition: each of the four pieces has a distinct resonance and each resonance is depicted by a different open shape. It is critical to note that each piece gives rise to a different quasi-periodic timing pattern which overlaps in time. To uncover the factors underlying the perception of bouncing versus breaking, Warren and Verbrugge (1984) generated several hybrid variations. In (a) and (b) [for (a)–(d) see this page], there was one quasi-periodic pattern. If each impact yielded a different resonance, the perception was of breaking. On the other hand, if each impact yielded the identical sound, although created by the addition of individual resonances, the perception was of bouncing. In (c) there were overlapping quasi-periodic sequences. If the sound of each impact was identical (created by the addition of individual resonances), the perception was of bouncing. In (d), there was one periodic sequence. The perception was neither bouncing nor breaking.

terning (e.g., temporal patterning for bouncing with the spectral patterning for breaking). Imagine that the object breaks into four parts and that we measure the resonances of each part (see figure 8.10).

1. Using the single-bouncing damped quasi-periodic sequence, as in bouncing, each successive impact was represented by different spectra of alternating parts, as in breaking (panel a). This destroyed the perception of bouncing: the identity of the impacts over time is necessary to signify the unity of a single object bouncing.

2. Again using the single-bouncing sequence, each impact was represented by the identical sound, created by the summation of the spectra of the four pieces (panel b). This did lead to the perception of bouncing: the identity of impacts, even if they represent multiple pieces, signifies bouncing.

3. Now using the overlapping damped quasi-periodic sequences representing the pieces of a broken object, each impact was constructed to have the identical spectra, as in bouncing (panel c). This destroyed the perception of breaking: distinct spectral properties of successive sounds are necessary to signify the multiple pieces of broken objects.

4. A strict periodic sequence in which the impacts are equally timed destroyed the perception of bouncing (panel d). An accelerating rhythm of impacts is necessary to perceive bouncing. Surprisingly, bouncing was still perceived if the intensity of each impact was identical.

Overall, both the spectral and temporal patterns determine the percept. It is the time-varying spectral patterns that convey information about the events.

What does all this mean? First, and most important, it reaffirms that there are multiple possibilities for identification. For example, listeners can identify a speaker on the basis of vocal-fold vibration, vocal tract resonance, rate of speech, and any other idiosyncratic gesture. Second, hybrid instrument and hybrid voice experiments reaffirm the importance of the sound-body resonance modes. Although the speaker experiments suggest that the resonance/formant function is predominant, fundamental frequency may be more important in natural settings. Third, research on natural events reaffirms that frequency patterning over longer temporal intervals strongly affects perception.

8.5 Overview

This chapter has taken a broad look at identification. The emphasis has been on the qualities (timbre) that distinguish voices, instruments, and events, for these qualities must form the basis for successful identification. Research primarily concerned with identification has not been stressed, because it should be clear by now that there is no answer to the question of how "good" identification is. Performance is a function of so many variables that any level of performance is both possible and plausible.

In general, the results reported here support the notion of the multiplicity of factors influencing timbre. The attack/decay transients, the more time-independent spectral energy distribution, as well as the rhythmic patterning affect timbre, and each can be successfully used for identification. There are other specific aspects of timbre I have not discussed here. For example, researchers (e.g., Glenn and Kleiner 1968; Su and Li 1974) involved in machine recognition of speakers have utilized measures of the nasal spectrum and nasal coarticulation (e.g., mi, me, ni, ne). They have argued that these sounds have strong speaker-dependent characteristics that are not modified in natural speech. It is unclear whether listeners tend to pay attention to timbre qualities that are intrinsically due to mechanical properties and thus are less easily disguised. Brown (1981), cited above, does argue for this conclusion. Brown claims that acoustic properties that are due to the length, shape, and damping of the larynx are less likely than properties like speaking rate or frequency variation to change under the varied natural conditions, and therefore that listeners will attend to these properties first. I am not persuaded by this contention. Across the gamut of experiments, listeners adapt their strategies to the kinds of variation found among speakers (or instruments or natural events). There is no evidence that there are timbre qualities that are naturally preferred and naturally utilized first to identify any source.

Moreover, there is a general correspondence between speaker, instrument, and event identification. The various methodologies and simulation techniques, though not always equally useful, have been used for all sources. There do not seem to be any outcomes that suggest that voice timbre is judged fundamentally differently from instrument timbre or event timbre or that speaker identification follows principles different from those for instrument or event identification. It is my impression that future research should focus on acoustic information spanning longer temporal intervals. This information may be crucial for the perception of timbre. We next turn to the identification of speech sounds and instrumental notes. It is at this level that the controversy has raged over whether speech is perceived differently from the way nonspeech is perceived.

Further Reading

Erickson (1975) explores the nature of timbre in music. This very interesting book is relevant also to chapters 7 and 10. Plomp (1976) provides a psychophysical approach to the perception of timbre. The discussion of complex tones is relevant also for chapter 10.
Erickson, R. (1976). *Sound structure in music.* Berkeley: University of California Press.
Plomp, R. (1975). *Aspects of tone sensation.* London: Academic.

Chapter 9
Phonemes: Notes and Intervals

It is the immense difference between the physical acoustic signal on the one hand and the perceptual-cognitive world on the other hand that has frustrated theorists and researchers. The acoustic signal and perceptual world seem to bear no simple one-to-one resemblance to each other. I believe that this lack of correspondence is true for both speech and music; in fact I believe it is true for any ongoing behavior in which there are parallel, overlapping actions. Liberman (1982) elaborates on this discrepancy for speech: "The diverse, continuous, and tangled sounds of speech are automatically perceived as a scant handful of discrete and variously ordered segments. Moreover, the segments are given in perception as distinctly phonetic objects, without the encumbering auditory baggage that would make them all but useless for their proper role as vehicles of language" (p. 148).

As discussed previously, the inability to make direct connections between the acoustic signal and speech segments (consonants and vowels) has led some theorists to argue for a unique speech (or phonetic) perception mechanism. When the claim is made that the speech mode is unique, there are two obvious questions. First, what aspect or aspects of speech are unique? There are many aspects of speech that could be unique (e.g., acoustic structure, production constraints, communicative function). However, the vast majority of research investigating this claim involves the perception of isolated synthetic syllables. The synthetic syllables are abstract representations evolved from the examination of spectrograms (as discussed in chapter 5). The goal of this work is to demonstrate that the perception of these sounds as speech cannot be explained by traditional auditory mechanisms and that the perception of these sounds as speech differs from the perception of these same sounds as nonspeech. Second, what is the contrast? The speech mode is unique as opposed to what? The "what" are results obtained from experiments using discrete, nonvarying tones and experiments using complex tones resembling speech sounds— that is, traditional psychophysical experiments (see section 2.5). This kind of contrast has led to labeling the differences as an auditory-phonetic dichotomy. Phonetic (speech) perception supposedly involves processes that do not occur in nonspeech (auditory) perception. But nonspeech covers a great deal of territory: pure sine-wave tones, frequency- and intensity-modulated complex tones produced by an instrument, tone combinations in a musical interval or chord, nonspeech sounds produced by the vocal tract (laughs, cries, hums, coughs), and so forth. It is thus not clear how to buttresss the claim that speech perception is unique, because it might differ from the perception of one type of nonspeech sound but not differ from the perception of a different type of nonspeech sound.

What has happened over the past fifteen to twenty years is that speech researchers have discovered phenomena that do not seem to have obvious nonspeech counterparts or obvious auditory explanations. After the dust settles, research begins to emerge that demonstrates that the phenomenon is due to a specific experimental methodology or that the same phenomenon will occur with nonspeech stimuli that match the time-varying properties of the speech signal. The nonspeech sounds composed of pure tones and noise bands seem "speech-like," but they are not perceived as speech. This demolishes the speech-specific claim and leads to the search for other phenomena that cannot be matched by nonspeech stimuli or explained by auditory perception. Thus, the ground on which the auditory-phonetic distinction is based continually shifts.

The fact that the phenomena may not unambiguously support an auditory-phonetic distinction, however, does not mean that they are uninteresting. We can consider various phenomena for the information they may provide about the perception of complex, naturally occurring auditory events. Several that have been used to explore the characteristics of speech perception will be discussed below in order to illustrate properties of auditory perception in general.

9.1 Categorical Perception

In general, categorization refers to processes in which different objects and events are placed or sorted into a small number of categories. Objects and events within a single category share a common property, although they differ on other irrelevant properties (e.g., a door will open or close a passageway, though it may be constructed of different materials, it may be different sizes and shapes, and it may be hinged or sliding). Many categories are based on obvious physical characteristics; others are based on conventions or subtle distinctions. Categorizing is a ubiquitous perceptual-cognitive process found in all domains and is in no way specific to speech, of course. Repp (1984) has written an exhaustive review of categorical perception, and the following owes much to his discussion.

Categorical perception in speech specifically concerns the descriptive categories evolved by linguists. As detailed in chapter 5, each speech sound can be described in terms of articulatory features. Stop consonants, for example, are characterized in terms of voicing and place of articulation. If these descriptive categories are perceptually real, then we might expect that sounds are perceived in terms of the articulatory movements and that all sounds with the same movements are perceived as identical. For example, the unvoiced /t/ and the voiced /d/ have the identical place of articulation. In normal speech, the voice onset time boundary that separates voiced from unvoiced consonants (that is, the lag in voicing onset at which voiced and unvoiced percepts are equiprobable) is about +30 msec. It is possible to create a continuous series of consonants in which the voice onset time varies from −20 msec (prevoicing: voicing preceds the brust) to +80 msec. If these simulated segments are perceived categorically, then the segments should break into two discrete categories at one voice onset time boundary. The segments within each category would be perceptually equivalent, and all segments in one category would be clearly dissimilar to all segments in the second category. To put it differently, each segment would be unambiguously an unvoiced /t/ or a voiced /d/; there would be no middle cases. Listeners could not discriminate among various segments labeled /t/ and could not discriminate among other segments labeled /d/. If this were the case, then the phonetic labels generated by articulatory differences would perfectly predict the perceptual organization into discrete speech segments. This is the *strong* version of the theory of categorical perception, in which phonetic categories completely dominate perception. Others place more importance on acoustic differences, and in these versions alternative instances of one phonetic category can be discriminated. Before the research outcomes are presented, a historial perspective may prove helpful.

Discrimination
One of the basic concerns in the development of psychology has been the relationship between physical intensities and psychological magnitudes. Although some research has been aimed at describing various perceptual qualities (e.g., "warmth," "volume," "smoothness"), most work has investigated the sensitivity of a sensory system. The impetus for this comes from Gustav Fechner, who may be said to have founded experimental psychology. His *Element der Psychophysik*, published in 1860 (reprinted 1966), laid out most of the concepts and methods used up to the present day.

Fechner's enduring legacy was to emphasize that psychological magnitudes could be measured by means of the ability to discriminate between stimuli of nearly identical energy levels. The measurement of the amount of energy required to produce perceptible auditory differences is not easy, even for simple sinusoid tones, as section 2.5 pointed out. Overall, however, the auditory system is remarkably sensitive. Typically, individuals can discriminate between two tones separated by only 0.5 to 2.0 Hz (for example, between 400 and 402 Hz) at low and middle frequencies and can distinguish between two tones separated by a 12% (0.5 dB) change in intensity across a wide range of frequencies and intensities (see section 2.5).

These small differences, given the wide range of auditory sensitivity, suggest that a vast number of sounds can be discriminated. The intensity range of the ear extends from 0 dB to 110 dB. Even if we were to increase the difference threshold of 0.5 dB to 1.0 dB, it would still suggest that a listener could discriminate more than 100 steps of intensity. Similarly, the frequency range is about 12,000 Hz. Even using a high estimate of 25 Hz for the difference threshold for frequency, there are still about 500 different frequencies that can be discriminated. Combining the figures for intensity and frequency generates the astonishing, and yet underestimated, figure of 50,000 discriminable sounds (this does not include discriminations based on duration or other variables). Using more realistic estimates, Denes and Pinson (1963) suggest that there are 280 perceptually different intensity levels and 1400 perceptually different frequency levels, yielding—if both intensity and frequency are varied—between 300,000 and 400,000 discriminable tones.

This figure is in sharp contrast to the 90 or so phonetic units used to describe speech and the 90 or so musical notes of Western music. Why is the discrepancy so large? To understand this, we must compare the ability to discriminate between two stimuli to the ability to identify which of many possible stimuli occurred at a specific instant. Notice how different the two tasks are. In a discrimination task, an individual compares and listens for differences between two stimuli presented in close temporal proximity. In an identification or absolute judgment task, the individual listens to one stimulus at a time and tries to connect that perceptual sound to one in his or her memory that has a particular name or label. It should not be surprising that identification judgments are much more difficult, or that memory and judgment processes generate a real bottleneck to perceiving. What is surprising is the extent of this bottleneck and the relatively small number of stimuli that people can identify accurately.

Identification
In absolute judgment experiments, one of a specified set of sounds is presented on each trial. The sounds usually vary along one dimension. If the sounds vary in frequency, then the intensity, duration, onset, and so on are identical for all sounds. The subject attempts to identify that stimulus by label. If there are only two stimuli, except for cases in which the stimuli are nearly identical, perfect performance is expected. As the number of stimuli increases, we expect most errors to occur between similar, adjacent tones. For example, if there were five tones, A, B, C, D and E, such that

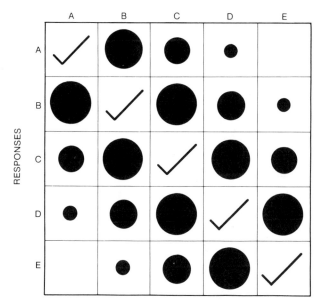

Figure 9.1
A stimulus-response confusion matrix. Adjacent stimuli (e.g., A and B) are maximally similar, and end-point stimuli (A and E) are maximally dissimilar. The subject is presented one of the five stimuli and must label that stimulus. Correct identifications, portrayed by checkmarks, lie on the major diagonal. Incorrect identifications are pictured by the filled circles; the size of the circle portrays the relative number of errors. The majority of errors occur between similar stimuli (e.g., identifying stimulus C as D). In contrast, very few errors occur between dissimilar stimuli (identifying B as E).

adjacent tones were most similar, the majority of errors would be because of confusion between A and B, B and C, C and D, and D and E. Fewer errors would be due to confusion between A and C, B and D, and C and E, and even fewer confusions would occur between A and D, B and E, or A and E. The probability that any two stimuli will be confused decreases as they become more different (see figure 9.1).

It is necessary to develop statistical measures that can be used to compare performances. For example, suppose an observer has a 10% error rate with 10 stimuli, but 25% with 20 stimuli: which represents better performance? Intuitively, the increased complexity of a set of 20 stimuli suggests that performance has actually improved, despite the fact that errors have increased 2.5 times. Absolute judgment experiments are evaluated by predicting how many stimuli an observer can identify without any errors. In other words, on the basis of the pattern of correct identifications and confusions, it is possible by statistical procedures to calculate the maximum number of stimuli that can be identified without error (i.e., each labeled correctly). This number is termed the measure of information transmission.

Research using absolute judgments has led to the rather stark conclusion that individuals can identify only about five to nine stimuli that vary along one attribute. Thus, people may identify seven tones that differ only in frequency, or six tones that differ only in intensity. (The number of stimuli that can be identified is a function of the attribute; for example, only two or three temporal intervals can be identified.) Remember that discrimination tasks suggest that 200 intensities and 1500 frequencies can be discriminated. The ability to identify stimuli that vary along one dimension is severely limited. The differences between stimuli are not critical. For frequency identification, performance is only slightly better if the stimulus range is from 100 Hz to 8000 Hz rather than from 100 Hz to 500 Hz—the improvement is on the level of subjects being able to identify eight rather than seven stimuli (Garner 1962).

These numbers are all out of proportion with our experiences in recognizing faces, words, or melodies. The difference is due to the fact that absolute judgment experiments utilize stimuli that vary along only one dimension. Faces, melodies, or words vary on many dimensions: size, shape, intensity, frequency, duration, and/or rhythm. We can conduct absolute judgment experiments with stimuli that vary on several dimensions at once. The stimuli in such an experiment can vary independently in intensity, frequency, and duration. For example, the first stimulus could be 50 dB, 1000 Hz, 100 msec; the second stimulus could be 50 dB, 1000 Hz, 500 msec; the third stimulus could be 50 dB, 500 Hz, 100 msec; the fourth stimulus could be 75 dB, 500 Hz, 500 msec; and son on. The results of these experiments demonstrate that each additional dimension aids identification. Pollack and Ficks (1954) used eight auditory dimensions involving noise plus tone stimuli—frequency of tone, frequency range of noise, intensity of tone, intensity of noise, rate of interruption, ratio of noise duration to tone duration, total duration, and apparent sound direction—and found that observers could identify about 125 different sounds. This number seems more appropriate to perceptual abilities but is still much less than our sensitivities imply is possible.

The main issue here is the nature of speech and music perception. This research tells us that individuals are extremely sensitive in discriminating even minute differences in sensory energy between two stimuli. In contrast, individuals find it difficult to identify stimuli that differ along one dimension. The confusions are usually between similar stimuli, and the physical difference between two stimuli predicts the number of confusions. Obviously, though, the musical and speech events in the real world differ on more than one dimension. Differences are due to frequency, intensity, duration, attack transient, harmonic and formant structure, and so forth. Individuals can make use of the independent variation on each dimension, and we would expect listeners to be able to identify a large number of sounds; thus we cannot distinguish on that basis whether music and speech sounds are unique. The distribution of confusions or errors, however, has been found to be a useful tool to characterize music or speech sounds.

Categorical Perception versus Continuous Perception
To review the argument, for sinusoid tones of varying frequencies and intensities, listeners will confuse similar tones, and the probability of a confusion (or the ability to distinguish between two tones) can be predicted by the physical similarity between two tones. The results for speech and music sounds may not follow this pattern. Speech sounds may have evolved to be maximally different, both in physical articulatory characteristics and in resulting perceptual outcomes. In an identical way, instruments may have evolved to utilize the possible mechanisms of sound production (blowing into or across a tube; blowing through a vibrating reed; striking, plucking, or bowing a string or membrane; hitting a plate or block) and thereby maximize the differences among the resulting perceptual outcomes. Moreover, even within the playing range of a single instrument, the acoustic properties between individual notes change in complex ways (see chapters 4 and 8). There is not a gradual change, which would occur when changing the intensity or frequency of a pure tone. On top of this, we hear meaningful speech segments, musical notes, and environmental events, not acoustic segments or the frequency and intensity of complex tones. It is very hard to hear speech as nonspeech. Similarly, to the musically trained it is very hard to hear intervals and chords as frequency ratios, and to the normally experienced listener, it is very hard to hear events as acoustic energy. Events name themselves. The properties of the acoustic energy that supports a meaningful percept may be available only with extreme difficulty. Normally, we are not even aware of these acoustic properties. We listen to meanings, and irrelevant perceptual differences are ignored. Alternative acoustic realizations of the same events are categorized and treated as functionally equivalent.

This suggests one way in which listening to speech and music may be different from discriminating pure tones. For pure tones, discrimination is based on the physical difference. For speech and music, discrimination is based primarily on the functional label (meaning) of the two sounds. This leads to the paradoxical result that if all pairs of elements are equally different physically, two elements that are perceived as being representatives of the same speech or the same musical class cannot be discriminated from each other at all, and yet two sounds that are perceived as being representative of different speech or different musical classes are discriminated with nearly 100% accuracy. Listeners are unable to pay attention to the physical properties of the sounds. They hear the sound (or sounds) as a /p/ or a musical fifth interval; they do not hear the /p/ as transitions plus formants or the fifth as a pair of frequencies. Listeners hear the categories of speech or music.

Experimental procedures   To determine whether speech and music sounds are perceived categorically as perceptual entities or are perceived continuously as varying acoustic sounds, two procedures are typically used. In the first procedure, one stimulus element is presented individually, and subjects are required to label or categorize that stimulus; for example, is it from category 1 or 2? In the second procedure, three elements are typically presented sequentially. The first two are different sounds—A and B—and then one of the first two sounds is repeated. Thus, a trial could be either ABA, ABB, BAA, or BAB. The subject judges whether the third element matches the first (as in the sequence ABA) or the second (as in the sequence ABB). If a listener cannot make the discrimination and guesses, the percentage correct will be 50%. This procedure has been termed the *ABX format*.

For example, suppose we have six square-wave tones that vary the attack transient length. The attack times are equally spaced on a linear scale: 20 msec, 60 msec, 100 msec, 140 msec, 180 msec, and 220 msec (diagrammed at the top of figure 9.2). Furthermore, suppose that elements A (20 msec), B (60 msec), and C (100 msec) are typically categorized as I, and D (140 msec), E (180 msec), and F (220 msec) are typically categorized as II. If these elements are perceived categorically, then in the identification experiment, elements A–C ought to be labeled I with nearly 100% agreement; elements D–F ought to be labeled II with nearly 100% agreement. Now consider the outcome if the six elements are perceived continuously. If this is the case, then the end points—A and F—will still be labeled with 100% agreement. However, the intermediate elements—B and C plus D and E—would be more ambiguous. One possible outcome is that B would be labeled I for 80% and II for 20% of the time, while C would be labeled I for 60% and II for 40% of the time. The converse labels would occur for elements D (II, 60%; I, 40%) and E (II, 80%; I, 20%). For categorical perception, the identification function would show a steep shift at one element; in contrast, for acoustic perception, the identification function would be a smooth continuous curve. These two possibilities are shown in figure 9.2, panel a.

Differences also occur in the ABX discrimination test. If these elements are perceived categorically, then discrimination ought to be at the chance level if the two sounds in each pair lie within the same category (comparisons A/B, B/C, A/C, as well as D/E, E/F, D/F). Although the two stimuli differ acoustically, the meaningful categorical perception will be identical,

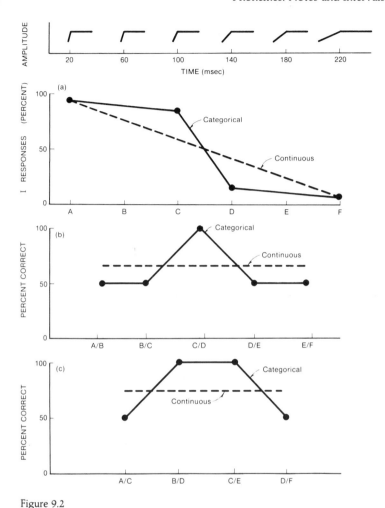

Figure 9.2

Theoretical outcomes distinguishing categorical and continuous perception. The six tones are portrayed at the top of the figure. Theoretical results for the identification or labeling experiment are shown in (a). For categorical perception, stimuli A, B, and C ought to be labeled I nearly 100% of the time, and stimuli D, E, and F ought to be labeled I rarely (they would be labeled II nearly 100% of the time). For continuous perception, the end-point stimuli, A and F, ought to be labeled with nearly 100% consistency, but the middle stimuli ought to be labeled I and II an equal number of times. The outcomes for a one-step discrimination between adjacent stimuli are shown in (b). Each comparison is labeled on the x-axis. For categorical perception, stimuli in different categories are easy to discriminate, but stimuli in the same category are difficult to discriminate. For continuous perception, each pair of stimuli are equally easy to discriminate (the actual level of performance depends on the stimulus differences). The results for a two-step discrimination between alternating stimuli are shown in (c). For categorical perception, stimuli in different categories are easy to discriminate, but stimuli in the same category are difficult to discriminate. What is critical is that between-category discrimination is better than within-category discrimination. For continuous perception, each pair of stimuli is equally easy to discriminate. We might expect two-step discrimination to be better than one-step discrimination.

and subjects will not be able to discriminate among them. Discrimination ought to be nearly perfect if the two elements come from different categories (comparisons A/D, A/E, A/F, B/D, B/E, B/F, C/D, C/E, C/F). In contrast, if perception is based on acoustic differences, then the difficulty of discrimination should be related to the differences in attack time. Discrimination should be poorest between adjacent pairs A/B, B/C, C/D, D/E, and E/F. Discrimination should be better for tones two steps apart (e.g., A/C, B/D, C/E, D/F) and should continue to improve as the attack time of the two stimuli becomes more different. The stimulus pairs that distinguish between categorical and auditory perception are those that are physically similar but on opposite sides of the category boundary (e.g., C/D, C/E, B/D). Because the two stimuli fall in different categories, categorical listening should yield excellent discrimination. Because the two stimuli are physically similar, auditory listening should yield poor discrimination. For categorical perceiving, the event is heard directly; the acoustic properties of the sound are recovered from memory. For auditory perceiving, the acoustic properties are heard directly; the perceptual events are deduced.

Speech   Notions concerning the significance of categorical versus auditory perception distinction have undergone dramatic change. Originally, consonants were thought to be perceived categorically, and vowels and nonspeech sounds were thought to be perceived continuously. This outcome meshed with the auditory nature of each sound: each consonant is created by specific articulatory movements that restrict the vocal tract, and it may be physically impossible to create sounds between two consonants—that is, the articulations and resulting speech sounds are discontinuous. In contrast, vowels are distinguished by an open vocal tract and by more constant formant frequencies, and it seems possible to "shade" from one vowel to another (e.g., diphthongs). For these reasons, vowels were thought to be perceived acoustically and continuously.

This characterization of categorical perception is overly simplified. First, categorical perception can be found when judging vowels, musical intervals, and nonspeech stimuli as well as consonants. Second, categorical perception is not a fixed, unalterable perceptual process. Categorical perception depends on the task and on the memory and judgment of the listener. Each of these issues will be discussed below in an effort to determine what insights categorical judgments can give to the nature of perceiving.

We will begin with a traditional example of categorical perception in consonants, in which the stimulus variation was the second formant transition that distinguishes among the voiced stop consonants /b/, /d/, /g/ (Liberman et al. 1957). A schematic spectrogram illustrating different second formant transitions is shown in figure 9.3.

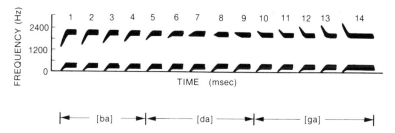

Figure 9.3
Spectrogram representations of variations of the second formant transitions. The syllable typically perceived is labeled below the spectrogram (adapted from Liberman, Harris, Hoffman, and Griffith 1957).

In the identification task, each possible sound is presented alone, and subjects were required to name the sound. The results are shown in figure 9.4. The important outcome is that the changeover from hearing /b/ to /d/ and the changeover from hearing /d/ to /g/ occurs very rapidly, taking about two steps in the second formant transition. Identification functions are also shown for vowels in which the frequency of the second formant was varied. Here, the changeover between two adjacent vowels is slower and smoother. It takes about three steps to go from one vowel to the next.

This, however, is just half of the story. To demonstrate categorical perception, observers should not be able to discriminate between sounds that are placed in the same category (i.e., labeled the same). All sounds labeled /b/ should be indistinguishable, as should sounds labeled /d/ or /g/. Listeners should be able to distinguish among adjacent sounds if they are labeled differently and fall into different categories. (A weaker criterion is that listeners should be able to make more accurate discriminations between categories than within categories.) As shown in figure 9.4, this was the case. Subjects could not discriminate between stimuli 1/2 or 2/3 (stimuli 1, 2, 3 were labeled /b/); but subjects could discriminate between stimuli 3/4 (stimulus 3 is typically labeled /b/ and stimulus 4 is typically labeled /d/). The same outcome also occurred in even more striking fashion at the boundary between /d/ and /g/. Vowel perception is "weakly" categorical. Listeners can discriminate between vowels within the same category, but they discriminate more accurately at the boundaries, as shown by the peaks at these points. This sort of research seemed to demonstrate clearly that perception of the dynamic stop consonants differed from the perception of other auditory stimuli. Phonetic segments in different categories could be discriminated; segments in the same category could not, because they are perceptually equivalent.

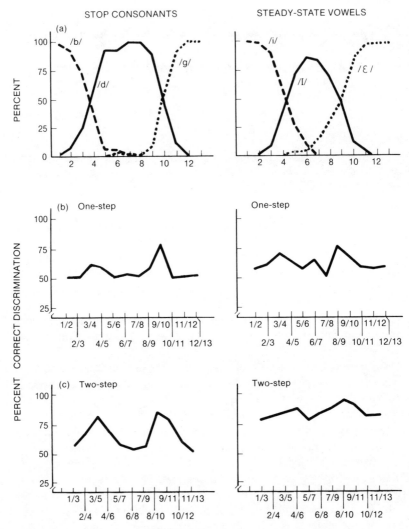

Figure 9.4
Identification and discrimination functions for stop-consonants and vowels. The results from the identification experiment is pictured in (a). Subjects labeled the stop consonant sounds as either /b/, /d/, or /g/ and labeled the vowel sounds as either /i/, /ɪ/, or /ɛ/. The results for the one-step and two-step discriminations are displayed in (b) and (c), respectively. The one-step and two-step discriminations are labeled along the x-axis. Chance performance is 50% (adapted from Pisoni 1971).

Nonspeech analogues   This view proved to be overly simplified, at best. It soon became clear that categorical perception was the outcome of a complex set of perceptual processes. This led to extensive experimentation attempting to uncover the factors that led to categorical perception. One approach was to simulate speech segments with nonspeech analogues. If categorical perception were demonstrated here and if a psychoacoustic explanation could be found, then categorical speech perception would be merely an example of basic auditory perceptual functioning. Experiments of this sort were performed by Miller et al. (1976) and by Pisoni (1977). Miller et al. (1976) simulated voice onset time, which is one distinguishing feature between voiced and unvoiced consonants (i.e., the time delay in first formant voicing). A nose burst simulated the stop consonant release and aspiration, and a buzz (a short pulse repeated 100 times per second) simulated the voicing. To create a voice onset time (VOT) continuum, at one extreme the buzz onset preceded the noise onset by 10 msec (VOT = − 10 msec; prevoicing), and at the other extreme the buzz onset came after the noise onset by 80 msec (VOT = 80 msec; unvoiced). To demonstrate that categorical perception could be due to timing asynchrony using pure tones, Pisoni (1977) used a sinusoid tone of 500 Hz as the first partial and a sinusoid tone of 1500 Hz as the second partial. The sounds were speech-like but did not resemble speech. Examples of the stimuli illustrating the timing variation are shown in figure 9.5a.

To demonstrate categorical perception, subjects labeled each sound in an identification experiment and then attempted to discriminate among each pair of adjacent sounds. If categorical perception occurred, a sharp change in identification as a function of asynchrony time was expected, and discrimination performance ought to be better for points of sounds labeled as being in different categories. A schematic representation of the results are shown in figure 9.5b. Clearly, based on the two criteria described above, perception was categorical: the Miller et al. (1976) and Pisoni (1977) data show that the transition between labeling the sounds into categories occurred within two 10-msec steps. Pisoni's date suggest that the tonal stimuli were perceived in three categories: (1) sounds in which the lower frequency component preceded the upper frequency component by 20 msec or more; (2) sounds in which the onset difference between the two components was 20 msec or less; (3) sounds in which the higher frequency component preceded the lower frequency by 20 msec or more. Moreover, discrimination was best between sounds that were labeled differently— that is, al onset delay times at which the sounds underwent a categorization (around 50%). Discrimination did, however, tend to be better than chance for sounds *within* a category for noise/buzz stimuli, but discrimination between stimuli in the same category was close to chance level for two sinusoidal stimuli.

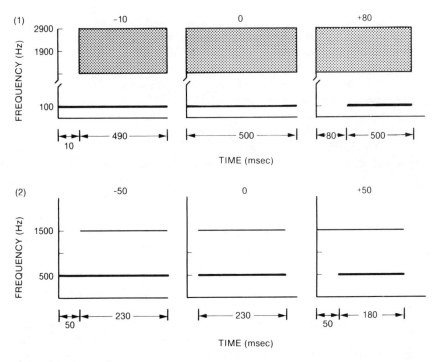

Figure 9.5(a) (this page)
Nonspeech analogues used to investigate categorical perception. In (1), a noise burst (dotted rectangle) is presented along with a 100 Hz pulse that simulates voicing (Miller et al., 1976). At one extreme, the voicing precedes the noise burst by 10 msec (voice onset time = −10 msec). At the other extreme, the noise precedes the voicing by 80 msec (VOT = 80 msec). In (2), two sinusoid tones are presented. The 500 Hz tone is more intense; that frequency line is drawn darker and thicker. The 500 Hz and 1500 Hz tone may differ in onset asynchrony from −50 msec to +50 msec (Pisoni 1977).

Figure 9.5(b) (facing page)
Results for both types of nonspeech stimuli. The results for the noise/buzz stimuli for experienced listeners are presented in (1). The solid lines represent the percentage of identifications in which the buzz preceded the noise. The identification curves are "categorical"; there is a sharp, rapid change in identification. The vertical dotted line gives the timing at which the two labels are 50–50. The dashed line represents the discrimination performance between pairs of adjacent stimuli. Discrimination is best about when the identification shifts from buzz noise to noise buzz, which demonstrates that discrimination is better between categories. The light horizontal line is chance discrimination performance (33% in this case) (adapted from Miller et al. 1976). The results from the two sinusoid tone stimuli are presented in (2). The solid and dashed lines portray the identification task. The solid lines are the percent of judgments that the lower tone leads, and the dashed lines are the percent of judgments that the higher tone leads. These identification functions are categorical; there is a sharp, rapid change in labeling. The 50–50 points are indicated in msec in each graph. The dotted line portrays the two-step discrimination performance. Again, the performance is categorical: discrimination is best between stimuli in different categories. That is, discrimination is best straddling the point where the two labeling curves cross (adapted from Pisoni 1977).

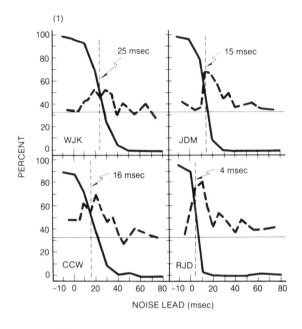

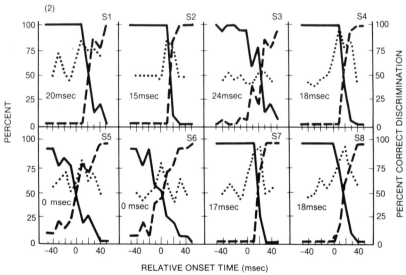

These two similar experiments lead to the same conclusion, that categorical perception can occur for nonspeech sounds. Why does categorical perception occur for these stimuli and not for others? One possibility is that there are natural auditory sensitivities or discontinuities, so that continuous, equal acoustic changes are not perceived continuously. In other words, a change of 10 msec in onset delay may not be perceivable at some values of lag time but may lead to distinct perceptual changes at other values of lag time. Because of the temporal properties of the auditory neural system, there may be distinct changes in timbre even between two stimuli that differ in voice onset time only by 10 msec. For example, longer voice onset times may lead to the perception of two tones (Rasch 1978, discussed in chapter 7) or may lead to the perception of successive tones (Hirsh 1959). Shorter voice onset times may lead to the perception of one "richer" complex tone or the perception of simultaneous tones. The ability to discriminate among sounds falling in different categories would result from the different quality (timbre) of the sounds in different categories.

Now imagine pairs of sounds like those used by Pisoni. Given a neural limitation of the auditory system, it may be difficult to discriminate between two sounds in one category in which the two harmonics seem to be two separate tones, or between two sounds in a second category in which the two harmonics seem to fuse. However, because of the timbre change, it may be easy to discriminate between two sounds in different categories. In this case, the identical difference in onset synchrony between two sounds can have different outcomes: two sounds that fall in one category are difficult to discriminate, but two sounds that fall in different categories are easy to discriminate. The natural sensitivities of the auditory system generate categorical perception.

These results illustrate categorical perception for nonspeech sounds that mimic speech sounds. The question still remains whether acoustic/perceptual discontinuities discussed here can completely explain categorical perception. My evaluation of the research outcomes is that it cannot. For example, Rosen and Howell (1987) argue that there are no discontinuities in the perception of onset asynchrony. They propose that the ability to perceive whether the onset of two tones is simultaneous or successive is a simple function of the amount of asynchrony. Moreover, the voice onset times that characterize phonemic differences vary among languages and often do not match the perceptual discontinuities found in psychophysical experiments. We will return to this issue at the end of this section.

Music   Another approach taken to study categorical perception is to investigate other domains, such as music, that do not possess psychophysical discontinuities. If categorical perception is found for music, a "learned" continuum, then the argument for the generality of categorical perception across all kinds of auditory events becomes much stronger. The basic frame for musical scales is the octave: two tones with frequencies in the ratio of 2 to 1. Each octave is divided into twelve steps so that adjacent notes are related to each other by a constant frequency ratio. The spacing between adjacent notes is termed a *semitone* and is identical to adjacent keys on a piano. The difference between two notes is further divided into 100 cents. Western music is based on the intervals between two notes. One technique for teaching the intervals instructs musicians to conceptualize each interval as a qualitatively distinct entity. One interval might be though of as "tinny," a second one as "steady" or "calm," another as "desolate." Alternatively, musicians are instructed to associate each interval with a familiar melody. The aim of these approaches is to make each interval a unique event (like a phoneme), in contrast to thinking of the intervals as a continuum of frequency ratios.

Categorical perception can arise for individual notes and for individual intervals. Listeners with "perfect" pitch ought to perceive individual notes categorically, because the continuous range of frequencies is labeled according to the discrete frequencies of the scale notes. This means that the identification function should show a sharp change in labeling from one note to the next as frequency moves from one note toward the other, and discrimination of acoustic changes that straddle the boundary between two notes should be better than equivalent changes around one note (i.e., notes should be like stop consonant syllables). Listeners with relative pitch ought to identify the standard tonal intervals provided by a musical scale categorically, because the continuous range of frequency ratios is labeled according to the musical intervals generated by the notes of the scale. The labeling of intervals should show a sharp change in going from one interval to the adjacent interval, and discrimination between intervals that straddle boundaries ought to be better than discrimination between intervals within boundaries (i.e., intervals should be like stop consonant syllables).

Experiments by Siegel and Siegel (1977a, b) and Burns and Ward (1978) have shown these predictions to be correct. For example, Burns and Ward have demonstrated categorical perception of musical intervals by musicians with relative pitch. In this work, subjects were presented pairs of notes that varied across three musical intervals: (1) 262 Hz to 311 Hz, a minor third (m3); (2) 262 Hz to 330 Hz, a major third (M3); (3) 262 Hz to 349 Hz, a fourth (4). An identification task revealed categorical labeling: there was a sharp and distinct transition in labeling the intervals (top panel of figure 9.6). In the discrimination task, the musicians were presented two intervals and were asked to judge which one was wider. The difference between the intervals was 1/4 semitone (25 cents or roughly 5 Hz), 3/8 semitone (37.5 cents or roughly 7 Hz) or 1/2 semitone (50 cents or roughly 10 Hz). The results, shown in figure 9.6, illustrate that discrimination was maximum

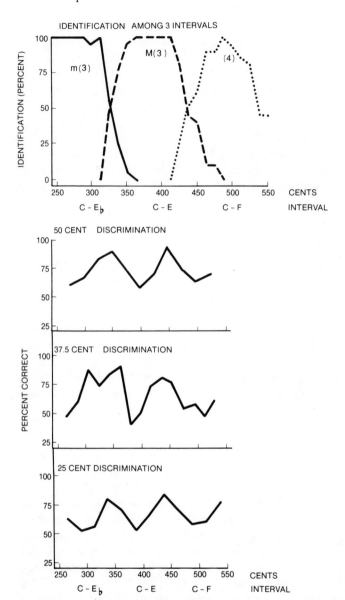

Figure 9.6

Categorical perception of musical intervals by a musically trained subject. The top panel portrays the identification of three intervals. The labeling of the C–E♭ interval is represented by the solid line, the C–E interval by the dashed line, and the C–F interval by the dotted line. The difference between any pair of adjacent notes is defined as 100 cents. Therefore, the C–E♭ interval equals 300 cents. Identification is categorical; the transition between each interval is sharp and rapid. The discrimination between two intervals that differed in frequency separation is pictured below for three frequency differences. For each curve, discrimination is highest when the two intervals straddle the interval identification boundary (i.e., around 350 and 450 cents) and discrimination is poorest in the middle of each interval (i.e., around 300, 400, and 500 cents) (adapted from Burns and Ward 1978).

at the boundaries between the musical intervals where each test interval was perceived and labeled as being a different musical interval. It was difficult to discriminate between two intervals perceived as being the same musical interval. (Remember that each discrimination test was between two intervals that differed by the same frequency.) Nonmusically trained subjects did not show categorical perception.

In addition, Siegel and Siegel (1977a) have shown that listeners with absolute pitch categorically label individual notes. They assign scale names to nonscale frequencies so that any frequency is labeled reliably as one of the scale notes. The evidence for categorical perception comes from the sharpness of the labeling of the individual frequencies in the identification task. In the same fashion, listeners with relative pitch categorically label intervals. They assign interval names to nonmusical intervals so that any frequency ratio is labeled reliably as one of the common musical intervals. Data from nonmusical subjects do not show any evidence for categorical performance, because they do not reliably label individual notes or intervals as being of one sort. The results for absolute pitch are shown in figure 9.7.

Siegel and Siegel (1977a) did not perform the discrimination task. However, they did ask musicians to describe intervals that were sharp or flat (Siegel and Siegel 1977b). Surprisingly, even trained musicians were unable to do this. They tended to rate out-of-tune intervals as being in tune and were unable to distinguish sharp from flat. Siegel and Siegel (1977b) presented the intervals in isolation, and this might have produced the poor performance. To create a musical context, Wapnick, Bourassa, and Sampson (1982) presented intervals at the end of a ten-note passage. In this situation, musicians were more able to distinguish out-of-tune intervals (58% in a musical context versus 51% in isolation) although the percentage of incorrect judgments was still very high. Even trained musicians in a musical context make within-category discriminations with difficulty. This suggests that musical intervals are perceived categorically.

Experimental variations   Categorical perception is thus not restricted to one class of auditory events. It is found when there is no conceivable auditory-system discontinuity, which illustrates that categorical perception can be an acquired, attentional disposition. Categorical perception represents one way of encountering our environment. In adapting to and understanding the unpredictable perceptual world, normally it is unnecessary to make fine distinctions among events. In listening for meaning, it is of little importance to discriminate among the acoustic versions of [pa].

If categorical perception represents a strategy for unpredictable and difficult perception, we might simplify the discrimination task and/or provide enhanced feedback about the relevant acoustic differences among events within a category, in order to "weaken" the degree of categorical

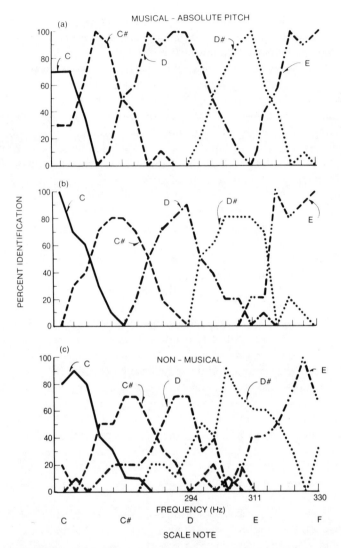

Figure 9.7
Categorical perception of individual notes by musically trained listeners with absolute pitch. Panels (*a*) and (*b*) portray the identification of individual notes by two listeners with absolute pitch. The identification curves are categorical; the curves are relatively narrow and there are relatively sharp, rapid changes in the labeling between adjacent notes. Panel (*c*) portrays the labeling of notes by a listener without absolute pitch. The results are not categorical; the identification curves are wide and erratic (adapted from Siegel and Siegel 1977a).

perception experimentally. Both types of experimental variations have been tried. Consider first the more difficult ABX discrimination task; the listener does not know which particular stimuli will be presented on any trial (i.e., low predictability), and the listener must make the difficult double comparison of A to X and B to X, which taxes the auditory memory. Categorical perception is thus likely to occur. In contrast, the AX (same-different) discrimination task is simpler. Experiments using the AX task yield far better within-category discrimination, which indicates more continuous perception (Crowder 1982). Furthermore, if the discrimination task is simplified so that there is little uncertainty as to which stimuli will be presented, categorical perception is not found for stop consonant voice onset time or for nonspeech analogues as used by Miller et al. (1975) (Kewley-Port, Watson, and Foyle 1988). Consider now the effects of acoustic training on categorical perception. Normally, listeners search for meaning units (phonemes) and are unaware of the sorts of acoustic differences that occur among examples of the same segment. Teaching the relevant acoustic differences by means of clear examples, providing feedback on each trial, and using the simple AX discrimination task improves performance on speech sounds to such a degree that it resembles continuous acoustic discrimination. It is even possible by these means to introduce a new discrimination not normally found in the native language (Carney, Widin, and Viemeister 1977; Jamieson and Morosan 1986; Pisoni et al. 1982).

Implications of Categorical Perception
Where does this leave us? Categorical perception demonstrates two aspects of audition. Sensory-auditory perception involves fine-grained discriminations between acoustic signals. Categorical event perception (phonetic, musical note, and interval) involves identification of speech or musical segments or other types of events. When categorical perception is found, it illustrates the dominance of the second mode: event perception takes precedence over sensory perception. The physical energy must generate an acoustic signal that gives rise to the categorical percept, yet the acoustic stimulus is relatively unavailable to the consciousness. The sensory information is not completely lost; with appropriate training procedures, it is possible to learn to make fine-grained discriminations.

Why should categorical perception occur? From one perspective, categorical perception is necessary for meaning perception to occur at all. Across all domains, the same event is represented by a range of vastly different acoustic signals. In speech, this is due mainly to coarticulation. Categorical perception might appear to be a simplified style of perception that throws away subtleties in the signal. However, the time pressure of discourse makes categorical perception imperative. Listeners must make rapid discriminations between sounds in different categories, or normal connected conversation cannot occur. Similar issues occur in music. The same note may be represented by different acoustic signals in different contexts. Part of these differences are due to the physical processes that underlie music production. Part of these differences are due to human performance. The performance of even highly skilled instrumentalists and singers is very variable. There are gross pitch deviations in any musical performance, and yet listeners are unaware of them. Seashore ([1938]/1967) comments: "The hearing of pitch is largely a matter of conceptual hearing in terms of conventional intervals" (p. 269).

Feature detectors   How does categorical perception come about? Until the early 1980s, categorical perception was assumed to be unique to speech, and the accepted theory was that there were "feature detectors" in the auditory system. These detectors were thought to be maximally sensitive to the complex distinctive features that underlie the contrasts among speech sounds. For example, the difference between the voiced (e.g., /b/, /d/, /g/) and the unvoiced stop consonants (e.g., /p/, /t/, /k/) might be coded by the time delay for the onset of vocal cord vibration. The notion was that there were sets of specific detectors, some of which "fired" maximally when the voicing was simultaneous with the burst (voiced) and others that fired maximally when the voicing was delayed (unvoiced). The perception of voiced or unvoiced consonants depended on which set of detectors fired more rapidly. The original view was that these feature detectors were innate, because categorical perception of the voiced-unvoiced distinction had been found in very young infants.

The feature detector notion stems from the theoretical position that phonetic differences can be described by distinctive features (voiced-unvoiced; place of articulation; stops-fricatives, etc.), and that there are separate detectors for each distinctive feature. Supporting the possibility of such detectors has been physiological research in animals that has discovered single cells that appear to detect complex stimulus events. Various stimuli are presented to the animal, and the goal is to find the environmental events that maximally stimulate a cell to fire. When this is determined, the individual cell is said to be tuned to that event or to be a detector of that event. Vision research has found cells responsive to bars of light in specific orientations, responsive to movement in one direction, and responsive to complex forms. One of the most elegant demonstrations of the power of this technique was performed on frogs by Lettvin et al. (1959). They found a set of cells that responded to small, dark, convex objects that moved jerkily with respect to the background. They termed this cell, for obvious reasons, a bug detector. Given the nativistic position of many linguists (Chomsky 1965), it seemed natural for them to speculate that specialized detectors had evolved to decode language.

Although the idea of feature detectors is undeniably appealing, there are many objections to its plausibility. First of all, few important speech or music characteristics are based on one stimulus characteristic. In an article critiquing the notion of feature detectors, Diehl (1981) lists nine acoustic variables that affect the voicing-nonvoicing distinction: (1) voice onset time (as discussed above); (2) duration of voiced formant transitions; (3) first formant onset frequency; (4) onset frequencies and directions of second and third formant transitions; (5) spectral characteristics of the following vowel; (6) duration of the following vowel; (7) duration of aspiration; (8) intensity of aspiration; and (9) direction of fundamental frequency change at voicing onset. It seems unlikely that there are independent feature detectors for each one of these variables. In addition, context (e.g., speaking rate) would affect the magnitude of many of these variables. Each detector would have to vary its output on the basis of the overall context. This in turn would destroy the simple idea of a passive detector that directly perceives one distinctive feature. On top of these problems, to postulate feature detectors as a general explanation for categorical perception in other auditory domains would require an implausible variety of detectors (e.g., musical note, musical interval). Feature detectors therefore seem to be an inappropriate explanation for categorical perception.

Auditory discontinuities   In the sense that feature detectors were hypothesized to account for the supposed uniqueness of categorical perception for speech, an alternative model based on natural acoustic functioning was hypothesized to account for the supposed common occurrence of categorical perception across all domains. This view hypothesizes that the sharp shifts in labeling and the within-category versus between-category discriminations reflect discontinuous changes in auditory sensitivity. These changes in auditory sensitivity do not occur along single dimensions. The data presented in chapter 2 illustrate that the sensitivity to attributes like frequency or intensity changes in a gradual fashion throughout the range. Discontinuous changes occur in stimulus complexes when each component can vary against the context provided by the other part. At various points, the perceived sound undergoes Gestalt-like perceptual changes, and these points generate the sharp labeling denoting the various categories. Discriminations within a category would be difficult, and discriminations between sounds that straddle the boundary would be relatively easy because of the enhanced perceptual difference.

Consider two examples of this process. The first comes from the research of Miller et al. (1976) and Pisoni (1977), discussed previously. In that work the onset asynchrony of two "partials" of a complex signal was varied systematically, and a continuous series of stimuli was broken into perceptual categories by listeners. The second is hypothetical and stems from experiments in which the direction of the second formant transition is varied as illustrated in figure 9.3. Here the transition ranges from rising in frequency, to remaining constant in frequency, to decreasing in frequency. Again there is a series of stimuli separated by equal physical changes that may perceptually cleave into classes or categories because of the changing relationships between the transition and the steady-state section. Work on the perception of frequency glides has suggested that the perception of upward and downward frequency glides is not symmetric (Pols and Schouten 1987). If the rate of frequency change is low, listeners hear upward and downward frequency glides as decreasing in pitch. Only if the rate of frequency change is high do listeners hear an upward frequency glide increasing in pitch. This difference may be due to neural adaptation.

To summarize, an auditory theory points out that small variations at specific points along physical dimensions can produce sharp jumps and qualitative changes in perceptual outcomes, although equal variations at other points yield only small changes. In order for these qualitative changes to be perceptually relevant, they must mesh with acoustic changes caused by variations in the production process. For example, the voiced-unvoiced production process generates differences in the onset times of the formants. This acoustic consequence becomes perceptually important because differing onset times can create a qualitative perceptual change. In the same way, the place of the articulation production process generates formant transitions of different directions. The transition direction is relevant because it can create a qualitative perceptual change. In other words, categorical perception can be understood by juxtaposing acoustic changes due to physical production variations with qualitative perception changes due to auditory system functioning. Although I have emphasized the match between production and perception in yielding categorical perception, it may be that categories emerge solely because of the qualitative changes brought about by physical variation or solely because of changes brought about by the functioning of the nervous system. I imagine an evolutionary model here. Out of the multiplicity of sounds that a human can make, those that "stuck" as speech sounds possessed a fit between production and perception. Diehl (1987) uses the term "mutually enhancing." The speech sounds that are selected must be easy to discriminate, and discrimination is maximized by utilizing acoustic contrasts that are enhanced and maximized by the normal functioning of the nervous system. Possibly for these reasons, frequency or pitch is not universally used as a speech feature. Frequency is continuous and perception of pitch is continuous, and thus frequency would not work very well as a feature.

This is a psychophysical theory relating physical properties to psychological ones. It is an applicable to vision or taste as it is to audition. It resembles Gibson's (1979) notion of affordances in which perceptual systems and the physical world are attuned. But does it help us to understand categorical perception? I think the answer is yes and no. At a simple level, categorical perception does depend on the ability to distinguish between sound segments. Thus perceptual sensitivities can generate possibilities for categorization. By the same token, production processes that yield qualitatively different acoustic signals can generate possibilities for categorization. However, there is impressive evidence that most examples of categorical perception cannot be easily explained on the basis of auditory sensitivities. Even the case of voice onset time, which we have discussed extensively, is inconsistent. First, the finding of categorical perception is contingent on the experimental conditions. Second, the use of voice onset time as a speech feature varies across languages and rarely coincides with any psychoacoustic estimate of the detection for onset asynchrony. For example, there are boundaries in Spanish (e.g., a voice onset time at 0 msec) different from English and still different boundaries in Thai (e.g., a voice onset time at 40 msec). Bilingual individuals switch their boundaries and resulting categories as a function of the language context. This would be impossible if there were fixed perceptual sensitivities.

Summary of Categorical Perception
I think it is best to conceptualize categorical perception as a multifaceted phenomenon, not explainable solely in terms of specific production mechanisms or solely in terms of specific auditory discontinuities. All perceiving comes from acoustic patterning, and all perceiving can yield both the categorization and the auditory detail. Acoustic information is usually ambiguous and supports many possibilities. The best perceptual strategy would be to retain as much acoustic information as possible for as long a time as possible to allow surrounding information to influence the percept. Extensive experience and practice may lead to shortcuts, to an emphasis on the categorical information most useful for natural events. This is true for the average language user and for the trained musician. In extremely overlearned and overpracticed domains it may be quite difficult to switch attention to the acoustic details, but it is obviously possible. Without the ability to switch among perceptual levels, our perceptual capabilities would be static, and we would be unable to tune to the properties of the stimulation.

9.2 Context Effects

Perception occurs in a context; the meaning of any acoustic segment depends on the signal in which it is embedded. Event perception requires integration. There are multiple sources of information concerning any perceptual event, and the perceiver must, in some way, combine that information. To judge climbability, you must integrate slope, height, and traction and also consider equipment, skill, and fatigue. A steep slope can be climbed if there is enough traction, but a shallow slope cannot be climbed if it is a sheet of ice.

One means of distinguishing among various kinds of context effects is based on temporal relationships. Following a distinction espoused by Repp (1982), one type of context effect is termed a *trading relationship*. A trading relationship exists among variables that specify the same contrast. For "climbability," slope and traction enter into a trading relationship. Change in one environmental variable that would lead to a perceptual switch can be countered or compensated by variation in a different variable in order to maintain the original percept (e.g., an increase in perceived slope that might lead to the perception that it is unclimbable can be countered by an increase in perceived traction, foot and hand holds, etc.). Trading relationships, therefore, are due to the production of a contrast and occur at one point in time.

A second type of context effect may be termed a *surround relationship*. A surround relationship exists when the surrounding variation influences the perception of one type of contrast, although these variations do not enter into the production of the contrast. For example, shoes, climbing equipment, skill, and fatigue would influence perceived climbability, but these factors do not enter into the perception generated by the mountainside. In the same way, speaking rate can influence the perception of stop consonants, and overall speech pitch can influence the perception of vowels (see chapter 5). In none of the cases are the actual properties of the event varied (as in trading relationships); rather, the perception of the same physical signal is altered and determined by its surrounding context.

Given that events generate complex interrelationships among physical energies, the perception of events in all modalities and within one modality should involve context relationships. In what follows I will concentrate on speech perception, because the demonstration of trading relationships and surrounding context effects has been an important part of theory construction. Comparable context effects that have been investigated in nonspeech and music contexts will also be considered. (Many of the following results were discussed briefly in section 5.3.

Trading Relationships
The one-to-many and many-to-one relationships between the acoustic signal and the percept are characteristic of all aspects of speech. The same acoustic cue can generate different phonetic contrasts, and conversely, different acoustic cues can lead to the same phonetic contrasts. Our interest lies in the many-to-one relationship: a particular articulator movement yields several acoustic cues (the many) to a speech segment (the one). Each

cue is sufficient, but not necessary, so that listeners can use only one in isolation to identify the particular segment. Alternatively, listeners can use the interrelationships among the cues created by the articulation so that a change in one acoustic cue leading to a phonemic change can be offset by a change in a second acoustic cue reinstating the original phonemic percept.

A simple example may clarify the trading relation concept. Suppose we asked individuals to judge comfortableness for different combinations of temperature and humidity. In an experimental chamber, the temperature (10° C to 38° C) and humidity (50% to 100%) is varied independently. There will be a trade between temperature and humidity; this relationship is plotted in figure 9.8. The x-axis is temperature and the y-axis is humidity. A line connects combinations of temperature and humidity that are judged to be equally comfortable. All combinations above the curved line are judged less comfortable, and all combinations below the line are judged more comfortable. It is possible to trade temperature for humidity; a higher temperature can be compensated by a lower humidity. I think it is quite

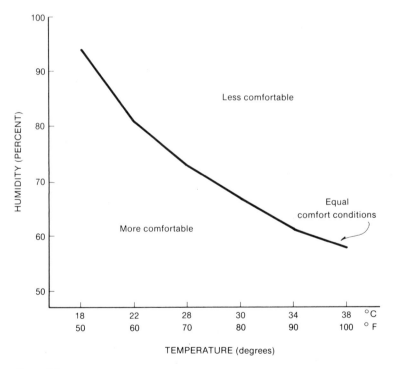

Figure 9.8
A hypothetical trading relationship involving humidity and temperature. The solid line represents combinations of humidity and temperature that are judged equally comfortable.

plausible that the judges could not judge temperature and humidity independently (although they could probably verbalize the tradeoff abstractly).

Speech   An example of a trading relationship in speech concerns the voiced-voiceless distinction. Research has shown that both the voice onset time and the onset frequency of the first formant transition contribute to the distinction between a voiced and voiceless consonant. For a voiceless stop consonant, the voicing is delayed (T_2 in figure 9.9), and the first (voicing) formant (F_1) will begin at a higher frequency because of the delayed initiation of the F_1 transition (see figure 9.9). As the voicing is delayed further, the onset frequency will continue to increase.

Summerfield and Haggard (1977) asked listeners to distinguish whether a sound segment more resembled a voiced /g/ or voiceless /k/. Shorter voice onset times should lead to the perception of the voiced /g/; longer voice onset times should lead to the perception of the voiceless /k/. A lower F_1 onset frequency should lead to the perception of the voiced /g/; a higher F_1 onset frequency should lead to the perception of the voiceless /k/. The trading relation thus becomes: (1) if F_1 onset frequency is lowered (to signal a voiced stop), then voice onset time must be lengthened (to signal a voiceless stop) to maintain the same phonemic percept; (2) similarly, if F_1 onset frequency is raised (to signal a voiceless stop), then voice onset time must be shortened (to signal a voiced stop) to maintain the same phonemic percept. Summerfield and Haggard found that voice onset time could be traded for F_1 onset frequency. If F_1 frequency was 200 Hz, then voice onset time to achieve equal judgments of /g/ and /k/ was 34 msec; if F_1 frequency was increased to 400 Hz, then the voice onset time time to achieve equal judgments of /g/ and /k/ must be reduced to 23 msec. These results are depicted by the solid line in figure 9.9. One cue can compensate for another.

A second example involves the distinction between [sei] and [stei] (Best, Morrongiello, and Robson 1981). The acoustic consequences of the complete closure for the stop /t/ are the introduction of a silent gap and a lower F_1 onset frequency. We might expect the trading relation to work in the following way. Because a longer gap and lower F_1 onset frequency both signal [stei], we would need to lengthen the silent interval to maintain the perception of [stei] if the F_1 onset frequency were increased. This is the analogous relationship to that described previously for the voice-voiceless distinction. Experimentally, this indeed was the outcome: when the F_2 onset frequency was increased from 230 Hz to 430 Hz, then the silent interval required for the perception of [stei] needed to be increased from 32 msec to 57 msec.

These researchers went a step further to demonstrate that alternative stimuli generated by means of a trading relation ($F_1 = 230$ Hz, silence =

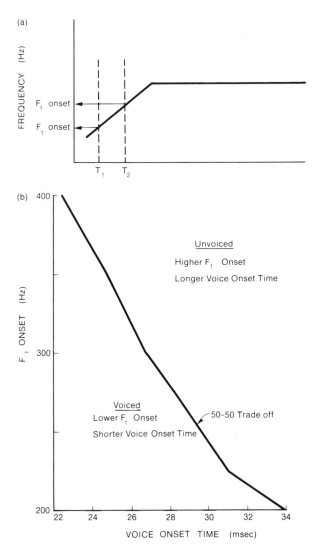

Figure 9.9
Voiced-unvoiced trading relationship. The first formant is pictured in (a). At longer voice onset times, T_2 as opposed to T_1, the F_1 onset frequency increases. Therefore, it is possible to trade the F_1 onset frequency against voice onset time. Voiced stop consonants will be characterized by lower F_1 onset frequencies and shorter voice onset times (combinations in the lower left corner in b); unvoiced stop consonants will be characterized by higher F_1, onset frequencies, and longer voice onset times (combinations in the upper right corner in b). Identification data for this trading relationship is shown in (b). The solid line shows the combinations of onset frequency and voice onset time that give rise to equal probabilities of voiced and unvoiced judgments (adapted from Summerfield and Haggard 1977).

32 msec; $F_1 = 430$ Hz, silence $= 56$ msec) are perceptually indistinguishable. Listeners found it difficult to discriminate between two sounds, one characterized by a low F_1 frequency [stei]–short silent gap [sei] and one characterized by a high F_1 frequency [sei]–long silent gap [stei]. Although the discrimination task minimized memory requirements, listeners were not given feedback to allow isolation of relevant stimulus differences, which in other cases has proved critically important to improving within-category discrimination.

Finally, to demonstrate that trading relationships are unique to the speech mode, Best, Morrongiello, and Robson constructed analogous stimuli composed of sinusoid tones that could be perceived as nonspeech sounds. Each formant was replaced by a sinusoid tone that had the same frequency transitions as the speech replicas. These sinusoid analogues were indeterminate; some listeners heard them as speech but others heard them as nonspeech (i.e., chimes, ringing qualities, etc.). What is important here is that listeners who heard the sounds as speech displayed a trading relationship: length of silent interval could be traded by onset frequency of F_1. On the other hand, listeners who heard the sounds as nonspeech did not display the same trading relationship. In fact, half of these listeners paid attention to only one cue at a time: some discriminated solely on the basis of the temporal interval between the /s/ hiss and the remainder of the sound, and others discriminated on the basis of the quality of the sinusoid tones. These listeners did not integrate the two kinds of acoustic information —gap duration and spectral information—although listeners who heard these sounds as speech did integrate them.

On the whole, results concerning perception of nonspeech analogues tend to be contradictory. The analogues are ambiguous, and many aspects of the experiment—instructions, practice, demonstrations, and exemplars —lead subjects to use different perceptual strategies. This generates different outcomes; in some cases there is equivalence between speech and nonspeech analogues, in others, there is not. (This issue will be discussed later in the chapter.)

Trading relationships illustrate that one acoustic cue can compensate for another. A different way of stating this outcome is that the interpretation of one cue depends on the value of another cue. The interpretation of voice onset time depends on the interpretation of the F_1 onset frequency. For some values of the F_1 onset frequency, a variation in voice onset time brings about a perceptual change; for other values of the F_1 onset frequency, the identical variation in voice onset time does not bring about a perceptual change.

Nonspeech analogues Trading relationships can also be found for nonspeech analogues. Parker, Diehl, and Kluender (1986) studied the trading relationship that distinguishes the voiced /b/, as in [aba] or "rabid," from the voiceless /p/, as in [apa] or "rapid." Two significant articulatory acoustic variables are: (1) the duration of the stop closure: short closures characterize voiced consonants and long closures characterize voiceless consonants; (2) vocal cord vibration: presence of vibration characterizes voiced consonants and absence characterizes voiceless consonants. The trading relationship exists because a longer closure time (leading to a voiceless percept) can be compensated by the presence of vocal cord vibration (leading to a voiced percept).

Parker, Diehl, and Kluender constructed a set of speech and nonspeech analogues ranging from [aba] to [apa]. To construct the speech stimuli, the vowel speech segments were replicated by computer and silent intervals ranging between 20 msec and 120 msec were inserted. Vocal cord "buzzing" was inserted within the silent intervals. To construct the nonspeech analogues, square-wave vowel segments were generated with timing identical to that of the speech segments, and silent intervals (20 msec to 120 msec) were inserted. Square-waves do not sound like speech formants, and no subjects reported hearing the analogues as speech. The vocal cord buzzing was identical to that used for the speech stimuli. In some square-wave analogues there was a falling frequency glide into the silent interval and a rising frequency glide out of the silent interval (see figure 9.10). The preglide "aimed" toward the lower frequency vocal cord vibration and the postglide aimed back toward the final square-wave harmonics.

There was a clear trading relationship for the speech stimuli. The closure duration at which the percept switched from [aba] to [apa] increased if vocal cord buzzing was present. The same trading effect occurred for the fall-rise frequency glide square-wave stimuli although there was no effect for the steady-state square-wave stimuli. However, the shift in duration was three times greater for the speech stimuli (about 18 msec) than for the square-wave stimuli (6 msec).

The authors suggest that vocal cord vibration reduces the perceived duration of the gap, which means that the duration must be increased (if the vibration is present) to yield a voiceless percept. However, the vocal cord vibration will not be integrated into the ongoing sound and generate the trading relationship unless its frequency is similar to the adjacent vowel segments, because of stream segregation. Without frequency contiguity, the vocal cord vibration will form a separate stream and not affect the phonemic contrast. For this reason, a trading relationship was found for the fall-rise square-wave analogue because the trajectory aimed toward the vocal cord buzzing leading to integration. A trading relationship was not found for the steady square-wave analogue because the buzzing was perceived as a separate event (see chapter 7).

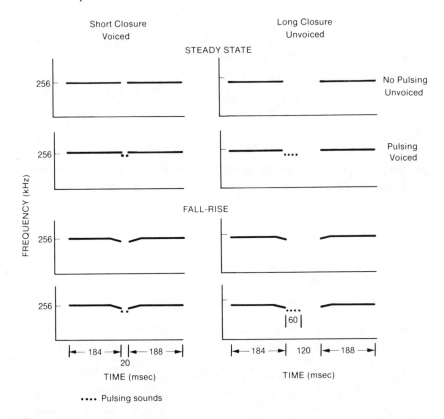

Figure 9.10
Trading relationship for a nonspeech analogue. Voiced consonants are characterized by short closure durations and vocal cord vibration; unvoiced consonants are characterized by long closure durations and the absence of vocal cord vibration. The analogues are created by using a square wave with a fundamental frequency of 256 Hz. (only the 256 Hz fundamental is shown). The square waves have the identical timing as the speech sounds, but they do not have the same formant frequencies. Steady-frequency analogues are pictured in the top four panels; fall-rise frequency analogues are pictured in the bottom four. For the fall-rise analogues, the transitions pointed toward the pulsing (88 Hz). All analogues in the left column had a closure duration of 20 msec; all analogues in the right column had a closure duration of 120 msec. The pulsing is represented by filled dots. The pulsing filled the 20 msec closure and filled one-half the 120 msec closure (adapted from Parker, Diehl, and Kluender 1986).

Summary of trading relationships   Trading relationships often involve fundamentally different kinds of articulatory/acoustic cues. The relationship may equate a temporal cue (voice onset time or silent interval duration) to a spectral cue (F_1 onset frequency or vocal cord buzzing); it puts both on a common perceptual scale. The seeming noncomparability of temporal and spectral factors has led some speech researchers to argue that trading relationships demonstrate that speech perception is based on articulatory gestures. However, the demonstration of trading effects with nonspeech stimuli, understandable from psychoacoustic principles, suggests that trading relationships are general perceptual phenomena. Moreover, data measuring adaptation and recovery of neural firing rates over time suggest mechanisms that connect the two kinds of factors. This will be discussed in chapter 12.

Surround Context Effects
Four types of surround effects that influence the categorization of a phoneme will be discussed: (1) preceding and following speech segments; (2) vocal tract physiology; (3) speaking rate (similar effects will be illustrated for nonspeech by varying perceived rate); and (4) the visual patterning of the mouth and lips due to articulatory movements.

Speech segments   The surrounding speech context affects the acoustic signal for a phonemic segment, and listeners must compensate for these coarticulation effects. One example involves the /sh/–/s/ distinction when followed by vowels /a/ or /u/. The vowel /u/ tends to invoke anticipatory lip rounding, which has the effect of lowering the frequency of the fricative noise. The vowel /a/, in contrast, does not bring about a lowering of the fricative frequency. Listeners must compensate in order to "capture" the fricative. As an example, suppose that the first spectral peak frequency for /sh/ is 2500 Hz and that the same spectral peak frequency for /s/ is 2800 Hz. If the lip rounding lowers the frequency by 200 Hz, then [shu] is 2300 and [su] is 2600 Hz. A 2600 Hz formant is thus representative of /sh/ when /a/ follows but representative of /s/ when /u/ follows. On this basis, when listeners hear the following /u/, they mentally "bump up" the formant frequencies, and this would bring about a higher percentage of /s/ responses and a lower percentage of /sh/ responses. Mann and Repp (1980) have shown this to be the case using synthetic stimuli. In fact listeners overcompensated: the perceptual correction (in terms of changes in categorization as a function of frequency change) was nearly twice as large as the actual frequency change in production.
    A second experiment investigated the effect of the liquid consonants /l/ and /r/ on the perception of stop consonants and vice versa (Mann 1980). The stimuli consisted of two-syllable utterances: alda, alga, arda, arga.

These two-syllable stimuli demonstrate context effects in two directions: (1) the production of the liquid (/l/ and /r/) affects the production and subsequent perceptual categorization of the stop consonant (/d/ and /g/), a left-to-right effect; and (2) the production of the stop consonant affects the production of the liquid (particularly the part of the liquid that overlaps the stop).

The rationale is as follows. The production of /l/ in the front of the mouth makes it more likely that production of the coarticulated stop consonant will also move toward the front of the mouth. Stop consonants following [al] are thus more likely to have acoustic characteristics of the front stop consonants ([da]) than of the back stop consonants ([ga]. To compensate, listeners must interpret ambiguous coarticulated stop consonants differently, depending on whether [al] or [ar] precedes. Following [al], listeners should interpret the resulting formants as coming from a stop consonant articulated farther back in the mouth. In fact, for the identical formants, listeners gave more [ga] responses (back of mouth) following [al] than following [ar]. Moreover, the context effects also worked right to left. Suppose anticipatory articulation of the following stop consonant affected the noise spectrum of the prior liquids. Then the [al] in "alga" should differ from the [al] in "alda" and for the same reason [ar] should differ in "arga" and "arda." We might expect the "imprint" of the stop consonant to change the liquid. On this basis listeners should be able to guess whether the bisyllable was "alga" or "alda" (arga or arda) solely from the liquid segment. This was the outcome; listeners were able to identify the missing stop consonant from the articulatory changes caused by the consonants in the prior syllable. The right-to-left context effect is a direct result of coarticulation-induced variation. In contrast, the prior left-to-right context effect was a compensation for the coarticulation.

Speakers Speakers affect the acoustic signal because of their vocal architecture—the size, shape, and damping of the vocal apparatus—and their speaking rate. There are large differences among individuals in their speaking pitch. The formant frequencies of children can be 50% greater than that for adult males. Moreover, the frequency differences are not consistent across formants, consonants, or vowels. As the vocal tract grows it also changes shape, and this in turn moves the formants around to varying degrees (Fant 1960). Traditionally, as explained in chapter 5, it was thought that listeners utilized the formant frequencies of "cardinal" vowels to induce information about the vocal tract to interpret the speech signal. These cardinal or point vowels—/i/, /a/, and /u/—represent unique extremes in the acoustic and articulatory vowel space, and they are acoustically stable for small changes in articulation (Stevens 1972).

However, a model for compensation based on point vowels is probably incorrect. In research investigating vowel identification, investigators presented vowels embedded in consonant-vowel-consonant syllables. Listeners were able to identify a high proportion (about 85%) of vowels, even with random presentation of the unknown speakers. Presentation by only one speaker improved identification just slightly. Moreover, experience with the point vowel sounds did not improve identification (Shankweiler, Strange, and Verbrugge 1977). It could be that the syllable, containing formant transitions both into and out of the vowel, allows the listener to map out the speaker's unique vocal tract resonances. In fact, work with "vowel-less" syllables created by eliminating the center portions of consonant-vowel-consonant syllables demonstrated that the transitions were sufficient for identification (Parker and Diehl 1984). Vocal tract compensation may not be necessary because the syllable provides enough information for the vowel independent of talker variation. Each vowel may have a unique onset and offset formant transition as well as duration, which would allow identification of the vowel across different speakers. The issue remains open.

We can illustrate speaker normalization in the perception of consonants. Mann and Repp (1980), in the process of investigating the effect of a vowel following a fricative (discussed above in the subsection on speech context), utilized male and female speakers. They created hybrid syllables by combining a synthetically produced fricative noise with a lower frequency male- or higher frequency female-generated vowel. Listeners interpreted the fricative noise spectrum on the basis of the inferred vocal tract size induced from the vowel and therefore perceived a different fricative for lower and higher pitch vowels. The identical fricative burst would be perceived as a higher frequency /s/ for a lower pitch male vowel, but would be perceived as a lower frequency /sh/ for a higher pitch female vowel.

Speaking rate   To investigate the effect of speaking rate on consonant categorization, experiments have attempted to demonstrate that the perception of a phonemic contrast is influenced by the duration of the syllable itself or is influenced by the perceived articulatory rate induced by the surrounding context.

Summerfield (1981) has investigated the effect of speaking rate information on the voiced-voiceless contrast. First, Summerfield demonstrated that the voice onset time of the voiceless stops was strongly affected by rate. As speaking rate increased, the voice onset time delay between the burst and voicing onset for the voiceless consonants decreased as much as 20 msec. This makes the difference in voice onset time between voiced and voiceless consonants smaller at faster speaking rates. Summerfield has further illustrated that when categorizing stop consonants listeners compensate for the change in voice onset time due to speaking rate. Summerfield created a common set of synthetic stop consonant syllables (like [ba] or [pa]) in which the voice onset time was systematically varied from about 10 msec to about 45 msec. The simulated articulatory rate was varied by changing the duration of the steady-state, roughly vowel portions of a preceding phrase, "A bird in the hand is worth two in the bush." At slow rates, the boundary between voiced and voiceless consonants occurred at a voice onset time of 35 msec or more; at the fast rate this transition occurred at 25 msec or more. The categorization data thus mirror the production data: in production and in perception, at faster articulatory rates shorter voice onset times distinguish between voiced and voiceless consonants. The major influence of rate information occurred in the time period in which the speaker was articulating the stop consonant itself. The ability to push the voice onset time around by rate variation suggests that the simple auditory resolution theory proposed previously to explain categorical perception can be only part of the answer concerning the rationale underlying the use of voice onset time as a phonemic contrast.

Miller and Liberman (1979) also investigated the effect of duration on the categorization of syllables. The contrast between stop consonant syllables (e.g., [ba]) and semivowel syllables (e.g., [wa]) can be signaled by the duration of the consonant formant transitions. Faster transitions (16 msec to 40 msec) tend to lead to the perception of the stop consonant [ba]; slower transitions (40 msec to 64 msec) tend to lead to the perception of the semivowel [wa]. In a series of experiments, Miller and Liberman varied not only the duration of the transition but also the overall duration of the syllable. In the first experiment, they varied the syllable duration by extending the steady-state formants (representing the vowel) as shown in figure 9.11. A longer syllable suggests a slower articulatory rate, which in turn suggests that the transition duration would also be slower. At slower articulation rates, therefore, the perceptual change from [ba] to [wa] should occur at longer transition durations, and at faster articulation rates the change should occur at shorter durations. The results indicate that as the syllable duration increased from 80 msec to 296 msec (i.e., from a fast to a slow, simulated articulatory rate), the transition durations for the 50–50 point of [ba]/[wa] judgments increased from 32 msec to 47 msec. Listeners expected the [wa] transition to be longer because of the slower articulation.

This outcome is shown in a slightly different way in figure 9.11. In (a) the entire syllable is 80 msec, representing a fast articulatory rate. A transition of 40 msec (one-half of the syllable) is perceived to be a slow transition so that the percept is [wa]. In (b) the entire syllable is 160 msec, representing a slow articulatory rate. The identical transition of 40 msec

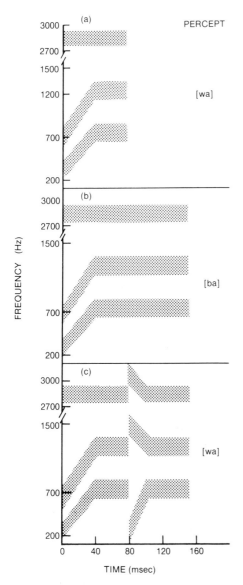

Figure 9.11
Effect of perceived articulation rate on [ba]/[wa] identification. Faster transitions lead to the perception of [ba], slower transitions to the perception of [wa]. The transitions are not perceived absolutely, but within the context of the entire syllable or syllables. In (a), the overall duration of the syllable is short. Therefore, the transition is perceived to be longer and the percept is [wa]. In (b), the overall duration of the syllable in long. Therefore, the identical transition is perceived to be shorter and the percept is [ba]. In (c), the overall duration is identical to that in (b). However, the last 80 msec represents the syllable [da]. The initial [wa] or [ba] is then assumed to be articulated in the first 80 msec, as in (a), and the percept shifts back to [wa] (adapted from Miller and Liberman 1979).

(now one-quarter of the syllable) is perceived to be a fast transition so that the percept switches to [ba].

In the second experiment, Miller and Liberman increased the overall duration by adding a 72 msec formant transition appropriate for an ending [da] to create a "bada-wada" continuum (in c). Listeners interpreted the [da] ending as specifying a faster articulatory rate, even though the overall syllable duration equaled the duration of syllables with the extended steady-state formant. On this basis, listeners perceived a transition of 40 msec as [wa]. Syllable duration in itself is obviously not the critical determinant. Adding steady-state information shifted categorization in one direction; adding a final transition shifted it in the opposite duration. It is the internal structure that determines the perceived rate and the perceived syllable.

These results illustrate that perceived articulatory rate has a marked effect of phonemic categorization. In all instances, the acoustic contrast, which remained the same, was interpreted differently as a function of perceived rate.

Nonspeech analogues   These findings for speech stimuli have led to experiments replicating these results using nonspeech sounds. Pastore (1983) investigated the ability to discriminate differences in onset and in offset asynchrony between two sine-wave components. He argued that this task was analogous to judging the voice-voiceless contrast. Pastore reasoned that listeners would judge a consonant as voiced when they could not perceive the delay in voicing—that is, when all the formants appeared to begin together. Listeners would judge a consonant as voiceless when they could perceive the delay—that is, when they could perceive that the formants started at different times. This task was therefore an attempt to probe the capacity to make this distinction. The important result here was that the ability to discriminate the onset and offset asynchronies decreased at longer overall durations. When the stimulus duration was 10 msec, subjects could discriminate an onset asynchrony of 4 msec or more, but when the stimulus duration was 300 msec, subjects could discriminate an onset asynchrony of 12 msec or more (parallel results were found for offset asynchronies). In a similar vein, Kelly and Watson (1986) have shown that it is much more difficult to distinguish a low-high frequency sequence from a high-low frequency sequence when the pair is followed by a trailing tone (analogous to the vowel component). The trailing tone interferes with the discrimination of temporal order and can create a trading relationship.

These results with nonspeech stimuli are analogous to those found for synthetic speech: namely, the voiced-voiceless contrast is a function of syllable duration. Speech theorists attribute the change to listeners correcting for articulation rate (as in Summerfield's work, described above). However, Pastore's results offer a psychoacoustic interpretation. The longer

syllable duration makes it more difficult to perceive the asynchrony specifying a voiceless consonant, and therefore judgments of voiced consonants
increase (this may be due to the increased energy masking the initial
segment of the syllable). The voice onset time must thus be increased to
yield a voiceless consonant. Although psychophysical data of this sort
do not provide a complete explanation of context effects, they do point
out that general psychoacoustic processes may lead to understanding many
of these effects.

Pisoni, Carrell, and Gans (1983) have replicated all of the [ba] to [wa]
tradeoff results of Miller and Liberman (1979) using nonspeech analogues.
The nonspeech analogue consisted of four or five sinusoid tones, each of
which represented the middle frequency of one formant. Each sinusoid tone
mimicked the frequency contour—onset transient, steady state, offset
transient—of the formant (see figure 9.12). Pisoni and his colleagues (1983)
demonstrated that the transition between the perception of rapid spectrum
changes (as in /b/) and slower spectrum changes (as in /w/) changed as a
function of overall duration and, moreover, that the internal structure of the
stimulus (as found by Miller and Liberman) also affected the judgments.
The authors argue on this basis that context effects are not peculiar to the
perception of speech signals, but may reflect general psychophysical principles underlying categorization.

Implicit so far is the idea that articulatory rate information supplies the
context that allows the listener to interpret one durational cue that distinguishes between the two possible consonants. However, it can be difficult
to understand how the context and cue can be identified and separated.
What part of the acoustic signal is cue and what part is context? In an
experiment, we can keep one part constant and vary another. We then
argue that the constant part represents the cue and the variable part
represents the context. In ongoing speech, however, this distinction becomes untenable; both the cue and context are simply parts of the same
unified speech signal. Possibly it would be better to give up the notion of
a cue interpreted in a context and replace it with the concept of an event
perception. The categorization of a phonemic contrast is based on the
listener's sensitivity to the timing of spectral information specifying identity.
It appears that the important temporal information spans the interval
required for the articulatory events involved in the production of the
consonant itself. This temporal spectral information is not ambiguous; there
is no need to interpret it in a context. Rather, the syllable is articulated at a
given rate and the acoustic signal gives us the perception of both the
phonemic element and the articulatory rate at the same time. It should
be noted, however, that though an event perception theory can explain
changes intrinsic in the syllable itself, it cannot explain perceptual changes
caused by the rate of more distant speech.

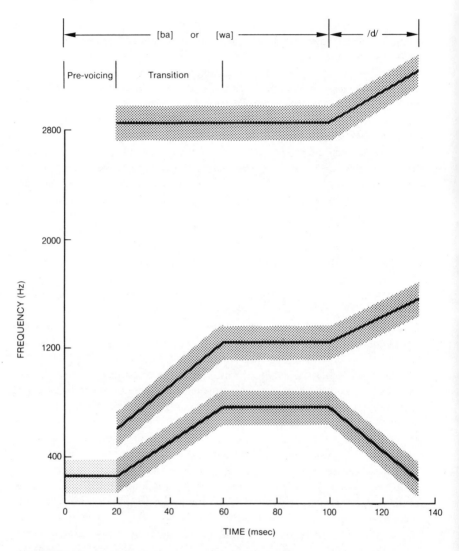

Figure 9.12
Nonspeech analogues used to investigate the effect of overall duration on stimulus identification. The speech formants are portrayed by the stippled areas. Sinusoid tones at the
middle frequency of the formants are used to create the analogues. The sinusoids are
portrayed by the solid lines in the middle of the formants (adapted from Pisoni, Carrell, and
Gans 1983).

Visual articulation information   We usually think of vision as being the dominant perceptual system for moving and orienting in space. It is the change in visual information over time that gives us knowledge about the spatial world. When we come to speech, the role of vision is less clear. Lip reading is very difficult. Although there are roughly 40 phonemes, Summerfield (1983) estimates that there are about 12 distinct visual configurations of the mouth, lips, jaw, and teeth. Thus 63% of sounds are invisible to sight. Nonetheless, visual articulation information can be very helpful in difficult, noisy conditions. Improvements of as much as 50% have been reported (Sumby and Pollack 1954).

Speaking brings forth both visual and acoustic structure concerning the articulatory production of speech sounds. To experience a coherent event (one speaker uttering one message), the visual and auditory information must be integrated into one percept; there must be some information received that the visual and acoustic energies result from the same event, and some common time-keeping system that keeps the two sources of information in step with each other. In other words, observers must have some way to relate what they see to what they hear. (Even two- to four-month-old children show distress if the auditory and visual signals are desynchronized; see Dodd 1979.) In general, there should be a bias toward perceiving simultaneous bimodal (visual plus auditory) information as signifying a single event. On the one hand, if the bimodal information can signify two or more different events, the built-in flexibility of the perceptual systems could lead to the perception of the "average" event, the "common denominator" event, the fusion event, or the event specified by one modality with the information specified by the other modality "misperceived" to fit the dominant percept. On the other hand, if the bimodal information drastically conflicts, it may overwhelm the tendency to single-event perception and yield disparate auditory and visual events (analogous to stream segregation).

In a striking example of audiovisual integration, MacDonald and McGurk (1978) and Summerfield (1979) visually presented a person saying simple consonant-vowel syllables coupled with a synthetic acoustic recording of the same type of syllable. In some cases, the visual and acoustic syllables were identical, in others the two conflicted. Surprisingly, few adults commented that the visual and auditory information conflicted; they (mis)perceived one syllable. In some responses, one or the other modality signal predominated, usually the visual. In others the percept was a syllable not presented in either. The interplay between the modalities was strongest when the acoustic and visual information was ambiguous.

For example, if an acoustic [ba] was synchronized with a visual [ga], the majority of listeners reported [da]. If, however, an acoustic [ga] was synchronized with a visual [ba], listeners reported [ga] or the hybrid [b'ga]. The first outcome can be rationalized as follows. The articulation of [ba] requires closing the lips completely. When the visual display of [ga] does not show a complete lip closure, listeners do not categorize the acoustic sound as a [ba]. Instead, they reported a different voiced stop consonant ([da]), which does not require lip closure (less frequently, listeners will report the correct acoustic signal [ga]). In the second case, the visual input [ba] displayed a lip closure. Lip closure can occur for stop consonants articulated at the back of the mouth like [ga], so that there was a possibility that [ga] had been articulated. The other articulatory possibility is the combination [b′ga] with the /b/ signaled by the visual lip closure and the [ga] by the acoustic signal. These two possibilities account for the predominant percepts. The influence of conflicting visual information may be strong only with simple acoustic syllables. Other work (Easton and Basala 1982) utilizing simple words found little or no effect from the visual articulation information.

In an interesting analogy to the research on the effect of speaking rate, Green and Miller (1985) combined visual information generated by fast or slow articulation rates with a constant acoustic pattern. Listeners compensated for the visually perceived articulation rate in the same way that they compensated for auditory articulation rate: they shifted the voice onset time and discriminated voiced from voiceless stop consonants as a function of the visually perceived rate.

Visual and auditory information is also integrated in nonspeech perception. Massaro (1987) generated a set of sounds ranging from a simulated pluck (short rise times) to a simulated bow (long rise times), as well as one visual scene of a clear pluck and one scene of a clear bow. As found for speech, even when the auditory and visual information conflicted, there was a coherent percept. The dominant modality tended to be the less ambiguous one.

These results illustrate that listeners combine the visual and acoustic information specifying events. There is a subtle synthesis of the two domains to yield a unified percept. Both the visual and acoustic physical energy represent the same act, and they are interchangeable for that very reason. It is the patterning of information that leads to phonemic perception (or, in general, event perception). Speech perception is not based solely on acoustic analysis and thus may be better understood in a more general theory.

9.3 Implications of Categorical Perception and Context Effects

Comparisons among Speech, Nonspeech, and Music

The production and perception of speech (and nonspeech) is enormously complicated, and this material only skims the surface. To provide some overview, various perceptual effects are "crossed" with speech, nonspeech analogues, and musical stimuli in table 9.1. Many of the combinations have been discussed in this chapter. For other combinations, I have suggested equivalent phenomena. Still other combinations have been left blank, because the comparable phenomena are unclear.

The leftmost column represents speech stimuli. What is common to all the diverse perceptual phenomena is that each requires the listener to integrate information over time or across different kinds of physical energies. What can make all the speech outcomes coherent is an appeal to the dynamic, overlapping, and continuous articulatory events that underlie the signal. If we merely refer to acoustic cues or features in isolation (e.g., voice onset time, first formant onset frequency, second formant transition duration), then many of the perceptual phenomena become incomprehensible. That features are important in speech perception has been taken for granted, but we must remember that all features are embedded in a continuous flow and that it is the temporal relationships that give each feature its meaning. There are many features that affect any phonemic contrast, and the evaluation of each must depend on the magnitudes of all the others. The number of computations seems overwhelming. For this reason, the categories of speech may be perceived without recourse to the abstracted features. The categories may be perceivable because of acoustic invariants created by the constraints on production. Features may reflect only scientific abstractions. From this perspective, context effects are examples of higher-order invariants.

The middle column represents nonspeech stimuli, which are modeled after speech stimuli. Typically, a formant is replaced by a single sinusoid tone. These nonspeech analogues tend to be ambiguous: some listeners hear them as speech, others hear them as speechlike, and still others hear them as nonspeech.

Overall, the results are puzzling. In some instances, the results resemble those for speech stimuli, in other instances the results do not. This outcome should not be surprising, because the ambiguous sound of the nonspeech analogues allows for different perceptual strategies. There are instances in which combining information from several dimensions would yield a more accurate perception, but there are also situations in which judgments along one physical dimension would be preferred. For example, if we need to judge weight, we should not be influenced by the size or shape of the object. The experimental context (e.g., instructions, training procedures, expectations of the researcher) restricts to some degree the way subjects respond to the nonspeech analogues and thus helps determine the outcomes.

The final column represents musical stimuli. Much of this column is empty. Categorical perception occurs for individual notes and intervals, but

Table 9.1
Comparison of Perception of Speech, Nonspeech Analogues, and Music

Phenomenon	Domain		
	Speech	Nonspeech analogue	Music
Categorical perception	Stop consonants /b/–/d/–/g/	Buzz–sine wave combination; asynchronous sine wave tones	Relative pitch for musical intervals
Context effects			
Trading	Voice onset time traded for F_1 onset frequency	Closure duration traded for low frequency pulsing	Spectral dimension traded for inharmonicity to determine timbre*
Surround			
Coarticulation	/sh/–/s/ distinction cued by formant shifts brought about by following vowel		Identification of notes or chords changes due to overlapping acoustic energy created by instrument or performer*
Pitch	Fricative distinction cued by frequency of vowel formants	Perception of frequency glides affected by surrounding steady frequencies	
Duration	[ba]–[wa] formant duration contrast cued by vowel duration	Glide duration contrast cued by steady tone duration	
Audiovisual Integration	Identification of stop consonants		Music perception affected by perceived movements of performer (violin bowing)

*Hypothesized.

it is harder to specify and demonstrate the various kinds of context effects. We can imagine a trading relationship for the timbre of an instrument. In the previous chapter, timbre was described in terms of three dimensions. Thus it might be possible to trade the magnitude in one dimension for the magnitude in a different dimension. For example, the amount of initial inharmonic energy could be traded with the degree of synchrony of the partials to maintain instrument identity. Other context effects, such as player, instrument, and rate normalization, must also occur, but these phenomena have not been addressed. In the same way that the speech signal reflects many of the subtleties of the articulatory acts, so must the musical signal reflect the subtleties of playing.

A Biologically Distinct Speech Mode?

The unraveling of the context-dependent, coarticulated acoustic signal into speech is an extraordinary accomplishment. However, I do not believe that we need to appeal to a specialized cortical module to explain the perception of phonetic units. Instead of conceptualizing phonetic and auditory perception as alternate modes, I think the critical issue is how phonetic perception is constructed out of auditory perception.

Consider the effect termed *duplex perception,* based on an experimental procedure designed to illustrate a distinct phonetic mode. The essence of this procedure is to demonstrate that a single part of a sound can be perceived as integrated into a phonetic unit and simultaneously perceived as a nonspeech "chirp." A demonstration by Whalen and Liberman (1987) made use of the third formant transition, which can be used to create a distinction between [da] and [ga]. As shown in figure 9.13, a downward frequency transition leads to the perception of [da]; an upward frequency transition leads to the perception of [ga]. In this experiment, the third formant was simulated by a sinusoid tone so that the transition by itself sounded like an upward or downward whistle. To create the duplex perception, the third formant transition is varied in intensity relative to the rest of the syllable. At low intensities of the formant transition, the percept was purely phonemic: listeners heard [da] or [ga] depending on the transition, but they could not hear a whistle. At higher intensities, the percept was duplex: listeners heard [da] or [ga] and also an upward or downward whistle. The perception of the whistle was veridical in the sense that listeners could discriminate accurately between upward and downward frequency transitions.

Whalen and Liberman argue that because at the lower intensities corresponding to natural speech the transition is integrated into the phonetic unit, the processing of sound as speech has priority. Only after the speech signal is extracted is any excess acoustic energy processed. In their words, the phonetic mode takes precedence over the auditory mode. Notice that

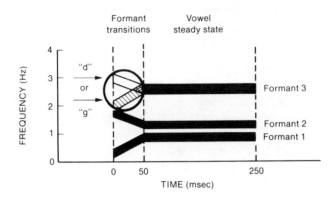

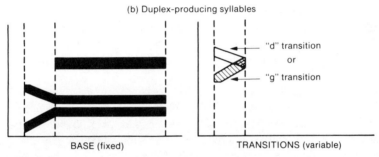

Figure 9.13
Duplex perception: priority of the speech (phonetic) mode. In a normal syllable (a), a downward or upward third formant transition generates the perception of [da] or [ga], respectively. In Whalen and Liberman's study, the intensity of transition was varied independently of the base (b). At low intensities, only the correct [da] or [ga] syllable was heard. At high intensities, both the correct syllable and a (correct) upward or downward whistle were heard (from Whalen and Liberman 1987 by permission; copyright © 1987 AAAS).

we discussed a similar experiment in chapter 7. Darwin (1984) increased the intensity of the first formant of a vowel and found that listeners did not integrate all of the added intensity into the vowel percept. The "extra" energy was heard as a second stream in exactly the same way the extra intensity of the third formant transition is heard as a separate whistle stream.

The fact that duplex perception can be seen as an example of stream segregation does not address the main issue of why the third formant transition is integrated into a phonetic unit or, more basically, why the parts of the signal are integrated into a single stream (that is, into a phonetic unit at all). One could argue from a perspective of stream organization: (1) the formant transition ending on the steady-state formant is an instance of good continuation, so the transition and steady state are likely to form one event; (2) the formants occur at harmonics of the voicing frequency so the formants are likely to form one complex tone; and (3) the onsets and offsets of the formants are synchronous so the formants are likely to form one complex tone. It is the harmonic and temporal structure that leads to the unified percept. In addition, one could argue that the perception of the transition as a separate whistle is also due to stream segregation. The change in the transition intensity at the steady-state formant onset creates an offset asynchrony.

To achieve a better perspective, it may be helpful to turn to demonstrations in visual perception (in part because these are easier to illustrate on a printed page). We can start with a simple example of a light placed on the rim of a wheel. If the wheel is rolled in a darkened room so that the wheel is invisible, people report seeing a "cycloid" movement, shown in figure 9.14. This movement is the combination of rotational motion around the wheel center and the linear motion from left to right. If a second light is placed at the center of the wheel, the perception of the rim light often changes. Observers see the rim light rotating around the center light as it moves left to right. This is not the only percept. Some observers still see a cycloid movement of the rim light along with a horizontal movement of the center light, and still other observers see a stick defined by the two lights "tumbling" in space (see Cutting and Proffitt 1982). What is important is that the percept of one light on a rim can undergo drastic changes when embedded in a configuration of lights, and equally important, the two lights can join into one motion. The perceptual system abstracts the related motions among the points. By analogy, the percept arising from one formant may be a chirp or a whistle and can be quite different from the phonetic percept arising from the coherence of two or more formants. The perceptual system abstracts the relationships among the formants. We do not hypothesize a specialized wheel-detecting perceptual mode, even though any single light does not lead to a wheel-like percept. By the same

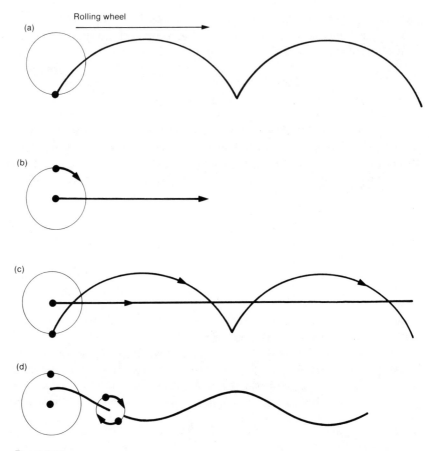

Figure 9.14
Reorganization of visual elements in a configuration of elements. A single light on a wheel rim appears to move in a cycloid motion (a). If a center light is added, the motion of the rim light changes. The rim light may be perceived circling the center light (b), the rim light still may be perceived moving in a cycloid motion (c), or the rim light and center light may be perceived tumbling along an oscillating path (d).

token, we need not hypothesize a specialized speech mode even though any single formant does not lead to a phonetic percept.

We should expect that "more" structure will result in less ambiguous percepts. For example, two or three lights spaced around the rim along with the center light should result in the stronger perception of a wheel, and a coarticulated speech sound should result in a stronger phonetic percept than a simplified replica. For example, Remez and colleagues have simulated speech sounds by replacing the formants with pure sinusoid tones having the same frequency and amplitude variation of the formants (Remez et al. 1987). What is missing is the voicing, the broadband formant structure, and the nonharmonic components. Although naive listeners hear the sounds as overlapping tones, only two-thirds of the listeners can hear these time-varying stimuli as speech if asked to listen for a linguistic message. Thus, although coherent variation in the sinusoids can lead to phonetic perception, the reduction in structure leads to a weaker sense of speech.

The emergence of phonetic elements from nonspeech components has a parallel in visual perception. The emergence of duplex perception— speech and nonspeech perception from the same element—also seems to have a parallel in visual perception. Imagine a swaying tree or a moving person. We can put lights on the various limbs of the tree or the various joints (elbows, knees, etc.) of the person. If the lights are stationary, one does not see trees or people; the lights appear at random positions. As the lights move, most viewers report seeing trees or bushes or seeing people jumping, climbing, or walking. The lights appear to follow space/time trajectories associated with simple movements (Cutting 1982; Johansson 1973). Now suppose we add extra movement to a light attached to a tree limb or joint. I suggest that the percept would change into a duplex mode: there would be the coherent swaying and people movements, plus the residual movement as a separate component. Extra movement of a tree limb would create the perception of a tree swaying plus the perception of a limb whipping back and forth as if the limb were broken or attached to something. Extra movement of a joint would create the perception of walking plus the perception of a jerky component. The perceptual system would abstract the coherent swaying or people movement, and the leftover motion would be the second part of the duplex percept. We could also imagine a poorly played clarinet or violin note in which one or more partials are too intense. The percept might well be one of correct timbre plus extra sound. The "unused" part of the signal would create a separate sound. (Bregman [1987] offers a different explanation of duplex perception that is worth careful study.)

What the visual analogies tell us, I believe, is that the perceptual systems pull out the coherent relationships among the parts, and that a single motion can be part of a common movement among all parts (like the syllable percept) and yet also represent a unique movement (like the chirp percept). In a way, we are peeling away layers of the problem and leaving the crux. Why are the three formants heard as a syllable? Does this imply a biologically specialized speech center? At the present time, these sorts of questions must remain unanswered. All I am arguing here is that there appear to be no perceptual outcomes unique to speech stimuli.

9.4 A Psychophysical Perspective

The perception of speech, nonspeech, and musical stimuli is limited by the sensitivity of the auditory system. Some of these limitations may be understood from a different perspective in considering the perception of a stop consonant. Various psychophysical relationships affect the translation of the physical energy into a psychological percept. A beginning stop consonant consists of a period of silence, a noise burst, initiation of the voicing, and the formant transitions, leading to the final steady-state formants typical of the following vowel. Before considering each component in turn, it is important to consider various psychophysical relationships that are common to all of them.

Psychophysical Constraints

Sensory discrimination   The difference threshold (i.e., the amount of energy that must be added or deleted from a stimulus to produce a perceptual change) is proportional to the intensity. The ratio between the change in intensity required to yield a perceptual difference and the stimulus intensity is constant across a wide range of intensities. (This is named Weber's ratio, after the physiologist who discovered it around 1830.) Thus, absolute sensitivity decreases as the stimulus intensity increases. If the difference threshold is 1/20, then a 1-unit change at 20 or a 5-unit change at 100 is necessary to yield a perceptual change.

The issue of discriminative ability is found for all aspects of the acoustic signal. For example, the intensity of the burst, the duration of the silence, the fundamental frequency, and the first formant onset frequency, among others, all signal phonemic contrasts. At this point, we do not have comprehensive data that indicate the discrimination threshold among values of these factors within an ongoing signal. For example, the frequency difference threshold for complex tones is equal or better than that for pure tones, because information is combined across all the harmonics (Henning and Grosberg 1968). But, compared to sustained synthetic vowels, the frequency difference threshold for rising or falling fundamental frequency tones is five to ten times poorer (Klatt 1973); the difference threshold for rising or falling fundamental frequency within a spoken sentence is ten to fifty times poorer (Harris and Umeda 1987), and the difference threshold for which frequency glide covered the wider frequency range was more than ten times poorer ('t Hart 1981). The context may decrease the resolution due to interference from other parts of the speech signal, or the context may enhance the resolution, because of comparison with "reference" or unchanging parts of the signal.

Masking   When the presence of one stimulus interferes with the perception of another stimulus, we say that one stimulus has masked the other. There are several procedures that generate masking.

1. The masking or interfering sound may occur simultaneously with the target sound (*simultaneous* masking), or the masking sound may precede or follow the target without overlapping in time (termed *forward* or *backward* masking). For simultaneous masking, the two sounds are superimposed so that the mask degrades the target by energy overlap. For forward and backward masking, the masker interferes with the processing of the target sound. The masker may interfere with the memory of the target, may summate with some aspect of the target, or may create an incorrect referent.

2. The masking sound may be the same type of sound as the target (e.g., sinusoid tone masker with sinusoid tone target), or the masking and target sounds may be of different types (noise masker with sinusoid tone target).

3. The task may require the listener to state merely whether the first stimulus was present or to identify which of several possible stimuli was presented.

The factors that affect masking are far from clear. Nonetheless, masking is an important factor in the perception of speech sounds. The burst, each formant transition, and each steady-state formant have the potential to mask another component, and of course external sounds have the potential to mask any part of the speech sound. For example, the burst may forward mask the formant transition. Miller et al. (1976) and Pisoni (1977) both suggest that categorical perception found for voice onset timing may be partially due to backward masking of the first component by the more intense second component.

Temporal discrimination   The nature of the acoustic signal makes temporal resolution and integration fundamental to perception.

1. The spectrum is a function of duration. The frequency range (bandwidth) of a signal is inversely proportional to the duration. As the

duration decreases, the bandwidth increases and the signal is smeared across a wide range of frequencies (see Section 2.1). This may be an important factor limiting frequency discrimination in short duration signals.

2. The auditory system can integrate energy over varying time periods. At the shortest time periods (about 2 msec), the listener can discriminate between the quality (i.e., timbre) of complex sounds without being able to label the components. At the longest time periods (about 200 msec), the listener can discriminate between the temporal order of events (Hirsh 1974).

3. The auditory system does not have perfect temporal resolution. The discrimination among durations of transitions, steady states, and silences should be related to the overall duration, as specified by Weber's ratio; the difference threshold will increase at longer durations. (Another factor determining resolution will be the segregation of the auditory wave into events, as described in chapter 7.)

A different aspect of temporal resolution is that of the perception of onset asynchrony. The discrimination of asynchrony is important for the voiced-voiceless contrast as well as for other delays of one formant relative to another. This resolution will vary as a function of other acoustic properties, such as overall duration or intensity (as in Pastore's [1983] work).

Spectral discrimination   The auditory system acts like a set of overlapping bandpass frequency filters. Essentially, sound energy within a frequency range is integrated or summed together (see section 2.6). The width of the *critical band* (the range of frequencies that are integrated) increases at higher frequencies (indicating tighter coupling or damping) and decreases at lower frequencies (indicating looser coupling or damping). The concept of the critical band was broad consequences. On the one hand, at low frequencies, where the critical bands are narrow (loose coupling, high Q), individual harmonics can be resolved. However, loose coupling implies a slower response time (i.e., it takes longer for the vibration to reach its maximum amplitude after stimulus onset and similarly to decay after stimulus offset). Thus, the output from these bands will "smear" temporal changes. On the other hand, at high frequencies, where the critical bands are wide (tight coupling, low Q), individual harmonics are not resolved. The superposition of the harmonics creates a complex wave in which the frequency of the amplitude modulation may match the fundamental frequency. (As described in chapter 12, this amplitude modulation [i.e., the periodicity of the wave] can have specific effects on auditory pathway fibers that can generate a sense of pitch.) However, the tight coupling implies a faster response time which means that temporal change of the higher frequencies will be detected. Moreover, sounds within a critical band combine in masking situations. The effective masking intensity is the sum of the energy within the critical band. The notion of the critical band is important acoustically, because it provides a basis for explanations of the degree of masking, loudness summation, and possible interaction of formants.

Espinoza-Varas (1987) points out that perception is always at several levels of detail. A listener can hear the gross labeling acoustic cues for the phoneme or syllable, but the listener can also hear the acoustic cues for duration, amplitude variation, frequency variation, and/or spectral variation. He argues that this may be understood in terms of the degree of spectral integration (and degree of temporal integration). Judgments of timbre involve integrating across a very wide range of frequencies (i.e., across many critical bands); judgments of phonetic category involve integrating across a narrower range of frequencies (i.e., across several critical bands); judgments of specific auditory properties involve integrating across a very narrow range of frequencies (i.e., across one critical band). Espinoza-Varas argues that all of these levels exist simultaneously and that the listener can vary the degree of integration in order to "zoom" in and out to examine the auditory detail. In the same manner, Gordon (1988) suggests that speaker-rate context effects can be based on lower-level, coarser acoustic variables.

Constraints on Speech Perception
With these general acoustic concepts in hand, we will now consider the various acoustic components of a stop consonant.

The silence   The duration of the silent interval is an important speech cue. It can lead to the incorporation of a stop consonant into a perceived syllable, as going from "slit" to "split," and distinguish between voiced and voiceless stop consonants, as in "rabid" versus "rapid." The perception of the length of silent intervals is affected by the rate and duration of surrounding elements (a "movement illusion") as well as by the similarity of the surrounding elements (a silent interval is judged more accurately when the elements form a single stream). The ability to discriminate among durations tends to determine how many values of silence can be utilized for speech contrasts.

The burst   The burst consists of a short duration of broadband noise energy. The perceived duration, intensity, and frequency of the burst provide phonemic contrasts. On this basis, energy integration, temporal resolution, and the critical bands surrounding the frequencies of the noise energy limit and determine the perceived contrasts. Moreover, the backward masking stemming from the formant transitions and masking sounds in the environment also affect the ability to discriminate the burst characteristics.

Formant transitions   The initial part of the formants provides a diverse set of phonemic cues: (1) the rate of the transitions; (2) the onset frequencies of the transitions; (3) the direction of the transitions (upward or downward); and (4) the differences in onset timing among the transitions. What is common to the burst, silence, and formant transitions are the general acoustic issues of temporal resolution, integration, critical bands, and in particular, simultaneous masking. What is unique to the formant transitions is the perception of frequency glides that terminate on a steady frequency. Research, though limited, has shown that the perceived pitch of a glide is not a simple function of the initial and terminal frequency: the pitch quality is changed by duration (Nábělek, Nábělek, and Hirsh 1970). Moreover, slower glides seem to be perceived differently from the way faster glides are perceived (Schouten 1986).

The masking of frequency glides is not well understood. The masking of a glide by noise is a function of glide duration as well as of the direction and frequency shift of the glide. It is unknown how one glide masks another. For example, does an upward glide mask another upward glide more than a downward glide? All in all, even though the formant transition is thought to be a key cue in speech perception, the psychophysical relationships underlying the perception of glides are so poorly understood that it is nearly impossible to speculate on the role of these general principles in speech and nonspeech perception.

Steady-state formants   The steady-state formants end a consonant-vowel syllable. The frequencies and durations of the steady state provide the vowel contrasts, the durations provide a cue to articulatory rate, and the frequencies further provide an end referent for the transitions. On the one hand, by serving as a perceptual anchor, the steady-state frequencies may allow for more accurate discrimination of other stimulus attributes. On the other hand, the steady-state component may backward mask the initial transient and affect the ability to determine the relative onset and offset of the formants.

Jamieson (1987) has demonstrated that the perception of frequency transitions is significantly affected by a steady-state following tone. Jamieson varied the duration of the frequency transitions and asked subjects to determine if two transitions were identical. If the transitions were presented alone, discrimination followed Weber's law: discrimination was maximum at shorter durations (10–30 msec). However, if the transitions were followed by a steady tone, discrimination was maximum at intermediate durations (40–60 msec). The steady tone interfered with the perception of shorter transitions.

Summary of Psychophysical Perspectives

What this all means is that the speech (or music) signal displayed on a spectrogram is not the signal that is transmitted to the auditory cortex. The auditory nervous system stands between the external acoustic signal, the physiological signal, and the internal psychological percept. Various fine acoustic differences may not be discriminable, and other differences may be integrated; some contrasts may not be perceived because of "smear" of masking, and other contrasts may be enhanced. Clearly, there may be acoustic explanations for categorical perception or some trading or context relationships in auditory perception. What is important in the future is to determine how the perceptual signal allows the listener to recapture the message out of the acoustic signal.

9.5 Overview

Up to this point, we have considered the perception of individual speech and non-speech elements. This emphasis has allowed us to describe the interactive nature of the acoustic variables and to illustrate how the active auditory system can make use of and even capitalize on the interactions to perceive the element. The focus on individual elements, though used, has many shortcomings, particularly because the perceptual information is found throughout the context provided by the entire signal. For these reasons, the next chapter will discuss the perception of longer passages—sentences and melodies—and how the structure of the longer passages influences the perception of the individual elements.

Chapter 10

Grammars of Music and Language

One of the most striking phenomena in the perception of speech is the degree to which our conscious experience follows the semantic intention of the speaker. Our conscious perceptual world is composed of greetings, warnings, questions, statements, while their vehicle, the segments of speech, goes largely unnoticed and words are subordinated to the framework of the phrase or sentence. Nor is this "striving after meaning" a mere artifact confined to situations in which we want to understand rather than to analyze, since our ability to analyze speech into its components is itself influenced by higher-level units
—Darwin 1976, p. 175.

We listen to events and meanings, not to acoustic sound waves. The context in which we listen profoundly affects what we perceive. We make use of all the knowledge we have: knowledge about the language, the speaker, the topic, the intent, the situation, and so on. We understand with little or no effort, yet if we tape-record an utterance and then attempt to identify each word in isolation, performance is quite poor (Pollack and Pickett 1964). The acoustic signal itself is not sufficient for communication. We understand musical events in an identical fashion. The musical context and our experience, understanding, and knowledge, in addition to the notes, affect what we perceive. The notes themselves do not generate themes, melodies, variations, or emotional responses.

The goal of this chapter is to describe the perception of melodies and sentences. However, musical notes and speech segments are not merely strung together like beads. There are rule structures that govern the order and interpretation of the elements, and production and under-standing function within these bounds. The first task will be to lay out these hypothesized structures that underpin our understanding of speech and music. Only then can we evaluate the implications of the experimental research. The structures have supplied both the rationale for initiating the research as well as the models against which to evaluate the outcomes.

10.1 Linguistic and Music Universals

As a beginning, we might ask what features are common to all languages, what features are common to all musical systems, and whether the two sets of features are identical. The goal here is to distinguish language and music from other communicative systems like mating calls or territorial signals. Linguists (e.g., Hockett 1963) have produced a list of design features of the structures required for language. These features distinguish human language from animal communication systems. All are found in every human language; in contrast, at least one is missing from every animal communication system. Although the list was generated solely from linguistic analysis, it can also be used to outline the features of the structures required for music. Five features are important here.

1. Discreteness. The messages in language are built out of a limited set of units (i.e., phonemes). Similarly, the messages in music are built out of a limited set of units (i.e., scale notes). This means that the units of speech and music should differ in sharp and discrete ways. Our restricted ability to identify and categorize stimuli and the contextual variation due to coarticulation and musical overlapping suggest that efficient communication can only occur with a relatively small set of nonconfusable elements. A small number of scale notes provides a stable framework to allow the rapid perception of melodic movement and to allow comparisons between different tunes. Discreteness, then, allows rapid and efficient communication, circumventing our limited perceptual capabilities.

2. and 3. Arbitrariness and Semanticity. An element in language is meaningful because it stands for something (semanticity). However, there is no physical or geometrical resemblance between the language unit and the thing it stands for (arbitrariness). Any sound unit(s) can stand for "dog"; there are no restrictions. There are language units in which the sounds tend to portray the thing they represent (animal sounds like "moo"), but these are the exception.

The translation of this linguistic universal to music is not obvious. To do so, we must think about the notes of a phrase as having a meaning. Within a phrase a note may be ambiguous; it may allow several tonal interpretations. The surrounding context serves to fix the meaning. That is, a note might be the focus of a phrase (termed the *tonic*, like the subject), or the note might induce an expectation so that other notes bring the phrase to a resolution. If we take this point of view, which follows the intuitions of music theorists, we can see that any given note does stand for something. This would be the musical analogue of semanticity (e.g., any note may represent a specific musical meaning). The fundamental difference is that language refers to an external thing; music does not. We might think of language having an internal and an external meaning, but music having only an internal meaning.

4. Openness. Linguistic messages can be constructed without end. There is no limit to the number of sentences. Music is also open. New compositions based on historical formulas as well as based on unique idioms are constantly being created. Musical phrases can be transformed melodically or rhythmically; they can be embedded in the middle of other phrases; and they can be expanded by adding material to the end.

5. Duality of patterning. Language is the relation between sound and meaning: the connection between the sequences of physical energy and the organized meanings in consciousness.

The design features of discreteness, arbitrariness, and openness imply that the sound system is made up a small set of meaningless sounds. These sounds combine in different ways to make meaning units that stand for things, and these units can be combined further to produce an unlimited set of messages. Half of the duality is the phonological system, the rules that restrict the permissible ways in which the meaningless sound elements can be combined into meaning units. The other half is the semantic system, the rules that attach meanings to the phonological units. Between the phonological system and the semantic system is the syntactic system, the rules that restrict the permissible ways in which the meaning units can be combined into messages. Since the openness feature allows a phonological unit to stand for different things depending on context, the syntactic system must be systematic and complete so that sounds can be translated into meanings.

Duality is also a design feature of music. On the one hand, there are the meaningless acoustic elements generated by discrete frequencies. On the other hand, there is the internal musical meaning. The notes take on meaning by reference to an internal representation of musical structure. It is the relationships among the notes, as specified by this music structure, rather than the physical values in and of themselves, that give each note a meaning.

Obviously, language and music are not identical in all design features. Some design features seem particular to language: (1) displacement: linguistic messages may refer to things remote in time and space; and (2) truthfulness: linguistic messages can be false and they also can be meaningless. The possibility of polyphonic construction seems to be unique to music. In polyphonic music, two or more notes or themes are played simultaneously. Therefore, each note may act in two ways, as a melodic element as well as a harmonic element.

There are several psychological consequences of these design features. Openness implies that we can never learn a language by memorizing all the utterances. Moreover, most words never have one fixed meaning, so that we can never learn a language by memorizing each word. The explanation of linguistic and musical understanding must shift to the cognitive structures inside individuals. Heredity may supply potential perceptual structures that experience with language and music adjusts to the linguistic and musical conventions of the community. These potential structures allow for the ease of learning language and music, and permit alternative linguistic and musical conventions.

10.2 Linguistic and Music Theory

For both linguistic and music theory, the goal might be to mirror the intuitions of an educated listener (Chomsky 1965; Lerdahl and Jackendoff 1983). The intuitions express what the listener understands when listening to a sequence of speech or musical sounds. The intuitions represent a grammar, a model of the listener's knowledge of language and music. Without such intuitions, listeners would be unable to distinguish grammatical from ungrammatical sequences (in both speech and music), to recognize sequences as repetitions or equivalences (paraphrases), and to understand and create an infinitely large number of novel sentences. These educated listeners are experienced and familiar with the language and music of the culture. They need not be experts or have formal training in linguistic or music theory.

We can put it another way. On one hand there is the surface level, the sounds of the sequences. On the other hand, there is the meaning of the sequence. It is the listeners' internal structures or grammars that make the sounds into meanings. The listeners impose a structure that yields the acoustic segments and yield the relationships among the segments. The segments and relationships are within the listeners, not the sounds. Figure 10.1 provides an analogy using a visual figure. In the figure there are eleven straight line segments. In themselves, the eleven are meaningless. However, their visual spatial grammars lead the vast majority of viewers to see not lines but a bar piercing through a triangle. We impose a structure on the line elements. There are other possibilities shown in figure 10.1, but these are unlikely to be perceived. Researchers use examples of this sort to discover the grammars of vision by cataloguing the possible visual figures that are perceived and the equally possible visual figures that are not perceived. In the same way, auditory sequences can be used to discover the grammars of music and speech. Each visual and/or auditory example is ambiguous; each allows for a variety of meanings and understandings. That

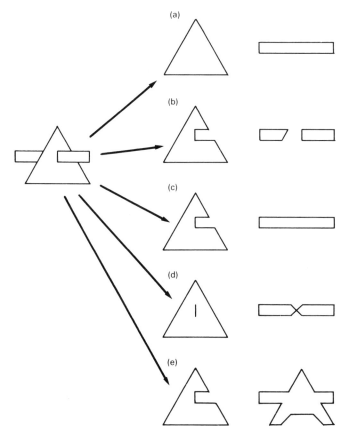

Figure 10.1
"Visual grammars" lead us to perceive one out of many possible organizations of the line elements. Typically we "see" a bar piercing a triangle (a), but there are many other geometrical possibilities. A few of these are illustrated (b, c, d, e).

we do not normally perceive the alternatives is a mark of the pervasiveness and ubiquity of our grammars.

A detailed description of musical and language grammars is beyond the scope of this book. Here I will emphasize the grammars and intuitions underlying Western music in order to make comparisons with our more firmly developed linguistic intuitions.

10.3 Music Grammars: Tonality and Harmony

Notes

Octaves   The vast majority of (if not all) musical cultures use discrete pitch elements (discrete notes would be a design feature). Although discrete notes are not logically necessary, sensory and/or memory limitations tend to rule out musical systems based on continuous variation of frequency. Given that music is based on a set of notes, the pivotal relationship that seems to organize the elements is that of the octave (one tone has twice the frequency of the other tone). In nearly all cultures, tones separated by an octave are considered to be musically equivalent.

The reason that octave tones are perceived as equivalent is unclear. The traditional hypothesis is that the overtones are identical. For example, the harmonics of a 150 Hz tone are 150 Hz, 300 Hz, 450 Hz, 600 Hz, and so on; the harmonics of a 300 Hz tone are 300 Hz, 600 Hz, 900 Hz, and so on. There is a perfect matching of the even harmonics of the 150 Hz tone to each harmonic of the 300 Hz. Tones separated by a octave have the greatest number of matching harmonics, and traditionally the number of matching harmonics has been used as a measure of the musical "goodness" of the interval between a pair of tones. For example, two tones in a $3:2$ frequency ratio have also been given musical precedence (this is termed a fifth). Here, every third harmonic of the lower frequency tone matches every second harmonic of the higher frequency tone (e.g., 300, 600, 900, 1200, 1500, 1800 Hz, etc.: 450, 900, 1350, 1800 Hz, etc.).

Any octave therefore defines a pitch interval, and the construction of a musical scale consists of filling the interval with intermediate tones. Which tones should be used to fill in the octave interval? The decision represents the compromise between two conflicting impulses. The first impulse is to choose tones such that simultaneous pairs sound smooth, without a sense of roughness. The second impulse is to create enough tones for composition to occur. A small number of tones can be chosen so that each pair sounds consonant, but this will be at the cost of simplistic and childlike pieces of music. On the other hand, a large number of tones can be chosen that allow intricate compositions, but this will be at the cost of some rough or dissonant intervals between pairs. Across a wide range of musical cultures, the possible number of tones per octave ranges from 5 to 24. In actual practice, the number of tones within each octave in any composition ranges from 5 to 7. This number is about at the limit of the ability to identify individual tones as measured in absolute judgment experiments.

Musical notes   We can imagine the entire scale to be made up of adjacent octaves. Starting with a bottom note of 100 Hz, the first octave would be from 100 Hz to 200 Hz, the second octave would be from 200 Hz to 400 Hz, the third octave would be from 400 Hz to 800 Hz, and so on. Now suppose we arbitrarily choose a second note of 150 Hz. To maintain the same relationships, this second note should be 300 Hz within the second octave and should be 600 Hz within the third octave, so that the ratio of the second note to the lowest frequency of any octave always is 3 : 2, or 50% greater. Notice that this procedure produces an octave relationship for the second note: 150 Hz, 300 Hz, 600 Hz, etc. What this means is that if we construct a scale based on octave equivalences, the notes in each octave segment bear an identical relationship to each other. Thus a simple 100 Hz, 133 Hz, 166 Hz first octave becomes a 200 Hz, 266 Hz, 332 Hz second octave, which becomes an 800 Hz, 1064 Hz, 1328 Hz fourth octave, and so on. The notes in the second octave are two times the frequencies of the notes in the first octave; the notes in the third and fourth octaves are four and eight times the frequencies of the notes in first octave, and on it goes. If we specify the notes of the first octave, all the other notes of higher octaves are completely determined.

The historical development of the choice of scale notes is somewhat chaotic. Moreover, there is little consistency across musical cultures in the precise notes chosen. In spite of this, one historical principle in Western music that provides some semblance of coherence is choosing notes so that playing any two notes simultaneously will result in a harmonious, consonant sound. Consonant pairs of notes occur when the maximum number of harmonics match. If the harmonics do not match in frequency, then the resulting beats (review section 2.1) produce a pulsating roughness that yields a dissonant interval. (The perception of consonance is quite complex: acoustic consonance, musical consonance, and perceived consonance are not identical. A good review is provided by Pierce 1983.)

To maximize the number of matching harmonics, the frequency ratios between the fundamentals should be expressible as a ratio of small whole numbers (e.g., 3 : 2, 4 : 3, 5 : 3, 5 : 4). If the frequency ratio between two tones is expressible as two whole numbers, then some of the harmonics will match. For a 4 : 3 ratio, every third harmonic of the higher frequency tone matches every fourth harmonic of the lower frequency tone. For example, if the tones are 300 Hz and 400 Hz, then the fourth harmonic (1200 Hz) and the eighth harmonic (2400 Hz) of 300 Hz match the third harmonic (1200 Hz) and sixth harmonic (2400 Hz) of 400 Hz. The smaller the whole numbers (3:2 as opposed to 4:3), the higher the proportion of harmonic matches.

Two strategies have been used to select consonant notes for a scale. The first is to use only the 3:2 interval ratio and generate the scale notes by successive 3/2 multiplications and octave equivalences. The second is to choose notes so that the frequency ratios between scale notes are the smallest possible whole number ratios. Neither of these strategies works perfectly. There are always discrepancies between the ideal consonant frequencies and the generated frequencies.

Consider first constructing all the scale notes by means of the smallest numbers (and highest consonant) 3:2 ratio. (This is sometimes termed Pythagorean tuning.) If the first note of the octave is 240 Hz, the second note will be 360 Hz (240 × 3/2). The third note obtained by a 3/2 multiplication will be 540 Hz (360 × 3/2), but since 540 is outside the 240 Hz to 480 Hz octave, its lower octave equivalent, 540/2 or 270 Hz, becomes the scale note. Continue this process twelve times—multiply by 3/2 and if outside the octave divide by 2—and it will generate the twelve notes within the octave. However, the final iteration should bring us to 480 Hz, the next octave, but it does not. The calculated octave (486 Hz) is higher than 480 Hz. Moreover, the frequency ratio between adjacent notes also varies, which can be seen in figure 10.2. Basically, a pure 3/2 harmonic ratio and a pure 2/1 octave ratio cannot exist in the same scale.

Consider next a scale construction technique, termed *just tuning* based on small number ratios (the discussion below follows Benade 1976). Starting with any note, the first tone selected would be the 2:1 ratio, the octave. The second tone selected would be the 3:2 ratio tone; the third tone selected would be the 4:3 ratio tone; the fourth tone selected would be the 5:4 ratio tone; and the fifth tone selected would be the 5:3 ratio tone. A pictorial representation appears in figure 10.2.

Up to this point, everything works out fine. All the selected notes are simply related to the lowest reference note, and moreover, each selected one is related to every other one. For example, the third tone (4:3) forms a 4:5 ratio with the fifth tone (5:3), since 4:3 divided by 5:3 equals 5:4. The difficulties arise when we try to insert more notes into the octave while still maintaining simple frequency ratios. For example, we might try to fit a note between the base note and the 5:4 tone. Thinking of simple ratios, we could start with the first selected tone (the 3:2 or "fifth") and reduce its frequency by a 3:4 ratio to produce a 9:8 tone. This possibility makes the 9:8 tone simply related to both the 3:2 and 4:3 tone but not to the 5:3 and 5:4 tone. Alternatively, we could start with the 5:3 tone and reduce it by a 2:3 ratio to yield a 10/9 tone. Now the 10/9 alternative

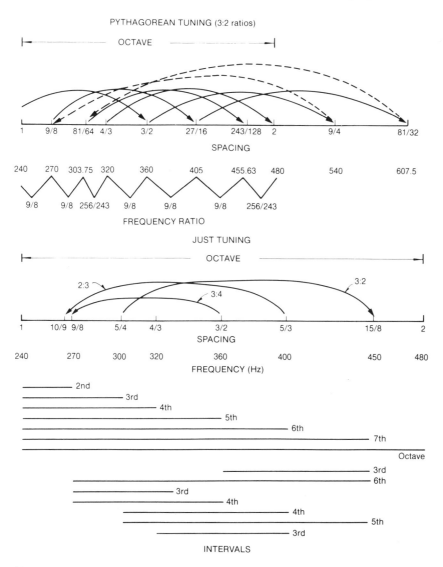

Figure 10.2
Pythagorean and just tuning: Musical scale construction based on simple numerical ratios. Pythagorean scale notes are generated by using the consonant 3:2 ratio. Each new note is generated by multiplying the previous frequency by 3/2. In the top panel, the solid arrows show the generated notes, and the dashed arrows show the octave equivalents necessary to keep the scale notes within a single octave. As shown below the notes, the frequency ratio between adjacent notes is not the same across all possible pairs. Just tuning notes are generated using small whole number ratios in the bottom panel. Difficulties arise when fitting in extra notes. There are two possibilities shown for the second note. Other notes (some sharps and flats) also cannot be defined unambiguously. The intervals beginning with the first note of the scale and intervals beginning with different notes of the scale are shown at the bottom of the figure.

would be simply related to both the 5:3 and 3:2 tone, but not the 4:3 or 5:4 tone. If the base tone is 240 Hz, then the 10:9 tone is 266.67 Hz and the 9:8 tone is 270 Hz, a difference of 3.33 Hz, which can bring about a sense of dissonance.

We can press on, selecting the 9:8 tone, and try to insert a tone just below the octave. We get this tone by starting with the 5:4 note and increasing it by 3:2 to generate the 15:8 tone. This gives a set of seven notes: 1, 9:8, 5:4; 4:3; 3:2; 5:3; and 15:8. These are termed the *whole* tones and represent the white keys of the piano. The twelve whole notes obtained by using the small whole number ratio intervals are termed the *diatonic* notes, and each note is named by a syllable (i.e., solfeggio). This is shown in table 10.1.

However, there are several problems. The ratio between adjacent notes varies from 9:8 (270 Hz to 240 Hz) to 10:9 (300 Hz to 270 Hz). There is no way to satisfy the simple ratio criterion. Moreover, any other scale constructed by starting from another note of the scale will result in mismatched frequencies. For example, if starting at 270 Hz, the second note will be 303.75 Hz, which differs by 3.75 Hz from the third note of the 240 Hz scale (300 Hz). Thus, for each possible starting note, you would need to tune the instrument to the different intervals of that scale.

Although some theorists have described scales based on frequency ratios as more "natural" than other scales, measurements of actual concerts do not bear out the contention that musicians tend to play intervals to conform to the mathematically pure intervals. Historically, the need to be able to move easily from scale to scale led to the adoption of the equal tempered scale. In the equal temperament system, the octave interval is broken into intervals so that the frequency ratio between all adjacent notes is identical (this is not true for the intervals described above). Consider the simplest case: dividing the octave interval into two segments by introducing one note. If we use the octave 240 Hz to 480 Hz, we need to find the note such that the ratio of note/240 equals 480/note. Alternatively, we can start with 240 and multiply it by a constant number to get the next scale note. We then take the derived scale note and multiply it again by the same constant to get 480. We cannot simply take the average of 240 and 480 because 360/240 = 1.5, which does not equal 480/360 = 1.33. We need to find the square root of 240 × 480, which is approximately 339. Now 339/240 = 1.41, and 480/339 = 1.41. Alternatively, 240 × 1.41 = 339, and 339 × 1.41 = 480. Notice that the 1.41 ratio is equal to the square root of 2; thus to split two octaves in two, multiply the lower frequencies by the square root of 2. The next simplest case would involve splitting the octave into three equal intervals by introducing two notes. Working through the algebra, the notes are 240 Hz, 302 Hz, 381 Hz, 480 Hz. The constant multiplier is 1.26, or the *cube* root of 2.

Table 10.1
Pythagorean, Just, and Equal Temperament Tuning Systems

Interval name	Solfeggio	Letter notation	Pythagorean tuning (PT)			Just intonation (JI)			Equal temperament (ET)	
			Numerical origin	Frequency ratio	Cents	Numerical origin	Frequency ratio	Cents	Frequency ratio	Cents
Unison	DO	C	$1:1$	1.000	0.0	$1:1$	1.000	0.0	1.000	0
Minor second		D♭	$2^8:3^5$	1.053	90.2	$16:15$	1.067	111.7	1.059	100
		C♯	$3^7:2^{11}$	1.068	113.7	$16:15$	1.067		1.059	100
Major second	RE	D	$3^2:2^3$	1.125	203.9	$10:9$	1.111	182.4	1.122	200
						$9:8$	1.125	203.9		
Minor third		E♭	$2^5:3^3$	1.186	294.1	$6:5$	1.200	315.6	1.189	300
		D♯	$3^9:2^{14}$	1.201	317.6	$6:5$	1.200	315.6	1.189	300
Major third	MI	E	$3^4:2^6$	1.265	407.8	$5:4$	1.250	386.3	1.260	400
Fourth	FA	F	$2^2:3$	1.333	498.1	$4:3$	1.333	498.1	1.335	500
Tritone		G♭	$2^{10}:3^6$	1.407	588.3	$45:32$	1.406	590.2	1.414	600
		F♯	$3^6:2^9$	1.424	611.7	$64:45$	1.422	609.8	1.414	600
Fifth	SO	G	$3:2$	1.500	702.0	$3:2$	1.500	702.0	1.498	700
Minor sixth		A♭	$2^7:3^4$	1.580	792.2	$8:5$	1.600	813.7	1.587	800
		G♯	$3^8:2^{12}$	1.602	815.6	$8:5$	1.600	813.7	1.587	800
Major sixth	LA	A	$3^3:2^4$	1.688	905.0	$5:3$	1.667	884.4	1.682	900
Minor seventh						$7:4$	1.750	968.8		
		B♭	$2^4:3^2$	1.788	996.1	$16:9$	1.777	996.1	1.782	1000
		A♯	$3^{10}:2^{15}$	1.802	1019.1	$9:5$	1.800	1017.6	1.782	1000
Major seventh	TI	B	$3^5:2^7$	1.900	1109.8	$15:8$	1.875	1088.3	1.888	1100
Octave	DO	C	$2:1$	2.000	1200.0	$2:1$	2.000	1200.0	2.000	1200

SOURCE: Burns and Ward 1982 and Martin 1962 by permission of publisher.

To break the octave interval into smaller intervals, the constant that relates adjacent notes is obtained by taking a root of 2. To split the interval into five parts using four notes, take the fifth root of 2 (the fifth root of 2 is 1.15; the notes would be 240 Hz, 276 Hz, 317 Hz, 365 Hz, 419 Hz, 480 Hz). In Western music, the octave interval is broken into twelve parts using eleven notes. The constant that relates the adjacent notes is the twelfth root of 2, or 1.06. Using this constant we can generate each note of the scale by multiplying successively by 1.06.

The twelve intervals and twelve notes of the musical scale are shown in table 10.1. The 3 : 2 numerical ratios that give rise to each interval for Pythagorean tuning, the whole number ratios that give rise to each interval for just intonation, and the successive 1.06 frequency ratios that give rise to each interval for equal temperament are listed. For both Pythagorean and just tuning, there are often two possible values for a single note (e.g., the alternative 10/9 and 9/8 D described previously). To provide a common unit, each ratio step in equal temperament is defined to be 100 cents; thus an octave is 1200 cents. It is possible to compare the three tunings by means of this common unit of 1200 cents per octave.

Equal temperament represents a compromise. None of the intervals are simple ratios, and therefore on this basis all intervals are out of tune. Nevertheless, each perfect interval is closely approximated and the differences are not readily noticeable. The equal temperament scale allows for easy transitions between keys because the frequency ratio between adjacent notes is identical, and for this reason it has been the standard for the past two hundred years.

Up to this point, I have described the process of defining all the possible notes in the Western scale. In any one composition, of course, not all notes are utilized, and the selection process imposes musical as well as psychological constraints and "intuitions." The note selection provides a tonal focus and suggests the importance and dynamic tendencies of each note (Zuckerkandl 1959).

Musical Keys: Structuring the Notes

Major and minor scales   The twelve notes that compose the octave generate 12 equal intervals, termed semitones, which do not create a tonal structure. In order to create a tonal focus or reference framework for all notes, a subset of notes (and resulting intervals) is selected. In Western music, there are two predominant ways of selecting the notes and intervals: the major and minor scales. The scale types are really abstractions, the result of reflection about the notes used in melodies.

The first type of scale is termed a *major* scale. One major scale is represented by the white keys of the piano (see figure 10.3). If we start at

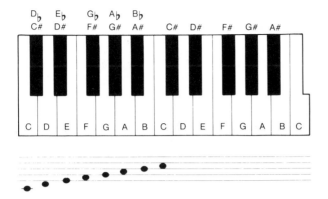

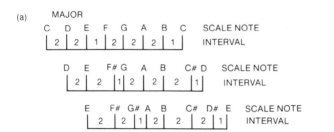

Figure 10.3
Major and minor scales. Two octaves on the piano keyboard are sketched at the top. Each black key has two possible note names: the sharp above the lower white key and the flat below the upper white key (e.g., C♯/D♭, D♯/E♭, etc.). Major scales beginning on the first three white keys are illustrated in (a). The scale note and the interval size are indicated. The minor scale beginning on the first white key is illustrated in (b). The equivalence of one major and one minor scale is illustrated in (c). The sixth note of the major scale is the first (or tonic) note of the minor scale.

the C key, then progress up to the C one octave above, we will hit seven keys including the initial C. Remember that the interval between each pair of adjacent notes (white to black or white to white, e.g., B to C) on the keyboard is an identical semitone. But the intervals between white keys do not represent equal steps, so the semitone intervals of major scales are 2, 2, 1, 2, 2, 2, 1. The intervals represent the *diatonic* order, the tonal sequence underlying Western music. We can begin a major scale with any note, and in the process utilize a different set of notes. For example if we start with D, the second white key from the left, the notes of the major scale would be D, E, F-sharp (to achieve a two-step interval), G, A, B, and C-sharp. Here, we would need two black keys in order to yield the required intervals between notes of the major scale. Major scales can be started at any note and in this process all twelve notes of the octave would be needed. Major scales starting with the first three white keys are shown in figure 10.3.

The second type of scale is termed the *minor* scale. The minor is characterized by semitone steps of 2, 1, 2, 2, 1, 2, 2. A diagram of the minor scale on the piano keyboard is also shown in figure 10.3. As is true for the major scales, we can start the minor scales at any note and thereby utilize all the notes. The major and minor scales represent two alternative versions of the diatonic order: the major is found in the minor and vice versa. We can see this by laying out the notes of a major and minor scale and moving one relative to the other until all the notes match. As shown in figure 10.3, the scales are identical when the first (or *tonic*) note of the minor scale is the sixth note of the major scale. Thus, the major and minor scales represent alternative versions of one diatonic order.

Tonal movement   Why these diatonic intervals? Traditionally, the most popular explanation has been based on consonance due to the identity of overtones. This argument was used above to yield the white keys of the piano in terms of the system of just intonation. A different type of explanation focuses on the properties of the semitone intervals themselves. First, the pattern of intervals in the diatonic scales is asymmetric. Second, the diatonic scales create a variety of one- and two-semitone intervals and also create all possible semitone intervals; for example, the interval between C and A is nine semitones. To create all such intervals, a minimum of seven notes is required. Third, each note has a different pattern of semitone intervals with all the other notes. Only one note can be the tonic. Each note can then be said to have a unique structural function (Balzano 1980). The principles of tonal relationships are probably not found in the physical properties of complex tones or in the properties of physiological mechanisms underlying hearing. Neither can account for the diversity of tonal relationships within one culture or across different cultures. And, although some researchers (Helmholtz [1863] 1954) have believed that tonal relationships are freely and arbitrarily selected principles of style, I do not believe this to be the case, either. It may be impossible to provide a convincing rationale for the emergence of diatonic scales, but we can make use of the intuitions of music theorists to state some of the more important perceptual consequences of the existence of diatonic scales.

Within a musical context, each tone has a direction or balance. Beginning with the major scale, we can analyze the quality of each tone. If we start with the tonic note, we "hear" the second, third, and fourth notes as pointing back to the tonic. There is a tension: a tendency to return to the tonic. The fifth note is a pivot. The fifth note marks the greatest distance from the tonic. Yet it is somewhat balanced; it can fall back to the tonic or it can bounce ahead to the eighth note, an octave above the tonic. The sixth note can move to the fifth note or move toward the seventh note and from there to the eighth note, an octave above. A representation of these tendencies is shown in figure 10.4.

If we try to analyze minor scales in the same fashion, we find there are difficulties. Although the first five elements have the same dynamic quality

MAJOR SCALES

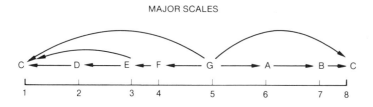

MINOR SCALES

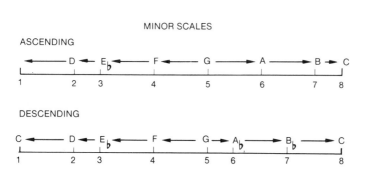

Figure 10.4
Movements between notes in major and minor scales. For major scales, the fifth (G) is a pivot. Notes up to G tend to return to the tonic; notes above G tend to move to the next octave. For minor scales, there are different movements for ascending and descending progressions. The sixth and seventh notes are moved to create the correct intervals (adapted from Zuckerkandl 1959).

of pointing back toward the tonic, the sixth and seven elements do not point toward the octave. What we need to do is to shift those elements around, putting them in the same position as for the major scale (see figure 10.3). Thus, there are really two minor scales: (1) the diatonic minor usually associated with the descending direction, and (2) the melodic minor incorporating different sixth and seventh notes usually associated with the ascending direction (see figure 10.4).

The tonic is the strongest dynamic center, and the fifth and third notes are weaker centers. There are simple movements that reveal the tonic center: an upward scale beginning at the tonic and ending at the octave above the tonic; or an upward and then downward movement beginning and ending at the tonic. Movement to the tonic represents balance.

Scale relationships   When we select the seven (diatonic) notes for a major or minor scale and select one note as the tonic, we are defining the key. Each key is named by the tonic note and the type of scale, e.g., B-flat major, C-sharp minor. Different keys can be related in three ways.

1. For every major scale, there is one minor scale that, although offset, shares the same seven tones (see figure 10.3). The two scales are termed the *relative* major and minor.

2. For every major scale, there is one minor scale that has the same tonic, e.g., C major and C minor. These two keys have different sets of notes, but the identity of the center ties them closely together.

3. For every scale, there are two different scales that have six of their seven notes in common. Consider the C-major scale shown in figure 10.5(a). To generate a second scale that shares six notes, there are only two options; we can move the fourth note up one step so that the original 2212221 intervals become 2221221, which is also a major scale, or move the seventh note down one step so that the 2212221 intervals become 2212212, which is also a major scale. Moving the fourth note up one step, to F sharp, makes G the tonic. Moving the seventh note down one step, to B flat, makes F the tonic. Following this same strategy, we then take the G scale and consider the two possibilities obtained by moving the fourth note up one step *or* the seventh note down one step. Moving the seventh note down brings us back to the original scale; moving the fourth note up brings us to the scale beginning with D, containing two sharps. Alternatively, we take the F scale and raise the fourth note *or* lower the seventh note. Raising the fourth note returns us to the original scale; lowering the seventh note brings us to the scale beginning with B flat, containing two flats. The entire process is drawn out for eight keys in figure 10.5(a) and (b). After passing four flats or four sharps, each key can be

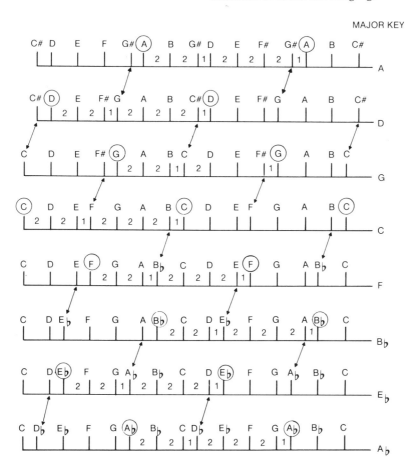

Figure 10.5(a)
Generation of the circle of fifths. One major scale can be transformed into another scale by
shifting the fourth note up one semitone or by shifting the seventh note down one
semitone. Continuing this process eleven times (in one direction) will generate all of the
major and minor scales and the twelfth step will recycle back to the original key. The tonic
note of each scale is circled.

Figure 10.5(b)
The circle of fifths portrays each key change around a circle. Each combination of sharps and flats creates one major and one minor key. Keys with more than four sharps or flats can be written either as a set of sharps or a set of flats. Figure 10.5(a) illustrates eight of the twelve possible keys (from Zuckerkandl 1959 by permission).

written either as a set of sharps or as a set of flats. This occurs because each black key can be thought of as the sharp of the white key below or the flat of the white key above, and in places where there is not a black key (where two white keys are adjacent), the lower white can be conceptualized as the flat of the upper white and the upper white as the sharp of the lower white (see figure 10.3).

What this means is that the scale or key transformations come back on themselves. The flat scales transform into sharp scales and vice versa, so that all the possible musical keys can be systematically represented in a circle, termed the circle of fifths, shown in figure 10.5(b). Each key can be transformed into two other keys; for one key the tonic is a fifth above the tonic of the original key (e.g., D is a fifth above G), for the other key the tonic is a fifth below the tonic of the original key (e.g., C is a fifth below G). The fundamental relationship between the base note and the fifth note thus becomes reflected in the relationships among keys.

Harmony
In general, harmony refers to the relationship among tones played simultaneously, the vertical axis of music. The search for physical or mathematical

explanations for harmonic relationships has proved largely fruitless. Harmony is a cultural phenomenon, and musical experience leads to harmonic expectations.

Intervals   It is traditional to describe notes in terms of the intervals separating them. It is the movement between notes, not the frequencies of the individual notes themselves, that defines the musical quality. The intervals are shown in figure 10.6. Each interval is labeled by the number of the note above the tonic. If the upper note is a note of the scale, then it is a major interval (in the case of octaves, fifth, fourths, and unisons, the term *perfect* is used). A major interval, made a semitone smaller, becomes a minor interval. The stability or strength of any interval is derived from the strength of the individual notes. The fifth and the major third are thus the most stable intervals.

Chords   Harmony is based on chords, in the same sense that melody is based on notes. To push the analogy further, harmony is the movement of chords; melody is the movement of notes. The strongest chord is the major triad obtained by the superposition of two thirds: the first, third, and fifth tone of the scale (see figure 10.6). The first or tonic note is termed the root, which functions as the center of the chord. According to music theory, it does not matter whether the third or fifth note of the triad is lower in frequency than the root. The root obtains its status by scale position.

Each note of a scale can function as the root of a triad. In figure 10.7, the seven triads for a major scale are shown. Each triad is labeled by the scale position of the root note and is characterized by the interval between the root and the third and by the interval between the root and the fifth.

Chord movement   Harmony is the progression of chords. The dynamic quality of the chord stems from the tonal property of the root note, and the quality of each root note is determined by its position in the scale. (The preferred chord progressions are termed *voice leading* techniques.) Perhaps the most important chord progression is that from V to I. The I triad is termed the tonic chord, and the V triad is termed the dominant chord. Since the V triad appears to point toward I more than any other triad does, it must be harmonically closest to I. In general, two chords are harmonically closest when the root notes are separated by fifths. The normal way for triads (harmony) to move is by fifths; in contrast the normal way for notes (melody) to move is by seconds (i.e., adjacent notes).

Using the fifth as the building unit, we can build a graph of harmonic progressions, in which arrows point in the direction of movement, as shown in figure 10.7. Zuckerkandl (1959) describes chord progressions as a I ... V → I sequence. Starting with I, there is a open-ended movement away

340   Chapter 10

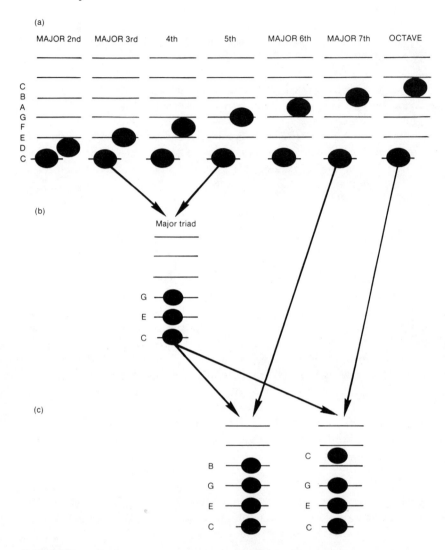

Figure 10.6
Intervals and chords of tonal music. The seven intervals are illustrated in (a). The major third and the (perfect) fifth intervals are combined to form the major triad (b). In turn, the major triad is combined with the major seventh interval or with the octave interval to form four-note chords (c).

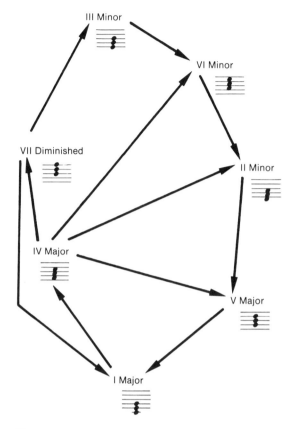

Figure 10.7
Chord progressions. The movement tendencies among the seven triads (one for each note) of major scales is illustrated. Chord movement often starts at I, moves to another chord, and returns to I by way of V. Alternatively, the chord progression may return to I by way of VII (adapted from Zuckerkandl 1959).

from the tonic, then a jump to the dominant V, and finally a return to I. The common harmonic sequence is to begin at I, progress through intermediate triads (IV, VI, II), move to the dominant (V), and then end with I. There is an optional, open-ended initial component as well as a fixed, obligatory closing.

Harmonic polyphonic music is often conceived as a four-part texture. The four parts customarily are named for the classes of singing voices: soprano, alto, tenor, and bass. Each part is meant to represent an ideal quality, a human voice or instrument. Since a triad contains only three notes, the four-part harmony needs to be completed. The fourth note can be the octave above the root or the fourth note can be the seventh of the chord, another third above the fifth note (refer to figure 10.6). This four-tone chord is termed the seventh chord. The major triad and seventh chords are the main constituents of harmony. All other chords are related to these.

Tonality: Melody and Harmony

The notion of tonality was originally defined to cope with the emergence of harmonic Western music, which is based on the triad with a clear tonal center. However, there are many music systems in which there is a clear tonal center and yet the notes of the scales bear little relationship to a harmonic (diatonic) series. This has led to a more general view of tonality, as in its definition in the Harvard Dictionary of Music (Apel 1972): "Loyalty to a tonic, in the broadest sense of the word. One of the most striking phenomena of music is the fact that, throughout its evolution—in non-Western cultures, in Gregorian chant, and in harmonized music—practically every single piece gives preference to one tone (the tonic), making this the tonal center to which all other tones are related" (p. 855).

This does not mean that a certain tone will be perceived as the tonal center throughout a piece. In nearly all compositions, the tonal center shifts; the scale notes change. These shifts are not arbitrary, because they reflect specific relationships to the original tonic. The original tonic provides a constant reference across all the tonal shifts.

In "melody and harmony" music, we do not hear two separate movements. We hear an integrated motion. Not only do the notes of the melody relate; the chords of the harmony relate, and the "corresponding" note and chord relate. In some cases, the note and chord have the same dynamic quality: both point to resolution or incompleteness. In other cases, the chord progression (i.e., the harmony) may interpret the melody. In all cases, tonality provides the frame that gives each component its relational meaning. It is a *relational* meaning, because without the framework provided by the tonic (tonality in general), a note or chord is not integrated and remains merely a sound.

10.4 Music Theory and Perceptual Psychology

We have been following the language of music theorists. These theorists speak psychologically: they talk of movement, resolution, integration, tensions, centers, moving toward, loyalty, and so on. These terms could have been lifted from a theory of personality. Individual notes and individual chords are perceived in relation to a key. The key is induced or discovered by means of the sequence of notes and chords; the sequences follow rules and therefore provide clues to the dominant key and ultimately to the tonal center.

How do the tonal relationships bring about the sense of music? To investigate these concepts psychologically is a complex undertaking. We need to find ways to tease out the musical intuitions or grammars listeners are using to "understand" a passage. These would include interval, chord, scale, and key relationships. A pure sine-wave tone in isolation does not bring about "musical" perception, but this does not mean that a full orchestra is required. All that is necessary is to provide a musically relevant context and structure. Unfortunately, this may be difficult to achieve in practice. Several experimental approaches are used to investigate the underlying cognitive musical intuitions. Each technique can provide insights, and several techniques converge to the same conclusions.

1. Recognition of familiar passages. In this approach, a well-known tune ("Oh Susannah" or "London Bridge Is Falling Down") is distorted in differing ways and the listener is asked to identify it. The percentage correct despite the distortion should measure the importance of the distorted variable. For example, the rhythm of a song might be changed to make the duration of each note equal and the timing between the onset of each pair of notes identical. If listeners can no longer correctly name the tune, then we can infer that the rhythmic structure is necessary. If listeners can still identify the tune, then we can infer that the rhythm is not of great importance. Or, the melodic sequence can be distorted by raising or lowering individual notes by an octave (the entire melody is not transformed by the same amount; rather, each note is changed differently). If listeners can still identify the melody, then this provides evidence that notes having the same scale position in different octaves are perceived as being equivalent. If listeners cannot identify the distorted melody, this argues against the psychological reality of octave equivalence in spite of the physical identity of the harmonics.

2. Errors in recognition or matching. In this approach, a first passage is presented to the listener. After a short delay, a second passage is presented. The subject must state whether the two passages are identical or equivalent in some specified way. The second passage might

be perfectly transposed to a different key so that all the interval sizes are identical, or it might be transposed to a different key so that some of the interval sizes are changed. The listener would thus be required to distinguish perfect transpositions from incorrect transpositions. The ability to discriminate between correct and incorrect transpositions measures the importance of interval size in the perception of melodies. In general, discrimination errors give information about the perception of musical structures and transformations.

3. Errors in memory or reproduction. In this approach, a passage is presented, and after a delay the subject is required to reproduce that sequence (either by transcription, direct playback, or some other technique). It might be expected that sequences that are musically "correct" (i.e., those that fit musical grammars) would be easiest to remember and reproduce. Moreover, reproduction errors for sequences that do not fit musical conventions might tend to create a sequence that is more musically correct. The reproductions would be more "grammatical."

4. Direct judgments of "appropriateness" or "similarity." In this approach, subjects are asked to make judgments concerning some aspect of musicality. Listeners might judge how "appropriately" a note ends a sequence, for example, or listeners might be presented two notes or two chords and asked to judge how similar they appear to be. In contrast to the previous approaches, there are no correct answers and subjects are free to choose their own criteria. The goal is to discover the complex grammars and intuitions listeners are using to perceive music. This is exactly the same procedure used for discovering the dimensions of timbre. As discussed in chapter 8, the open-ended nature of the judgments paradoxically ensures that the most relevant perceptual attributes will emerge.

A survey of psychological research in the general area of tonality follows. The material roughly traces the theoretical development above. The relationship among notes will be discussed first, then the formation of melodic sequences and the formation of chords and chord sequences. We will finish with research concerning the relationships among keys.

10.5 Perception of Music Grammars

Notes and Scales

Perception of octaves   Tones that are separated by an octave are considered to be musically and perceptually equivalent (they are given the same name) in the scales of nearly all but one or two musical systems. The belief in the reality of octave equivalence is deep seated. From a physical point of view, the octave is the only interval in which the harmonics will coincide exactly. For this reason, two notes separated by octaves cannot create dissonance, if dissonance is due to beats among harmonics. Although the physical argument for the uniqueness of the octave is compelling, the actual perceptual evidence is weaker. On the whole, the results of many varied studies suggest that octave equivalence is perceived by experienced musical listeners in all contexts but is perceived by less-experienced listeners only in a musical context and not when using isolated tones.

Several studies have asked subjects either to make direct judgments about the similarity between two tones or to choose a second tone that is most similar to a given, fixed tone (Thurlow and Erchul 1977; Ward 1954). Typically, the tones are presented in isolation. Relatively few of the subjects, even with musical training, were able to judge octave equivalence: the percentage of accuracy ranged from 33% to 50%. Experienced musical subjects did judge two tones separated by an octave as more similar than other pairs. Moreover, these subjects were able to identify scale intervals for sinusoid tones correctly, even when one tone was replaced by its octave equivalent (the interval 400 Hz−1200 Hz was perceived as a fifth, namely 400 Hz−600 Hz). Subjects who were able to produce octave equivalences tended to make the octave slightly sharp, with a ratio greater than 2 : 1. This corresponds to the cross-cultural evidence that octaves tend to be slightly greater than 2 to 1 (Dowling 1978). The low percentage of subjects who showed octave generalization may have been due to the weak musical context created by the isolated tones. In experiments to be discussed in the next section, Krumhansl and Shepard (1979) and Krumhansl and Kessler (1982) found that within a musical context, musically inexperienced subjects (as well as experienced subjects) displayed octave equivalence; in fact, this was the only tonal feature utilized by inexperienced subjects.

If tones separated by one octave (or several octaves) are perceptually equivalent, then it should be possible to replace a note by an octave equivalent and still retain the identical percept. (As mentioned previously, music theorists make this assumption when naming triads and chords.) In several experiments, a simple melody was distorted by replacing each note with an octave equivalent. If listeners hear the tune in spite of the octave replacements, this is evidence for the perceptual equivalence of octaves. An example is shown in figure 10.8. The original tune and two possible octave transformations are presented. The first transformation preserves the contour of the melody: if adjacent notes in the tune increase in frequency, then the octave replacements also increase in frequency. (A similar restriction occurs when notes decrease in frequency.) The second transformation does not preserve the contour. The octave equivalent is chosen randomly so that

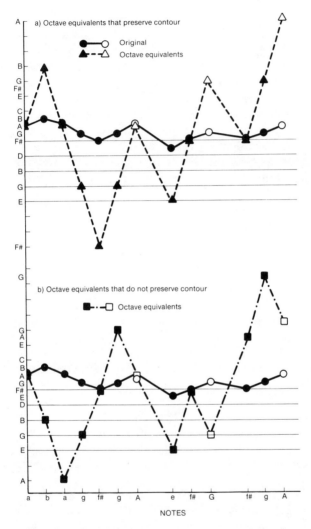

Figure 10.8
Octave equivalents. Contour-preserving and non-contour-preserving transformations. The original version of "London Bridge" is drawn in circles connected by a solid line. The scale notes of the piece are labeled along the horizontal axis. The actual notes are drawn in musical notation and are labeled along the vertical axis. An octave equivalent melody that preserves the up-and-down contour of the original melody is drawn in (a), using triangles. Each note in the transformed melody is an octave equivalent of the original note. This can be verified by comparing the notes along the vertical axis. An octave-equivalent melody that does not preserve the up-and-down contour of the original melody is drawn in (b), using squares. For example, the first two notes of the original increase (in frequency) going from A to B. The octave equivalent decreases (in frequency) going from A to the lower-octave B. (For all melodies, open symbols represent two time beats and are labeled by capitals along the horizontal axis; filled symbols represent one time beat.) (Adapted from Kallman and Massaro 1979).

though adjacent notes in the original tune increase (or decrease) in frequency, the octave equivalent can either increase or decrease in frequency.

The results from several experiments suggest that octave-equivalent melodies that do not preserve the contours cannot be identified correctly (reviewed by Dowling 1984). Melodies are not perceived directly in terms of the abstracted scale positions of the notes. However, if listeners are told the title of the melody beforehand, then they can identify the octave-equivalent melodies. To do this successfully, listeners must make use of octave equivalence in order to compare the scrambled octave melody with their memory of the correct melody. Octave-equivalent melodies that preserve contours are identified better than non-octave-equivalent distorted melodies that also preserve contours. Octave equivalents thus improve identification beyond that achievable from the contour alone (all conditions are poorer than identification of undistorted melodies).

These results imply that the direct perception of octave equivalence is remarkably sensitive to context. Experienced musicians can judge single-note equivalence without a musical surround, but inexperienced listeners can judge single-note equivalence only within a musical surround. For all listeners, octave equivalence in melodic passages is derived. Listeners must generate the equivalents from a memory representation and then compare it to the presented melody.

Note/scale relationships   The twelve notes within each octave are thought to play specific roles within a scale. Seven notes will make up the scale (the diatonic notes), and five other notes will not belong to the scale (the non-diatonic notes); some notes are stable, and other notes are weaker and unstable. Experiments exploring these musical concepts have suggested that if musically sophisticated listeners are provided a musical context, their judgments reflect the tonal structure. However, if listeners are presented isolated tones, judgments tend to be made purely on the physical dimensions of frequency and intensity.

In one experiment, musically sophisticated subjects judged the similarity between pairs of notes presented sequentially (Krumhansl 1979). In order to achieve a musical context, subjects were presented either the ascending or descending major scale or the major triad before each judgment. Based on the context generated by that scale or triad, subjects were asked to judge how similar the first tone was to the second tone.

The similarity ratings were equivalent across the three contexts: ascending scale, descending scale, and major triad chord. Given that the ratings were equivalent, the similarity judgments were averaged across the three contexts. The average similarity judgments then were considered to be the distances between notes, and the notes were placed in a geometric space so that the distances between stimuli reflected as accurately as possi-

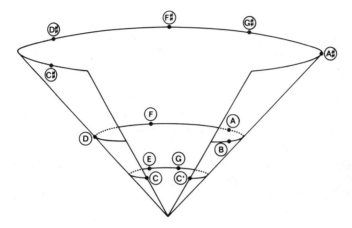

Figure 10.9
Spatial configuration of the scale notes. The notes can be represented around the surface of a cut open ice-cream cone. The notes of the major triad are at the base; the diatonic notes fall around the middle, and the nondiatonic notes fall around the top rim. The cut symbolizes the octave equivalence (C' is one octave above C)(from Krumhansl 1979; reprinted by permission of publisher).

ble the judged similarities. The positions of the notes resemble an ice-cream cone, as shown in figure 10.9. Overall, these spatial positions derived from the similarity judgments provide evidence for the cognitive reality of several musical ideas.

1. The tones making up the major triad chord (C, E, G) form a set of closely related tones toward the base of the cone. Other diatonic tones making up the C-major scale also form a set of related tones and are adjacent to the major triad diatonic tones. The nondiatonic notes are more spread out, reflecting the weaker relationships among these tones themselves and between the nondiatonic tones and the diatonic tones.

2. Subjects judged tones differing by an octave as being highly similar, demonstrating octave equivalence. The cone wraps around in a circle so that tones differing by an octave are in close proximity.

3. Tones close in frequency tend to be judged more similar than tones further separated in frequency.

This can be summarized by pointing out that the strength of the similarity between two notes was multiply determined: by frequency separation, by octave equivalence, and also by the relationship of the notes within the tonal context. In addition, the similarity judgment changed as a function of the order of the two notes, which also indicates the importance of the tonal context. (The judgment was how similar the first tone was to the second tone.) Here, a nonscale note to scale note movement (e.g., G-sharp to C) is judged more similar than a scale note to nonscale note movement (C to G-sharp). In other words, there is a tendency to move down the cone toward the more central notes, from less stable to more stable notes. Music analysts have been unanimous in attributing the motion of music to this tendency. Starting with the stable notes to establish the tonal context, a musical passage shifts to nondiatonic notes to create the feeling of incompleteness and then reverts back to the diatonic tones to achieve a sense of closure.

These results demonstrate the complex intuitions underlying the scale notes. Other research by the same authors used a different approach (Krumhansl and Kessler 1982). Musically sophisticated listeners were presented first with a musical element, such as an ascending scale, to generate a context. Following that, a single note from the chromatic scale was presented. The listeners were asked to judge how well the single tone "fit into" or "went with" the musical elements heard first. Specifically, on one trial the listener might be presented a C-major scale (the white notes on the piano), followed by a nondiatonic note like B-flat. On the next trial, the listener might be presented with the identical scale followed by a diatonic note F. Across a sequence of twelve trials, all twelve notes of the octave were presented. The ratings generated a profile that measures the degree to which each element fits into a musical key.

The results demonstrated that for the most part listeners' judgments were the same whether the key was suggested by a scale, a chord, or a cadence of chords. The average results are shown for a major and a minor key in figure 10.10. For both major and minor scales, the major triad notes (i.e., the tonic, the fifth, and the third) were judged to fit best. The other diatonic notes were judged to fit next best, and nondiatonic notes were judged to fit poorly.

Both studies suggest that the tonic, fifth, and third are the most closely related elements and provide the "foundation" for the scale. The other diatonic elements are perceived to fit into this structure, and the nondiatonic elements are perceived to be more distant and unrelated. It is also noteworthy (no pun intended) that scales, chords, or chord cadences provide equally strong musical contexts.

Geometrical models   These kinds of data have led to spatial and geometrical models representing the perceptual relationships among the notes. These models attempt to account for the various aspects of note perception, such as: (1) tone height: perceived pitch is a function of frequency, and as the frequency difference (i.e., the frequency ratio) between two notes increases, the notes usually are judged more dissimilar; (2) octave equivalence: two

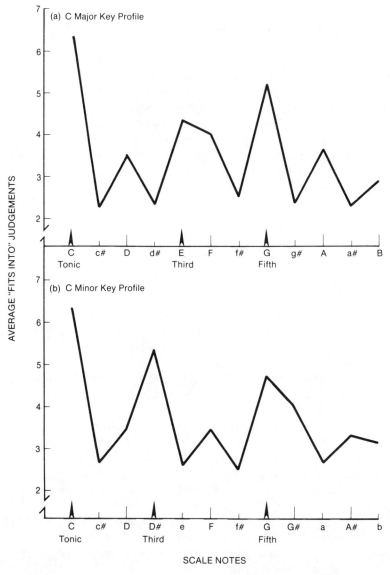

Figure 10.10
Perceptual structure of major and minor scales. The average judgments of how well scale notes fit a tonal context are denoted for a C-major key context (*a*) and a C-minor key context (*b*). Notes are displayed along the horizontal axis. Notes of the scale are indicated simultaneously by capital letters and by longer vertical tick marks. The notes of the major triad are indicated by vertical arrow heads. The results show that the notes of the scale are judged to fit better than nonscale notes and that the notes of the major triad receive the highest judgment (adapted from Krumhansl and Kessler 1982).

tones related by an octave are judged to be more or less equivalent (the term *chroma* has been used to signify the common perceptual quality shared by notes separated by an octave; all of the C notes have one chroma and all the D notes have a different chroma); (3) fifth interval: two tones related by a fifth (a 3:2 relationship) tend to be heard as particularly harmonious, the fifth completes the major triad chord, and keys that share the greatest number of notes are separated by fifths; and (4) major third interval: the third is perceived to be one of the important scale intervals, and the major triad is composed of two thirds.

Each of these aspects of note perception introduces one more abstract musical intuition. As each is incorporated into a geometrical model, it imposes new restrictions, makes the model more complex, and in mathematical terms requires more dimensions.

Perhaps the best starting point is to conceptualize a model that combines tone height and octave equivalence (chroma). To do this, we need to distort the simple graph of pitch versus frequency (e.g., figure 2.27) and transform it into a helix or spiral as shown in figure 10.11. What we do is take the pitch-frequency graph and make one complete turn per octave.

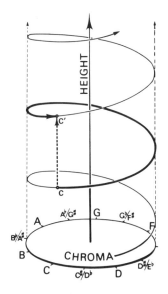

Figure 10.11
Spatial representation of tone height and tone chroma. To represent the perceptual equivalence of notes separated by an octave, the notes are twisted into a helix so that notes separated by an octave (with the same chroma) occur at the same radial position. A vertical line dropped from one note would intersect the same note in lower octaves (illustrated by dashed line for C′ to C) (from Shepard 1965 by permission of publisher).

Because of this rotation, notes that are separated by an octave will fall in a vertical straight line (on top of each other) and thus are physically closer, representing their musical similarity (e.g., Ruckmick 1929). To make octave equivalents even closer in space, we can squash the helix. If we imagine collapsing the entire helix down, then all tones with the same chroma (notes with the same name) will fall at the same point around the chroma circle. This representation more clearly separates the two components of pitch: tone height, represented by the vertical dimension, and tone quality or tone chroma, represented by the circular dimension of the helix.

If we attempt to integrate the similarity of notes separated by a fifth into a geometric model, the complexity of the model increases dramatically. For example, if we combine pitch height with the circle of fifths, the appropriate geometrical model is a double helix, shown in figure 10.12. (Shepard 1982). Around the circle at the base is the circle of fifths. Each ascending helix contains alternative notes of the chromatic scale so that pitch height is represented vertically, and equivalent notes in each octave fall in the same vertical column around the cylinder to generate octave equivalence.

These models are helpful in characterizing pitch relationships in a musical context. Nonetheless, subjects were judging each individual note as a perceptual event. Outside of the laboratory, people rarely perceive individual tones as events. Instead, pitch is a medium, the means by which musical (as well as nonmusical) patterns can be constructed (Attneave and Olson 1971). It is necessary to investigate the role of musical grammars in perceiving tunes and melodies.

Notes within tonal and atonal sequences   Tonality should provide a reference frame that allows listeners to determine whether two notes, or two passages separated in time, are identical or different. Tonal sequences are defined as those in which each note comes from one diatonic scale (each note is a member of one key). Atonal sequences are defined as those in which the notes cannot have come from one diatonic scale. This definition of atonal is used consistently in psychologically oriented research on tonal structure. Music theorists are wary of such a definition. Butler (1986), for example, points out that whether a passage has a tonal structure depends on the definition of tonal structure. It is possible to derive some reasonable harmonic interpretation from nearly any passage. As a first approximation, the simple definition of atonal is probably sufficient. However, the simple dichotomy of tonal versus atonal will need to be refined in future work.

Krumhansl (1979) demonstrated that the memory for a single note is determined by the musical context. The experimental procedure was as follows: on one trial, a single tone termed the standard was presented for 0.5 sec. The standard was followed by an eight-note melody lasting 4.0 sec,

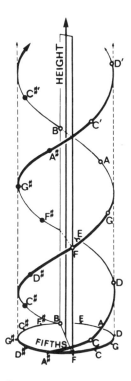

Figure 10.12
Spatial representation of pitch height, pitch chroma, and the circle of fifths. The circle of fifths is represented around the oval base (see figure 10.5). Pitch height is represented vertically, and pitch chroma is represented by rotating the notes around a helix so that octave-equivalent notes line up vertically. The twelve notes lie along two intertwined helixes. The six notes along each helix are separated by two semitones. The white notes to the right of the vertical plane are diatonic notes within the scale; the black notes to the left of the plane are nondiatonic notes out of the scale (from Shepard 1982 by permission of publisher).

which was expected to affect the memory for the standard, and then a single comparison tone was presented for 0.5 sec. The comparison tone could be identical to the standard or be one semitone above or one semitone below the standard. The task was to judge whether the standard and the comparison tone were the same.

The interpolated musical passage was tonal or atonal. On the basis of the tonal or atonal melodic sequences, the standard notes were classified as being diatonic (a note of the key) or nondiatonic. Diagrams of the four possibilities are shown in figure 10.13.

An interpolated diatonic sequence aided performance by generating a consistent reference; it was easier to discriminate between notes within the scale than outside the scale. However, if the standard was not a scale note, then the interpolated diatonic sequence hindered performance by generating a competing reference. Therefore, in a tonal context, notes were internally represented by subjects as scale notes. In contrast, with an interpolated atonal sequence it was actually easier to discriminate between nondiatonic notes outside the scale.

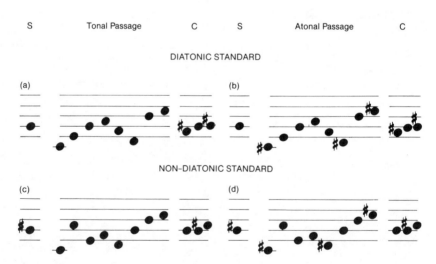

Figure 10.13
Identification of notes within tonal and atonal contexts. On each trial, subjects were presented the standard (S), a short eight-note passage, and then one of the three possible comparison notes (C). The comparison was either the same as the standard (a correct match) or was one semitone higher or lower (an incorrect match). The four variations of the standard note (diatonic vs. nondiatonic) and interpolated passage (tonal vs. atonal) are illustrated in (a)–(d). In addition, the three possible comparison stimuli are displayed (adapted from Krumhansl 1979).

The effect of tonal context on the perception and identification of individual notes within a melody has been demonstrated by Cuddy, Cohen, and Miller (1979). These researchers constructed a seven-element sequence by surrounding a consistent three-note kernel (positions 3, 4, and 5) with two sets of two notes (positions 1, 2 and 6, 7). In the first condition, the four surrounding notes were diatonic and the last two notes formed a musical V to I final cadence. In the second condition, the four surrounding notes were randomly chosen diatonic notes. In the third condition, the four surrounding notes were nondiatonic so that the sequence was atonal. In every trial a seven-note sequence was presented first. Then two alternative transposed sequences were presented (the alternatives were transposed in order that subjects could not merely match tones). One sequence was a perfect match; the other sequence differed by one semitone because of changing one of the three kernel notes. The identical change in a kernel occurred for each of the three conditions.

The results indicated that subjects were most accurate in detecting the correct transposition in the diatonic and cadence condition and least accurate in the atonal condition. Moreover, changing a kernel note to a nondiatonic note made detection easier in a tonal context. These results demonstrated quite clearly that tonality aids identification. The tonality acts to limit the number of the possible sequences and allows for the easier detection of nontonal notes. A verbal analogy would be to create a kernel like OGR. A tonal sequence with a musical ending cadence might correspond to a word like PROGRAM. A diatonic sequence might correspond to a wordlike segment that follows phonological rules, like GLOGREB. An atonal sequence might correspond to a seven-letter segment that does not follow phonological rules, like LGOGRBE. By analogy, it should be easiest to detect a letter change in PROGRAM (e.g., PROLRAM), harder in GLOGREB, hardest in LGOGRBE.

Tonal and atonal melodies   The definition of a melody must be psychological; melodies are sequences of tones that are perceived as a single and unified entity (Mursell 1937, p. 102). There must be an internal structure that is picked up by the listener. To derive a theory of melody perception, we can isolate features of the melody and then assess their relevance and importance in perception and memory.

1. The first feature is the up-and-down patterning between adjacent notes, which is termed the *contour* of the melody. We can describe the contour in terms of three values: $+$, 0, $-$. The "$+$" value indicates that for two adjacent notes, the following note increases in pitch; the "$-$" value indicates that the following note decreases in pitch; and the "0" value indicates that the two notes have the identical pitch (the note repeats itself). The contour is, therefore, the sequential pattern of

+, −, and 0. For example, the contour of the beginning of the melody "Three Blind Mice" is −−+−−, as shown in figure 10.14. Experimentally, we can take such a short passage and preserve the contour although changing each and every note, as in panel (b). Alternatively, we can take the same passage and change the contour, as in panel (c). We might expect that changes in direction of the contour (from going up to going down) are critical for identification. Vision can provide an analogy. The changes in contour direction are analogous to visual angles, and angles, far more than connecting lines, define a visual figure.

2. The second feature is the pattern of the size and direction of the semitone intervals between successive notes. The pitch change can be labeled as −2 or +4, indicating a two-semitone pitch decrease or a four-semitone pitch increase (see figure 10.14). Given the intervals, the contour can be recovered.

3. The third feature is the pattern of scale steps in a tonal framework. Each note is represented by its position within the scale (from 1 to 7). In other words, each note is defined abstractly with respect to tonic and scale type (see figure 10.14). Given the scale steps, the semitone intervals and contour can be recovered.

4. The fourth feature is the notes actually played. Given the sequence of notes, all other features can be recovered.

What is typical of classical and folk music is the repetition of melodic themes using different pitch levels, interval sizes, and keys. There are many options open to the composer. The theme can be played in a different octave, in a different key while maintaining the exact interval sizes, or in the same key but varying the interval sizes. The ability of listeners to perceive these repetitions as being different and yet fundamentally equivalent leads to hearing the composition as a unified whole.

Dowling and co-workers (reviewed in Dowling and Harwood 1986), as well as others, have attempted in a series of experiments to specify exactly what it is that listeners pick up when they listen to short melodic themes. In a typical experiment, a sequence of notes is first presented as the standard, and then this standard is followed by a comparison sequence. The comparison sequence might be a perfect transposition in which the sequence of intervals is identical. Alternatively, the comparison sequence might be an incorrect "lure," in which the size of one or more intervals is altered while the identical contour is maintained. The subject's task is to decide whether the comparison is an exact transposition or a transposition lure. If the comparison sequence is not transposed, it is easy to reject comparison stimuli that do not share the same notes. (Dowling has used lures that change the contour, but these are usually easy to reject.) Using "Twinkle, Twinkle, Little Star" as the original standard, an example of a

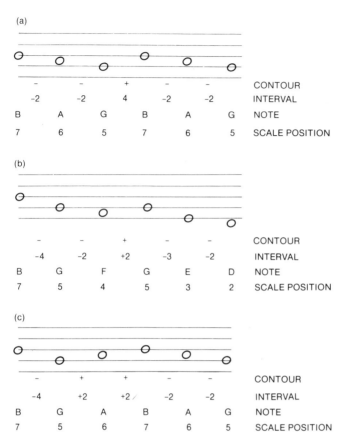

Figure 10.14
Properties of melodic sequences. Passages can be characterized in terms of the melodic contour, the size of the interval, the actual note, and the position of that note within the key. The first six notes of "Three Blind Mice" are shown in (a). A transformation that maintains the identical contour (−−+−−) while altering the interval, note, and scale position is shown in (b). A transformation that does not maintain the identical contour is shown in (c).

correct transposition in the original key, a correct transposition in a different key, an incorrect transposition in a different key, an incorrect transposition in the original key that changes the interval size (termed a *tonal lure*), and an incorrect atonal transposition are shown in figure 10.15. All of these have a contour identical to that of the standard.

The results for this task are complex: they depend on the type of sequence, the experience of the listener, and the details of the task. The original research (Dowling and Fujitani 1971) used five-note atonal sequences. For atonal sequences, subjects could not distinguish between exact transpositions and transposition lures that had the same contour. In other words, if the comparison was a lure that maintained the same contour, subjects often described the lure as being a correct transposition. This means that in an atonal context, listeners are unable to make use of the exact intervals between notes; all listeners can do is utilize the pattern of ups and downs. The atonal context "disallows" the intuitive musical grammars that a listener would normally use, and it forces listeners to a cruder and simpler level of perception—the pattern of ups and downs. Here, in fact, inexperienced subjects do better.

In a tonal context, interval and scale information is available to the listeners. For example, with a tonal sequence, subjects distinguish between the exact transposition of that tonal melody and a transposed atonal melody "lure" with the same contour (as noted above, listeners were unable to distinguish this case for atonal melodies). Experienced subjects performed much better than inexperienced subjects on this comparison, although inexperienced subjects still performed better than chance. However, experienced and nonexperienced subjects were unable to distinguish exact tonal transpositions, which maintained the size of each interval, from tonal transposition "lures" in the same key, which varied the size of each interval. Both transpositions sound "natural" as opposed to the unnatural sound of atonal transpositions. In addition, subjects may have been confused by the possible note identities in the transposition (Dowling 1978).

These results suggest that there is greater reliance on the harmonic structure of the interval sizes (or on the exact scale notes themselves) for more familiar or natural passages. For familiar songs, Bartlett and Dowling (1980) found that adults could distinguish between exact transpositions and lures, which preserved only the contour, in the same key. (Subjects could not make this distinction for novel melodies, as described in the previous paragraph.) Even inexperienced subjects can produce an exact transposition for a highly overlearned tune, e.g., the NBC chimes used in the 1960s (Attneave and Olson 1971).

These results illustrate that both the type of short melodic sequence and the experience of the listener influence the features used to perceive the

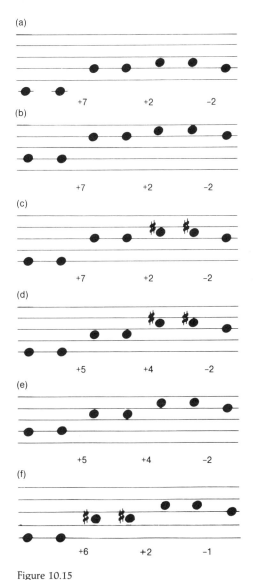

Figure 10.15
Transpositions of simple melodies. The original melody, "Twinkle, Twinkle, Little Star," is represented in (a). The interval sizes between notes are shown. Any exact transposition must maintain the identical sizes of the intervals. An exact transposition in the same key is represented in (b). An exact transposition in a different key is represented in (c). An incorrect tonal transposition in a different key is represented in (d). The interval sizes are different. An incorrect tonal transposition in the original key is represented in (e). Again, the interval sizes differ from the original. An incorrect atonal transposition is represented in (f). The notes do not correspond to any scale.

sequence. Another factor is the length of the sequence. Edworthy (1985) demonstrated that contour was predominant for short sequences, but that interval information was predominant for longer sequences. Edworthy argues that when the melody is transposed, initial tonal information about intervals is "shaky." The ongoing melody increasingly stabilizes the tonal structure, which allows the apprehension of interval information. Still another factor that influences identification is the temporal delay. At short delays between the standard and comparison, contour information dominates, but at longer delays interval information dominates (Dowling and Bartlett 1981).

In sum, atonal sequences, tonal sequences, and familiar tonal melodies bring about different levels of musical understanding and processing. With atonal sequences, listeners seem to be restricted to perceiving the contour of the sequence: interval information is unavailable because expectations and intuitions based on the common musical structures are consistently violated. With novel tonal sequences, listeners can utilize contour and tonal information. Listeners distinguish between transpositions and atonal sequences with identical contour, but they cannot distinguish between exact transpositions and tonal contours in the same key that do not preserve interval size. Finally, with familiar tonal sequences, listeners utilize interval information and scale notes to distinguish between exact transpositions and identical contours in the same key. With the exception of atonal sequences, experienced musicians tend to perform better than inexperienced listeners. Musicians can vary the way they utilize the musical structures. This seems to suggest that contour is most important in nonmusical contexts (in the same way that simple frequency differences between two notes are most important in nonmusical contexts). Interval size information and/or scale position information is most important in tonal contexts (in the same way that scale relationships among notes are most important in musical contexts). Moreover, contour information is probably most important in discriminating between melodies; interval information is probably most important in identifying one melody.

Consider an analogy from visual perception. If you needed to judge whether two faces in different orientations were the same person, an overall shape feature analogous to contour (e.g., size, angularity) might take precedence. However, if you needed to identify one face, then more detailed facial information, analogous to intervals, would be necessary to select that face from all others in your memory. You would probably have stored several faces with the identical size and angularity. The same situation occurs in melody perception: listeners must use interval or scale-note information to identify melodies, because many melodies have the identical contour.

Overall, in a tonal context, the grammar and intuitions of Western music influence the perception of individual notes, intervals, and melodies. The tonal context creates an implicit cognitive/perceptual structure that affects the perceived belongingness of individual tones, the perceived similarity between pairs of tones, and the ability to perceive melodic relationships. The ability to pick up this musical structure is determined in part by the experience of the listener and in part by the experimental task.

Parallels in language   At this point it is worthwhile to consider some parallels in language. This treatment is necessarily sketchy, because of space limitations.

1. It has been demonstrated many times that comprehension and understanding is faster in a grammatical context than in a non-grammatical context.

In a classic experiment, Miller and Isard (1963) demonstrated that grammatical and semantically meaningful sentences ("pink bouquets emit fragrant odors") were easier to understand than grammatical but meaningless sentences ("pink accidents cause sleeping storms"), and both were easier to understand than ungrammatical sentences ("around accidents country honey and shoot").

In a similar demonstration, Tulving and Gold (1963) showed that words were more quickly recognized when they were congruent to the sentence meaning. For example, "collision" is identified more easily in the congruent sentence, "Three people were killed in a terrible highway collision," than in the incongruent sentence, "She likes red fruit and jams of strawberry and collision." The grammar leads to reasonable predictions about what will follow. The grammar serves to restrict the range of possibilities in the same way that tonal grammars restrict the range of possible notes.

There are two kinds of restriction rules. The first, termed *subcategorization* rules, refers to the choice of words that are grammatical in the context of other words. For example, the construction "dalmatians eat talk" is disallowed because it is ungrammatical. This appears analogous to tonality rules that specify the grammatical elements, the diatonic notes. The second, termed *selection* rules, refer to the choice of words that are *semantically* meaningful. For example, the utterance "flower chewed a bone" is not easily understood. (I doubt if there are any non-meaningful utterances. All can be interpreted metaphorically or by a change in context. "Flower" could be the name of a dog.) Language selection rules appear analogous to musical cadence rules that yield "meaningful" note sequences. (As above, I doubt that there are nonmeaningful musical passages. It may take many repetitions, but eventually an organization will emerge.)

In similar experiments, both Ganong (1980) and Massaro and Cohen (1983) demonstrated that linguistic knowledge will influence the categorization of speech sounds. Ganong varied the voice onset time to produce a voiced /d/ to unvoiced /t/ continuum. These stop consonants were used as initial consonants to generate a "dash" to "tash" continuum and a "dask" to "task" continuum. Subjects made more "dash" responses for the "dash-tash" continuum but more "task" responses for the "dask-task" continuum. Knowledge of the words in the language influenced the perception of phonetic segments.

2. It appears that it takes about twice as long to recognize a word in isolation (350 msec) as in a context (200 msec) (Marslen-Wilson and Welsh 1978). In context, listeners can identify a word after the initial consonant-vowel syllable, long before the end of the word. Since many words have the same initial syllable, listeners must be using the context to restrict the set of possible words. Several researchers have suggested that in meaningful contexts, words can be recognized without recognizing the individual syllables, but in nonsense contexts (or in isolation), words can be recognized only after recognizing and encoding the individual syllables (see review by Samuel 1986). By analogy, in tonal contexts, experienced listeners might be able to perceive directly harmonic sequences plus cadences and extrapolate to the following notes, while in atonal contexts, even experienced listeners must perceive the entire passage before being able to achieve a sense of organization.

3. It is obvious that a listener's understanding of any utterance is affected by attention, experience, and prior knowledge as well as by the grammar of the utterance. Furthermore, listeners do not remember the actual utterance. They paraphrase, induce logical implications, and add material to make the utterance meaningful. The comprehension and memory for speech is a joint function of the material and listener (Bransford 1979).

We find the same results in the research of Cuddy and co-workers and Dowling and co-workers. Both the experience of the listener and the structure of the notes determines performance. Experienced musicians can better cope with tonal sequences, but highly familiar, overlearned songs can make up for inexperience. In all cases, however, the listener is perceiving the structure among the elements, not the actual physical sequence itself. The perceptual and cognitive strategies for listening to speech and to music are very similar.

Chords and Harmony

What distinguishes Western music from the music of other cultures is its characteristic harmonic structure. Although the use of simultaneous notes must date back to the beginning of music, the movement between chords composed of unified notes began only in the 1700s. It was the use of the major triad as a "pivot" that led to the development of Western classical music. Although we describe the harmonic structure in terms of chords, the same harmonic analysis arises when the notes forming the chord are not played simultaneously but follow one another as a harmonic progression. The three or four tones making up the chord or progression are conceptualized as creating the identical context.

To review, chords made up of three notes can be constructed at each position of the scale. Starting at each note of the scale (the root of the chord), alternate successive notes in the scale are utilized to form the chord. According to music theory, the I (tonic), IV (subdominant), and V (dominant) chords take the central role in establishing the sense of tonality and key. The harmonic progression I-V-I is a typical sequence moving from the tonic to the dominant and then returning to the tonic. The remaining triads are thought to play more peripheral harmonic roles and to create a demand for resolution.

As should be clear by now, there is an analogy between the structuring of notes and the structuring of chords. Certain notes and certain chords are perceived as central and as bringing about a sense of resolution. Other notes and other chords are way stations in the movement toward the more stable tonic. Still other notes and other chords are very peripheral and rarely occur in the music. The central notes and chords give rise to a more defined sense of tonality and key. This makes good sense: the stability of a triad must be due to the stability of the three intervals separating pairs of notes, and therefore relationships among triads should be based in some fashion on the relationships among tonal intervals. It is no surprise, therefore, that psychological experiments investigating harmonic structure are analogous to those investigating tonal structure. These experiments tend to utilize similarity or musical "goodness" judgments or recognition or memory paradigms.

Chord relatedness and similarity   One experiment investigated the relatedness of two chords in a musical context (Krumhansl, Bharucha, and Kessler 1982). The musical context was created by playing an ascending scale, and this was followed by two chords. The subjects were asked to rate how well the second chord followed the first chord in the context of each scale. Three different scales and thirteen different chords were used. The three scales were C major, G major and A minor. G major is closely associated with C major; the two scales differ in only one note. The A-minor scale is

Table 10.2
Chords and Their Relationship to Three Keys

| | | Key | | |
| | | C | G | A |
Chord	Notes	major	major	minor
C major (C)	C E G	I	IV	
D minor (d)	D F A	II		IV
E minor (e)	E G B	III	VI	
F major (F)	F A C	IV		VI
G major (G)	G B D	V	I	
A minor (a)	A C E	VI	II	I
B diminished (b°)	B D F	VII		II
D major (D)	D F♯ A		V	
F♯ diminished (f♯°)	F♯ A C		VII	
B minor (b)	B D F♯		III	
E major (E)	E G♯ B			V
G♯ diminished (g♯°)	G♯ B D			VII
C augmented (C+)	C E G♯			III

SOURCE: From Krumhansl, Bharucha, and Kessler 1982 by permission of the American Psychological Association.
NOTE: Roman numerals refer to scale position of root of triad.

the relative minor of C major and contains exactly the same scale notes except that it begins on A (figure 10.5). The thirteen chords are listed in table 10.2.

The relatedness judgments were treated as if they represented the similarity between each pair of chords. The similarities were then used to create a geometrical model in which the distance between each pair of chords stood for the judged similarity. The geometrical solution across all three scale contexts is shown in figure 10.16. What is important to see is that for all three contexts, the harmonically significant chords, namely I, V, and IV, lie close together in the center. In addition, chords within a single key are perceived to be more related than chords in different keys; they tend to be located in one area of the spatial representation. The judgments can be combined across the three keys to generate one spatial representation (figure 10.16, panel b). The I and V chords are most closely related (they are bound together in the innermost concentric oval). The IV chord is most closely related to the I and V chords (the I, V, and IV chords are combined in the second innermost oval). The VI, II, III, and VII chords are increasingly less related to the central chords, and each in turn falls within a more peripheral oval. There was also a tendency for subjects to judge a chord movement to more stable chords (nonmajor to major) as more related than chord movement to less stable chords (major to nonmajor). (As

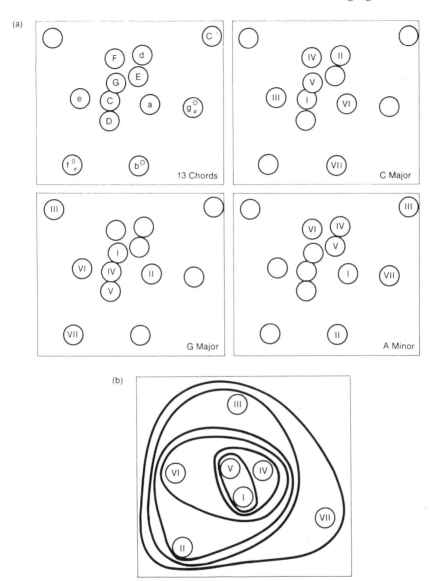

Figure 10.16
Spatial representation of the relatedness or similarity among chords of a scale. The spatial configuration for all thirteen chords is shown in the upper left panel in (a). The remaining three panels show the seven chords of each key separately. The spatial configurations for each key depict the I, V, and IV chords in the middle of the set of chords. This positioning conveys the importance of these chords. The geometrical configuration of the seven scale chords averaged across the three keys is shown in (b). The concentric ovals portray the degree of relatedness among the chords (from Krumhansl, Bharucha, and Kessler 1982 by permission of the American Psychological Association).

described previously, the identical asymmetry was found for judgments of individual notes.)

Experiments based on remembering and identifying sequences of chords provide converging evidence that the structures uncovered in the relatedness experiments are indeed psychologically relevant (Bharucha and Krumhansl 1983). Here, a sequence of seven chords was presented as the standard. Then a second sequence was presented that was either identical to the original standard sequence or differed because one chord was changed. The chord sequences were either harmonic, using chords within a single key, or random, using chords drawn from different keys. The results demonstrated that sequences of chords following conventional harmonic rules created such a unified, stable cognitive representation that listeners found it difficult to distinguish exchanges of one diatonic chord for another. Just about any triad based on scale notes appeared to "fit," and it therefore became difficult to distinguish between two harmonic but nonidentical sequences. In addition, it was much easier to detect a diatonic to nondiatonic change than a nondiatonic to diatonic change. We can think about this result in the following way. A nondiatonic element would be "jarring" and easily seen as being different against the stable referent of the diatonic sequence. A random sequence containing nondiatonic chords would not create a very stable representation. Listeners might therefore find it more difficult to distinguish the original nondiatonic sequence from the subsequent incorrect but diatonic comparison.

Taken together, these two experiments illustrate the cognitive-perceptual structure underlying Western harmony. Listeners have a "feel" about the appropriate sequences of triads and how these sequences will change as a function of the overall musical context. In one context, a certain chord movement should occur; in another context, a different chord movement should occur. A chord generates an expectation about what will follow. It activates or primes related chords (Bharucha and Stoeckig 1986). Context dependency is thus as much a part of music perception as it is a part of speech and language perception.

Chord/key organization and recognition   The musical structure brought about by the major triad may be generated in several ways. The triad may be performed as a chord, or the notes of the triad may be presented sequentially, so that the structure is brought about by a single line of notes in which no chords appear. According to music theory, each of the six sequential orders of the major triad (e.g., C-E-G; C-G-E; E-C-G; E-G-C; G-E-C; G-C-E) is assumed to generate the identical context. One task of musical analysis, therefore, is to take an ongoing passage and group the notes into three- or four-note harmonic chords. A single note need not be restricted to a single chord; it may be the terminal note of one chord and the initial note of the next chord. The analysis may occur in two steps: (1) identification of the key or tonality; and (2) assignment of the notes to a particular chord. These two steps are often intertwined; key identification may be based on the possible chord sequences and vice versa. Recent work has suggested that the order of the triads does affect the perceived key. Listeners tend to focus on the terminal triad and perceive the key signaled by that triad. For example, suppose a sequence alternated triads from two different keys. The sequence A_1, B_1, A_2, B_2, A_3, B_3 would be perceived as being in key B, but if the sequence were reversed it would be perceived as being in key A (Deutsch 1984).

There are several possible ways of splitting a passage into harmonic units. Musical analysis is problem solving; different possibilities are tried until one is found that best seems to match the element sequence (this is similar to our conception of stream segregation). Some passages appear to be quite easy to structure: all notes belong to one key, the first and last notes are the tonic, and the triad sequences are traditional. Other passages appear to be more ambiguous, because the sequence of notes does not fit the common conventions of music.

The distribution of the notes themselves often provides the strongest cues to the key. Across a wide variety of music, the percentage of time each note appears is a strong reflection of the key. The tonic note has the greatest frequency and overall duration, the fifth note has the second greatest frequency and duration, and other diatonic notes (e.g., the third) tend to have occurrences proportional to their importance in the key (Hughes 1977). For this reason, a listener can discover the key by attending to the most prominent notes (in terms of frequency or duration). Moreover, the more stable notes usually begin and end phrases and are placed at accent points. In Indian music, the tonic and fifth often become drone tones that are played continuously throughout the passage (Castellano, Bharucha, and Krumhansl 1984).

The first study investigated the ability of experienced listeners to identify the key of a short musical passage (Cohen 1982). The passages were taken from the forty-eight preludes and fugues of the *Well-Tempered Clavier* of J. S. Bach. Bach wrote forty-eight pieces in all twenty-four major and minor keys to demonstrate the versatility of the then new equal-tempered tuning system. The first four notes begin with the tonic note and include only scale notes. After hearing only these four notes, the percentage correct in identifying the correct major key was 83% and the percentage correct in identifying the correct minor key was 55%. The last four bars typically resolve or come back to the tonic. For a different group of listeners who heard only the final four bars, the percentage correct for the major and minor keys was 87% and 33% respectively. As the musical passage evolves, there is typically a change or modulation to a new key (the new key is usually adjacent to the original key, as shown by the circle of fifths). Thus it should be more difficult to identify the key after four or eight bars; for a third group of listeners who heard four or eight bars, the percentage correct for the major and minor keys dropped to 48% and 31% respectively. This study therefore demonstrated that trained listeners are able to identify the key from only a few introductory diatonic notes.

If listeners can pick up the key (or tonality) after even a few notes, then sequences that are simple and harmonically unambiguous should be easier to organize than sequences that are harmonically ambiguous. To study the correspondence between the theoretical structures of music analysts and the perceptions of listeners, two experiments have been performed. In the first experiment, musicians wrote out the harmonic structure of various seven-note passages. In the second experiment, different listeners judged the same sequences for "musical keyness" or "completeness." The results showed an excellent correspondence between musical analysis and perceptual judgments. Passages that were consistently broken into harmonic units were judged by listeners to be musically complete. It is doubtful that the listeners performed the analysis consciously; it is much more likely that these judgments reflect the intuition that passages that follow harmonic progressions represent more conventional contemporary music. Passages that violated the greatest number of harmonic conventions were judged the least musical (Cuddy, Cohen, and Mewhort 1981).

The discussion of music theory above began with scale construction and then progressed to harmony, the structure and transitions among chords. In that material I argued that musical theory makes claims about the centralness of and transitions among certain triad chords. The psychological research presented to this point attempts to investigate these claims. The work of Krumhansl and associates directly investigated the perceived relatedness of chords and the perception of sequences of chords. The work of Cuddy and associates investigated the perception of passages in which the triad notes are played one after the other. Both types of experiments lead to the identical conclusion that the grammars of music function perceptually. Listeners use their musical intuitions and understandings in judgments of chord similarity and of musicality.

Keys: Harmonic Relationships
A Western musical composition typically undergoes one or more key changes before returning to the original key at the close. The notes change, which leads listeners to perceive a different tonic and different relationships among chords. Music theory suggests that some key changes or key modulations are easy to bring about perceptually and that other key changes are quite difficult. Theorists equate the ease of modulation with the distance between keys. Three measures have been used to specify key

distance (all order the distances identically): (1) the number of identical tones in the two keys; (2) the difference in the number of sharps or flats in the key signature; and (3) the distance around the circle of fifths (see figure 10.5).

The psychological research has involved two goals. The first has been to demonstrate that the ease of moving between two keys is a function of the distance (as defined above) between those keys. The second has been to investigate the effect of key distance on the recognition of note or chord sequences.

Key similarity   The first goal is to derive musical intuitions concerning the distance or similarity between keys. One procedure is to utilize the task in which subjects judged how well a single note fit in a musical context. Krumhansl and Kessler (1982) asked the subjects to make the judgments for each of the twelve notes in the chromatic scale for each major and minor key context. To review (see figures 10.9 and 10.10), the three notes making up the major triad were judged to fit best, the other notes in the key were judged intermediate, and the nondiatonic notes were judged to fit poorest. For every key, each of the twelve notes has a "fit-into" rating.

We can define the similarity (or distance) betwen two keys as the equivalence of these judgments. The similarity of two keys is therefore based on the equivalence of the tonal functions of the individual notes. Consider an example. In figure 10.17, I have generated hypothetical profiles of the "fit" for the twelve notes in five keys. On the one hand, the "fit" pattern is somewhat similar for key 1 and key 2; the identical notes have high and low judgments. By the same reasoning, the "fit" pattern is somewhat similar for key 3 and key 4. On the other hand, keys 1 and 2 seem dissimilar to keys 3 and 4, because different notes have high and low judgments. Key 5 seems "in between" all of the other keys. If we were to construct a spatial representation, then keys 1 and 2 would be close together, keys 3 and 4 would be close together, but keys 1 and 2 would be distant from keys 3 and 4. Key 5 would fit somewhere between the two pairs. Using all the profiles, multidimensional scaling could be used to place all the keys in a geometric space so that the similarities among the note profiles determined the positions of all the keys in this space.

Krumhansl and Kessler (1982) used the equivalence among the note profiles as the measure of the distance between keys, and these distances then were used to construct a spatial model representing the similarities among keys. The spatial representation, shown in figure 10.18, illustrates that keys that are adjacent around the circle of fifths are close together in the space. These keys share the maximum number of scale notes and differ in only one sharp or flat. This means that the distance between any two keys can be derived from the equivalence of tonal functions. The tonic, the

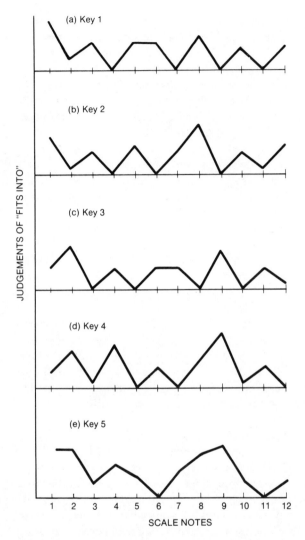

JUDGEMENTS OF "FITS INTO"

SCALE NOTES

Figure 10.17
Key similarity based on tonal similarity. The graph for each of five hypothetical keys shows the degree to which each note of the scale is judged to "fit into" that key. We would expect that the tonic and the fifth would have the highest ratings for all keys. Krumhansl and Kessler (1982) used these kinds of judgments to create a spatial configuration of keys.

PERCEPTUAL STRUCTURE OF KEYS

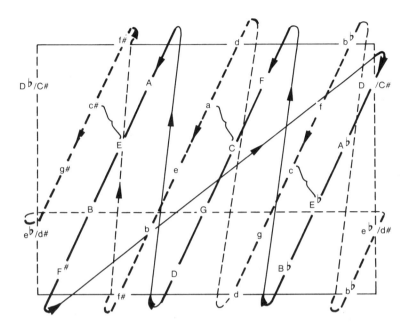

Figure 10.18

Spatial configuration of keys. The appropriate spatial configuration is technically termed a *torus*, which is like an inner tube for a tire. Imagine cutting a circular tube to produce a long cylinder. Each end (although separated by the length of the tube) is identical (because they were adjacent before being cut), and this is the reason the left vertical and the right vertical dashed lines in the figure have the same keys (D♭/C♯ and e♭/d♯). Take the tube and cut one seam along the length. The tube will open up and be a rectangular sheet in which the top and bottom are identical. That is the reason the top solid line and bottom solid line have the identical keys (f♯, d, b♭). The major keys (in uppercase letters) wind their way around the torus following the order of the circle of fifths (see figure 10.5) and eventually come back on themselves. The solid lines track the order of the major keys. (The unbroken solid lines denote going around the back of the torus.) The minor keys (lowercase letters) also wind their way, parallel to the major keys, around the torus. The dashed lines track the circle of fifths for the minor keys. The dashed lines denote going around the back of the torus (adapted from Krumhansl and Kessler 1982).

third, and the fifth notes are critical. Any two keys that share these critical notes will be judged similar. For example, if two keys are separated by a fifth, the fifth of one key is the tonic of the second key. That the identical note is a focus for both keys makes the keys musically and perceptually similar and allows a relatively easy transition between the keys.

Chord/key relationships   The key creates the context for the perception of individual chords. The perceived similarity or relatedness between two chords should depend on the context. Overall, we might expect that two triads in the same key will be judged as being more related than two triads coming from different keys. Moreover, two chords within one key will be perceived as maximally similar when "their" key is perceived as providing the context, but the identical chords will be perceived as being more dissimilar when a different key is perceived as the context. This prediction can be tested by using the same set of seven chords from one key while utilizing differing key contexts (the differing key contexts could be generated by playing scales in different keys). The subject reports "how well" the second chord follows the first chord in the context of the scale.

In one experiment the subject was presented the seven triads formed from the seven notes of a C-major scale and the seven triads formed from the seven notes of an F-sharp major scale (Bharucha and Krumhansl 1983). The keys of C major and F-sharp major are maximally different in terms of the fewest number of common notes and greatest difference in sharps and flats (none versus six sharps). The results of the experiment are shown in figure 10.19. The center panel provides the spatial solution when there was no context. In this case, the triads from the C-major scale were separated from the triads of the F-sharp scale. Moreover, for each set, the core triads—I, V, and IV—are found in the center of the seven triads. What the context does is to change the similarity between triads. Triads that are in the context key are perceived as being more related, and triads that are in a distant key are perceived as being less related. Thus when the context key is C major, triads in C major become more similar and appear closer together in the spatial model, and triads in the distant F-sharp major key become less related and appear further apart in the spatial model. The reverse effect occurs when the context key is F-sharp major—F-sharp major triads become more similar and C-major triads become more dissimilar. One final point should be made. Remember that when we discussed the perception of individual notes, we pointed out that two notes—one in the key and one outside the key—were perceived as more related when the order was outside to inside than when the order was inside to outside. The same effect is found for triad chords: movement into the context key is judged as creating a better sense of relatedness or fit than movement out of the key.

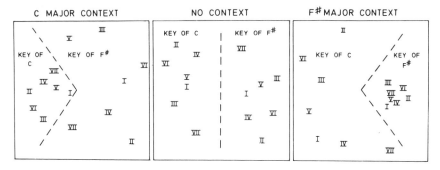

Figure 10.19
The relatedness of chords in a key context. The spatial configuration for the seven chords from the key of C and the seven chords from the key of F♯ when there is no context is illustrated in the center panel. The chords tend to fall on different sides of the configuration, but the similarity among the C chords is roughly equal to the similarity among the F♯ chords. In a C-major context (left panel), the perceived similarity among the C-major chords increases; they are closer together in the configuration. Conversely, the perceived similarity among the F♯-major chords decreases; those chords are spread farther apart in the configuration. The reverse occurs in an F♯-major context: the F♯-major chords are perceived to be more similar and the C-major chords are perceived to be more dissimilar (from Bharucha and Krumhansl 1983 by permission).

The perceived relatedness between triads depends on the context generated by the key. Two chords from one key are perceived as maximally related in that key context and less related as the context key gets more distant. Similarity among chords cannot be solely a function of the frequencies of the notes. The context key brings about a sense of expectation about the sounds that will occur. Notes and triads that fit these expectations are judged as being related, and those that are "jarring" to these expectations are judged as being less related. Movements between notes or chords into the context key are perceived as fitting and appropriate; movement out of the key is seen as inappropriate.

Key movement   As already stated, Western music is characterized by changes in key that serve to bring about a contrast of mood or mark boundaries within a movement. Typically a change in key is achieved by means of a pivot chord that is found in both keys. The musical passage moves to the pivot chord, and the pivot chord is followed by the strong triads of the new key (I, IV, and V) to bring about the perception of the change.

A single triad by itself cannot bring about the perception of one key, because a triad occurs in several keys; any triad will have multiple possibilities. For example, an F-major triad (F-A-C) is the IV chord of a C major, the V chord of B-flat major, and the VI chord of A minor (see table 10.2 for examples). According to music theory, this harmonic ambiguity represents the range of possible perceptual referents. Successive triads in one key bring about the strengthening of the perception of that key and the weakening of the perception of alternative keys (to the extent that all those successive triads could not occur in one of the alternative keys). From this perspective, a sequence of triads that is found in two keys should lead to the simultaneous perception of both keys (although one key might be stronger than the other), and it should therefore be easy to go from one key to the other. The sense of key should smoothly shift from the first to the second. The common triads "prime" the second key. Similarly, two distant keys share few triads; the triads from the first key will not prime or suggest the second key, and the change from one key to the other will be difficult and abrupt (Krumhansl and Kessler 1982).

Key similarity and melody perception On this basis, the musical context should affect the perception of a melody. The context will restrict the listener to expect the notes, chords, and customary sequences from one or more closely related keys. Listeners may make "false positive" identifications; they will be more likely to perceive two nonidentical melodies as being equivalent if the melodies are presented in closely related keys.

Research using the experimental procedures described above has varied the key distance between the standard melody and the exact transposition or contour lure (Bartlett and Dowling 1980). The exact transposition or contour lure was played in either a near key (G or D, separated by one or two steps from the standard C) or a far key (E or B, separated by four or five steps from the standard C). The results showed that listeners were more able to reject far-key lures than near-key lures. For near keys, the melody and contour lure sounded like true transpositions because they shared more notes. For far keys, the melody and contour lure did not share many notes and listeners were not misled. As might be expected, listeners were more able to detect interval changes in familiar, well-learned melodies, regardless of key. The scale notes, interval sizes, and contour for these melodies are in long-term memory.

Parallels in language The relationships among chords and among keys are similar to the relationships among individual notes. For this reason, many of the parallels between language and music described previously also have relevance here. There are three other parallels between language and music that deserve mention.

1. Scales and chords act to bring about a sense of context: the listener expects a specific set of notes, chords and modulations to adjoining keys. A part of the listener's musical knowledge has been "activated."

We might therefore expect the listener to be able to recognize or identify those musical units more rapidly than musical units coming from unactivated parts of the listener's knowledge. The same "priming" effect occurs in language. If subjects are presented words like "doctor" and "hospital," they will perceive other medical words (e.g., "nurse") faster than nonmedical words. The original words prime the subjects' "medical" knowledge in the same way that triads prime a key (Meyer and Schvaneveldt 1971).

2. Any single triad is ambiguous; it is a member of several keys and therefore by itself can suggest several possibilities. The triad is understood in the context of all the other elements. Composers can increase or resolve the sense of ambiguity by the sequence of elements. Words also have multiple meanings, and listeners must figure out the speaker's intention. Whether deliberate or inadvertent, ambiguity makes understanding far harder. Ambiguity can occur because of word choice (He took the *right* turn at the intersection), because of sentence structure (Steve or Ron and Bill will come), and/or because of grammatical ambiguity (Shooting hunters can be dangerous). Surprisingly, listeners typically report coming up with only one meaning, but it does take them longer to interpret the ambiguous utterance than the nonambiguous utterance. Obviously, context must be used to resolve the ambiguity, but how is that accomplished? One possibility is that word recognition and context information are independent: all meanings of an ambiguous word are activated to some degree and then context is used to select the appropriate meaning. The second possibility is that word recognition and context information are interactive: the context limits the initial meaning activation to the appropriate contextual sense (see review by Simpson 1984). If the second possibility is correct as suggested by the work of Glucksburg, Kreuz, and Rho (1986), we might expect that the tonal movement (equivalent to the sentence context) limits the possible harmonic meaning of any note or chord.

3. For both language and music, many different physical sequences yield the same meaning. As described above, the sense of tonality can be brought about in many ways: a major triad, a cadence of triads, or a sequence of notes. Similarly, the same idea can be expressed linguistically in many ways. This outcome is due to the open-ended design characteristic of language and music.

10.6 Listening to Music

The research just discussed encompasses a broad range of intuitions concerning tonality. It is unfortunate that the focus on tonality has led to experiments based on short, single-voice musical passages that isolate and study one facet of possible tonal relationships. The music we listen to is extended and polyphonic. Typically, a recurrent theme is elaborated in several ways—harmonically, melodically, rhythmically—which means that each variation can be seen as both different from and similar to the original theme. The ability to perceive a recurring motif within the stream of elements is what gives coherence to a piece of music. The meaning of a passage is determined by what may have occurred much earlier. In turn, the structure of the piece of music provides a framework for identifying each of the variations.

Abstraction of Musical Themes

It may well be that the features involved in listening to short melodies—contour, interval sizes, scale notes—allow listeners to identify the theme and variation plan. For example, contour may not be sufficient to re-create a melody accurately, but contour may be sufficient to allow recognition of a variation of a previously heard theme. Research concerning the perception of musical themes has been sporadic. Some of this work will be presented below to give a sense of the issues and methodologies.

One study investigated the abstraction of themes in a full musical context (Pollard-Gott 1983). The Sonata in B minor by Liszt is composed of two themes that undergo independent variation. The sonata is not simple, and the variations are subtle, even for experienced musicians. Four variations of each theme can be identified, so that in total there are eight critical segments. In the experiment listeners first heard an entire twelve-minute selection, containing themes and variations, from the sonata. Second, they were presented all possible pairs of the eight critical segments and were asked to make similarity judgments between each pair (28 in all). To track the development of the two theme concepts, the listeners returned twice within a week and followed the identical procedure.

The major result was that it took several listening sessions for the listeners to abstract each theme and its variations. After the first session, judgments of similarity were based on physical features like pitch and loudness. Only in sessions 2 and 3 did listeners perceive the theme-and-variation form of the musical passages. Then, they judged the variations of themes A and B as similar and judged the variations of A as different from variations of B. (Their judgments still reflected the physical features; the theme component was added to these others.) Experienced musicians were more likely to use the theme differences in making their judgments, particularly after sessions 1 and 2. The most expert musicians used only the theme feature; they did not use any of the possible physical features. What may be surprising is the inability to abstract the themes; the Liszt sonata is a difficult piece of music.

This research demonstrated that listeners could uncover the theme structure, but because of the complex passages of the sonata it was impossible to specify the features listeners were using to organize the themes. To discover which features are predominant, other research has systematically manipulated the construction of variations. For example, Halpern (1984) found that tunes with the same rhythm and/or contour were judged most similar and were most likely to be confused in a recognition task; tunes with different rhythms and/or contours were judged least similar and least likely to be confused in a recognition task. Musicians were sensitive to variations due to major versus minor key; nonmusicians hardly used this feature at all. Thus, even in a nonmusical context, listeners were quite adept at discovering the features that can create variations of a theme. Rhythm and contour categorize the tunes into themes for all listeners; scale type categorizes the tunes only for musically experienced listeners.

These studies illustrate that the musical concepts studied in experiments on short melodic passages are relevant in more natural situations. Listeners can abstract recurring themes within an ongoing sequence of notes, and the features that lead to this achievement are those inherent in the tonal-rhythmic structure. The ability to perceive music structurally is sharpened and enhanced by experience and knowledge of these possible relationships, as would be expected for all perceptual events.

Polyphonic and Contrapuntal Music
Before concluding, it is interesting to consider the perception of music in which there are two or more ongoing harmonically related melodic themes (termed *contrapuntal*) or music in which there is text and melody. In contrapuntal music, the simultaneous notes coming from each melodic line are harmonically related. The progression of chords formed by the simultaneous notes provides the harmonic framework for each of the melodic lines. From research on stream formation, we might expect that listeners can pay attention to one of the melodic lines but not to two or more at one time. Sloboda (1985) suggests that the musical harmonic relationships aid the perception of a coherent passage. This seems quite plausible, because research on stream segregation demonstrates that tones that are harmonically related and that have the identical temporal pattern tend to form one complex tone. This allows the melodic lines to reinforce each other so that at any point in time, one line is the focus and the other lines become background harmony. As Sloboda remarks, a wrong note will stick out because it creates a jarring harmony (and may lead to a splitting of the chord), but it may be difficult to pinpoint the error if one is not attending to the appropriate melodic line.

A similar situation occurs with songs, the combination of an apparently separate text and melody. Although it seems natural to imagine each component individually—a different text can be combined with a melody and two different texts can be combined with the same melody—several anecdotal sources suggest that a text and melody form an integrated event. For example, it is difficult to recognize that two songs with different words have the identical melody, e.g., "Twinkle, Twinkle, Little Star," the "Alphabet Song," and "Baa, Baa, Black Sheep." Moreover, it is often extremely difficult to recite the text of a well-known song without singing it.

To investigate whether text and melody are independent or integrated components, Serafine, Crowder, and Repp (1984) first presented a set of songs to listeners. We can represent the set of songs as M1T1, M2T2, M3T3, where M1 is the melody of song 1 and T1 is the text of song 1. They then scrambled the melody and text to produce new songs, such as M1T3, M2T1, M3T2, and tested the recognition for the melody and the text. They found that the text and melody were integrated: remembering the words depended on remembering the melody and vice versa. There was an asymmetry: memory for words was more independent of melody than melody from text. In particular, memory for melody was at the chance level unless the original text was present.

The authors point out that a melody can exist without words, but words always have a tune created by the intonation of spoken language. In a song, the melody becomes the intonation and can create the meaning for the text. Normally, we remember not the intonation per se, but only the meaning conveyed by that intonation (e.g., a question as opposed to a statement). From this perspective, the reason that melody is poorly remembered is the same reason that intonation is poorly remembered. Melody and intonation have been incorporated within the text meaning.

Major and Minor Keys
A chapter on music structure would be incomplete without a brief discussion of the tradition that major keys are thought to be "happy" and minor keys are thought to be "sad." This distinction is confounded by the tendency for pieces in a minor key to be lower in pitch and slower, which makes it difficult to attribute the emotion unambiguously to the minor key. Crowder (1984) argues nevertheless that the evidence for this characterization is strong, because even isolated major and minor chords reflect this affective dimension. There are two proposed explanations. The physical explanation is based on the fact that harmonics of the notes of major triads tend to match better (at lower harmonics) than the harmonics of the notes of minor triads. Thus, the major triads may be perceived as more consonant or more pleasant. The cultural explanation is that the major/minor distinction is merely convention and socialization: it is nothing more than an accident that major keys became associated with happiness and minor keys became associated with sadness. Whatever the explanation, the major

versus minor scale distinction is psychologically important, because it taps into one of our basic emotions.

10.7 Overview and Hesitations

The comparison between the perception of language and music is extremely difficult. Several authors (e.g., Bernstein 1976) have tried to evolve specific equivalences: phonemes to notes, words and/or sentences to phrases, linguistic deep structure to music harmonic structure. Ultimately these attempts fail, possibly because of the creative use of both language and music. Instead of trying to equate linguistic and musical levels or processes (either learned or innate), it is more useful to illustrate that music perception and understanding follow the general design characteristics for language perception and understanding. Music perception does involve arbitrariness and semanticity, duality, context dependence, and creativity.

We can think of music structure existing at three levels: notes, chords, and keys. There are structural relationships among elements within each level (e.g., among notes, among chords, and among keys), and there are structural relationships among elements in different levels (e.g., between notes and chords, between notes and keys, and between chords and keys).

At the level of notes, judgments of similarity reflect both the frequency difference and the harmonic relationships. In musical contexts, the tonic, the fifth, and the third are perceived as the closely related core notes; other diatonic notes are less closely related. These peripheral tones are perceived as resolving toward the core notes.

At the level of chords, both the harmonic relationships and the key context affect judgments of similarity. In a musical context, the tonic chord I, the dominant chord V, and the subdominant chord IV are perceived as the closely related core, with other diatonic chords less closely related. The peripheral chords are perceived as resolving toward the core chords, and the chord sequences ending with the V to I cadence appear to define the key. Thus, the within-level organization for both notes and chords is similar. At both levels there is a resolution toward the core, and at both levels the similarity judgments are a function of the musical key. The similarity between notes and chords changes as a function of the key: two notes or chords that are perceived as being closely related in one key context will be perceived as being distant in another key. In sum, the kind of organization is invariant across contexts, but which elements are seen as related and unrelated is a direct consequence of the key.

At the level of musical keys, the match between notes and chords determines the similarity and ease of movement between keys. Two keys that have the identical core notes are perceived as similar, and two keys that have a different set of core notes are perceived as dissimilar. Each chord, being a member of several keys, has a multiple identity; any chord can be the pivot in a change of key.

The relationships between levels appear cumulative, with each level built upon the previous one. It is possible to argue that the relationship among notes is primary. The two core notes of the scale—the tonic and the fifth—are the root notes of the two primary triad chords. Moreover, the number of identical scale notes predicts the distance between keys. But the similarity judgments between two notes are not context independent: the similarity between a pair of notes separated by the same interval depends on the scale positions of the notes. For this reason, there are no physical frequency relationships that uniquely determine note similarity, and therefore in turn there are no physical frequency relationships that uniquely determine chord and key similarity.

Musical listeners have constructed a set of intuitions or grammars about the structure of music as a consequence of their experience with music. The listener expects to hear a particular set of harmonic relationships, expects certain chords to resolve to others, and expects the notes of one key to modulate to the notes of another key. The listener possesses an open structure, within which the particular notes of a composition are understood; this is not different conceptually from the open structures of language. Jordan and Shepard (1987) have suggested that we think of the tonal structures as semirigid templates, with the distance between holes in the template set at the spacing of the major diatonic scale: 2, 2, 1, 2, 2, 2, 1. They imagine that when trying to perceive the musical meaning listeners slide this template up and down until the musical tones fit into its holes. The unevenness of the tonal spacing should result in a unique fit. The fit determines the role (e.g., tonic) of each note. Jordan and Shepard (1987) demonstrated experimentally that tones that do not fit the diatonic scale are perceived incorrectly. The notes are perceived according to the supposed spacing of the template rather than according to their true frequency intervals.

Yet I have misgivings. Fundamentally I am concerned whether experimentation has taken us too far from the experience of music. As Darwin (1976) states in the quotation at the beginning of this chapter, the segments of speech go unnoticed, subordinated to the intentions of speaker and hearer. Similarly, in music listening, the notes, chords, and key are subordinated to the perception of a cohesive unit. Music occurs "out of the blue" (Davies 1978), and for a novel melody the listener must discover the tonal framework as the melody unfolds. There is a constant back-and-forth listening in time, because past notes are required to give meaning to the present and future notes.

The research I have presented may be challenged in two ways.

1. The experiments typically use experienced subjects. The subjects usually have an extensive musical background, even though they may not have had formal training (surprisingly, there is very little research using very competent musicians). All of the research finds that the experienced subjects more closely approach the theoretical musical concepts, and the degree of experience predicts the fit. We can be uncharitable and argue that these results merely demonstrate the training of the subjects. These subjects are schooled in the conventions of music, and the experimentation is just a measure of their learning. On this basis, it is no wonder that the judgments match the theoretical constructs, and it raises the question whether these constructs are valid for untutored listeners.

There are several counterarguments. First, the differences between inexperienced and experienced listeners is one of degree. Inexperienced listeners do the same things as experienced listeners but not as well. Second, even Western children in the eight- to ten-year-old range display a harmonic sense. These children prefer endings using diatonic notes to endings using nondiatonic notes, are better able to distinguish errors in tonal sequences than in atonal sequences, are able to distinguish changes in contour and interval, and are able to distinguish near- from far-key transpositions (Krumhansl and Keil 1982; Trehub, Morrongiello, and Thorpe 1985). This is not to say that musical knowledge is innate; all it says is that sensitivity to music conventions is acquired early in life without formal training, just as language is (see Trehub 1987 for a review).

Overall, the contention would be that to capture the grammar of music one *needs* to utilize experts. After all, to capture language intuitions one needs to use expert language users, and it should be no different for music. What differs between language and music is that the average language user is an expert because of the immense amount of exposure the average person experiences. This is not the case for music; many have only a limited, passive involvement.

My feeling is that using musically experienced subjects does not seriously invalidate this research. Suppose we were interested in studying athletic skills. It would make most sense to experiment with world-class athletes. The world-class athlete would provide the timing, muscular strength, coordination, and so on that are required to optimal performance. This could provide baselines to discover why performance might diminish. If we started with average athletes, we might never know what factors were necessary for optimal performance (or what optimal performance was). At the very least, this work provides a set of possible perceptual skills against which other performances can be compared.

2. The experiments on notes, chords, and keys stem from only one music tradition or style, and that style is of relatively recent origin. Moreover, the musical concepts of this style, such as discrete notes, octave equivalences, tonic resolution, and key modulation, represent reflections and abstractions about that music. Prior to 1550 there was no harmony as we know it, and yet clearly there was music. There were composers, musicians who interpreted a composition, and listeners who understood a composition. Even now there is a diversity of styles, ranging from classical music written according to the above rules, to twelve-tone music based on different compositional techniques, to electronic synthetic music that may not be characterized by discrete pitches at all (Serafine 1983).

People listen, enjoy, and respond to all these kinds of music. But listeners do not necessarily hear the compositions in the same way that the composer intended. What this means is that though notes, chords, and keys serve as powerful ways of notating and describing music, there is no guarantee that they reflect the proper way to describe listening to music. Serafine (1983) argues: "They are not themselves the elements of music. They are at best powerful analytic inventions, but they are not the cognitive building blocks from which music is created or heard." This same issue arises in theories of speech perception. Are the speech sounds—the phonemes—the building blocks of speech, or are they after-the-fact abstractions, obtained only from highly trained linguists?

I do not believe that there is a *single* fundamental unit. From my perspective, it is the organizing tendencies of people, making sense of the events of music and speech, that result in *music* and *speech*. It is clear that a full understanding of perception will come only from an understanding at all perceptual levels. Although notes and chords as conceptualized in music theory may not be *the* building block, they are inherent in the music and must enter into our understanding of it. As discussed in the very first chapter, there are many levels of analysis. The elements are one level cohere to create a higher level and in turn are made up of elements of a lower level. There is no single level of explanation. From this somewhat hesitant perspective, I believe these outcomes concerning Western tonality are valuable. Thus to describe the cognitive structures underlying harmony does not "miss" the point. It is the description of one of several possible points.

Further Reading

Dowling, W. J., and Harwood, D. L. (1986). *Music cognition.* Orlando, Fla.: Academic.

Sloboda. J. A. (1985). *The musical mind: The cognitive psychology of music.* Oxford: Oxford University Press.

Chapter 11
Rhythm

Rhythmic organization is an inherent part of all human activity. Rhythm energizes, structures, creates, and expresses temporal quality. It is as important in hammering a nail or playing basketball as it is in speech, music, or dancing. Time is not merely the passive medium within which events occur. Rather, time acts to shape and determine all phenomena. Moreover, rhythmic organization exists at all levels of activity. Bill Russell, the former basketball star, talks about an individual's rhythm in shooting or dribbling, a team's rhythm in executing a play, and a game's rhythm in terms of the ebb and flow of intensity and momentum.

What musicians, carpenters, basketball players, and dancers have in common is an appreciation of rhythmic levels. The rhythm of a game emerges from the rhythm of individuals, the rhythm among team members, and the rhythmic contrasts between opposing teams. In the same way, musical rhythm emerges from the lines of each instrument or instrumental section. Each line might be simple or complex, and yet, in a very real sense, the rhythm cannot be found at any one of these levels. In the same way, speech rhythms emerge from diverse rhythmic levels; there is the rhythm of the words, phrases, and sentences, the rhythm portraying emotions, the rhythm used for emphasis, the rhythm unique to a regional dialect, and so on. As has been found for musical rhythms, the way one speech rhythmic level operates depends on the value of the other levels. The emergent rhythm is multifaceted. There is the beat or meter, the pace or tempo, the accent rhythm, the timing rhythm, and the melodic or intonation rhythm (Ladd 1980; Radocy and Boyle 1979). These aspects are not independent in much the same way that the rhythmic levels of a basketball game are not independent. They support each other and allow each to emerge.

It is difficult to disentangle all of the uses and meanings of the term rhythm. We could define rhythm in terms of the objective physical stimulus. From this perspective, we would attempt to identify those aspects of the physical wave, such as frequency, duration, intensity, or silence, that serve acoustically to segment the sounds in time. Alternatively, we could define rhythm in terms of the perceptual response. The response might be emotional, as in hearing a "dancing," "exciting," or "calm" rhythm, or the response might be behavioral, as in clapping, swaying, or toe-tapping, or the response might be physiological, as in changes in heart rate or muscular movements. Finally, we could define rhythm in terms of a notated system. The system would systematically mark the rhythm in terms of strong-weak, heavy-light, or filled-unfilled.

It seems appropriate to focus on the rhythmic experience. After all, a rhythm is emergent; it arises from a context, it is within the person. Thus it makes sense to talk about the acoustic characteristics or notational characteristics that may bring about a rhythmic perception. It makes sense, however, only within the context of the phenomenal experience of rhythm. We do not have a rhythm center in the brain, nor do we have specialized time receptors. There is no component of the acoustic signal that can uniquely specify the rhythm.

The experience of rhythm involves movement, regularity, grouping, and yet accentuation and differentiation. There is the experience of regular movement between more strongly accented elements; weaker elements belong to stronger elements, resulting in a sense of groups of elements. There is differentiation between the groups. In addition to the perceptual component, there is a distinct synchronization of the body to the strong accents.

Given the very apparent body reactions to rhythm along with the numerous spontaneous regular rhythmic actions—breathing, walking, sucking—it is no wonder that the initial psychological theories of rhythm centered on physiological processes. It was once claimed that periodic functions, such as heart or respiration rate, underlay the rhythmic response: tempos above these rates were considered fast, tempos below these rates were considered sluggish, and tempos that matched these rates were considered just right. In addition, it was claimed that rhythmical structures must initiate muscle movements in order for the impression of rhythm to emerge. It is quite clear, however, that although movements usually accompany rhythmic experience, they are not the cause of it (Fraisse 1982; Ruckmick 1913; Stetson 1905).

Subsequently, research shifted to investigate rhythm as a perceptual grouping or organization. These studies have emphasized the relationship between the timing of elements and the perceived rhythm. The term *timing* is used in a general sense. It includes the order of elements as well as the duration of each element and the duration of silent intervals between successive elements. This research, using simple sequences, can provide a background against which to understand the complex rhythms of music and speech.

11.1 The Rhythm of Sequences of Individual Tones

Natural Timings

If we conceptualize rhythm as the perception of the grouping and ordering of elements, it is appropriate to start by considering the "natural" timings that underlie the perception of rhythm. Suppose we begin with a single series of identical elements separated by equal time intervals. There are no acoustic differences among elements or among the intervals separating the elements to specify any grouping physically.

The first question we might ask concerns the succession of the elements. At one extreme, we can shorten the interval between the onsets of adjacent elements. If the interval is short enough, the elements are no longer perceived as one element following another but as continuous. Although there is no single absolute value for the required interval separating the elements, 50 msec (0.05 sec) is a rough estimate of the minimum interval needed to hear one element following another. At the other extreme, we can lengthen the interval between the onsets of adjacent elements. If the interval is too long, the individual elements are no longer perceived as following one another but as single, isolated events. The notion of rhythm is of a regular succession; separating the elements destroys the cohesion. Again, there is no single absolute value, but a rough estimate is that at intervals greater than 1.5–2.0 sec the percept changes from a regular unified sequence to a series of isolated elements (Fraisse 1978).

Is there is a preferred time interval, equivalent to a preferred tempo (that is, number of elements per second)? To answer this question, subjects have seen asked to tap at their preferred rate. This has been termed the *personal* tempo or *spontaneous* tempo (Fraisse 1963). As might be expected, there is a great deal of variability across individuals. The spontaneous tempo ranges from intervals of 200 msec (5.0 taps/sec) to 1.4 sec (0.7 taps/sec); the majority of individuals fall between 200 msec (5.0 taps/sec) and 900 msec (1.1 taps/sec), and a representative value would be 600 msec (1.7 taps/sec). Although there are large differences across individuals, each individual tends to have a stable tempo that occurs for various actions. (The spontaneous rhythms of identical twins are very similar; in contrast, the spontaneous rhythms of fraternal twins are no more similar than between unrelated people, which might suggest that the spontaneous tempo is biologically determined.) The spontaneous tapping rhythm closely matches the preferred perceptual rhythm in experiments in which subjects were required to adjust the presentation rate of tones to yield their most preferred rhythm.

What comes out of this is the conception that although rhythmic activities can occur over a wide range of timing, preferred rates occur from 200 msec (5.0 elements/sec) to 900 msec (1.1 elements/sec). Supporting evidence for this contention comes from two other sources:

1. When subjects are asked to reproduce temporal intervals, they tend to overestimate short intervals (making them longer) and underestimate long intervals (making them shorter). At an interval of about 500 msec to 600 msec, there is little over- or underestimation. This suggests a movement toward this latter "indifference" interval. Moreover, the accuracy of judging intervals is maximum around 500–600 msec and the accuracy declines for longer and shorter intervals (Fraisse 1963).

2. There are many spontaneous motor movements that occur at the rate of approximately 2/sec, such as walking, sucking in the newborn, and rocking. Although it is tempting to argue that motor movements determine the peception of rhythm, it is more likely that rhythm and movement patterns are indicative of a general timing sense.

In sum, below a certain time interval, separate events are perceived as continuous, and the regularity inherent in rhythm does not emerge (the continuous percept despite discrete elements is probably due to their neural persistence). Above a certain interval, elements are perceived as single, unconnected events, not of ongoing regularity. There seems to be a preferred range of timings from roughly 4 elements/sec to 1 element/sec. I do not believe that there is a rhythmic constant or temporal "moment." There is simply too much variation among individuals and within a single individual across tasks. There is, however, a relatively small range of spontaneous and/or preferred rhythmic intervals.

"Subjective" Rhythms

Now let us consider the perceptions of sequences of equally spaced, identical elements, termed *isochronous pulse trains*. As early as the 1890s, published research demonstrated that pulse trains appear to group into units of two or three or four despite the physical identity of the elements and despite the equal intervals between elements. The first note of each group is perceived as stronger and accented, and the following elements are perceived as weaker and unaccented. The authors termed these *subjective* rhythms, because there was no physical rhythm to perceive (Bolton 1894; Woodrow 1909). To them, the perception of a rhythmic organization was surprising. From our present perspective, the use of the term "subjective" was unfortunate, because all rhythms are subjective; events in the physical world merely follow one another. Subsequent research has suggested that there is a slight preference to organize into groups of four, but groups of three and two are nearly equal in popularity (see figure 11.1, panel a). In all cases, the initial element was perceived to be accented, and the time intervals between elements within each group appeared shorter than the

STIMULUS   PERCEPT

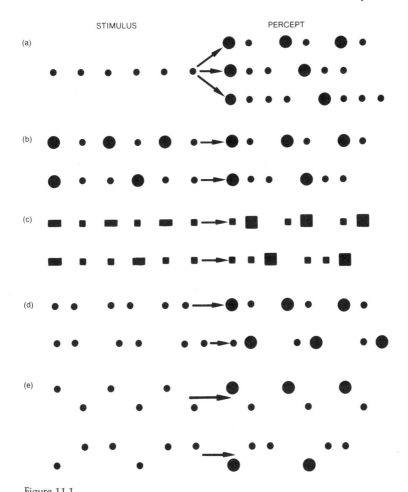

Figure 11.1
"Subjective" rhythm. A series of equally timed elements (i.e., equal temporal intervals
between the onset of successive identical elements) is perceived as rhythmical. A series of
identical elements, as in (a), is perceived to form groups of 2, 3, or 4 elements. The initial
element of each group is perceived to be accented (represented by a bigger filled circle), and
the time intervals between elements do not appear equal. If every second or third element is
more intense, as in (b), the elements are perceived to form groups so that the more intense
elements begin each group and there appear to be longer intervals between groups. If every
second or third element is longer, as in (c), the elements are perceived to form groups so
that the longer duration elements are the last elements of each group, the longer duration
elements appear accented, and there appear to be longer intervals between groups. If
every second interval between two elements is increased so that the elements form groups
temporally, as in (d), then the first elements of each group appears accented if the longer
interval is slightly greater than the other intervals, but the last element of each group
appears accented if the longer interval is much greater than the other interval. If the
elements are different frequencies, as in (e), then the elements are perceived to form groups
so that the higher-pitch element begins each group and appears accented, and the interval
between groups appears longer. If one note occurs less often, it may appear to be accented
and begin each group.

time intervals between the final element of one group and the initial elements of the next group. Surprisingly, the effect of presentation rate is small. As the elements speed up (say from 3 elements/sec to 5 elements/sec), the size of the group increases only slightly (Harrell 1937).

Subsequent research varied the sequence by making some elements louder, or by making some intervals longer in order to investigate the effect on rhythm perception. Some of these results are as follows:

1. Intensity accentuation. If alternative elements are accentuated by increasing their intensity, then the elements are perceived grouped into twos so that the accented element begins the group. The interval following the louder note seems shorter; the interval preceding the louder note seems longer. Similarly, if the intensity of every third note is increased, then the sequence is perceived grouped into threes, with the accented element starting the group. The two intervals following the louder note seem shorter and the interval preceding the louder note seems longer. Thus, the intensity context brings about a temporal reorganization—the intervals are no longer perceived as being identical (Fraisse 1956). Instead, the intervals within a group are assimilated and perceived as shorter, and the intervals separating groups are differentiated and perceived as longer (see figure 11.1, panel b).

2. Duration accentuation. If every second or third element is lengthened, then the elements are perceived in groups of two or three, with the shorter elements beginning the group. The perception of the sequence changes: the longer element is perceived to be accented, the intervals within a group are perceived to be shorter, and the intervals separating groups are perceived to be longer (Woodrow 1951). We might summarize by stating that intensity leads to group-beginning accentuation and duration leads to group-ending accentuation (see figure 11.1, panel c).

3. Interval differences. If the interval between every second or third element is lengthened, then listeners hear the sequence grouped into twos or threes. If the difference between the length of the intervals is small, then the initial element of each group appears to be accented. However, if the difference between the lengths of the intervals is large, then the final element of the group appears to be accented (Povel and Okkerman 1981) (see figure 11.1, panel d).

4. Frequency differences. The pitch of elements can affect the perceived grouping in several ways. First, the higher pitch elements tend to be perceived as the accented element of a group. Second, the least frequent element is usually perceived as the initial accented element of a group (see figure 11.1, panel e). Third, the "turn-around" pitch in an

up-down contour

        C
    b   b

tends to be perceived as accented (Thomassen 1982). Fourth, the initial element following a pitch "jump" tends to be perceived as accented (Jones 1981b), as in note B in

            e
        d   d
    c   c
        B

   Each of these factors may reinforce or conflict with another. For example, it is possible to "pit" intensity against interval to yield the perceived rhythm. Starting with a particular intensity difference yielding loud-soft rhythmic groups, the interval between the soft and loud elements can be lengthened until the rhythm shifts to soft-loud groups because of the interval timing. Then the intensity difference can be increased to reverse the grouping, and so on. Alternatively, small intensity and interval length differences may combine and yield a particular grouping, although neither alone would yield that outcome.

Rhythmic Organization
What can we take away from this work?

   1. It seems clear that listeners spontaneously organize auditory elements—musical notes, speech sounds, environmental events—into rhythmic groups. The formation of auditory streams can be conceptualized as the first step of this organization. Each stream is then further organized rhythmically. This should not be understood to imply a rigid sequence—stream formation and then rhythm organization. The timing among elements affects the stream segregation.
   2. In order for individual elements to emerge as rhythmical accents, the onset-to-onset tone interval must be within certain bounds; beyond about 1.5 sec, two elements lose a sense of coherence and appear unrelated.
   3. It seems most natural to group the elements into twos, threes, or fours. It is more difficult to group into fives or sevens. Longer rhythmic groups often have weaker perceptual accents that act to split the longer unit into groups of two or three. For example, a group of eight might be perceived as having the strongest accent on the first element, a strong accent on the fifth element, and weaker accents on the third and seventh elements.

4. The rhythmic grouping can be induced by many possible physical variables: intensity, duration, pitch, interelement timing, and timbre, among others. There seem to be distinct grouping rules; for example, the most intense element begins the group, but the longest element ends the group. All the variables act jointly to determine the perceived grouping. If two or more variables lead to different ways of splitting the elements, then the relative strength of each determines the rhythmic outcome.

5. It is critically important to realize that the perceptual grouping brings about a reorganization of the entire sequence. If only the intensity of elements is varied, this generates a change in the perceived interval between elements; likewise, if the interval between elements is varied, this generates a change in perceived intensity; and if the duration of elements is varied, this generates a change in the perceived intensity and the perceived intervals. These outcomes are therefore identical to nearly all other events: any single change affects the entire percept. It tells us that the perceived accent at one point may be the result of an acoustic change in another part of the sequence. It also points out the lack of correspondence between the characteristics of the physical acoustic wave and the perceived rhythm and accentuation.

6. Given the restructuring of the sequence, we must conceptualize rhythm as relative timing. The timing and accentuation of any single element is determined relative to the timing and accentuation of all other elements, adjacent ones as well as nonadjacent ones.

We might question whether rhythmic principles coming out of such simple auditory sequences can have relevance to the complex rhythms of music and speech. Initially, I was skeptical. Right now I feel that although these sequences cannot capture all of the aspects of rhythm, the notions of grouping into equal size units, competition among grouping cues, perceptual reorganization, and internal rhythmic structure can provide a foundation for the understanding of more complex rhythmic sequences.

11.2 Theories of Rhythm

When we move from repetitive sequences of identical elements, the perceived rhythm is determined not only by the features (e.g., pitch) of the individual elements but also by the structural relationships across the entire musical passage or linguistic utterance. The perception of the segments of speech and music is inherently context dependent, and I believe that the perception of the rhythms of speech and music is no less context dependent. This means that an understanding of the emergent rhythm must take into account several levels of analysis and that each level is in turn dependent on every other level. This also means that it is unlikely that it will be possible to develop a context-free procedure that, given the acoustic wave, can induce the perceived rhythmic structure. To start off, we must consider each rhythmic level separately.

Meter and Beat
Beats refer to the sense of equally spaced temporal units. Beats are often marked by the onset of individual sounds, but the sense of beats can occur even without physical elements. *Meter* is the sense of a regular, periodic sequence of subjectively stronger and weaker beats that characterizes music and many languages. When we tap in time with a record we are beating out the meter, when we dance we are moving in time with the meter, and when we parade we are stepping in time with the meter. I would guess that meter is what most people think of as rhythm.

A theory of rhythm must account for the sense of meter, the alternation of strong and weak beats. It must also account for which notes become strong beats and which notes become weak beats. Finally, it must account for the grouping of beats, for which strong and weak beats go together. Before the factors that affect beat assignment can be discussed, it is necessary to generate an abstract representation of meter.

The alternation of strong and weak beats occurs at several tempos. We can tap in synchrony to every note or syllable, but typically we tap every second, third, or fourth element, and we tap every fourth, sixth, or eighth element more strongly. Thus we need to think of the levels of meter: there are faster meters at lower levels (strong beats every second note) and slower meters at higher levels (strong[er] beats every fourth or even every eighth note). It is the combination of the meters at different levels that gives rise to the perceived strength of any beat. It is the fact that the meter is perceived as layered in both music and speech that has led theorists to describe meter as hierarchical (Martin 1972; Yeston 1975).

In general, a hierarchical structure is composed of individual items such that a set of items at one level may be split up into smaller sets at a lower level (e.g., the set of elements "abcde" may be split into one set, "abc", and another set, "de") and such that two sets of items at one level can combine to form a larger set at a higher level. The process of creating the hierarchy determines the relationships among the levels and among the groups at each level. If we consider a country, the first lower level might consist of the provinces or states, and the next lower level might consist of the cities within each province or state. Each lower level is a political (or functional) subdivision of the higher level. Alternatively, we might first slice the country down the middle, north to south (thereby splitting some states). Then we could slice the western region in half and likewise slice the eastern region in half. In this case, each lower level is a geographical subdivision of the higher level. Returning to musical and language meter, each level becomes a pattern of beats. Each lower level is a subdivision of the interval between beats in a higher level. If the beats occur every four time units in the higher level, the beats might occur every two time units in the lower level.

Meter and Grouping

To achieve a complete theory of rhythm, Lerdahl and Jackendoff (1983) argue that we need to create two hierarchies. The meter hierarchy will represent the strength of each beat. The grouping hierarchy will represent the organization of stronger and weaker beats into chunks, phrases, or units (e.g., phrases like strong-weak or weak-weak-strong). It is important to realize that there are many possible meter and grouping hierarchies, because the strong beat can be assigned to different elements and the beats can be grouped in different ways. Lerdahl and Jackendoff reduce this ambiguity in two steps. The initial step is to define "well-formedness rules," which specify the shape and form of all possible hierarchies. The second step is to define "meter preference rules" and "grouping preference rules," which specify the perceptual tendencies and inclinations of the listener. The preference rules lead to the perception of one of the possible "well-formed" meter hierarchies and one of the possible "well-formed" grouping hierarchies. The well-formedness rules are identical for music and speech; the meter preference and grouping preference rules will differ for the two domains.

Well-formedness rules: meter hierarchies   The well-formedness rules act to limit the possible hierarchies to musically appropriate ones. One proposed rule limits the meter at each level to equally spaced beats. At the lowest level of the hierarchy, each *equal* time unit receives one beat. If each eighth note receives one beat, then a half note (equal to four eighth notes) receives four beats and the combination of two sixteenth notes (each equal to one-half an eighth note) receives one beat. Each successive upward level represents a slower meter in which the beats are further separated in time. At each level, however, the beats are equally timed and occur in synchrony with beats at the lower level (Martin 1972).

In traditional Western music, beats at the higher levels tend to occur on every second (or third beat) of the lower levels. Thus, at higher levels the beats occur every second, fourth, or eighth (or every third, sixth, or twelfth) beat. In the figures here, the beats at each metrical level (a single row) are represented by dots below the strong elements or notes. The lowest meter is found right below the elements: there is a beat (dot) at each time point. The first higher meter is found one row down: there is a beat at every other time point. The next higher levels are represented by lower and lower rows: there is a beat every fourth or eighth time point. This notation has been used to draw a meter hierarchy for the sequence A1B2C3D4 in figure 11.2. For each level of the hierarchy, there is one level of the meter.

An example written in musical notation is also shown in figure 11.2. Here, the sequence is eight time units long but elements have different duration values. The sequence is made up of sixteenth notes (4/time unit), eighth notes (2/time unit), quarter notes (1/time unit), and half notes (2 time units). At the lowest level of the meter hierarchy, the representation of the timing is based on the shortest element, the sixteenth note, so that there are four beats per time unit. (The half note is thus represented by eight beats.) Each higher level of the meter represents a doubling of the time unit. Therefore the second level represents eighth notes (2 beats/time unit), the third level represents quarter notes (1 beat/time unit), and continuing down the fifth level represents whole notes (1 beat/4 time units). Again, there is a one-to-one match between the levels of the hierarchy and the levels of the meter.

The beats at each level are equally strong, and the relative strength of each note/beat is indicated by the number of levels at which the beats appear. The onsets of the first and fifth time units are perceived to be the strongest beats because they receive beats on five levels, and the onset of the third and seventh time units are perceived to be the secondary beats because they receive beats on four levels. Notice that the strength of any beat is relative; it depends on the structure of the hierarchy.

Well-formedness rules: grouping hierarchies   The proposed rules include: (1) only adjacent elements may form groups and an element cannot be skipped over; (2) with rare exceptions, an element may be in only one group at a single level; and (3) the relation between levels does not change in moving from level to level.

Preference rules   The well-formedness rules cannot identify which meter or grouping will emerge. There are many possible meters and groupings that satisfy these rules. To provide a concrete example for meters, imagine a repeating twelve-unit passage made up of notes with identical timing, e.g., abcdefghijklabcdefghijkl etc. There are permissible meter hierarchies based on triples, and there are hierarchies based on duples. In addition, there are alternative ways that the stronger beats at different levels can be assigned. If the passage is organized by threes, then the beats on the second level may occur in three ways: AbcDefGhiJkl or BcdEfgHijKla or CdeFghIjkLab. At the next level, the strong beats could be assigned in two ways:

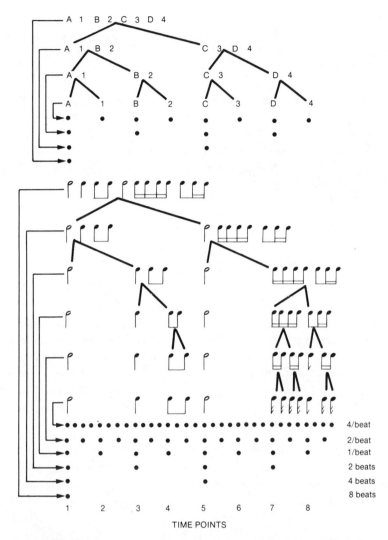

Figure 11.2
Meter hierarchies. The meter hierarchy for the sequence A1B2C3D4 is portrayed at the top. Each element is assumed to be one beat long. The sequence is split into two groups of 4, four groups of 2, and ultimately eight groups of 1 at the lowest level of the hierarchy. At the lowest level, each element receives one beat, represented by a dot placed under the elements. At the next highest level, the first element of each group receives a beat so that there are four beats. One level further up, the first element of each group again receives a beat so that there are two beats. At the highest level, only the first element receives a beat. A musical meter hierarchy is illustrated next. Each level from the top represents the partitioning of the entire phrase into equal subunits of time. At the lowest level, each sixteenth note (the shortest element) is given one beat. At each higher level, the time scale expands by a factor of 2 until at the highest level only the first note receives a beat.

using AbcDefGhiJkl, either on elements A̲ and G̲, or on elements D̲ and J̲. If the beat assignment is A̲bcDefG̲hiJkl, at the highest level, the strongest beat could be assigned in two ways: A̅bcDefG̲hiJkl, or A̲bcDefG̅hiJkl. Thus there are twelve possible meters if the passage is broken into groups of three. In addition to this, the grouping of strong and weak notes can be done in three ways: (Abc) (Def) (Ghi) (Jkl), or (bcD) (efG) (hiJ) (klA), or (cDe) (fGh) (iJk) (lAb). By the same reasoning, there are twelve possible meters if the passage is broken into groups of two and four. To provide a concrete example for grouping, imagine a simple repeating sequence, e.g., 12341234 etc. The elements can be placed into two groups in seven ways: (12) (34); (23) (41); (13) (24); (123) (4); (1) (234); (2) (341); or (3) (412). The well-formedness rules only disallow groupings like (13) (24), (134) (2), or (124) (3), in which groups are not composed of adjacent elements (as might occur in stream segregation).

The preference rules compensate for this ambiguity by proposing perceptual rules for predicting which of the possible meters (i.e., which elements will be perceived as strongly accented) and which groupings will take precedence. These rules resemble the Gestalt principles of visual organization (discussed in chapter 7). One way to think about meter preference rules is to start with a metric grid of strong and weak beats, as derived in figure 11.2, and to imagine sliding that grid along a musical passage or utterance so that the strong beats will fall on different elements as the grid moves. What preference rules do is suggest which assignment of strong beats to elements is musically "best" according to the conventions of Western music. (It is impossible to define "best" unambiguously. It is much like the Gestalt psychology concept of Prägnanz, discussed in chapter 7, for which I similarly argued no definition was adequate.) The rules are not laws; they do not prescribe what organization should occur. Listeners do differ, and this leads to alternative rhythmic perceptions.

The preference rules for meter and grouping hierarchies are of different sorts and apply to different aspects of the sequence.

1. The first set of rules applies to sequences of identical elements separated by different-length silent intervals, such as xx-xx-xxxxx- (the x's represent elements, the hyphens represent blank intervals). For meter hierarchies, Povel and Essens (1985) suggest preference rules such as: (a) a strong beat should not occur on a silence or rest; (b) a strong beat should occur on the first or last element of a run of adjacent identical elements; (c) strong beats should occur at the same place in repeating phrases; (d) strong beats should occur in a two-beat meter—strong, weak, strong, weak—or in a three-beat meter—strong, weak, weak, strong, weak, weak. For grouping hierarchies, elements close in time will be placed in same group. Silences (musical

rests) partition the elements. (Slurred elements also will tend to be placed in the same group.)

One repeating twelve-element sequence is shown in figure 11.3. For that sequence (xx-xx-xxxxx-) we need to consider various strong-weak-weak and strong-weak meters. The best fit is a strong-weak-weak, three-beat meter. For any three-beat meter, the stronger beats would be spaced six beats part (e.g., 1 and 7, or 2 and 8, or 3 and 9, etc.) and the strong beats would be three beats apart, splitting the stronger beats. The problem is to fit a three-beat meter to the pattern. Theoretically there are twelve possibilities, because the strongest beat could fall on any element (or empty interval). The best fit is shown in panel (a). Strong beats would be felt on elements 1, 4, 7, and 10; stronger beats would be felt on elements 1 and 7; and the strongest beat would be felt on elements 1 or 7. In this case the strong beats occur at the beginning of runs of elements (with one exception); the strong beats do not occur on silent elements; and the strong beats occur at the same elements in parallel units (e.g., elements 1 and 4). No other possible meter works as well. The elements would be unambiguously grouped by the silent elements into groups of three and then groups of six as shown by the brackets underneath (a). This creates runs of 2, 2, and 5 elements. For this rhythm, the best meter and best grouping are identical: the stronger beats occur at the beginning of runs of elements. The meter in panel (b) is a possible alternative, yet the second stronger beat falls in the middle of a run of elements. For other meters shown in panels (c) and (d), strong beats fall on weaker elements. There is still an unresolved question: should element 1 or 7 receive the strongest beat? To resolve this, we need additional preference rules: for example, a rule that longer runs come at the end of the phrase.

It is important to realize that the meter affects the perception of the entire sequence. Povel and Essens (1985) constructed twelve-element sequences of this sort and accompanied each sequence with a drum tap that occurred every three time elements or every four time elements. Listeners were unable to recognize that the two sequences were identical when played in different meters. This result is analogous to those in the previous chapter concerning the "locked-together" memory for text and melody in songs.

2. The second set of rules applies to sequences in which the elements vary in intensity and duration. For meter hierarchies, strong beats would occur on the more intense or longer duration elements; also, strong beats would occur at the beginning of changes in accentuation, as in going from forte (loud) to piano (soft); at the beginning of changes in articulation, as in going from four notes per beat (sixteenth

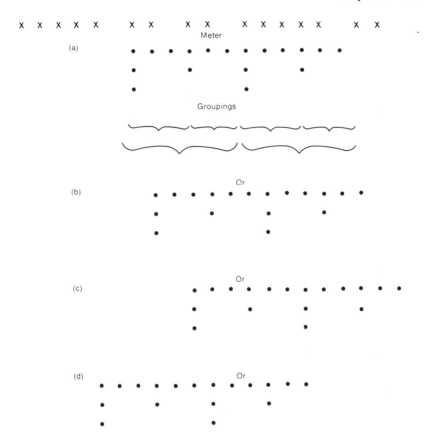

Figure 11.3
Fitting a meter to a rhythm. The rhythm xx-xx-xxxxx- is 12 elements long. The beat meter
is a 3-beat; strong-weak-weak. The best way to fit a 3-beat meter is indicated in (a). The
grouping of the elements is indicated by brackets. No other grouping into threes or fours is
as good. The strong beats fall at the beginning of runs of elements. Other possible ways of
fitting a meter are shown in (b), (c), and (d). None of these is as good as (a) in terms of
matching the meter preference rules.

notes) to two notes per beat (eighth notes); or at the beginning of notes that are slurred together. For grouping hierarchies, more intense and longer duration notes partition the elements into groups (exactly as found for subjective rhythms). Moreover, changes in acoustic qualities like articulation, length, timbre, and intensity partition elements. Similar elements will be placed in one group, and the boundaries between groups occur at changes of these qualities.

3. The third set of rules applies to sequences in which the notes vary in frequency. Here, the strong beats of the preferred meters occur at points of large changes in pitch, at points of changes of harmony, and at points in the traditional Western cadences (as explained in chapter 10). In addition, the lower pitch notes tend to be more important to the perception of the meter than higher pitch tones. Thus one more preference rule would be to prefer meters with strong beats on the bass notes. With respect to grouping, the notes within each group should be similar in one way. For example, each group could be composed of identical elements, alternating elements, or ascending or descending progressions. The repeating sequence 111234333456 is probably grouped as (111) (234) (333) (456) rather than (112) (343) (334) (561).

The groupings may be hierarchically organized in the same fashion that beats can be hierarchically organized (Jones 1987). Two adjacent groups at a lower level can be combined into a single group at a higher level. For example, the sequence 111234333456 could be initially grouped by threes at the lowest level: (111) (234) (333) (456). Then the sequence could be grouped by sixes at the second level: [(111) (234)] [(333) (456)]. And the sequence could be grouped into a single unit of twelve at the highest level: {[(111) (234)] [(333) (456)]}.

4. One overall grouping principle that must be mentioned, common to all perceptual and cognitive functioning, is to place elements into equal-sized groups and to avoid groups of one or two items (Imai 1966). Thus, with twelve notes (or twelve syllables), people prefer to make three groups of 4, four groups of 3, or possibly two groups of 6. People tend not to make six groups of 2, or to place differing numbers of elements in each group (e.g., a 5/4/3 split).

To summarize, meter preference rules attempt to account for the placement of accentuation, for stronger beats alternating with weaker beats. Some meter preference rules parallel the research on auditory subjective rhythm. Strong beats are equally spaced, strong beats occur on louder elements, and strong beats occur on the first element of a run of elements. Other preference rules parallel the research on Western tonality. Strong beats occur at harmonic (key) changes and at ending cadences. Still other preference rules parallel general research on cognitive organization. Strong beats occur at the same point in parallel units. Grouping preference rules attempt to account for the linking of stronger and weaker beats into groups. Elements with similar acoustic qualities like frequency, timbre, or intensity are placed in one group; elements in close temporal proximity are placed in one group; and elements that form progressions, alternations, or Western tonal cadences are placed in one group. The meter structure can be said to punctuate the notes of the melody, the strong beats accentuating the important notes and the weak beats providing the connection among the stronger beats. The grouping of stronger and weaker beats brings about the completion of the rhythmic interpretation. These groupings are combined with the meter/beat structure. Neither is primary.

Bringing the meter and grouping structures together begins to express the complexity of music. In a musical passage, the meter and grouping structures interact. The melodic phrases may be in phase with the meter structure so that the initial, important elements of the phrase occur on the strongest beats, or the melodic phrases may be out of phase so that the important notes fall on weak beats. For example, in the simple eight-element pattern "xxxooooo," the meter structure would create stronger beats on the first and fifth element, but the grouping structure would partition the three x's from the five o's. Thus, the meter and grouping are out of phase. Moreover, a weak beat is sometimes heard as an upbeat and sometimes heard as a downbeat, because of the relation of the weak beat to the strong beat in terms of the grouping structure. Lerdahl and Jackendoff (1983) speculate that in short time spans (close to the musical surface), it is the meter hierarchy that imposes the perceived strength of the elements. The elements are heard with respect to the strong and weak beats. Yet in longer time spans, the grouping hierarchy organizes the piece into phrases, themes, and sections. At the higher grouping levels, units are found that repeat or rephrase the tonal motion. The elements are heard with respect to the beginning and end of the themes. It seems intuitive that different levels of analysis might require different perspectives. We will come to the same conclusion for speech rhythms, namely that the interplay between meter and grouping determines rhythm. The meter of speech rhythms underlies the perception in English of the alternation of strong and weak syllables, and the grouping and melody of speech underlies the organization of major pitch changes, which signify various emotional, informational, emphatic, and attitudinal components.

11.3 Experimental Research on Music-Like Rhythms

Rhythm simultaneously creates a sense of accentuation and of grouping; rhythm partitions and organizes the ongoing sequence. The theoretical discussion of rhythm in the previous section distinguished meter from grouping in order to emphasize the interlocking parts of rhythmic experience. The perception of a rhythm structure yields both the meter and the grouping at one time, however, and I doubt that it is possible to separate them in experience. The meter and the grouping are based on the identical sound sequence. The majority of research has not attempted to distinguish between the two but has attempted instead to study the ways in which different acoustic characteristics lead to rhythm perception.

This review of the experimental work is organized into three subsections. The first covers research in which the notes are physically identical, but the timings among notes are varied. These may be termed patterns "of time." The second covers research in which the timing among notes is identical, but the frequency (or intensity) patterning among notes is varied. These may be termed patterns "in time." Third covers research that combines timing with frequency patterns. The goal of these experiments is to investigate how the temporal pattern and the frequency (or intensity) pattern combine to create the perception of rhythm.

Patterns of Time

One rhythmic line   Meter has been defined as the periodic alternation of strong and weak beats. As described previously, Povel and Essens (1985) argue that in a sequence of identical elements, the single elements, the second element of a pair, and the first and last elements of a run are naturally perceived as accented, exactly as was noted above when discussing "subjective" rhythm. They argue that if the strong accented elements are equally spaced in time, then a stable meter will quickly emerge to fit the natural accents. Such a pattern should be easy to reproduce. If, however, the accents are not equally spaced in time, then any meter (the regular progression of strong beats) will fall on some accented elements, some weak elements, and possibly some silent intervals. There will be no stable meter, and the pattern should be difficult to perceive and to reproduce. For patterns with sixteen temporal units (either a tone or a silence), a four-beat meter would divide the pattern evenly. Strong beats would occur on elements 1, 5, 9, and 13 (the pattern would repeat on element 17). Examples of sixteen-unit sequences with natural accents on elements 1, 5, 9, 13, 17, etc., that fit a four-beat meter and examples of sixteen-unit sequences that do not fit a four-beat meter are shown in figure 11.4.

The experimental results clearly demonstrated that sequences in which the natural accents occurred every fifth element, matching a four-beat meter, were easier to grasp and identify than other sequences in which the accents did not fit a four-beat meter. For the easy sequences in which accents formed a meter, subjects were able to repeat the patterns to dupli-

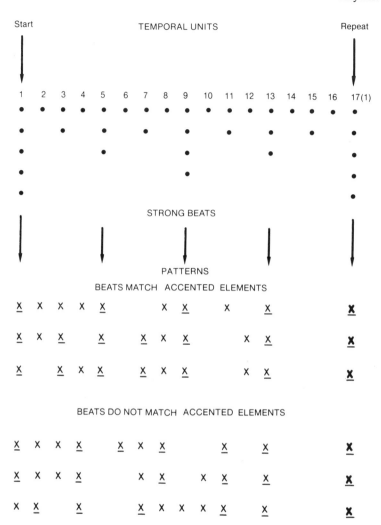

Figure 11.4
Patterns in time. The pattern of stronger and weaker beats that would occur when a 4-beat
meter is used to organize a 16-unit repeating pattern is pictured at the top of the figure. The
strongest beats occur at time points 1 and 9, and slightly weaker strong beats occur at time
points 5 and 13. Repeating 16-unit patterns composed of 9 elements are shown below. The
naturally accented elements, according to Povel and Essens (1985), are underlined. For the
first three patterns, the strong beats fall on the accented elements, which means that these
patterns should be easy to perceive and reproduce. For the second three patterns, the strong
beats do not fall on the accented elements; these patterns should be difficult to perceive and
reproduce.

cate the interval timing between elements closely. As can be seen in figure 11.4, the silent interval between elements could be one to four units long, and with a stable meter listeners were able to reproduce the different interval lengths accurately. On the other hand, for the difficult sequences in which the accents did not form a meter, subjects were unable to reproduce the length of silent intervals accurately. Instead of hearing the sequence in terms of the timing, they tended to hear the sequence in term of the element grouping. For example the fifth pattern figure 11.4 would be: a four-element group, silent interval, two-element group, silent interval, two-element group, silent interval, one-element group, silent interval. The groups of elements become the figure, not the timing between groups; the relative timing of the intervals is lost. Subjects tended to reduce the various intervals to two kinds—a short one between elements within a group and a long one between groups.

It should be no surprise that listeners tend to simplify rhythms. What may be surprising is the degree to which the intervals from the onset of one note to the onset of the next note are reduced to two or three values. Studies by Fraisse (1956) and Povel (1981) have shown that subjects spontaneously use only two intervals such that the shorter one is roughly one-half the length of the longer one. The duration of the shorter interval is less than 400 msec—from 150 msec to 400 msec (about 7 to 2 elements/sec)—and the duration of the longer interval is 300 msec to 860 sec (about 3 to 1 elements/sec). When listeners are asked to reproduce temporal patterns, they tend to simplify the original intervals by making the similar intervals more identical and making the longer intervals equal to twice the shorter intervals. The short interval leads to the perception of succession, a series of notes. The longer interval leads to the perception of grouping and separation, a differentiation between notes. For example, a pattern with the onset-to-onset intervals 300–450=450 (in msec) was reproduced as 270–560–530 (in msec), which thereby makes the ratio between the short and long interval closer to 2 to 1. For a second example, a 180–690–450 pattern is reproduced as 170–670–550, which thereby makes the length of the two longer intervals more similar. Dauer (1983) reports similar results for speech: pauses within a sentence were roughly one-half the length of pauses between sentences (roughly 0.5 sec to 1.0 sec).

The simplification of timing can be seen in a different way by examining the use of different note durations in Western music. The duration of a note can extend from a sixty-fourth note (1/16 of a beat) to a whole note (4 beats): seven possibilities exist, because each type of note is twice the length of the previous type. In addition, the duration of each type can be increased 50% by means of dot notation, so that overall there are fourteen possible durations. Nonetheless, Fraisse (1956) counted the frequency of different durations in compositions ranging from Beethoven to Stravinsky to Bartók and found that these composers tended to use only two durations extensively in any piece. Two durations account for over 85% of the notes in one composition. The ratio of the two durations is 2 to 1 (e.g., quarter note to eighth note, or eighth note to sixteenth note), and the shorter duration is more frequent (59% to 27%).

The experimental results and music conventions converge. In reproducing temporal intervals, subjects are able to use only two intervals accurately. All shorter and all longer intervals tend to become more similar, and the ratio between the shorter and longer intervals tends toward 2 to 1. These adjustments act to reinforce the sense of meter, in which the stronger beats falling on elements are equally spaced in time. Musical compositions use the identical timing conventions for the duration of notes. The short durations are equivalent, the long durations are equivalent, and the ratio is 2 to 1. These timing constraints may be imposed by perceptual limitations. For example, in absolute judgment experiments (discussed in chapter 9), subjects could judge accurately only two or three tone durations. Thus, the dominance of duple meter in Western music may not be due merely to convention. However, we would expect professional musicians to have far better control of timing and to produce different timings for expressive reasons.

Multiple rhythmic lines   Although the results from Western music tend to portray a simple meter structure for rhythm, the music of Africa, based on the interplay of different rhythmic lines, provides a different picture. Basically, Western music has one beat (the conductor's beat), and all the rhythmic lines that bring about the sense of meter are divisions or multiples of that beat. In contrast, African drum rhythms are composed of simultaneous rhythmic lines that are not simply related to each other. Moreover, each rhythmic line may be irregular, with the intervals changing between notes. The notes of each line usually do not occur at equal time intervals, and therefore it is impossible to construct a meter in which beats do not fall at an empty interval. For example, A. M. Jones (1959) and Pressing (1983) have identified standard patterns that are common to much of African rhythm: X-X--X-X-X--X-X--X-X-X-- and X-X-X--X-X-- X-X-X--X-X--. Both patterns consists of twelve units with the notes (hand claps) of the first pattern falling on 1, 3, 6, 8, and 10 (and then again on 1) Each clap is identical; none is stressed. Patterns are typically tapped at a rapid rate; the twelve units taking about 2 seconds or less. Because of this rapid rate, the pattern is probably perceived as one unit. Pressing (1983) suggests that the inability to create a stable meter makes the patterns rhythmically interesting. There are alternative ways of perceiving the pattern; the rhythm never settles into one stable, repeating unit.

African drum rhythms are made up of several rhythmic lines. It is very helpful to conceptualize each line as related to a fast regular pulse in the background. Thus, a song with one clap every three units and a different clap every four units would be conceptualized in twelve units as shown in figure 11.5. In an actual composition, some of the rhythmic lines will be regular (isochronous), such as tapping every three, four, or six elements, and other lines will be irregular, such as the X-X--X-X-X-- pattern described above. There has been very little research on the perception of rhythms composed of two or more lines, and the research that has been done has used only uniform pulses that are dissonant (e.g., a two-line polyrhythm might be 3 against 5 where 3 indicates three notes per time unit and where 5 indicates five notes per time unit, or a three-line polyrhythm might be 3 against 4 against 5). In this work a polyrhythm composed of two or three lines is presented, and the subject is asked to tap along with the perceived meter. The perceived meter is nearly always one of the rhythmic lines, and the subject will tap in synchrony to each element or possibly every other element of that rhythmic line (Handel 1984).

The results of this research give insights into the choice of meter in Western music, even though Western compositions based on dissonant rhythmic lines are atypical.

1. The first factor determining the choice of meter is the onset-to-onset interval betwen elements of one rhythmic line. If the elements are separated by more than 800 msec, the elements appear unconnected and disjointed and are thus unsuited to serve as the meter. If the elements are separated by less than 200 msec, the elements appear grouped with subjectively accented and unaccented elements; here also the elements cannot serve as the meter to provide a regular beat. This means that the perceived meter will change as a function of the overall tempo. Consider a 2 against 7 polyrhythm. If a measure takes 3 seconds, then the seven-element rhythm line will be chosen as the meter, because the two-element line is too slow (1.5 sec between elements). However, if a measure takes one second then the two-element line will be chosen as the meter, because the seven-element line is too fast (143 msec between elements). These limits are context dependent and not absolute, because they are a function of the overall composition.

2. The second factor is the pitch of the elements of one rhythmic line. (In all cases the elements of one line were identical.) Typically, the meter chosen was the rhythmic line with the lower pitch or the

PATTERN (LENGTH)   ELEMENTS

Pattern (Length)	1	2	3	4	5	6	7	8	9	10	11	12	13	14	15	16	17
ISOCHRONOUS PATTERNS																	
2(2)	X		**X**														
3(3)	X			**X**													
4(4)	X				**X**												
NON-ISOCHRONOUS																	
332(8)	X			X			X		**X**								
2223(9)	X		X		X		X			**X**							
22233(12)	X		X		X		X			X			**X**				
22323(12)	X		X		X			X		X			**X**				
23223(12)	X		X			X		X		X			**X**				
2223223(16)	X		X		X		X			X		X		X			**X**
33424(16)	X			X			X				X		X				**X**

POLYRHYTHMS

Start   Repeat

ELEMENTS

3 x 4 (repeats on element 13)

Line	1	2	3	4	5	6	7	8	9	10	11	12	13
3	3				3				3				3
4	4			4			4			4			4

ELEMENTS

2 x 3 x 7 (element markers printed: 1, 10, 20, 30, 43)

Line	Beats (value at elements)
1	markers: 1, 10, 20, 30, 43
2	2 at elements 1, 22, 43
3	3 at elements 1, 15, 29, 43
7	7 at elements 1, 7, 13, 19, 25, 31, 37, 43

ELEMENTS

2 x 5 x 7 (element markers printed: 1, 18, 36, 54, 71)

Line	Beats (value at elements)
1	markers: 1, 18, 36, 54, 71
2	2 at elements 1, 36, 71
5	5 at elements 1, 15, 29, 43, 57, 71
7	7 at elements 1, 11, 21, 31, 41, 51, 61, 71

Figure 11.5

Rhythmic patterns that are used in the drum music of Africa. Typically several rhythmic lines are played simultaneously, and often a master drummer improvises on top of the repeating rhythmic patterns. Polyrhythms are defined as the simultaneous presentation of two isochronous patterns that do not share a common denominator. Three examples are shown. The element at which the polyrhythm repeats can be calculated by multiplying the number of elements in each line together (e.g., the pattern 2 × 5 × 7 ends on the 70th element and repeats on the 71st element).

contrasting pitch, if two or more rhythmic lines had the identical frequency. Using a different procedure based on similarity judgments, Pitt and Monahan (1987) suggest that pitch information can be independent of the rhythmic information.

3. The third factor is the configuration of the polyrhythm. For example, a meter based on the seven-element rhythmic line was preferred for a 2 against 3 against 7 polyrhythm, but a meter based on the two-element rhythmic line was preferred for a 2 against 5 against 7 polyrhythm. The polyrhythm as a whole acts to highlight or focus one of the rhythmic lines (see figure 11.5).

4. The fourth factor was the intensity of the elements. Invariably the louder rhythmic line was chosen as the meter, though this was affected by the timing and frequency of the rhythmic lines.

All in all, these results portray a consistent pattern of outcomes. Meter is regularity, the regular alternation of stronger beats with weaker beats. Which elements are perceived to be the strong beats is based on the tempo and the timing among the elements as well as on the acoustic qualities of the elements. The regular strong beat—weak beat timing of a meter has clear functional use. If the important notes occur on the strong beats, then listeners can plan to "hear ahead" and direct their attention to the important upcoming notes. This allows listeners to be more efficient in the face of competing notes and allows for the lapses of attention that are inevitable (M. R. Jones 1976; Martin 1972). For speech, it is clear that being able to predict when important words will occur can be of immense help in communication.

Overall, I believe that music theory underestimates the effect of timing and tempo on meter organization. On the one hand, there are constraints because of the inability to distinguish more than two or three durations, and the inability to perceive a meter easily outside of onset-to-onset intervals between 200 and 800 msec. This has probably lead to the building up of the strong and weak beats out of two or three timing units that are multiples of each other. On the other hand, there is the question of whether rhythmic organization is independent of tempo. At first glance, it seems that speeding up or slowing down the tempo is equivalent to transposing a musical passage up or down in frequency. But changing the tempo changes the size of the timing intervals, and different rhythms may emerge. (This would be analogous to expanding or contracting the size of the frequency intervals.) In several studies, changes in tempo are the major factor determining perceived dissimilarity (e.g., Gabrielsson 1973). I am sure that it would be possible to take a melody and, without any note changes, produce a slow version that could not be recognized as being identical to a fast version (Sink 1983).

Patterns in Time
Even if the notes are equally intense and equally spaced, the frequency
pattern of the notes leads to a sense of rhythm, with subjectively stronger
and weaker beats and subjectively longer and shorter intervals between
notes. Here we will be concerned with the principles that underlie the
grouping of the elements and thus determine the perceived beats.

Binary patterns   The simplest situation uses patterns made up of just two
elements. Garner (1974) and his co-workers constructed eight-element patterns composed of two elements differing in frequency. The patterns
were presented over and over again without pause (i.e., recycled). A
pattern like XXXOXOOO, for example, would generate the sequence
XXXOXOOOXXXOXOOO etc. Subjects listened to the sequence and,
when they felt ready, described the pattern in terms of the X, O sequence.
They could describe the sequence as XXXOXOOO, or OXOOOXXX, or
OOOXXXOX. In fact, there are eight ways to describe the sequence,
starting at each one of the eight pattern elements.
    At faster rates, typical of music (2 elements/sec or faster), the patterns
tend to be perceived with little sense of trying to figure it out; the pattern
is perceived as a whole. Subjects hear one element as the figure and one as
the ground. The pattern XXXOXOOO can be represented as:

$$X \; X \; X \; \_ \; X \; \_ \; \_ \; \_ \; X \; X \; X \; \_ \; X \; \_ \; \_ \; \_$$
$$+$$
$$\_ \; \_ \; \_ \; O \; \_ \; O O O \; \_ \; \_ \; \_ \; O \; \_ \; O O O$$

Subjects hardly ever break apart a run of elements; what varies is how
subjects order the runs of elements. The subject's preferred organization of
the figure element is to start with the longest run of identical elements
(XXX _ X _ _ _ , rather than X _ _ _ XXX _). The subject's preferred
organization of the ground element is to end with the longest run
(_ _ _ O _ OOO, rather than OOO _ _ _ O _). For this pattern,
the preferred organization for both the figure and the ground elements are
compatible, and therefore the highly preferred organization of the entire
pattern should be OOOXOXXX if O is the figure element (and X is the
ground element) or XXXOXOOO if X is the figure element (and O is the
ground element). If the organization for the figure and ground conflict,
then the overall organization is more variable; the listener may organize by
the figure, the ground, or some compromise.
    Separately, the figure elements and the ground elements form patterns
in time (analogous to patterns shown in figure 11.4). Each consists of runs
of identical elements with differing onset-to-onset intervals. The initial
element of each run often appears to be accented, as would be predicted.
We can hypothesize that the figure or ground pattern will be easy to pick

up when the accented elements occur at equally spaced points in time, exactly as demonstrated by Povel and Essens (1985); see figure 11.4. In contrast, the pattern will be difficult, and will even appear unrhythmical, if the accents occur irregularly. In fact, the folk music of Yugoslavia, Bulgaria, and Turkey is deliberately constructed so that the accented elements do not fall at equal time points (e.g., *XxxXxxxXxxx*, where *X* and *x* represent accented and nonaccented elements). This may generate a pleasing, pulsating rhythm (as suggested for African rhythms).

In similar work, Fraisse and Oleron (1954) have shown essentially the same results. Subjects will tend to reorganize sequences of tone elements so that runs of identical elements are kept together (i.e., LSSL will be reproduced as LLSS, where L and S stand for loud and soft). Although subjects in Garner's work consistently tended to prefer either the high or the low pitch element as the figure element, subjects in Fraisse and Oleron's work often made the less frequent element the figure element.

These results point out two important principles. First, listeners will spontaneously reorganize ongoing sequences. The initial elements will not be heard as strong beats beginning the pattern unless they lead to a simple, structured rhythm. In musical compositions, the first note can be heard as an upbeat, an embellishment, or the initial note of a repeating theme. How it will be perceived is a function of its role in the continuing melody. Second, listeners easily pick up repetitions of the recycling pattern. Although there are many possible recycling patterns within the ongoing sequence, listeners will "lock onto" one pattern that is structurally simple. For patterns composed of two elements, listeners organize based on runs of identical elements. Strong beats begin each run.

Frequency patterns   If we consider temporal patterns composed of many different elements, the specific organizing rules will be more complex. The majority of research has utilized simple frequency patterns. For example, one repeating pattern might be 2354334522212354334522221, where the numbers 1–5 represent different frequencies ranging from low to high. Patterns of this sort can be conceptualized as being made up of subgroups that are linked together hierarchically. The notes beginning the subgroups become the strong beats and define the melodic meter. But as described previously, there are several ways of breaking the sequence into subgroups (e.g., 354/334/522/212) so that preference rules are necessary. All other things constant, the preferred subgroups might be: (1) runs of identical elements (e.g., 222); (2) scale progressions (e.g., 123 and 543); or (3) alternations (e.g., 2323). The boundaries between the subgroups can be defined by jumps in pitch (e.g., 123567 is split into [123] [567] by the pitch jump), by changes in contour (543345 is split into [543] [345] by the downward to upward reversal), or by changes in alternation (12122323 is split into

[1212] [2323] (Jones 1981a, b; Restle 1970). The above pattern can be simply broken into the four three-element subgroups, (123) (543) (345) (222). In tonal contexts, a movement to the tonic may make the tonic note a strong beat. Listeners will reorganize ongoing sequences to achieve a simple organization.

Two points are important. First, subjects are able to use various types of relationships to break a pattern into groups. Listeners can use the relationship between groups (using transposition, 123234 is split into [123] [234]), or the relationships of Western tonal music (place all notes of a cadence in one group), or the relationships of melodic movement (place all notes of a progression in one group). Some relationships involve the elements within each group (e.g., runs of identical elements, frequency progressions); others involve the parallel relationships across different groups (e.g., transposition, complementation, so that 122221 becomes [122] [221]). Second, the different relationships compete to determine the perceived grouping. Notice that in many of the above sequences, runs of identical elements were split apart. Placing the identical elements together would have eliminated other grouping relationships and led to a more complex structure overall. This multiplicity of possibilities helps explain differences among listeners.

Results from less musically oriented tasks provide supporting evidence for the organization of sequences. These tasks use either a string of lights for visual presentation or very slow presentation of atonal music sequences. Across this work, sequences based on transformations that progress in an orderly fashion (12235667) are easier to learn than sequences constructed from transformations that progress randomly (12672356) and are much easier to learn than sequences constructed from a random order of the elements (6125267). Thus subjects were able to utilize the transformation to parse the sequence into related subunits, and difficulty became a matter of the predictability of the transformations (Jones 1981a, b).

Rhythmic interpretation has been discussed in two sections. The first involved timing factors that lead to a sense of meter. The second involved frequency (melodic) factors underlying element grouping that lead to a sense of meter. The emergent rhythm is the result of the interplay between these factors along with general perceptual factors (e.g., groups of equal size). Some aspects of rhythmic organization must be a function of the knowledge and skill of the listener (e.g., groupings based on chords), but others must be a function of general perceptual principles and therefore relatively independent of experience.

Patterns "of Time" and "in Time"
The separate discussion of timing meter and frequency (melodic) rhythm is necessarily artificial, because the emergent rhythm is the joint function of both. (To simplify the writing, I will use the terms "melodic rhythm" and

"melodic meter" to mean the perception of stronger and weaker beats brought about by the frequency pattern.) Yet without this simplification it would be impossible to determine some basic principles. We will now consider the three types of experimental studies that attempt to study the interplay between timing and melody. In the first, the experimenter artificially forces the meter timing to be incompatible with the melodic grouping rhythm, and the effect of the conflict is studied. In the second, a musical passage is presented as written, and the effect of both timing and melody on the perceived rhythm is studied. In the third, a performance is analyzed temporally in order to study how the performer varies the meter timing to account for the melody.

Incompatible timing and melody rhythms   The simplest experiments pitting the timing meters against melody meters have utilized auditory patterns made of two elements differing in pitch. In one experiment (Handel 1973), an eight-element repeating pattern (e.g., XXOOXOXOXXOOXOXO) was broken up temporally into groups of three or nine by placing a silent interval after every third or ninth element (e.g., if the pattern is broken into groups of three elements the sequence would be XXO-OXO-XOX-XOO-XOX-OXX-OOX-OXO-XXO- and so on). As can be seen, the silent interval travels through the pattern; each block of three elements is different, until it begins to repeat after eight blocks. The sequence appears to be continuously changing. Thus, the timing is in units of three while the melodic grouping is in units of two (XX) (OO) (XO) (XO). The results demonstrated that the incompatible timing made it very difficult to identify the pattern correctly. If an eight-element pattern was compatibly broken into temporal units of two or eight elements (XX-OO-XO-XO), the percentage correct was roughly 90%. However, if the eight-element pattern was incompatibly broken into temporal units of three or nine, the percentage correct was roughly 50%. In fact, 33% of the descriptions were of a pattern nine elements long, the correct eight-element pattern plus the first element tacked on at the end (e.g., the pattern XXOOXOXO might be described as XXOOXOXOX). Thus the strength of the timing meter led to the misperception of the frequency pattern.

The rhythm that dominates is the simpler. For example, we can temporally split the simple pattern XXXXOOOO into the sequence XXX-XOO-OOX-XXX-OOO-OXX-XXO-OOO-. In this case subjects organize the sequence by the melodic grouping determined by the pitch shift between the runs of identical elements, not by the timing as found above. The melodic meter based on XXXXOOOO ([XXXX] [OOOO]) is simpler than the temporal meter based on three elements, so the melodic meter dominates. However, the temporal meter based on three elements is simpler than the melodic meter based on XXOOXOXO (e.g., [XX] [OO] [XO] [XO]), so the temporal meter dominates. It is a truism that there is no perceptual principle, whether auditory, visual, or tactual, that always dominates. The percept always is the outcome of competing organizations (Handel 1974).

Jones (1987) has elaborated a dynamic pattern theory that overlays temporal and melody accents. The two kinds of accents jointly lead to a higher-order temporal structure. Notes at which the two accents coincide become the strongest beats, and notes at which only one accent occurs become the weaker beats. If the temporal and melodic accents coincide, strong beats will alternate with weak beats, and a regular meter will emerge. If the two accents do not coincide, there will be an irregular pattern of beats and a meter will not emerge. Consider simple examples from Deutsch (1980), composed of three-note or four-note repeating melodic patterns; examples are shown in figure 11.6. The pitch jumps separating the phrases lead to the perception of a melodic accent on the leading note of each phrase. Each pattern is broken into groups of three or four by inserting a silent interval after every third or fourth element. The silent interval leads to the perception of a timing accent on the initial element of each temporal group. A temporal grouping into threes will yield a compatible timing-melodic meter when the melodic phrase is three elements long but will yield an incompatible timing-melodic meter when the melodic phrase is four elements long. The outcomes will be reversed if the temporal grouping is into fours (see figure 11.6). The results from Deutsch's experiment confirmed that incompatible rhythms produced poorer reproduction than compatible rhythms.

Timing meters and melodic meters represent alternative rhythmic organizations. The timing and melodic meters compete, and the emergent rhythm represents the interplay between the two kinds of possibilities. In Western music the timing meter, based on twos (strong/weak) or threes (strong/weak/weak), is invariably simpler than the meter based on the melody. It is for this reason that the timing meter usually takes precedence.

Timing and melodic rhythms in music   Other researchers have investigated the timing/melody interplay in classical Western music. When listening to music, people break up the continuous flow of elements into structural units (musical measures) so that the initial note of each unit is perceived to be accented. These structural units form the regular, repeating meter organization (i.e., a "frame") that allows listeners to abstract the theme and variation process that underlies music. The perceived units are not necessarily the same ones the composer wrote in the musical score, however.

Vos (1979) used passages from Bach's *Well-Tempered Clavier* to discover the principles listeners used to induce the musical measure and whether the notated time signature corresponded to the listener's perception of the

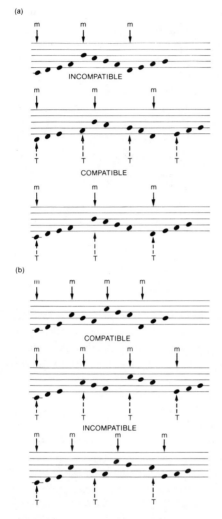

Figure 11.6
Construction of compatible and incompatible melodic and temporal rhythmic accents. In (a), a 12-note sequence is composed of 3 progressions; there are 3 melodic accents (indicated by m) on the first element following each pitch jump, which results in a reversal between an upward and downward progression. Below the isochronous sequence, the sequence is broken into subgroups of 3 elements or 4 elements by placing a silent interval between two elements. Temporal accents fall on the first element of each subgroup (indicated by T). For incompatible rhythms, the melodic and temporal accents fall on different elements. For compatible rhythms, the melodic and temporal accents fall on the same elements. In (b) the 12-element sequence is composed of 4 progressions. There are 4 melodic accents. Below that, the sequence is broken into subgroups of 3 or 4 elements by means of silent intervals. Temporal subgroups of three elements create compatible melodic and temporal accents, but temporal subgroups of four elements create incompatible accents (adapted from Deutsch 1980).

musical measures. The results obtained by Vos are difficult to summarize concisely, because the results for each passage differ. What can be said is that the melodic sequence does in large part determine where the listener perceives the beginning and end of measures. The temporal limits on beat intervals described previously, however, seem to restrict the listener to measures of intermediate duration.

Consider passage (a) in figure 11.7. This passage is written in 3/4 time (three beats per measure; each quarter note gets one beat) and the average measure takes 3 seconds. However, none of the subjects heard the measures as written. The vast majority heard the measure in two beats, not three. The grouping into two beats has two consequences. First, it allowed the listeners to utilize a counting scheme based on units of two and in this case the subjects reported using four counts per measure (a one-and-two-and count). Second, the four counts per measure reduces the interval between counts to 500 msec (2 counts/sec) and thus brings the meter within the preferred limits.

The second example is pattern (b). This passage was written in a 9/8 time signature (nine beats per measure; each eighth note receives one beat), and a measure lasts 2 seconds on the average. This passage yielded the greatest variety of organizations. Only 10% of the subjects heard the measures as notated. The majority of subjects heard measures consisting of six beats, 2/3 of the notated measure. Most of the perceived six-beat measures cut across the notated measure and placed the longer elements at the end of the perceived measure. Subjects counted in sixes, yielding a measure about 1.5 seconds long and an interval between counts of 250 msec. This is at the upper limit for a beat, but because eighth notes are the fastest notes, it does not pose any problems. It is important to note that every subject heard the passage grouped in threes, a function of the melodic sequence.

Although it is impossible to state any invariant rules from this research, some generalizations can be made. First, the perceived count, beat, meter, and measure are the joint function of timing constraints and element patterning (see Deliege 1987 for similar conclusions). I believe the emergent rhythm is the result of both aspects acting in parallel, not of one taking precedence. Second, there seem to be preferred timing intervals, and subjects are likely to prefer element organizations that are compatible with those constraints. These timing constraints may reflect cognitive limitations. It may be that listeners find it hard to keep passages of more than one to 2 seconds in their memories (particularly in the midst of ongoing music) and thus look for regularities at shorter intervals. Third, the rules concerning simple sequences seem applicable to more complex passages, as long as we recognize that these rules may be "bent" by the overall context.

(a)

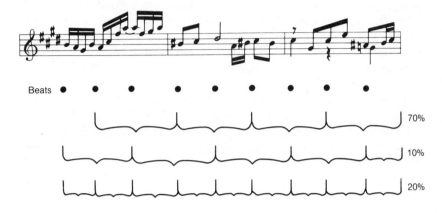

(b)

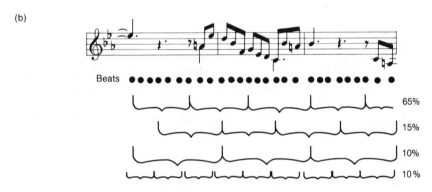

Figure 11.7
Rhythmic organization into measures. Listeners were asked to organize the recorded passages into measures. For each passage, the perceived beats are depicted by filled circles and the organization into measures is shown by the brackets. The percentage reporting each organization is shown at the right (adapted from Vos 1979).

Rhythmic variation   Up to this point, we have not really discussed rhythm performance, the sense that one performance "swings" or the sense that one rhythm makes it easier to understand the theme. As Bengtsson and Gabrielsson (1977) ask, "what is it in the music stimulus that brings about the different rhythm characters"? One possible strategy is to record instrumentalists playing different kinds of rhythms and measure the various note durations and various intervals between notes. The performances are then compared to the notated timing, a mechanical production. A half note (2 beats) followed by a quarter note (1 beat), for example, or a quarter note followed by an eighth note (1/2 beat), should be played in a 2 to 1 ratio. Deviations from that ratio should signify how a performer conveys a rhythmic or emotional quality or highlights a melodic feature of the piece. Across a range of rhythms and players, it should be possible to discover the factors that lead to different kinds of rhythmic experience.

For the performer, the musical score with its notated melody and timing is only the beginning. To it, the performer adds musical knowledge about the piece (melodic repetitions and variations, cadences, rhythmic subdivisions, key shifts) as well as musical knowledge about the general style and period. The goal is to portray the hierarchical levels of the structure to the listener. The levels involve individual notes, beats, measures, short phrases (i.e., groups of measures), and longer phrases formed from several shorter phrases. These rhythmic variations may also be those of an expressive hierarchy, with each level building on top of others to match the structural hierarchy of the score.

Bengtsson and Gabrielsson (1983) have examined simple Swedish folk songs. The folk song is shown in the middle of figure 11.8 and consists of a series of alternating half notes (2 beats) and quarter notes (1 beat). The tune can be broken into two phrases of eight measures. Panel (a) illustrates the deviation of each note from mechanical regularity. The half notes are shortened (from 2.0 beats to 1.95 beats) and the quarter notes are lengthened (from 1.0 beat to 1.1 beats). Thus the ratio between a half and a quarter note is about 1.75 : 1.0, below the notated ratio of 2.0 : 1.0. The dotted half note (3 beats) in measure 8 is lengthened to approximately 3.15 beats at the end of the first eight-measure phrase. Panel (b) shows the deviation for each measure. For both the first and the second phrases, the middle measures are played quickly and the final measure(s) are played much more slowly. This slow timing at the end sets off each phrase (the same pattern occurs for speech). The rhythmic changes at the phrase level are overlaid on the rhythmic changes at the note level.

The authors took another step and synthesized differing versions of the same piece that varied the ratio of the half note to the quarter note. When listeners were asked to rate each version, half note/quarter note ratios between 1.7 : 1 and 2.0 : 1 were equally preferred, and ratios outside these

416   Chapter 11

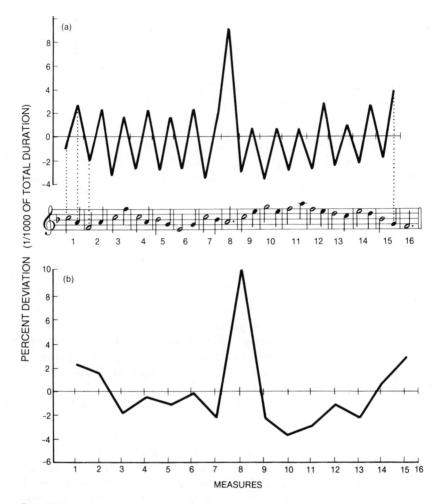

Figure 11.8
Rhythmic performance of a simple folk song. The folk song is composed of half notes (open circles) equaling 2 beats, quarter notes (filled circles) equaling 1 beat, and dotted half notes (open circles followed by a dot) equaling 3 beats. The actual folk song is shown in the middle of the figure. Panel (*a*) displays the performance of the individual notes. The vertical axis represents the deviation from perfect mechanical timing. A positive deviation means that the note was played longer than notated; a negative deviation means that the note was played shorter. There is a regular pattern: the half note is played shorter and the quarter note is played longer than notated. Panel (*b*) displays the performance for the individual measures. Positive deviations mean that the measure as a whole was longer than notated, and negative deviations mean that the measure was shorter than notated. Measures at the end of phrases tend to be extended (which, as shown in figure 11.10, is also true for speech) (from Bengtsson and Gabrielsson 1983 by permission).

boundaries were judged rhythmically poorer. Thus the aesthetic preferences match the actual expressive changes in performance. Even within the
preferred region, however, as Bengtsson and Gabrielsson point out, the
"motion" character changes.

Viennese waltzes provide another example. Typically the first beat is
shortened and the second beat is lengthened, i.e., the second beat "starts"
too early. Bengtsson and Gabrielsson (1983) constructed several versions
of the waltz rhythm that varied the timing of the first and second beat. At
one extreme, the duration of each beat was equal (i.e., the first and second
beats each took 33% of the measure), and at the other extreme, the duration
of the first beat was 23% of the measure, and the duration of the second
beat was 44%. (In all versions, the tone duration for the first beat was
longer and the tone duration was shorter for the second and third beats to
create a sense of stress.) The timings are illustrated in figure 11.9. As shown
in panel (b) of figure 11.9, experienced listeners preferred the 27%/40%
version, which is close to the measured values of many performances. On
the other hand, nonexperienced listeners tended to prefer the more even
durations (i.e., the more mechanical production). Variation at the note and
beat level does generate distinct rhythmic effects. The preference for an
effect, however, is influenced by experience.

Clarke (1985), by means of an analysis of a piano performance, suggests
that it is the beats that are explicitly and precisely timed. Individual notes
are collected together within rhythmic units and specified in terms of the
beat positions. Clarke suggests that performers develop overlearned "procedures" for dividing a beat. Procedures dividing the beat into equal size
units may be quite precise, although procedures dividing the beat into
unequal size units may use simple duration categories like long and short.
Clarke illustrates two kinds of timing variation. The first alters the beat
intervals, either slowing down or speeding up the piece as a whole. The
second alters the division within one or more beats, either increasing or
decreasing the long/short difference. The expressive component alters the
structural relations (i.e., the beats and subdivision of the beats), but it must
operate within the bounds of the abstract representation of the piece.
Otherwise the expressive timing variation could not reveal the relationship
among features of the music.

The research of Bengtsson and Gabrielsson and of Clarke illustrates how
expressive features are molded around structural features, particularly at
the level of the beat and meter. At a higher level, Todd (1985) has illustrated how a performer's tendency to slow down at a phrase boundary (i.e.,
phrase-final lengthening) is used to reflect the underlying musical structure.
Using a variety of classical Western music, Todd was able to generate a
hierarchical representation to estimate the strength or importance of each
phrase ending. Todd then measured the amount of phrase lengthening at

(a)

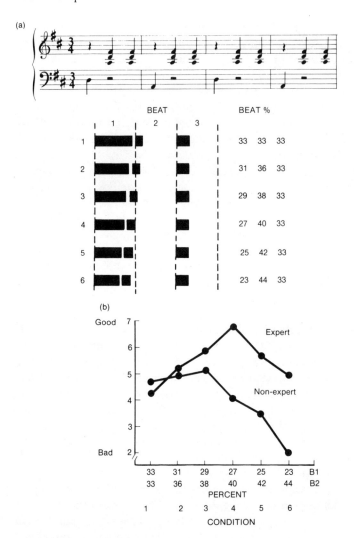

(b)

Figure 11.9
Timing variation and listening preferences for waltz rhythms. The score of the waltz is shown in (a). Each measure has three beats. To create different rhythms, the onset of the second beat was varied. A schematic of the beat structure is sketched below the score. The first example represents regularity: each of the three beats is equal. The percentage of the measure for each beat is listed to the right. The percentages are calculated from the onset of one note to the onset of the next note. The sixth example represents the most extreme variation: the duration of the first beat decreased by 10% and the duration of the second beat increased by 10%. The aesthetic ratings of the six rhythmic variations by expert and nonexpert judges appear in (b). The six variations are arrayed along the horizontal axis and the judgments are arrayed along the vertical axis. The rating "2" is between very bad and rather bad and the rating "7" is rather good (from Bengtsson and Gabrielsson 1983 by permission).

each ending and found that roughly, the greater the importance of the break, the greater the lengthening at a boundary. The phrase lengthening was maximum at the most important boundaries (and this is also true for speech).

Finally, Bengtsson and Gabrielsson (1983) have presented a hierarchical analysis of a waltz composed of thirty-two measures. They point out that two measures (three beats apiece) are combined to create a complete dancing cycle or turn. These units in turn are replicated at higher levels to create the entire musical structure. For example, two dancing cycles form what Bengtsson and Gabrielsson call a phrase, two phrases form a half period, two half periods form a period, and two periods form the piece. Each of these levels will induce a timing change to emphasize that unit. The overall timing will be the summation of the effects at each level, and the phrase lengthening will reflect the combination of all the levels (exactly like the results of Todd 1985 discussed above). The greatest phrase lengthening will occur at those endings that are found at all levels, in exactly the same way that the strongest beats occur on the notes that have beats at all levels.

Summary of Research on Music-Like Rhythms
These results illustrate the kinds of timing and melodic factors that influence the perception of rhythm. These factors affect each other so that one factor must be interpreted with respect to changes brought about by all the others. The production and interpretation of rhythm is context dependent. We see the same type of context effects and trading relationships that are involved in speech perception (chapter 9). This makes the acoustic analysis of rhythm difficult, because the same lack of invariance found for speech perception is found for rhythmic perception.

Speech rhythms will be considered next. Although the organization of the material differs, we will come to the identical conclusion that rhythmic experience comes out of the interaction of different rhythmic lines.

11.4 Speech Rhythms

All observers comment on the rhythm of speech. Some sounds are marked from others, for example, as louder, longer, or higher in pitch, and occur in certain time relationships to each other and to sounds that are softer, shorter, or lower in pitch. We refer to this marking of sounds as *stress*, and to the relationships between successive stressed and unstressed sounds as a *stress pattern*, although stress may not always correspond to physical measures of acoustic intensity, duration, or frequency. There is no automatic correspondence between the perceived stress and any acoustic measure. This is true for speech as much as it is true for music. This outcome should not be surprising, because the perception of rhythm is relative.

Speech rhythms refer to the perception of a regular ordering of stronger and weaker elements. (Musical meter has been discussed above in the same way.) It is clear that the production of both speech and musical rhythms must be constrained by our ability to order and sequence our movements in time. Movements are periodic. There are preferred intervals between movements, movements tend to cycle between tension and relaxation, and strong and weak movements often alternate. The movement constraints are probably not terribly significant when playing a clarinet, but the constraints are severe when talking. Speech involves the complex coordination of many articulatory components, and each component has its own set of dynamic movement constraints and possibilities. The lips, tongue, jaw, and glottis cannot open, close, or move instantaneously, because of inertia, muscular slack, and limitations of the neuromuscular system. This implies constraints on the possible speech rhythms; some rhythms simply may be impossible to achieve. It is for this reason that ultimately our understanding of speech rhythms must refer to articulatory dynamics. It may be that language capitalizes on the articulatory constraints to generate distinctions between elements. At present there is not enough data even to guess at this. Moreover, it is difficult to determine which aspects of rhythm are "physiologically" predetermined and which are "culturally" selected.

As found for musical rhythm, the perceived speech rhythm is the joint function of stress assignments at many levels. For example, at the segment level, the quality of the vowel (high versus low, tense versus lax) may determine its acoustic frequency, duration, and intensity. At the sentence level, a speaker may assign higher stress to new information (assumed not to be known by the listener). What should be emphasized is that the levels are not ordered from higher to lower. The levels are of different types. Some levels can be conceptualized as being part of the utterance (e.g., vowel quality). Yet other levels are not part of the utterance itself (e.g., newness of information). The stress assignments from one level are not merely superimposed on the stress assignment from a second level. Instead, the manner in which the rules of stress assignment operate at one level *depend upon* what happens at other levels. The detailing of stress assignment rules is far beyond the scope of this book. I will attempt to illustrate some of the stress rules in English and then attempt to illustrate the similarities between musical and speech rhythm.

Acoustic Determinants of Perceived Stress
Traditionally, stress has been assumed to be correlated to the perceived loudness, duration, and pitch of speech syllables. Although the term *syllable* is commonplace, it is difficult to come up with one single definition. The speech syllable is not the same as word divisions given in dictionaries, it

is not the same as a phoneme, and it is not the same as a vowel. We can roughly define a syllable physically as a *sonority* or loudness peak surrounded by segments with progressively decreasing sonority values (Selkirk 1984). Alternatively, we can define a syllable phonologically as a phoneme combination with a vowel center bounded by a permitted consonant or consonant combination (O'Connor and Trim 1953). Each permitted combination creates a possible template or hierarchical structure for syllables (Selkirk 1984). Each language may have a different set of allowable syllables.

Experiments dating back to the late 1950s have demonstrated that intensity, duration, and pitch influence stress judgments (Fry 1958). These experiments used ambiguous words like "object" and "insult." These words will be heard as the nouns OBject and INsult, if the first syllable is perceived as stressed and as the verbs obJECT and inSULT, if the second syllable is perceived as stressed. Starting with a neutral version, the first (or second) syllable was increasingly stressed by progressively making that syllable louder, longer, or higher in pitch. If these factors influence stress, then the percentage of noun judgments should increase when the property of the first syllable is incremented and the percentage of verb judgments should increase when the property of the second syllable is incremented. Experimentally, all three factors determined stress. Overall, it appears that fundamental frequency is the dominant stress cue in English and that duration is a stronger stress cue than intensity (this clearly goes against our intuition, since we perceive stressed vowels to be louder). Although there are exceptions, intensity, frequency, and duration generally covary in speaking. In articulating a stressed syllable, speakers expel a greater volume of air, and this physical act simultaneously increases intensity and fundamental pitch and (typically) duration. Here is one example of how the articulation system constraints the variation among the factors determining stress.

The perception of stress would be easy if the neutral physical magnitudes of loudness, duration, and pitch were identical for all speech sounds; then the stressed element would be the one with the greatest magnitude. But unstressed speech sounds have different magnitudes; a stressed "weak" sound may be lower acoustically than an unstressed "strong" sound. The listener must therefore judge stress in relation to the neutral magnitude.

Consider duration, one of the primary cues for stress. The duration of stressed vowels is roughly twice the duration of unstressed vowels, and in certain situations the ratio increases to 8 to 1 (Klatt 1976). However, speech sounds naturally differ in duration, and stress perception must compensate for these inherent differences. For example, other things being equal, a low vowel (e.g., bad, 300 msec in duration) is longer than a high vowel (e.g., bed, 80 msec in duration). The greater duration of the low vowels may be due to the greater articulatory movements required for their production. Moreover, there is a tendency for vowels to be shorter if followed by a voiceless consonant than if followed by a voiced consonant. The average duration of short vowels was 33% shorter before the voiceless /t/ than the voiced /d/. In addition to these factors, syllables at the end of a word are somewhat longer in duration. This change in duration is distinct from those above because the position of the syllable within the word, and not the syllable itself, determines the duration. This means that the longest vowel or syllable is not necessarily the stressed segment. Whether a given duration signifies a stressed syllable must be judged with respect to durational changes that occur naturally because of articulatory dynamics and constraints.

Now consider frequency, possibly the most important cue for stress. Many factors influence the fundamental frequency of the syllable vowel and therefore also affect the perceived stress. Vowels differ in their intrinsic pitch, with higher vowels having a greater fundamental pitch (e.g., 183 Hz for /i/ as in "beet" versus 163 Hz for /ae/ as in "bat"; Lehiste and Peterson 1959). Moreover, the preceding consonant influences the fundamental frequency of the following vowel so much that the value of the fundamental frequency can reverse. The fundamental frequency of /i/ following /v/ or /z/ drops 20 Hz to roughly 164 Hz (as opposed to 183 Hz); the fundamental frequency of /ae/ following /t/ or /p/ increases 10 Hz to roughly 172 Hz (as opposed to 162 Hz). Coarticulation brings about frequency changes that must be compensated for in the perception of stress. Often, it is not pitch itself that signifies the stress but a change in frequency. Bolinger (1958) terms this a *pitch accent*, a relatively rapid up or down pitch movement from a smooth contour. Thus, even though the fundamental frequency of a stressed vowel may be 25% higher than if unstressed, that vowel still may not be the highest frequency vowel in a phrase.

To summarize at this point, the cues for stress and accent include frequency, duration, and intensity. To perceive stress, however, it is not sufficient to recognize merely the highest pitch, the longest syllable, or the loudest syllable, because the intrinsic value of different syllables varies. The listener must filter out the factors that influence duration and frequency in order to perceive the speaker's intended stress. Stress perception is yet another example of a context effect. We should expect frequency, duration, and intensity to be in a trading relationship in the same way that other articulatory constraints are, as discussed in chapter 9. For example, we can hear stresses in whispers where there is no voicing (i.e., there is no fundamental frequency). In English, at least, frequency, duration, and intensity tend to increase together when syllables are stressed and similarly decrease together when syllables are unstressed. For this reason, when I discuss lexical, semantic, syntactic, and performance factors influencing stress, I will simply use the term *stress* without specifying the exact acoustic cues.

Prosody, Intonation, Suprasegmentals

Up to this point, I have discussed those factors influencing perceived stress that could be said to reflect the functioning of the articulatory system. Roughly speaking, these factors influence individual speech syllables. However, to study the rhythm of speech we must shift our focus to features that span more than one segment. The terms *prosody*, *intonation*, and *suprasegmentals* have been used to define those features (Lehiste 1976). The meanings of these terms overlap, and I will use them interchangeably. Although some theorists have defined intonation solely as pitch movement (i.e., changes in fundamental frequency), here intonation and prosody include patterns of pitch, loudness, duration, pitch range, tempo, and any other factors that affect the perception of stress and rhythm. Prosodic features do not change the denotative meaning of a word (i.e., the difference between INsult and inSULT is not a prosodic feature).

There have been two approaches to the study of prosodic phenomena. The concrete approach attempts to discover the specific acoustic factors that lead to the perception of stress and the perception of distinct intonational meanings like "anger," "impatience," and/or "emphasis." The set of acoustic factors are supposed to be context independent and to lead invariably to the same percept. The prosodic features are peripheral, an added-on "accompaniment" to the linguistic message. The abstract approach views prosody as being reflected in the linguistic structure and defines prosody broadly as "any phenomena that involve phonological organization at levels above the segment" (Ladd and Cutler 1983). From this perspective, it is unlikely that there is any direct connection between the acoustic signal and the contextual meaning. The same contour or intonation may express different grammatical and emotional messages, depending on the context. Moreover, although the concrete approach views stress as being directly determined by the cues of pitch, loudness, and duration, the abstract approach views stress as being a "possibility," and that possibility is determined by the prosodic structure as a whole unit. The structure—not syllable features—determines the perceptual cues.

Prosodic features affecting stress   As has been elaborated throughout this chapter, stress assignment occurs at many diverse levels. At the word level, some syllables are stressed and some are unstressed. Stress assignment may be partially due to articulation, because syllables with tense vowels (or diphthongs) (SOfa, VEto, aROma) tend to be stressed. Moreover, there is a tendency for "heavy" syllables containing many consonants (c) and vowels (v) (e.g., cvcc, ccvc, cvccc) to be stressed and "light" syllables (cv, vc) to be unstressed. On top of these factors there is a tendency to alternate stressed and unstressed syllables within a word, much like musical meter. Other aspects of word stress are culturally determined. This is easily seen when the same word has a different stress pattern in different dialects (e.g., garAGE in the United States versus GARage in Britain or inSURance versus INsurance in different parts of the United States). The grammatical category of a word also influences stress; in fluent speech, nouns, adjectives, and verbs receive stress and "function" words, such as articles, prepositions, and conjunctions, do not (Pike 1945).

Compared to isolated vowels, unstressed vowels are shorter in duration and their formant frequencies move toward the average value across all the vowels. The vowel sound becomes less distinctive; it takes on a neutral quality. When speakers are talking quickly, stressed syllables also become shorter in duration, but the change in spectra characteristic of unstressed syllables does not occur. On this basis, it is possible to distinguish durational changes attributable to stress from those attributable to speaking rate (Gay 1978).

In phrases and sentences, both semantic and syntactic factors influence intonation. The basic unit has been variously termed an intonation group, a tone-unit group, a breath group, or a phonological phrase. Roughly, it is the successive sounds within a single acceptable intonation pattern. There is no single cue, however, that will always signify the boundary between groups. One possible representation of an intonation group is created by plotting fundamental frequency against time (see figure 11.10). This can illustrate several ways in which frequency and duration influence the grouping of speech elements into words and phrases and influence the perception of contrastive stresses.

Grouping   The grouping of speech elements into units is conveyed by fundamental frequency, silent pause length, and syllable duration. Characteristically, the frequency starts at a value slightly above the average frequency and then undergoes a frequency oscillation that gradually decreases in central frequency (Gårding 1983). As portrayed in figure 11.10, the range of oscillation becomes narrower across the phrase. At the beginning of the next phrase, the frequency resets to the original value and then follows roughly the same trajectory. The frequency variation can signal two aspects of the structure. First, there is the grouping of the segments into the overall phrase signaled by the frequency rise and lowering, followed by the resetting of the frequency serving as the boundary marker. This resetting of pitch level typically occurs between unaccented syllables. Second, there is the grouping of the segments into words signaled by the frequency oscillation. One up-and-down (or down-and-up) frequency cycle defines an entity, a stress group. If each word is

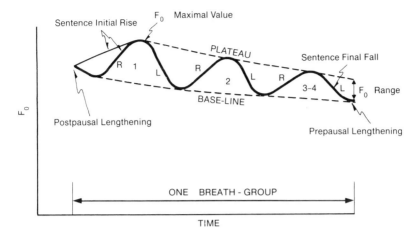

Figure 11.10
A schematic representation of one breath group. There is a tendency for the voice fundamental frequency (F_0) to oscillate between two abstract lines, with the up-and-down range of the oscillation decreasing toward the end of the breath group. A prosodic word is often indicated by an F_0 rise (R) and lowering (L). The rise and lowering marked by 1 and 2 portray one word; the rise and lowering marked by 3–4 portray two words. In addition, the first phoneme and final syllable tend to lengthen to mark the beginning and end of a group (adapted from Vaissière 1983).

pronounced carefully, each word will undergo one oscillation. Several syllables can also be combined into a single stress group in which there is a single increase and decrease in frequency. A stress group of this sort might occur when a speaker is trying to indicate a close tie among words.

Cooper, Tye-Murray, and Eady (1985) have demonstrated that listeners use the pitch contour in perceiving sentences. They argue that declarative sentences invariably have a rising fundamental frequency contour on the first syllable or word. The authors constructed a pair of identical sentences (with the exception of the intonation) by starting with two sentences like "White corn is extra sweet this year" and "Corn is extra sweet this year."

                    e corn is extra sweet this year.
                 t
                i
              h
           w
                        n is extra sweet this year.
                    r
                  o
                c

They then electronically deleted the word "white" in the first sentence to produce two versions of "corn is extra sweet this year." In the version from which "white" was removed, "corn" did not have the correct rising frequency contour, because it was not the true first word. In the experiment, subjects were asked to judge whether a word had been deleted from each sentence. For sentences in which the intonation contour had been altered by deleting the first word, over 50% of subjects judged that a word had been deleted. For the identical control sentence in which the intonation was appropriate, about 20% of subjects judged that a word had been deleted. The contour allowed listeners to discover the structure of the sentence.

Syllable duration is also an importance acoustic cue to grouping. There is a strong tendency to lengthen the final vowels at boundaries between words, clauses, phrases, or sentences. The increase in duration is greater at the end of phrases than at the end of words (exactly as found for musical performance; see discussion of Todd 1985) and occurs even in the absence of an actual silent pause. Examples of duration change can be illustrated by comparing two sentences with the identical syllable sequence but different syntactic structure:

1. The cowboy and the *badman* led the carriage.
2. The clumsy and the *bad man*gled the carriage.

In sentence 2, the boundary is between bad/man; in sentence 1, the boundary is between badman/led. The duration of the syllable "bad" in sentence 2 at the boundary is 300 msec; the duration of the syllable "bad" in sentence 1 before the boundary is 180 msec (Klatt 1976). Typically, the duration of the vowel in the final syllable before a boundary may increase between 60 and 200 msec.

Silent pauses quite obviously mark boundaries between intonation groups. Speakers tend to pause at the end of conceptual units, and the pauses tend to be longer between larger units—for example, pauses between sentences are longer than pauses between clauses within sentences. The vast majority of intonation pauses are due not to breathing requirements but to marking boundaries between clauses and between subject and predicate (Cruttenden 1986). We breathe when we pause. But pauses do not always signify boundaries (e.g., hesitation and planning pauses), and pauses that should occur between clauses may be filled (e.g., to prevent interruptions). Thus a pause is not an invariant marker.

In sum, fundamental frequency, syllable duration, and pause all act to segment the roughly continuous speech signal into linguistic units. In English, these cues tend to act in concert, although there are instances where they may conflict. In other languages, these same factors are used to mark boundaries, but the particular mechanism may differ. In French, for example, the final syllable at a boundary is lengthened in duration, but the intensity is decreased and frequency variation occurs only after a period of constant fundamental frequency (Wenk and Wioland 1982).

Emphasis and contrast   Speech rhythms not only aid the listener in segmenting the ongoing acoustic signal into meaningful units but also signify what the speaker is trying to communicate. The speaker imagines what the listener knows or expects, and changes the stress and rhythmic pattern to convey the information. For example, speakers stress information not known to the listener as opposed to information assumed to be known by the listener. The speaker can deaccent information that is obvious from the previous context. For example, one might accent the word "write" in "I need a TOOL to WRITE with" but not in "I need a PENcil to write with." It is generally known that pencils, but not tools, are for writing, so that in the second sentence the verb "to write" does not need to be accented. In addition, speakers stress information that contrasts or specifies an event (e.g., the GRAY dog as opposed to the BROWN dog but the gray DOG as opposed to the gray CAT). Speakers may also stress general social or emotional meanings, such as challenge or sarcasm. An example is the response to "I need a long vacation" (Brazil, Coulthard, and Johns 1980):

$$\begin{array}{ccc} & \text{we A} & \diagdown \\ \text{Don't} & \text{L} & \diagdown \\ & & \text{L} \searrow \end{array}$$

The speaker adjusts the accents to go on the "point of information focus, or on the items of contrast or emotional highlighting" (Bolinger 1972, p. 635).

Accent is conveyed acoustically by both fundamental frequency and duration. As described above, the overall tendency for the fundamental frequency of a simple phrase is to decrease and, for the small-scale oscillations in frequency, to decrease in range. Accent is acoustically portrayed by a frequency shift of the entire phrase as well as by a larger frequency oscillation, superimposed on the overall phrase contour. Thus, the frequency of a stressed syllable and the frequency variation of a stress element must be perceived in relation to the normal values. The same absolute frequency at the beginning of the phrase may signal de-emphasis; at the end of the phrase, that frequency may signal stress.

Another acoustic cue to emphatic or contrast stress is syllable or word duration. Typically a stressed element increases in duration by 10% to 20% or more. Klatt (1976) provides an example of new information stress by comparing the duration of the word "raisin" in the two sentences:

1. There were no raisin cakes left, so I bought *raisin* bread.

[370 msec]

2. There were no loaves of rye bread left, so I bought *raisin* bread.

[500 msec]

In the first sentence, "raisin" appears in the initial phrase, so it is less informative in the second phrase. In the second sentence, "raisin" is stated for the first time in the second phrase. The duration of "raisin" in sentence 1, where it is less informative, was 370 msec; the duration of "raisin" in sentence 2, where it is novel, was 500 msec.

In addition to frequency and durational effects on words or phrases, there are effects that span sentences and are thus an additional component of the rhythmic structure. Possibly the best-known frequency effect is the rise in fundamental frequency at the end of a sentence, which distinguishes questions from statements. Across many languages, yes-no questions are conveyed by eliminating the fundamental frequency drop or by adding a short upward glide at the end. But there are other characteristic frequency contours that portray sentence-level information. Several linguists have characterized a "calling" contour:

John \ Din \
  ny \   ner \

or a stylized frequency drop for "reminders":

Look out for the broken ste \
  p \

(if the broken step is known to all), as opposed to a frequency fall for more dangerous situations:

Look out for the broken s \
  t \
  e \
  p \

(if the step has just broken). There are also duration effects that extend over many units. Speakers slow the overall rate for important sentences and tend to speak the last sentence of a paragraph more slowly.

Intonation: Timing and Melodic Rhythms
For music, we argued that both the timing rhythms and the melodic rhythms influence the structure of the beats perceived by the listener. For speech, the same distinction between timing and melodic rhythms will prove helpful. The timing rhythms account for the potential for any syllable within the sentence structure to be stressed. The timing rhythms yield the hierarchical representation of meter, exactly as suggested for musical meter. The melodic or intonational rhythms, based on changes of funda-

mental frequency, act to bring one or more of the potential stresses to the forefront, to make that syllable perceived as the sentence center or focus. Simultaneously, the melodic contour provides "semantic" information in terms of the pattern of the fundamental frequency. The contour may display surprise, anger, contrast, or resignation. But as argued for musical rhythms, the meaning of the sentence should not be thought of as being based on the word- and sentence-structure meanings, with the intonation adding the emotional tone or attitude. Instead the words, syntax, rhythm and intonation form a gestalt, in which each aspect changes the other.

There have been two approaches to intonation. The first, in the physical tradition, emphasizes the acoustic magnitudes of individual syllables; each syllable is given an absolute value, independent of the values given to other syllables, to be used in generating the stress and pitch contour pattern. The second, in the abstract tradition deemphasizes the magnitudes of individual syllables and argues that stress comes from the relationships among syllables. A syllable does not have a fixed stress, because adding stress to one syllable can have the effect of weakening the stress on a second syllable. The stress of one syllable must be defined in terms of the stress of other syllables; the stress of one syllable in isolation is unknown and undefinable.

Let me take this position a step further, because it is quite important. The relational approach contends that the perception of stress comes from the rhythmic structure. The perceived stress falls on the beat. The stress of any syllable is based on its position within the rhythm, that is, its relation to the rest of the syllables. The stress pattern is not heard because of the changes in pitch, duration, or intensity; rather, these changes induce us to hear a particular rhythmic structure in which given syllables become prominent. It is true that pitch rises or duration increases usually occur on the stressed syllable. However, these acoustic changes are associated or correlated with syllable stress; these acoustic changes are not the cause of syllable stress. Pitch and duration intonation can bring different syllables into prominence; this in turn will signal the listener to perceive a different interpretation.

The starting point for theories of prosody is the *appearance* of equal time intervals between prominent syllables in English, among other languages. This is termed *stress timing*. The linguistic stress is analogous to the musical meter. The fundamental hypothesis is that linguistic stress is based on a hierarchical organization of beats in time, so that strong and weak beats roughly alternate. Following a discussion of the derivation of the rhythmic stress pattern, I will describe the concept of an intonational "melodic" contour. The relationship of the rhythmic stress pattern and the intonational contour yields the meaning of the utterance in exactly the same way that the meter and grouping preference rules yield the organization of a musical theme.

Rhythmic stress   Theoretical developments concerning stress and linguistic rhythms began about fifteen years ago with the work of Martin (1972), M. Y. Liberman (1975), Liberman and Prince (1977), and Selkirk (1980), among others. As Liberman and Prince (1977) state, much of the previous accounts of stress stemmed from three observations. First, the typical stress pattern of a phrase emphasizes the last word (three COWS, John SKIED); the typical stress pattern of a compound emphasizes the first component (BLACKboard, COWboy). Second, the relative stress within a phrase tends to be maintained when it is embedded in a longer phrase. Liberman and Prince give the example "WHALE-oil," which, when embedded in the phrase "WHALE-oil LAMP," retains the strong-weak relation between whale and oil although the primary stress falls on lamp. Third, there are instances in which the relative stresses shift if embedding occurs. Two examples are used extensively in linguistics: (a) thirTEEN, with the relative stress on the second syllable, but THIRteen MEN, in which the stronger stress shifts from the second to the first syllable in thirteen; (b) tenneSSEE, with the relative stress on the third syllable, but TENNessee AIR, in which the stronger stress shifts from the third to the first syllable in Tennessee. What is important is that the stress of a syllable changes as a function of the surrounding context. These considerations lead to representing relative stress hierarchically, with each level of the hierarchy representing one level of the stress assignment. The levels of the hierarchy represent syllables, feet (a combination of syllables), words, phrases, and sentences.

Liberman and Prince portray the structure of the stress assignment using only the binary strong-weak relation. At each level of the hierarchy (between two syllables, or between two feet), there is one strong branch and one weak branch. At the syllable level, the strong branch terminates on a stressed syllable, and the weak branch terminates on an unstressed syllable. At higher levels, there are various rules that determine the strong and weak branch; they will be discussed below. The pattern of weak and strong branches that terminates on any syllable determines the relative stress value of that syllable.

This can be seen in simple two-syllable words like LAbor, MOdest, and balLOON. (Here, I will assume that the stressed and unstressed syllables are known beforehand; a short discussion of stress rules was given in a previous section.) For each word, there is a simple binary hierarchy, with the strong branch going to the stressed syllable and the weak branch going to the unstressed syllable (shown in figure 11.11). The point at which two branches converge is termed a *node*. The node might be a syllabic foot, a word, a phrase, or sentence. Now consider longer yet still simple words like "missiSSIPPi," which has 4 syllables in a simple strong-weak alternation. It is possible to begin the hierarchy by combining the strong-weak pairs into two sets of branches (see figure 11.11). Although it is possible to combine

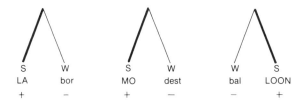

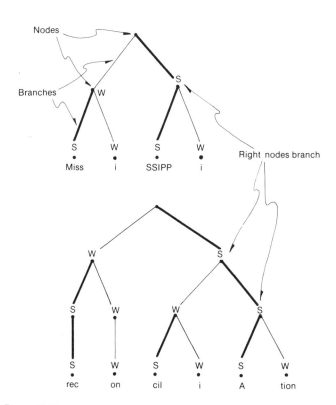

Figure 11.11
Stress hierarchies for binary strong-weak branches. A stress hierarchy consists of levels of
nodes. Each node splits into two branches; each branch terminates on one lower node. One
branch always leads to a strong node (S) and one branch always leads to a weak node (W).
The branch leading to the strong node is portrayed by a darker line. The right node branch
rule proposes that the right node is strong if, and only if, it branches into two nodes at a
lower level (examples from Hayes 1984; Liberman and Prince 1977).

the two sets of branches into a higher level branch, it is unclear which of the higher-level branches is strong and which is weak. A rule that generally predicts relative stress within a word is that the rightmost node (or pair of branches) receives the stronger stress if and only if it branches into two syllables, and the leftmost node (or pair of branches) receives the stronger stress if the rightmost node does not branch. The rightmost node does branch, so that the third and fourth syllables receive the stronger higher-order branch. The word "reconciliAtion" is also shown: it contains three pairs of alternating strong-weak syllables so that there are three levels in the hierarchy. At both higher levels, the rightmost node branches and the right branch is the strong one.

More difficult cases arise when pairs of stressed-unstressed syllables do not alternate: consider the words PAmela, vaNILLa, and aMERica (see figure 11.12). PAmela consists of three syllables: strong, weak, weak. Two branches connecting to one node must alternate strong-weak, and therefore the first step is to combine "PA" (strong) and "me" (weak) into a node. At the next level, combine the "PA + me" node with the "la" branch. The word rule above stated that the right side is strong only if it branches. Here the right side does not branch, so it is weak; the resulting hierarchy is shown in figure 11.12. The second case is vaNILLa, which contains an unstressed, stressed, unstressed syllable alternation. The "NIL" and "la" syllables are first combined into a strong-weak branch and then the first syllable "va" is conjoined. Here the rightmost node is strong, because it branches. The third case is aMERica, an unstressed, stressed, unstressed, unstressed pattern. First, combine the middle two syllables into a strong-weak mode; then apply the word rule to make the next level of branches strong-weak because the right branch does not split; and finally the highest branches become weak-strong, because the right branch further splits into two lower-level branches.

These rules construct a binary hierarchy for single words. There are similar rules that allow the construction of hierarchies conjoining single words into compound words and single words into phrases. At the phrase level, the second word in a phrase (or the second phrase in a longer phrase) receives the strong branch. This yields "tennessee AIR," "mississippi LEGislature," and "thirteen MEN," as shown in figure 11.13.

Rhythmic timing: metrical grid   Each hierarchy represents linguistic stress, a pattern of segments in terms of salience. But the linguistic stress does not give us the pattern of streses in time. We do not know the timing between strong and weak beats. We can, however, use the linguistic hierarchy to generate the rhythmic stress, the beat of the utterance. This has been termed the "metrical grid" and is constructed in the following steps, illus-

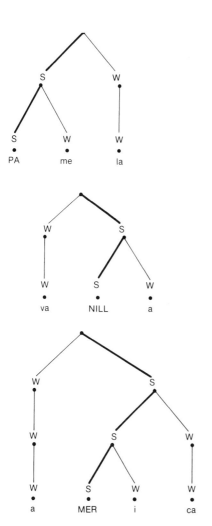

Figure 11.12
Stress hierarchies for words in which stressed and unstressed syllables do not alternate
(examples from Liberman and Prince 1977).

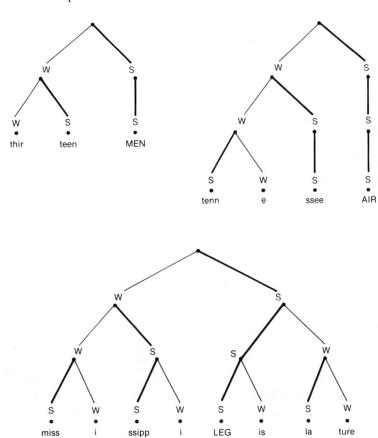

Figure 11.13
Stress hierarchies for two-word phrases. The second word in the phrase receives the strong branch (examples from Hayes 1984; Liberman and Prince 1977).

trated in figure 11.14:

1. Construct a hierarchical tree as described above to represent the stressed-unstressed syllables (strong-weak branches) of the phrase.

2. Place a marker below every syllable. This merely serves to mark each syllable. It is equivalent to marking the beginning of each time unit when constructing the musical grid.

3. Place a marker under every stressed syllable. The only confusion occurs because a one-syllable word receives a marker even if it ends on a weak branch. This is true for "grow" in "Belgian farmers grow turnips." This step constructs the first higher level, exactly as done for the musical meter (figure 11.3).

4. Now place additional markers under the strongest syllable of each word and grouping to indicate the strong branch of every higher level. Thus, in figure 11.14(a) there is a marker under "far" (in farmers) and "TUR" (in turnips) to reflect the second level of the hierarchy and an additional marker under "tur" to reflect the third level of the hierarchy.

This process is also illustrated for 'thirteen men," Tennessee air," and "Mississippi Mabel" in figure 11.14(b), and "a hundred thirteen men" in figure 11.14(c). Higher levels in the linguistic hierarchies are represented by lower levels in the metric grid. There is a horizontal symmetry. The similarity between the metric grid for speech (figure 11.14) and for music (figure 11.2) is obvious. The metrical grid represents the relative stress of the individual syllables. The stronger stresses have more markers. The number of markers, however, should be interpreted only in terms of more or less. Four markers do not represent twice the stress of two markers and the difference in stress between three and two markers may or may not be equal to the difference in stress between two and one markers.

Stressed and unstressed syllables naturally tend to alternate, but when two stressed syllables are adjacent there are rhythmic pressures to move stresses around to return to an alternation. Rhythmic clashes between two stressed syllables are easily seen with the use of the grids. The stress clash exists because the more prominent syllables are adjacent, without less prominent syllables to supply an alternation of strong and weak syllables. Thus, there are stress clashes between "teen" and "men" in "thirteen men," between "see" and "air" in "Tennessee air," between "sip" and "Ma" in Mississippi Mabel," and between "teen" and "men" in a "hundred thirteen men." The stress clashes are shown by dashed rectangles in figure 11.14.

The stress clash provides the impetus to change the prominence of syllables to improve the strong-weak alternation. Liberman and Prince deal with the clash by relabeling two branches—switching the strong-weak prominence. The two prominent syllables that clash are not equal: "men" is

(a)

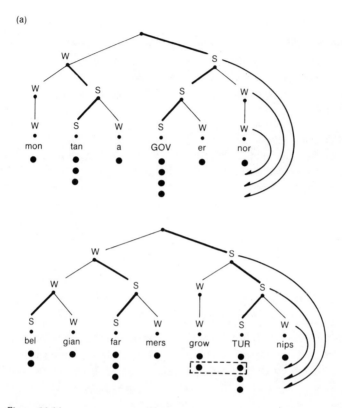

Figure 11.14
The construction of metrical grids and the identification of stress clashes. In (a) (this page), metrical grids are constructed for two phrases. Each level in the stress hierarchy creates one level in the metrical grid. Stress clashes occur when two stressed syllables are not separated by an unstressed syllable. The stress clashes are enclosed by dashed rectangles: "grow" and "TUR" represent a stress clash. In (b) (facing page), the resolution of stress clashes is illustrated. The stress clash is enclosed in the metrical grid on the left and the revised stress hierarchy that eliminates the clash is drawn on the right. In (c) (verso of facing page), the resolution of the stress clash in "one hundred thirteen men" is illustrated. Two switches in the stress hierarchy are necessary (examples from Hayes 1984; Liberman and Prince 1977).

(b)

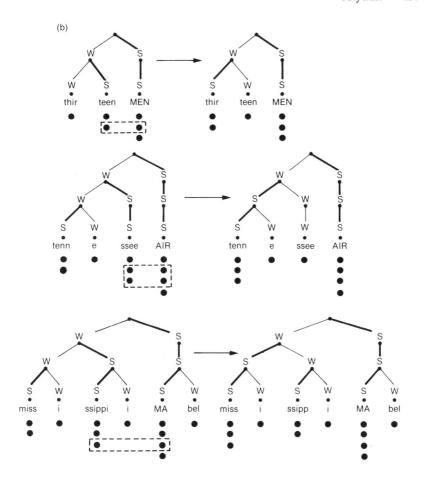

(c)

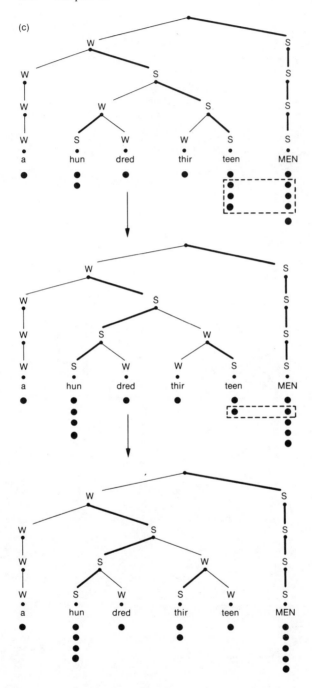

stronger than "teen," "Ma" is stronger than "sipp," and so on. Liberman and Prince create a strong-weak reversal for the weaker of the two strong syllables at the level of the stress clash. This pushes the "weaker" strong syllable further away from the "stronger" strong syllable and places a truly weak syllable in between. "Ma" is stronger than "sipp," so the weak-strong branch at level 2 of Mississippi Mabel is reversed to eliminate the clash. This improves the stress rhythm by making the stress pattern more regular.

The hierarchical tree structure, as we have seen, represents the linguistic stress relationships among the elements. Syllables are stressed or unstressed depending on various factors, such as the type of vowels, consonant clusters, and position. The syllables are then joined into words, words into compound words, words into phrases, and so on. At each higher level, there are linguistic rules that specify the strong and weak branches and that allow the construction of the entire tree. In turn, the tree generates a representation of stresses in the metric grid. Stress clashes between stronger syllables found in the grid result in reversals in the linguistic stress assignment of the hierarchical tree, and this in turn changes the metrical grid so that the clash no longer occurs. The goal is to achieve an alternation of strong and weak stresses.

Hayes (1984) and Selkirk (1984) take this argument further by hypothesizing that there are universal timing rules, no different than any other kind of rhythmic activity, that create further pressures to change the stress assignments. There are natural rhythmic, tense-relax predispositions, and the stress rhythm is optimized when there is a grid level at which stresses occur every four syllables and stresses at lower levels evenly divide the stresses at the higher levels. These rules tend to bring the linguistic stress rhythm into a simple alternation, four beats per measure in musical terms. Hayes (1984) presents examples like "twenty-seven Mississippi legislators" and "Mississippi-Alabama rivalries" to illustrate the application of these timing rules (see figure 11.15). In fact, Hayes speculates that although the timing rules are presently based on syllables, it might be more appropriate to base them on actual physical time. This would suggest that speakers lengthen or shorten syllables or that speakers insert silent pauses in order to make the stresses more evenly spaced in time (in the same way this is achieved by stress exchange). For English speakers, the interval between stresses ranges between 0.2 sec (5 beats/sec) to 1.0 sec (1 beat/sec). Notice that these are nearly the identical timing restrictions for music meter (see section 11.3), which reinforces Hayes's contention that these timing roles are universal. Stress occurs anywhere from 1 syllable/stress to 8 syllables/stress, with a rough average of 3 syllables/stress based on a speaking rate ranging from 5 to 8 syllables/sec.

These timing rules lead to the conclusion that a simple binary or trinary alternation would be the ideal rhythm for English. Yet most speech does

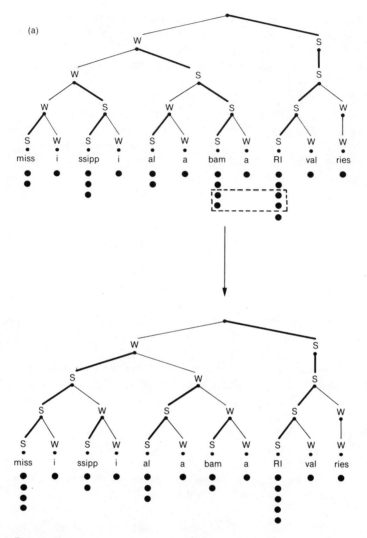

Figure 11.15
Stress rhythms based on a strict alternation of strong and weak beats. The stress assignment is changed until the stronger and weaker beats strictly alternate (examples from Hayes 1984).

(b)

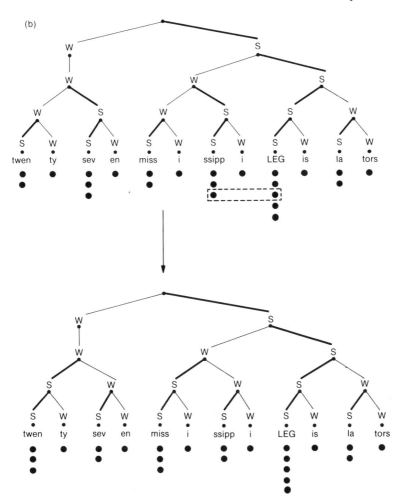

Figure 11.15(b)

not follow this pattern. There are many reasons for this: speakers may not plan far enough ahead and therefore make mistakes or hesitate; the text itself cannot be forced into that timing; and most important to us, stress in English can serve nonmetrical rhythmic ends. The rhythm can serve to focus, contrast, and group constituents. A short discussion of these factors follows.

Melodic rhythms   Intonation is the melody of language. It is the combination of changes in frequency (pitch), duration, loudness, tempo, voice register, and timbre. Bolinger (1955) defines intonation as the "melodic line of speech, the rising and falling of the 'fundamental' or singing pitch of the voice." Intonation may be said to be categorical (a "surprise" intonation as opposed to a "contradiction" contour) as well as continuous ("really" surprised as opposed to "mildly" surprised).

Traditionally, intonation has been considered not quite language proper. It is something that is added to the syntax and semantics of language. A recurring phrase is that "intonation is around the edge of language." Communication can occur without intonation, as books prove. Nevertheless, intonation can change the "meaning" from expressing surprise to expressing derision, from statements to questions, and so on. An intonational contour or an intonational inflection (a rise or fall in pitch on a syllable) may change the semantics of the sentence in much the same way that a mustache, beard, or hair style may change the appearance of other facial features. I believe intonation must be studied and conceptualized in the same way that other aspects of language are examined.

Intonation combines with the pattern of strong and weak stresses coming from the stress hierarchy. The stress hierarchy and metrical grid reveal the possibilities for stress: the syllables ending on strong branches. The intonation selects and accentuates one of the strong syllables and acts to group the syllables (analogous to the grouping rules of Lerdahl and Jackendoff 1983). The intonation may accent a single-syllable word or one syllable of a multiple-syllable word. In both cases, the hierarchy continues to reflect the relative strength of the other syllables of the sentence.

Two issues stand out in attempts to describe the nature of intonation. The first issue concerns the level at which intonation occurs. On the one hand there is the view that intonation is a global construct. Thus one should study the intonation pitch contour—the pattern of ups and downs—which extends across many units of the utterance. The absolute values of pitch are of secondary importance. Proponents of this view attempt to characterize the meaning of different contours. Contours are categorized into classes, each with its own "dictionary" meaning. On the other hand, there is the view that intonation should be studied at the level of individual speech segments. From this perspective the absolute pitch or loudness of a segment is the critical aspect for the perception of the intonation, and the overall contour is of secondary importance. Perhaps the contours yield the categorical meaning, and the absolute pitches determine the strength, the more or less aspect, of meaning. Notice that the music research by Dowling and others (reviewed in section 10.5) comparing melodic contour to intervals is directly parallel. That work seemed to suggest that contour was dominant for novel melodies, although the actual intervals and key became more important over time, for experienced musicians, and for well-learned melodies.

The second issue concerns the principles for generating the intonation contour. Here again there are two major perspectives. On the one hand, some linguists propose that intonation arises from the operation of grammatical rules. The syntax and semantics of the sentence bring forth the intonation by means of a set of generative rules (e.g., Chomsky and Halle 1968). The same rules apply in all circumstances. On the other hand, other linguists claim that intonation cannot be predicted from grammar, and that intonation reflects the intention of the speaker. "Accent is predictable, if you're a mind reader," writes Bolinger. By this he means that accent is created by the speaker to communicate a meaning. Without knowing that intended meaning, it is impossible to predict the accent.

Intonation can be used to convey emotional "messages" as well as semantic messages. Many of the following examples of the emotional and semantic functions of intonation come from Ladd (1980).

Emotional messages   Intonation can serve to reveal specific emotions and attitudes. If a child asks for a piece of candy, there is a big difference between the reply

> n \
>   o ↓

and the reply

> n \
>   o ↓

The latter is far more firm and assertive. Similarly, the surprised response

>   did ↗
> she /

is not as surprised as

>   d. ↗
>   i /
> she d /

In both of these cases, the degree of pitch change indicates the strength of the emotion (the more or less component).

In other cases, shifts in intonation reveal opposite emotions. For example,

is a compliment but

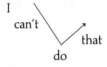

is decidedly not a compliment. For a second example,

I can't

is questioning, but

I
   can't
          that
      do

is contradicting.

It should be clear that emotions and attitudes are conveyed by the congruence between the semantics and intonation. A polite semantic (e.g., please, could you …) uttered with a hostile intonation produces only confusion. The listener must decide which "signal" is really meant, given the context. Other languages make use of special particles, honorifics, and inflectional categories to convey attitude. In contrast, English makes use of intonation to convey "the way" we say things, and this may allow inconsistencies to arise.

Research into the communication of emotion by means of intonation has been relatively extensive. However, the results seem to be marked more by inconsistency than by regularities that organize the findings (Frick 1985; Scherer 1986). Scherer (1986) has proposed a theoretical model that views emotion as a process (not a steady state) that adapts a person to ongoing events in the world. The person evaluates each event according to criteria such as novelty, pleasantness, goal/need, and difficulty of coping. Each of these criteria represents one emotional feature, and each feature has an effect on the nervous system. The arousal of the nervous system will control muscle action and tension, and this will affect the acoustic output. In a fearful situation, for example, the arousal of the nervous system will lead to increased muscle tension, constriction of the vocal tract, decreased salivation, and an increase in respiration. Increased muscle tension will lead to an increase in fundamental frequency and possibly will lead to increased variation in the bandwidth frequency of noise components, because the vocal-fold vibration breaks down under increased tension. Constriction of the vocal tract will change the resonant frequencies and should lead to increased energy at higher frequencies; a decrease in salivation will decrease the damping of the vocal tract and will also tend to increase the higher frequency energy; and finally an increase in respiration may yield increased air pressure in the lungs, which can result in an increase in fundamental frequency and intensity.

I think Scherer's model is notable for its attempt to tie emotional changes to articulatory changes by means of nervous system functioning. Given the complexity of emotional influences, the complexity of the nervous system, and the complexity of articulation, it should be clear that no single acoustic change can possibly predict the perception of an emotion. Given this complexity, it is remarkable that listeners are able to discriminate between emotion portrayed by prosodic cues with high accuracy. It must mean that the information about emotion involves a set of interrelated articulatory changes.

Grammar

Phrasing and ambiguity   We have already discused the use of pitch contours to distinguish among statements and questions and the use of pauses and duration changes to mark syntactic boundaries. In addition, a lowering of pitch is often used to indicate a parenthetical phrase.

```
                                         i
                                       f
                          bout    get
  John                   is a      to    red
                 told
         don't tell him I     u
      and                   o
                     y
      [←—parenthetical phrase—→]
```

Even within the parenthetical phrase, intonational contours may occur to signify emphasis or attitude.

Finally, intonation can serve to clarify ambiguous phrases. Three examples are given below.

　　　　　　　　　an
1. They don't admit　 y students [they are picked carefully] *or*
　　　　　　　　　　　stu
   They don't admit any　　dents [no students were picked]
　　　　　　struc
2. I have in　　tions to leave [dropping off the instruction] *or*
　　　　　　　　　　　lea
   I have instructions to　　ve [to go away]
3. light housekeeper [tidy up] *or*
   lighthouse keeper [Coast Guard employee]

For the first two examples, the pitch contour serves to distinguish between the alternatives; for the third example duration changes serve to distinguish between the alternatives. To create the phrase "light housekeeper," speakers delay the onset of "house." To create the phrase "lighthouse keeper," speakers speed up the onset of "house."

Semantics   Possibly the most important function of the intonation contour is to emphasize or de-emphasize a word or phrase, or to indicate a contrast or shift in meaning. Accent is therefore independent of sentence structure. Accent is placed on the point of information in the sentence, on items of contrast, or is used as "emotional highlighting"; the speaker adjusts the accents to suit his or her meaning.

Consider the question below and the identical reply with three possible accents

　　When was the last time you saw any of your relatives?
　　1. My MOTHER called me yesterday—does that count?
　　2. My mother CALLED me yesterday—does that count?
　　3. My MOTHER called ME yesterday—does that count?

In each answer, the accent acts to focus on one part of the answer. The tag question "Does that count?" asks the speaker whether the focus signaled by the accent satisfactorily answers the question. In 1, the speaker is asking whether mother is an acceptable relative; in 2, the speaker is asking whether a telephone conversation is acceptable or whether personal contact is necessary; in 3, the speaker is asking whether it is acceptable if another person initiated the contact. In each answer, the intonation pattern provides a focus; it leads the listener to pay attention to one possible aspect of the answer.

In other cases, the intonation contour acts to downgrade or de-emphasize a noun. For example:

1. Harry wants a Volkswagen, but his wife would prefer an AMERICAN *car*.
2. Has John read Slaughterhouse-Five? No, John doesn't READ *books*.

The de-accented words (*car* and *books*) would normally be accented, but in these cases those words are predictable and do not provide new information. In another example of de-acccenting known information,

```
        bomb had
A               wrecked
                        i
                        t
```

seems to imply that bombs are somewhat commonplace or not unusual, but

```
        bomb
A       had wre
            c
            k
            e
            d it
```

seems to imply that bombs are unlikely and improbable. In the first sentence, "bomb" has been de-accented by means of eliminating the pitch rise on the word.

We can conceptualize accenting and de-accenting as opposite sides of the same coin. De-accenting one item has the effect of emphasizing an alternate item, because the stress hierarchy and accentuation are based on the relationships among the items. As argued previously, all rhythmic phenomena are relational, and changes at one point generate changes throughout the structure.

Several experiments on sentence comprehension have indeed demonstrated the helpfulness of stressing appropriate words of a sentence. In these experiments, if focus words were stressed, this led to faster comprehension. The stress could occur in a prior sentence and provide the listener with the appropriate context to understand the following sentence. Alternatively, the stress could occur in the present sentence and provide the focus of information (Bock and Mazzella 1983).

Before finishing, it is fun to consider some of the stylized conventional intonation contours used in English. One stylized contour has been termed the *calling contour* and consists of stepping down from one fairly level pitch to another, as in

```
come and get \
        it. \
```

Ladd (1980), however, argues that the calling intonation is not for calling, but signals a stereotyped or conventional situation. He mentions as an example that

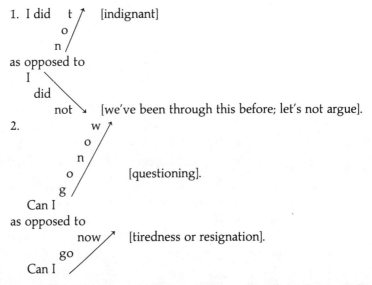

is o.k. (conventional) if you want to pass by someone, but you need

if you create a mess on the floor. Stylized intonations include:

1. I did   t ↗   [indignant]
        o
      n

as opposed to

    I
      did
        not ↘   [we've been through this before; let's not argue].

2.   w ↗
           o
         n
       o ↗   [questioning].
     g
   Can I

as opposed to

           now ↗   [tiredness or resignation].
        go
   Can I

The question of whether stylized intonations indeed have fixed meanings is an open one. There are strong disagreements about whether one contour means the same thing for different utterances in different contexts. It is clear, however, that the intonation is chosen to convey a message-in-context. The choice of contour is free and is not determined by other semantic and syntactic components.

Summary of intonation   The major points are:
1. Intonation contours are the melodies of language. The contours can portray emotions, reveal grammatical constructions, and highlight or emphasize meaning. Moreover, although this has not been discussed, the contours can reflect regional, cultural, and possibly individual personality characteristics.

2. The pitch contour induces a perception of rhythm in the same way that pitch alternations, melodic progressions, and pitch jumps induce a sense of rhythm for melodic sequences in music.

3. Both the stress and the intonation patterns reflect the relational nature of rhythm. Changes at one point result in perceptual consequences throughout the utterance. The intonation contour accentuates and groups the stressed elements and changes the listener's perception of all the stress relationships.

4. It is unclear whether intonation patterns are the same across languages. Bolinger (1978) argues that there are innate patterns cutting across languages, dialects, and individual differences. For example, Cruttenden (1986) suggests that falling pitch at the end of intonation groups usually signifies assertive and continuing statements and that rising pitch usually signifies tentative or questioning statements.

5. Finally, stress and accent are in the "head." Acoustic characteristics do *not* uniquely determine the accent. The acoustic wave induces us to hear a rhythmic pattern, but the acoustic wave does not directly signal that pattern. Householder (1957) comments: "Machines don't hear like people, because people hear things that aren't there, but the machines do hear very well all the factors which induce us to hear what isn't there" (p. 244).

Speech Rhythm in General
As mentioned previously, much of research and theory has stemmed from the observation that there are equal intervals between stressed syllables in English. For this reason, English and many other languages have been termed *stress-timed*. Other languages, like French, have been termed *syllable-timed* because syllables recur at regular time intervals (stress timing may be irregular). The distinction between stress-timed and syllable-timed languages would imply that for phrases with differing numbers of syllables, speakers using a stress-timed language would shorten the duration or spacing between the syllables to ensure that the stresses would occur at roughly equal time intervals. In contrast, speakers using a syllable-timed language would maintain the same timing so that each phrase would require a different amount of time to say.

It is clear now that this distinction is unwarranted. All languages have accents and stresses, and these accents and stresses do tend to occur at roughly equal intervals (although there is wide variation in the measured intervals). Listeners exaggerate the equality of the timing and report hearing stresses as more equidistant than measurements indicate. Languages termed stress-timed are structurally different from languages termed syllable-timed. Stress-timed languages contain a wide variation in syllable type, their unstressed vowels tend to become uniform acoustically (more in the center, in terms of formant frequencies), and they tend to display greater freedom in intonation and accent placement. But, once again, all languages display a tendency for stresses to occur at constant intervals (Wenk and Wioland 1982).

This rhythmic tendency is obviously advantageous. The accents occur at equal intervals, and speakers can make the important words fall on the accents. Listeners can direct their attention ahead to guarantee picking up important content words in the future. By the same token, violations of the equal-interval timing provide cues about the speaker's intentions. It is this performance issue that will now be considered. What kinds of rhythm variation do speakers and performers use, and how do these change our perception?

11.5 The Performance of Rhythm

Actually, all the preceding material in this chapter has concerned rhythmic performance. Speakers use duration changes to mark syntactic boundaries and pitch changes to mark the informational focus of an utterance. Musicians vary the interval and duration timing to mark theme boundaries and to create various expressive effects. Rhythmic performance requires a representation of the output, a set of motor commands that can generate the output sequence, and a set of timing and movement goals. Performance requires preparation and planning, because the rhythmic structure is relational. The rhythm cannot be achieved by letting the elements run off mechanically, one after the other. Without planning an overarching structure, continuity of rhythmic movements would be impossible. What tends to characterize skilled rhythmic performance is a sense of fluency, automaticity, and smoothness. The abrupt stops and starts, hesitations, and jerkiness that characterizes much of our unplanned movements are eliminated in skilled performance.

In order to achieve this sense of fluency inherent in rhythm, the coordinated movements must be preplanned and pretimed. This suggests the need to hypothesize some sort of internal timing mechanism. The timing mechanism, clock, or timekeeper can serve two functions. The first function is to trigger a movement at specific times, the "3, 2, 1, fire" function. The second function is to provide a temporal goal, a time point to which movements are coordinated (e.g., moving faster or slower to reach a point to cut off a rolling ball, or moving two hands to arrive at one spot simultaneously). Here, the timer is anticipating a goal and can adjust the rate of various movements to reach that goal. The coordination necessary for speech and music rhythms will be discussed below.

Speech

Speaking involves both planning and execution. Speakers must plan what they are going to say and then execute that plan in terms of motor movements that yield segments, syllables, words, and phrases, and so on. Planning and execution occur simultaneously. Speakers are executing what they have planned and are simultaneously planning what to say next. There must be some constraint on what is planned by what can be executed. It makes no sense to plan a long complex structure if the speaker cannot execute that sentence because of motor or memory limitations.

Much of our knowledge about speech execution comes from speech errors. Clark and Clark (1977) suggest that there are two kinds of errors. The first arises from difficulties in simultaneously planning and executing. Speakers hesitate, correct, or insert *uhs* when they need to do further planning. (Musicians do not have this luxury.) In all probability, listeners learn to ignore these interruptions, since they are often filled by interjections like oh, ah, or well or word "repeats" with which the speaker signals the listener what he or she is planning to say next. The listener must "close up" the utterance in order to to discover the stress structure.

The second arises from difficulties in creating the motor program that brings about the articulation itself. From a study of speech errors, it is possible to lay out a rough five-stage model: (1) meaning selection; (2) syntactic outline selection; (3) content word selection; (4) function word selection; and (5) phonetic segment selection. Speaking errors can give hints of the processes at each stage.

The syntactic outline specifies a succession of word slots and indicates which slots will receive accentuation. This conclusion is based on errors such as: "a maniac for WEEKENDS" [instead of "a weekend for MANIACS"]. The outline of this sentence may be: noun + preposition + (noun + [plural] + [stress]). The features of plural and stress occur in the syntactic outline; any word that falls in that slot will be pluralized and stressed. "Weekend" and "maniac" were reversed; each was placed in the wrong slot. Nevertheless, [plural] + [stress] stay with the slot. Since [plural] + [stress] go with a slot, not with a word, "weekends" becomes plural and stressed even though it is the wrong word. This suggests that the syntactic outline is chosen first and then words are selected to fill the slots. However, other results suggest that the choice of words precedes accent placement. For example, a word might be de-accented because it appeared previously:

If you have a hundred dollars, then SPEND a hundred dollars.

I had a headache, but fortunately it wasn't a BAD headache.

In both of the examples, the final word(s), which would normally be stressed, are not stressed because they already appear in the sentence.

Speakers would not have been able to make this accent adjustment if the choice of words did not affect the syntactic stress (Cutler 1984).

It is probable that the mental representation of a content word includes its stress pattern. This conclusion is based on errors such as:

Now the paradigm involves PREsenting [instead of preSENting].
I need the number of the psyCHOL. [instead of PsychoLOGical corporation].

For all errors of this sort, the incorrect stress pattern is that of another related word.

Phonetic slips of the tongue occur most commonly in stressed words, and moreover, anticipations (bake my BIKE [instead of take my BIKE]) are three times as frequent as perseverations (pulled a PANTRUM [instead of pulled a TANTRUM]). What is being anticipated is a segment for an accented word giving new information. These results can be understood if accented words, being most important in the sentence, are chosen first. The accented words are more available and, therefore, may more easily "intrude." Notice that the substitutions tend to be between equivalent syllables. Stressed syllables replace stressed syllables but stressed syllables do not replace unstressed syllables. The fact that syllables are interchanged has led MacNeilage (1985) to argue that the syllable structure must be represented independently in production. This reinforces the claim that the rhythm of speech should be based on the syllable.

The articulatory program attempts to capitalize on regular patterns and is disrupted when regular and irregular patterns are mixed. Tongue twisters illustrate this point.

In "She sells sea shells," the initial consonants are patterned A(sh) B(s) B(s) A(sh) but the final consonants are C(ee) D(ells) C(ee) D(ells). The two patterns differ—ABBA versus CDCD—and this produces the stumbling. Speakers often articulate incorrectly: She sells she sells. The initial consonants are forced into the same alternation as the final consonants so that A(sh) always goes with C(ee) and B(s) always goes with D(ells).

In "rubber baby buggy bumpers," there are four conflicting patterns. The initial consonants are A(r) B(b) B(b) B(b); the next vowels are C(u) D(a) C(u) C(u); the middle consonants are E(labial b), E(labial b), F(velar g), E(labial mp) (refer to chapter 5 for the labial-velar articulatory differences); and the final vowels are G(er), H(y), H(y), G(er). All four patterns conflict, and the inability to create parallel patterns generates errors.

Schourup (1973), (cited in Clark and Clark 1977) argues that the critical reason these phrases are tongue twisters is that each word has the identical stress pattern. In the first example above, each word is heavily stressed; in the second, each word consists of strong-weak syllables. The rhythm will reinforce regular articulatory patterns but will disrupt irregular patterns.

Because the articulatory patterns of the tongue twisters are irregular, the rhythm induces the speaker to make the patterns more regular and this leads to the simplifying errors.

This discussion of speech rhythms has emphasized the planning of the utterance. The speech errors tell us that speakers set up abstract representations of what they are trying to say, fill this abstraction up with stressed and unstressed syllables and words, add function words, and then generate a motor program to produce the articulatory elements. The stress pattern of the utterance enters at all levels: stress assignments are notated in the abstract representation, the choice of words affects the stress, and rhythm influences the ease of articulation. Notice that we have not even considered intonation contours, which would increase the complexity even further.

Music
Consider the problems faced by a piano performer. The piece of music to interpret may have four voices (i.e., melodic lines) that the pianist must play simultaneously and "in time." Each voice contains notes of different pitches, different durations, different dynamics, and so on. The pianist must play each melodic line in its notated pattern (at least roughly), must keep each line in the appropriate temporal relation to each other, and must be aware of the expressive aspects of each line. Merely playing mechanically is not sufficient; the player must make use of expressive variation in timing. The performer will "shade" notes by playing them off the beat so that strict regularity is overcome. Otherwise the player is accused of not having "rhythm." (Parenthetically, this is an odd accusation because rhythm is out there to be heard; it is a perceptual experience on the part of the listener.) Thus musical rhythm can give insights into the control of timing, particularly into how different hands act independently to generate the variability, which paradoxically leads to the perception of rhythmic eloquence.

Shaffer (1981) has studied the timing of experienced, skilled musicians using difficult pieces of music. Each piece requires differing movements in each hand in positioning, striking, and actual movement, and the main point to come out of Shaffer's study is the independence of timing movements that a skilled performer can employ. The first piece was a Chopin study consisting of three equal notes per measure in the right hand against four equal notes per measure in the left hand. Playing 3 notes against 4 notes is not simple; without extensive practice, very few people are able to keep the two different rates going. The pianist studied not only was able to play the polyrhythm accurately but in addition was able to vary the timing to achieve two types of rhythmic variations. In the first variation, the pianist changed the tempo of both rates (both hands) together. Measures could be changed in overall duration, and the notated beats within each measure could be varied so that, for instance, the first and third beats could be lengthened and the second and fourth beats could be shortened. What is important, though, is that the 3-note and 4-note patterns were preserved in their correct timing relationships across any sort of variation. In the second variation, the pianist changed the timing of one hand relative to the other. In other words, the notes of the 3-note pattern were shifted in time relative to the notes of the 4-note pattern.

These kinds of results lead to the conclusion that separate time-keeping levels exist. The fact that the timing of the 3-note pattern can shift relative to the 4-note pattern leads to the conclusion that there is a separate clock or time-keeping system for each hand. The fact that the timing of each hand can change in parallel leads to the conclusion that there is a higher-level "control" clock. Typically the higher-level clock locks the two lower-level clocks together (this is often termed *entrainment*) and is, therefore, responsible for timing changes that affect each hand in the same way. Moreover, this higher-level clock is necessary to allow each lower-level clock (each hand) flexibility, because the higher-level clock provides a regular target to allow the player to get back in time. This flexibility and independence was further illustrated when the pianist made an error in one hand. Here the pianist made timing adjustments in the "error" hand, but the timing in the other hand was unaffected. Shaffer's pianists were exceptional. Other work (Peters 1985) using experienced pianists found large performance decrements when playing contrasting rhythms. Possibly the performers studied by Shaffer had so overlearned the procedures for timing (to use Clarke's [1985] expression) that interference between hands was minimized.

The second piece was a Bach fugue. The pianist must play four different voices, two voices with each hand, at the same time. The four voices must be in time yet distinct, as is necessary for polyphonic music. The pianist used intensity differences (in addition to the different frequencies) to contrast the polyphonic voices. The bass (softest), tenor, alto, and soprano (loudest) were played at different intensity levels. The pianist was able to preserve the relative intensities of each voice even though each voice could be played by different fingers or even different hands throughout the performance. The motor programming was not in terms of muscular groups but in terms of musical patterns.

What Speech Production Tells Us about Music Production and Vice Versa
The sections on speech and music are complementary. The material on speech details some aspects of constructing the utterance. The material on music details some aspects of producing the score. Nonetheless, the planning for music must be analogous to the planning for speech and the production of speech must be analogous to the production of music.

There are three parallels between music and speech planning. The first is that performers initially lay out a general plan for the output. For speech, this would be the general intention and the general sentence structure; for music this would be the general historical style as well as the expressive interpretation as notated by composer or as conceptualized by the performer. That the speaker has a plan is illustrated by such errors as, "he threw the WINDOW through the clock," transposing "window" and "clock." The stress that would have been on "clock" in the correct version (He threw the clock) remains in that position, yielding a stress on "window." That the musical performer has an "overall view" of a piece is illustrated by a pianist who played the Bach fugue without previous practice. The pianist was knowledgeable about the structure of similar pieces and was an expert sight reader. It is nonetheless striking that he was able to play the piece nearly perfectly on the first run-through. This ability must be based on a sense of the composer's intent, musical style, and the overall conventions of harmony. Moreover, when the performer played the piece a second time, there was a marked similarity in style, demonstrating that there was a consistent view and intention.

The second parallel is that elements are labeled in terms of abstract characteristics. In speech, words in the "mental dictionary" may be labeled regarding syllables, stress, type, plural, and so on. In music, notes may be labeled in the same way regarding their harmonic functions. Shaffer (1981) found that many errors tended to be explainable in terms of harmonic substitutions, that is, replacing one note by another note of the major triad. Slips of the tongue often involve substitutions of words by other similar-sounding or -meaning words, but within the constraints of the language, just as notes are constrained by the harmonic system. "Slips of the tongue" can become "stips of the lung" but not "tlips of the sung" because the sound [tl] is not allowed at the beginning of English words.

The third parallel is that errors often indicate intrusions from other parts of the output. In speech, there are anticipation errors, where stressed syllables of future words replace equivalent syllables of prior words. In music performances, intrusion errors sometimes seem to come about when a note to be played by one hand is inserted into the notes played by the other hand. It is as if the performer lost track of what was to be performed in each hand, and notes incorrectly moved from one motor program to the other. The theory underlying speech errors suggests that stressed words are selected first, which makes them more available and thus most likely to intrude. The theory underlying music suggests that diatonic scale notes are most available and thus most likely to intrude. In polyphonic music, there would be parallel programs.

In turn, there are parallels between speech and music production. Speech sounds are created and produced by motor movements. Coarticulation demonstrates that the movements proceed in parallel, and in addition, stress and intonation patterns are constructed in parallel. In the same way that music production can utilize timing programs that are both dependent and independent of each other, so can speaking. After all, speaking is probably our most highly practiced complex skill, and there are instances in which all aspects of the utterance undergo the identical time variation and other instances in which coarticulation, stress, and intonation follow different timing trajectories. What this means is that speaking involves several independent "clocks," each timing one aspect of the utterance. Some theory even goes so far as to suggest independent timing for consonants and vowels (Fowler 1986). None of the components of language is truly independent, however, and all components must be related to one higher-level clock.

11.6 The Experience of Rhythm

The discussion of rhythm to this point has been almost all technical; nowhere have we discussed the experience of rhythm. Emotional responses are always difficult to study, because they are private and thus difficult to compare across individuals.

The research on rhythmic experience has used techniques of multi-dimensional scaling to uncover the underlying attributes. Extensive research by Gabrielsson (1973) has used three experimental procedures. In the first, subjects were asked to judge the similarity between two rhythms. In the second, subjects were asked to judge rhythms according to a set of attributes such as complexity, syncopation, regularity, and intricacy. In the third, subjects were asked to give verbal descriptions of how they experienced the rhythms. Gabrielsson used monophonic rhythms performed on the piano or drum, polyphonic rhythms generated electronically, and real music. Across all instances, the rhythmical samples tended to be simple.

Although the specific dimensions or attributes differed from experiment to experiment on the basis of subjects, stimuli, context, and type of judgment, three groups of dimensions appear to be common and important. Rhythms that are representative of two of the dimensions are shown in figure 11.16.

> The cognitive-structural dimension distinguishes rhythm on the basis of (1) meter: two, three, or four, etc., beats per measure; (2) degree of accent on the first beat; (3) type of underlying pattern: whether the rhythm may be perceived as a "variation or filling out" of an underlying basic pattern; (4) clearness of marked basic patterns: whether the perceptually strong accents are clear, and the prominence of instruments carrying the pattern; (5) uniformity-variation, simplicity-complexity: typically, a uniform rhythm is perceived as simple.

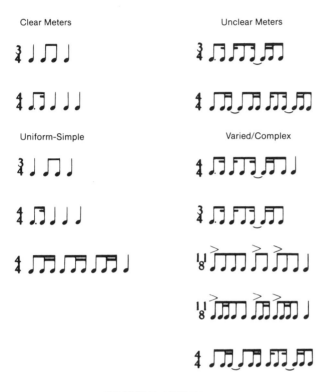

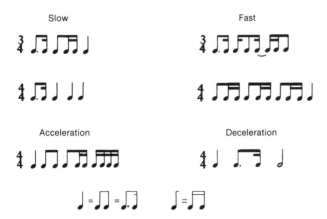

Figure 11.16
Representative rhythms for the cognitive-structural and the movement-motion dimensions. The time signature for each rhythm is indicated. A 4 in the denominator indicates that each quarter note receives one beat; an 8 in the denominator indicates that each eighth note receives one beat (adapted from Gabrielsson 1973).

The movement-motion dimension distinguishes rhythms on the basis of (1) rapidity and tempo: rapidity refers to the rhythm as a whole and is closely related to number of elements per time unit, and tempo refers to the rate of the underlying beat; (2) forward movement/motion: refers to rhythms that appear to accelerate within the measure, and is related to the distribution of elements within a measure; (3) movement/motion: refers to a sense of motion in relation to the rhythm, and is reflected in a number of bipolar dimensions such as dancing-walking, rocking-knocking, graceful-thumping, flexible-rugged, solemn-swinging, and others.

The emotional dimension distinguishes rhythms on the basis of (1) vital (high rapidity/tempo)–dull; (2) Excited (high rapidity/tempo, pronounced syncopation)–calm; (3) rigid (monotonous, static, and mechanical)–flexible; and (4) solemn–playful.

These three dimensions fit previous thinking in distinguishing among the structure, movement, and emotional components of rhythm (Fraisse 1974). The performers' rhythmic variations act to highlight (and possibly create) these rhythmic factors. They create the accent pattern, emphasize the theme and variations, change tempo, and interpret the notated timing.

11.7 Overview

"Every investigator . . . in his definition of rhythm is very certain and unequivocal as to its complexity. This is practically the only point that all are agreed on" (Isaacs 1920, p. 295). Isaacs's comment, made over sixty-five years ago, appears to be perfectly apt today, unfortunately. There is very little agreement on the nature of rhythm, the appropriate way to study rhythm, or the usefulness of rhythm in the construction of theories. A good performance, whether in speech, music, or tennis, is marked by acoustic and motor complexity. But a good performance is not perceived as complex; it is perceived as natural.

To adequately portray rhythm, one must shift from descriptions based on traditional acoustic variables to one based on diverse interactive levels. It is clear that the overall patterning of the acoustic wave brings about the perception of a rhythm, but the rhythm cannot be attributed to any single part of the wave. Without this conceptualization of rhythm as being composed of many levels, we are left with an overly simplified version. Speakers and musicians have a large "arsenal" of rhythmic possibilities at their disposal. Yet these possibilities must fit within production timing and motor constraints as well as the auditory perceptual constraints. It is the independent production of the various rhythmic levels that allows the elasticity, the *rubato* of music, as well as the independence of stress and accent in speech and the independence of meter and grouping in music. In the same way, it must be the parallel perception of these levels that allows for the perception of rhythm.

Further Reading

Cooper and Meyer (1960) is the classic study of rhythm in music. Longuet-Higgins and co-workers have developed formalized theories of musical rhythm. Hogg and McCully (1987) give an extended treatment of meter in speech.

Cooper, G., and Meyer, L. B. (1960). *The rhythmic structure of music.* Chicago: University of Chicago Press.

Hogg, R., and McCully, C. B. (1987). *Metrical phonology: A coursebook.* Cambridge: Cambridge University Press.

Longuet-Higgins, C., and Lee, C. (1982). The perception of musical rhythms. *Perception,* 11, 115–156.

Longuet-Higgins, C., and Lee, C. (1984). The rhythmic interpretation of monophonic music. *Music Perception,* 1 (4), 424–441.

Chapter 12
The Physiology of Listening

In chapters 2–6, we discussed the auditory environment: what information there is to perceive. In chapters 7–11, we discussed auditory perceiving: what acoustic information appears to underlie perception. Taken together, what kind of framework does all of this provide? First of all, the production of extremely diverse kinds of sounds can be understood by a source-filter model. The acoustic pattern varies in time; the temporal patterning among the partials and/or formants creates the relevant information. Second, listening to speech and music employs similar perceptual and cognitive mechanisms. This is due partly to the homologies in production across the various domains of sound and partly to the homologies in formal properties of speech and music. Third, listening is an active process. Auditory information is context dependent; the significance of any part of the signal varies as a function of the values of other parts of the signal. This makes it unlikely that perception is based on the value of any single attribute considered in isolation.

Obviously, it is possible to analyze the auditory nervous system part by part (and we will do just that below), but we should not expect listening to be the sum of these parts and properties. The mechanisms that emerge will depend on the tests used to measure them (Jenkins 1984). For example, physiological data based on pure tones in isolation may not be applicable to dynamic events in a noisy environment. Our understanding is also limited by our technology, which restricts the ways in which we conceptualize physiological processes. The problem is not merely lack of sensitivity or inability to make multiple measurements.

The evolution of the auditory system has been debated for many years. Biologists originally traced the vertebrate ear back to the lateral line in fish. The lateral line detects water movement by means of the movements of "hair" cells within a trough along the side of the fish. Although the lateral line shares many features with the vertebrate ear, it is now hypothesized that the vertebrate ear is an outgrowth of the vestibular balance system.

Regardless of its actual origin, the auditory system appears to have been the last sensory system to evolve. It is characteristic of vertebrates above the fishes—amphibians, birds, primates, humans—which live a portion of their life on land. We can speculate that the emerging auditory system was useful for detecting and localizing predators, prey, and mates. The auditory system became an event or movement detector, especially sensitive to the identification and localization of brief transient sounds created by other animals.

If significant sounds in the environment were continuous or slowly changing, our exterior auditory ystem might have consisted of one movable ear. The sound could be localized by turning the ear to maximize sound intensity. Localization information is transitory and brief however, and accurate localization must depend on the phase, intensity, and spectral comparison of two signals, each generated by one ear. To enhance localization, the evolution of the ear led to a greater sensitivity to intensity differences at higher frequencies and to a greater ability to resolve sound blends, while the evolution of brain structures led to a greater ability to detect timing and spectral differences between the ears. It is somewhat humbling to conjecture that mundane survival requirements led to an auditory system capable of communication, whether by grunts, sound gestures, or a language. It is clear, however, that without the increased capabilities brought about by survival requirements, speech and music could not exist.

It is worthwhile to contrast the neural pathways underlying vision and audition. The eye is formed out of brain cells There are roughly 130 million light-sensitive receptors in the retina of each eye. The receptors converge onto roughly one million fibers of the visual nerve, which in turn stimulate 100 million neurons in each side of the visual cortex. In contrast, the ear is formed out of skin cells. There are roughly 15,000 receptors in each ear, which converge on roughly 15,000 fibers of the auditory nerve. The pathway to the auditory cortex has many nuclei in which the fibers converge and then diverge. At each such center, the number of auditory neurons increases so that there are about 100 million auditory cells in each side of the auditory cortex. The number of visual and auditory cortical cells is therefore identical, although the number of receptor cells and their origin are as different as possible. The number of subcortical "way stations" of the auditory pathways compensate for the humble origins of the ear.

Traditional descriptions of the auditory system distinguish the ear, the peripheral neural pathways leading to the cortex, and the cortex itself. Before each component is detailed, it will be useful to present the conceptual issues concerning each part.

The analysis of the ear concerns the transformation of the air molecule vibrations into the neural firing of specialized cells (termed *hair cells*). The fundamental issue is the neural coding of frequency (pitch) and intensity (loudness).

The analysis of the neural pathways concerns the transformation of the neural firing of individual hair cells in the cochlea into firing patterns of neurons running toward the cortex. The auditory system has the most extensive interconnections of diverse neurons at various brain nuclei, and these interconnections may yield higher-level neurons tuned to specific characteristics of an auditory signal. The basic idea is that progression toward the cortex yields more complex detectors, tuned to more abstract properties of the event. The fundamental issue is to determine if such cells exist, and if they do, to identify the stimulus properties that excite the cells.

The analysis of the auditory cortex concerns the localization of function within the left and right hemispheres. The issue of localization is immensely complicated because of the level of analysis. At the simplest level, the auditory nerve does conduct to specific regions of the cortex. At these regions, the nerve unravels and connects in specific ways to the brain cells. It is possible to map the auditory cortex in order to discover whether there is a simple relationship between the spatial position of a cell in the cortex and its maximal sensitivity to acoustic attributes like frequency. At more abstract levels, the idea of localization implies specialization for higher-level functioning. We could argue that localization encompasses large domains, e.g., language areas distinct from music areas. We might even argue that there are distinct neural areas that are specifically "wired" to interpret semantics as distinct from syntax or specifically wired to interpret rhythm as distinct from harmony. The notion that brain organization is based on domains or "modules" has been termed *vertical* organization by Fodor (1983). Vertical organization is characterized by being genetically determined, by being localized in distinct neural structures, and by being "computationally autonomous" in the sense that the output is automatic and is not affected by other cognitive processes. In contrast to the view that the brain is organized by vertical domains, we could assume that the brain is organized by horizontal processes—remembering, judging, comparing, and associating, among others. Here, the very same cognitive processes act on all sorts of inputs: visual images, speech sounds, odors, musical sounds, and so on. The faculty of "comparing" is context- and domain-free; it operates in the identical way for all inputs. The fundamental issue is to determine the degree and type of localization at each cortical level.

This threefold partition of ear, neural pathways, and cortex will serve as the basis for the rest of the chapter. Only the barest outlines of the incorporation of information from the environment into consciousness is understood. Nonetheless, what is known will be presented below, noting where the conclusions are most tentative. Nearly all the data come from rodents, cats, and primates, and the question of generalizability always arises.

12.1 The Structure of the Ear

The ear can be broken down into three parts: the outer ear, the middle ear, and the inner ear.

Outer Ear

The outer ear consists of the pinna and the hollow resonant cylinder called the ear canal. The ear canal terminates at the eardrum (the alternative term is the tympanic membrane). Together, the pinna and ear canal seem like a brass horn, the pinna resembling the flare and the ear canal resembling a roughly straight piece of tubing. It is a backward instrument, aiding in the capture of sound energy.

The pinna, with its intricate construction of swirls, is most developed in humans. As discussed in chapter 3, the pinna aids front-to-back localization: it funnels sounds in front of and shadows sounds behind a listener. In addition, the shape of the pinna creates a frequency filter so that as a sound source moves vertically from below the head to above the head, different frequency bands are accentuated and diminished. These changes provide the localization information for elevation.

The ear canal is quite irregular in shape, the walls are not rigid, and the length is roughly 2.3 cm (about 1 in). It is a hollow tube closed at one end. The resonant frequency corresponds to 1 divided by 4 times the length, or about 3500–4000 Hz. Because of its construction, the ear canal is moderately damped (medium Q); we would expect a wide resonant band rather than a sharp resonance. Direct measurement has, in fact, found a broad region extending from 2000 Hz to 5000 Hz.

It is possible to measure the combined effect of the head, pinna, and ear canal. The combination of all effects at different positions around the head are shown in figure 12.1. Notice that the general effect is to produce an acoustical gain between 1500 Hz and 7000 Hz. In the region between 2000 Hz and 4000 Hz, pressure at the ear drum may be as much as six times stronger (15 dB) than in the surrounding free field. It should be remember that the major part of speech and musical energy fall at those same frequencies.

Middle Ear

The middle ear provides the bridge between the vibration of the ear drum at the outer ear and the vibration of the oval window at the inner ear. The middle ear is needed because of the mismatch in density and compressi-

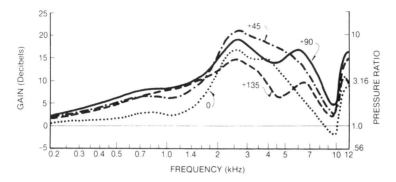

Figure 12.1
The change in pressure at the ear drum due to the head, pinna, and ear canal. If the head and outer ear had no effect; the pressure gain at all frequencies would be 0 (light horizontal line). Zero degrees is straight ahead (adapted from Shaw 1974).

bility between air (at the ear drum) and water (at the oval window). This mismatch limits the degree to which an air vibration can excite a water vibration.

Impedance matching   Impedance (R) is a measure of the density and compressibility of a medium. The percentage of power transferred between two mediums is equal to $4R_1 R_2/(R_1 + R_2)^2$. If the impedances are equal ($R_1 = R_2$), then all the incident power is transferred. However, if the impedances are quite different, the percentage of energy transferred rapidly drops off. For example, if $R_1 = 100\ R_2$, then only 4% of the power is transmitted. The nontransmitted power (96%) is reflected back into the original medium. The impedance of water is 3750 times greater than air, so only about 1/1000 of the power in the air is transmitted to the water.

What this means is that if air molecule vibration were to hit the fluid-filled cochlea directly, only about 1/1000 of the power would be effective in creating fluid movement. The remaining part would be uselessly reflected back to the air. Snakes do not possess the intricate structure of the middle ear; therefore they cannot hear the air-borne vibration of the flute of the charmer. Snakes "hear" ground-based vibrations. The impedance of the ground more closely matches that of water, so when resting its head on the ground, the jawbone of the snake picks up and transmits the vibration to the fluid-filled inner ear.

Three factors, enumerated below, improve the transfer of air vibration energy into fluid vibration energy. To help visualize these mechanisms, a diagram of the middle ear is shown in figure 12.2. As can be seen, the eardrum (tympanic membrane) is connected to the oval window by three

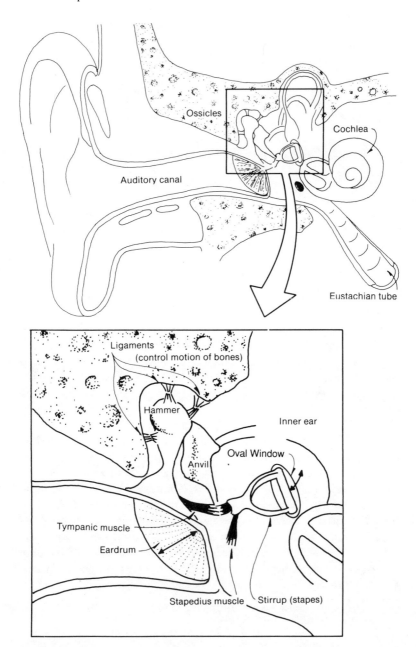

Figure 12.2
A schematic view of the outer, middle, and inner ear, and a detailed view of the middle ear. The back-and-forth movement of the eardrum results in a "swinging door" movement of the stapes against the oval window of the cochlea. The stapedius and tympanic muscles control the acoustic reflex by loosening the connections among the middle ear bones.

connected bones. Because of their shapes, the bones are commonly called the hammer (malleus), anvil (incus), and stirrup (stapes).

1. The most important factor is that the size of the tympanic membrane is roughly thirty times greater than the size of the oval window. The vibratory pressure at the eardrum is funneled and concentrated on the oval window. The pressure on the smaller area is increased by the ratio between the areas, about 35 to 1.
2. The three bones act as a lever and thereby increase the pressure at the oval window. The lever arm from the eardrum is roughly 1.15–1.30 times longer than the lever arm driving the oval window. This effectively increases the pressure at the oval window by the same amount.
3. Instead of moving as a stable membrane, the eardrum buckles in the middle, which tends to increase the pressure at the oval window by a factor of 2.

It is possible to combine these three factors by multiplication—35 × 1.15 × 2—to yield an overall pressure ratio of 80.5. Thus the effect of the middle ear structure is to increase the pressure impinging on the inner ear 80-fold and thereby increase the amplitude of the fluid vibration. The maximum gain occurs between 500 Hz and 8000 Hz (measured for the cat). It is unclear how much the middle ear compensates for the impedance mismatch. The calculations are complicated and need to be based on physical values that are not firmly established. The estimates range from 65% to 100%, which suggests that at least two-thirds of the mismatch is overcome.

For the middle ear to function properly, the air pressure behind the eardrum surrounding the bones must be equal to the natural air pressure. The eustachian tube opens briefly when swallowing or yawning, and this serves to equalize the pressure. If the pressures not are equal, the effect of the middle ear matching decreases. This is a common occurrence when descending or ascending in altitude—the sense of hearing grows poorer until our ears "pop" to equalize the pressures.

Acoustic reflex   The three bones are held in place by two pairs of muscles, the tympanic muscle attached to the hammer and the stapedius muscle attached to the stirrup (see figure 12.2). When stimulated by high intensity sounds, the stapedius muscle contracts reflexively (termed the *auditory reflex*). The muscular contraction stiffens the bony chain, attenuating the low frequency (below 1000 Hz) vibration that reaches the oval window of the inner ear. The strength and timing of the reflex is a direct function of intensity. The reflex is initiated at relatively modest sound levels (about 65 dB, or moderate speaking levels) and affects hearing at all intensities above 90dB (moderate traffic noise). At higher intensities, the latency until the reflex begins is shorter, and it reaches its maximum value in a shorter time period. Surprisingly, the reflex adapts to long duration tones and therefore the low frequency attenuation weakens (Pickles 1982).

The acoustic reflex is too slow to protect the inner ear structures against intense, rapid transients. The reflex can reduce the transmission of low frequency tones by a factor of 1/10 to 1/100. The reflex thus tends to compress the amplitude change for slowly varying signals but does not attenuate short transients. (This fact reinforces the notion that transients carry the majority of auditory information.) Action of the reflex does improve hearing, particularly at higher intensities. Low frequency sounds tend to mask high frequency sounds, and therefore by attenuating low frequencies the reflex can make the high frequency sounds that are so critical for speech perceptions more detectable. At intensities greater than 90 dB, which normally trigger the reflex, patients with a defective reflex do show a decrement in speech perception.

The contraction of the pupil when exposed to intense light and the contraction of the stapedius muscle seem analogous. Although it is a widely held idea, the purpose of the pupil is not to protect the eye from bright light (the change in pupil size is much too small). The closing of the pupil increases the depth of field so that a greater part of the field of view is in focus. By the same token, the purpose of the stapedius reflex is not to protect the ear but to enhance perception by attenuating the low frequency components.

Inner Ear
The cochlea is responsible for the transformation of the middle ear fluid vibration into neural firings. The cochlea is a coiled, fluid-filled structure containing hair cells (*cochlea* means snail in Latin). Movement of the hair cells generates the neural impulses. The cochlea is a tube about 35 mm (1 1/3 inch) in length and makes about two and one-half coils, about the size of a small bean. The cochlea is split up the middle by two membranes that form a triangular-shaped partition. The hair cells lie within the partition fixed to the bottom membrane. The air vibration, magnified by the middle ear, creates a pressure wave in the fluid, which distorts the bottom membrane of the middle partition. The distortion of the membrane bends hair cells, which leads to those hair cells firing.

Cochlea   We can understand how the cochlea functions by turning to simplified models. The simplest representation begins with a fluid-filled short cylinder with an elastic covering at each end (see figure 12.3). The cylinder represents the cochlea, and the two elastics represent the oval and round windows (A). Now we connect the stirrup to the one elastic representing the oval window, and we place a third elastic membrane in the

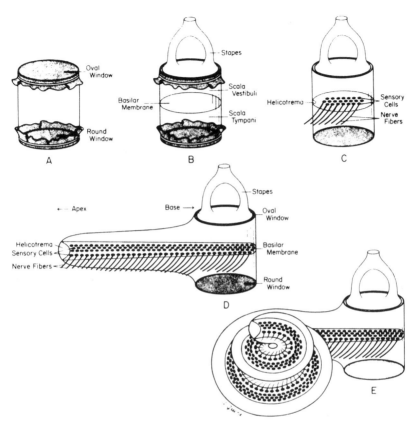

Figure 12.3
Simplified representations of the cochlea. The simplest representation, *A*, consists of a short fluid filled cylinder with an elastic membrane covering each end. Movements of the top membrane will result in equivalent movements of the bottom membrane. More complex representations, *B* and *C*, include an elastic membrane containing sensory cells to stand for the basilar membrane in the center of the cylinder. A replica stapes sets the fluid within the cylinder into motion and thereby moves the basilar membrane. The most complex representations, *D* and *E*, extend and lengthen the basilar membrane. Regions along the extended basilar membrane can be tuned to different frequencies. Coiling the cochlea (*E*) results in a compact inner ear (from Kiang 1975 by permission; copyright © 1975 Raven Press).

middle of the cylinder to represent the partition along the cochlea (B). Assume that this membrane is attached to the walls by bones or muscles. Moving the stirrup up and down will create pressure differences in the top half, which will distort the middle membrane. The induced pressure differences will be released or compensated by movement of the bottom elastic representing the round window. If, as in (C), hair cells are represented on the middle membrane, we get a crude inner ear. The movement of the membrane will bend (or shear) the hair cells and generate neural impulses. To increase the sensitivity of the ear, the membrane can be lengthened and the surrounding cylinder can be extended perpendicular to the oval and round windows (D). The tubing gets narrower as it extends outward, but the membrane widens as the attaching bones and muscle become narrower. Moreover, in the human ear the membrane reduces in stiffness. The membrane does not extend the complete length; there is a hole (the helicotrema) at the end so that fluid can escape from above the membrane (this ensures that the membrane can return to its resting position if the stapes undergoes a forward or backward movement). As the stapes vibrates back and forth it will create a wave pattern in the fluid, but the position along the middle membrane that undergoes the maximum movement will depend on the frequency of the vibration as well as on the physical properties of the membrane. Finally, we can take the elongated tubing and twist it into a coil to make it more compact (E). In doing so, we can now identify inner hair cells along the inside curve and outer hair cells located along the outside curve. Again, different vibration frequencies of the stapes will bring about the maximum movement of the middle membrane at different points along its length.

This schematic ear represents the essentials of the inner ear. We now focus briefly on the anatomy and physiology of the partition extending through the cochlea. The partition is wedge-shaped, bounded by two elastic membranes, resembling a triangle. The top membrane (Reissner's membrane), is quite light and delicate. It is the movement of the bottom membrane (basilar membrane) due to the fluid pressure that is the important motion. Within the triangular wedge is the complex structure known as the organ of Corti (named after its discover, Alfonso Corti). The organ of Corti sits on the basilar membrane and contains the hair cells that are the actual receptor cells. As shown in figure 12.4, supporting cells rest on the basilar membrane and the hair cells sit on these supporting cells. Arching over the hair cells is the tectorial membrane. The cilia or hairs of the outer hair cells appear to be embedded in the underside of the tectorial membrane, but the cilia of the inner hair cells are not embedded. The basilar membrane and the tectorial membrane can move independently of each other, and this produces a sideways shearing motion of the cilia.

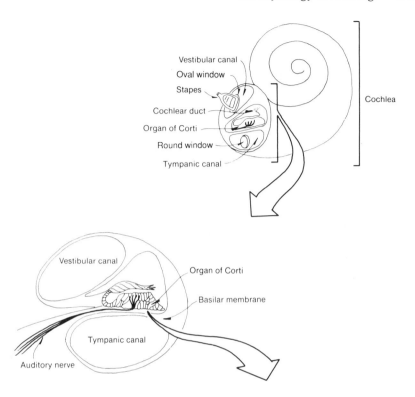

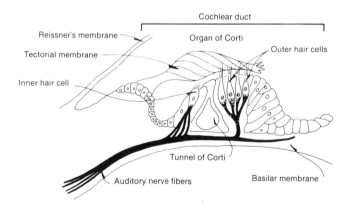

Figure 12.4
Three views of the inner ear. The *top view* shows the coiled cochlea divided into three roughly triangular tubes. The *middle view* shows a detailed cross-section. The *bottom view* zooms in on the center segment, bounded by Reissner's membrane on the top and the Basilar membrane on the bottom. Note that each inner hair cell is connected to several nerve fibers and that several outer hair cells converge on one nerve fiber.

There are roughly 3500 inner hairs arrayed in a single row along the length of the basilar membrane. There are many more outer hair cells, roughly 12,000, and these are arrayed in three rows. Surprisingly, 90% to 95% of the fibers of the auditory nerve connect to the inner hair cells. Many outer hair cells converge on a single auditory nerve fiber while each inner hair cell may excite up to twenty auditory nerve fibers (see figure 12.4). The outer hair cells act to enhance the selectivity of the cochlea mechanisms by changing the mechanical properties of the basilar membrane. The outer hair cells change the coupling of the basilar membrane so that the actual movement pattern is restricted to a smaller part of the membrane (the Q increases). If the outer hair cells are selectively damaged, there is a striking loss of sensitivity (Pickles 1986).

To review, the shearing movements of the cilia of the hair cells generate the nerve impulses. This shearing movement is brought about by the movement of the basilar membrane caused by the wave motion of the fluid within the cochlea. From this perspective, to understand further how the ear works, it is necessary to investigate the motion of the basilar membrane, particularly as a function of frequency.

Basilar membrane   Historically, there have been two general theories about the basilar membrane. In the first, termed a *place theory*, different points along the basilar membrane are assumed to undergo maximum displacement as a function of frequency. Hair cells located at the point of maximum displacement undergo the greatest distortion and, therefore, fire at the highest rate. Each hair cell would code a specific frequency based on its position along the cochlea. In the second, termed a *timing* or *frequency theory*, the basilar membrane is assumed to move up and down in synchrony with the pressure variation of the sound wave caused by the movement of the stapes at the oval window. Each up-and-down movement results in one neural firing, so that frequency is coded directly by the rate of firing: a 200 Hz tone results in hair cells firing 200 times per second and a 1000 Hz tone results in hair cells firing 1000 times per second. For frequencies beyond the firing rate of individual cells (roughly 1000 times/sec), the firings of many cells are integrated to create the correct firing rate.

The initial investigation of basilar membrane function was due to the work of Georg von Békésy (1960). Studying the basilar membrane is incredibly difficult because of its small size, its location within the hardest bones in the head, and the fact that it is surrounded by fluid. Von Békésy had the basic insight that the physical properties of the basilar membrane determined the manner in which the membrane vibrated. Starting with some known properties of the basilar membrane, namely that the stiffness decreases a hundredfold from the base at the oval window to the apex at the helicotrema, von Békésy discovered that by varying the overall stiffness of the membrane and the coupling between adjacent parts of the membrane, the identical vibration pattern at the stapes could yield very different patterns of motion on a simulated basilar membrane. In simple terms, coupling means the degree to which vibration at one point on the membrane affects the vibration at other parts.

We will use a simple illustration to represent these ideas (see figure 12.5). The model uses a rubber sheet that increases in width and decreases in stiffness toward the end to mimic the physical properties of the basilar membrane. The sheet is cut across the width into strips that, because of the physical changes in width and stiffness, have different resonant frequencies. The coupling is varied by the interconnections among the strips. To represent light coupling, the strips are loosely connected (or unconnected altogether) so that vibration in one strip will have little effect on adjacent strips; to represent medium coupling, the strips are more tightly connected so that vibration in one strip will bring about some vibration in adjacent strips (light lines); to represent stiff coupling, the strips are very tightly connected so that vibration in one strip will bring about nearly identical vibration in adjacent strips (dark heavy lines).

Imagine that the rubber sheet is set into motion by a sinusoidal vibration. For loose uncoupled systems, only the strip with the resonance frequency identical to the driving frequency will begin to vibrate up and down; this leads to a pure place system (a). On the other hand, for stiff, highly coupled systems, all the strips will vibrate together at the driving frequency; the entire membrane will vibrate as one unit. This leads to a pure frequency system (c). For intermediate coupling, the vibration will create a traveling wave which propagates down the system from the stiffest, narrowest section to the most compliant, widest section (b). The point of greatest vibration amplitude will occur at the strip that has a resonant frequency matching the driving frequency. At high frequencies, the maximum will occur in the stiff region at the base; at low frequencies the maximum will occur in the flexible region at the apex.

The fact that the motion of the basilar membrane is determined by its physical properties does not explain what kind of motion occurs. To discover this, von Békésy spend twenty years improving techniques until he could study the basilar membrane in post-mortem human cochleas. He discovered that stimulation with a constant frequency resulted in a traveling wave that progressed down the basilar membrane. Because of the physical changes along the membrane, the shape of the wave is not constant. The amplitude grows to a maximum at one point and then rapidly decreases. The maximum amplitude occurs near the oval windows for high frequencies and occurs near the apex for low frequencies. Moreover, as the wave travels down the membrane its speed decreases, particularly in the region of maximum displacement. Thus the mechanical properties of

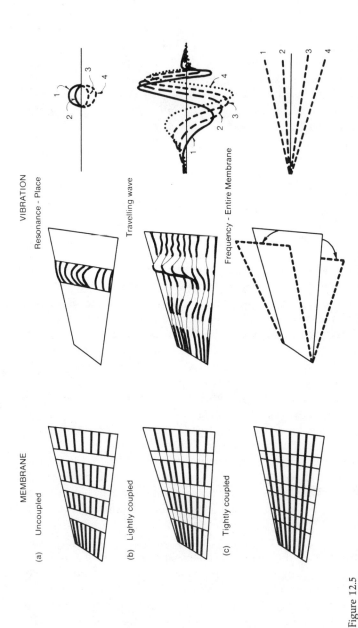

Figure 12.5
A simulated model of the basilar membrane based on a rubber sheet. The coupling between strips is portrayed by the thickness of the lines connecting the strips. As the coupling within the rubber sheet is increased so that the segments become more strongly interconnected, the vibration pattern shifts from a localized resonance to a traveling wave, and then to a movement of the entire membrane as a unit. Because the basilar membrane is held along its edges, the vibration amplitude will be maximum in the middle. This is shown most clearly for the traveling wave. The *second column* shows the vibration pattern along the top of the membrane; the *third column* shows the vibration pattern from the side of the membrane at four time points.

the basilar membrane act to focus the different frequency components of the input signal at different points along the membrane. Consider different stimuli:

1. For a single cycle, there will be one traveling wave pattern that moves down the membrane.

2. For a continuous, sinusoidal vibration, the vibration on the basilar membrane will be a series of traveling waves. I imagine waves approaching a beach; the height of the waves changes because of the ocean bottom (sandbars), and after a certain point the wave just collapses. (This analogy breaks down, however, because the wave motion on the basilar membrane is due to the compressive waves on the fluids; the basilar membrane is not moved directly.)

3. For a click (theoretically consisting of all frequencies), the high frequency components are "captured" and generate maximum displacement near the oval window while the low frequency components are captured and generate maximum displacement toward the far end. Thus there will be displacement along the entire length of the membrane. As the wave progresses along the basilar membrane, lower and lower frequencies are filtered out of the traveling wave. The vibration at each point on the basilar membrane is at its resonant frequency, and the decay is most rapid at the higher frequencies.

4. For typical speech, music, or environmental sounds consisting of several partials, the traveling wave will stimulate different points, corresponding to the frequency of each partial, along the basilar membrane. The basilar membrane spreads out the frequencies along its length.

Frequency selectivity   There are two ways of measuring the sharpness of the frequency selectivity on the basilar membrane. The first is to measure the displacement amplitude along the basilar membrane for a sound of constant frequency. As shown in figure 12.6, the point of maximum displacement moves toward the helicotrema or apex as the frequency decreases. An alternative way of representing the sensitivity is to measure the displacement at one point on the membrane as a function of frequency. The relative amplitude is shown as a function of frequency for constant stapes displacement and constant stapes velocity in figure 12.7. The basilar membrane acts as a low-pass filter. At any point, all frequencies up to a certain value lead to a relatively constant displacement; frequencies above this value lead to drastically smaller displacements.

These Nobel Prize discoveries of von Békésy form the foundation of our knowledge of cochlea functioning. What was puzzling in von Békésy's work was the rather broad tuning (or selectivity) along the basilar mem-

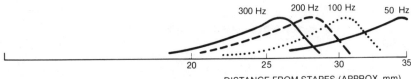

DISTANCE FROM STAPES (APPROX. mm)

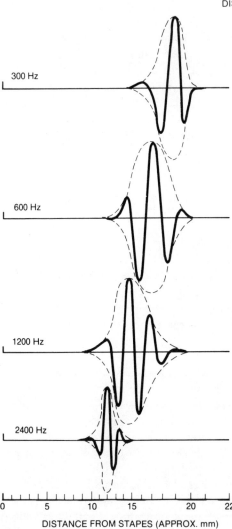

DISTANCE FROM STAPES (APPROX. mm)

Figure 12.6
The traveling wave pattern on the basilar membrane. In the top panel, the amount of
displacement along the membrane is shown for tones of differing frequencies (adapted from
von Békésy 1960). In the next four panels, the traveling wave pattern is shown for different
frequencies. The light lines touching the peaks display the displacement envelopes (from
Pfeiffer and Kim 1975 by permission). The displacements shown in the top panel are
equivalent to the top half of the envelopes.

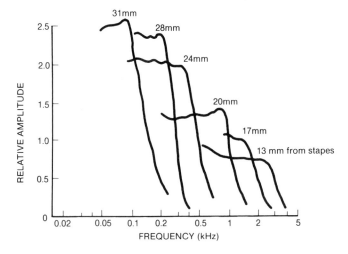

Figure 12.7
The amplitude of movement at different points along the basilar membrane as a function of frequency. The amplitude at any point is essentially constant for a range of frequencies up to a cutoff value and then drops to zero for all higher frequencies. The membrane acts as a low-pass filter: each point responds to frequencies below a certain value. Near the stapes it responds up to higher frequencies; near the base it responds only up to lower frequencies (from Eldridge 1974 by permission).

brane. The crude tuning did not seem capable of supporting the superb frequency discrimination of less than 1 Hz. Von Békésy and others were forced to hypothesize filters or neurological circuits capable of sharpening the gross tuning. However, more refined measuring techniques have demonstrated that the selectivity of the cochlea is far greater than von Békésy's measurements suggested. Von Békésy was forced to use high intensity pressure waves to measure the displacement from ears of human cadavers. Newer techniques can record directly from the hair cells of live rodents at much lower intensities. The evidence suggests that the mechanical functioning of the basilar membrane itself creates the necessary selectivity (e.g., Khanna and Leonard 1982). The enhanced selectivity is partly due to the properties of the basilar membrane itself and partly due to the mechanical action of the outer hair cells and tectorial membrane that sharpen the movement. For example, the outer hair cells might expand or contract physically, and because of their connection to the tectorial membrane they might change the vibration pattern, or the tectorial membrane itself might resonate at different points along the membrane because of the driving frequency (Hudspeth 1985; Pickles 1986). There is an extremely important caveat, however. These measurements were taken using stimulation at threshold levels, far below normal listening levels. At intensity levels approximating normal listening, frequency selectivity tends to completely break down. The entire membrane vibrates, and no region can be singled out. We will return to this problem.

The final issue is the generation of neural impulses by the hair cells. Although the hair cells look symmetrical, opposite movements along the same axis of motion have dramatically different effects (these results come from analyses of hair cells along the lateral line in fish, where they can be investigated readily). Mechanical distortion in one direction leads to increased firing rates; distortion in the opposite direction leads to decreased firing rates. This implies that hair cells fire in time or in phase with one particular motion of the basilar membrane.

Summary of the Ear
To review, the ear analyzes any complex wave into frequency components, because of the physical structure of the basilar membrane and the mechanical properties of the hair cells. Each frequency generates maximum movement at a different point along the basilar membrane, and therefore different bundles of hair cells are stimulated. Moreover, the firing of each hair cell occurs at one specific point in the movement of the membrane. Thus the firing rate matches the stimulating frequency (or some fraction if the hair cell fires on alternate cycles). There are two kinds of information: (1) place on basilar membrane correlated to frequency; and (2) timing of neural impulses correlated to frequency.

Finally, we should not lose sight of the fact that the ear is yet another instrument. It possesses resonant modes, coupled systems, and so on. The ear filters the source so that the energy distribution transmitted to the cortex differs from the energy distribution in the air. At least on a global level, the filtering seems to be helpful, enhancing sound energy at the frequencies necessary for speech perception.

12.2 The Peripheral Nervous System

The auditory system has the most complicated set of interconnections of any sensory system. The majority (70%) of nerve pathways are contralateral, crossing from one ear to the auditory cortex on the opposite side. The remainder are ipsilateral, ascending from one ear to the cortex on the same side. There are nerve pathways passing through four or five relay stations before going to the auditory cortex. Other nerve pathways skip nuclei and make direct contact with "higher-level" nuclei. As discussed previously, this complexity seems necessary to compensate for the small number of hair cells in the mechanical cochlea. A schematic representation is shown in figure 12.8.

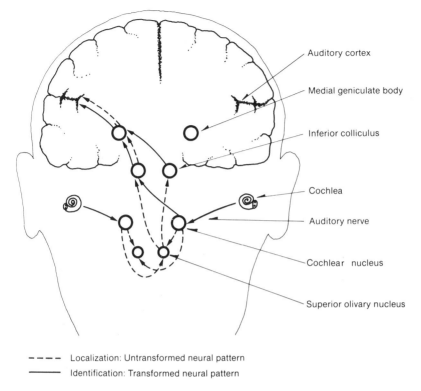

Figure 12.8
The auditory pathways from the cochlea. Pathways from both ears primarily involved in localization converge on the superior olivary nucleus and then project to the ipsilateral and contralateral inferior colliculus. Pathways from each ear primarily involved in recognition and identification of events go from the cochlear nucleus directly to the contralateral inferior colliculus. All pathways intermix at the inferior colliculus and then travel to the ipsilateral and contralateral medial geniculate body and on the auditory cortex.

What is the general orientation of the auditory system? What are the perceptual goals? Above all, the auditory system must yield the identity of the event as well as its location; the what and the where. We need to uncover the relevant acoustic information (based on physical and psychological experimentation) and to discover whether there are neurological mechanisms "tuned" to this information. There must be a correspondence between the acoustic information and sensory functioning, if only because the mechanisms of the auditory system solely determine what we can perceive.

First consider identity. In the preceding chapters we have seen that much of the important "what" perceptual information occurs in the dynamic changes across time of frequency, intensity, resonance, spectrum, noise, and so on. These changes clearly occur in a context, and an event must therefore be defined both by the steady-state value and by the transient. In fact, the context is necessary to define the physical properties of the transient. At first glance, this conceptualization of an auditory event matches the organization of the auditory system. At every level of the auditory system there is tonotopic organization: different frequencies are represented spatially in each nucleus, which suggests that the absolute frequencies are consistently coded. Moreover, at each nucleus there are cells that are responsive to changes in frequency and/or intensity and are relatively unresponsive to steady sounds. The pathways most concerned with the representation of the event are shown with solid lines in figure 12.8. Unfortunately, there are many gaps in our understanding. Research to this point has only described the diversity of cells in the auditory nuclei. There appears to be little relationship among cells at the same nuclei and little relationship among cells at different levels. In addition much of our knowledge is based on the recording of firing patterns of single nerve fibers or cells, although the important neural information may lie in the patterning of firing among different cells or group of cells.

Now consider location. In the eye, retinal cells code spatial position directly. This is not true for the ear. The basilar membrane vibration is based on frequency and intensity, not location. To recapture location, stimulation to each ear must be compared, and this requires distinct nuclei where fibers from each ear converge. Recall from chapter 3 that the two basic cues to location are interaural differences in time due to the separation between the ears and interaural differences in intensity due to the sound reflections of the head and body. If there is a parallel between physical differences and physiological coding, then there should be cells that respond only to these interaural differences. Here there does seem to be a good parallel between the physical and psychological information and the organization of the auditory system. There are distinct nuclei and pathways dedicated to the calculation of interaural differences. These are indicated by dashed lines in figure 12.8.

In what follows, I will emphasize the physiological coding in the auditory nerve. There has been rather extensive research on the firing patterns of individual nerves to simulated speech sounds. Following this, the results from higher-level auditory nuclei will be considered. Here the results are more diverse and spotty.

Auditory Nerve Fibers
The first point in the peripheral auditory system is the eighth nerve, which contains the fibers connected to the inner hair cells. Overall, the response characteristics of nerve fibers are remarkably consistent across several species, and the research findings are probably a good reflection of human functioning.

In the typical experiment, the animal is anesthetized, and a microelectrode is inserted into the auditory nerve until a single fiber is impaled. The firing pattern of that fiber is recorded for various combinations of frequency and intensity. The test tone may be presented up to 100 times to generate an accurate picture. The results can be plotted in two ways. In the first, the firing rate/sec is plotted against frequency and intensity to portray the sensitivity and selectivity or tuning. In the second, the intervals between individual firings are plotted against the timing of the stimulating tone to portray the degree to which the firings are synchronized to one point of the tone.

Firing rate   First consider the measurement of sensitivity and selectivity. A sinusoid tone is swept up and down in frequency at varying intensities. The firing rates are recorded for each possible combination of frequency/intensity. The results for one nerve fiber are shown in figure 12.9. There is a "best" frequency around 10,000 Hz, at which the fiber is maximally sensitive: the fiber fires at this frequency at the lowest intensities. This frequency is termed the *characteristic frequency*. As the intensity is increased, the fiber fires at a wider range of frequencies until at the highest intensities, the fiber will fire at frequencies ranging from 1000 Hz to 11,000 Hz. This range of frequencies is a measure of selectivity. Highly selective fibers will fire only to a narrow range. A frequency tuning curve is the frequency-intensity region within which the firing rate increases by some percentage over the baseline firing rate and is illustrated to the right of the experimental data.

The tuning curves obviously are asymmetrical. At frequencies above the characteristic frequency, the response rate is low, even at high intensities. At frequencies below the characteristic frequency, the response rate increases at higher intensities. The low frequency tails occur at intensities of

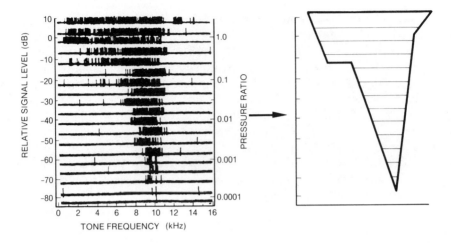

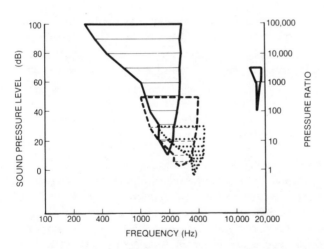

Figure 12.9
Frequency-intensity response areas for single auditory fibers. In the *top left panel*, the actual firing record is shown for different combinations of frequency and intensity. Each vertical line represents a spike and black regions represent high firing rates (adapted from Evans 1972). A schematic representation is shown on the *right*, enclosing all combinations of frequency and intensity that yield a 20% increase in firing rate. In the *bottom panel*, response areas for four fibers with different characteristic frequencies are shown (adapted from Galambos and Davis 1943).

real world sounds and suggest that many high frequency fibers will fire in response to low frequency partials. The asymmetrical shape is a consequence of the mechanical properties of the basilar membrane, which is arrayed from high (oval window) to low (helicotrema) frequency; each point captures a high frequency component and only the lower frequency components will be transmitted onward. Thus intense higher frequency partials will be captured; they cannot "reach" and cannot change the physical displacement of the lower frequency end of the basilar membrane. In contrast, high intensity, lower frequency partials will change the motion of the entire basilar membrane. This will affect the firing of all hair cells and affect the firing rate of all nerve fibers. Tuning curves for other fibers are also shown in figure 12.9.

The tuning curves do not display actual firing rate. In one possible representation, frequency is plotted against firing rate (spikes/sec). Each curve represents the outcome at a different intensity (see figure 12.10, panel a). The same picture emerges: as intensity increases, the range of frequencies to which the nerve is responsive dramatically increases. At 40 dB, the frequency range is 1750 Hz to 2300 Hz; at 80 dB, the range is 300 Hz to 2700 Hz. Obviously, any single firing rate, say 65 spikes/sec, can be brought about by many different combinations of frequency and intensity. In a second possible representation, intensity is plotted against firing rate. Each curve now represents the firing rate at a different frequency (figure 12.10, panel b). What is most important here is that the firing rate reaches its maximum at relatively low intensities; higher intensities do not increase the firing rate. The fiber shown has a characteristic frequency of 1300 Hz. For a sinusoid tone at the characteristic frequency of 1300 Hz, the firing rate begins to increase at 40 dB and then reaches its maximum at 75−80 dB. At other frequencies, the nerve fiber begins to increase its firing rate at 50 dB and reaches its maximum at 90 dB (at the 40 dB range, the pressure ratio equals 100).

It is not clear how intensity is coded in the nervous system. The simplest mechanism would be the number of nerve impulses per second. However, as shown above, the majority of nerve fibers cannot consistently increase their firing rate to track increases in physical intensity. Approximately 85% of the nerve fibers have relatively low thresholds, high spontaneous firing rates, and firing rates that go from the spontaneous rate to the maximum rate (termed the saturation level), over a pressure increase of 100 to 1 (equal to a 40 dB increase). This functional range is far less than required; the loudness range of normal hearing spans a 10 million to 1 pressure increase (equal to a 140 dB increase). Changes in firing rates of these fibers clearly cannot provide adequate information for intensity discrimination at higher levels. There are a small number of fibers (approximately 15%) with higher thresholds, a higher saturation level, and a low spontaneous firing

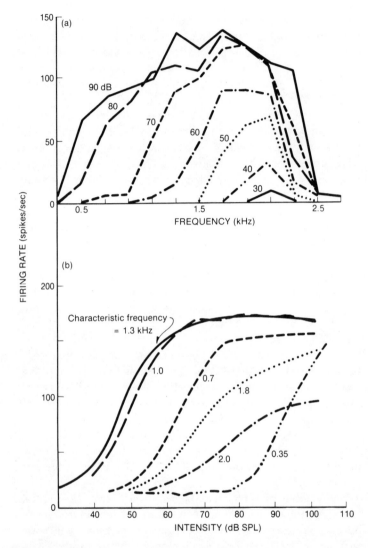

Figure 12.10
Response areas for single auditory fibers. The results in panel (a) illustrate that as the intensity of the stimulus tone is increased, the fiber fires to a wider range of frequencies. The fiber loses its "tuning" (adapted from Rose et al. 1971). The results in panel (b) illustrate that above a certain stimulus intensity, the firing rate saturates. That is, the firing rate increases to its maximum valve over a relatively small intensity range and does not increase further at higher intensities (which are still within the normal range) (adapted from Sachs and Abbas 1974).

rate that may take over at higher intensities (M. C. Liberman 1978). Intensity might be portrayed by the number of nerve fibers firing above a certain rate, or by those fibers with higher thresholds and higher saturation levels. Alternatively, intensity might be portrayed by the timing between firings (described below). Right now, there is no conclusive evidence.

Timing of impulse firings   Now consider the temporal pattern of the nerve impulses. Remember that points on the basilar membrane will oscillate at the frequency of the driving vibration. At one extreme, the nerve fiber can fire randomly throughout the basilar membrane oscillation, and at the other extreme, the nerve fiber can fire at only one point in the movement. In this latter case, we would say that the firings are *phase-locked* to one point of the sound wave. A continuous sinusoid wave with neural spikes drawn underneath is shown in figure 12.11.

One way to display the temporal firing pattern is to measure the time between each pair of successive spikes without regard to the stimulating wave. These *interresponse* intervals create *interval histograms* in which the x-axis represents the time interval between successive spikes and the y-axis represents the number of such intervals. Interval histograms determine the regularity of the firings but cannot show if the spikes occur at one point in the wave pattern. A second way to display the firing pattern is to measure the interval between a fixed point on the stimulating wave and the first following spike (this of course requires a periodic wave). Again, we cumulate the number of spikes occurring in each interval to create *period* histograms. The x-axis is the time interval (in msec) between the fixed wave point (typically, the upward zero-crossing beginning the wave) and the first spike; the y-axis is the number of spikes in each such interval. If spikes tend to occur at one point of the waveform, then the majority of spikes ought to occur at one time interval. A simple example generating both interval and period histograms is shown in figure 12.11.

An example of experimental interval histograms for a single fiber is shown in figure 12.12(a). The characteristic frequency for this fiber is 1000 Hz, and the figure includes interval histograms for sinusoid tones ranging from 412 Hz to 1600 Hz. This fiber tends to fire once per period. For a stimulus of 412 Hz (period equals 2.5 msec, indicated by dots on the time axis), the intervals between spikes are multiples of 2.5 msec. At 1000 Hz, the intervals between spikes are multiples of 1 msec, which is the period of that tone. The fact that there are several peaks demonstrates that the fiber does not fire for every cycle. The first peak represents the number of firings in which the fiber fired on successive periods (roughly 25% for a 1000 Hz stimulus). The second peak represents the number of firings in which the fiber fired, did not fire during the next cycle, and then fired

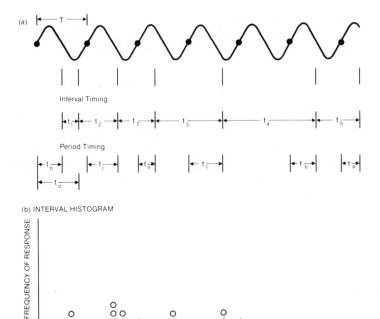

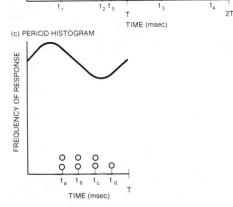

Figure 12.11
Construction of interval and period histograms. Panel (a) shows a sinusoidal vibration. The beginning of each period is marked by a large dot (the length of the period is T). The vertical lines below indicate each firing spike. The interval timings (t_1, etc.) are time intervals in milliseconds between successive spikes irrespective of the stimulus wave. The period timings (t_a, etc.) are the intervals between the onset of each period (0° phase angle) and the firing within that period. If the fiber does not fire within a cycle, the initial point is shifted to the onset of the next period. Period timings always are measured within one cycle. An interval histogram is constructed in (b). The x-axis represents time, and T is the period. The two intervals (t_3 and t_4) that are longer than T indicate that the fiber did not fire on one cycle. (A real fiber may not fire for several cycles.) A period histogram is constructed in (c). The waveform above the histogram can be used to determine at what point in the wave the fiber usually fires.

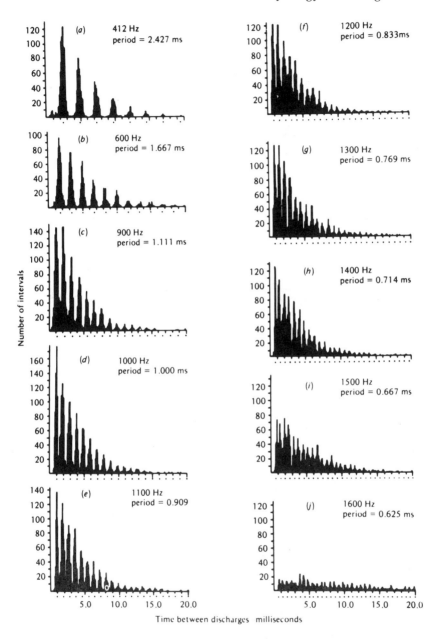

Figure 12.12(a)
Interval histograms for individual auditory nerve fibers. Interval histograms are shown in panels (a)–(j). The x-axis is time and the dots underneath indicate each period. The y-axis is the number of firings that occur in each temporal interval. The regular peaks in firing frequencies up to 1500 Hz indicate that the fiber fires at multiples of the period. The fiber fires once each cycle, although it does not necessarily fire every cycle (from Rose et al. 1967 by permission).

488   Chapter 12

(b) PERIOD HISTOGRAMS

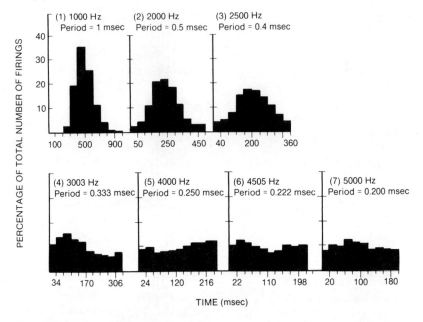

Figure 12.12(b)
Period histograms are shown in panels (1)–(7) for a different fiber with a characteristic frequency of 4000 Hz. The stimulus frequency ranged from 1000 Hz to 5000 Hz. At frequencies up to about 3000 Hz, the firings are clumped into one part of the cycle. Above 4000 Hz, the firings are evenly distributed throughout the cycle (from Rose et al. 1967 by permission).

during the following cycle (roughly 18% for 1000 Hz). All peaks can be interpreted in the same way.

Examples of period histograms of a single nerve fiber (characteristic frequency = 4000 Hz) to sinusoid waves of differing frequencies are shown in figure 12.12(b). At 1000 Hz, there is distinct phase locking, since 96% of the spikes fall in half of the cycle. At higher frequencies, the degree of phase locking diminishes and by 3000–4000 Hz, spikes occur equally often at all points of the wave.

What do period and interval histograms demonstrate?

1. Most important, there is a high degree of phase locking in auditory nerve fibers. The frequency limit to phase locking occurs at roughly 5000 Hz.
2. The probability of a fiber firing to each cycle of the test stimulus is constant. That is, regardless of whether the fiber has just fired, the probability of firing in the next cycle remains at the same value.

3. Phase locking occurs for both simple and complex periodic waves as well as for clicks and white noise, which are made up of energy across a wide frequency range. For all sounds, each fiber will fire at its characteristic frequency in response to the acoustic energy at that frequency. What this means for event perception is that the results at the auditory nerve found for simple tonal stimuli are applicable to complex stimuli composed of different mixes of partials.

4. It appears that the temporal characteristics, phase locking in particular, are more resistant to intensity saturation. The degree of phase locking increases as the pressure increases over a range of 70–80 dB (a 10,000-fold increase in pressure). The firing rate is an ambiguous cue to intensity because it increases only over a limited pressure range of 40 dB; if pressure increases further, the firing rate remains constant. Thus the degree of phase locking may be a better measure of intensity.

These represent the two major ways—average firing rate and phase-locking synchronization—for describing the firing patterns of auditory nerves. There are two other factors that affect the firing pattern—adaptation and two-tone suppression—and we will consider each in turn. After this, it is possible to understand results of research using simulated speech as the sound source.

Adaptation
Traditionally adaptation has been studied by presenting a constant tone with an instantaneous onset against a silent background and then measuring the decline in response rate (i.e., the spikes/sec) over the length of the tone. As can be seen in figure 12.13, when the tone is turned on, there is an onset firing burst, followed by a rapid initial decrease in firing rate, which transforms into a steady gradual decrease. It is best to conceptualize adaptation as a two-stage process: a very rapid adaptation lasting 2–5 msec, and a following short-term adaptation lasting up to 40–50 msec.

This distinction between rapid and short-term adaptation may help explain the neural coding of intensity. We previously pointed out that the average firing rate of nerve fibers saturated over a restricted intensity range; differences among average firing rates, therefore, cannot code the immense variation that is discriminable in intensity. This average firing rate corresponds to the short-term adaptation firing rate, and indeed the short-term rate does reach a maximum over a restricted intensity rate (see figure 12.13, panel a). However, research has demonstrated that the onset burst and rapid adaptation firing rate to the sound more accurately tracks changes in intensity (Delgutte 1980; Smith, Brachman, and Goodman 1983). In other words, the operating range—the ratio of the intensity at

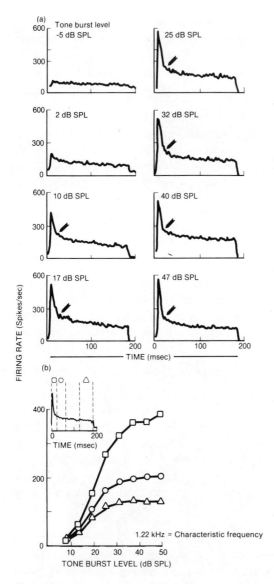

Figure 12.13
The adaptation of firing rate over the duration of a tone. In (a), the firing rate is shown at different intensity levels. At all but the lowest intensity, there is an initial firing burst followed by a rapid drop in rate, which transforms into a gradual decrease in firing rate. The transition between rapid and short-term adaptation is marked by an arrow. In (b), the firing rate at different time points in the signal is shown at different intensity levels. At the very beginning of the tone (open squares), increasing signal intensity generates an increase in firing rate. However, at later time points in the signal (open circles or triangles), increasing signal intensity generates only a small increase in firing rate (from Delgutte 1980 by permission).

which the fiber reaches its maximum firing rate to the intensity at which the fiber begins to fire—is greater for the tone onset than for the tone steady state. A comparison of the firing rate for the steady-state portion of the tone and the initial onset is shown in figure 12.13, panel (b). The steady-state portion has an operating range of 10-fold (+10dB to 30dB). However, the onset portion has an operating range of 300-fold or more (40 dB). These results demonstrate that much more of the intensity variation in the environment is coded, at least in the onset firing rate, than previously measured.

For tones with the longer onset transients (40 msec) typical of environmental events, the effects of adaptation are more complex. Since the intensity builds up relatively slowly, the amount of adaptation increases gradually over the duration of the onset and will change the maximum response to different intensities (Smith, Brachman, and Goodman 1983). This effect can be seen in figure 12.14. In the first panels (a), a simulation models the firing pattern as a function of intensity for a tone that reaches maximum intensity over a period of 50 msec. The initial response grows as a function of intensity although the steady-state response tends to be constant. The slow onset allows the initial firing response to "sneak" by the adaptation. The second panels (b) compare the response to tones with long and short onsets. For tones with short onsets (right column), the initial and steady-state response saturate at relatively low intensity levels. In contrast, for tones with longer onsets (left column), the initial response continues to grow as the intensity increases although the steady-state response remains constant.

Another important case of adaptation occurs when two tones are presented simultaneously. In one procedure, an adaptation (or background) tone is presented first, and then the test tone is added to or presented over the adapting tone after a time delay. The results are shown in figure 12.15(a). Compared to the response to the test tone when there is no background noise, shown in panel (a1), the background tone has two effects on the test-tone response: (1) it reduces the increase in firing rate when the test tone is added, and (2) it reduces the total number of responses to the test tone, as shown in panel (a2). The incremental response to the added test tone, however, was independent of the time delay between the onset of the background and the onset of the test tone. This has the effect of bringing about a neurological enhancement of the intensity transients characteristic of speech and music as follows. Remember that the background tone also is adapting over time, and its firing rate will thus decrease. The fact that the incremental response is constant means that the incremental response is independent of the adaptation level. Therefore the ratio of the incremental response (which is constant) to the background response increases over time (because the background response is de-

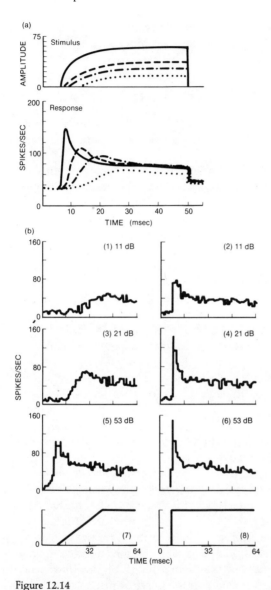

Figure 12.14
The effects of onset (attack) time on neural adaptation. In (a) a simulation is used to predict
the neural response for a tone with a relatively slow onset time. The amplitude envelope is
shown for four different maximum intensity levels in the top panel; the neural response is
shown below for each of the four amplitudes. In (b), panels (1)–(6), the response to tones
with a long and a short onset time is graphed at three intensity levels. A representation of
the long and short amplitude envelopes are shown in panels (7) and (8) respectively. The
response to the long onset tone (left column) continues to increase when going from 21 to
53 dB (pressure ratio = 40). In contrast, the response to the short onset tone (right column)
is maximum at 21 dB and does not increase at the greater intensity (from Smith, Brachman,
and Goodman 1983 by permission of New York Academy of Science).

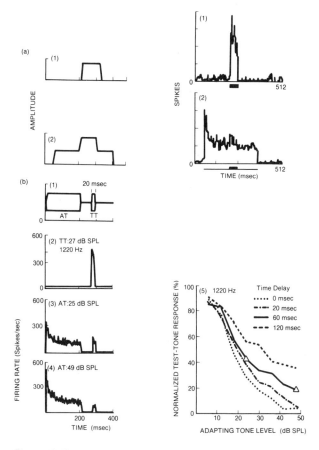

Figure 12.15
Adaptation due to simultaneously presented tones and adaptation due to preceding tones. The effect of simultaneous tones is illustrated in (a). The left column is a representation of two amplitude envelopes. The right column portrays the neural response to both stimulus conditions (from Smith, Brachman, and Goodman 1983 by permission). The stimulus is represented by lines and boxes under the graph. In (a1), the stimulus is presented over a silent background; in (a2), the stimulus is presented over a sound background. The effect of an adapting tone (AT) that precedes the test tone (TT) is shown in (b). In the left column. The fiber's response is shown to the adapting tone and the text tone at different intensities of the adapting tone. The tones are presented at the characteristic frequency of the fiber— 1200 Hz. Panel (b1) is a schematic representation of the timing of the adapting tone, the silent interval separating the adapting and test tone, and the test tone. Panel (b2) depicts the response to the test tone (TT) when the adapting tone is omitted. The firing to the test tone is the baseline; no prior adaptation occured. Panels (b3) and (b4) depict the response to the adapting tone (AT) and test tone at two different intensities of the adapting tone. Clearly, the response to the test tone decreases. At the right, the adaptation due to different intensities of the adapting tone and to different time delays between the AT offset and TT onset is graphed. The vertical axis is the firing rate following the adaptation tone divided by the firing rate at the same intensity without an adaptation tone. The two outcomes shown in (b3) and (b4) are represented by open triangles (from Delgutte 1980 by permission).

creasing). For example, it is easier to perceive vowels in background noise if the noise begins before the vowel than if the noise and vowel begin simultaneously (see Summerfield, Sidwell, and Nelson 1987). The initial noise has adapted to some degree, making the vowel more perceptible.

The final case of adaptation occurs because of an adapting sound preceding a test tone; see figure 12.15(b). The amount of adaptation increases with the duration and intensity of the adapting tone and decreases with the silent interval between the adapting tone and the test tone. Even a moderately intense adapting tone can reduce the firing rate of the test tone to zero if the two tones immediately follow each other. There is an strong asymmetry; adaptation builds up more rapidly to an adapting tone than it dissipates to a silence. It takes an adapting tone of 45 msec to reduce the firing rate by 63%, but it takes a silent interval of 90 msec to recover that 63% reduction. Adaptation and recovery from adaptation probably represent different processes. To summarize the important point here, adaptation will change the firing rate to any tone or speech sound in an ongoing context, because of the buildup and decay of adaptation resulting from prior stimulation. The change in firing rate will be a function of the precise timing relationships.

What does all this mean? On short time scales, adaptation creates a transient firing pattern yielding information about onset timing and onset intensity, while maintaining a fixed firing rate across a wide range of steady intensity levels. On longer time scales, adaptation can change the firing rate to individual tones because of the buildup of adaptation created by the intensity and timing of previous tones. It may well be that many trading effects thought to be unique to phonetic perception are due to adaptation at the auditory nerve and are therefore the same for all auditory events.

Two-Tone Suppression
Single tones produce only excitation in auditory nerve fibers. However, a second tone can inhibit or suppress the excitation of one tone. This effect is demonstrated in figure 12.16. The onset of the second tone produces a large reduction in firing (although this reduction gradually weakens because of adaptation of the suppressing tone). The time interval between the onset of the second tone and the suppression of the firing rate is nearly equal to the time interval between the onset of a tone and the beginning of excitation firings. The fact that these latencies are equivalent leads to the conclusion that suppression is due to a mechanical effect of the hair cells in the cochlea. Suppression does not seem to be due to inhibition among neurons or due to feedback from higher levels in the nervous system.

The degree of suppression is a function of the frequency and intensity relationships between the two tones. To plot this relationship, we start with a nerve fiber and map out the excitation area. Then the frequency and

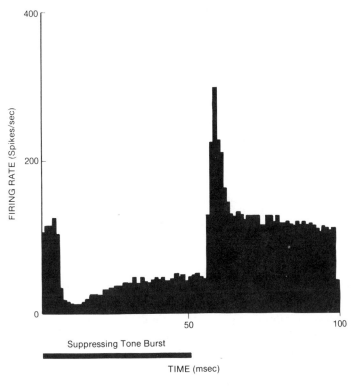

Figure 12.16
Suppression of the firing of one fiber by the onset of another tone. The suppressing tone burst is represented by the dark bar under the x-axis. When the suppressing tone begins, there is a lag before the firing rate begins to decrease. By the same token, when the suppressing tone ends, there is a lag before the firing rate begins to increase. Following this lag, there is the typical onset firing burst followed by a normal steady response (from Kiang et al. 1965 by permission of MIT Press).

intensity of one tone (the probe tone) is fixed, and the second suppressing tone is presented at various frequencies and intensities. The suppression region consists of all frequency-intensity combinations (of the second tone) that produce a 20% decrease in firing rate of the probe tone. An example is shown in figure 12.17. For tones above the characteristic frequency, the suppression region is narrow; suppression begins at relatively low intensities, but the suppression disappears at higher intensities. For tones below the characteristic frequency, the suppression region is wide; suppression begins at higher intensities and the suppression in firing rate increases at greater intensities until the fiber nearly stops responding. Unfortunately, there is one further complication. Suppression is maximum for high threshold, low spontaneous rate fibers and minimum for low threshold, high spontaneous rate fibers. The same factors that influence suppression by a single tone also influence suppression by noise made up of a broad band of frequencies: noise below the characteristic frequency produces a greater decrease in firing rate, particularly for high threshold fibers (Sachs and Young 1980).

The second effect of suppression is to reduce the degree of temporal synchronization (phase locking) of a neural fiber. This has been termed two-tone synchrony suppression. An example of this effect is shown in figure 12.18. Panel (a) and panel (b) show the response of one fiber to single tones of 768 Hz and 1152 Hz. The characteristic frequency of this fiber is 1240 Hz. In both cases, the fiber accurately tracks the tone, it fires at one point in the wave. Therefore, there are six peaks for the 768 Hz tone and nine peaks for the 1,152 Hz tone in 8 msec. If the two tones are presented together at lower intensities, the fiber is phase locked mainly to the 1152 Hz tone which is closer to its characteristic frequency: there are nine peaks. However, if the two tones are presented together at higher intensities, the fiber becomes phase-locked mainly to the lower frequency 768 Hz tone: there are six peaks. The lower frequency tone captures the fiber at the expense of the higher frequency tone. Synchrony suppression almost always is a result of a response to a lower frequency component displacing the response to a higher frequency comonent, even if the higher frequency component is at the characteristic frequency of the fiber.

At this point we have reviewed all the major results concerning the firing pattern of nerve fibers. These include: (1) frequency tuning curves; (2) firing rate saturation; (3) phase locking; (4) adaptation at onset and at steady state; and (5) two (or more) tone suppression of firing rate and synchronization. We will now investigate experiments using speech and simulated speech. The goal will be to illustrate how the principles outlined above account for firing patterns in the auditory nerve fibers to speech-like stimuli.

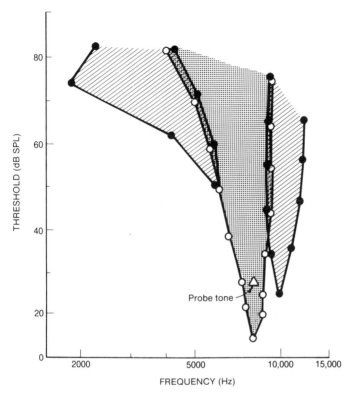

Figure 12.17
Excitation and suppression regions for a single fiber. The excitation region is dotted. All frequency-intensity combinations within the excitation region yield an increase in firing rate. To test for suppression, a test or probe lying in the middle of the excitation region is used to excite the fiber. The probe tone is presented simultaneously with other single tones that vary in frequency and intensity. The suppression region (shaded) is defined by all tones that reduce by 20% the firing rate initiated by the probe tone (adapted from Arthur, Pfeiffer, and Suga 1971).

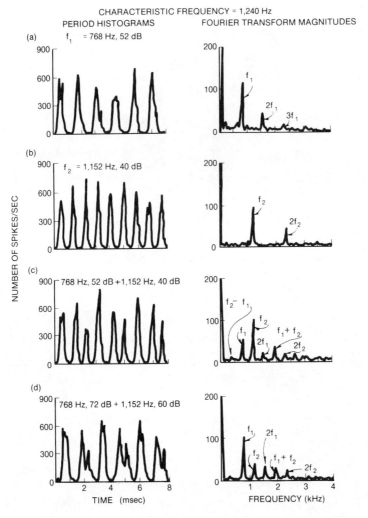

CHARACTERISTIC FREQUENCY = 1,240 Hz

Figure 12.18
Suppression of temporal synchronization (phase locking) of a nerve fiber to one tone by a second lower frequency tone. The period histograms are shown in the left column. The length of the x-axis is the period of the fundamental of 128 Hz (7.8 msec). Panels (a) and (b) show the response to individual sinusoid tones of 768 Hz and 1152 Hz. The peaks in the period histograms demonstrate that the fiber fires once per cycle for each harmonic. The Fourier magnitudes demonstrate that the synchronization is primarily at the frequency of the harmonic. Panel (c) shows the response when the two tones are combined at a low intensity. Here the strongest response is to the 1152 Hz tone, which is closest to the characteristic frequency of the fiber; there are nine peaks in the histogram and the largest Fourier component is 1152 Hz (f_2). Panel (d) shows the response when the two tones are combined at a higher intensity. In this case, the strongest response shifts to the lower frequency 768 Hz tone: there are six peaks in the histogram and the largest Fourier component is 768 Hz (f_1) (adapted from Sachs and Young 1980).

12.3 Speech and Speech-Like Stimuli

To study the nerve fiber response, a simulated vowel or consonant-vowel syllable is presented repetitively, and the firing of individual fibers is recorded. The stimulus is presented at several intensity levels ranging from threshold (about 50–60 dB) to normal levels (80–100 dB). Cats are usually used as the experimental animals.

Vowels
Vowels are created by periodic voicing (source) imposed on a vocal tract configuration (filter), which typically generates a sound composed of two or three energy peaks (formants) in the spectrum. Although experiments on using "vowel-less" vowels (see chapter 5) suggest that steady-state formant frequencies are not required for vowel identification, the neural representation of the formant frequencies is still an important issue.

Firing rate   The simplest model suggests that the formant frequencies are coded by high firing rates of fibers with characteristic frequencies that match the formant frequencies. The greater physical amplitudes at formant frequencies would excite those fibers to a greater degree. Experimentally, the first step is to determine the characteristic frequency of each fiber, using pure tones. The firing rate of that fiber for the synthesized vowel is then found. The characteristic frequency of the fiber is plotted on the horizontal axis and the firing rate of the fiber is plotted along the vertical axis. (In the figures presented, the vertical axis is the ratio between the increase in firing rate to the vowel divided by the maximum increase for pure tones at the characteristic frequency.) The results for vowels /ɛ/ (as in bet), /a/, and /ɪ/ are shown in figure 12.19. For each vowel, the formant frequencies are represented by vertical arrows.

The firing rates for /ɛ/ are shown in (a) at three intensity levels. The solid line is the average firing rate for high firing rate fibers at each fiber's characteristic frequency (roughly 85% of the population). The dashed line is the average firing rate for the low firing rate fibers at each fiber's characteristic frequency (roughly 15% of the population).

At the lower intensity level, the distribution of the firing rates closely matches the energy levels of the vowel; the firing rate of fibers whose characteristic frequency matches the formant frequencies is maximum. However, at higher intensities the firing rate of all fibers with characteristic frequencies between 500 Hz and 3000 Hz become roughly equal, so that the firing rate maxima corresponding to the formant frequencies largely disappear. The representation from the low firing rate fibers still resembles the amplitude spectra to some degree, but it is likely that at still higher intensities (which are still within the normal range) the firing rates of different low firing rate fibers would also become equal, eliminating the

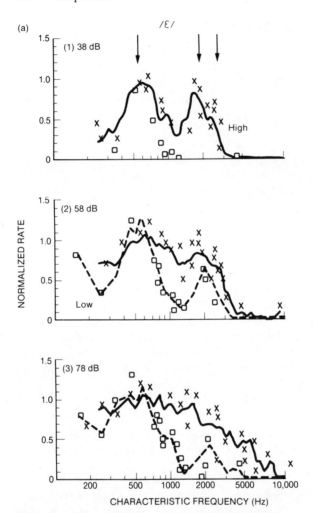

Figure 12.19
Firing rates to vowel-like stimuli. Panel (a) shows the results for the vowel /ε/. In the three graphs, the firing rate is shown at three different intensities. The vertical arrows represent the formant frequencies. The solid line (x's) represents the average response for high spontaneously firing rate fibers at each frequency, while the dashed lines (open squares) represent the average response for low spontaneously firing rate fibers at each frequency. Not all fibers are drawn; those drawn illustrate the response curves. Panel (b) shows the firing rate response to the vowels /a/ and /ɪ/. The vertical arrows represent the formant frequencies. For each vowel the average firing rate is shown at three intensities (the 20 dB difference represents a pressure ratio of 10) (adapted from Sachs, Young, and Miller 1982).

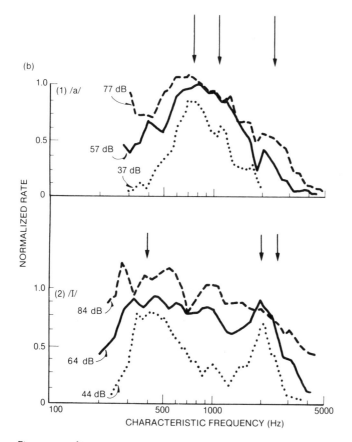

(b)

(1) /a/

77 dB

57 dB

37 dB

(2) /I/

84 dB

64 dB

44 dB

NORMALIZED RATE

CHARACTERISTIC FREQUENCY (Hz)

Figure 12.19(b)

formant peaks. Similar results are shown for the vowels /ɪ/ and /a/ in figure 12.19(b). For both vowels, at low intensities, the pattern of firing across frequency closely mimics the formant amplitudes, but at higher intensities the pattern of firing across frequency flattens out so that peaks in firing rate corresponding to formants disappear.

Why does this happen? The most obvious explanation is firing rate saturation. For roughly 85% of the fibers, the change in firing rate from threshold to the maximum rate occurs over only a 20 to 30 dB range. Thus fibers at or near formant frequencies, which fire at nearly maximum rates at the low intensities, cannot increase their firing rate as intensity increases. In contrast, fibers between formants or far from the formant frequencies are firing well below their maximum rates at low intensities. As intensity increases, firing rate of these fibers can increase (as shown by the tails of the tuning curves) and thereby equalize the firing rates across nerve fibers with different characteristic frequencies.

A second factor that affects the firing pattern is two-tone suppression. If a more intense tone below a fiber's characteristic frequency and a weaker tone at the characteristic frequency are presented simultaneously, the more intense tone can interfere with the firing of that fiber at the characteristic frequency. For vowels, the higher energy first formant can act to suppress the firing of nerve fibers tuned to the weaker second and third formants. Thus two-tone suppression does not lead to the sharpening of the energy spectrum; it leads to quite the opposite—a loss of upper formant peaks. Two-tone suppression does keep the neural representation compact, disallowing very high characteristic frequency fibers from firing at high rates as might be expected from the lower frequency tails of the tuning curves of those fibers.

Phase-lock timing   An alternative model suggests that formant frequencies are coded by timing, specifically by the interval between firing spikes. Research using pure tones has indicated that the firing is synchronous or phase-locked: the firing occurs at the same point (or phase) of each repetition of the stimulus pattern. With a complex stimulus wave, a single fiber might fire to only one partial or to combinations of several partials in the complex. A Fourier analysis can reveal to which partials the fiber synchronizes.

To simplify these ideas, consider the simple sawtooth wave pattern. A sawtooth wave consists of all harmonics (section 2.1), and the amplitude of each harmonic is inversely proportional to its number. Each nerve fiber may, therefore, phase-lock to one or more partials of the sawtooth wave, and the interval between spikes indicates to which partials the fiber is phase-locked. We will assume that all phase-locked firings occur at the positive peak of the wave (a 90° phase) and for simplicity we will assume that the fiber usually fires at every cycle. Furthermore, we will assume that the fundamental frequency is 100 Hz so that the period is 10 msec. In figure 12.20, the sawtooth wave is drawn at the top (a). Below that, hypothetical spike patterns are shown. The first fiber (b) is phase-locked to the fundamental; the period histogram has one peak centered around 2.5 msec and the Fourier transform would show a maximum response at the fundamental. The second fiber (c) is phase-locked to the third harmonic; the period histogram has three peaks centered around 0.83 msec, 4.25 msec, and 7.5 msec and the Fourier transform would show a maximum response at the third harmonic. The third fiber (d) fires at every positive peak of the second harmonic (1.25 and 6.25 msec) and 50% of the positive peaks of the fifth harmonic (0.5, 2.5, 4.5, 6.5, and 8.5 msec). The period histogram has small narrow peaks centered at 0.5, 2.5, 4.5 msec and 8.5 msec due to the fifth harmonic, a high wide peak centered at 6 msec due to both harmonics and a high narrow peak at 1.25 msec due to the second harmonic. The Fourier transform would show a large response at the second harmonic and a smaller response at the fifth harmonic. The fourth fiber (e) fires at random; it is not phase-locked to any harmonic. The period histogram is essentially flat, and the probability of firing at any time point is constant. The Fourier transform would show an equal response at all frequencies (the Fourier transform reflects the fact that all frequencies are equally probable).

The firing patterns of three fibers to one stimulus waveform are shown in figure 12.21 (Sachs and Young 1980). Each histogram covers one period of the stimulus (i.e., the time in msec along the x-axis equals the period). The fundamental frequency was 128 Hz, and the formant frequencies were 512 Hz, 1152 Hz, and 2432 Hz. A rough idea of the firing of each fiber can be obtained by counting and examining the peaks in each histogram. The number of peaks indicates the harmonic to which the fiber is synchronized. The first fiber is synchronized to the third harmonic and the second fiber is synchronized to the sixth harmonic. The shape of the peaks indicates the variation in the firing synchronization. If each peak is a perfect vertical line occurring at one time point, then the fiber is phase-locked to one point on only one harmonic. If the peaks are wider and more irregular in shape and height, then the fiber is phase-locked to several harmonics. On this basis, the second fiber (characteristic frequency = 770 Hz) has the most regular firing pattern because the peaks are narrow and uniform. Although the third fiber has the same number of peaks as the second fiber, the peaks are more irregular than those of the second fiber, which suggests the firing pattern is more irregular. The Fourier transform of the period histogram measures the strength of response to each harmonic. The Fourier amplitudes are then transformed into a synchronization index; for every fiber, there is one value of the index for each harmonic of the stimulus. The synchronization index reflects both the firing rate and the degree of phase

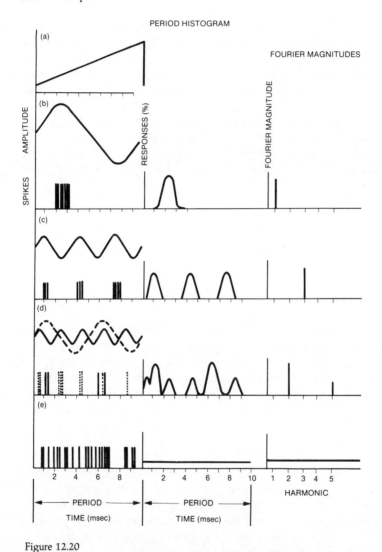

Figure 12.20
Phase locking to harmonics of a sawtooth wave. The sawtooth wave is shown in (a). The
fundamental is shown in (b). Below that, a simulated fiber that phase-locks to the fundamental is illustrated. The firing spikes, period histogram, and Fourier components are shown.
The third harmonic is shown in (c), with a simultated fiber that phase-locks to the third
harmonic below. The firing spikes, period histogram, and Fourier components are shown.
The three "humps" of the period histogram display the outcome; all spikes occur in
synchrony with one segment of each period of the harmonic. The second and fifth harmonic
is shown in (d), with a simulated fiber that phase-locks to both harmonics below. The spikes
to the second harmonic are illustrated by solid vertical lines; the spikes to the fifth harmonic
are illustrated by dashed vertical lines. The resulting period histogram and Fourier components are shown to the right. A random firing pattern is shown in (e). The flat period
histogram and flat Fourier components are shown to the right.

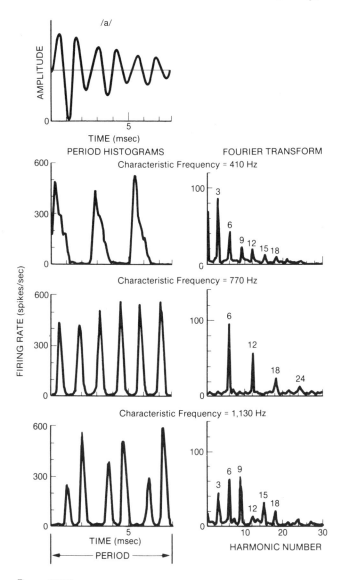

Figure 12.21
Phase locking of three fibers to a simulated /a/. The top panel portrays the pressure wave across one period. Below, the period histograms and Fourier transforms are shown for three fibers. For the two fibers with characteristic frequencies of 410 Hz and 770 Hz, the phase locking is maximum to the harmonic closest to the characteristic frequency. For the third fiber with a characterstic frequency of 1130 Hz, phase locking occurs to nearly all multiples of the third harmonic with maximums at the sixth and ninth harmonic (adapted from Sachs and Young 1980).

locking. For example, the Fourier transform for the second fiber shows maximum synchronization to the sixth and twelfth harmonics and very low synchronization to any other harmonic.

The results from the vowel /ɛ/ with formants at harmonics 4, 14, and 19 are shown in figure 12.22 (Young and Sachs 1979). Each graph shows the value of the synchronization index to one harmonic (y-axis) for fibers with different characteristic frequencies. These graphs illustrate several points:

1. At low intensity levels, the maximum response of each fiber was to harmonic components near that fiber's characteristic frequency. This can be seen in the first row (a): fibers with characteristic frequencies ranging from 400 Hz to 900 Hz synchronized to the fourth harmonic at 512 Hz, fibers with characteristic frequencies ranging from 1200 Hz to 1400 Hz synchronized to the tenth harmonic at 1280 Hz, and fibers with characteristic frequencies ranging from 1700 Hz to 1900 Hz synchronized to the fourteenth harmonic at 1792 Hz.

2. At moderate intensity levels, the majority of fibers fire in synchrony to the high amplitude harmonics. Turning to the second row (b) in figure 12.22, there is an increase in synchrony to the intense fourth and fourteenth formant harmonics and a decrease in synchrony to the weak tenth harmonic, which is not a formant. The high intensity lower frequency harmonics associated with the first formant captured auditory fibers with higher characteristic frequencies because of two-tone synchrony suppression; those nerve fibers now synchronize to the lower frequency harmonics. Remember that the nerve fibers are firing more rapidly, as shown in figure 12.19. But because the firing now is synchronized to the frequency of the harmonics of the first formant, it does not interfere with the identification of the vowel.

3. At the highest intensities, response synchrony to the higher formants may give way to response synchrony to the more intense lowest formant (c); a fiber that synchronized to the high frequency second formant at moderate intensities may come to synchronize to the more intense first formant. Again, this seems to be due to two-tone synchrony suppression. This effect is clearly shown in the bottom left of the figure. Many fibers with characteristic frequencies above 2000 Hz synchronize to the 512 Hz fourth harmonic. The synchronization of these fibers to the 1792 Hz second formant decreases as indicated by the smaller synchronization index in the bottom right graph.

We can make the following generalizations. Overall, if the characteristic frequency of a fiber matches a high energy formant, the major response occurs at the formant frequency (more precisely, at the harmonic closest to

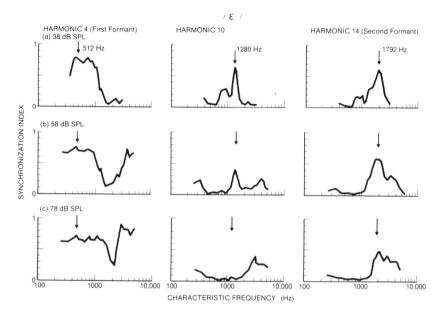

Figure 12.22
The average degree of phase locking to three harmonics at different intensities. Each panel represents the average synchronization to one harmonic by high and low threshold fibers with the same characteristic frequency. A high synchronization index indicates that fibers with that characteristic frequency are tightly phase-locked to the harmonic. Each panel comes from the same fibers, which means that each fiber is represented nine times. Thus the first column represents the amount of synchronization to the fourth harmonic and the second and third columns represent the amount of synchronization to the tenth and fourteenth harmonic for all fibers. The frequency of the harmonic is denoted by the vertical arrow. Each row represents the phase locking at a different intensity level. Consider the bottom row (78 dB). The graphs illustrate that fibers with characteristic frequencies between 100 Hz and 1000 Hz and with characteristic frequencies above 2000 Hz synchronize to the fourth harmonic (*left column*); fibers with characteristic frequencies between 1000 Hz and approximately 2000 Hz synchronize to the fourteenth harmonic (*right column*). Overall, as the intensity increases, there is an increase in synchronization to the fourth harmonic even for fibers with high characteristic frequencies. This is due to synchrony suppression (adapted from Young and Sachs 1979).

the formant). However, at greater intensities, because of two-tone suppression, fibers with high characteristic frequencies will begin to synchronize at the frequency of the first or second formant. In addition, fibers with both low and high characteristic frequencies may synchronize at the voicing fundamental frequency (again because of two-tone suppression). It is this synchronization to the voicing frequency that yields the perception of voice pitch.

Sachs, Young, and co-workers argue that the synchronized timings of the neural firings are more useful for speech perception because they do not degrade as intensity increases. In figure 12.23, an averaged synchronization rate for three vowels are shown across a 60 dB range (Young and Sachs 1979). The average synchronization rate is the strength of the synchronized response of each fiber at a small set of frequencies surrounding the characteristic frequency. The pattern is relatively constant; a neural code based in some way on the synchronized firings would be able to specify the vowel across a wide range of intensities. Two-tone synchrony suppression maintains the formant peaks because fibers with high characteristic frequencies begin to synchronize to low frequency formants.

To summarize, the neural coding of vowels is primarily accomplished by increased firing rates of fibers whose characteristic frequencies match one of the formant intensity peaks and by the phase-locking of fibers to the harmonics of the vowel's formants. It appears on the basis of rather limited studies that neural mechanisms involving the timing between spikes are more useful than average firing rate in providing a robust neural code for vowel discrimination. The average rate profiles rapidly flatten out at the maximum firing rates at even moderate intensities and therefore cannot unambiguously specify different vowels. There is experimental evidence that the onset response does not asymptote at such low intensities, but the usefulness of these firings is unclear. Similarly, the role of low spontaneously firing fibers is unclear. It is possible that vowel perception depends on the high firing rate fibers at low intensities and on the low firing rate fibers at high intensities.

There is strong evidence that the synchronization of individual fibers remains consistent across large changes in intensity. Two questions remain about phase-lock coding. First, is the relevant component of the phase locking the amount of synchronization at the characteristic frequency of the fiber? If the characteristic frequency of the fiber is 750 Hz, then the relevant neural coding is assumed to be the synchronized component to stimulus energy at 750 Hz; the synchronized response at other harmonic frequencies, for example, is presumed not to affect the percept. Second, is there synchronized responding at higher levels in the auditory pathways and, if so, are there neural mechanisms that can "decode" or respond to the constant interval between spikes? Up to the present, the evidence is

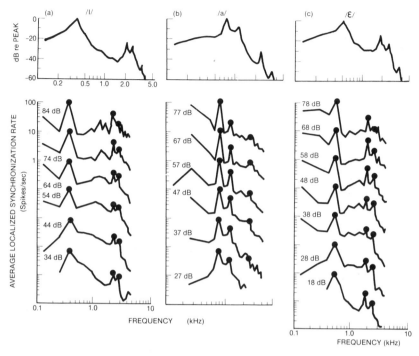

Figure 12.23
The localized frequency synchronization to three different vowels. The top row is the amplitude near the eardrum for each of the three vowels. The fundamental voicing frequency for all vowels is 128 Hz. Below that, the average synchronization of fibers with different characteristic frequencies is plotted at varying intensities. The curves are offset vertically to avoid confusion. The formant frequencies are shown as filled circles (adapted from Young and Sachs 1979).

that synchronization breaks down at higher levels, and there have been no findings of neurons that respond to specific timing intervals (Palmer, Winter, and Darwin 1986).

Consonants
Stop consonant syllables may be characterized by the rapid amplitude and frequency variation during the formant transitions as well as the steady vowel formants. Considering an entire stop consonant–vowel syllable, the formant transition may last 20 msec to 60 msec and then resolve into the steady component, which may last 50 msec to 200 msec. The formant transition is softer than the steady "vowel section." A schematic representation of the syllables [ba], [da], and [ga] appears in figure 12.24. The first 50 msec is the formant transition; the final 50 msec is the vowel segment. All syllables had a fundamental frequency of 125 Hz. As shown for vowels, the response of individual fibers can be measured either in terms of average firing rate or in terms of synchronization to a harmonic component (the synchronization index does in fact incorporate the firing rate).

Firing rate   Overall, average firing rates can provide information about the change in formant frequency and thus can provide information about the identity of syllables. Basically, a fiber fires at its maximum rate at time points when the formant frequency is near its characteristic frequency. Thus the fiber "tracks" the formant frequencies. This is shown for four fibers in figure 12.25. For fibers with low characteristic frequencies, the firing patterns were nearly identical for all syllables, because the first formants were identical. However, for fibers with high characteristic frequencies, the firing rates increased when the formant frequencies become more similar to the characteristic frequency. For example, in panel (c) and panel (d), the difference in the firing rate pattern between [ba] as opposed to [da] and [ga] at the syllable onset reflects the stronger F_2 and F_3 formants in this frequency region for [da] and [ga] (refer to figure 12.24).

Phase-lock timing   Now we turn to results in terms of synchronized firing rates. The results are unambiguous that fibers synchronize to energy peaks for each syllable and accurately track frequency changes through the transitions. This can be seen in figure 12.26. Panel (a) portrays the synchronization to the syllable [ba]. The characteristic frequency of the fiber was 880 Hz, so initially there was some synchronization to the second formant at 875 Hz. Over the duration of the transition, the second formant increased to 1500 Hz while the first formant increased to 800 Hz. The synchronized response switched to the first formant as it moved into characteristic frequency area of the fiber. Panel (b) portrays the synchronization to the syllable [da] for a fiber whose characteristic frequency

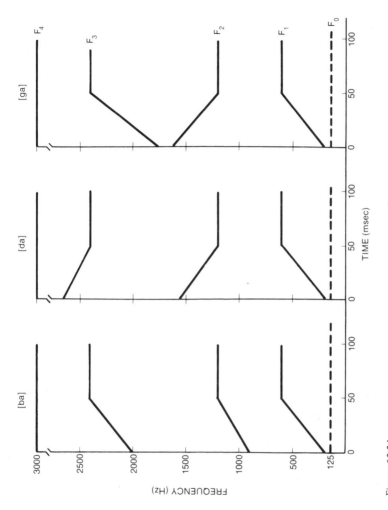

Figure 12.24
The formant transitions and steady state formant frequencies for three simulated consonant-vowel syllables (based on data in Sinex and Geisler 1983). F_0 is the fundamental voicing frequency, and F_1, F_2, F_3, and F_4 are the first four formants.

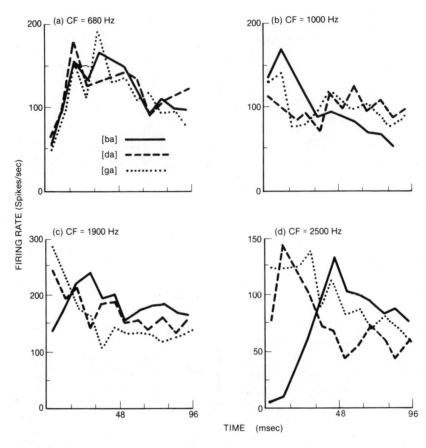

Figure 12.25
The firing rates of four different fibers to three simulated syllables. For each fiber, the average rate is shown at time points throughout the formant transition and steady state. Each fiber increases its firing rate at the times the formant frequencies are near the fiber's characteristic frequency. Conversely, each fiber decreases its firing rate when the formant frequencies diverge from its characteristic frequency (adapted from Sinex and Geisler 1983).

equals 1900 Hz. This fiber tracked the change in frequency of the second formant and synchronized at the harmonic frequency of the formant. The synchronization occurs at the *instantaneous* frequency of the formant.

The synchronization of seven fibers with different characteristic frequencies (originating from different regions of the cochlea) to formant frequencies of the three syllables is shown in a different way at the bottom of Figure 12.26. At the syllable onset, the fibers synchronize to the starting formant frequencies, with the exception of fibers with characteristic frequencies falling between the frequencies of the first and second formants at syllable onset. The fibers that fell between the first two formants tended

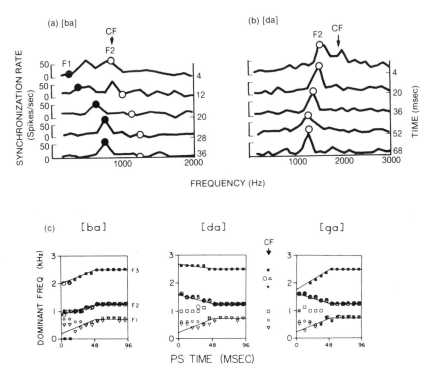

Figure 12.26
Phase locking to consonant-vowel syllables. In panels (a) and (b), the first two formant frequencies are represented at five time points by the filled (F1) and unfilled (F2) circles. The formant frequencies change throughout the transition. The results in both panels demonstrate that the fiber synchronizes to the formant frequency near its characteristic frequency at each time point. There is a synchronized firing peak at the formant frequency. In panel (c), the formant transition and steady-state frequencies are shown for three syllables, identical to those drawn in figure 12.24. The dominant synchronization frequency is shown for seven fibers whose characteristic frequency is portrayed between the graphs for [da] and [ga]. Each of the seven fibers begins to phase-lock to one of the formant frequencies and changes its synchronized response to match the formant frequencies (from Sinex and Geisler 1983 by permission).

initially to synchronize to harmonics near their characteristic frequency. However, within 30 msec all fibers became dominated by a frequency component near one of the first two formants and then synchronized to the nearest harmonic at that instant and for the remainder of the syllable.

All in all, these results are very convincing that synchronized phase-locked neural firings can accurately convey auditory information relevant to speech (and music) perception. However, phase locking is limited by the refractory period of the neural discharge to frequencies of less than 3000–4000 Hz in auditory nerves. Moreover, at higher neural centers, the frequency limit to phase locking is much lower. How then are fricatives, which may have energy between 5000 and 10,000 Hz, coded? Phase locking is clearly impossible for these sounds.

Fricatives
Most of the energy in fricatives is located in frequency bands; discrimination between fricatives could thus be based on the frequencies of these bands. We would imagine that fibers with characteristic frequencies matching the frequencies of high energy bands would respond with the highest firing rates so that each fricative would excite a different set of fibers.

The average discharge rate does appear to be a relatively accurate indicant of fricative identity. As found for vowels, the average rate becomes somewhat ambiguous at higher intensities because of saturation (although since fricatives are softer than vowels, fewer fibers reach saturation and the problem is somewhat less). However, the onset response is more immune to rate saturation. The rate profiles across fibers with different characteristic frequencies at a representative intensity are shown in figure 12.27. As can be seen, the maximum response tends to occur at frequency regions of maximum energy. There are clear differences among the fricatives in the response profile, and theoretically the fricatives could be distinguished on this basis. The production of fricatives does not produce low frequency harmonics corresponding to the voicing fundamental frequency, and therefore two-tone suppression does not distort the firing rates.

Adaptation and Context Dependency
Adaptation may explain aspects of the context dependency (e.g., trading relationships) of speech and by implication may explain aspects of the context dependency of music and environmental events. Two aspects of short-term adaptation are relevant: (1) the effect of prior context on the response to the current stimulus; and (2) the effect of stimulus onset duration on the initial neural response.

Let us start with the effect of prior context on the neutral response to a current stimulus. As described in section 12.2, a prior adaptation tone can

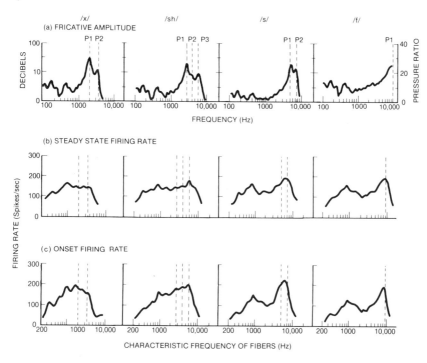

Figure 12.27

Firing rate profiles to different fricatives. The top row presents the amplitude at different frequencies for four fricatives (/x/ as in the German Ba*ch*). The amplitude peaks are represented by dashed vertical lines. The second row presents the average steady-state firing rate for fibers with different characteristic frequencies. The firing rate pattern tends to resemble the amplitude pattern of each fricative in the sense that fibers with characteristic frequencies that match amplitude peaks fire most rapidly. The third row presents the average onset firing rate for fibers with different characteristic frequencies. The onset firing rate pattern closely mimics the amplitude pattern of each fricative (adapted from Delgutte and Kiang 1984). Note that the frequency scale differs from (*a*) to (*b*) and (*c*).

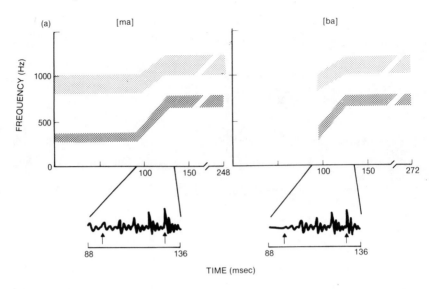

Figure 12.28
Adaptation in simulated speech stimuli. The formants for [ma] and [ba] are shown in (a). The pressure variation for the formant transition for [ma] and [ba] are shown below. The transition occurs between the arrows, both transitions are quite similar. A comparison of the firing rates between [ma] and [ba] for five fibers is shown in (b). A comparison of the firing pattern for each fiber makes it obvious that the initial formants drastically changed the firing pattern to the formant transition for fibers with low characteristic frequencies (from Delgutte 1980 by permission).

reduce the firing rate to the following tone by 50% or more. This effect can be significant for speech. For example, consider a simulated [ba] consisting of two formants, as illustrated in figure 12.28(a). This syllable consists of a formant transition ending on formants appropriate for /a/. If the simulated [ba] is preceded by steady formants at the initial frequencies of the transition, the percept is the nasal [ma]. The low frequency components change the percept, even though the [ba] segment is identical. In this example, the low frequency [ma] formants are thought of as the adapting tone and the [ba] transition plus steady state is thought of as the test tone.

The firing patterns for [ma] and [ba] are shown in figure 12.28(b). The low frequency nasal components adapt fibers with low characteristic frequencies so that the response pattern to the equivalent parts of the syllables is not equal. This adaptation eliminates the firing peaks associated with the formant transitions for fibers with characteristic frequencies of 350 Hz, 600 Hz, and 2000 Hz that fall within the [ba] transition. (Note that the response to the /a/ is hardly changed.) The response is identical only for fibers whose characteristic frequency fall far above the formant frequencies. In all instances, the effect of preceding context is to change the firing rate;

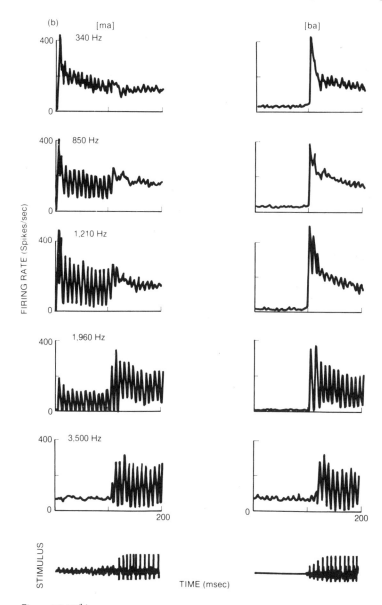

Figure 12.28(b)

the context does not affect the synchronization of the fibers (Delgutte 1980).

Adaptation clearly changes the neural response to speech-like stimuli over the time span of a typical syllable. Because adaptation depresses the response to particular frequency components, the overall effect must be to increase the contrast between successive parts of the utterance separated by an abrupt change in frequency spectrum.

Now we will turn to the effect of adaptation on the neural response to stimulus onset. There are two aspects of adaptation which affect the neural firing to the stimulus onset. The first factor is the onset duration. A short onset generates an immediate large firing burst (see figure 12.14). The second factor is the silent duration between the previous tone and the stimulus onset. A short silent duration reduces the initial rapid firing burst more than a long silent duration does (see figure 12.15). The type of onset firing burst can be used to classify speech sounds. For example, fricatives (like /sh/) are characterized by a weak burst (flat) response. There is a gradual stimulus onset that is not generally preceded by a silent interval. In contrast, affricatives (like /ch/ as in chaw) are characterized by a strong initial firing burst. There is a rapid stimulus onset that is generally preceded by silence. The strength of the initial burst is affected by the duration of the silent interval as well as by the onset duration, so it appears likely that silent duration and onset duration could be "traded" as described in chapter 9. Decreasing the silent interval or increasing the onset duration leads to a weak burst denoting the fricative; increasing the silent interval or decreasing the onset duration leads to a large burst denoting the affricative.

Simulations using a model of a nerve fiber based on results from adaptation experiments are shown in figure 12.29. The stimuli ranged from [asha] to [acha]. The initial voiced part of the stimulus was the vowel /a/. The simulated /sh/ or /ch/ followed after a silent interval. Prototypical fricatives occur in the upper left—0 msec silence duration and 80 msec rise time—and yield a flat firing rate response at the onset of the fricative. Prototypical affricatives occur on the lower right—100 msec silence durations and instantaneous rise time—and yield a sharp firing rate peak at onset. The peak sharpens as the silence duration increases (to the right) or as the rise time decreases (downward) illustrating the trading relationship between a temporal cue (silence duration) and a spectral cue (rise time).

There are many kinds of context effects in speech, and clearly short-term adaptation cannot account for them all. However, short-term adaptation and two-tone suppression both tell us that the understanding of pereptual mechanisms must rest on an appropriate stimulus analysis. The unit of analysis cannot be the spectrum at an instant; it is not the auditory equivalent of a snapshot. Instead, the unit of analysis is a time fragment considered across the evolving spectrum; the overlapping temporal effects of

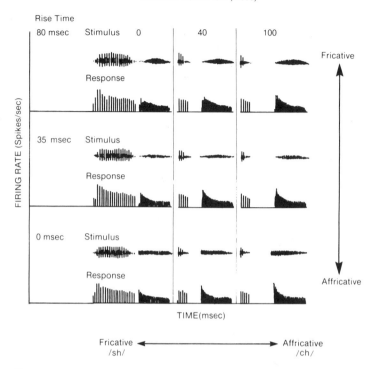

SILENCE DURATION (msec)

Figure 12.29

A trading relationship for onset firing burst based on two aspects of adaptation: rise time can be traded for silence duration. The initial part of each stimulus consisted of the voiced vowel /a/. Following the offset of the vowel, there was a variable silent duration followed by the consonant stimulus. The silent durations, created by delaying the onset of the consonant, equaled 0, 40, or 100 msec and are represented by the three columns. The rise times of the consonant equaled 80, 35, or 0 msec and are represented by the three rows. For the slow 80 msec rise time, the consonant stimulus reaches its maximum roughly in the stimulus middle. For the fast 0 msec rise time, the consonant stimulus reaches its maximum at the onset. The response pattern of importance is the onset of the second component. In the upper left, the 80 msec rise time–0 silence duration yields a relatively equal, flat response rate, which is perceived as a fricative. There is no initial firing burst. In contrast, in the lower right, the 0 msec rise time–100 silence duration yields a large firing burst at onset, which is perceived as an affricative. The peakiness of the firing pattern is a trading relation between the silence duration and rise time (adapted from Delgutte 1982).

adaptation and the overlapping spectrum effects of neural suppression requires a reconceptualization of the stimulus.

Summary of Speech and Speech-Like Stimuli
A first impression of these results is that the firing patterns of nerve fibers to speech stimuli follow the same principles found for simple tone stimuli. The relation between firing rate and intensity, firing rate saturation over rather small intensity ranges, two-tone rate and synchrony suppression, and adaptation all follow the same principles across stimuli of different complexity. The complex profile of firing rate across the frequency range of the nerve fibers seems to be due merely to the many interacting components, rather than to any new principles specific to speech-like stimuli. I am led to the conclusion that the encoding of acoustic energy is identical for speech, music, and environmental events.

A second impression is the diversity, partial overlapping, and even inconsistency of the hypothesized processing schemes. Speech perception could be based on:

1. The firing rates of fibers with different characteristic frequencies. The pattern of firing rate across fibers with different characteristic frequencies seems able to portray all speech sounds at low intensities around threshold and to portray differences among fricatives at greater intensities. Low spontaneously firing fibers may underlie perception at higher intensities. The perceptually relevant fibers would change as a function of intensity (see Delgutte 1987).

2. The firing of fibers with different characteristic frequencies during the onset of sounds. The logic here is identical to that above; the restriction to onset is an admission that saturation and adaptation act to restrict firing rate at higher intensities and thus equalize the firing rate across fibers with different characteristic frequencies. The pattern of onset firing clearly sharpens differences among fricatives and may be able to extend the intensity range for the unambiguous perception of vowels and stop consonants. Dynamic cues generating the firing peaks may provide unique auditory information.

3. The profile of neural firing across all fibers. In this scheme, all that is required is that each individual speech phoneme or syllable yields a distinct profile of firing rates across fibers with different characteristic frequencies. Experimental results suggest that profiles indeed are different. However, unless the profiles are invariant (or similar looking) for different intensities, this would seem to create an insurmountable recognition problem, because profiles at each intensity would be unique and would need to be encoded individually.

4. The degree of synchronization (phase-locking) to frequency components at each fiber's characteristic frequency. This has been termed a temporal-place model, because the relevant neural code is the regu-

larity of firing (temporal) at the characteristic frequency (defined by place). Responses of fibers with similar characteristic frequencies are usually averaged together to yield a localized synchronized response. A synchronization model has been used successfully to represent the properties of vowels and stop consonants, although it cannot represent fricatives because of the very high frequency energy, which precludes phase locking.

I come away from this work with an uneasy feeling. It seems to me that there are three possible conclusions. The first is simply that there are different mechanisms used to encode the various speech sounds. Encoding by synchronization, by average rate, or by both would occur for all sounds, and be attributed to neural constraints. However, on logical grounds, this conclusion seems inelegant and uneconomical. The second is that the neural firing pattern over time represents all of the information—the onset and average firing rate, the synchronization at characteristic frequencies, and the rate profile across fibers. There really is no need to postulate priority based on indices at the nerve fiber. The firing pattern will be transformed as it progresses toward the auditory contex, and the "true" neural code may be quite different than any found at the auditory nerve. The third is that our conceptualization of speech is incorrect. A set of notions built on formants and energy bands may simply be an incorrect way to portray the physical signal. By the same reasoning, a physiological model based on the firing rates of individual fibers (even if considered as part of a profile) may be incorrect. The initial paragraphs of this chapter warned against reification, against making the outcomes of one type of measurement become reality. My sympathies at this point are with the third conclusion. I think the ambiguities described here are due to an incorrect conceptualization of the relevant physical realization in the stimulus. Given this, it is nearly impossible to discover the relevant neural variation. Basically, we do not yet have a theory of auditory perceiving.

12.4 Auditory Pathways

There are a large number of relay stations in the auditory pathway where firing patterns could be transformed to reflect certain characteristics of the stimulus event. It seems to me there are several overarching principles:

1. Beginning at the cochlear nucleus, there are different combinations of excitatory and inhibitory connections to produce cells that fire to particular aspects of the stimulus (e.g., stimulus onset). Each cell at a lower level connects to several cells at a higher level, which means that there is an increase in the number of fibers toward the cortex.

2. Cells tend to respond to the dynamic parts of the stimulus (e.g., onset, offset, amplitude, and frequency modulation), and the percen-

tage of cells that respond only to stimulus changes increases going up the central pathways.

3. However, there seems to be a straight excitation class of cells that may be necessary for accurate localization.

4. Each type of cell seems to be located in a particular region of each nucleus, a spatial organization by function. Yet in the cortex, the regions are interleaved so that functional organization is minimized.

5. Within each region, normally there is tonotopic organization. There is at least one direction on the surface in which the best (characteristic) frequencies of the cells increase or decrease in regular order.

Cochlear Nucleus

Ipsilateral fibers coming from the auditory nerve first terminate in the cochlear nucleus, and the interconnections yield a variety of cell types. All auditory nerve fibers are qualitatively similar, though they differ with respect to characteristic frequency, spontaneous firing rate, and threshold. In contrast, cells in the cochlear nucleus have qualitatively different firing patterns. Moreover, the firing rate of one cell may be reduced below the spontaneous rate by presentation of a different tone with a frequency slightly different from the characteristic frequency. All of these outcomes are thought to be due to neural inhibition. Quite simply, when a nerve fiber fires, the output may not only excite a subsequent fiber to increase its firing rate by means of an excitatory connection or synapse but also inhibit another fiber to decrease its firing rate by means of an inhibitory synapse.

In general, each fiber is stimulated by several excitatory and inhibitory inputs so that the resultant firing rate and firing pattern is a function of the sum of all the inputs. Inhibitory effects are used to explain firing patterns that are not simple functions of the stimulation. For example, inhibition is assumed if the firing rate begins to increase with an increase of intensity and then begins to decrease with a further increase in intensity; or if the firing pattern to a steady tone is a burst of spikes followed by a period of no firing. The degree of inhibition depends on the similarity of characteristic frequencies. Given a cell with a characteristic frequency of 5000 Hz, the inhibition from cells with characteristic frequencies around 4500 Hz will be greater than from cells with characteristic frequencies around 3000 Hz. Until it is possible to record simultaneously from many cells at different levels, it will be impossible to detail the intricacies of the inhibitory circuits.

Let us start with the basic anatomy of the three-part cochlear nucleus. Each incoming auditory nerve splits in two; one branch goes to the anteroventral division and the other branch goes first to the posteroventral cochlear nucleus and then to the dorsal cochlear nucleus (see figure 12.30). What is important is that each nerve fiber simultaneously conveys the

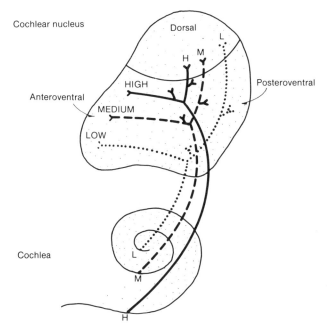

Figure 12.30
A schematic representation of the connection between the cochlea and cochlear nucleus. The tonotopic organization in the cochlea is maintained in all three subdivisions of the cochlea nucleus.

identical firing pattern to each of the three parts of the cochlear nucleus. We could expect that each section of the cochlear nucleus would show different response properties, depending on the way in which the excitatory and inhibitory inputs converge on the cells in each section.

Ventral cochlear nucleus   The vast majority of cells in the ventral nucleus give excitatory responses to tones and noise at all intensity levels (Shofner and Young 1985; Young 1987). The simplest neurons are purely excitatory and have discharge patterns similar to those found for auditory nerve fibers. These neurons seem to be the "bushy" cells that receive inputs from one to four auditory nerves and that make direct connections to the superior olivary nucleus, which is responsible for binaural comparisons yielding localization. These bushy cells appear to fire in response to every firing of any nerve fiber forming the synapse. The temporal pattern closely mimics the pattern on the auditory nerve fibers—an initial burst that adapts to a steady rate—and may be very irregular. Thus, the bushy cells seem designed to transmit precise temporal and intensity information required for sound localization to the superior olivary cortex. An example of this type of cell is shown in figure 12.31.

The more complex neurons are excitatory but have an irregular "chopper" discharge pattern. The firing pattern oscillates, yielding a regular variation in firing rate. These neurons appear to be the "stellate" cells that receive inputs from many auditory nerve fibers. The firing pattern, reflecting the integration of many fibers, is very regular. The firing of the stellate cells may convey intensity information important for event identification (stellate cells do not appear to connect to the superior olivary nucleus). An example of a chopper stellate cell is also shown in figure 12.31.

Dorsal cochlear nucleus   The dorsal cochlear nucleus might be termed the 'coding" area, as nearly all cells show a transformation of the nerve fiber excitation. In a 1985 study (Shofner and Young 1985), not one of over a hundred cells showed a simple excitation pattern.

The majority of cells show excitation and inhibition frequency regions to tones and noise. Most of these cells have a chopper discharge pattern, though some possess a "pauser" pattern: an initial excitatory response, followed by a pause in activity (duration greater than 5 msec), followed by a gradual buildup of response.

Another type of cell, found only in the dorsal nucleus, responds to pure tones at the characteristic frequency but does not respond to noise stimuli. The intensity firing rate function is nonmonotonic. As intensity increases, firing rate first increases and then decreases. The firing pattern is variable: some cells show a chopper response, but others are hard to classify.

Still another type of cell found only in the dorsal nucleus is characterized by excitatory responses to tones and noise, by inhibitory responses to frequencies around the characteristic frequency, and by a firing rate output that does not increase monotonically with increases in intensity. At low intensities around threshold, the cell fires throughout the stimulus tone or noise. At intermediate intensity, there is pauser response: excitatory, response silence, buildup of excitatory response. At the highest intensities, some cells fire only at onset and offset; others fire only at onset.

Other research   These outcomes depend on an accurate localization of the cells as well as on an accurate specification of the response patterns. Other work, equally important, contains information about the response to dynamic changing stimuli, but unfortunately in this research the anatomical location of the cells within the cochlear nucleus was not specified.

Møller (1983 for review) has investigated the firing patterns of cells in the cochlear nucleus of rats to tonal stimuli that are frequency modulated. These stimuli begin at a frequency below the characteristic frequency,

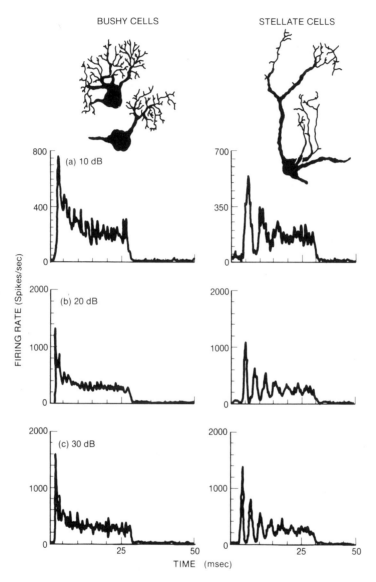

Figure 12.31
"Bushy" and "stellate" cells of the ventral cochlea nucleus. Bushy cells are purely excitatory, and the firing pattern has an initial firing burst that adapts and transforms into a more continuous steady response. Stellate cells are excitatory, but the firing pattern often has a regular variation in rate that can be seen clearly at stimulus intensities of 20 dB and 30 dB. This is termed a "chopper" response (adapted from Shofner and Young 1985 and from Young 1984).

increase in frequency over a short time period, and decrease back to the starting frequency over the identical time period and then repeat. In an experiment, the time period for the frequency transition is varied and the firing response of that cell is recorded for each period. Møller found that cells had maximum firing rates at specific rates of the frequency modulation. Two examples of these outcomes are drawn schematically in figure 12.32. For both "triangular" and trapezoidal modulation, the maximum response of these cells occurs when the frequency modulation sweeps up and down about 10–15 times per second, and this sensitivity holds across a wide variety of intensities. Other cells have different optimal modulation rates. What this all demonstrates is that cells in the cochlear nucleus are more sensitive to frequency *change* than auditory nerve fibers are. The pattern of interconnections of auditory nerves yields cells that are tuned to the temporal pattern of the auditory nerve fiber firings. The frequency modulation often makes the cells respond to a smaller range of frequencies than when presented with discrete steady-state tones. The modulation increases the selectivity.

Møller (1983, a review of his previous work) further demonstrated that cells in the cochlear nucleus respond to changes in intensity. Imagine a steady tone at the characteristic frequency. The amplitude of the tone is now modulated at different rates. At a modulation rate of 10 per second, the amplitude would oscillate at the rate of 10 times per second. Møller found that cells in the rat are maximally sensitive to modulations between 50 Hz and 200 Hz (see figure 12.32). Amplitude changes of 10% can result in a 50% change in firing rate. This large change in response rate occurs at intensities at which the response rate to steady tones saturates. These results once again demonstrate that cells in the auditory pathway can respond to changes in stimulation even when their discharge rate is constant for steady-state sounds.

Summary of cochlear nucleus   The cochlear nucleus illustrates in clear detail some of the general principles underlying the central auditory pathways: (1) there is tonotopic organization; (2) the incoming neural pattern is transmitted simultaneously to multiple areas; (3) the incoming neural signal is transformed in various ways so that the outgoing neural signals possess different temporal firing patterns; and (4) the maximum firing rate tends to occur at points of spectral change. This means that any event is coded by the configuration of firings across the different kinds of neural patterns. No single type of cell "detects" the event. Moreover, the neural pathways operate conservatively. The nervous system appears to retain as much of the information in the input signal as possible. An unprocessed, original signal as well as transformed variants are transmitted "upward." There is

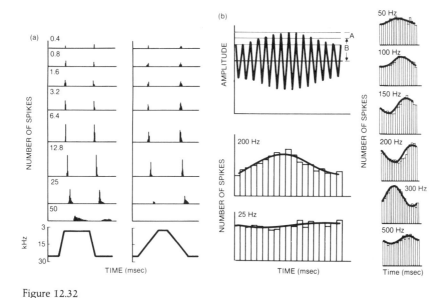

Figure 12.32

Cells in the cochlea nucleus may respond only to frequency- or amplitude-modulated signals. The effect of frequency modulation is shown for two cells in panel (a). The "shape" of the frequency modulation is shown in the bottom row of (a). The period histograms for different sweep rates (indicated by numbers to the left) are shown above. The maximum response occurred at 12.8 sweeps per second. That is, the frequency would sweep down and back up 12.8 times per second (the duration of one sweep is 78 msec). The effect of intensity modulation is shown in panel (b). The left column shows one cycle of a modulated wave. The amplitude of the wave is B, and the amplitude of modulation is A; the intensity modulation is described by its frequency. Thus a modulation frequency of 25 Hz means that the signal undergoes one rise and fall in intensity every 40 msec. Period histograms are used to detect whether the fiber fires consistently at one point in the intensity modulation. The period histograms in the left column suggest that the fiber synchronizes to a 200 Hz modulation, because the number of spikes systematically increases and decreases across one cycle of the modulation. The fiber does not synchronize to a 25 Hz modulation because the number of spikes is nearly identical across one cycle (i.e. the histogram is flat). Data from other fibers are shown in the right column. These data suggest that phase locking occurs for intensity modulation between 100 Hz and 500 Hz. The representation of one cycle of the modulation is shifted to most closely match the period histograms (from Møller 1983 by permission).

little evidence to support the idea that frequency coding is "sharpened" as the signal progresses toward the auditory cortex.

Surprisingly, the development of the different cell types in the cochlear nucleus is quite rapid (Brugge and O'Conner 1984). All basic cell types are found within two weeks of birth (in the cat). The development of these cells is independent of firing inputs generated in the auditory nerve by normal acoustic events. The development of the ability for phase locking occurs over a longer time interval. Originally, cells show phase locking only up to 600–1000 Hz, but by the end of three weeks most cells demonstrate phase locking up to 3000 Hz. It may be that phase locking in the cochlear nucleus requires phase locking in all the lower excitatory connections.

Superior Olivary Complex
The olivary nucleus appears to underlie the perception of localization (see review by Masterton and Imig 1984). Location is based mainly on the comparisons of the temporal and spectral patterns between the two ears, and the superior olivary complex is the lowest level at which information from the two ears converges. The primary "bushy" nerve cells from the ventral cochlear nucleus project to the superior olivary complex. These primary nerve cells compose the pipeline transmitting the short latency signal faithfully representing the temporal pattern.

Three subparts can be identified within the olivary complex (see figure 12.33). The medial nucleus is a relay bringing inputs from the contralateral cochlear nucleus to the lateral superior olivary nuclei. The lateral superior olive also receives inputs from the ipsilateral cochlear nucleus. The medial superior olive receives direct inputs from the cochlear nuclei of both sides. We will now consider the lateral and medial superior olive nuclei in more detail, because the medial trapezoid body appears to be a simple relay.

Lateral olivary complex   Each cell of the lateral superior olivary nuclei receives an excitatory input from the ipsilateral cochlear nucleus and an inhibitory input from the contralateral cochlear nucleus (relayed through the medial nucleus). The cells are arrayed tonotopically so that the excitatory and inhibitory fibers converging on one tree-like cell in the lateral superior olivary nuclei are matched in characteristic frequency. On this basis, we can imagine that these cells respond to the difference between the inputs at specific frequencies from each ear. In other words, these cells metaphorically subtract the intensity at one ear from the intensity at the other ear. If the ipsilateral ear input at a particular frequency is greater, then cells tuned to that frequency would increase their firing rate; if the contralateral input is greater, those cells would decrease their firing rate (Tsuchitani 1988). Intensity differences due to sound shadows would be created by the head and upper body, and intensity differences would

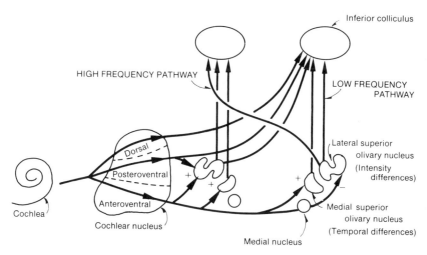

Figure 12.33
Pathways from the cochlear nucleus to the superior olivary nucleus and subsequently to the inferior colliculus. The pathways carrying the interaural intensity differences from the lateral olivary complex split. The high frequency differences travel contralaterally to the inferior colliculus; the low frequency differences travel ipsilaterally.

therefore be maximum at the higher frequencies (i.e., shorter wavelengths). The high frequency "difference" response most useful for localization crosses over and ascends the contralateral side of the brainstem; the less useful low frequency "difference" response ascends the ipsilateral side of the brainstem. Thus intensity location information is found in the contralateral cortex. The size of the lateral superior olivary nucleus in different species is correlated with high frequency sensitivity, which supports the conclusion that this nucleus is tuned to high frequency differences. The lateral superior olivary nucleus is small in large primates (e.g., gorillas and humans), which have relatively poor high frequency hearing, but well developed in dogs and cats, which have good high frequency sensitivity. In sum, these results suggest that the lateral superior olivary nuclei is responsible for localization based on high frequency intensity differences (or high frequency spectral differences in general).

Medial olivary complex   The large majority of cells in the medial olivary nucleus receive excitatory inputs from each cochlear nucleus; stimulation of either ear will lead to an increase in firing rate. However, when both ears are stimulated, the firing rate will be maximum when the excitation spikes from each ear converge at the same time (in phase), and the firing rate will be minimum when the spikes from each ear converge at alternate times (out of phase).

Let us consider the excitation process in more detail. From the source onset, the time for an excitation spike to arrive at a medial cell consists of (1) the time for the sound to travel to one ear; plus (2) the time for that neural response to travel to the medial cells. Consider a sound off the right ear. It takes longer for the airborne sound to reach the left ear [$(t + y)$ msec] than the right [(t) msec], a time difference represented by y milliseconds. In addition, it takes longer for the nerve impulse to travel contralaterally to the left nucleus [$(n + x)$ msec] than ipsilaterally to the right nucleus (n msec). Any contralateral medial cell will fire maximally when the added airborne sound time delay (y msec) equals the added neurological travel time delay (x msec), because the nerve impulses from the two ears will arrive synchronously at the medial cell. To make this model work, we need to assume that cells in the medial complex have different travel times. Then a given cell will fire maximally for sounds at one spatial position. At that location the airborne sound delay due to the distance around the head will equal the neural delay due to transmission contralaterally and, therefore, will yield synchronized arrival times. Across the distribution of cells in the medial area, we would expect groups of cells responsive to different orientations. The output from the contralateral medial nucleus ascends ipsilaterally directly to the contralateral cortex.

This model depends on phase locking of the firing of hair cells to the stimulating waveform. Only then can the firing occur at distinct time points. The required phase locking occurs only at low frequencies and, therefore, we might expect cells in the medial nuclei to show the greatest response to low frequency stimuli. It is true, in fact, that animals without a medial region (hedgehogs) cannot localize low frequency tone blips; animals with highly developed medial regions (e.g., humans, cats) can easily localize low frequency tone blips.

Summary of the superior olivary complex   The output from the superior olivary body appears able to provide information necessary to construct a "spatial map." Cells in the lateral superior olivary body systematically respond to intensity differences at high frequencies, and cells in the medial superior olivary body systematically respond to temporal differences between the ears. Both the intensity and temporal differences change as a function of spatial location. In addition, the outputs of many of these cells are relatively constant for different intensities and/or sound qualities. However, except in the owl, there is little evidence that a neural spatial map actually exists.

Research with barn owls has demonstrated a map of sound direction (Knudsen 1984). In one brain area, there are cells with specific receptive fields; that is, cells that fire to sound stimulation from a specific region in space. The receptive fields generate a two-dimensional place map of sound direction; each spatial location is represented by a restricted region of neural activity in the brain. Research has demonstrated that the auditory map is aligned to spatial direction by visual information (Knudsen and Knudsen 1985). In other words, visual sightings teach the owl the direction associated with neural firing in a particular point in the neural auditory map. Because of the fact that heads grow in size, a particular time disparity representing the extra time to travel around the head will signify different orientations as head size increases. Thus the auditory map must be able to recalibrate itself, and this is accomplished visually. The same problem occurs for humans; as a child matures, head size increases and the time disparity due to any spatial position will increase (Bower 1974). For humans, the visual modality also may serve as the referent as it does for owls.

The results for cats are quite different and may be more representative of human functioning. There does not seem to be a place map of sound direction. The pathways from the superior olivary nuclei proceed to the inferior colliculus, and then on to the auditory cortex, but at no point is there a neural map of the external space (Jenkins and Merzenich 1984).

Inferior Colliculus
The inferior colliculus contains a wide variety of cells. This is to be expected, because the inferior colliculus is the point of convergence of the binaural cells from the superior olivary nucleus and the monaural cells from the dorsal cochlear nucleus (remember that these cells tend to have complex response patterns such as onset, onset-offset, or delayed response). It is estimated that between 65% and 80% of the cells can be binaurally stimulated; the remainder can be stimulated only through one ear. For both classes, the stronger response occurs to contralateral stimulation. Typically there is an onset response to tones, and a sustained discharge to complex sounds that may signal phase changes among the harmonics. Phase locking is infrequent, and only occurs below 1000 Hz (Kuwada et al. 1984). It is estimated that 30% to 40% of the cells respond to sound sources in one region in space. These cells usually respond to all directions left of or right of one spatial direction. For example, one cell might respond to all orientations to the left of the midline. The cells displaying directional sensitivity, however, are spread out nonsystematically throughout the inferior colliculus (Aitkin, Gates, and Phillips 1984).

Similar results are seen in the higher structures of the colliculus and the auditory cortex. There are directionally sensitive cells, but there are no spatial maps. For the cat at least, it is clear that destruction of cortical tissue results in the loss of ability to localize specific frequencies (Jenkins and Merzenich 1984). Sound directions may be represented along a strip of cortical tissue that is maximally responsive to one frequency (an isofrequency strip). The evidence suggests to me that localization is not represented by individual cells arrayed within a neural spatial map but by the pattern of firings of groups of cells.

Summary of Auditory Pathways
What generalizations can be made? Most important, there seem to be parallel sensory channels that are based on the type of synapse, type of neuron, and type of interconnection. The output from each level is divergent. The same hair cell firing pattern is conveyed to different populations of cells, where different properties of the firing pattern are abstracted. The derived firing patterns are then transmitted along other independent circuits. These circuits converge at the inferior colliculus, where spatial information from the olivary complex is joined to spectral information from the cochlear nucleus. For the cat, it is estimated that there are twelve or more functionally distinct input sources at the colliculus. Similarly, the outputs from the inferior colliculus are transmitted to distinct subregions of the auditory thalamus (the medial geniculate) and in turn one or more regions of the medial geniculate transmit impulses to each region of the auditory cortex.

The neural connections preserve frequency selectivity. Cells with one maximum frequency sensitivity connect to other cells with the identical sensitivity, and there is no mixing of frequency information. However, within groups of cells with the same frequency sensitivity, the connections are divergent and many to many. Each cell connects to many other cells in the target nucleus, and in turn each receptor cell is influenced by the firing patterns of many cells. Merzenich, Jenkins, and Middlebrooks (1984) state that "at every level, interlevel projections are highly divergent and convergent. Information is repeatedly combined and then widely redistributed in a complex, ascending interlevel cascade" (p. 406).

12.5 Central Nervous System: Auditory Cortex

Up to this point, I have no doubt that the principles of auditory system functioning found in rodents, monkeys, and cats will be nearly identical to that in humans. When we study the cortex, I become uncertain about the comparability across species. With this in mind, I will sketch some broad principles and forgo details of the cortical organization of different species.

Traditionally, psychologists have distinguished among sensation, perception, and higher-order processes and have imagined that the cortex is organized in the same way. The model would include a single sensory region that would receive inputs directly from the lower centers. These "sensory firings" would be sent onward and "upward" to be interpreted into percepts, and finally would be sent to nonsensory association areas for integration with other information. It is a serial, step by step, interpretive model to match the classical distinction between sensation and perception. Each level is more complex, and evolution progressively adds levels of analysis and control.

Two objections come to mind. First, the sensation to perception progression seems to be an inappropriate way to conceptualize the active search for event information. By the same reasoning, a sensation to perception model of cortical organization would be inappropriate. Second, the fact that the auditory pathways and subcortical centers are organized into a set of parallel representations would suggest that the cortex is also organized into a set of parallel, distributed representations. Otherwise, there would be no use for that type of organization.

Following Merzenich and Kaas (1980), we can set forth some general principles for cortical organization.

1. There are multiple representations of sensory information in the auditory cortex. Some representations are tonotopic. Other representations are not, and the characteristic frequencies are scattered across the surface. In the macaque monkey, there seem to be six representations spatially organized by frequency and possibly one representation not organized by frequency. In the cat, there seem to be four representations spatially organized by frequency and three other representation not organized by frequency. (The cortex is mapped by placing electrodes at different cortical points of anesthetized animals. Typically, sinusoid tones of varying frequencies are presented. Each cortical cell is then characterized by frequency, namely the frequency for which the cell has the lowest threshold.)

2. The number of cortical fields increases in advanced mammals. Lower animals with "smooth" cortexes like hedgehogs, opossums, and rats have few sensory representations; higher mammals with large convoluted cortexes like cats and monkeys (and presumably humans) have many sensory representations.

Why should the cortex be organized into separate representations? Why not one large complex representation with interspersd functions? One reasonable explanation is that neural functioning depends on the simultaneous activation of groups of interconnected neurons and not on the activation of an individual neuron. Unless the appropriate neurons are spatially close, the "circuits" will not function. If new functions are needed, then additional representations can be easily realized, located in close spatial proximity to the original representations. Connections between representation regions can be made by the axons of nerve cells, which can travel relatively long distances. What we end up with is a group of interconnected regions, each

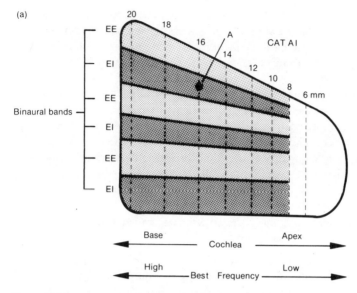

Figure 12.34
The organization of area AI in the auditory cortex of the cat. Panel (*a*) is a schematic representation of tonotopic organization and binaural organization. Different regions of the cochlea are represented along vertical tracks. The numbers in the figure represent the distance from one end of the cochlea. Binaural bands are represented along alternating horizontal tracks. In the excitation EE bands, cells increase their firing rate to sounds in either ear. In the excitation/inhibition EI bands, cells increase their firing rate to sounds in the contralateral ear but decrease their firing rate to sounds in the ipsilateral ear (or vice versa in IE inhibition/excitation bands) (adapted from Merzenich, Colwell, and Anderson 1982). The mapping of a small region in AI is shown in panel (*b*). The isofrequency contours are shown by dashed lines. An IE binaural band is located in the center. For this band, contralateral stimulation suppresses the firing rate (adapted from Brugge 1985).

(b)

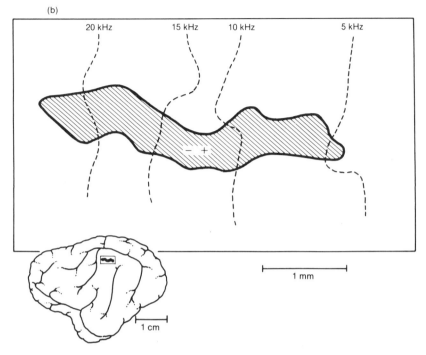

Figure 12.34(b)

region affecting and being affected by all the rest. On the other hand, if the neurons for each function are spread throughout the cortex, then the continued addition of more neurons for additional functions necessarily would spread out the original neurons. This increased distance would make it difficult for the original circuits to continue to function (Kaas 1982).

3. Each representation is fed by a different mix of fibers from the lower cortical centers. Each representation is therefore simultaneously activated, and each representation is specialized to some degree, reflecting the different mix and pattern of the inputs. Unfortunately, even in the cat, the most extensively studied animal, there is little information about the role of each representation.

4. All representations seem to be interconnected, and there are often reciprocal connections between pairs of representations.

5. The sensory representations vary in organization, and the end result is a mixture of inherent organization modified by sensory experience. We can use the major auditory field in the cat (AI) to illustrate this proposition (see figure 12.34). The AI area is roughly

trapezoid in shape, and the dotted lines represent equal cochlea positions and therefore isofrequency contours: all cells falling along one dotted line are maximally sensitive to the same frequency. These isofrequency lines seem to be genetically determined, because there is little variation across individuals.

Perpendicular to the isofrequency lines are bands of cells with the identical binaural characteristics. Cells in the white EI bands are excited by the contralateral ear and inhibited by the ipsilateral ear (or vice versa in IE regions). Cells in the grey EE bands are excited by both ears. Thus cells at point A increase their firing rate to a signal presented to the contralateral ear but reduce their firing rate to a signal presented to the ipsilateral ear. What characterizes the binaural bands is an extensive variability across individuals. Although the bands are drawn very neatly in figure 12.34, panel (a), they actually swoop in and out at random within one animal and are quite different across animals. An example of an irregular IE band appears in figure 12.34, panel (b). Merzenich and colleagues hypothesize that this variability comes from the dense anatomical projections from the medial geniculate body to the cortex (see figure 12.35). To simplify it somewhat, each EI region and each EE region in the medial geniculate body projects to every binaural band in the cortex. Each cortical band is therefore the result of the convergence of many pathways. Along an isofrequency contour, there is virtually an all-to-all connection. Merzenich speculates that the patterns of firing due to sensory stimulation can increase the size of some binaural regions and decrease other binaural regions. Thus the variability in the binaural bands is a result of sensory experience taken in over the life of the animal (Schreiner and Cynader 1984).

There are more neural connections in infants than adults, and this difference cannot be explained simply by cell death due to aging. There is growing evidence that there is competition among the neural connections, and the ones excited by environmental events survive. There is far more flexibility and plasticity in the nervous system than previously imagined (Easter et al. 1985). In sum, the frequency (tonotopic) organization is fixed, but the binaural representation is modified by experience. If each of the bands makes a unique contribution, then the perceptual differences among individuals could be explained at least in part by these cortical differences.

What can we learn from these organizational principles? First, perception must arise from the parallel, simultaneous activation of the cortical representations. The representations will interact and modify the firing patterns of each other. Second, each cortical representation is the end result of convergence from diverse auditory pathways. The complex properties (i.e.,

(a)

Primary Auditory Cortex

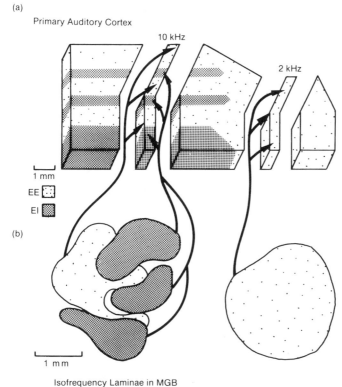

10 kHz

2 kHz

1 mm

EE

EI

(b)

1 mm

Isofrequency Laminae in MGB

Figure 12.35
The connections between the medial geniculate body and the auditory cortex are "many to many". All EI regions in the medial geniculate project to all EI regions in the auditory cortex, and all EE regions in the medical geniculate project to all EE regions in the auditory cortex. Tonotopic organization is maintained for all connections, so each frequency region in the medial geniculate body projects to the same frequency region in the cortex. The tonotopic organization is invariant across cats, but the EI and EE bands differ dramatically between cats and seem to be the outcome of early experience (adapted from Merzenich, Jenkins, and Middlebrook 1984).

features) that could be abstracted by the lower centers are not kept separate in the cortex but are anatomically superimposed.

12.6 Cortical Organization in Humans

The specific cortical representations found in the cat will clearly not match those in humans, but I do believe that multiple representations will be found in the human cortex. The basic question concerns the functional properties of each representation. We could think of each representation as a domain module—one for speech, one for music, and so on. The massive neural convergence suggests that a single cortical area might have sufficient capabilities. Each module would need to be self-contained: able to localize sources, compensate for context effects, integrate over long time spans of the signal, and so on. In other words, each module would need to be capable of all the functions necessary for understanding. Another possibility is to imagine the domain modules as being only the tonotopic representations. The nontonotopic representations would be nonspecific and would be recruited to serve each domain as needed.

Given the pattern of neural connections found in the cat and the monkey, I believe it is implausible that one (or more than one) cortical representation is uniquely a language (or music) module. All sounds are analyzed by frequency at the ear, and frequency information is kept separate all the way up the auditory pathways. The auditory pathways do not know if they are listening to speech or music. Speech and music perception depend crucially on the timing among differing frequency components over longer time spans. This perception would necessarily depend on the firing pattern *within* one tonotopic representation and *across several* tonotopic representations. Conversely, the specific organization within any one representation and the specific organizations across representations will have emerged because of the particular sensory experience. Typically, these organizations will have been determined by the neural patterning brought about by sounds in longer time spans, because those sounds will produce overlapping neural impulses. Moreover, the organization of typical events (e.g., one spatial location, common patterns among frequency partials in timing, duration, modulation) probably yields neural firings within particular regions of each representation and thus creates the greatest possibility for cortical reorganization. The very plasticity of the interconnections ensures that each representation can be tuned to the sounds of any speech and music system.

Instead of each representation being a specifically speech or nonspeech module, each might be involved in general perceptual processes that cut across domains. For example, one representation would involve localization (and in fact Jenkins and Merzenich [1984] argue that area AI in the cat underlies localization), one would involve frequency patterning (either in speech intonation or in music melody or Doppler effects), and another would involve timing in all domains. Speech, music, and event perception would necessarily require the integration of all the representations.

Localization of Function
We can get a glimpse of cortical organization by studying localization of function. In simplest terms, localization of function is based on the simple idea that specific areas of the brain are responsible for certain functions. Even though Egyptians recorded instances of head injuries that led to speech disorders, it took many years to recognize that the brain had the central role in intellectual activity. Yet it was (and still is) unclear whether the brain should be conceptualized as one relatively holistic unit or conceptualized as a series of somewhat independent domains. Historically, research in the late 1800s shifted the prevailing view to one of localization of function.

Methods for assessing localization   We can probe the functioning of the brain in several ways.

1. The first depends upon brain lesions or brain damage. In lesion studies, localized damage to the brain appears to result in particular behavioral deficits. From this correlation of brain area to functional deficit, we infer that the basic skills underlying a higher function are localized in that area. For example, in split-brain operations the corpus callosum is cut, so that there is no direct connection between the left and right hemispheres of the cortex (see below, figure 12.36, panel a). It is possible to present stimuli so that they arrive only at one hemisphere and thereby investigate the performance of that hemisphere alone. In hemispherectomy operations, one entire cortical hemisphere is removed. In these relatively rare individuals, it is possible to study the functioning of the remaining cortex.

The outcomes from all of these studies should be viewed with caution. Fundamentally, this research is based on a small number of clinical cases in which cortical damage may be widespread and unknowable. The split-brain cases have attracted much attention. It is important to keep in mind that the individuals in those cases had intractable epilepsy throughout their lives and therefore both hemispheres had probably suffered unknown damage. Although specific lesions might appear to offer the best possibility for discovering the localization of differing skills, it is often difficult to pinpoint the location of the actual lesions and the damage is often more widespread than originally believed.

2. The second depends on physiological studies in normal sub-jects. These studies have used measurements such as cerebral blood flow or electrical responses to record the activity in different parts of the cortex. Subjects are typically asked to do a task—e.g., singing a song, whistling—and it is postulated that cortical areas with increased blood flow or increased electrical activity are involved in that task. These results should also be considered with caution. There are tech-nical difficulties in making these measurements, and at best the phys-iological indices provide only crude localization information.

3. The third utilizes experimental techniques with normal subjects. The dichotic listening procedure involves the simultaneous, competi-tive presentation of auditory material in each ear. The assumption is that in competitive situations, the ipsilateral pathways are suppressed by the bigger, more efficient contralateral pathways. Thus right ear material is carried to the left hemisphere, and left ear material is carried to the right hemisphere. (If material is transferred between hemispheres, it is across the corpus callosum.) Suppose speech stimuli presented in the right ear are identified more accurately than speech stimuli presented in the left ear. This outcome would suggest that the left hemisphere is specialized for language. However, these sorts of results also must be viewed with caution. First, the ipsilateral path-ways are not suppressed, because they are needed for spatial localiza-tion and subjects rarely misreport which ear the words were pre-sented in. Also, subjects often create ear blends, combining "back" to one ear with "lack" to the other ear and reporting "black." The ipsilateral pathways are probably weaker than contralateral pathways, but they are not completely suppressed. Thus performance on stimuli presented to each ear is the result of varying combinations of left and right cortical involvement. Second, performance is often a function of the strategies used by the subject. The subject can direct attention to either ear, can vary the order of report of the items, and might employ different perceptual modes. These factors can either inflate or deflate performance differences between the ears.

Outcomes from localization studies   The results from studies of cortical lo-calization come from an immense variety of observations and anecdotes as well as from controlled and uncontrolled experiments. I do not believe that the results lead to any simple conclusions, for the inconsistencies are difficult to resolve. Some of the outstanding outcomes can be summarized as follows.

1. The first question to be asked is whether there is localization of any sort. For speech, there is a consensus that the perception and

processing are carried out in the left hemisphere. For music, the results are much more ambiguous; there does not seem to be a dominant hemisphere, and there seems to be a wide distribution of abilities across individuals. On the whole, the right hemisphere is more involved in the perception of unfamiliar melodic sequences and timbre, with the left hemisphere becoming more involved with the naming of familiar tunes (a language function).

Each hemisphere has the potential to take on the typical functions of the other. In children born without left hemisphere, for example, the development of language proceeds normally. However, some research has suggested that language mastery is never complete in the right hemisphere (Searleman 1983). Probably there are "preferred" localizations that can be compensated for in varying degrees in other cortical regions.

We know that apparent differences between speech and nonspeech perception are often due to differences in the complexity and structure of the sounds. I think this set of research findings on the lateralization of speech and nonspeech perception suffers from the same defect. For example, Efron, Koss, and Yund (1983) report that more complex nonspeech sounds that more closely approximate the complexity of speech sounds require left hemisphere analysis. Thus differences between hemispheres may be due not to the speech-nonspeech distinction but to the complexity of sound.

2. The second question is more specific, and it hinges on a positive response to the general question of localization. If there is localization, is the speech or music domain subdivided so that subprocesses are found in specific locations? To do this, it is important to find specific speech or music deficits that are closely correlated to specific cortical areas. Only studies of clinical patients with "mappable" cortical damage would allow for this correlation.

The first cortex area implicated in speech was discovered by Broca in 1861. Broca, quite by chance, studied a patient who was unable to speak but could understand spoken language (we do not know, however, the extent of the understanding). Within a few weeks the patient died, and an autopsy revealed damage in one region of the left cortex. It has been named Broca's area, and patients with damage there are characterized by slow, labored, and slurred speech combined with phonemic and phonetic errors: a deficit of motor control. A few years later, Wernicke identified a different area of the left cortex associated with the inability to understand speech, although the ability to speak appeared normal. There seemed to be one cortical area for speaking and a different area for understanding.

(a)

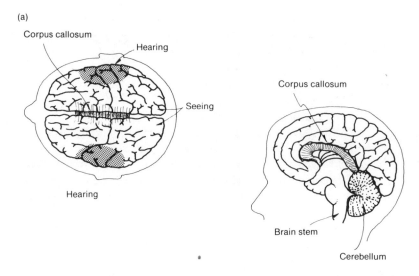

(b)

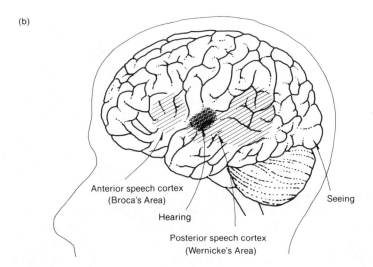

Figure 12.36
Simplified representation of cortical localization. The corpus collosum is depicted in
panel (a). If the corpus collosum is surgically cut, the left and right hemispheres cannot
communicate directly. The general localization of auditory areas in the left side of the cortex
are shown in panel (b).

It soon became clear, however, that the deficits associated with each lesion site are not simple. Patients with Broca's aphasia have agrammatical speech; they drop plural and past-tense markers, and they have difficulty understanding embedded sentences like "The man greeted by his wife was smoking a pipe." They can make use of semantic constraints (e.g., red apple) but not syntactic constraints. Patients with Wernicke's aphasia have fluid speech, but it is often nonsensical and meaningless.

Given that specific lesions have a variety of language consequences, one strategy is to look for a different way of understanding the defects. For example, Zurif (1984) suggests that damage in Broca's area produces a syntactic grammatical deficit, a linguistic problem, and that damage in other areas might produce an external referential deficit, an inability to connect a word to an event or object. In other words, we define the function of cortical area by the configuration of deficits. Another strategy is to give up the notion that cortical areas are specific to one domain. For instance, Broca's area might be involved with motor control, an input-output component. This area might have evolved because of the enhancement of a cortical area already specialized for motor control (e.g., respiration or feeding) or might have evolved because of the emergence of another representation to cope with the increased difficulty of articulation.

The evidence seems to suggest that perception of music (or of events in general) is not localized to the same degree as speech. Different regions have not been found for music perception. Zatorre (1984) suggests that the frontal area of the right cortex (i.e., temporal area) is most involved in the processing of timbre and short melodic sequences, and he took an important analytic step by using the techniques of Dowling (see section 10.5) to discover which aspects of melody (contour, intervals, key) were affected by lesion damage. The results were inconclusive, but if we are to learn something about the relationship between cortical sites and music perception, we will need to invoke more sophisticated concepts about music perception.

My reading of the research reports is thus that areas of the brain are specialized, but the specialization is not simply by domain or by function. For example, multilingual individuals who have brain damage often show different speech deficits in each language (Paradis 1977, 1987). A colleague told me his grandfather had difficulty with the words (semantics) in one language and the grammar (syntax) in another language. Since there are a multiplicity of neural connections and since the cortex is organized by sensory experience to some extent, any single cortical region might serve different functions in varying contexts. This adaptability may help explain why some studies report that experienced musicians show a left cortex localization for music.

3. The third question is whether there are processing differences in cortical regions. The cortex is not homogeneous, and there are areas of distinct "architecture." The type, distribution, and interconnections of the cells differ. On the face of it, this would imply that each architectural region functions differently. However, at this point our knowledge is much too limited to infer the relation of architecture, function, and domain.

Let me summarize this discussion of the auditory cortex. The classical version of cortical organization is hierarchical. At the top of the hierarchy is the decision maker, the little man in the head. This version of organization seems untenable because there is no "top." Anatomically, each representation of the auditory cortex is interconnected, and there are large overlaps in the fibers transmitted from lower centers. From research in cats and monkeys, we know that frequency information is maintained throughout the pathways. Other aspects of the organization emerge out of "degenerate," nonspecific wiring. Neurophysiologists talk of distributed systems, networks of cells that act together to yield perception. Given such a parallel system of representations, it is undeniably appealing to postulate that each representation underlies one domain and then to assign different sides of the cortex to different kinds of domains. The left hemisphere is verbal, analytic, linear, rational; the right hemisphere is nonverbal (music, global, parallel, emotional). But from what we know about anatomy and about auditory event perception, these labels at best misrepresent physiology and perceiving.

12.7 Overview

This chapter covers the gamut of the physiology of listening, from mechanical processes in the middle ear, to the timing of firings in the auditory nerve, to neural assemblies in the auditory regions of the cortex. When I first imagined writing this book, I thought there would be elegant connections between perceptual variables and physiological cells. I thought that it would be possible to discover acoustic features (which might be quite complex) for events and to discover physiological analyzers that signal these features. But as I began to appreciate the inherent context dependency of perceiving, it dawned on me that a fundamentally different model of cortical functioning was necessary. Because of the complexity of the acoustic signal, a relatively static organization into centers would be inadequate and inappropriate. A flexible organizational system, able to capitalize on the regularities in the acoustic signal caused by the constraints on production, would be necessary. Giving up the concept of a hierarchical organization leaves the problem of how the multiple representations yield a coherent percept. That is still a mystery.

Chapter 13
Finally

For G-d bounded His wisdom in language, in words, and therefore, ultimately, in sounds . . .

Every type of wisdom, according to its category and level, has its own particular song and melody.

Faith also has its own song and melody, particular to Faith.
—Rabbi Nachman of Breslov (1762–1809)

The book has centered on the psychophysics of listening, the relationship between the objective (physical) and subjective (psychological) experience. Throughout, I have been hesitant and cautious. The inherent context dependency of the physical world and the inherent context dependency of the perceptual world preclude a simple one-to-one relationship. I often wonder how perception can occur at all.

This emphasis on the psychophysics has left two gaps. The first gap is the role of the listener's knowledge and experience and of the listener's goals and intentions in representing the world. No one is "naive," and our expectations constrain and control our percepts in complex ways. The transparency of the perceptual world hides the ubiquity of these representations.

The second gap is the experience of listening, the experience of being in the auditory world, listening to one's self and to the world. Although there are equivalent expressions—looking at and listening to—listening, more than looking, puts us in the world. Looking makes each of us a focused observer, listening makes each of us a surrounded participant. My sense is that I am part of my auditory world but that I am looking into my visual world. It is perhaps for this reason that music is so closely tied to religious experience. The rhythm and melody of music bonds the experience in ways that I am at a loss to explain.

And that is why I would rather be blind than deaf.

Glossary

ABSOLUTE JUDGMENT TASK One of a predetermined set of stimuli is presented, and the observer tries to identify or recognize it using its name or number. The pattern of correct and incorrect responses is analyzed by means of information theory to determine the number of different stimuli that can be correctly identified without error. The number is termed the *information transmission*.

ACCENT A note or chord that is emphasized or perceived as stronger. The accent may be acoustic (greater amplitude, higher pitch) or may be due to the listener's perception of the musical movement. (The term *accent* usually refers to music; the analogous term *stress* usually refers to speech.)

ADAPTATION The reduction, caused by prior or continuing stimulation, in the firing rate of neurons.

ADDITIVITY The physical principle that the amplitude of the combination (superposition) of two or more sound waves at any time point is the algebraic sum of the amplitudes of the individual sound waves at that time point.

AFFORDANCE Properties of things with respect to the observer. The affordances are specified in the invariant acoustic information and allow the perceiver to function in the environment. There is one affordance for each possible action with a thing.

AMPLITUDE For harmonic vibrations, the maximum displacement during one cycle. For airborne sounds, amplitude refers to the maximum change in air pressure.

AMPLITUDE MODULATION Variation in amplitude (loudness) for a tone of constant pitch. If the modulation is a repetitive oscillation, it can be described in terms of modulation frequency (Hz) and by the change in amplitude (depth).

ANTINODE Any point on a standing wave that undergoes maximum displacement.

ARTICULATION, MANNER OF A feature used to classify consonants in terms of the manner in which the airflow is restricted.

ARTICULATION, PLACE OF The point in the mouth that is constricted, blocking the flow of air. Necessary for the production of consonants.

ARTICULATORY The pattern of movements involved in the production of speech sounds.

ARTICULATORY FEATURE There are three features of the physical process of speaking—manner of articulation, place of articulation, and voicing—that can be used to classify the speech sounds.

ASYNCHRONY Two sounds or the harmonics of one sound that do not have the identical onset or offset time (i.e., lack of coincidence). Measured in milliseconds.

ATONAL/TONAL Experimentally, atonal sequences contain notes that do not come from one major or minor scale; tonal sequences contain notes from only one scale. Musically, atonal music does not follow the conventions of tonality, the dominant-tonic relationship.

ATTACK The part of the sound in which the amplitude is increasing. The attack time may be measured in terms of the time required for the sound to increase from 10% of the maximum amplitude to 90% of the maximum amplitude. Each harmonic (or partial) of a complex tone may have a different attack (and decay) time. Also termed *rise time*.

AUDITORY RESTORATION The perception of continuous sound even if segments have been obliterated or interrupted by louder sounds of similar frequency. It is possible to delete parts of a sound and maintain the perception that the sound is continuous if noise is inserted in the silent parts.

BEATS (ACOUSTICAL) The oscillation in amplitude (rise and fall in loudness) when two tones of slightly different frequencies occur simultaneously. The frequency of the amplitude oscillation (i.e., beat frequency) is equal to the difference in frequency between the two tones.

BEATS (RHYTHMIC) Equal temporal units (from note onset to note onset) of a composition. Each beat is equivalent to an up-and-down movement of the conductor's hand. The duration of the beat determines the tempo: at a slow tempo (metronome = 50), there are 50 beats/minute; at a fast tempo (metronome = 140), there are 140 beats/minute.

BRANCH The splitting of superordinate groups into subordinate groups in a hierarchy. Each branch represents the relationship between the two levels of the hierarchy.

CADENCE A sequence of notes or chords that is used at the end of a compositon to mark the conclusion (relaxation of tension). Each musical style has a limited number of cadences, and the traditional cadences have changed historically.

CATEGORICAL PERCEPTION A style of perceiving defined by accurate discrimination between events in different categories and poorer discrimination between events within a single category.

CHARACTERISTIC FREQUENCY (ACOUSTICAL) The frequency of maximum movement amplitude for a vibration mode (i.e., the resonant frequency).

CHARACTERISTIC FREQUENCY (PHYSIOLOGICAL) For an auditory nerve fiber, the frequency at which the fiber is most easily excited (i.e., the frequency at which the threshold is minimum).

CHROMA The equivalence of notes due to their identical position within the scale at different octaves (e.g., all A's have the same chroma).

CIRCLE OF FIFTHS A representation illustrating that twelve successive steps of a fifth (a 3:2 ratio of frequency) return to the original note (given octave equivalence). Because each note is the initial note of a scale, the circle represents the relationship among scales.

COARTICULATION The simultaneous production of two or more speech sounds due to the overlapping of articulatory movements.

CONSONANCE The perceptual sense that the combination of two or more tones appears smooth or pleasant.

CONTEXT DEPENDENT Situations in which production and/or perceptual processes are affected by prior and subsequent events.

CONTEXTUAL A theoretical point of view that the perception of an acoustic signal depends on the preceding and following signals within which it is embedded.

CONTOUR The up-and-down frequency pattern of a note sequence. Upward frequency movements may be represented by a plus sign; downward frequency movements may be represented by a minus sign. The size of the movement is not indicated.

CONTRALATERAL FIBERS Fibers that cross the body midline; fibers from the right ear that terminate in the left side of the brain (and vice versa).

COUPLING The process by which a driving vibrator (e.g., a string) can excite another vibrator (e.g., the sound body of a violin). See DAMPING.

CRITICAL BAND A range of frequencies that is integrated by the neural system, equivalent to a band-pass filter. The ear can be said to be a series of overlapping critical bands, each responding to a narrow range of frequencies.

CYCLE One complete repetition of a vibration pattern.

DAMPING A damped oscillation will lose energy and die away because of sound radiation and friction. A highly damped oscillation will die away quickly, will be excited rapidly by a driving vibration, and will reach the same amplitude across a wide range of frequencies. Conversely, a lightly damped oscillation will die away slowly, will be excited slowly by a driving vibration, and will reach maximum amplitude at only a narrow range of frequencies.

DECAY The part of the sound in which the amplitude is decreasing. Decay time may be measured in terms of the time required for the tone to decrease from 90% of maximum amplitude to 10% of maximum amplitude.

DECIBELS A unit of the difference between two sounds in terms of the ratio between sound pressures. Each $10:1$ sound pressure ratio is equal to 20 decibels (dB), so that a $100:1$ ratio is equal to 40 decibels.

DESIGN FEATURE Characteristics of human language that distinguish it from communication systems used by animals.

DIFFRACTION Process by which sound waves spread out in all directions after passing through an opening; also the process by which sound waves fill in behind an object.

DIMENSION A perceived characteristic of a sound (or object), e.g., loudness, pitch, beat rate, and so on. In simple scaling situations, the observer abstracts out the dimension and rates the magnitude of that property. In multidimensional scaling, the observer is presumed to judge the difference between two sounds on the basis of all perceived dimensions, and the task of the statistical analysis is to discover the number of dimensions and, for each sound, to measure the magnitude on each dimension.

DIPHTHONGS Vowels that are combinations of two sounds. For example, the sound /eɪ/ as in bait and /au/ in bout.

DISSONANCE The sense of roughness or unpleasantness created by two or more simultaneous tones.

DISTAL The stimulus object or event in the environment. The object or event stimulates the receptors by means of intervening sound waves.

DOPPLER EFFECT The change in the frequency of sounds because of movement toward and away from the listener.

DUALITY OF PATTERNING The organized patterns of sound segments and the organized patterns of meanings. Language is the relation between the two levels of patterning.

ELASTIC MEDIUM A material in which the force to return to equilibrium is proportional to the displacement from equilibrium. Vibration of an elastic medium will yield simple harmonic motion.

ENVELOPE The pattern of the amplitude of a vibration across time (i.e., the line connecting the peaks of the oscillation).

FIGURE-GROUND ORGANIZATION The tendency to perceive part of the visual or auditory scene as "tightly" organized objects or events (the figure) standing out against a diffuse, poorly organized background (the ground).

FILTER A device that selectively transmits a range of frequencies. A low-pass filter transmits frequencies below a specified frequency, a high-pass filter transmits frequencies above a specified frequency, and a band-pass filter transmits frequencies within a band defined by a lower and higher frequency.

FISSION The splitting of the acoustic signal into perceptual events or streams, each presumed to represent a different sound source.

FORMANTS A broad resonance frequency region (medium damping) that amplifies any harmonic component falling within its range.

FORMANT TRANSITION The frequency change from the onset of a consonant to the steady vowel frequency. The transition is due jointly to the places of articulation for the consonant and for the vowel.

FOURIER ANALYSIS A mathematical theorem that any periodic vibration can be analyzed into a set of simple sinusoid waves. In turn, the superposition of the sinusoid waves will reproduce the original vibration.

FREQUENCY The number of times per second that the vibration pattern repeats, i.e., the number of cycles per second. Measured in hertz (Hz).

FREQUENCY MODULATION Oscillation in frequency around a center value. The modulation frequency can be specified in Hz if the oscillation is periodic.

FREQUENCY SEPARATION The ratio (in Hz) between the fundamental frequency of two tones.

FREQUENCY SPECTRUM The specification of the sinusoid components of a complex vibration in terms of frequency, amplitude, and phase of the harmonics.

FREQUENCY STREAMING The splitting apart of the acoustic signal on the basis of the frequency separation of the sounds.

FREQUENCY THEORY The general idea that pitch perception is based on the rate of neural firing (or on the interval between neural spikes).

FRICATIVE Consonants produced by a turbulent airflow, resulting in acoustic energy spread over a wide frequency range.

FUSION Perceiving a set of simultaneous frequency components as one complex tone.

GESTALT PRINCIPLES Relationships among elements that lead to the perception of objects or events (which include those elements). These principles lead to the perception of figures.

GLIDES (SEMIVOWELS) Created by rapid movements of articulatory system, e.g., /w/, /r/, /y/.

HAAS (PRECEDENCE) EFFECT The perception of object location is determined by the direction of the first sound wave (typically the direct wave). The subsequent reflected waves do not affect localization and in this sense are inhibited, but they do affect the quality or timbre of the sound.

HARMONIC MOTION The vibration pattern that occurs in an elastic medium. The amplitude of the movements traces a sinusoid curve.

HARMONICS The set of vibration modes of an object. For a harmonic series, the natural frequencies of the modes are simple integer multiples of the fundamental frequency.

HARMONY The structure of the musical chords (i.e., notes played simultaneously); the sequences and cadences of chords with respect to the tonic.

HIERARCHY An organization in which adjacent elements are organized into subgroups. In turn, adjacent elements within each subgroup are organized into smaller subgroups. Various rules are employed to determine how to place the elements into subgroups.

HIGHER-ORDER VARIABLES A variable that emerges due to the organization of the individual elements, e.g., symmetry. Alternatively, a variable whose value is a function of the combination of other variables, e.g., timbre.

IDENTIFICATION An experimental procedure in which one stimulus is presented and the observer must name that stimulus. Sometimes all the possible stimuli are known to the observer; sometimes the possible stimuli are not disclosed beforehand.

INHARMONICS Sets of vibration modes in which the natural or resonant frequencies are *not* multiples of the fundamental frequency.

INTENSITY Average rate of sound energy falling on a unit area.

INTERAURAL DIFFERENCES Differences in the acoustic signal from the two ears. These include intensity, phase, spectral, and arrival time differences.

INTERFERENCE Because of additivity/superposition of sound waves, the combination of sound waves can lead to the reinforcing or canceling of the amplitude of the combined wave.

INTERRESPONSE INTERVAL The time, usually in milliseconds, between two successive neural impulses.

INTONATION Patterns of pitch, loudness, or other qualities spanning more than one speech segment. Intonation may refer to consistent meanings based on the up-and-down pitch patterns.

IPSILATERAL Nerve fibers that remain on one side of the body midline. Ipsilateral fibers from the right ear terminate in the right auditory cortex.

ISOCHRONOUS A series of tonal elements such that the onset of each element is separated by equal intervals of time.

KEY MODULATION The transition from one key to another within a composition. This modulation is accomplished by means of notes that are found in both keys.

LATERALIZATION The finding that specific kind of perceptions (e.g., speech perception) are localized in the left or right side of the cortex.

LEVELS The subdivisions possible in a hierarchical representation. All subgroups at one level are conceptualized to be equivalent in complexity.

LEXICAL Roughly, the meaning of a word.

LINEARITY A relationship between two variables that can be represented by a straight line, for example, $y = 3x + 4$. Here any increase in x generates a $3x$ increase in y (if x increases from 3 to 6 or from 4 to 7, y increases by 9).

LOCALIZATION The perceptual ability to determine the position in space (orientation and distance) of a sound source. Since the ear is not organized spatially, localization normally depends on interaural differences.

LONGITUDINAL WAVE The back-and-forth movement of molecules in the same direction as the propagation of the wave.

MELODY A sequence of notes that is perceived to be organized into a coherent phrase. Melody is defined perceptually.

MELS The unit of perceived pitch.

METER Sense of the regular alternation of stronger and weaker beats.

MOTOR PROGRAM A set of prestructured muscle commands prepared in advance of the movements. It theoretically contains the order of the movements, the overlap of the movements, and the relative force of the movements. Motor programs are assumed to underlie skilled, rapid performances in which there is not sufficient time to select successive movements.

MUSIC INTERVAL The pitch relationship (distance) between any two notes within one octave. The name indicates the number of notes of the scale within that interval.

NASALS Consonants formed by closing the mouth at one point and opening the nasal cavity (e.g., /m/, /n/).

NODE A point on a standing wave pattern that remains stationary.

NOISE A random oscillation that is not periodic. At any point in time all frequencies have an equal probability of occurring. The amplitude of each frequency is also probabilistic. For white noise, the probability of any amplitude follows the normal curve, and over time all frequencies would have the same power. Some experiments use band-pass white noise in which all frequencies within a frequency range have equal probability and equal power.

NOTATED TIME SIGNATURE The vertical arrangement of two numbers such that the upper number indicates the number of beats within a measure (i.e., the number of beats within one repetition of the meter). The lower number indicates the time value, or note value, that receives a beat.

OCTAVE A pair of tones such that the fundamental frequency of the higher is twice the fundamental frequency of the lower.

OFFSET See DECAY.

ONSET See ATTACK.

OSCILLATION The back-and-forth movement of a vibration across time (i.e., within a cycle).

PARALLEL TRANSMISSION In general, the idea that one segment of acoustic energy conveys, at the same time, information about many attributes of the event. In speech production, each acoustic element conveys information about the surrounding speech segments.

PARTIALS The frequency components of one complex tone that do not have a simple whole number relationship among the frequencies (e.g., 100, 180, 225 Hz ...). The term "harmonics" usually is restricted to frequency components that do have a simple whole number relationship (e.g., 100, 200, 300 Hz ...).

PERIOD The time interval required to repeat one cycle of a repeating vibration pattern.

PERIODIC A vibration that repeats over and over again.

PHASE A measure of the position along the sinusoidal vibration. One complete cycle contains 360°, and a phase angle of 0° is said to occur when the vibration beginning at equilibrium moves toward positive displacement. Similarly, a phase angle of 90° occurs when the vibration beginning at the maximum positive displacement moves toward equilibrium. The phase angle between two sinusoid waves reflects the difference in phase between the two waves.

PHASE-LOCKED The firing of a single neuron at one distinct point in the vibration cycle. (The neuron need not fire on every cycle, but each firing would occur at the same point in the cycle.)

PHONEME Smallest difference in sound that creates a meaning. An abstract underlying representation yielding the articulatory features that generate meaning differences. Phonemes are surrounded by slashes (e.g., /d/).

PHONETICS The analysis and categorization of the naturally occurring speech sounds in a language. A description of the pronunciation of a segment.

PHONOLOGICAL Description of the speech sounds as a system of language. The rules determining which sounds and sound sequences are allowable in one language.

PHONS The magnitude of the perceived loudness of any sound.

PLACE THEORY The idea that pitch perception depends on which nerve fibers are excited. Because the fibers are arrayed along the basilar membrane, different patterns of movement of the membrane will excite different fibers.

PRÄGNANZ The gestalt principle that percepts always tend toward "as good a figure" as the stimulus object will permit. Although "as good as" is not formally defined, the percept will tend to be highly organized, simple, enclosed, symmetrical, and so on.

PRESSURE A measure of the concentration of force applied to a surface.

PROFILE In theories of pitch perception, the pattern of firing rates of auditory fibers connected to different frequency regions of the basilar membrane i.e. the pattern of firing rates for fibers with different characteristic frequencies.

PROGRESSION A series of notes that increase (or decrease) in frequency, going up or down the scale.

PROSODIC Patterns of acoustic qualities spanning more than one segment that affect the perception of stress and the perception of meaning.

PROTOTYPE A representation of some event in memory. Recognition occurs when the stimulus representation generated by the auditory system is matched to one of the prototypes. Also called *template-matching*.

PROXIMAL The stimulus energy at the receptors. See DISTAL.

PULSE TRAIN A series of isochronous, precisely equivalent stimuli. Each pulse marks off an equal temporal interval.

Q The quality factor, a measure of the damping. A high Q represents a system with light damping.

QUALITY Used as a synonym for timbre, distinguishing among sounds. Also used as a synonym for dimension, a characteristic of a sound or object.

RECOGNITION See IDENTIFICATION.

RECYCLED A melodic or rhythm pattern that is repeated continuously without intervening pauses. E.g., *abaca*, if recycled, would generate *abacaabacaabaca....*

REFLECTION The bouncing back of a sound wave off a surface. Sound waves of all frequencies are assumed to be reflected identically.

RELATIONAL A perceptual theory that postulates that the meaning and interpretation of any acoustic magnitude depends on the magnitudes of other acoustic variables. In other words, the identical magnitude may result in different perceptions as a function of the magnitudes of other variables.

RESONANCE Any vibration mode. Each mode has a natural frequency.

REVERBERATION Persistence of sound in an enclosed space, due to multiple reflections of the sound wave.

RISE TIME See ATTACK.

RUN OF ELEMENTS A continuous sequence of identical elements. The pattern *AAAABBACCC* could be described as a run of four A's, a run of two B's, a run of one A, and a run of three C's.

SCALE An abstraction based on the notes used in a musical composition. The diatonic scale used in European music is based on a sequence of semitone and whole tone intervals.

SCALE STEPS Designating notes in terms of their position in a major or minor scale.

SEGMENT The series of sounds roughly equivalent to letters, forming words. Phonetic segments are based on pronunciation differences; phonological segments are based on meaning differences.

SEMANTICS The meaning (internal to the listener) of words and sentences.

SEMITONE The interval between two adjacent musical notes. For equal tempered scales, the frequency ratio is roughly 1.06 for *all* pairs of adjacent notes.

SEMIVOWELS See GLIDES.

SINUSOID The displacement against time pattern for simple harmonic vibration.

SOURCE-FILTER A model for sound production in which a complex driving vibration excites a sound body that radiates the sound. The output is determined by the frequencies of the complex driving vibration, the frequencies of the vibration modes of the sound body, and the coupling between the driving vibration and the sound body. The driving vibration is the source. The sound body is the filter; the sound body changes the relative strengths of the components of the driving vibration.

SPECTROGRAMS Representations of the amplitude and frequency of the component vibrations composing a complex oscillation (by Fourier analysis).

STANDING WAVE A stationary vibration pattern, generated by the superposition of reflected traveling waves.

STEADY STATE The part of a tone during which the amplitude is relatively constant. Nonetheless, the amplitudes of individual harmonics may be rapidly changing.

STOP CONSONANTS Consonants characterized by a brief, complete blocking of the airflow through the vocal tract.

STREAM SEGREGATION The perceptual organization of a complex acoustic signal into separate acoustic events. Each stream will represent one sound source or event.

STRESS Any sound that is perceived as "prominent" or "marked." There may not be a simple relation between stress and an acoustic variable.

STRESS-TIMING Languages in which there tend to be equal time intervals between the onset of one stressed syllable and the onset of the next stressed syllable.

SUPERPOSITION The acoustic result that the resultant wave from a set of simultaneous sounds is the sum of the amplitudes at each point in time.

SUPRASEGMENTAL Acoustic features that extend over more than one segment (a segment is roughly equal to a letter).

SURFACE LEVEL The sounds, phonological representations, making up an utterance. Typically the surface level refers to the words and their order in a sentence.

SURROUND RELATIONSHIPS The perceptual result that the interpretation of an acoustic segment as one speech sound as opposed to another will be a function of the magnitudes of other acoustic segments.

SYLLABLE-TIMING Languages in which each syllable is thought to take an equal temporal interval.

SYNCHRONIZATION Neurologically, the repeated firing of a auditory nerve fiber at one point in the waveform (see PHASE-LOCKED).

SYNTAX The rules relating sounds to meanings. These rules include grammatical relationships and transformations; syntax restricts the ways words can be arranged in sentences.

TEMPO The rate of presentation or production of the elements. Metronome timing is stated in terms of beats per minute.

TIMBRE The quality of a sound disregarding frequency and intensity.

TONAL See ATONAL/TONAL.

TONALITY Musical compositions in which all notes appear to be related to a single note, the tonic. This is a broad definition, making nearly all music tonal. Alternatively, tonality can be used more restrictively and be applied to music written in one key.

TONE HEIGHT Roughly, the frequency of a note. Tone height distinguishes between tones of equivalent chroma in different octaves.

TONIC The central note of a musical piece; the first note of a key.

TONOTOPIC Neurological organization such that cells responding to different frequencies are laid out anatomically from low to high frequency.

TRADING RELATIONSHIPS Any event will result in several acoustic variables. A trading relationship implies that changes in one variable may be compensated by "opposing" changes in another variable, which results in the identical perception.

TRANSIENT Any part of a longer sound that undergoes rapid change (e.g., the attack and decay).

TRANSVERSE WAVE Oscillations in which the elements move at right angles to the direction of the waves. For ocean waves, the water particles move up and down while the wave travels right to left (or vice versa).

TRAVELING WAVE Wave motion in which the peaks and zero points move through the medium. For example, traveling waves move down the basilar membrane. In contrast, for a standing wave the peaks and zeros (nodes) remain at the same position.

TRIAD A chord of three notes consisting of a root (i.e., the tonic), the note representing the third, and the note representing the fifth. The basis of harmony.

TWO-TONE SUPPRESSION The firing pattern of one auditory nerve fiber due to a single tone is changed when a second tone is presented simultaneously. The firing rate is decreased, and the firings are less accurately synchronized to the wave pattern of the first tone.

UNIVERSALS Characteristics of language that are common to all human languages.

VIBRATION MODE The pattern of oscillation or vibration that occurs at a characteristic frequency of the object.

VIBRATO A small up-and-down variation in frequency for aesthetic purposes. The frequency change effects the amplitude of each partial so that the tone changes quality.

VOICED/UNVOICED A distinctive feature of consonant production. The onset of first formant voicing distinguishes among consonants with the same manner and place of articulation.

WAVELENGTH The distance of one repetition (cycle) of a vibration.

References

Abberton, E., and Fourcin, A. J. (1978). Intonation and speaker identification. *Language and Speech*, 21 (4), 305–318.

Aitkin, L. M., Gates, G. R., and Phillips, S. C. (1984). Responses of neurons in inferior colliculus to variations in sound-source azimuth. *Journal of Neurophysiology*, 52 (1), 1–17.

Allport, F. H. (1955). *Theories of perception and the concept of structure*. New York: Wiley.

American National Standards Institute (1973). *Psychoacoustical terminology*. S3.20. New York: American National Standards Institute.

Ammons, C. H., Worchel, P., and Dallenbach, K. M. (1953). "Facial vision": The perception of obstacles out of doors by blindfolded and blindfolded-deafened subjects. *American Journal of Psychology*, 66 (4), 519–553.

ANSI. *See* American National Standards Institute.

Apel, W. (1972). *Harvard dictionary of music*. 2nd ed. Cambridge, Mass.: Harvard University Press.

Arthur, R. M., Pfeiffer, R. R., and Suga, N. (1971). Properties of two-tone inhibition in primary auditory neurones. *Journal of Physiology*, 212 (3), 593–609.

Attneave, F., and Olson, R. K. (1971). Pitch as a medium: A new approach to psychophysical scaling. *American Journal of Psychology*, 84 (2), 147–166.

Austin, J. L. (1962). *Sense and sensibilia*. Oxford: Oxford University Press.

Backus, J. (1974). Input impedance curves for the reed woodwind instruments. *Journal of the Acoustical Society of America*, 56 (4), 1266–1279.

Backus, J. (1976). Input impedance curves for the brass instruments. *Journal of the Acoustical Society of America*, 60 (2), 470–480.

Backus, J. (1977). *The acoustical foundations of music*. 2nd ed. New York: W. W. Norton.

Balzano, G. J. (1980). The group-theoretic description of twelvefold and microtonal pitch systems. *Computer Music Journal*, 4 (4), 66–84.

Bartlett, J. C., and Dowling, W. J. (1980). Recognition of transposed melodies: A key-distance effect in developmental perspective. *Journal of Experimental Psychology: Human Perception and Performance*, 6 (3), 501–515.

Bashford, J. A., and Warren, R. M. (1987). Multiple phonemic restorations follow the rules for auditory induction. *Perception & Psychophysics*, 42 (2), 114–121.

Bassett, I. G., and Eastmond, E. J. (1964). Echolocation: measurement of pitch versus distance for sounds reflected from a flat surface. *Journal of the Acoustical Society of America*, 36 (5), 911–916.

Benade, A. H. (1960). *Horns, strings, and harmony*. Garden City, N.Y.: Anchor Books.

Benade, A. H. (1976). *Fundamentals of musical acoustics*. London: Oxford University Press.

Benade, A. H., and Larson, C. O. (1985). Requirements and techniques for measuring the musical spectrum of the clarinet. *Journal of the Acoustical Society of America*, 78 (5), 1475–1498.

Bengtsson, I. and Gabrielsson, A. (1977). Rhythm research in Uppsala. In *Music, Room, Acoustics* (pp. 19–25). Publications issued by the Royal Swedish Academy of Music, No. 17, Stockholm.

Bengtsson, I., and Gabrielsson, A. (1983). Analysis and synthesis of musical rhythm. In J. Sundberg (ed.), *Studies of music performance* (pp. 27–60). Publications issued by the Royal Swedish Academy of Music, No. 39, Stockholm.

Beranek, L. L. (1962). *Music, acoustics, and architecture.* New York: Wiley.

Berger, K. W. (1964). Some factors in the recognition of timbre. *Journal of the Acoustical Society of America,* 36 (10), 1888–1891.

Bernstein, L. (1976). *The unanswered question: Six talks at Harvard.* Cambridge, Mass.: Harvard University Press.

Best, C. T., Morrongiello, B., and Robson, R. (1981). Perceptual equivalence of acoustic cues in speech and nonspeech perception. *Perception & Psychophysics,* 29 (3), 191–211.

Bharucha, J., and Krumhansl, C. L. (1983). The representation of harmonic structure in music: Hierarchies of stability as a function of context. *Cognition,* 13 (11), 63–102.

Bharucha, J., and Stoeckig, K. (1986). Reaction time and musical expectancy: Priming of chords. *Journal of Experimental Psychology: Human Perception and Performance,* 12 (4), 403–410.

Bismarck, G. von (1974). Timbre of steady sounds: A factorial investigation of its verbal attributes. *Acustica,* 30 (3), 146–159.

Björk, E. A. (1985). The perceived quality of natural sounds. *Acustica,* 57 (3), 185–188.

Blauert, J. (1983). *Spatial hearing: The psychophysics of human sound localization.* Cambridge, Mass.: MIT Press.

Blauert, J., and Lindemann, W. (1986). Auditory spaciousness: Some further psychoacoustic analyses. *Journal of the Acoustical Society of America,* 80 (2), 533–542.

Bock, J. K., and Mazzella, J. R. (1983). Intonational marking of given and new information: Some consequences for comprehension. *Memory and Cognition,* 11 (1), 64–76.

Bolinger, D. L. (1955). The melody of language. *Modern Language Forum,* 40 (1), 19–30.

Bolinger, D. L. (1958). A theory of pitch accent in English. *Word,* 14 (2–3), 109–149.

Bolinger, D. L. (1972). Accent is predictable (if you're a mind reader). *Language,* 48 (3), 633–644.

Bolinger, D. L. (1978). Intonation across languages. In J. P. Greenberg, C. A. Ferguson, and E. A. Moravesik (eds.), *Universals of human language. Vol. 2: Phonology* (pp. 471–524). Stanford: Stanford University Press.

Bolton, T. L. (1894). Rhythm. *American Journal of Psychology,* 6 (2), 145–238.

Boomsliter, P. C., and Creel, W. (1972). Research potentials in auditory characteristics of violin tone. *Journal of the Acoustical Society of America,* 51 (6, part 2), 1984–1993.

Boring, E. G. (1942). *Sensation and perception in the history of experimental psychology.* New York: Appleton-Century-Crofts.

Boring, E. G. (1950). *A history of experimental psychology.* 2nd ed. New York: Appleton-Century-Crofts.

Bower, T. G. R. (1974). *Development in infancy.* San Francisco: Freeman.

Bransford, J. D. (1979). *Human cognition: Learning, understanding, and remembering.* Belmont, Calif.: Wadsworth.

Brazil, D. C., Coulthard, M. R., and Johns, C. (1980). *Discourse intonation and language teaching.* London: Longman.

Bregman, A. S. (1978a). The formation of auditory streams. In J. Requin (ed.), *Attention and performance VII* (pp. 63–75). Hillsdale, N.J.: Erlbaum.

Bregman, A. S. (1978b). Auditory streaming is cumulative. *Journal of Experimental Psychology: Human Perception and Performance,* 4 (3), 380–387.

Bregman, A. S. (1978c). Auditory streaming: Competition among alternative organizations. *Perception and Psychophysics,* 23 (5), 391–398.

Bregman, A. S. (1981). Asking the "what for" question in auditory perception. In M. Kubovy and J. R. Pomerantz (eds.), *Perceptual organization* (pp. 99–118). Hillsdale, N.J.: Erlbaum.

Bregman, A. S. (1987). The meaning of duplex perception: Sounds as transparent objects. In M. E. H. Schouten (ed.), *The psychophysics of speech perception* (pp. 95–111). Dordrecht: Nijhoff.

Bregman, A. S., and Campbell, J. (1971). Primary auditory stream segregation and perception of order in rapid sequences of tones. *Journal of Experimental Psychology*, 89 (2), 244–249.

Bregman, A. S., and Dannenbring, G. L. (1973). The effect of continuity on auditory stream segregation. *Perception & Psychophysics*, 13 (2), 08–312.

Bregman, A. S., and Dannenbring, G. L. (1977). Auditory continuity and amplitude edges. *Canadian Journal of Psychology*, 31 (3), 151–159.

Bregman, A. S., and Pinker, S. (1978). Auditory streaming and the building of timbre. *Canadian Journal of Psychology*, 32 (1), 19–31.

Bregman, A. S., and Rudnicky, A. I. (1975). Auditory segregation: Stream or streams? *Journal of Experimental Psychology: Human Perception and Performance*, 1 (3), 263–267.

Bregman, A. S., and Steiger, H. (1980). Auditory streaming and vertical localization: Interdependence of "what" and "where" decisions in audition. *Perception & Psychophysics*, 28 (6), 539–546.

Bricker, P., and Pruzansky, S. (1976). Speaker recognition. In N. Lass (ed.), *Contemporary Issues in Experimental Phonetics* (pp. 295–326). New York: Academic.

Broadbent, D. E. (1958). *Perception and communication*. Oxford: Pergamon.

Brown, R. (1981). An experimental study of the relative importance of acoustic parameters for auditory speaker recognition. *Language and Speech*, 24 (4), 295–310.

Brugge, J. F. (1985). Patterns of organization in auditory cortex. *Journal of the Acoustical Society of America*, 78 (1), 353–359.

Brugge, J. F., and O'Conner, T. A. (1984). Postnatal functional development of the dorsal and posteroventral cochlear nucleii of the cat. *Journal of the Acoustical Society of America*, 75 (5), 1548–1562.

Brunswik, E. (1956). *Perception and the representative design of psychological experiments*. Berkeley: University of California Press.

Burns, E. M., and Ward, W. D. (1978). Categorical perception-phenomenon or epiphenomenon: Evidence from experiments in the perception of melodic musical intervals. *Journal of the Acoustical Society of America*, 63 (2), 456–468.

Burns, E. M., and Ward, W. D. (1982). Intervals, scales, and tuning. In D. Deutsch (ed.), *The psychology of music*, pp. 241–269. New York: Academic Press.

Butler, D. (1986). [Review of *Musical structure and cognition*.] *Music Psychology*, 4 (2), 235–240.

Carney, A. E., Widin, G. P., and Viemeister, N. F. (1977). Noncategorical perception of stop consonants differing in VOT. *Journal of the Acoustical Society of America*, 62 (4), 961–970.

Castellano, M. A., Bharucha, J. J., and Krumhansl, C. L. (1984). Tonal hierarchies in the music of North India. *Journal of Experimental Psychology: General*, 113 (3), 394–412.

Charbonneau, G. R. (1981). Timbre and the perceptual effects of three types of data reduction. *Computer Music Journal*, 5 (2), 10–19.

Cherry, C. (1957). *On human communication*. Cambridge, Mass.: MIT Press.

Chomsky, N. (1957). *Syntactic structures*. The Hague: Mouton.

Chomsky, N. (1965). *Aspects of the theory of syntax*. Cambridge, Mass.: MIT Press.

Chomsky, N., and Halle, M. (1968). *The sound pattern of English*. New York: Harper & Row.

Ciocca, V., and Bregman, A. S. (1987). Perceived continuity of gliding and steady state tones through interrupting noise. *Perception & Psychophysics*, 42 (5), 476–484.

Clark, H. H., and Clark, E. V. (1977). *Psychology and language: An introduction to psycholinguistics.* New York: Harcourt Brace Jovanovich.

Clarke, E. F. (1985). Some aspects of rhythm and expression in performances of Erik Satie's "Gnossienne No. 5." *Music Perception,* 2 (3), 299–328.

Clarke, F. R., and Becker, R. W. (1969). Comparison of techniques for discriminating among talkers. *Journal of Speech and Hearing Research,* 12 (4), 747–761.

Cohen, A. J. (1982). Exploring the sensitivity to structure in music. *Canadian University Music Review,* 3 (1), 15–30.

Cole, R. A., and Scott, B. (1973). Perception of temporal order in speech: The role of vowel transitions. *Canadian Journal of Psychology,* 27 (4), 441–449.

Coleman, P. D. (1963). An analysis of cues to auditory depth perception in free space. *Psychological Bulletin,* 60 (3), 302–315.

Cooper, G., and Meyer, L. B. (1960). *The rhythmic structure of music.* Chicago: University of Chicago Press.

Cooper, W. E., Tye-Murray, N., and Eady, S. J. (1985). Acoustical cues to the reconstruction of missing words in speech perception. *Perception & Psychophysics,* 38 (1), 30–40.

Couper-Kuhlen, R. (1986). *An introduction to English prosody.* London: Edward Arnold.

Crowder, R. G. (1982). The communality of auditory sensory storage in perception and immediate memory. *Perception & Psychophysics,* 31 (5), 477–483.

Crowder, R. G. (1984). Perception of the major/minor distinction. I. Historical and theoretical foundations. *Psychomusicology,* 4 (1 and 2), 3–12.

Cruttenden, A. (1986). *Intonation.* Cambridge: Cambridge University Press.

Cuddy, L. L., Cohen, A. J., and Mewhort, D. J. K. (1981). Perception of structure in short melodic sequences. *Journal of Experimental Psychology: Human Perception and Performance,* 7 (4), 869–883.

Cuddy, L. L., Cohen, A. J., and Miller, J. (1979). Melody recognition: The experimental application of musical rules. *Canadian Journal of Psychology* 33 (3), 148–157.

Culver, C. A. (1956). *Musical acoustics.* 4th ed. New York: McGraw-Hill.

Cutler, A. (1984). Stress and accent in language production and understanding. In D. Gibbon and H. Richter (eds.), *Intonation, accent, and rhythm* (pp. 77–90). Berlin: De Gruyter.

Cutting, J. E. (1982). Blowing in the wind: Perceiving structure in trees and bushes. *Cognition,* 12 (1), 12–44.

Cutting, J. E., and Proffitt, D. R. (1982). The minimum principle and the perception of absolute, common, and relative motions. *Cognitive Psychology,* 14 (2), 211–246.

Darwin, C. J. (1976). The perception of speech. In E. C. Carterette and M. P. Friedman (eds.), *Handbook of Perception.* Vol. 4: *Language and Speech* (pp. 175–216). New York: Academic.

Darwin, C. J. (1984). Perceiving vowels in the presence of another sound: Constraints on formant perception. *Journal of the Acoustical Society of America,* 76 (6), 1636–1647.

Dauer, R. M. (1983). Stress-timing and syllable-timing reanalyzed. *Journal of Phonetics,* 11 (1), 51–62.

Davidson, B., Power, R. P., and Michie, P. T. (1987). The effects of familiarity and previous training on perception of an ambiguous musical figure. *Perception & Psychophysics,* 41 (6), 601–608.

Davies, J. B. (1978). *The psychology of music.* Stanford: Stanford University Press.

Delgutte, B. (1980). Representation of speech-like sounds in the discharge patterns of auditory-nerve fibers. *Journal of the Acoustical Society of America,* 68 (3), 843–857.

Delgutte, B. (1982). Some correlates of phonetic distinctions at the level of the auditory nerve. In R. Carlson and B. Granstrom (eds.), *The representation of speech in the peripheral auditory system* (pp. 131–149). Amsterdam: Elsevier/North Holland.

Delgutte, B. (1984). Speech coding in the auditory nerve. II. Processing schemes for vowel-like sounds. *Journal of the Acoustical Society of America*, 75 (3), 879–886.

Delgutte, B. (1987). Peripheral auditory processing of speech information: Implications from a physiological study of intensity discrimination. In M. E. H. Schouten (ed.), *The psychophysics of speech perception* (pp. 333–353). Dordrecht: Nijhoff.

Delgutte, B., and Kiang, N. Y. S. (1984). Speech coding in the auditory nerve. III. Voiceless fricative consonants. *Journal of the Acoustical Society of America*, 75 (3), 887–896.

Deliege, I. (1987). Grouping conditions in listening to music: An approach to Lerdahl and Jackendoff's grouping perference rules. *Music Perception*, 4 (4), 325–360.

Denes, P. B., and Pinson, E. N. (1963). *The speech chain.* Murray Hill, N.J.: Bell Telephone Laboratories.

Dennis, M. (1983). Syntax in brain-injured children. In M. Studdert-Kennedy (ed.), *Psychobiology of language* (pp. 195–202). Cambridge, Mass.: MIT Press.

Deutsch, D. (1975). Two-channel listening to musical scales. *Journal of the Acoustical Society of America*, 57 (5), 1156–1160.

Deutsch, D. (1980). The processing of structured and unstructured tonal sequences. *Perception & Psychophysics*, 28 (5), 381–389.

Deutsch, D. (1984). Two issues concerning tonal hierarchies: Comment on Castellano, Bharucha, and Krumhansl. *Journal of Experimental Psychology: General*, 113 (3), 413–416.

Diehl, R. L. (1981). Feature detectors for speech: A critical reappraisal. *Psychological Bulletin*, 89 (1), 1–18.

Diehl, R. L. (1986). Coproduction and direct perception of phonetic segments: A critique. *Journal of Phonetics*, 14 (1), 61–66.

Diehl, R. L. (1987). Auditory constraints on speech perception. In M. E. H. Schouten (ed.), *The psychophysics of speech perception* (pp. 210–219). Dordrecht: Nijhoff.

Divenyi, P. L., and Blauert, J. (1987). On creating a precedent for binaural patterns: When is an echo an echo? In W. A. Yost and C. S. Watson (eds.), *Auditory processing of complex sounds.* Hillsdale, N.J.: Erlbaum.

Dodd, B. (1979). Lip-reading in infants: Attention to speech presented in- and out-of-synchrony. *Cognitive Psychology*, 11 (4), 478–484.

Dorman, M. F., Cutting, J. E., and Raphael, L. J. (1975). Perception of temporal order in vowel sequences with and without formant transitions. *Journal of Experimental Psychology: Human Perception and Performance*, 104 (2), 121–129.

Dowling, W. J. (1973a). The perception of interleaved melodies. *Cognitive Psychology*, 5 (3), 322–337.

Dowling, W. J. (1973b). Rhythmic groups and subjective chunks in memory for melodies. *Perception & Psychophysics*, 14 (1), 37–40.

Dowling, W. J. (1978). Scale and contour: Two components of a theory of memory for melodies. *Psychological Review*, 85 (4), 341–354

Dowling, W. J. (1984). Musical experience and tonal scales in recognition of octave scrambled melodies. *Psychomusicology*, 4 (1 and 2), 13–32.

Dowling, W. J. (1986). Context effects on melody recognition: Scale-step versus interval representations. *Music Perception*, 3 (3), 281–296.

Dowling, W. J., and Bartlett, J. C. (1981). The importance of interval information in long-term memory for melodies. *Psychomusicology*, 1 (1 and 2), 30–49.

Dowling, A. P., and Ffowes Williams, J. E. (1983). *Sound and sources of sound.* Chichester: Ellis Horwood.

Dowling, W. J., and Fujitani, D. S. (1971). Contour, interval, and pitch recognition in memory for melodies. *Journal of the Acoustical Society of America*, 49 (2, part 2), 524–531.

Dowling, W. J., and Harwood, D. L. (1986). *Music cognition.* Orlando, Fla.: Academic.

Dowling, W. J., Lung, K. M-T., and Herrbold, S. (1987). Aiming attention in pitch and time in the perception of interleaved melodies. *Perception & Psychophysics*, 41 (6), 642–656.

Duifhuis, H., Willems, L. F., and Sluyter, R. J. (1982). Measurement of pitch in speech: An implementation of Goldstein's theory of pitch perception. *Journal of the Acoustical Society of America*, 71 (6), 1568–1580.

Durlach, N. I., and Colburn, H. S. (1978). Binaural phenomena. In E. E. Carterette and M. P. Friedman (eds.), *Handbook of perception*. Vol. 4: *Hearing* (pp. 365–466). New York: Academic.

Easter, S. S., Jr., Purves, D., Rakic, P., and Spitzer, N. C. (1985). The changing view of neural specificity. *Science*, 230 (4725), 507–511.

Easton, R. D., and Basala, M. (1982). Perceptual dominance during lipreading. *Perception & Psychophysics*, 32 (6), 562–570.

Edworthy, J. (1985). Interval and contour in melody processing. *Music Perception*, 2 (3), 375–388.

Efron, R., Koss, B., and Yund, E. W. (1983). Central auditory processing. IV. Ear dominance-spatial and temporal complexity. *Brain and Language*, 19 (2), 264–282.

Eldridge, D. H. (1974). Inner ear—cochlear mechanics and cochlear potentials. In W. D. Keidel and W. D. Neff (eds.), *Handbook of sensory physiology*, vol. 5/1, pp. 549–584. Berlin: Springer.

Elman, J., and McClelland, J. (1986). Exploiting lawful variability in the speech wave. In J. S. Perkell and D. H. Klatt (eds.), *Invariance and variability in speech processes* (pp. 360–385). Hillsdale, N.J.: Erlbaum.

Erickson, R. (1976). *Sound structure in music*. Berkeley: University of California Press.

Espinoza-Varas, B. (1987). Levels of representation of phonemes and bandwidth of spectral-temporal integration. In M. E. H. Schouten (ed.), *The psychophysics of speech perception* (pp. 80–90). Dordrecht: Nijhoff.

Essens, P. J., and Povel, D. J. (1985). Metrical and nonmetrical representations of temporal patterns. *Perception & Psychophysics*, 37 (1), 1–7.

Evans, E. F. (1972). The frequency response and other properties of single fibers in the guinea pig cochlear nerve. *Journal of Physiology* (London), 226 (1), 263–287.

Fant, G. (1960). *Acoustical theory of speech production*. The Hague: Mouton.

Fechner, G. T. ([1860] 1966). *Elements of psychophysics*. Ed. D. H. Howes and E. G. Boring, trans. H. E. Adler. New York: Holt, Rinehart, and Winston.

Fedderson, W. E., Sandel, T. T., Teas, D. C., and Jeffress, L. A. (1957). Localization of high frequency tones. *Journal of the Acoustical Society of America*, 29 (9), 988–991.

Fodor, J. A. (1983). *The modularity of mind*. Cambridge, Mass.: MIT Press.

Foss, D. J., nd Hakes, D. T. (1978). *Psycholinguistics*. Englewood Cliffs, N.J.: Prentice-Hall.

Fowler, C. A. (1986). An event approach to the study of speech perception from a direct-realist perspective. *Journal of Phonetics*, 14 (1), 3–28.

Fraisse, P. (1956). *Les structures rythmiques*. Louvain: Publication Universitaires de Louvain.

Fraisse, P. (1963). *The psychology of time*. New York: Harper & Row.

Fraisse, P. (1974). *Psychologie du rythme*. Paris: Presses Universitaires de France.

Fraisse, P. (1978). Time and rhythm perception. In E. C. Carterette and M. P. Friedman (eds.), *Handbook of perception*. Vol. 8: *Perceptual coding*. New York: Academic.

Fraisse, P. (1982). Rhythm and tempo. In D. Deutsch (ed.), *The psychology of music* (pp. 149–180). New York: Academic.

Fraisse, P., and Oleron, G. (1954). La structuration intensive des rythmes. *L'Année Psychologique*, 54 (1), 35–52.

French, A. P. (1971). *Vibrations and waves*. New York: W. W. Norton.

Frick, R. W. (1985). Communicating emotion: The role of prosodic features. *Psychological Bulletin*, 97 (3), 412–429.

Fry, D. B. (1955). Duration and intensity as physical correlates of linguistic stress. *Journal of the Acoustical Society of America*, 27 (4), 765–768.

Fry, D. B. (1958). Experiments in the perception of stress. *Language and Speech*, 1 (2), 126–152.

Gabrielsson, A. (1973). Similarity ratings and dimensional analyses of auditory rhythm patterns. I and II. *Scandinavian Journal of Psychology*, 14 (2 and 3), 138–160, 161–176.

Gabrielsson, A. (1985). Interplay between analysis and synthesis in studies of music performance and music experience. *Music Perception*, 3 (1), 59–86.

Galambos, R., and Davis, H. (1943). Responses of single auditory nerve fibers to acoustic stimulation. *Journal of Neurophysiology*, 6 (1), 39–57.

Ganong, W. F., III (1980). Phonetic categorization in auditory word perception. *Journal of Experimental Psychology: Human Perception and Performance*, 6 (1), 110–125.

Gårding, E. (1983). A generative model of intonation. In D. R. Ladd and A. Cutler (eds.), *Prosody: Models and measurements* (pp. 1–25). Berlin: Springer-Verlag.

Gardner, M. B. (1969a). Image fusion, broadening, and displacement in sound localization. *Journal of the Acoustical Society of America*, 46 (2), 339–349.

Gardner, M. B. (1969b). Distance estimation of 0° or apparent 0° oriented speech signals in anechoic space. *Journal of the Acoustical Society of America*, 45 (1), 47–53.

Gardner, R. B., and Darwin, C. J. (1986). Grouping of vowel harmonics by frequency modulation: Absence of effects on phonemic categorization. *Perception & Psychophysics*, 40 (3), 183–187.

Garner, W. R. (1962). *Uncertainty and structure as psychological concepts*. New York: Wiley.

Garner, W. R. (1974). *The processing of information and structure*. Potomac, Md.: Erlbaum.

Gay, T. (1978). Effect of speaking rate on vowel formant movements. *Journal of the Acoustical Society of America*, 63 (1), 223–230.

Geldard, F. A. (1970). Vision, audition, and beyond. In W. D. Neff (ed.), *Contributions to sensory physiology*, Vol. 4 (pp. 1–17). New York: Academic.

Gibson, J. J. (1966). *The senses considered as perceptual systems*. Boston: Houghton Mifflin.

Gibson, J. J. (1979). *The ecological approach to visual perception*. Boston: Houghton Mifflin.

Glenn, J. W., and Kleiner, N. (1968). Speaker identification based on nasal phonation. *Journal of the Acoustical Society of America*, 43 (2), 368–372.

Glucksberg, S., Kreuz, R. J., and Rho, S. H. (1986). Context can constrain lexical access: Implications for models of language comprehension. *Journal of Experimental Psychology: Learning, Memory, and Cognition*, 12 (3), 323–335.

Gordon, J. W., and Grey, J. M. (1978). Perception of spectral modifications on orchestral instrument tones. *Computer Music Journal*, 2 (1), 24–31.

Gordon, P. C. (1988). Induction of rate-dependent processing by course-grained aspects of speech. *Perception & Psychophysics*, 43 (2), 137–146.

Green, D. M. (1976). *An introduction to hearing*. Hillsdale, N.J. Erlbaum.

Green, K. P., and Miller, J. L. (1985). On the role of visual rate information in phonetic perception. *Perception & Psychophysics*, 38 (3), 269–276.

Grey, J. M. (1977). Multidimensional perceptual scaling of musical timbres. *Journal of the Acoustical Society of America*, 61 (5), 1270–1277.

Grey, J. M. (1978). Timbre discrimination in musical patterns. *Journal of the Acoustical Society of America*, 64 (2), 467–472.

Grey, J. M., and Gordon, J. W. (1978). Perceptual effects of spectral modifications on musical timbres. *Journal of the Acoustical Society of America*, 63 (5), 1493–1500.

Grey, J. M., and Moorer, J. A. (1977). Perceptual evaluations of synthesized musical instrument tones. *Journal of the Acoustical Society of America*, 62 (2), 454–462.

Haas, H. (1972). The influence of a single echo on the audibility of speech. *Journal of Audio Engineering Society*, 201 (2), 145–159.

Hall, D. E. (1980). *Musical acoustics: An introduction.* Belmont, Calif.: Wadsworth.

Halpern, A. R. (1984). Perception of structure in novel music. *Memory and Cognition,* 12 (2), 163–170.

Hammarberg, R. (1976). The metaphysics of coarticulation. *Journal of Phonetics,* 4 (4), 353–363.

Handel, S. (1973). Temporal segmentation of repeating auditory patterns. *Journal of Experimental Psychology,* 101 (1), 46–54.

Handel, S. (1974). Perceiving melodic and rhythmic auditory patterns. *Journal of Experimental Psychology,* 103 (5), 922–933.

Handel, S. (1984). Using polyrhythms to study rhythm. *Music Perception,* 1 (4), 465–484.

Handel, S., and Todd, P. (1981). The segmentation of sequential patterns. *Journal of Experimental Psychology: Human Perception and Performance,* 7 (1), 41–55.

Handel, S., Weaver, M. S., and Lawson, G. (1983). Effect of rhythmic grouping on stream segregation. *Journal of Experimental Psychology: Human Perception and Performance,* 9 (4), 637–651.

Harrell, T. W. (1937). Factors influencing preference and memory for auditory patterns. *Journal of General Psychology,* 17 (1), 63–104.

Harris, M. S., and Umeda, N. (1987). Difference limens for fundamental frequency contours in sentences. *Journal of the Acoustical Society of America,* 81 (4), 1139–1145.

't Hart, J. (1981). Differential sensitivity to pitch distance, particularly in speech. *Journal of the Acoustical Society of America,* 69 (3), 811–821.

Hartmann, W. M. (1983). Localization of sound in rooms. *Journal of the Acoustical Society of America,* 74 (5), 1380–1391.

Hayes, S. P. (1941). *Contributions to a psychology of blindness.* New York: American Foundation for the Blind.

Hayes, B. (1984). The phonology of rhythm in English. *Linguistic Inquiry,* 15 (1), 33–74.

Hebrank, J., and Wright, D. (1974). Spectral cues used in the localization of sound sources on the median plane. *Journal of the Acoustical Society of America,* 56 (6), 1829–1834.

Hecker, M. (1971). Speech recognition. *American Speech and Hearing Association.* Monographs. Number 16.

Heise, G. A., and Miller, G. A. (1951). An experimental study of auditory patterns. *American Journal of Psychology,* 64 (1), 68–77.

Helmholtz, H. von ([1863] (1954)). *On the sensations of tone.* Trans. A. J. Ellis. New York: Dover.

Henning, G. B., and Grosberg, S. L. (1968). Effect of harmonic components on frequency discrimination. *Journal of the Acoustical Society of America,* 44 (5), 1386–1389.

Hirsh, I. J. (1959). Auditory perception of temporal order. *Journal of the Acoustical Society of America,* 31 (6), 759–767.

Hirsh, I. J. (1974). Temporal order and auditory perception. In H. R. Moskowitz, B. Scharf, and J. C. Stevens (eds.), *Sensation and Measurement* (pp. 251–258). Dordrecht: Reidel.

Hockett, C. F. (1955). *A manual of phonology.* Baltimore: Waverly Press.

Hockett, C. F. (1963). The problem of universals in language. In J. H. Greenberg (ed.), *Universals in Language* (pp. 1–29). Cambridge, Mass.: MIT Press.

Hogg, R., and McCully, C. B. (1987). *Metrical phonology: A coursebook.* Cambridge: Cambridge University Press.

Holmes, J. N., Mattingly, I. G., and Shearme, J. N. (1964). Speech synthesis by rule. *Language and Speech,* 7 (3), 127–143.

Holmgren, G. L. (1967). Physical and psychological correlates of speaker recognition. *Journal of Speech and Hearing Research,* 10 (1), 57–66.

Householder, F. (1957). Accent, juncture, intonation, and my grandfather's reader. *Word,* 13 (2), 234–245.

Hudspeth, A. J. (1985). The cellular basis of hearing: The biophysics of hair cells. *Science*, 230 (4727), 745–752.

Hughes, M. (1977). A quantitative analysis. In M. Yeston (ed.), *Readings in Schenker analysis and other approaches* (pp. 144–164). New Haven: Yale University Press.

Hutchins, C. M. (1962). The physics of violins. *Scientific American*, 207 (5), 79–93.

Hutchins, C. M. (ed.) (1975). *Musical acoustics*. Part 1: *Violin family components*. Stroudsburg, Pa.: Dowden, Hutchinson, & Ross.

Hutchins, C. M. (ed.) (1976). *Musical acoustics*. Part 2: *Violin family functions*. Stroudsburg, Pa.: Dowden, Hutchinson, & Ross.

Ihde, D. (1976). *Listening and voice: A phenomenology of sound*. Athens: Ohio University Press.

Imai, S. (1966) Classification of sets of stimuli with different stimulus characteristics and numerical properties. *Perception & Psychophysics*, 1 (2), 48–54.

Isaacs, E. (1920). The nature of rhythm experience. *Psychological Review*, 27 (2), 270–300.

Jamieson, D. G. (1987). Studies of possible psychoacoustic factors underlying speech perception. In M. E. H. Schouten (ed.), *The psychophysics of speech perception* (pp. 220–230). Dordrecht: Nijhoff.

Jamieson, D. G., and Morosan, D. E. (1986). Training non-native speech contrasts in adults: Acquisition of the English /ð/–/θ/ contrast by francophones. *Perception & Psychophysics*, 40 (4), 205–215.

Jenkins, J. J. (1984). Acoustic information for places, objects, and events. In W. H. Warren and R. E. Shaw (eds.), *Persistence and change: Proceedings of the first international conference on event perception* (pp. 115–138). Hillsdale, N.J.: Erlbaum.

Jenkins, W. M., and Merzenich, M. M. (1984). Role of cat primary auditory cortex for sound-localization behavior. *Journal of Neurophysiology*, 52 (5), 819–847.

Jenkins, J. J., Strange, W., and Edman, T. R. (1983). Identification of vowels in "vowelless" syllables. *Perception & Psychophysics*, 341 (5), 441–450.

Johansson, G. (1973). Visual perception of biological motion and a model for its analysis. *Perception & Psychophysics*, 14 (10), 201–211.

Jones, A. M. (1959). *Studies in African music*. London: Oxford University Press.

Jones, M. R. (1976). Time, our lost dimension: Toward a new theory of perception, attention, and memory. *Psychological Review*, 83 (5), 323–355.

Jones, M. R. (1981a). Music as a stimulus for psychological motion. Part I: Some determinants of expectancies. *Psychomusicology*, 1 (2), 34–51.

Jones, M. R. (1981b). A tutorial on some issues and methods in serial pattern research. *Perception & Psychophysics*, 30 (5), 492–504.

Jones, M. R. (1987). Perspectives on musical time. In A. Gabrielsson (ed.), *Action and perception in rhythm and music* (pp. 153–175). Publications issued by the Royal Swedish Academy of Music, No. 55, Stockholm.

Joos, M. (1948). Acoustic phonetics. *Language*, 24 (supplement), 1–137.

Jordan, D. S., and Shepard, R. N. (1987). Tonal schemas: Evidence obtained by probing distorted musical scales. *Perception & Psychophysics*, 41 (6), 489–504.

Judd, T. (1979). Comments on Deutsch's musical scale illusion. *Perception & Psychophysics*, 26 (1), 85–92.

Julesz, B., and Hirsh, I. J. (1972). Visual and auditory perception: An essay of comparison. In E. E. David, and P. Denes (eds.), *Human communication: A unified view* (pp. 283–340). New York: McGraw-Hill.

Kaas, J. H. (1982). The segregation of function in the nervous system: Why do sensory systems have so many subdivisions. In W. D. Neff (ed.), *Contributions to sensory physiology*, Vol. 7 (pp. 201–240). New York: Academic.

Kallman, H. J., and Massaro, D. W. (1979). Tone chroma is functional in melody recognition. *Perception & Psychophysics*, 26 (1), 32–56.

Keller, H. (1954). *Story of my life*. New York: Doubleday.

Kellogg, W. N. (1962). Sonar system of the blind. *Science*, 137 (3528), 399–404.

Kelly, R. E. (1974). Musical pitch variations caused by the Doppler effect. *American Journal of Physics*, 42 (6), 452–455.

Kelly, W. J., and Watson, C. S. (1986). Stimulus-based limitations on the discrimination between temporal orders of tones. *Journal of the Acoustical Society of America*, 79 (6), 1934–1938.

Kelso, J. A. S., Saltzman, E. L., and Tuller, B. (1986). The dynamical perspective on speech production. *Journal of Phonetics*, 14 (1), 29–59.

Kendall, R. A. (1986). The role of acoustic signal partitions in listener categorization of musical phrases. *Music Perception*, 4 (2), 185–214.

Kent, E. L. (ed.) (1977). *Musical acoustics: Piano and wind instruments*. Stroudsburg, Pa.: Dowden, Hutchinson, & Ross.

Kessler, E. J., Hanson, C., and Shepard, R. N. (1984). Tonal schemata in the perception of music in Bali and in the West. *Music Perception*, 2 (2), 131–165.

Kewley-Port, D., Watson, C. S., and Foyle, D. C. (1988). Auditory temporal acuity in relation to category boundaries; speech and nonspeech stimuli. *Journal of the Acoustical Society of America*, 83 (3), 1133–1145.

Khanna, S. M., and Leonard, D. G. B. (1982). Basilar membrane tuning in the cat cochlea. *Science*, 215 (4530), 305–306.

Kiang, N. Y. S. (1975). Stimulus representation in the discharge patterns of auditory neurons. In D. B. Tower (ed.), *Human communication and its disorders* (pp. 81–96). New York: Raven Press.

Kiang, N. Y. S., Watanabe, T., Thomas, E. C., and Clark, L. F. (1965). *Discharge patterns of single fibers in the cat's auditory nerve*. MIT Research Monographs, No. 35. Cambridge, Mass.: MIT Press.

Klatt, D. H. (1973). Discrimination of fundamental frequency contours in synthetic speech: Implications for models of pitch perception. *Journal of the Acoustical Society of America*, 53 (1), 8–16.

Klatt, D. H. (1976). Linguistic uses of segmental duration in English: Acoustic and perceptual evidence. *Journal of the Acoustical Society of America*, 59 (5), 1208–1221.

Knudsen, E. I. (1984). Synthesis of a neural map of auditory space in the owl. In G. M. Edelman, W. E. Gall, and W. M. Cowan (eds.), *Dynamic aspects of neocortical function* (pp. 375–396). New York: Wiley.

Knudsen, V. O., and Harris, C. M. (1978). *Acoustical designing in architecture*. New York: American Institute of Physics.

Knudsen, E. I., and Knudsen, P. (1985). Vision guides the adjustment of auditory localization in young barn owls. *Science*, 230 (4725), 545–548.

Koenig, W. (1950). Subjective effects in binaural hearing. *Journal of the Acoustical Society of America*, 22 (1), 61–62.

Koffka, K. (1935). *Principles of Gestalt psychology*. New York: Harcourt, Brace, & World.

Kohler, W. (1969). *The task of Gestalt psychology*. Princeton: Princeton University Press.

Krumhansl, C. L. (1979). The psychological representation of musical pitch in a tonal context. *Cognitive Psychology*, 11 (3), 346–374.

Krumhansl, C. L., Bharucha, J. J., and Kessler, E. J. (1982). Perceived harmonic structure of chords in three related musical keys. *Journal of Experimental Psychology: Human Perception and Performance*, 8 (1), 24–36.

Krumhansl, C. L., and Keil, F. C. (1982). Acquisition of the hierarchy of tonal functions in music. *Memory & Cognition*, 10 (3), 243–251.

Krumhansl, C. L., and Kessler, E. J. (1982). Tracing the dynamic changes in perceived tonal organization in a spatial representation of musical keys. *Psychological Review*, 89 (4), 334–368.

Krumhansl, C. L., and Shepard, R. N. (1979). Quantification of the hierarchy of tonal functions within a diatonic context. *Journal of Experimental Psychology: Human Perception and Performance*, 5 (4), 579–594.

Kubovy, M. (1981). Concurrent pitch segregation and the theory of indispensable attributes. In M. Kubovy and J. R. Pomerantz (eds.), *Perceptual organization* (pp. 55–98). Hillsdale, N.J.: Erlbaum.

Kuwabara, H., and Ohgushi, K. (1987). Contributions of vocal tract resonant frequencies and bandwidths to the personal perception of speech. *Acustica*, 63 (2), 120–128.

Kuwada, S., Yin, T. C. T., Syka, J., Buunen, T. J. F., and Wickesberg, R. E. (1984). Binaural interaction in low frequency neurons in inferior colliculus of the cat. IV. Comparisons of monaural and binaural response properties. *Journal of Neurophysiology*, 51 (6), 1306–1325.

Ladd, D. R. (1980). *The structure of intonational meaning: Evidence from English*. Bloomington: Indiana University Press.

Ladd, D. R., and Cutler, A. (1983). Introduction, models and measurements in the study of prosody. In D. R. Ladd, and A. Cutler (eds.), *Prosody: Models and measurements* (pp. 1–10). Berlin: Springer-Verlag.

Ladefoged, P. (1975). *A course in phonetics*. New York: Harcourt, Brace, & Jovanovich.

Lahiri, A., Gewirth, L., and Blumstein, S. E. (1984). A reconsideration of acoustical invariance for place of articulation in diffuse stop consonants. *Journal of the Acoustical Society of America*, 76 (2), 391–404.

Lehiste, I. (1976). Suprasegmental features of speech. In N. Lass (ed.), *Contemporary issues in contemporary phonetics* (pp. 225–239). New York: Academic.

Lehiste, I., and Peterson, G. E. (1959). Vowel amplitude and phonemic stress in American English. *Journal of the Acoustical Society of America*, 31 (4), 428–435.

Lenneberg, E. H. (1967). *Biological foundations of language*. New York: Wiley.

Lerdahl, F., and Jackendoff, R. (1983). *A generative theory of tonal music*. Cambridge, Mass.: MIT Press.

Lettvin, J. Y., Maturana, H. R., McCulloch, W. S., and Pitts, W. H. (1959). What the frog's eye tells the frog's brain. *Proceedings of the Institute of Radio Engineering*, 47, 1940–1951.

Liberman, A. M. (1970). The grammars of speech and language. *Cognitive Psychology*, 1 (4), 301–323.

Liberman, M. Y. (1975). On the intonational system of English. Doctoral dissertation, MIT. (pub., New York: Garland Press, 1979).

Liberman, M. C. (1978). Auditory-nerve responses from cats raised in a low noise chamber. *Journal of the Acoustical Society of America*, 63 (2), 442–455.

Liberman, A. M. (1982). On finding that speech is special. *American Psychologist*, 37 (2), 148–167.

Liberman, A. M., Cooper, F. S., Shankweiler, D. P., and Studdert-Kennedy, M. (1967). Perception of the speech code. *Psychological Review*, 74 (6), 431–461.

Liberman, A. M., Harris, K. S., Hoffman, H. S., and Griffith, B. C. (1957). The discrimination of speech sounds within and across phoneme boundaries. *Journal of Experimental Psychology*, 54 (5), 358–368.

Liberman, A. M., and Mattingly, I. G. (1985). The motor theory of speech perception revised. *Cognition*, 21 (1), 1–36.

Liberman, M. Y., and Prince, A. (1977). On stress and linguistic rhythm. *Linguistic Inquiry*, 8 (2), 249–336.

Liberman, A. M., and Studdert-Kennedy, M. (1978). Phonetic perception. In R. Held, H. W.

568   References

Leibowitz, and H. L. Teuber (eds.), *Handbook of sensory physiology*. Vol. 8: *Perception*. New York: Springer-Verlag.

Lieberman, P. (1977). *Speech physiology and acoustic phonetics*. New York: Macmillan.

Lieberman, P. (1984). *The biology and evolution of language*. Cambridge, Mass.: Harvard University Press.

Lindblom, B. E. F., and Studdert-Kennedy, M. (1967). On the role of formant transitions in vowel recognition. *Journal of the Acoustical Society of America*, 42 (4), 830–843.

Longuet-Higgins, C., and Lee, C. (1982). The perception of musical rhythms. *Perception*, 11, 115–156.

Longuet-Higgins, C., and Lee, C. (1984). The rhythmic interpretation of monophonic music. *Music Perception*, 1 (4), 424–441.

Luce, D., and Clark, M., Jr. (1967). Physical correlates of brass-instrument tones. *Journal of the Acoustical Society of America*, 42 (6), 1232–1243.

McAdams, S., and Bregman, A. S. (1979). Hearing musical streams. *Computer Music Journal*, 3 (4), 26–43, 60.

MacDonald, J., and McGurk, H. (1978). Visual influences on speech perception processes. *Perception & Psychophysics*, 24 (3), 253–257.

McIntyre, M. E., Schumacher, R. T., and Woodhouse, J. (1983). On the oscillations of musical instruments. *Journal of the Acoustical Society of America*, 74 (5), 1325–1345.

McIntyre, M. E., and Woodhouse, J. (1978). The acoustics of stringed musical instruments. *Interdisciplinary Science Reviews*, 3 (2), 157–173.

McNally, K. A., and Handel, S. (1977). The effect of element composition on streaming and ordering of repeating sequences. *Journal of Experimental Psychology: Human Perception and Performance*, 3 (3), 451–460.

MacNeilage, P. F. (1985). Serial-ordering errors in speech and typing. In V. A. Fromkin (ed.), *Phonetic linguistics: Essays in honor of Peter Ladefoged* (pp. 193–201). Orlando, Fla.: Academic.

Mann, V. A. (1980). Influence of preceding liquid on stop consonant perception. *Perception & Psychophysics*, 28, 407–412.

Mann, V. A., and Repp, B. H. (1980). Influence of vocalic context on perception of the /sh/–/s/ distinction. *Perception & Psychophysics*, 28 (3), 213–228.

Marks, L. E. (1978). *The unity of the senses*. New York: Academic.

Marslen-Wilson, W. D., and Welsh, A. (1978). Processing interactions and lexical access during word recognition in continuous speech. *Cognitive Psychology*, 10 (1), 29–63.

Martin, J. G. (1972). Rhythmic (hierarchical) versus serial structure in speech and other behavior. *Psychological Review*, 79 (6), 487–509.

Massaro, D. W. (1987). Psychophysics versus specialized processes in speech perception: An alternative perspective. In M. E. H. Schouten (ed.), *The psychophysics of speech perception* (pp. 46–65). Dordrecht: Nijhoff.

Massaro, D. W., and Cohen, M. M. (1983). Evaluation and integration of visual and auditory information in speech perception. *Journal of Experimental Psychology: Human Perception and Performance*, 9 (5), 753–771.

Masterton, R. B., and Imig, T. J. (1984). Neural mechanisms for sound localization. *Annual Review of Physiology*, 46, 275–287.

Matsumoto, H., Hiki, S., Sone, T., and Nimura, T. (1973). Multidimensional representation of personal quality of vowels and its acoustical correlates. *IEEE Transactions on Audio and Electroacoustics*, AU–21, 428–436.

Mershon, D. H., and King, E. (1975). Intensity and reverberation as factors in the auditory perception of egocentric distance. *Perception & Psychophysics*, 18 (6), 409–415.

Merzenich, M. M., Colwell, S. A., and Anderson, R. A. (1982). Thalamocortical and corticothalamic connections in the auditory system of the cat. In C. N. Woolsey (ed.),

Cortical sensory organization. Vol. 3: *Multiple auditory areas* (pp. 43–57). Clifton, N.J.: Humana Press.

Merzenich, M. M., Jenkins, W. M., and Middlebrooks, J. C. (1984). Observations and hypotheses on special organizational features of the central auditory nervous system. In G. M. Edelman, W. E. Gall, and W. M. Cowan (eds.), *Dynamic aspects of neocortical function* (pp. 397–424). New York: Wiley.

Merzenich, M. M., and Kaas, J. H. (1980). Principles of organization of sensory-perceptual systems in mammals. In J. M. Sprague and A. N. Epstein (eds.), *Progress in Psychobiology and Physiological Psychology.* Vol. 9 (pp. 1–41). New York: Academic.

Meyer, J. (1972). Directivity of the bowed-string instruments and its effect on orchestral sound in concert halls. *Journal of the Acoustical Society in America,* 51 (6, part 2), 1994–2009.

Meyer, D. E., and Schvaneveldt, R. W. (1971). Facilitation in recognizing pairs of words: Evidence of a dependence between retrieval operations. *Journal of Experimental Psychology,* 90 (2), 227–234.

Michaels, C. F., and Carello, C. (1981). *Direct perception.* Englewood Cliffs, N.J.: Prentice-Hall.

Middlebrooks, J. C., Dykes, R. W., and Merzenich, M. M. (1980). Binaural response-specific bands in primary auditory cortex (AI) of the cat: Topographical organization orthogonal to isofrequency contours. *Brain Research,* 181 (1), 31–48.

Miller, G. A. (1951). *Language and communication.* New York: McGraw-Hill.

Miller, G. A. (1981). *Language and speech.* San Francisco: Freeman.

Miller, J. E. (1964). Decapitation and recapitation: A study of voice quality. *Journal of the Acoustical Society of America,* 36 (11), 2002 (A).

Miller, G. A., and Heise, G. A. (1950). The trill threshold. *Journal of the Acoustical Society of America,* 22 (5), 637–638.

Miller, G. A., and Isard, S. (1963). Some perceptual consequences of linguistic rules. *Journal of Verbal Learning and Verbal Behavior,* 2 (3), 217–228.

Miller, J. L., and Liberman, A. M. (1979). Some effects of later occurring information on the perception of stop consonant and semivowel. *Perception & Psychophysics,* 25 (6), 457–465.

Miller, M. I., and Sachs, M. B. (1983). Representation of stop consonants in the discharge pattern of auditory-nerve fibers. *Journal of the Acoustical Society of America,* 74 (2), 502–517.

Miller, J. D., Wier, C. C., Pastore, R. E., Kelly, W. J., and Dooling, R. J. (1976). Discrimination and labeling of noise-buzz sequences with varying noise-lead times: An example of categorical perception. *Journal of the Acoustical Society of America,* 74 (2), 502–517.

Møller, A. R. (1983). *Auditory physiology.* New York: Academic.

Moore, B. C. J. (1982). *An introduction to the psychology of hearing.* 2nd ed. New York: Academic.

Moore, B. C. J., Glasberg, B. R., Peters, R. W. (1985). Thresholds for hearing mistuned partials as separate tones in harmonic complexes. *Journal of the Acoustical Society of America,* 80 (2), 479–483.

Moorer, J. A., and Grey, J. M. (1977a). Lexicon of analyzed tones. Part 1. A violin tone. *Computer Music Journal,* 1 (1), 39–45.

Moorer, J. A., and Grey J. M. (1977b). Lexicon of analyzed tones. Part 2. Clarinet and oboe tones. *Computer Music Journal,* 1 (2), 12–29.

Moorer, J. A., and Grey, J. M. (1978). Lexicon of analyzed tones. Part 3. The trumpet. *Computer Music Journal,* 2 (2), 23–31.

Moral, J. A., and Jansson, E. V. (1982). Eigenmodes, input admittance, and the function of the violin. *Acustica,* 50 (5), 329–337.

Murray, T., and Singh, S. (1980). Multidimensional analysis of male and female voices. *Journal of the Acoustical Society of America*, 68 (5), 1294–1300.

Mursell, J. L. (1937). *Psychology of music*. New York: W. W. Norton.

Nábělek, I. V., Nábělek, A. K., and Hirsh, I. J. (1970). Pitch of tone bursts of changing frequency. *Journal of the Acoustical Society of America*, 48 (2, part 2), 536–553.

Neisser, U. (1966). *Cognitive psychology*. New York: Appleton-Century-Crofts.

Noble, W. (1983). Hearing, hearing impairment, and the audible world: A theoretical essay. *Audiology*, 22 (4), 325–338.

Nooteboom, S. G., Brokx, J. P. L., and de Rooij, J. J. (1978). Contributions of prosody to speech perception. In W. J. M. Levelt and G. B. Flores d'Arcais (eds.), *Studies in the perception of language* (pp. 75–107). New York: Wiley.

O'Connor, J. D., Gerstman, L. J., Liberman, A. M., Delattre, P. C., and Cooper, F. S. (1957). Acoustic cues for the perception of initial /w, j, r, l/ in English. *Word*, 13 (1), 25–43.

O'Connor, J. D., and Trim, J. L. M. (1953). Vowel, consonant, and syllable: A phonological definition. *Word*, 9 (2), 103–122.

Öhman, S. E. G. (1966). Coarticulation in VCV utterances: Spectrographic measurements. *Journal of the Acoustical Society of America*, 39 (1), 151–168.

O'Shaughnessy, D. (1986). Speaker recognition. *IEEE Acoustics, Speech, and Signal Processing*, 3 (4), 4–17.

Palmer, A. R., Winter, I. M., and Darwin, C. J. (1986). The representation of steady state vowel sounds in the temporal discharge patterns of the guinea pig cochlear nerve and primarylike cochlear nucleus neurons. *Journal of the Acoustical Society of America*, 79 (1), 100–113.

Paradis, M. (1977). Bilingualism and aphasia. In H. A. Whitaker, and H. Whitaker (eds.), *Studies in neurolinguistics*. Vol. 3 (pp. 65–121). New York: Academic.

Paradis, M. (1987). The neurofunctional modularity of cognitive skills: Evidence from Japanese alexia and polyglot aphasia. In E. Keller and M. Gopnik (eds.), *Motor and sensory processes of language* (pp. 277–289). Hillsdale, N.J.: Erlbaum.

Parker, E. M., and Diehl, R. L. (1984). Identifying vowels in CVC syllables: Effects of inserting silence and noise. *Perception & Psychophysics*, 36 (4), 369–380.

Parker, E. M., Diehl, R. L., and Kluender, K. R. (1986). Trading relations in speech and nonspeech. *Perception & Psychophysics*, 39 (2), 129–142.

Pastore, R. E. (1983). Temporal order judgment of auditory stimulus offset. *Perception & Psychophysics*, 33 (1), 54–62.

Perrott, D. R., and Buell, T. N. (1982). Judgments of sound volume: Effects of signal duration, level, and interaural characteristics on the perceived extensity of broadband noise. *Journal of the Acoustical Society of America*, 72 (5), 1413–1417.

Peters, M. (1985). Performance of a rubato-like task: When two things cannot be done at the same time. *Music Perception*, 2 (4), 471–482.

Peterson, G. E., and Barney, H. C. (1952). Control methods used in a study of vowels. *Journal of the Acoustical Society of America*, 24 (2), 175–184.

Pfeiffer, R. R., and Kim, D. O. (1975). Cochlear nerve fiber responses: Distribution along cochlear partition. *Journal of the Acoustical Society of America*, 58 (4), 867–869.

Pickles, J. O. (1982). *An introduction to the physiology of hearing*. London: Academic.

Pickles, J. O. (1986). The neurophysiological basis of frequency selectivity. In B. C. J. Moore (ed.), *Frequency selectivity in hearing*, (pp. 51–122). London: Academic Press.

Pierce, J. R. (1983). *The science of musical sound*. New York: Scientific American Books.

Pike, K. L. (1945). *The intonation of American English*. Ann Arbor: University of Michigan Press.

Pisoni, D. B. (1971). On the nature of categorical perception of speech sounds. *Supplement to status report on speech research* (pp. 1–101), SR–27. New Haven: Haskins Laboratories.

Pisoni, D. B. (1973). Auditory and phonetic memory codes in the discrimination of consonants and vowels. *Perception & Psychophysics*, 13 (2), 253–260.

Pisoni, D. B. (1977). Identification and discrimination of the relative onset time of two component tones: Implications for voicing perception in stops. *Journal of the Acoustical Society of America*, 61 (5), 1352–1361.

Pisoni, D. B., Aslin, R. N., Perey, A. J., and Hennessy, B. L. (1982). Some effects of laboratory training on identification and discrimination of voicing contrasts in stop consonants. *Journal of Experimental Psychology: Human Perception and Performance*, 8 (2), 297–314.

Pisoni, D. B., Carrell, T. D., and Gans, S. J. (1983). Perception of the duration of rapid spectrum changes in speech and nonspeech signals. *Perception & Psychophysics*, 34 (4), 314–322.

Pisoni, D. B., and Luce, P. A. (1987). Trading relations, acoustic cue integration, and context effects in speech perception. In M. E. H. Schouten (ed.), *The psychophysics of speech perception* (pp. 159–172). Dordrecht: Nijhoff.

Piston, W. (1947). *Counterpoint*. New York: W. W. Norton.

Pitt, M. A., and Monahan, C. B. (1987). The perceived similarity of auditory polyrhythms. *Perception & Psychophysics*, 41 (6), 534–546.

Plomp, R. (1975). *Aspects of tone sensation*. London: Academic.

Pollack, I., and Ficks, L. (1954). Information of elementary multidimensional auditory displays. *Journal of the Acoustical Society of America*, 26 (2), 155–158.

Pollack, I., and Pickett, J. M. (1964). Intelligibility of excerpts from fluent speech: Auditory vs. structural context. *Journal of Verbal Learning and Verbal Behavior*, 3 (1), 79–84.

Pollack, I., Pickett, J. M., and Sumby, W. H. (1954). On the identification of speakers by voice. *Journal of the Acoustical Society of America*, 26 (3), 403–406.

Pollard-Gott, L. (1983). Emergence of thematic concepts in repeated listening to music. *Cognitive Psychology*, 15 (1), 66–94.

Pols, L. C. W., and Schouten, M. E. H. (1987). Perception of tone, band, and formant sweeps. In M. E. H. Schouten (ed.), *The psychophysics of speech perception* (pp. 231–240). Dordrecht: Nijhoff.

Pomerantz, J. R., and Kubovy, M. (1981). Perceptual organization: An overview. In M. Kubovy and J. R. Pomerantz (eds.), *Perceptual organization* (pp. 423–456). Hillsdale, N.J.: Erlbaum.

Povel, D. J. (1981). Internal representation of simple temporal patterns. *Journal of Experimental Psychology: Human Perception and Performance*, 7 (1), 3–18.

Povel, D. J., and Essens, P. (1985). Perception of temporal patterns. *Music Perception*, 2 (4), 411–440.

Povel, D. J., and Okkerman, H. (1981). Accents in equitone sequences. *Perception & Psychophysics*, 30 (6), 565–572.

Pressing, J. (1983). Cognitive isomorphisms in pitch and rhythm in world musics: West Africa, the Balkans, Thailand, and Western tonality. *Studies in Music*, 17, 38–61.

Radocy, R. E., and Boyle, J. D. (1979). *Psychological foundations of musical behavior*. Springfield, Ill.: Charles C. Thomas.

Rakerd, B., and Hartmann, W. H. (1986). Localization of sound in rooms. III: Onset and duration effects. *Journal of the Acoustical Society of America*, 80 (6), 1695–1706.

Rakerd, B., Verbrugge, R. R., and Shankweiler, D. P. (1984). Monitoring for vowels in isolation and in a consonantal context. *Journal of the Acoustical Society of America*, 76 (1), 27–31.

Rasch, R. A. (1978). The perception of simultaneous notes such as in polyphonic music. *Acustica*, 40 (1), 22–33.

Rasch, R. A. (1981). *Aspects of the perception and performance of polyphonic music*. Doctoral dissertation, University of Groningen, The Netherland.

Remez, R. E., Rubin, P. E., Nygaard, L. C., and Howell, W. A. (1987). Perceptual normalization of vowels produced by sinusoidal voices. *Journal of Experimental Psychology: Human Perception and Performance*, 13 (1), 40–61.

Repp, B. H. (1981). On levels of description in speech research. *Journal of the Acoustical Society of America*, 69 (5), 1462–1464.

Repp, B. H. (1982). Phonetic trading relations and context effects: New experimental evidence for a speech mode of perception. *Psychological Bulletin*, 92 (1), 81–110.

Repp, B. H. (1984). Categorical perception: Issues, methods, and findings. In N. Lass (ed.), *Speech and Language.* Vol. 10: *Advances in basic research and practice* (pp. 244–335). Orlando, Fla.: Academic.

Repp, B. H. (1987). The sound of two hands clapping: An exploratory study. *Journal of the Acoustical Society of America*, 81 (4), 1100–1109.

Restle, F. (1970). Theory of serial pattern learning: Structural trees. *Psychological Review*, 77 (6), 481–495.

Restle, F. (1972). The role of phrasing. *Journal of Experimental Psychology*, 92 (3), 385–390.

Rice, C. E., and Feinstein, S. H. (1965). Echo detection and ability of the blind: Size and distance factors. *Journal of Experimental Psychology*, 70 (3), 246–251.

Risset, J. C., and Mathews, M. V. (1969). Analysis of musical instrument tones. *Physics Today*, 22 (2), 23–80.

Risset, J. C., and Wessel, D. L. (1982). Exploration of timbre by analysis and synthesis. In D. Deutsch (ed.), *The psychology of music* (pp. 26–58). New York: Academic Press.

Rock, I. (1975). *An introduction to perception.* New York: Macmillan.

Rodgers, C. A. P. (1981). Pinna transformations and sound reproduction. *Journal of Audio Engineering Society*, 29 (4), 228–233.

Roederer, J. G. (1975). *Introduction to the physics and psychophysics of music.* New York: Springer-Verlag.

Rose, J. E., Brugge, J. F., Anderson, D. J., and Hind, J. E. (1967). Phase-locked response to low-frequency tones in single auditory nerve fibers of the squirrel monkey. *Journal of Neurophysiology*, 30 (4), 769–793.

Rose, J. E., Hind, J. E., Anderson, D. J., and Brugge, J. F. (1971). Some effects of stimulus intensity on response of auditory nerve fibers in the squirrel monkey. *Journal of Neurophysiology*, 34 (4), 685–699.

Rosen, S., and Howell, P. (1987). Is there a natural sensitivity at 20 ms in relative tone-onset-time continua? A reanalysis of Hirsh's (1959) data. In M. E. H. Schouten (ed.), *The psychophysics of speech perception* (pp. 199–209). Dordrecht: Nijhoff.

Ruckmick, C. A. (1913). The role of kinesthesis in the perception of rhythm. *American Journal of Psychology*, 24 (3), 305–359.

Ruckmick, C. A. (1929). A new classification of tonal qualities. *Psychological Review*, 36 (2), 172–180.

Sachs, M. B., and Abbas, P. J. (1974). Rate versus level functions for auditory nerve fibers in cats: Tone burst stimuli. *Journal of the Acoustical Society of America*, 56 (6), 1835–1847.

Sachs, M. B., and Young, E. D. (1980). Effects of nonlinearities on speech encoding in the auditory nerve. *Journal of the Acoustical Society of America*, 68 (3), 858–875.

Sachs, M. B., Young, E. D., and Miller, M. I. (1982). Encoding of speech features in the auditory nerve. In R. Carlson and B. Granstrom (eds.), *The representation of speech in the peripheral nervous system* (pp. 115–130). Amsterdam: Elsevier.

Saldanha, E. L., and Corso, J. F. (1964). Timbre cues and the identification of musical instruments. *Journal of the Acoustical Society of America*, 36 (11), 2021–2026.

Samuel, A. G. (1981). Phonemic restoration: Insights from a new methodology. *Journal of Experimental Psychology: General*, 110 (4), 474–494.

Samuel, A. G. (1986). The role of the lexicon in speech perception. In E. C. Schwab and H. C. Nusbaum (eds.), *Pattern recognition by humans and machines*. Vol. 1: *Speech perception* (pp. 89–111). Orlando, Fla.: Academic.

Sasaki, T. (1980). Sound restoration and temporal localization of noise in speech and music sounds. *Tohuku Psychological Folia*, 39 (1–4), 79–88.

Saunders, F. A. (1937). The mechanical action of violins. *Journal of the Acoustical Society of America*, 9 (2), 81–98.

Scharf, B. (1975). Audition. In B. Scharf (ed.), *Experimental sensory psychology* (pp. 112–149). Glenview, Ill.: Scott, Foresman.

Schelleng, J. C. (1973). The bowed string and the player. *Journal of the Acoustical Society of America*, 53 (1), 26–41.

Scherer, K. R. (1986). Vocal affect expression: A review and a model for future research. *Psychological Bulletin*, 99 (2), 143–165.

Schiffman, S. S., Reynolds, M. L., and Young, F. W. (1981). *Introduction to multidimensional scaling: Theory, methods, and applications*. New York: Academic.

Schourup, L. (1973). Unique New York unique New York unique New York. *Papers from the Ninth regional meeting, Chicago Linguistic Society*, 587–596.

Schouten, M. E. H. (1985). Identification and discrimination of sweep tones. *Perception & Psychophysics*, 37 (4), 369–376.

Schouten, M. E. H. (1986). Three-way identifications of sweep tones. *Perception & Psychophysics*, 40 (5), 359–361.

Schreiner, C. E., and Cynader, M. S. (1984). Basic functional organization of the second auditory cortical field AII of the cat. *Journal of Neurophysiology*, 51 (6), 1284–1305.

Searle, C. L., Braida, L. D., Davis, M. F., and Colburn, H. S. (1976). Model for auditory localization. *Journal of the Acoustical Society of America*, 60 (5), 1164–1181.

Searleman, A. (1983). Language capabilities of the right hemisphere. In A. Young (ed.), *Functions of the right cerebral hemisphere* (pp. 87–111). New York: Academic Press.

Seashore, C. E. ([1938] 1967). *Psychology of music*. New York: Dover.

Selkirk, E. O. (1980). The role of prosodic categories in English word stress. *Linguistic Inquiry*, 11 (3), 563–605.

Selkirk, E. O. (1984). *Phonology and syntax: The relation between sound and structure*. Cambridge, Mass.: MIT Press.

Serafine, M. L. (1983). Cognition in music. *Cognition*, 14 (2), 119–183.

Serafine, M. L., Crowder, R. G., and Repp, B. H. (1984). Integration of melody and text in memory for songs. *Cognition*, 16 (3), 285–303.

Shaffer, L. H. (1981). Performances of Chopin, Bach, and Bartók: Studies in motor programming. *Cognitive Psychology*, 13 (3), 326–376.

Shankweiler, D. P., Strange, W., and Verbrugge, R. R. (1977). Speech and the problems of perceptual constancy. In R. E. Shaw and J. Bransford (eds.), *Perceiving, acting, and knowing: Toward an ecological psychology* (pp. 315–345). Hillsdale, N.J.: Erlbaum.

Shaw, E. A. G. (1974). The external ear. In W. D. Keidel and W. D. Neff (eds.), *Handbook of sensory physiology*. Vol. V/11 (pp. 455–490). Berlin: Springer.

Shepard, R. N. (1965). Approximation to uniform gradients of generalization by monotone transformations of scale. In D. I. Mostofsky (ed.), *Stimulus generalization* (pp. 94–110). Stanford: Stanford University Press.

Shepard, R. N. (1982). Structural representations of musical pitch. In D. Deutsch (ed.), *The psychology of music* (pp. 344–390). New York: Academic Press.

Shofner, W. P., and Young, E. D. (1985). Excitatory/Inhibitory response types in the cochlear nucleus: Relationships to discharge patterns and responses to electrical stimulation of the auditory nerve. *Journal of Neurophysiology*, 54 (4), 917–939.

Siegel, J. A., and Siegel, W. (1977a). Absolute identification of notes and intervals by musicians. *Perception & Psychophysics*, 21 (2), 143–152.

Siegel, J. A., and Siegel, W. (1977b). Categorical identification of tonal intervals: Musicians can't tell *sharp* from *flat*. *Perception & Psychophysics*, 21 (5), 399–407.

Simpson, G. B. (1984). Lexical ambiguity and its role in models of word recognition. *Psychological Bulletin*, 96 (2), 316–340.

Sinex, D. G., and Geisler, C. D. (1983). Responses of auditory-nerve fibers to consonant-vowel syllables. *Journal of the Acoustical Society of America*, 73 (2), 602–615.

Singh, P. G. (1987). Perceptual organization of complex-tone sequences: A tradeoff between pitch and timbre. *Journal of the Acoustical Society of America*, 82 (3), 886–899.

Sink, P. E. (1983). Effects of rhythmic and melodic alterations on rhythmic perception. *Journal of Research in Music Education*, 3 (2), 101–115.

Sloboda, J. A. (1985). *The musical mind: The cognitive psychology of music*. Oxford: Oxford University Press.

Smith, R. L., Brachman, M. L., and Goodman, D. A. (1983). Adaptation in the auditory periphery. In C. P. Parkins and S. W. Anderson (eds.), *Cochlear prothesis*. Annals of the New York Academy of Sciences, Vol. 405 (pp. 79–93). New York: New York Academy of Sciences.

Smith, J., Hausfeld, S., Power, R. P., and Gorta, A. (1982). Ambiguous musical figures and auditory streaming. *Perception & Psychophysics*, 32 (5), 454–464.

Steiger, H., and Bregman, A. S. (1981). Capturing frequency components of glided tones: Frequency separation, orientation, and alignment. *Perception & Psychophysics*, 30 (5), 425–435.

Stetson, R. H. (1905). A motor theory of rhythm and discrete succession: II. *Psychological Review*, 12 (5), 293–350.

Stevens, K. N. (1972). The quantal nature of speech: Evidence from articulatory-acoustic data. In E. E. David, Jr. and P. B. Denes (eds.), *Human communication: A unified view* (pp. 51–66). New York: McGraw-Hill.

Stevens, K. N., and Blumstein, S. E. (1981). The search for invariant acoustical correlates of phonetic features. In P. D. Eimas and J. L. Miller (eds.), *Perspectives in the study of speech* (pp. 1–38). Hillsdale, N.J.: Erlbaum.

Stevens, S. S., and Davis, H. (1938). *Hearing*. New York: Wiley.

Strelow, E. R. (1985). What is needed for a theory of mobility: Direct perception and cognitive maps—Lessons from the blind. *Psychological Review*, 92 (2), 226–248.

Strong, W. J., and Plitnik, G. R. (1983). *Music, speech, and high-fidelity*. Salt Lake City: Soundprint.

Su, L.-S., and Li, K.-P. (1974). Identification of speakers by use of nasal coarticulation. *Journal of the Acoustical Society of America*, 56 (6), 1876–1882.

Sumby, W. H., and Pollack, I. (1954). Visual contribution to speech intelligibility in noise. *Journal of the Acoustical Society of America*, 26 (2), 212–215.

Summerfield, Q. (1979). Use of visual information in phonetic perception. *Phonetica*, 36 (4–5), 314–331.

Summerfield, Q. (1981). Articulatory rate and perceptual constancy in phonetic perception. *Journal of Experimental Psychology: Human Perception and Performance*, 7 (5), 1074–1095.

Summerfield, Q. (1983). Audio-visual speech perception, lip-reading, and artificial stimulation. In M. E. Lutman and M. P. Haggard (eds.), *Hearing science and hearing disorders* (pp. 131–182). London: Academic.

Summerfield, Q., and Haggard, M. (1977). On the dissociation of spectral and temporal cues to the voicing distinction in initial stop consonants. *Journal of the Acoustical Society of America*, 62 (2), 435–448.

Summerfield, Q., Sidwell, A., and Nelson, T. (1987). Auditory enhancement of changes in spectral amplitude. *Journal of the Acoustical Society of America*, 81 (3), 700–708.

Sundberg, J. (1977). The acoustics of the singing voice. *Scientific American*, 236 (3), 82–91.

Sundberg, J. (1982). Perception of singing. In D. Deutsch (ed.), *The psychology of music* (pp. 59–98). New York: Academic.

Taylor, C. (1976). *Sounds of music*. New York: Charles Scribner & Sons.

Thomas, I. B., and Fitzgibbons, P. J. (1971). Temporal order and perceptual classes. *Journal of the Acoustical Society of America*, 50 (1), 86–87.

Thomassen, J. M. (1982). Melodic accent: Experiments and a tentative model. *Journal of the Acoustical Society of America*, 71 (6), 1596–1605.

Thurlow, W. R., and Erchul, W. P. (1977). Judged similarity in pitch of octave multiples. *Perception & Psychophysics*, 22 (2), 177–182.

Todd, N. (1985). A model of expressive timing in tonal music. *Music Perception*, 3 (1), 33–58.

Trehub, S. E. (1987). Infants' perception of musical patterns. *Perception & Psychophysics*, 41 (6), 635–641.

Trehub, S. E., Morrongiello, B., and Thorpe, L. A. (1985). Children's perceptions of familiar melodies: The role of intervals, contour, and key. *Psychomusicology*, 5 (1 and 2), 39–43.

Tsuchitani, C. (1988). The inhibition of cat lateral superior olive unit excitatory responses to binaural tone burst. II. The sustained discharges. *Journal of Neurophysiology*, 59 (1), 184–211.

Tulving, E., and Gold, C. (1963). Stimulus information and contextual information as determinants of tachistoscopic recognition of words. *Journal of Experimental Psychology*, 66 (4), 319–327.

Twersky, V. (1951). Physical basis of the perception of obstacles by the blind. *American Journal of Psychology*, 64 (3), 409–411.

Vaissière, J. (1983). Language independent prosodic features. In D. R. Ladd and A. Cutler (eds.), *Prosody: Models and measurements* (pp. 53–66). Berlin: Springer-Verlag.

Van Derveer, N. J. (1979). *Acoustic information for event perception*. Paper presented at the celebration in honor of Eleanor J. Gibson, Cornell University, Ithaca, N.Y.

Van Lancker, D., Kreiman, J., and Emmorey, K. (1985). Familiar voice recognition: Patterns and parameters. Part I: Recognition of backward voices. *Journal of Phonetics*, 13 (1), 19–38.

Van Lancker, D., Kreiman, J., and Wickens, T. D. (1985). Familiar voice recognition: Patterns and parameters. Part II: Recognition of rate-altered voices. *Journal of Phonetics*, 13 (1), 39–52.

Van Noorden, L. P. A. S. (1975). Temporal coherence in the perception of tone sequences. Doctoral dissertation, Institute of Perception Research, Eindhoven, Holland.

Verbrugge, R. R., and Rakerd, B. (1986). Evidence of talker-independence in formation of vowels. *Language and Speech*, 29 (1), 39–57.

Voiers, W. D. (1964). Perceptual basis of speaker identity. *Journal of the Acoustical Society of America*, 36 (6), 1065–1073.

von Békésy, G. (1949). The moon illusion and similar auditory phenomena. *American Journal of Psychology*, 62 (4), 540–552.

von Békésy, G. (1960). *Experiments in hearing*, ed. E. G. Wever. New York: McGraw-Hill.

von Békésy, G. (1967). *Sensory inhibition*. Princeton: Princeton University Press.

Vos, P. G. (1979). *Identification of metre in music* (Internal Report 0N07). Nijmegen: University of Nijmegen.

Walden, B. E., Montgomery, A. A., Gibeily, G. J., Prosek, R. A., and Schwartz, D. M. (1978). Correlates of psychological dimensions in talker similarity. *Journal of Speech and Hearing Research*, 21 (2), 265–275.

Wallach, H. (1938). Über die Wahrnehmung der Schallrichtung [On the perception of the direction of sound]. *Psychologische Forschung*, 22 (3/4), 238–266.
Wallach, H., Newman, E. B., and Rosenzweig, M. R. (1949). The precedence effect in sound localization. *American Journal of Psychology*, 62 (3), 315–336.
Wapnick, J., Bourassa, G., and Sampson, J. (1982). The perception of tonal intervals in isolation and in melodic context. *Psychomusicology*, 2 (1), 21–36.
Ward, W. D. (1954). Subjective musical pitch. *Journal of the Acoustical Society of America*, 26 (3), 369–380.
Warren, R. M. (1970). Perceptual restoration of missing speech sounds. *Science*, 167 (3917), 392–393.
Warren, R. M. (1984). Perceptual restoration of obliterated sounds. *Psychological Bulletin*, 96 (2), 371–383.
Warren, R. M., and Sherman, G. L. (1974). Phonemic restorations based on subsequent context. *Perception & Psychophysics*, 16 (1), 150–156.
Warren, W. H., Jr., and Verbrugge, R. R. (1984). Auditory perception of breaking and bouncing events. *Journal of Experimental Psychology: Human Perception and Performance*, 10 (5), 704–712.
Wedin, L., and Goude, G. (1972). Dimension analysis of the perception of instrumental timbre. *Scandanavian Journal of Psychology*, 13 (3), 228–240.
Weinreich, G. (1979). The coupled motions of piano strings. *Scientific American*, 240 (1), 118–127.
Weintraub, M. (1987). Sound separation and auditory perceptual organization. In M. E. H. Schouten (ed.), *The psychophysics of speech perception* (pp. 125–134). Dordrecht: Nijhoff.
Wenk, B. J., and Wioland, F. (1982). Is French really syllable timed? *Journal of Phonetics*, 10 (2), 193–216.
Whalen, D. H., and Liberman, A. M. (1987). Speech perception takes precedence over nonspeech perception. *Science*, 237 (4811), 169–171.
Winckel, F. ([1960] 1967). *Music, sound, and sensation*. Trans. T. Binkley. New York: Dover.
Woodrow, H. (1909). A quantitative study of rhythm. *Archives of Psychology*, 14, 1–66.
Woodrow, H. (1951). Time perception. In S. S. Stevens (ed.), *Handbook of Experimental Psychology* (pp. 1224–1236). New York: Wiley.
Worchel, P., Mauney, J., and Andrew, J. G. (1950). The perception of obstacles by the blind. *Journal of Experimental Psychology*, 40 (6), 746–751.
Yeston, M. (1976). *The stratification of musical rhythm*. New Haven: Yale University Press.
Yost, W. A., and Nielsen, D. W. (1985). *Fundamentals of hearing*. 2nd ed. New York: Holt, Rinehart, and Winston.
Young, E. D. (1984). Response characteristics of neurons of the cochlear nuclei. In C. I. Berlin (ed.), *Hearing science, recent advances* (pp. 423–460). San Diego: College-Hill Press.
Young, E. D. (1987). Organization of the cochlear nucleus for information processing. In M. E. H. Schouten (ed.), *The psychophysics of speech perception* (pp. 355–370). Dordrecht: Nijhoff.
Young, E. D., and Sachs, M. B. (1979). Representation of steady-state vowels in the temporal aspects of the discharge patterns of populations of auditory nerve fibers. *Journal of the Acoustical Society of America*, 66 (5), 1381–1403.
Zatorre, R. J. (1984). Musical perception and cerebral function: A critical review. *Music Perception*, 2 (2), 196–221.
Zuckerkandl, V. (1959). *The sense of music*. Princeton: Princeton University Press.
Zue, V. W., and Laferriere, M. (1979). Acoustic study of medial /t, d/ in American English. *Journal of the Acoustical Society of America*, 66 (4), 1039–1050.
Zurif, E. (1984). Neurolinguistics: Some analyses of aphasic language. In M. Gazzaniga (ed.), *Handbook of cognitive neuroscience* (pp. 211–226). New York: Plenum.

Author Index

Subject Index